The Theory of Commodity Price Stabilization

A Study in the Economics of Risk

DAVID M. G. NEWBERY
and
JOSEPH E. STIGLITZ

CLARENDON PRESS · OXFORD
1981

Oxford University Press, Walton Street, Oxford OX2 6DP
London Glasgow New York Toronto
Delhi Bombay Calcutta Madras Karachi
Kuala Lumpur Singapore Hong Kong Tokyo
Nairobi Dar es Salaam Cape Town
Melbourne Auckland
and associate companies in
Beirut Berlin Ibadan Mexico City

Published in the United States by
Oxford University Press, New York

© David M. G. Newbery and Joseph E. Stiglitz 1981

All rights reserved. No part of this publication may be reproduced,
stored in a retrieval system, or transmitted, in any form or by any means,
electronic, mechanical, photocopying, recording, or otherwise, without
the prior permission of Oxford University Press

British Library Cataloguing in Publication Data
Newbery, David M. G.
The theory of commodity price stabilization.
I. Title   II. Stiglitz, Joseph E.
338.5'28   HB255
ISBN 0-19-828417-9
ISBN 0-19-828438-1 Pbk

Typeset by Anne Joshua Associates, Oxford, England
and Printed in the United States of America

For
TERRY AND JANE

Preface

This book develops a methodology within which alternative proposals for stabilizing the prices of agricultural and other commodities can be evaluated. Many countries — the United States, Britain, and the Common Market among them — have had some form of domestic price stabilization scheme for selected agricultural commodities for a long time, but over the years there have been recurrent proposals for an *international* stabilization programme. The dramatic boom and bust of many primary commodities over the period 1973–5, and the success of OPEC in raising the price of one primary commodity, oil, have again awakened interest in such proposals. The fourth meeting of the United Nations Conference in Trade and Development held in Nairobi in May 1976 proposed an Integrated Programme for Commodities, which, among other recommendations, proposed setting up buffer stocks to stabilize the prices of ten 'core' commodities. This renewed interest in price stabilization, and in particular the proposals for price stabilization, provided the direct impetus for the present book.

The studies from which this book has evolved were undertaken at the behest of the World Bank and the Agency for International Development (US AID). When we undertook the studies, we thought it would be an easy task converting the 'received wisdom' on commodity price stabilization into a simple model within which the magnitudes of the costs and benefits could be assessed. As our work progressed, it became increasingly clear that much of the received wisdom was incorrect, and that the standard model used in most empirical work rested on such special assumptions as to make it of very limited use.

In retrospect, this should not have been too surprising: a complete analysis of commodity price stabilization programmes requires nothing less than a full general equilibrium model of an economy with uncertainty, but with imperfect risk markets. This is an area of research which — in spite of its importance — has only recently been studied, and which is an active area of current research.

As a result of our attempt to develop this theory and apply it to the problem, we have produced more than just a book about commodity price stabilization. It is a book about the behaviour of economies with risk and with imperfect risk markets, with results which we believe will have a variety of applications in other areas. We believe our results will be of interest to general economists, and particularly economic theorists, who have only limited interest in the specific problem of commodity price stabilization, and to agricultural economists, who have long recognized the importance of risk and have, over the years, made significant contributions to our understanding of economic behaviour under risk.

We have written this book with these three audiences — the policy economists interested in assessing the desirability of commodity price stabilization programmes, the agricultural economist interested in the development of more general techniques for analysing risk, and the general economist, interested in the general equilibrium analysis of market economies in the presence of uncertainty — clearly in mind. Naturally, the objective of reaching such a wide and diverse audience brings special problems, for each group has different problems in mind and possesses a different background in mathematics and economics. What is a commonplace for one group is not for another; what is a plausible, reasonable, and widely accepted assumption for one may seem totally arbitrary to another. Our solution has been to be inclusive rather than succinct, in the expectation that readers familiar with one section will be able to skim and jump to the next stage, while others who find our approach novel will not need to consult other texts. We therefore expect readers to make intelligent use of the Contents.

To make our book as accessible as possible to as many non-technically oriented readers as possible, we have presented extensive summaries of our results (in Part I) and extensive intuitive interpretations of our analysis in the introductions to each of the other parts of the book, and also in the introductory and concluding sections of most of the chapters. Those chapters which require a somewhat higher level of mathematical skill are denoted by an asterisk. Readers who find particular chapters or sections of chapters hard going — and there will be few who find all of the chapters easy — can skip to the concluding section and then move on to the next chapter without losing the thread of the argument.

As we mentioned earlier, the original impetus for this research was provided by a set of studies we did for the World Bank and the Agency for International Development of the US State Department and we are indebted to both organizations for their interest and support. We would, in particular, like to thank Lorenzo Perez of US AID and Charles Blitzer of the World Bank for their helpful comments on these earlier studies. In the two and a half years over which this book was written, financial support was also received from the National Science Foundation. The first draft of the book was completed in the autumn of 1978 (while Stiglitz held the Oskar Morgenstern Distinguished Fellowship at Mathematica) and was typed by Julia Martinez of Mathematica. Subsequent drafts have been typed by Shirley French in Cambridge and Jackie Rowley in Oxford, and parts have circulated with help from the British Social Science Research Council.

We should like to acknowledge the helpful comments of numerous individuals on various drafts of the chapters of this book, especially: Avi Braverman, Franklin Allen, Gordon Gemmill, Richard Gilbert, Ravi Kanbur, Steve Salant, and Gerhard Wagenhals. Parts of Chapters 17, 18, and 21 have already appeared in the *Economic Journal*, as Newbery and Stiglitz (1979b), and we are grateful to the publishers for permission to include them here. Finally, of course, we should point out that none of the supporting institutions is responsible for any of the views expressed in this book.

Contents

Sections and chapters marked with an asterisk contain more technical material.

LIST OF TABLES	xvi
A NOTE ON NOTATION	xvi
LIST OF ABBREVIATIONS AND SYMBOLS	xvii

Part I   INTRODUCTION AND SUMMARY

Introduction	1
1. INTRODUCTION	2
1.1 Background	2
1.2 The structure of the book	4
1.3 Chapter guide for the policy economist	5
1.4 Introduction for the economic theorist	5
1.4.1 Welfare analysis and the competitive paradigm	5
1.4.2 Contributions to the analysis of incomplete risk markets	6
1.5 Introduction for the agricultural economist	8
1.6 Caveats and limitations	10
2. THE MAIN ISSUES	12
2.1 Background to the problem	12
2.2 Objectives of commodity price stabilization schemes	12
2.2.1 Raising average prices and incomes	14
2.2.2 Market access and tariff reform	14
2.2.3 Reducing the risks faced by producers	15
2.2.4 Macro-stabilization and development	15
2.2.5 Reducing the risks faced by consumers	16
2.2.6 Revenue raising	16
2.3 Differences between our approach and earlier studies	17
2.3.1 The meaning, consequences, and costs of risk	18
2.3.2 Short-run versus long-run impacts	19
2.3.3 General equilibrium incidence of stabilization	19
2.3.4 Macroeconomic effects	19
2.3.5 Other market distortions	20
2.3.6 General functional specification and the biases of conventional parameterizations	20
2.3.7 Dynamic analysis	21
2.3.8 Partial versus complete stabilization programmes	21

	2.3.9	Distributional versus efficiency effects	21
	2.3.10	Information and expectations	21
	2.3.11	Comparison with other instruments	22

3. SUMMARY OF FINDINGS — 23

3.1 Perfect market hypothesis — 24
3.2 Benefits of price stabilization — 25
- 3.2.1 The meaning of risk and the effects of price stabilization on the riskiness of agricultural income — 26
- 3.2.2 The effects of price stabilization on the variability of output — 29
- 3.2.3 Effects of price stabilization on mean income — 30
- 3.2.4 Effects of price stabilization on consumers — 33
- 3.2.5 The infeasibility of total stabilization and the desirability of partial stabilization schemes — 34
- 3.2.6 Macroeconomic benefits — 35

3.3 The costs of commodity price stabilization schemes — 36
- 3.3.1 Responses of the private sector to a commodity price stabilization scheme — 37
  - 3.3.1.1 The substitution of public for private storage — 37
  - 3.3.1.2 Production decisions of farmers — 38
- 3.3.2 The costs of stabilization in a dynamic stochastic setting — 39

3.4 Some alternative proposals — 39
- 3.4.1 The establishment of better futures markets — 41
- 3.4.2 The income stabilization scheme — 42
- 3.4.3 The establishment of better borrowing facilities for producing countries — 43
- 3.4.4 The establishment of better credit markets within LDCs — 43

3.5 The empirical results — 43

4. STATEMENT OF THE PROBLEM — 47

4.1 The causes of price variability — 47
- 4.1.1 Demand variability — 49
  - 4.1.1.1 Systematic demand variability — 49
  - 4.1.1.2 Non-systematic demand variability — 49
- 4.1.2 Supply variability — 50
  - 4.1.2.1 Systematic supply variability — 50
  - 4.1.2.2 Non-systematic supply variability — 51
- 4.1.3 Arbitrageurs and speculators — 51
- 4.1.4 Government — 52

4.2 Consequences of commodity price stabilization — 52

Part II FUNDAMENTALS: SUPPLY AND DEMAND UNDER RISK

Introduction 57

5. COMPETITIVE SUPPLY WITH RISK-NEUTRAL FARMERS 59
   5.1 Introduction 59
   5.2 Competitive supply without risk 60
   5.3 Competitive supply with risk-neutral farmers 63
      5.3.1 Pitfalls in graphical analysis 67

6. SUPPLY WITH RISK-AVERSE FARMERS 69
   6.1 Introduction 69
   6.2 The meaning of risk aversion 69
      6.2.1 Measuring risk aversion 72
      6.2.2 Parameterizing utility functions 73
   6.3 Measures of risk 76
   6.4* Comparative statics of risk analysis 80
      6.4.1 Effect of risk on effort 81
      6.4.2 Effect of risk on welfare 83
      6.4.3 Stability and comparative statics 83
   6.5 Mean-variance analysis 85
      6.5.1* Properties of the log-normal distribution 88
      6.5.2 Quadratic approximations and Taylor series expansions 90
   6.6 Measuring the benefits of price and income stabilization 92

7. EMPIRICAL MEASUREMENTS OF PRODUCERS' ATTITUDES TO RISK 96
   7.1 Distinguishing among alternative hypotheses 96
      7.1.1 Risk-taking in a multi-period context 99
   7.2 Empirical evidence 100
   7.3 Experimental determination of attitudes to risk 101
      7.3.1 Interpreting the evidence 103
   7.4 Other empirical studies of attitudes to risk 105
   7.5 The magnitude of income risk 108

8. THEORY OF CONSUMER DEMAND 111
   8.1 Introduction 111
   8.2* Duality, indirect utility functions, and the expenditure function 112
   8.3* Attitudes towards risk 116
   8.4 The specification of demand risk and utility functions 118

9.* CONSUMER BENEFITS OF PRICE STABILIZATION 122
   9.1 Introduction 122
   9.2 Efficiency and transfer benefits 123
   9.3 Income variability alone 124

9.4	Supply variability alone	125
9.5	Combining demand and supply variability	126
	Appendix: Derivation of formulae	129

10. MARKET EQUILIBRIUM WITH RATIONAL EXPECTATIONS — 131
10.1 Introduction — 131
10.2 The nature of expectations — 131
10.3 The efficiency of rational expectations equilibria — 136
10.4 Simple models of rational expectations with supply risk — 137
10.5 Concluding remarks — 141

11. PRICE DYNAMICS, EXPECTATIONS, AND ADJUSTMENTS — 142
11.1 Introduction — 142
11.2 Two models of incorrect expectations — 143
    11.2.1 Ignoring correlations — 143
    11.2.2 Adaptive expectations and the cobweb — 148
11.3 Empirical tests of rational expectations — 152
11.4 Learning and reasonable expectations — 153
    11.4.1 Obtaining information — 154
    11.4.2 Processing information — 156
11.5 The efficiency of expectations — 157
11.6 Conclusions — 158

Part III   MARKET EQUILIBRIUM
Introduction — 161

12. SHARING AND REDUCING RISK — 163
12.1 Risk-sharing activities — 164
    12.1.1 Limitations on risk-spreading and risk-sharing — 165
    12.1.2 Mechanisms for risk-spreading — 167
    12.1.3 Implications for the assessment of price stabilization schemes — 168
12.2 Risk-reducing activities — 169
    12.2.1 The choice of technique — 170
    12.2.2 Crop diversification — 170
    12.2.3* Implications — 172
    12.2.4 Other actions which affect the risk borne by producers — 175
12.3 Conclusions — 175

13.* FUTURES MARKETS AND RISK REDUCTION — 177
13.1 Futures markets and storage — 178
13.2 The risk-reducing role of futures markets — 181
13.3 Futures markets — hedging and speculation — 183
    13.3.1 Futures markets for commodities with no storage — 183
    13.3.2 Equilibrium in the futures market — 185

			Contents	xi
		13.3.3 Comparisons with perfect price stabilization	187
		13.3.4 Future markets for continuously stocked commodities	188
	13.4	The supply response of introducing futures markets	190
	13.5	Conclusions	191
		Appendix: Properties of joint normal distributions	193
14.	STORAGE AND SAVINGS		195
	14.1	Storage	195
		14.1.1 The effect of storage on price stability	197
	14.2	The effects of private storage on public buffer stocks	199
	14.3*	Savings	201
		14.3.1 Asset integration and the perceived cost of risk	204
15.*	THE EFFICIENCY OF MARKET EQUILIBRIUM		207
	15.1	Introduction	207
	15.2	A simple model with identical farmers and consumers	212
		15.2.1 Farmers	212
		15.2.2 Consumers	213
		15.2.3 Market equilibrium	214
	15.3	The inefficiency of market equilibrium	214
		15.3.1 Introduction	214
		15.3.2 Constrained Pareto efficient allocations	215
		15.3.3 Redundancy of risk markets and constrained efficiency	217
	15.4	Conditions for constrained Pareto efficiency	218
		15.4.1 Necessary and sufficient conditions for redundancy of risk markets	218
		15.4.2 Necessary conditions for constrained Pareto efficiency	220
	15.5	Restrictions on technology which ensure efficiency	225
		15.5.1 Multiplicative risk	225
		15.5.2 Costless choice of techniques	227
	15.6	The magnitude of the distortions	228
	15.7	Optimal corrective tax policy	231
		15.7.1 Conclusions on market efficiency with identical producers	232
	15.8	Imperfectly correlated output risk	232
	15.9	Conclusions	235
16.	INFORMATION AND MARKET EQUILIBRIUM		238
	16.1	Introduction	238
	16.2*	Futures markets	239
	16.3	Implications	243
	16.4	Information and commodity price stabilization	244

Part IV PRICE STABILIZATION WITH NO SUPPLY RESPONSE

Introduction   247

17. THE THEORY OF PARTIAL PRICE STABILIZATION   249
17.1 The definition of price stabilization   249
17.2 The welfare effect of stabilization   252
    17.2.1 The welfare effects on the three participants 253
    17.2.2 Efficiency and distributional effects   254
17.3 The total efficiency benefits of price stabilization   255
17.4 Stabilizing variable demand   258

18.* DETERMINANTS OF THE DISTRIBUTIONAL IMPACT OF PRICE STABILIZATION   259
18.1 Benefits to risk-neutral producers   260
    18.1.1 Stabilizing price with supply variability   260
        18.1.1.1 The effects of a little price stabilization 261
        18.1.1.2 Effects of slight destabilization 261
        18.1.1.3 Total stabilization versus no stabilization 262
    18.1.2 Stabilizing price with variable demand   262
        18.1.2.1 Additive risk   264
        18.1.2.2 Multiplicative demand risk   264
        18.1.2.3 Multiplicative inverse risk   266
    18.1.3 Including buffer profits   266
18.2 Price stabilization with risk-averse producers   267
18.3 The consumer benefits of price stabilization   269
    18.3.1 Stabilizing price with variable supply   269
    18.3.2 Stabilizing price with variable demand   270
18.4 Conclusions   271

19. EFFECTS OF MARKET DISTORTION   272
19.1 Introduction   272
19.2 A simple linear model of distorted trade   276
    19.2.1 Linear trade policies   279
    19.2.2 Non-linear trade policy   280
19.3 Conclusions   282

20. ESTIMATES OF THE BENEFITS OF PRICE STABILIZATION   284
20.1 Introduction   284
20.2 Measurement problems   285
    20.2.1 The instability facing individual countries   289
    20.2.2 Summary   292
20.3 The benefits of price stabilization   293
    20.3.1 The costs of price stabilization   294
    20.3.2 The distributive and risk-reducing effects of price stabilization 294
        20.3.2.1 Producers   295

	20.3.2.2 Consumers	295
20.4	Alternatives to buffer stocks	297
20.5	Conclusions	298

Part V SUPPLY RESPONSES TO STABILIZATION

Introduction — 301

21.* THE SIMPLE THEORY OF SUPPLY RESPONSE TO PRICE STABILIZATION — 304

- 21.1 A model of supply under price risk — 304
  - 21.1.1 Equilibrium without price stabilization — 305
  - 21.1.2 The stability of equilibrium — 306
- 21.2 A general characterization of stabilization schemes — 308
- 21.3 The effects of equilibrium homothetic price stabilization schemes — 310
  - 21.3.1 The effect on consumers — 313
- 21.4 The evaluation of particular schemes — 313
  - 21.4.1 A small degree of stabilization — 313
  - 21.4.2 Small departures from complete stabilization — 314
- 21.5 The distributional impacts of stabilization with diverse producers — 315
- 21.6 Demand-induced variability — 316
- 21.7 Concluding remarks — 317

22. RISK AVERSION AND SUPPLY RESPONSE: A GEOMETRICAL ANALYSIS — 318

- 22.1 Introduction — 318
- 22.2 The model — 320
- 22.3 Outline of the diagrammatic approach — 320
  - 22.3.1 The producer's indifference curve — 324
  - 22.3.2 The iso-effort locus — 324
  - 22.3.3 The short-run feasibility locus — 325
  - 22.3.4 The long-run feasibility locus — 325
- 22.4 Effect on producers — 326
  - 22.4.1 The short-run impact on producers — 326
  - 22.4.2 The long-run impact on producers — 327
- 22.5 Consumers' welfare and Pareto optimality of the market equilibrium — 329
- 22.6* The allocation of buffer profits — 332
- 22.7 Concluding remarks — 334

23. PARETO-INFERIOR TRADE AND PRICE STABILIZATION — 336

- 23.1 Introduction — 336
- 23.2 Comparison of autarky and free trade — 339
  - 23.2.1 The model — 339

	23.2.2	Farmers' allocation of land	340
	23.2.3	Autarky versus free trade	342
	23.2.4	Welfare analysis	345
23.3	Multiple equilibria and stability		348
	23.3.1	Boundary equilibria	350
	23.3.2	Stability	350
	23.3.3*	Example: Risk-neutral farmers	350
	23.3.4*	Stability of symmetric equilibrium for infinitely risk-averse farmers	351
23.4	Partial versus general equilibrium analysis		352
23.5	Robustness of the analysis		353
	23.5.1	Alternative specifications of consumers' demand curves	354
	23.5.2	Alternative specifications of risk	355
	23.5.3	Alternative specifications of producers' utility functions	355
	23.5.4	Two factors and comparative advantage	355
23.6	Concluding remarks		356
	Appendix 1* Conditions for boundary equilibria		358
	Appendix 2* Stability analysis		360

24. **TRADE POLICY** — 362
    - 24.1 Introduction — 362
        - 24.1.1 Symmetric trade policies — 362
    - 24.2 Effect of allowing a small amount of trade — 367
    - 24.3 Effects of a small restriction on free trade — 368
        - 24.3.1 Quotas versus tariffs — 369
    - 24.4 Financial markets — 370
    - 24.5 Conclusions — 371

Part VI MACROECONOMIC REPERCUSSIONS

Introduction — 373

25. **EXPORT-LED PRICE INSTABILITY** — 377
    - 25.1 The model — 377
    - 25.2 Perfect wage and price flexibility — 379
    - 25.3 Price rigidities and unemployment — 381
        - 25.3.1 Minimum wage below critical level: full employment — 382
        - 25.3.2 Minimum wage above critical level: periodic unemployment — 384
        - 25.3.3 Fixing the minimum wage — 388
    - 25.4 A simple model of inflation — 388
    - 25.5 Lessons from the models — 389
        - Appendix: The feasible range for the minimum wage — 391

26.	BALANCE-OF-PAYMENTS POLICY	392
27.	EXPORT INSTABILITY AND GROWTH	395
28.	INTERNATIONAL INSTABILITY	399

Part VII DYNAMIC CONSIDERATIONS

Introduction 403

29. BUFFER STOCKS 406
   29.1 Buffer stocks as stochastic processes 406
   29.2 The choice of stock rule 409
      29.2.1 Implications of the competitive storage rule 412
      29.2.2 Some simple examples of stock rules 414
      29.2.3 The pure random walk model 416
      29.2.4 Famine stock rule 418
   29.3 Conclusions 420

30.* OPTIMAL COMMODITY STOCKPILING RULES 421
   30.1 Introduction 421
   30.2 Approximate solutions 423
      30.2.1 Average stock size 426
      30.2.2 The degree of price stabilization 426
      30.2.3 The cost of increased price stability 427
   30.3 The benefits of price stabilization 428
   30.4 The bias in the competitive stock rule 430
      30.4.1 Extensions 432
      30.4.2 Comparisons with alternative stocking rules 432
   30.5 Conclusions 433
   Appendix: Derivation of approximate stock rule 435

31. EPILOGUE 439
   REFERENCES 446
   INDEX 452

List of Tables

2.1	Recent declines in commodity prices for 'core' commodities	13
6.1	Benefits of stabilizing the cocoa price by 50 per cent	95
7.1	Results of Binswanger's experiments	101
7.2	Risk alternatives for representative unirrigated farm, India	108
7.3	Coefficient of variation of income of Minnesota farmers	109
13.1	Variability of prices 1952–68	180
20.1	Measures of price instability 1951–75	287
20.2	Instability facing Nigerian cocoa producers	288
20.3	Shares in total exports of six commodities for selected countries, 1970–3 average	290
20.4	Instabilities by country and commodity 1951–75	291
20.5	Income instability	292
20.6	Net efficiency benefits of total price stabilization	293
20.7	Storage costs and returns	295
20.8	Producer benefits of complete price stabilization	296
20.9	Consumers' residual stabilization benefit	297
20.10	Risk benefits from successful income stabilization	298
29.1	Probabilities of stock levels	419
29.2	Marginal costs and benefits of capacity expansion	419

A Note on Notation

The alphabet has a limited number of letters, so some necessarily stand for different variables in different places as the following list shows. Random variables are indicated with a tilde, $\tilde{q}$, where we wish to draw attention to the randomness, but not always where the variable is usually random, like price, p. Expected values, that is, averages, are indicated by a bar, and the expectation operator, which takes the average value of the expression to its right, is E. Thus $Ep = \bar{p}$ is the average price, $p(\bar{Q})$ is the price of the average quantity (usually different from $\bar{p}$). In general we work with coefficients of variation, CV, of random variables rather than variances, since they are, unlike variances, dimensionless. Thus $\sigma^2 = \text{Var}(Q)/\bar{Q}^2$ is typically the squared CV of output. Subscripts either refer to variables; σ_p is the CV of price, or derivatives: V_I is $\partial V/\partial I$, or indices (usually i, j, t) indicating the person, state, or date.

Ordinary derivatives are usually indicated by a dash: f', f'', and partial derivatives by subscripted letters: f_x.

List of Abbreviations and Symbols

ABBREVIATIONS

AC	average cost
Corr	correlation coefficient
CV	coefficient of variation
Cov	covariance
CS	consumer surplus
EUV	export unit value
IMF	International Monetary Fund
IPC	Integrated Programme for Commodities
LDC	less developed country
log	logarithm
MA	moving average
MAD	mean absolute deviation
MC	marginal cost
SD	standard deviation
Var	variance

SYMBOLS

$\simeq, \cong, \approx$	approximately equal
$\equiv$	definitionally equal
$\tilde{\theta}$	indicates θ is a random variable
$\bar{x}$	expected value of x
f', f''	derivatives
t', t''	different dates

Key to frequently recurring symbols

A	Coefficient of absolute risk aversion
e	Exponential
E	Expectation operator
R	Coefficient of relative risk aversion (of producer, R^c of consumer)
ϵ	Price elasticity of demand
θ	Risk, state of the world, random variable (usually supply risk)
Λ	Log normal variate
Π	Product notation
σ	Coefficient of variation, subscript refers to variable
Δ	Difference operator

Part I

Introduction and Summary

The book as a whole contains seven parts, each preceded by a short introduction. The first part of this book is, as its title suggests, intended to describe the structure and contents of the book, to guide the reader, and present a brief summary of the main findings in a non-technical language. Chapter 1 contains separate chapter guides for each of the three audiences who will be interested in our results — policy makers, economic theorists, and agricultural economists.

Since different people have very different ideas about the nature and objectives of commodity schemes, Chapter 2 discusses these various objectives, limits our study, and explains how it differs from earlier studies. Chapter 3 presents, in a fairly non-technical way, the major substantive conclusions of our study. Finally, Chapter 4 discusses the causes and consequences of price variability, and hence provides a framework for the subsequent analysis.

Chapter 1

Introduction

1.1 Background

This book is concerned with assessing the desirability of stabilizing agricultural commodity prices by means of a commodity buffer stock scheme. Agricultural commodities are extremely important to most of the less developed countries (LDCs) — in 1976 56 per cent of the non-oil exports of LDCs were primary products and roughly one-third of non-oil exports were produced in the agricultural sector. Moreover, these statistics understate the importance of commodity price instabilities as faced by particular countries: at least twenty-six LDCs depended on one commodity for at least 50 per cent of their export earnings during 1974-6 (excluding oil exporters) and a further eleven earned between 40 and 50 per cent from one commodity. At the same time, their prices have been — by any standard — extremely volatile. For instance, the decline in prices from the highest level attained in the period 1974 to August 1975 was 67 per cent for sugar, 58 per cent for sisal, more than 40 per cent for cotton and rubber, and more than 25 per cent for cocoa and jute.

For the thirty-seven LDCs heavily dependent on a single export commodity, the volatility in commodity prices may impose very large costs. As a basis of comparison, the largest post-war recession in the United States involved a reduction in national income from the preceding year of 8 per cent, and, if the 1946 downturn is excluded, only 2 per cent. The Great Depression involved a total reduction of national income of 29 per cent spread over a four-year period, with the largest annual decline of 15 per cent. But a farmer producing one of the crops mentioned above, if he had been able to avoid any other source of variation in his income and had stabilized his output, might have had a reduction in his gross income of between 25 and 67 per cent (depending on the difference between world and local producer prices), and a reduction in his net income of an even greater amount.

It is no wonder then that at least since the end of the First World War governments have been intensively concerned about the instability of primary prices. Periodic dramatic collapses in prices (such as occurred in the early 1920s and during the Great Depression) have typically precipitated discussions about international commodity schemes, and in the past fifty years there have been seventeen major agreements in nine commodities: sugar (4), coffee (3), cocoa (1), tea (1), rubber (2), copper (2), tin (1), bauxite (1), and wheat (2). (See McNicol, 1978.)

During the past few years, there has been increasing interest in the formation of a general commodity price stabilization programme, and it was this growing interest that provided the immediate impetus for this book. Although we discuss in passing a number of alternative schemes that have been proposed, we are mainly concerned with price stabilization by means of buffer stock schemes. These put a certain amount of output into storage in years in which there is a large harvest, thus increasing price from what it would have been; and sell output from storage in years in which there is a small harvest, thus reducing price from what it would have been.

Although we are concerned with forming a judgement about the specific proposals which have been put forward — our general conclusion is that it is unlikely that such schemes would have a significant beneficial effect on the developing countries, and it is quite possible that they may even be made worse off — we are more concerned with developing a *methodology* with which this and other important policy questions in which risk plays a critical role can be assessed.

Several alternative approaches have been employed in the literature, involving the use of econometric techniques and simulation exercises. It is our belief that these approaches can be very useful, but only after one knows what it is that one wants to measure when one wishes to form an assessment of the costs and benefits of such a scheme, and only after one knows what parameters are likely to be important in determining the magnitudes of those costs and benefits. As we shall show, the standard specification (e.g. of linear demand and supply curves) strongly *biases* the results which emerge from the analysis even before the empirical study is undertaken.

The approach that we take is to formulate the simplest model which we believe captures the features of the economy most relevant for the question at hand. After formulating the model, we subject it to analysis in a number of different ways. In some cases we parameterize the various functions, and attempt to obtain an explicit solution, to see how the market equilibrium changes, for instance, when the degree of commodity price stabilization changes. When we do this, however, we then attempt to see how sensitive the results are to the particular parameterization employed, either by employing a quite different parameterization, or, more generally, simplifying the model still further in some dimension (e.g. by assuming that there are only two states, a good harvest and a bad harvest) which allows us to analyse the model keeping a fair degree of generality in other dimensions (e.g. general utility functions). In all cases we attempt to test the robustness of the model to slight changes in the assumptions. As in many other problems in economics, the total effect is a compound of a number of different effects, not all of which work in the same direction. Some of the effects we identify are probably not very important, others are. It is thus imperative, in any work of this kind, to obtain some order-of-magnitude feeling for the kinds of numbers involved, and this we do throughout the book.

It is important, however, to keep in mind the reason for these calculations: they are not intended to provide refined estimates of the costs or benefits of a commodity price stabilization scheme. Rather, they are intended to provide some feeling for the relative importance of different factors and to provide some direction for future empirical research. That research should be directed to establishing more precise values for parameters which appear to be important on the basis of our rough estimates, hence the need to model and roughly quantify the different effects. Often our models will suggest particular econometric formulations which can be used in this research, or identify the way in which particular effects, such as risk, should be measured and included in the formulation.

1.2 The structure of the book

We had three different audiences in mind when we wrote the book — economic theorists, agricultural economists, and policy-makers — each with different interests and skills. In the next three sections we address each of these in turn in order to guide them through the book, identify the issues with which they will be most concerned, and mention the main contributions which the book makes. The final section of this chapter points to some of the more critical limitations of our analysis. Any respectable academic work must be accompanied by a list of caveats, in which the authors inform the reader that the authors are aware of the limitations of their analysis, and this is even more true when the book is directed towards policy-makers. The list provided in this chapter is not exhaustive, since we mention specific caveats at appropriate points in the body of the text.

The book as a whole is divided into seven parts, of which the first part is an extended introduction and summary. Since different people have very different ideas about the nature and objectives of commodity schemes, in Chapter 2 we discuss the different objectives and delimit our study. Even so delimited, our analysis of commodity price stabilization differs markedly from most of the earlier studies. It is important to understand the reason for this, and the remainder of the chapter is devoted to clarifying how and why our study differs from most of the earlier studies.

Chapter 3 presents, in a fairly non-technical way, the major substantive conclusions of our study. Finally, Chapter 4 discusses, in broad outline, the causes and consequences of price variability. The discussion is designed to provide a framework for the subsequent analysis.

Parts II and III present the fundamentals of market equilibrium in the presence of risk. Much of it can be viewed as an application of recent developments in the economics of risk to an analysis of agricultural markets, but several of the chapters present new developments. Part II presents the more basic supply and demand analysis, while the topics covered in Part III are somewhat more advanced, although no less essential for an understanding of the issues at hand.

Part IV is concerned with assessing the costs and benefits of price stabilization under the assumption that producers do not change their behaviour as a result of the price stabilization scheme, while Part V shows how these results have to be modified when producers can change their production decisions (choice of technique, level of inputs, crop mix, etc.). Most of the book is thus concerned with the analysis of competitive market equilibrium on the assumption that prices adjust quickly to equilibrate supply and demand at full employment; and stays within the confines of microeconomics. Obviously, this is an important restriction which should be examined, and so Part VI addresses some of the macroeconomic issues raised by commodity price instability.

Finally, it is clear that any buffer stock scheme introduces a dynamic element into the market, for it is specifically concerned to transfer goods intertemporally. Fortunately, many of the problems we are concerned with can be discussed within a static framework, but some problems, particularly the design of a set of rules for the stabilization programme, can only be discussed in a dynamic framework, and Part VII is devoted to these.

1.3 Chapter guide for the policy economist

In a sense the remainder of Part I is an extended introduction, summary, and chapter guide for the policy economist. In addition, we suggest reading the introductions to each part and chapter together with the following sections. We recommend a quick reading of Chapters 5 and 6, which introduce the main concepts for our analysis of production or supply under risk. Section 6.6 derives the formulae for the producer benefits of stabilization. Chapter 7 discusses the theoretical and empirical evidence for attitudes to risk in a not too technical way. Chapter 12 presents a general survey of the responses available to agents confronted with risk, while Chapter 16 discusses the important and complex relationships between information, prices (especially prices on futures markets), and market equilibrium. The definition of price stabilization is set out and examined in the first part of Chapter 17, while Chapter 18 examines the importance of different econometric specifications of supply and demand.

The centre-piece of the analysis from the policy viewpoint is Chapter 20, which estimates the benefits of price stabilization. Finally, Chapter 29 gives a simple introduction to the dynamic analysis which is needed for the derivation of buffer stock rules. These rules are derived in Chapter 30, in which we suggest reading sections 30.1 and 30.4 onwards. The Epilogue draws out some of the conclusions.

We now suggest you turn to the last part of this chapter where we discuss some important caveats to bear in mind on what follows, and then to the remaining chapters in Part I, though the remaining sections of this chapter should also help clarify the structure of the book.

1.4 Introduction for the economic theorist

1.4.1 *Welfare analysis and the competitive paradigm*

Over the past few years, two, quite opposing approaches to the analysis of important applied economic problems have developed. One approach begins with the presumption that the allocation of resources provided by the market is approximately competitive and hence Pareto efficient; the market should be interfered with only if a significant 'market failure' occurs, and then only with caution. In particular, redistributive policies should be designed to minimize any interference with otherwise competitive markets. Those who hold this view look askance at proposals involving systematic government intervention in the market of the kind envisaged by commodity price stabilization schemes.

The other approach believes that market failures are so extensive, and that the competitive equilibrium paradigm is so far from providing an adequate description of the workings of the economy, that to rely on it for policy guidance is mistaken. Although those who subscribe to this view are often hostile to theory, some theoretical support for the limited applicability of the perfectly competitive model is provided by recent results in the theory of the second best. This literature has been largely negative in spirit, suggesting how difficult it is to prescribe correct remedies when even a few of the critical conditions for optimality of the market equilibrium are not satisfied.

The view to which we subscribe is that the absence of the complete set of risk markets which are required for the optimality of market equilibrium is a sufficiently important market failure to cast serious doubt on the usefulness of the perfect market hypothesis for policy purposes, at least where the central policy concern is with the allocation of risk-bearing, as it is here. On the other hand, we believe that economic theory can shed considerable light on critical policy questions; we do not subscribe to the prevailing mood of atheoretical agnosticism.

1.4.2 *Contributions to the analysis of incomplete risk markets*

For the general economist, this book can be viewed as an exercise in the analysis — descriptive and normative — of an important class of second-best problems arising from the absence of a complete set of risk markets. There are several aspects of our analysis to which we would like to call attention.

(i) *Partial equilibrium analysis of price uncertainty*. Most of the economic analysis of uncertainty has focused on the implications of *income uncertainty*. Uncertainties about relative prices (including the relative price of consumption today versus consumption tomorrow, i.e. uncertainty about rates of return) are, however, extremely important and not very well understood. (See, especially Chapters 6 and 17.)

(ii) *General equilibrium analysis of uncertainty*. We develop in this book a simple general equilibrium analysis which has some interesting — perhaps surprising — results.

First, rational expectations equilibria are not in general Pareto efficient. This proposition, and the nature of the resulting biases are explicitly analysed in Chapter 15.

Second, free trade may be Pareto inferior to autarky, i.e. consumers and producers in each of two countries may be made worse off by opening trade between them; equivalently, restricting speculative activity *may* constitute a Pareto improvement (Chapters 23 and 24).

Third, the impact and long-run equilibrium effects of policies which affect risk, and in particular, price stabilization schemes, may differ not only quantitatively, but also qualitatively (Chapter 22).

(iii) *Macroeconomic implications of price rigidities.* Most of the models of uncertainty that have been analysed to date have been equilibrium models in which prices and wages are flexible. We develop some simple macroeconomic models in which the implications of rigidities can be explicitly analysed. The model provides a qualitative analysis of a 'fixed price economy' which is subjected to a particular class of exogenous shocks.

(iv) *Dynamic analysis of buffer stock schemes.* The analysis of optimal buffer stock schemes (in one version of the problem) is equivalent to the problem of optimal savings with borrowing constraints. Although the problem of optimal savings under uncertainty has been extensively studied, limitations on borrowing have usually been ignored. These constraints have a significant effect on the nature of the optimal savings rule. We develop a general technique for obtaining approximations to the optimal buffer stock, as well as analysing certain important qualitative aspects of the optimal rules. (See Part VII.)

(v) *General equilibrium incidence analysis.* In the theory of taxation, the importance of tracing out the full consequences of how a tax on a factor in one sector is borne by the same factor in other sectors, has long been appreciated. In general, the tax does not just affect the factor on which it is nominally levied, but typically part of it is borne by other factors and part of it is borne by consumers. Under particular conditions, it is possible to obtain a precise analysis of the incidence of any tax (Harberger, 1964 and for a somewhat more general treatment, see Atkinson and Stiglitz, 1980). This kind of incidence analysis is potentially equally important for any government programme. We show how such an incidence analysis can be performed for commodity price stabilization: it turns out in fact that the partial equilibrium or impact analysis which ignores repercussions elsewhere is not only quantitatively wrong, but it may also be qualitatively incorrect in predicting the direction of response (Chapters 6, 22, and 24).

(vi) *Methodological contributions to the analysis of risk.* Finally, we hope our techniques of analysis will be found useful in a variety of situations. We should, in particular, mention the diagrammatic techniques of Chapter 22 for analysing the impact and general equilibrium effects of a change in risk, and our analysis of the effects of uncertainty on trade in Chapter 24. The two-state diagrammatic approach can also be used, as in Chapter 15, to illustrate the sources of inefficiency. The analysis of Chapters 17 and 18 shows how general properties of convexity can be applied to the study of price risk.

(vii) *Methodological contributions: cost–benefit analysis of risk-related public policies.* It is also our hope that the general procedures we develop here for cost–benefit analysis under uncertainty will be applicable to a wide variety of situations where one of the explicit consequences of the policy is a change in the risk faced by various agents within the economy.

For instance, many decisions concerning the development of new energy technologies involve many of the kinds of considerations discussed in this work. These developments may alter in a significant way the probability distribution of prices which will prevail in the future, just as commodity price stabilization schemes alter the price distribution of agricultural commodities.

Even within agriculture there are a number of other problems for which risk analysis is central, e.g. the introduction of new seeds, and the application of fertilizers, pesticides, etc. We hope that readers will find some of our techniques of analysis useful in these other contexts.

1.5 Introduction for the agricultural economist

The economics of agriculture has long proved a fruitful source of insight into economics generally, with its concepts of rent and the margin of production. Markets for agricultural commodities lend themselves to the competitive story of homogenous products and individually unimportant agents each taking prices as given, while the pervasive government intervention in domestic agricultural markets provides many of the simplest examples of the distortionary effect of intervention in the competitive market.

Not surprisingly, agricultural economists were among the first economists to realize the importance of risk to an understanding of the functioning of the economy and to attempt to develop formal models for analysing its consequences. Heady (1952), for instance, devotes nearly a quarter of his classic text to the subject; and almost any recent issue of the *American Journal of Agricultural Economics* has at least one article related to the subject. Indeed, the absence of adequate insurance markets has provided a significant part of the rationale for government intervention, and particularly for government price stabilization programmes.

In spite of its importance, our understanding of the effect of risk on agricultural production remains limited. This is not surprising, for the concepts of risk and of risk aversion, although intuitive, are hard to define precisely. As a result, the literature has tended to employ special parameterizations. These parameterizations may, however, seriously bias the kinds of results obtained, and in any case limit the generality of the analysis.

In Chapter 6 we provide a precise definition of risk and risk aversion, which is both general and at the same time sufficiently concrete to enable us to obtain meaningful results concerning the effect of risk on agricultural production. It enables us to identify the special properties associated with the particular parameterizations which have been employed extensively in the literature.

The conventional treatment of risk is that it lowers the effective rate of return (by the 'risk premium') which would lead to lower work effort. But there is another argument which suggests that farmers work harder as a result of risk, attempting to provide a margin for error. Our definition of risk and risk aversion shows that both cases are possible, and a second contribution of this book is to characterize situations where risk is likely to lead to higher levels of effort, and contrast them with the conventional response of lower effort. (See Chapter 6.)

The means by which individual farmers can respond to changes in risk are varied. One of the objectives of our analysis is to discuss these various responses, and to show how the availability of these various methods for *sharing*, *reducing*, and *shifting* risk implies that the effect of a change in risk on the level of output of a particular crop may be markedly different from that which would have occurred had the farmer been limited, say, simply to varying the level of input, the choice of technique of production, or the choice of crops. Chapter 12 provides a general survey of these issues, and Chapters 13 and 14 specific examples.

Although the focus of our analysis is theoretical, our results have important implications for the estimation of agricultural supply functions. Not only do we argue that risk needs to be taken into account, but our analysis suggests that certain commonly employed specifications may be theoretically suspect. This applies both to the estimation of attitudes to risk (Chapter 7) and to the specification of risk itself, and of demand (Chapter 18).

Although much of agricultural economics has been concerned to develop our understanding of the behaviour of the individual farmer, recent discussions of commodity price stabilization serve to remind us that markets for most primary commodities are international. What happens in one country affects prices in another. In particular, although it has long been recognized that the market price is determined by the interaction of demand and supply, i.e. the demand from all countries and the supply from all producers, the fact that the price *distribution* is determined by the interaction of the *distribution* of the demand and supply functions does not seem so widely recognized. Thus, the magnitude and nature of the risk faced by any individual producer is, in part, a result of the variability in supply of some other group of producers. These interactions are complex — far more complex than the simple interaction of non-stochastic demand and supply curves; but any analysis of the effects of a major policy change such as the stabilization of prices requires that they be taken into account. We discuss their effect on producers in Chapters 5 and 6, on consumers in Chapter 9, and on the market in Chapters 10 and 11. In Chapter 19 we show how these impacts are modified by distortions, and in Chapter 23 we examine the interaction of different sources of risk through international trade.

One reason for the complexity of the interactions is that there are many important intertemporal aspects to the analysis: farmers' actions depend critically on their expectations concerning prices which are likely to prevail in the future. But those expectations are likely to have been influenced by prices which occurred in previous periods, which in turn depended in part on the earlier actions based on earlier beliefs about prices, and so on. It is therefore important to enquire how farmers form their expectations, how they learn that their estimation procedures are misleading, and how they modify their forecasts. Given the importance of expectations, we develop as a bench-mark the theory of rational expectations in Chapter 10, which has the characteristic that, given what the farmer can observe, no further learning can take place, and he would not wish to modify his method of forecasting or decision-making. We compare this bench-mark with alternative methods of forecasting in Chapter 11, where a stochastic version of a cobweb model is analysed. We show that the stability of the model depends explicitly not only on the shape of the demand and supply curves (as earlier discussions have pointed out) but also on the speed of learning (adaptation). Slow speeds of adaptation lead to stability, but the economy may be far from the rational expectations equilibrium most of the time; faster speeds of learning mean that the economy may be more efficient, if it converges to an equilibrium, but it is less likely to converge. Then, in Chapter 16, we discuss other sources of information, especially futures markets, which may assist the farmer in his decision-making.

Finally, although public policy towards agriculture has long been a subject of academic interest, the discussions have, for the most part, employed old Marshallian surplus analysis which we argue is particularly unsatisfactory in the presence of risk. Moreover, many of the earlier studies have used special parameterizations which prejudge the distributional issues, as we show in Chapter 18.

We set out the main differences between our approach and the conventional analaysis in Chapter 2, which also directs the reader to the places in the book where specific issues are taken up. In brief, our analysis is characterized by (a) an attempt to ascertain the incidence of any policy measure both in the short run and in the long run; and (b) an attempt to identify precisely the source of market failure which might necessitate government intervention in the market and the implications that this market failure has for the benefits and costs of the public programme. It is the absence of perfect risk and futures markets which, in our judgement, makes commodity stabilization schemes so potentially attractive, and it is, therefore, the effect of price stabilization on risk-bearing and risk-taking which provides the focus of our analysis.

1.6 Caveats and limitations

Any study with policy implications, such as this, needs to be hedged about with caveats and the overriding cautionary remark that the policy implications only follow if the models from which they derive are adequate descriptions of reality. Ours is no exception, but the caveats carry even greater force, for our aim is primarily methodological and theoretical. Ultimately, judgements concerning the desirability of any commodity price stabilization will depend on certain empirical magnitudes, and a theoretical study cannot, therefore, provide the final answer. But a theoretical study of the kind we have undertaken here can point the way to what numbers to look at; and it can distinguish between 'bad' arguments and 'good' arguments for commodity price stabilization. In some cases, order-of-magnitude estimates of the variables which the theoretical study suggests are critical can be obtained, and these order-of-magnitude estimates can be used to make an informed judgement on whether, with more refined techniques, it would appear that a commodity price stabilization would substantially increase or decrease welfare, or whether the welfare changes — positive or negative — are likely to be small. The empirical results reported in Chapter 20 are presented in that spirit: not as definitive calculations but as order-of-magnitude calculations which, in themselves, seem to us very enlightening.

The second point to stress is that, as in any theoretical study, there is a delicate balance between the generality, detail, and complexity of the model on the one hand, and its tractability on the other. We have opted for a model which is more complex than is generally found in simple policy studies, yet of less generality than is found in traditional general equilibrium analysis. We have attempted to formulate the simplest model which can, at the same time, capture what we consider to be the essential features of the markets being examined. Clearly, there is considerable scope for further development of the models presented here, and one of our aims is to provide the stimulus for further model building, particularly of macroeconomic models of the kind discussed in Part VI.

Third, we need to emphasize that the relative allocation of space devoted to various topics within this book is not only a reflection of our judgement concerning the importance of the topics. Three other considerations played a part: first, we devote more space to those topics on which we have something new to say than to those which have been discussed extensively elsewhere. Second, we devote more space to those topics which are more difficult: there are many important points which can be made simply, and we hope we have done that. Third, there are some topics which we think are probably extremely important but on which we are quite brief, especially macroeconomic and dynamic issues discussed in Parts VI and VII. We would have liked to have been able to say more about these, but at the moment our knowledge in these areas is still relatively undeveloped. We hope that our remarks will at least serve to stimulate further research.

Finally, and more as an apology, we should point out that the literature in this area has been growing rapidly, and although we have attempted to note those studies published before the first draft of this book was completed (December 1977), we have not attempted to reference much of the subsequent literature. We have, however, identified a few surveys and collections of articles which will guide the interested reader through the literature.

Chapter 2

The Main Issues

2.1 Background to the problem

Undoubtedly inspired by the success of the OPEC cartel in raising the price of oil, during the past few years producers of other primary products have brought increasing pressure for the creation of some scheme which would stabilize (it was hoped at a high level) the prices of the commodities which they sell. At the time this book went to press, these pressures had not yet been successful in establishing a commodity price stabilization scheme but resolutions calling for the establishment of an Integrated Programme for Commodities (IPC), covering the ten core commodities identified by UNCTAD as suitable for stockpiling, listed in Table 2.1, were passed in a special meeting of UNCTAD held in Nairobi in May, 1976.

Table 2.1, which is extracted from one of the key supporting documents presented to the conference, demonstrates (in, as we shall argue in Chapter 20, a rather exaggerated way) the magnitude of price instability facing producers of primary commodities. However, even if we take yearly deviations from trend (as opposed to monthly deviations) as an indicator of price variability, Fig. 2.1 demonstrates that the fluctuations for six selected agricultural products have been substantial, by any standard.

However, it is important to remember that the Integrated Programme was always intended to be more than a stabilization scheme. Although buffer stocks were recommended for all core commodities, in all but two cases — cotton and tea — these buffer stocks were to be coupled with supply management measures (UNCTAD, 1975a), typically involving the permanent use of export quotas and/or production controls. In this respect the IPC follows tradition, for most commodity schemes have attempted to control supply.

The debate on the desirability of commodity price stabilization has been confused by the variety of different objectives which such schemes might pursue. In this book we are only concerned with pure price stabilization schemes in which there is no attempt to restrict production or trade. In this chapter we first look at the various objectives which have been proposed for commodity programmes in order to contrast them with pure price stabilization schemes, and then list the ways in which our approach differs from and advances upon the traditional analysis.

2.2 Objectives of commodity price stabilization schemes

The broad objective of all commodity programmes is to improve the welfare of primary commodity producers, or, more generally, the producing countries. The

Table 2.1 *Recent declines in commodity prices for 'core' commodities*

Commodity	Highest price in period 1974–5		Prices in August 1975	Decline from peak	Instability index[a]
	Level (cents per lb)	Month reached	(cents per lb)	%	%
Sugar	56.6	Nov. 1974	18.7	−66.9	109.1
Coffee	88.5	Aug. 1975	88.5	–	22.9
Cocoa	117.2	May 1974	78.3	−33.2	45.9
Tea	71.1	Mar. 1974	60.9	−14.3	14.7
Cotton	103.8	Jan. 1974	59.6	−42.5	28.3
Jute	20.8	Oct. 1974	15.0	−27.8	21.0
Sisal	48.5	June 1974	20.0	−58.7	62.4
Rubber	49.2	Jan. 1974	27.2	−44.7	32.2
Copper	137.5	April 1974	58.0	−57.8	41.9
Tin	415.3	Sept. 1974	306.0	−26.3	42.2

[a] Coefficient of variation of prices over period 1950–74.
Source: UNCTAD (1975a): TD/B/C.1/195.

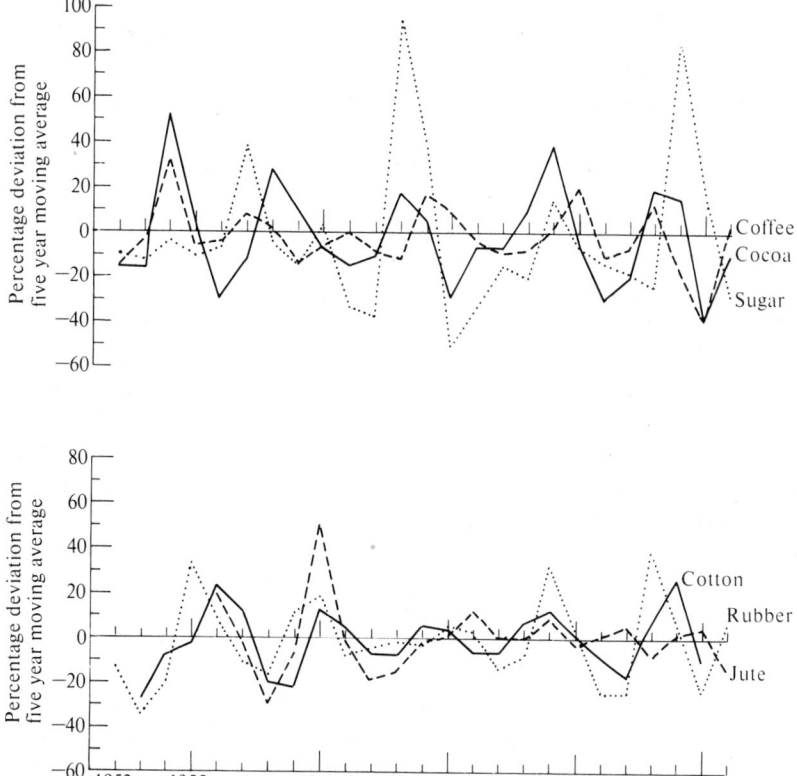

Source: World Bank (1979)

Fig. 2.1 Deviations of six 'core' commodity prices from trend 1952–75

IPC is directed to improving the welfare of LDCs in particular, though it is worth remembering that the developed countries export more primary commodities (excluding oil) than LDCs. Within this broad framework, several distinct objectives can be distinguished.

2.2.1 *Raising average prices and incomes*

One of the main objectives has been to raise the average price of primary commodities. Although it is now generally accepted that the terms of trade between primary commodities and manufactured goods has shown no long-run tendency to decline, there is a widespread belief that the prices of primary commodities, especially agricultural goods, are unjustly low because of the long-standing structure of protection by the importing countries. Not only do these tariffs depress the world price below the free trade level, but quotas and domestic support programmes also restrict the rate of growth of demand for many agricultural commodities. Faced with this market structure, exporting countries have two possible responses — to attempt a negotiated reduction of trade restrictions and/or to attempt to set up a countervailing cartel. Since these are quite distinct objectives, we consider the cartel approach first. The success of OPEC has encouraged other primary producers in the belief that co-operative action which restricted supply would improve their income and welfare. The problem is, of course, how to devise an acceptable agreement limiting output, since it will typically be in the interests of the smaller countries to expand production while benefiting from the raised prices. The other problem is that many LDCs also import primary commodities and would be adversely affected by such cartel action, while the developed countries would either benefit from the raised prices, or, if they opposed it, would undermine the cartel.

While there may be a case for such programmes (perhaps employing a uniform export tax on specific commodities, with the revenue allocated for development) our analysis is confined to pure price stabilization schemes in which there is no restriction on output or trade. As a result we avoid the problem of devising an acceptable agreement on supply restrictions. Nevertheless, we shall argue that even a pure price stabilization scheme will typically affect the level and pattern of supply and may also have significant distributional effects on producers and consumers. Indeed, much of our analysis will be concerned precisely with these distributional effects, which appear to be of the same order of importance as the net (efficiency) benefits of price stabilization.

2.2.2 *Market access and tariff reform*

As remarked above, protective policies against agricultural imports are of long standing, and particularly difficult to dismantle because of their intimate connection with domestic price policies and farm support programmes. Obviously, their removal should improve the revenues of the exporting countries, and in many cases would also improve the welfare of the importers if they could devise a satisfactory compensatory scheme for domestic producers.

Quite apart from their general desirability, such reforms bear on the issue of commodity price stabilization because it has been argued that the trade restrictions are in large part responsible for price instability. The logical approach to price stabilization is therefore to reduce the trade barriers which tend to fragment the world market. Market fragmentation means that small variations in supply can lead to wide fluctuations in the world price. Thus between 1972 and 1974 the US wholesale grain price more than tripled, while in the EEC it rose by 20 per cent, and in the USSR remained almost unchanged. Had the world market been unified (with the same market clearing spot price everywhere) the modest production shortfall need only have induced a small price rise.

Although we agree that tariff reform is the single most attractive approach to the problems facing the LDCs, it is quite distinct from the problem we discuss, which is to assess the impact of buffer stock schemes on the existing market structure. Nevertheless, the fact that trade in many primary commodities is distorted by protective policies raises some important issues for our approach which we discuss in Chapter 19.

2.2.3 *Reducing the risks faced by producers*

We are primarily concerned with the consequences of changing the variability in prices. One of our main arguments is that producers are concerned not so much with price variability as with income variability. There has been considerable confusion between the two alternative objectives of stabilizing prices and stabilizing income. Stabilizing prices might, as we shall see below, lead to increased income variability. This distinction is particularly important if farmers grow several crops whose returns, though individually unstable, are collectively relatively stable. A price stabilization programme for just one commodity might then induce large supply responses and have an adverse effect on prices and returns without reducing income risk.

Indeed, in Chapter 14 we go one step further, for it is not variability in income but in consumption that is ultimately important. We need to ask whether it is more efficient to have a buffer stock for *commodities* (or, at the margin, to subsidize such a buffer stock), to smooth prices, or to develop better methods of 'storing' *income* (or, at the margin, to subsidize the establishment of credit institutions) to smooth consumption directly. These distinctions between price, income, and consumption variability play an important role in our analysis.

2.2.4 *Macro-stabilization and development*

The consequences of price and income variability facing producers spill over to other sectors of the economy. In particular, they may lead to macroeconomic instability — unemployment and inflation — which we explore in Part VI. In addition, there is some concern that the variations in foreign exchange earnings resulting from price variability may have a deleterious effect on the development of LDCs (although the contrary argument, that variability in prices has no adverse effect on the level of investment, has also been put forward). In those countries in which domestic prices are insulated from international prices (e.g. where there is already an effective domestic price stabilization scheme) the macroeconomic effects (the induced instability in government budgets as well as in foreign exchange earnings) may be the primary source of concern. As we note in Part VI, when the primary objective of commodity price stabilization schemes is the elimination of the deleterious macroeconomic consequences of price variability, there probably exist less expensive programmes which are at least equally effective, such as the Compensatory Financing Facility of the International Monetary Fund and the Stabex programme of the Lomé Convention. On the other hand, these policies are not necessarily appropriate if the real concern is the risk borne by producers, for in the absence of domestic stabilization programmes policies designed for meeting the macroeconomic objectives (like IMF credits) may have little impact on the individual producer.

2.2.5 *Reducing the risks faced by consumers*

Most of the programmes do not have this as one of their explicitly stated goals, but if consumers are risk averse, their welfare may be adversely affected by price variability. Thus the reduction in risk provides one of the incentives for the co-operation of consuming nations in international agreements, one of whose objectives is price stabilization.

There may also be macroeconomic benefits for consuming countries similar to those described earlier for producing countries: clearly the variability of the price of oil is thought to be damaging to the users of oil. However, for most other commodities the macroeconomic effects are likely to be negligible since most commodities account for less than 1 per cent of consumers' expenditure, and thus will be ignored here.

2.2.6 *Revenue raising*

Finally, we should note that many programmes which go under the rubric of price stabilization in less developed countries really serve another function: raising revenue from the agricultural sector.

This is particularly noticeable where the commodity is purchased through a marketing board at government-regulated prices. A distinction should be made between the profits which might arise from a buffer stocking scheme − from buying at a low price, storing, and selling at a high price − the profits, in other words, associated with intertemporal arbitrage − and straightforward taxation of the agricultural sector. Again, although we are not primarily concerned with stabilization schemes as methods of raising revenue, we are concerned with the cost of running stabilization programmes and the need to raise enough revenue to cover such costs.

It is important to realize that although any programme may go some way in achieving all of these different objectives, different programmes may be relatively more successful in attaining particular objectives. For instance, programmes which increase the accessibility of LDCs to the capital market to offset the effects of variability in foreign exchange earnings may reduce the deleterious effects of price instability on macro-development, but the individual farmer within the country may receive no direct benefit from such programmes. On the other hand, the country could introduce an internal stabilization scheme, which would reduce the risk faced by farmers but which would have no effect on the instability of foreign exchange earnings and might, in fact, increase the instability in government deficits.

In conclusion, we shall be mainly concerned with the effect of pure commodity price stabilization schemes on the welfare of producers and consumers. Although our prime focus is on the producers, we discuss the effect of these schemes on the risk borne by consumers in Chapters 8 and 9, as well as drawing a careful distinction between the net benefits of stabilization and induced changes in the distribution of income between consumers and producers. The macroeconomic consequences of price instability may be at least as important as the microeconomic risk effects. We devote Part VI to analysing these macroeconomic effects. But it should be emphasized that the relatively limited allocation of space to this topic is more a reflection of the present state of knowledge of macroeconomics than our judgement of its relative importance.

2.3 Differences between our approach and earlier studies

When we began our study in 1976 the theoretical framework used in most empirical investigations of commodity price stabilization was the simple Marshallian analysis developed by Waugh (1944) and Oi (1961), and synthesized by Massell (1969, 1970). The appeal of this approach is that it lends itself to diagrammatic analysis, and makes strong predictions about the consequences of price stabilization. In the words of a recent empirical study, the Waugh-Oi-Massell approach assumes 'linear demand and supply schedules, instantaneous reaction of supply and demand to changes in market prices, additive stochastic disturbances and price stabilization at the mean of the prices that would have prevailed in an unstabilized market' (World Bank, 1977a).

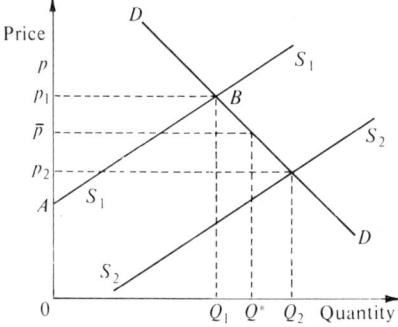

Fig. 2.2 Conventional analysis of supply-induced price variability

Fig. 2.2 illustrates the case of variable supply, and a corresponding figure would be drawn for variable demand. The schedules are linear, the source of risk generates short-run horizontal shifts in the schedules, and the price stabilization programme is assumed to perfectly stabilize the price at its mean level, $\bar{p}$, with no change in average supply. The benefits of price stabilization are measured by the change in average consumer and producer surplus, measured by the area between the supply and demand schedule.

The predictions of the model are readily derived by simple comparisons of areas under the schedules (see Fig. 3.1) and are quite precise:

(i) Producers gain and consumers lose from price stabilization if the source of instability lies on the supply side.

(ii) Consumers gain and producers lose from price stabilization if the source of instability lies on the demand side.

(iii) In both cases, gainers could afford to over-compensate the losers, so there are net benefits from price stabilization.

Although this approach has the attraction of simplicity, all three predictions depend sensitively on its very special assumptions, and can be criticized.

Thus, there are eleven main methodological differences between our study and this linear approach, which we list below and expand on in the next chapter. Since we began our study, other writers have drawn attention to some of the points raised below (see, for examples, the papers in Adams and Klein, 1978), and some important, but neglected, early studies have been rediscovered (Gustafson, 1958). Nevertheless, we believe ours is the first systematic account of the theory of commodity price stabilization which develops a general theoretical framework that allows an escape from the restrictions of too specific models.

2.3.1 *The meaning, consequences, and costs of risk*

Our analysis includes a more careful specification of what is meant by the risk faced by producers and consumers and the costs associated with this risk. One of the main benefits of a commodity price stabilization is the reduction in the risk borne by producers and by producing countries, yet none of the previous studies has taken this cost of risk-bearing into account.

We argue that it is variations in income, rather than variations in price, which are of concern to producers, that in certain (perhaps not uncommon) situations, a price stabilization scheme may destabilize incomes and hence increase the effective risk borne by producers.

Similarly, in the evaluation of the benefits to consumers, we have taken into account the correlations between income, the price of other commodities, and the price of the commodity being stabilized. We show that none of the earlier studies has adequately measured the consumer benefits of price stabilization when fluctuations in demand contribute to the price instability. We view this development of a methodology of cost–benefit analysis under risk as one of the major contributions of our study. (See especially Chapters 6, 9, 12, and 20.)

2.3.2 *Short-run versus long-run impacts*

Our analysis distinguishes between the short-run impact and the long-run equilibrium impact, where producers have fully responded to the change in risk. We show that stabilization may increase supply and could even increase the variability in output. This supply response will typically reduce the benefits which accrue to the producers and may increase the costs of running a price stabilization programme. In some cases, we can show that producers are eventually made worse off as a result of commodity price stabilization, even though the initial impact was favourable. (See especially Chapter 12 and Part V.)

We also distinguish between the *ex-ante* supply schedule at the start of the crop season, whose position depends on expectations about future returns, and the *ex-post* supply curve at the time of harvest, whose position depends on both inputs (*ex-ante* choices) and weather. We argue that the model of Fig. 2.2 is misleading both as a positive description of market equilibrium under risk and for a normative measure of producer benefit (Chapter 6).

2.3.3 *General equilibrium incidence of stabilization*

We also discuss the general equilibrium impact of price stabilization, and show that part of the cost of price instability may be borne by individuals within the producing countries who are not in the export sector, because variations in the income of the exporters generate variations in the income of other sectors within the economy. Thus, the beneficiaries of a commodity price stabilization scheme are not limited to those in the export sector. On the other hand, to the extent that the impact of the instability is spread through the economy, the aggregate benefit from stabilization may be reduced, since the more widely risks are spread the lower is the total cost of bearing the risk.

In other branches of public policy — especially in the analysis of taxation — it has long been recognized that the individuals ultimately bearing the cost or receiving the benefit of a government programme may be different from those who are nominally bearing the cost or receiving the benefits. For instance, a tax on the producer of a commodity may be shifted forward onto the customers of the firm in the form of higher prices; or it may be shifted backwards onto the suppliers of inputs (e.g. the workers) in the form of lower wages than they otherwise would have received. The analysis of the incidence of any tax is a complicated matter, but these general equilibrium responses are now recognized to be potentially of first-order importance. One of the primary objectives of this study is to extend such incidence analysis to a wider class of public programmes, particularly those designed to reduce risk. (See Chapters 12, 23, and 25.)

2.3.4 *Macroeconomic effects*

Although many economists have argued that the main benefits of price stabilization would be at the macroeconomic level, it has rarely been explained what precisely these benefits are, how they would flow from stabilization, and whether they could be obtained by alternative policies.

Although our primary concern is with microeconomic equilibrium models, Part VI is devoted to the macroeconomic impact of price stabilization. We develop models to show how price variability may result in the disequilibrium phenomena of unemployment and inflation. Obviously, a reduction in these would be of considerable benefit to most LDCs, but, to the extent that the major problems associated with price variability are macroeconomic in character, we suggest that macroeconomic policies (like lending policy) are likely to provide a better solution than price stabilization policies.

2.3.5 *Other market distortions*

World trade in many agricultural commodities, especially grains and sugar, is subject to tariffs, quotas, and a variety of domestic taxes and controls, whose presence might be argued to alter significantly the case for price stabilization. It is necessary to distinguish three senses in which this argument might be interpreted. It has been claimed that eliminating these distortions would generate much larger efficiency and distributional benefits than price stabilization, and would directly contribute to price stability. This seems likely, but is a quite distinct policy proposal which we do not consider. Second, it has been argued that the presence of distortions affects the size and distribution of benefits from price stabilization. We examine this argument in Chapter 19. Finally, it has been argued that price stabilization would precipitate tax and tariff changes which would affect the efficiency of international trade. We touch on these issues in Chapters 19 and 24.

2.3.6 *General functional specification and the biases of conventional parameterizations*

We have utilized more general specifications of the demand function, the supply function, and the stochastic processes involved than in earlier work. We are able to show that several results obtained earlier depend critically on the kinds of functional forms assumed, e.g. whether demand schedules are linear or have constant elasticity, and whether risk is additive or multiplicative. The particular specification of the econometric model to be used in estimating the benefits of a price stabilization programme may bias the results obtained in a significant way, and prejudge who gains or loses from price stabilization (Chapters 18 and 23).

In particular, we show that the linear model of Figure 2.2 is suspect both in its specification of risk (horizontal shifts in the schedules) and of the shape of supply and demand schedules, which together imply that it is feasible to stabilize prices at their mean, in which case average supply will not change. If, as seems likely, demand or supply schedules are non-linear it will be infeasible to stabilize price at its arithmetic mean — the buffer stock would steadily accumulate or decumulate. We shall argue that the emphasis on prices has been misplaced and that it is more logical (especially in short-run analysis) to consider holding mean supply constant. We therefore develop the theory of mean quantity preserving changes in price risk (Chapter 17).

2.3.7 Dynamic analysis

We have viewed the problem within a dynamic context, and in particular have analysed the buffer stock as the outcome of a stochastic process. As a result, we are able to show that many of the kinds of schemes proposed are likely either to involve extremely high costs or will, with a high probability, be unable to stabilize the price in the way intended.

Taking this dynamic view of the problem of commodity price stabilization leads naturally to the formulation of the problem as one of the design of optimal buffer stock (storage) rules. Under certain conditions the solution can be completely characterized and the required stocking rule calculated to the desired degree of accuracy. For moderate risk the approximate solution can be calculated quite easily. The results obtained from these approximations suggest that the optimal stabilization scheme would reduce price variabilies by a modest amount, but would achieve its effects at significantly lower cost than the popular alternative of keeping prices within a specified band width. (See Chapters 14, 29, and 30.)

2.3.8 Partial versus complete stabilization programmes

Since any stabilization programme which is economically feasible can only provide partial stabilization, we have developed a general analysis of the effects of partial stabilization schemes and show that, in certain circumstances, these may have a markedly different impact compared with that of the conventional (infeasible) bench-mark of complete price stabilization (Chapter 19).

2.3.9 Distributional versus efficiency effects

We have distinguished between the *distributional* and *efficiency* effects of any price stabilization scheme, and have divided the latter into arbitrage benefits and risk benefits. Arbitrage benefits are the benefits of transferring goods from dates of low value to dates of higher value, while risk benefits are the benefits of transferring real income between dates of differing value (different marginal utility of income). Earlier studies which have concentrated only on producers have failed to appreciate the difference between transfers which merely redistribute income and true efficiency gains, while none of the earlier empirical studies measured the risk benefits (Chapters 19 and 20).

2.3.10 Information and expectations

A price stabilization may generate additional benefits by improving the efficiency with which the economy collects and uses information. Our analysis of price stabilization assumes that agents have rational expectations about the relationships of their decisions and the resulting probability distribution of returns.

This is not because we believe this to be an accurate description of agricultural decision-making, but because it provides a bench-mark against which to measure the benefits of price stabilization. If expectations are not rational in this sense, then there may be additional gains of improved decision-making, for price stabilization typically reduces the sources of error and bias in forecasting. We also discuss the important question of the efficiency of the market economy in collecting and disseminating information useful for decision makers. (See Chapters 10, 11, and 16.)

2.3.11 *Comparison with other instruments*

Many other studies, in evaluating the desirability of buffer stock schemes, have not provided a comparative evaluation of the returns of this policy instrument relative to other instruments such as the improvement of futures markets. Although we have not provided as detailed a comparative evaluation as we would have liked, we do show how certain of the objectives of commodity price stabilization schemes can more effectively be accomplished by other means. (See Chapters 13 and 14.)

Our approach is to demonstrate the importance of each of these points by developing a theoretical framework capable of addressing these issues. Once their importance has been grasped the reader will be in a position to examine a particular market or commodity, identify its key features, and develop a simple but appropriate model with some feel for its merits and limitations. In the next chapter we continue our overview by summarizing the main conclusions of our study.

Chapter 3

Summary of Findings

The major result of our analysis is to question seriously the desirability of price stabilization schemes, both from the point of view of the producer and of the consumer. Our results show that the methods used in the evaluation of the costs and benefits employed in many of the earlier studies are seriously flawed; the costs tend to be underestimated and, although the direct benefits of risk reduction are usually completely ignored, the total benefits of stabilization are probably over-estimated. Moreover, it is not enough to measure the aggregative net benefits, for our analysis suggests that there are significant redistributive effects of price stabilization. Indeed, there seems a serious possibility that at least some of the LDCs will actually be worse off as a result of price stabilization and that the major beneficiaries of such programmes might be the developed countries. Moreover, there may be more effective methods of attaining the objectives of such schemes. In this chapter we attempt to summarize and explain our findings in a non-technical manner. Of necessity, we have had to rely on intuitive and heuristic arguments. The sceptical reader is referred to later chapters for a more complete but more technical analysis.

It is important to emphasize that our primary concern has been theoretical and methodological, with ascertaining the range of possible effects of such schemes, and, wherever possible, suggesting how one might go about quantifying the magnitudes involved. This approach is particularly useful for showing the mistakes and implicit (and unacceptable) assumptions of earlier studies.

Some of the more important effects are quantifiable, and we obtain order-of-magnitude estimates for these effects. There are, however, other effects for which the relevant quantitative information is, at present, not available. Some of these effects tend to reinforce our conclusions about the smallness of the benefits of commodity price stabilization, but others have consequences which are either ambiguous or which may run contrary to our conclusion. For instance, we suggest that commodity price stabilization may reduce the errors in resource allocation resulting from incorrect forecasting of future prices. We have not been able to quantify this effect, except in very simple models, but we believe that, were it possible to do so, it would not be likely to affect our over-all conclusions; though, of course, others may disagree. Moreover, we would argue that the benefits from the reduction in forecasting error might be attained more cheaply in other ways. At the very least, however, we hope we have provided a framework within which future analyses of the benefits and costs of price stabilization may be conducted.

The chapter begins with a discussion of the view that, because commodity markets are competitive, there is no case for any policy intervention such as price stabilization. Section 3.2 discusses the various benefits of price stabilization, section 3.3 their costs, section 3.4 considers some alternative policy measures, and the chapter concludes with the empirical results.

We begin with the 'perfect market hypothesis', according to which government intervention is not needed because markets already provide an efficient allocation of resources.

3.1 Perfect market hypothesis

Before developing a set of techniques for determining the benefits and costs associated with price stabilization schemes, we had to answer a fundamental question: if it is desirable to stabilize prices — and there are strong reasons in economic theory why it should be — why is it not profitable for private firms to do so? Whenever prices at two different dates or places are not equal, there is a potential profit in shifting the commodity from the low-price place or date to the high-price place or date. The arbitrageur purchases the commodity when the price is low, stores it, and sells it later at the high price. The difference in the price (less interest and storage costs) constitutes his profit. These costs mean that price stabilization will never be perfect. But why is there not here, as we usually assume in other aspects of economic behaviour, a congruence between social and private costs and benefits, so that the market provides the optimal degree of price stabilization? Is there some systematic market failure?

Many economists, following this line of reasoning, conclude that there is no convincing argument for, e.g., an international agency to intervene in the market in order to stabilize prices further. Put this way, the burden of proof appears to be on those who argue in favour of price stabilization schemes to identify an important source of market failure. Some of the more obvious sources, such as the non-competitive nature of certain commodity markets (the dominance, say, of a few chocolate-marketing firms) do not provide a convincing argument for price stabilization; the incentives for stabilization for a monopolist are not significantly different from those of a competitor.[1]

These economists begin with the presumption that the market allocates resources efficiently. This view, which dates back at least to Adam Smith's discussion of the market acting, as if with an invisible hand, to allocate resources for the 'general good', has received considerable analytical support in the last thirty years. Under certain conditions, the market can be shown to lead to a Pareto optimal allocation of resources: that is, there exists no alternative allocation of resources which would make everyone better off. All alternative allocations must make some individuals worse off, and it is in this sense in which

[1] The monopolist is, of course, concerned with stabilizing marginal revenues rather than prices, but if the elasticity of demand is approximately constant this yields approximately identical results. This argument must be qualified if the monopolist faces a limit price set by potential competition, in which case he may find it profitable deliberately to randomize his price (Newbery, 1978). While this may have some bearing on the behaviour of markets of natural resources, it seems of limited relevance to agricultural commodities.

the market economy has been shown to be efficient. The only assumption which appeared critical is that markets be competitive — a reasonable hypothesis for most agricultural commodities. There are of course other technical assumptions, such as non-satiation, which seem reasonable, and some important economic assumptions, such as the absence of externalities — the actions of any one farmer must not significantly affect the output of other farmers — which are not of primary importance in agriculture.

However, in the last few years it has become apparent that there are two assumptions which are critical to the validity of the theorem and which make its applicability to agriculture, or, indeed elsewhere, of doubtful validity.

First, there must be a complete set of futures and risk markets and there must be perfect information. These assumptions are clearly not satisfied, but their importance for the validity of the presumption that markets allocate resources efficiently has only recently been realized. (We have already discussed this in the Introduction in the part addressed to the general economist.)

For the moment we only wish to emphasize that in markets in which there is as much uncertainty and as much imperfection of information as characterizes those for many agricultural commodities, there is no presumption that the market allocates resources efficiently. Thus, there is a distinct possibility that government intervention, e.g. to stabilize prices, could improve economic efficiency. One cannot resolve this issue on *a priori* grounds alone, but must study the facts of each particular case. Therefore, a study such as this is necessary, even for economies in which prices adjust smoothly to clear markets which are competitive.

Second, the efficiency of the competitive economy requires perfect wage and price flexibility, which are obviously not present in any economy. A complete study of price stabilization thus requires an analysis of the effects of price rigidities elsewhere in the economy — in short, it requires a macroeconomic analysis such as that provided in Part VI.

At the same time, those economists who have emphasized the role of private markets in stabilizing prices do raise a fundamental point: it is imperative, in calculating the costs and benefits of a government programme, such as commodity price stabilization, to take into account the responses of the private sector. Their responses may reduce the benefits of the government programme and/or greatly increase the costs beyond the levels originally expected. We shall encounter this theme repeatedly in the following analysis.

3.2 Benefits of price stabilization

In assessing the benefits resulting from a price stabilization programme, we must distinguish between the effects on producers and those on consumers. Two types of effects may be distinguished, which we refer to as *transfer* effects and *efficiency* effects. The former represents the *distributional* impact of the programme; producers may gain or lose at the expense of consumers, or conversely.

The latter represents the gains (or perhaps losses) resulting from the increased (or decreased) efficiency with which the economy operates as a result of the stabilization programme. Crudely put, in terms of the conventional notions of consumer and producer surplus (which we shall attempt to refine in our subsequent discussion), the latter refers to the effect of the programme on the sum of producer and consumer surplus, while the former refers to the division of the total surplus between the two groups. Note that the programme could be desirable from the latter standpoint (i.e. total surplus could be increased), but not, without the appropriate redistributions, from the former (e.g. producers might be worse off; all the gains — and more — accruing to consumers).

Our analysis suggests that the efficiency benefits of a price stabilization programme might be less than has previously been thought, and also that the distributional impact may make the producers actually worse off. At the same time the major direct welfare gain of price stabilization, the reduction in risk borne by producers, has been ignored in earlier studies.

3.2.1 *The meaning of risk and the effects of price stabilization on the riskiness of agricultural income*

The basic argument of our analysis is that producers are not concerned with price variability itself, but with variability in consumption. The two differ in six important respects:

(i) First, income from the crop is the product of its price times the quantity, pQ. Suppose we measure income instability by the variance of the logarithm of income, then

$$\text{Var}(\log Y) = \text{Var}(\log pQ) = \text{Var}(\log p) + \text{Var}(\log Q) + 2\,\text{Cov}(\log p, \log Q).$$

Then, since for the world as a whole, price and quantity are inversely related, the variance in $\log Y$ is clearly different from the variance of prices. Eliminating the variance in p will not eliminate the variance in Y and may actually increase it.

To see this more clearly, consider the case where the only source of price variability is that induced by supply variability. Assume, moreover, that the demand schedule has constant elasticity, ϵ, so

$$p = Q^{-1/\epsilon}.$$

Thus, the income of the farmer is

$$Y = pQ = Q^{1-1/\epsilon}$$

and

$$\text{Var}(\log Y) = (1 - 1/\epsilon)^2 \text{Var}(\log Q).$$

After stabilization, we have

$$\text{Var}(\log Y) = \text{Var}(\log Q).$$

Whether stabilization reduces or increases the variance depends on whether

$$\epsilon \leq \tfrac{1}{2}.$$

Note that the case of $\epsilon = 1$ is a critical case, for then Y is constant (Var(log Y) is accordingly, zero). Note too that if $\epsilon < 1$, dates at which Q is low represent high-income states, i.e. income and quantity vary inversely. If supply fluctuations are the source of price variability, price stabilization actually increases income variability for commodities with a demand elasticity greater than 1/2.

This result applies to the world economy as a whole. For a single country, whose output Q_i is imperfectly correlated with that of the world, Q, we have, before stabilization,

$$\text{Var}(\log Y_i) = \text{Var}(\log Q_i) + \text{Var}(\log p) + 2\,\text{Cov}(\log p, \log Q_i).$$

With a constant elasticity demand schedule

$$\text{Var}(\log p) = (1/\epsilon)^2 \text{Var}(\log Q)$$

$$\text{Cov}(\log p, \log Q_i) = -(1/\epsilon)\text{Cov}(\log Q, \log Q_i).$$

Thus,

$$\text{Var}(\log Y_i) = \text{Var}(\log Q_i) + \text{Var}(\log p) - 2(1/\epsilon)\text{Cov}(\log Q, \log Q_i).$$

On the other hand, after stabilization,

$$\text{Var}(\log Y_i) = \text{Var}(\log Q_i).$$

Thus, the conditions under which stabilization reduces the variability of income for any particular small country (say where the covariance is close to zero) are less stringent; for those countries, price variability acts less like insurance and more like an additional source of 'noise'. This suggests that the benefits of pure price stabilization schemes are likely to be relatively more important for small countries and, correspondingly, are likely to be greater in total, the more widespread is the production of the commodity.

(ii) The income from a given crop is not the only source of income for many individuals. Usually they produce other crops; they may have other sources of income (e.g. wages); and they may store commodities, which they sell if the price turns out to be high (they are effectively speculating on the future price). Thus even if one were successful in reducing the variability of income generated by a particular crop, the effect of this on the welfare of the producer might be minimal. In the extreme, if the farmer is widely diversified and the income variability from the crop were uncorrelated with his other sources of income, then the variability in this source of income has a negligible effect on the welfare of the individual, and hence its elimination would have a negligible effect. For crops whose return is negatively correlated with income from all sources in the aggregate, the reduction in income variability would actually increase total income risk and hence have a deleterious effect on welfare.

Thus, the magnitude of the benefits accruing from stabilizing the price of a given crop to the individual farmer will depend on the total opportunities for diversification, including access to wages and income from other sources, his ability to store crops, and the opportunity to speculate on futures markets. Consequently, these benefits are likely to be larger in monoculture economies than in diversified economies (though futures markets are well developed for many of the commodities grown in monoculture economies).

(iii) Producer prices may differ from world market prices. Many countries engage in internal stabilization programmes via marketing boards.

(iv) There are futures markets, long-term contracts, and other means by which some of the risk can be transferred from the producer to others. In these cases, the farmer is protected from some of the variability in market prices. To the extent that he is, reducing the variability in market price may have little effect on the variability of his income. On the other hand, in these situations the risk may be borne by others; there may still be a social cost to the price variability. This is particularly true if wages and prices are rigid (Chapters 25 and 26).

(v) What the individual is concerned with is, of course, not nominal income, but real income, and the price of the commodities the individual purchases may be positively correlated with income from the given crop, so that the variability in real income is less than the variability of nominal income. Let us write real income, Y^*, for an undiversified farmer as

$$Y^* = pQ/\hat{p},$$

where $\hat{p}$ is the price paid for other commodities. But the price index of the goods consumed by the individual includes non-traded goods; since the demand for these goods is likely to rise with income in the given country, the price of such goods is likely to increase, and thus real income is likely to be less variable than nominal income (Chapter 25). This point is closely related to one which has been discussed elsewhere in connection with setting up a price stabilization scheme — the choice of a numeraire or of a basket of goods in terms of which the price should be stabilized. Indeed, it is even possible that stabilizing prices in terms of an international market basket would destabilize real income for some (or even all) producers.

(vi) Finally, it was argued that it was variability in consumption that mattered; the variability in that depends on (a) the longevity of individuals; (b) their access to the capital market; and (c) the rate of interest. At an extreme, if individuals were very long lived, had easy access to the capital market, and the rate of interest were zero, there would be no variability in consumption (provided the stochastic variables in the demand and supply functions were independently distributed over time). *Permanent* income would not vary. At the other extreme, if individuals have a planning horizon of only one year then the variability of consumption is equal to the variability in current income. In general, however, even if individuals cannot borrow freely they can save, and thus variability in consumption will be less than variability in income. (See Chapter 14.)

All of these arguments have been concerned with the risk borne by individuals; they suggest that reducing variability in prices is likely to have a relatively small (and perhaps perverse) effect on the welfare of the individual farmer. Similar arguments are relevant at the national level; some of them, such as the diversifiability of risk and the smoothing of the consumption pattern through borrowing and lending, apply with even greater force.

Although we have argued that the benefits accruing from risk reduction (the variability in real spendable income) are likely to be limited, it does not follow that they should be ignored altogether, as previous studies have. The reason for their small size is partly that price stabilization is a rather inefficient method of stabilizing income; our analysis suggests that different policies, directed specifically at income stabilization, may be quite potent.

We provide an order-of-magnitude estimate of these benefits in Chapter 20. Expressed as a percentage of the value of mean income they can be shown to be approximately equal to one-half the product of the degree of relative risk aversion (often thought to be of the order of magnitude of 1 to 2) times the change in the squared coefficient of variation in income. Table 20.10 provides estimates of this for six agricultural commodities chosen from the list of core commodities.

3.2.2 *The effects of price stabilization on the variability of output*

So far we have implicitly assumed variability in output will be unaffected by the price stabilization programme. Whether this is reasonable depends on the balance of two arguments, one suggesting that variability will increase, the other that it will decrease. If price stabilization reduces income risk, then producers might be more willing to adopt risky production techniques or less diversified cropping patterns. This kind of adjustment typically improves producer welfare in the short run, since it offers them options not previously available, but in the long run the relative prices of the various crops will change in response to these adjustments, and it is possible for producers to gain significantly less in the long run or even lose as a result of stabilization. It is likely, however, to increase the costs of a stabilization programme, perhaps substantially.

On the other hand, if producers are myopic in forecasting future prices, the resulting cobwebs may further destabilize incomes. Price stabilization may improve their forecasting ability and stabilize their production decisions, thus leading to a more stable pattern of supply.

Even when an argument can be made that a price stabilization programme would be desirable in the long run, there are short-term costs of introducing such a programme which may more than offset the long-run gains. For instance, if farmers initially had rational expectations concerning the price distribution, it might take them quite a long time to learn the characteristics of the new, stabilized equilibrium, and in the interim there may be systematic misperceptions giving rise to welfare losses. For example, they may believe that the stabilization authority is going to be successful at stabilizing prices at the mean price prevailing before the stabilization programme. The farmers may respond by greatly expanding supply which will eventually force the stabilization authority to stabilize the price around a lower level. Thus, at some date in the future, the

30 Commodity Price Stabilization

producers' anticipations will not be correct; they will be expecting a higher price than they rationally should; and this induces a welfare loss because of the excessive use of productive inputs and the excessive cost of an accumulating stockpile.

3.2.3 Effects of price stabilization on mean income

The traditional method of assessing the effect of stabilization programmes on the mean income of producers is to draw a demand curve, such as in Fig. 3.1, calculate the mean revenue generated by two prices p_1 and p_2 each occurring with probability 1/2, and compare that with the revenue accruing at the mean price, $\bar{p}$. In Fig. 3.1 it is clear that with a linear demand schedule the average revenue is higher with a stabilized price than with the random price.

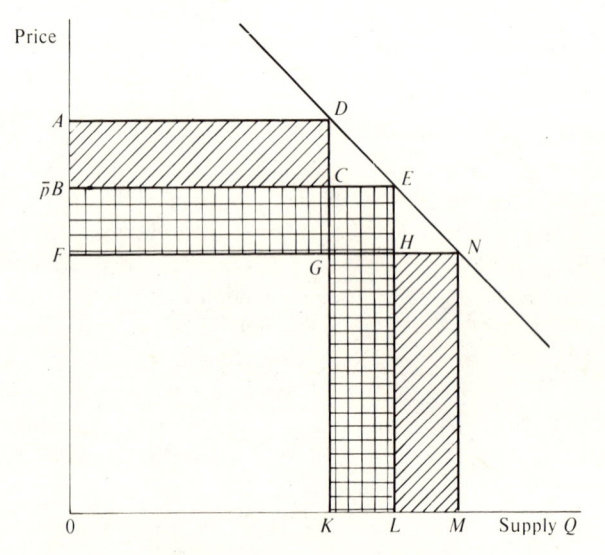

Fig. 3.1 Producer benefits of stabilizing variable supply
Loss from stabilization when price rises: $ABCD - CELK$
Gain from stabilization when price falls: $BFHE - HNML$
Average gain from stabilization: $CEHG$

This will also be the case if the *revenue* function is concave in *price*, i.e. if it has the shape shown in Fig. 3.2. (Convexity and concavity are defined in section 5.2. A concave function has a negative second derivative, while a convex function, as in Fig. 3.3, has a positive second derivative.) Using dashes to denote derivative, if

$$R = Q(p)p$$

then

$$R' = Q + pQ' = Q(1 - \epsilon)$$

Summary of Findings 31

(where ϵ is the elasticity of demand expressed as a function of price) and

$$R'' = Q'(1 - \epsilon) - Q\epsilon'.$$

Thus, if the demand curve has constant elasticity, ($\epsilon' = 0$), the revenue curve will be concave ($R'' < 0$) or convex ($R'' > 0$) as the elasticity of demand is less than or greater than unity. Increasing the dispersion of price lowers average revenue if the revenue function (as a function of price) is concave, as in Fig. 3.2; conversely if the revenue function is convex, as in Fig. 3.3.

This analysis is, however, misleading. First of all, assuming that mean price would remain unchanged is an unreasonable and unjustifiable assumption.

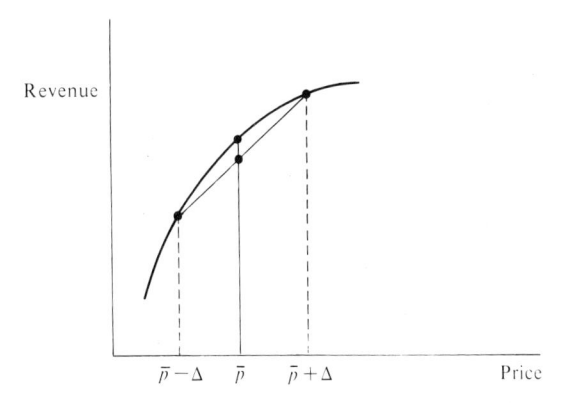

Fig. 3.2 Concave revenue function

Price dispersion decreases average revenue (example: constant elasticity demand curve with elasticity less than unity; linear demand schedule).

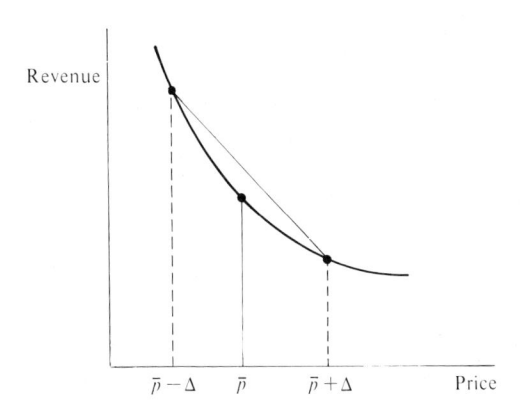

Fig. 3.3 Convex revenue function

Price dispersion increases average revenue (example: constant elasticity demand curve with elasticity greater than unity).

32 Commodity Price Stabilization

Keeping mean price constant has a strong implication for mean consumption: unless demand schedules are linear, it implies that average consumption is decreased for normal (i.e. convex) demand curves (see Fig. 3.4). For this to be feasible, of course, there must be a corresponding change in supply, and there is no reason to expect that the supply response will be of precisely the required amount. It seems far more reasonble to take, as our first working hypothesis, the assumption that there is no supply response: that is to consider what we refer to as mean output preserving reductions in price variability.

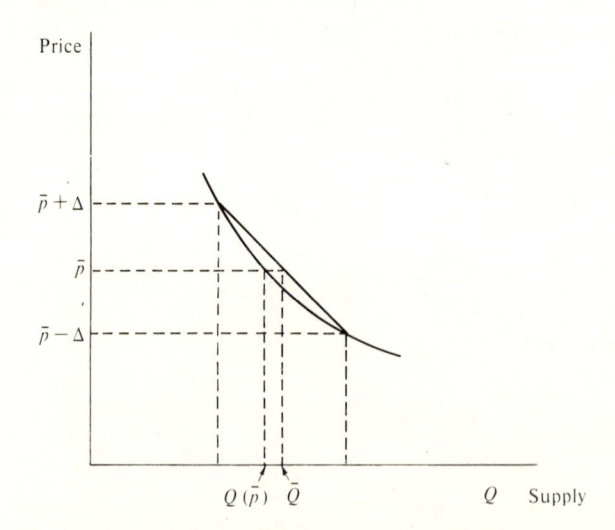

Fig. 3.4 Effect on mean demand of price stabilization

With normal demand curves, increasing the price by a given amount reduces demand by less than the amount that demand is increased when price is reduced by the same amount. Hence it is not feasible to change the dispersion of price holding the mean price and mean supply constant.

This has the advantage that it is feasible, and it is a natural bench-mark which can be thought of as the short-run impact. However, a complete analysis needs to take into account the long-run supply responses of the producers. This turns out to be a somewhat subtle and complicated task. There are a number of types of supply responses: the allocation of resources among different crops, the level of inputs (including labour), the choice of technique, and the number of farmers. It turns out that both the way in which expectations are formed and the nature of the price stabilization programme play a crucial role in determining the magnitude of these effects.

Consider for instance the choice of the level of inputs. (Similar arguments hold for the other decisions facing farmers.) A reduction in risk may be thought of as raising the effective return to growing the given crop and hence lead to greater inputs of, say, labour. This increases the mean output and lowers the average price. One would expect this to reduce the benefits accruing to producers somewhat, but not to reverse the direction of the benefit, or else farmers would reduce inputs and drive the price up again. The analysis of Chapters 6 and 22 shows that this intuitive argument is deficient on two grounds. First, it is possible that the reduction of uncertainty reduces output rather than increases it. For instance, if individuals are extremely risk averse, so that they are concerned with the minimum level of income they attain in the worst case, then reducing income variability reduces the level of inputs required to guarantee this minimum income level. Second, the effect on welfare depends on what happens to expected total utility, while the choice of effort (or inputs) depends on what happens to a weighted mean return, where the weights depend on *marginal* utilities. The two can vary in the same or in opposite directions, and thus it is possible to show under not unreasonable conditions that the supply response will be positive even when this makes the individual farmer worse off.

This can be seen more clearly if we consider the allocation between two different crops, one of which has a safe real return and a constant output per unit input regardless of scale, while the other is risky. Stabilizing the price of the risky crop will lead to a shift into the production of the risky crop, which will lower its price. If one could stabilize completely income generated by the risky crop by varying its price inversely with supply, then resources would shift into the crop until the mean return fell to that of the safe crop. If the demand for the safe crop is sufficiently elastic so that its price does not rise significantly (if, for example, it is traded in world markets), then price stabilization will make the individual farmer worse off than he was before because he could have originally chosen to produce only the safe crop, but he actually chose to produce some of the risky crop.

These responses on the part of producers can be shown to be of a distributional sort, i.e. they represent a gain to consumers at the expense of producers. In particular when there are no changes in (mean) output, the change in mean income can be shown to be purely distributional, the gain or loss to the producer being exactly offset by an equivalent loss or gain to consumers. There are, of course, in addition to these *transfer effects*, some effects arising from the change in the magnitude of risk borne by producers and consumers. We have already discussed the former so we now turn to the latter.

3.2.4 *Effects of price stabilization on consumers*

Considerations similar to those discussed in subsection 3.2.1 enable one to show that the efficiency gains arising from stabilizing the prices faced by consumers are overestimated by the traditional methods which measure the consumer surplus of a single commodity. The reason for this (set out more fully in Chapter 9) is that the price of a given commodity is likely to be correlated with income; hence the price variations actually serve to reduce the variability of consumers' real income. Indeed, if the major source of price variability were the variability of demand generated by income variability, it can be shown that the elimination of price variability would actually make consumers worse off. (To eliminate the variability of price, consumers would be forced to increase the variability of their consumption of the commodity.) The evidence, however, suggests that consumer price variability is markedly smaller than producer price variability, presumably because of activities of arbitrageurs in the consuming countries; indeed, consumer price variability is sufficiently small for most primary commodities in developed countries that its elimination would have limited social value. On the other hand, it appears that most of the consumer price variability for agricultural commodities is probably due to supply variability rather than variability arising out of income fluctuations; this implies that the net benefit from price stabilization, though small, is still probably positive. For sugar (of the crops examined, the one with the highest consumer price variability), if relative risk aversion were unity and the price elasticity of demand were 0.7 and income elasticity were near unity, then the net benefit to consumers from complete stabilization of consumer price would be approximately 0.05 per cent of the mean expenditure on sugar.

3.2.5 The infeasibility of total stabilization and the desirability of partial stabilization schemes

Most of the calculations of the benefits of price stabilization have assumed that these schemes could totally stabilize the price. There is some presumption that this is not feasible in a market economy except at very high cost. In any case it can be shown that such total stabilization is frequently undesirable from the point of view of the producer, even if average consumption were not lowered, as will generally be required for feasible price stabilization.

Assume the stabilization authority attempted to stabilize completely the price of a given commodity, and that the randomness in the price arose from the stochastic nature of output; moreover, assume that output fluctuations were uncorrelated over time. Then we can show that the stochastic process describing the buffer stock is a random walk, and that, accordingly, with probability 1 there will come a date at which prices cannot be stabilized because the stockpile is exhausted, or, if the price is set high stocks will grow without bound or must be destroyed. This means that total stabilization schemes are infeasible or inefficient. For this reason we shall be particularly concerned to develop the analysis of partial stabilization schemes.

Obviously, the gross benefits of partial stabilization are likely to be less than for complete stabilization but, less obviously, they may also differ in their distributional impact.

We also find that when we take account of both the costs and benefits of various degrees of stabilization, recognizing that both benefits and costs rise with the degree of stabilization, it will turn out that although some stabilization appears to be desirable, the amount of stabilization which is optimal seems to be very limited.

The set of dynamic price stabilization schemes which are feasible if private storage is allowed is further restricted if we allow private speculation. For if there is any price variability, but the government follows a rule which has the property that there is any systematic correlation in the price between two dates (perhaps dependent on some observable variable, such as the stock of the commodity already in the buffer stock), then speculators will eventually learn that relationship. There may be arbitrage profits for them to make, and they may take actions which significantly increase the cost of running the government buffer stock scheme (and may make it infeasible).

If the government announces a policy, such as that price will be completely stabilized, which is not feasible, it may face speculative pressures even in the short run: speculators, knowing that eventually (no matter how large the buffer stock) the buffer stock will run out, will hoard commodities, particularly as the stockpiles dwindle; there will be runs on the stock. Such speculative attacks on foreign exchange reserves or metal stocks are a recurrent feature of past attempts at price stabilization. It is thus conceivable that the government might actually increase price variability rather than reduce it.

3.2.6 *Macroeconomic benefits*

Many writers have advanced vague claims that the macroeconomic benefits of price stabilization are potentially large compared either with the microeconomic benefits, or, more relevantly, with the storage costs. Presumably the argument runs as follows. Suppose we ignore redistribution effects and focus simply on efficiency, i.e. on the level of national income. At full-employment competitive equilibrium the value of national output (ignoring distribution) is maximized, as at point A in Fig. 3.5. The effect of risk is to cause fluctuations in the level of output per unit of resource employed, but instead of graphing variable output

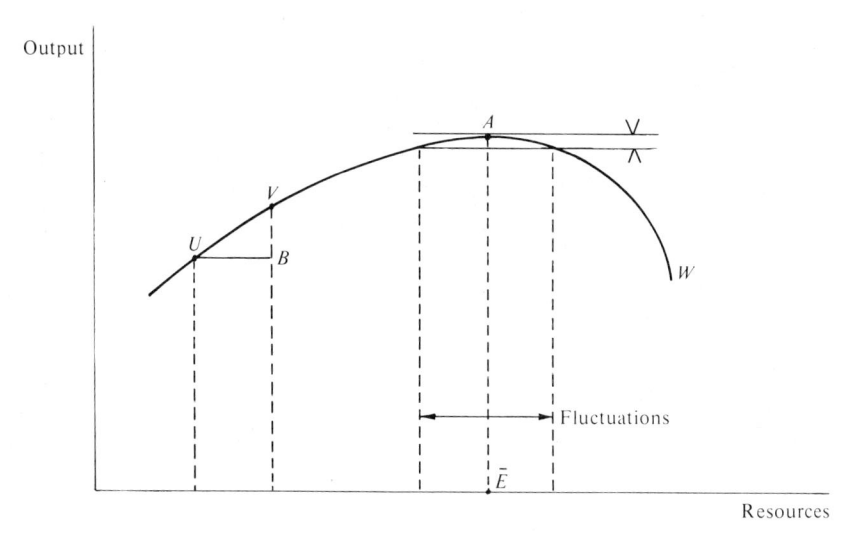

Fig. 3.5 Macro- and micro-gains from stabilization

for fixed resources, it is more convenient to assume fixed output possibilities and variable inputs. The microeconomic gains of stabilization assume full employment, and are then gains from the reduction of the fluctuations about A. Since the curve UAW is flat at A, these gains are typically small (shown arrowed).

If, on the other hand, instability leads to disequilibrium, the economy may be at a point such as U. Stabilization may reduce the extent of disequilibrium and move the economy to V, generating substantial gains VB. The reasons for the disequilibrium vary, but the following argument of Kaldor (1976) is representative. He disaggregates the world into 'primary' producers, whose products have market clearing prices, and 'secondary' producers, the advanced manufacturing countries, whose products have 'administered', or cost-determined prices. Changes in the demand for primary commodities lead to changes in prices, but for manufactured goods prices remain steady but output, and hence employment, varies. Thus, if commodity prices fall, incomes in the primary-producing countries fall, and so does demand for manufactured goods, leading to a recession and a loss of output. If, however, commodity prices rise too much, developed countries experience balance-of-payments difficulties and deflate, again causing recession. Reducing price instability reduces the average level of unemployment and is thus worth a significant percentage of GNP, far in excess of the required storage costs.

This argument is suggestive but rather inconclusive. The problem is that whereas equilibrium is well defined, disequilibrium is not. The microeconomic gains are thus relatively well specified and easily quantifiable compared with the macroeconomic gains, and it is more difficult to judge the validity of macroeconomic arguments. In this context one would want to know why exchange rates do not adjust to make manufactured goods prices variable on international markets, why exchange reserves do not buffer fluctuations in trade, and why macro-stabilizing (counter-cyclical) policies of governments do not eliminate unemployment. It is even difficult to identify how much unemployment is due to this cause, rather than more direct causes (such as the instability of investment). We are therefore sceptical that the macro-benefits of stabilization can be quantified even approximately, though we accept that they could be significant. Thus we have attempted to provide some tentative macro models to remedy the imprecision of earlier discussions but have not attempted to provide any empirical estimates of the magnitudes involved. Our claim that the benefits of price stabilization have been overestimated by other writers is thus a claim that the quantified, i.e. microeconomic, benefits have been overestimated, not that total benefits have been.

3.3 The costs of commodity price stabilization schemes

It is our conclusion that not only have the microeconomic benefits of commodity price stabilization schemes probably been overestimated, for the reasons we have set out in the previous section, but also that the costs have been underestimated.

There are two basic reasons for this:

(i) Most of the earlier studies assumed that there would be no change in behaviour by producers as a result of the introduction of a commodity price stabilization scheme. We detail below several likely responses; one of the main consequences of these responses is an increase in the cost of operating the buffer stock scheme.

(ii) Most of the estimates have not employed an explicitly dynamic model of the kind required for an accurate estimate of the cost of running a buffer stock scheme.

3.3.1 Responses of the private sector to a commodity price stabilization scheme

3.3.1.1 The substitution of public for private storage.
Many commodities are stocked in significant amounts by governments, producers, and traders. (Since the storage is widespread throughout the economy, it is hard to estimate the total magnitude involved.) Stabilization schemes will, to the extent to which they are effective, make such storage less attractive (since, by definition, a price stabilization scheme reduces the variability of price. The motivation, the economic return, for storage is provided by the difference in price between the date at which the commodity is bought and the date at which it is sold;[1] thus reducing the variability reduces the economic return to storage). To take an extreme case, assume that those who engaged in storage were risk neutral, and storage costs plus interest costs were equal to 10 per cent of the value of the amount stored. Assume that the average amount in storage was equal to 20 per cent of the average annual crop.

Consider two dates, say t and $t + 1$, such that, without government intervention, it is known that the price will be 10 per cent greater at the second than at the first. If the demand curve is stable and has an elasticity of ϵ, the quantity supplied on the market must be 0.1ϵ greater in the first period than the second. This is a 'typical' period, so 20 per cent of the annual crop is in storage with producers. Assume that the stabilization authority believes that the 10 per cent variation in price is excessive and wishes to reduce it by one-half. It believes it can do this by buying 0.025ϵ of the amount supplied and storing it for one period. (This will imply that the amount consumed in the two years will differ by 0.05ϵ rather than by 0.1ϵ, and hence the price variation is reduced by half.) In fact, of course, if the price rise falls below 10 per cent no private stockholder will be interested in holding onto his stocks, and thus all private stockholders will dump their total holding, that is, about 20 per cent of the total supply, on the market. To prevent the price falling the authority will have to buy this up, and so, instead of purchasing $0.025\epsilon Q$ it has to purchase $(0.025\epsilon + 0.2)Q$, which, if the demand elasticity $\epsilon = 0.5$ is 17 times as much. The partial equilibrium cost, ignoring the response of private storage, is only 6 per cent of the

---
[1] For risk-averse producers, storage may also serve an 'insurance' role, as described in Chapter 14. Commodity price stabilization may actually induce more private storage; in that case, the public cost of commodity price stabilization will be lower.

total cost. This suggests that the storage costs borne by the new buffer stock agency may be automatically underestimated by ignoring the response of other stockholders, though, of course, the *total* storage costs may not be overestimated. Again, it is important to distinguish between *transfer costs*, or reallocation of costs from private to public stock agencies, and net social costs.[1]

3.3.1.2 Production decisions of farmers. Conventional estimates of the cost (and benefits) of stabilization schemes may also be misleading because they fail to take account of the production response of producers. These include the producers' choice of techniques of production, levels of inputs (including labour supply), the number of farmers producing, and the mix of crops produced. The basic arguments are simple.

Consider first the question of the choice of crops produced. Assume that stabilizing a crop's price makes growing the crop more attractive (as one would expect). Then farmers will shift production into the given crop. This will have two effects — the benefits accruing to the producers of this crop will be reduced (and, as we remarked above, they even may be worse off), and the costs of operating the buffer stock scheme will be greater than without this shift. The second problem would be reduced if schemes were simultaneously introduced for crops which are alternatives from the point of view of producers, though this may be difficult if the alternatives have high storage costs.

Similarly, consider the question of the choice of technique. With price variability, risk-neutral producers have an incentive to use technologies which are negatively correlated with output elsewhere (positively correlated with price) (see, e.g., subsection 3.2.1). A region might find it profitable to grow a crop even when its average output per unit were lower than elsewhere; if its output and international price were positively correlated, expected income from growing such a crop would obviously exceed mean price times expected output. In effect, such a region obtains a return from providing a kind of 'social insurance' to the rest of the economy; this is both socially and privately profitable. Stabilizing the price will mean that such a region would no longer find it profitable to grow the crop, and as a result the amount of variability in output will be increased — thus imposing greater costs than anticipated on the stabilization authority.

Similarly, if producers are risk averse, they will adjust their choice of technique as a trade-off between mean income and risk. The reduction in risk consequent upon a price stabilization programme will lead them thus to choose riskier techniques so the amount of variability which the stabilization authority will have to absorb will increase and with it the cost.

---

[1] If private producers have a comparative cost advantage in storage, then there will be a real social cost associated with the displacement. To the extent that the storage costs represent the fixed costs of storage facilities, it may take a long time for the full adjustment from private to public storage to occur.

3.3.2 *The costs of stabilization in a dynamic stochastic setting*

We argued earlier that commodity price stabilization ought to be viewed as transferring commodities from dates at which their price was low to dates at which their price was high. Since the sequence of outputs and demands is stochastic, so is the sequence of prices; we showed earlier (subsection 3.2.5) that recognizing this severely restricted the set of feasible stabilization schemes; the benefits to be attained from the partial stabilization schemes which could be implemented are likely to be much smaller than the benefits associated with total stabilization.

Once we recognize the dynamic stochastic nature of any commodity price stabilization scheme, it also becomes apparent that the potential costs may be much larger than the earlier sample analysis suggested: the problem arises from the fact that there may be a run of good years (or a run of bad years). The buffer stock scheme has to have the capacity to store the excess product if there is a run of good years, and it has to have in storage a large enough stock to keep prices from rising if there is a run of bad years. Not only does this require maintaining a large permanent buffer stock (with associated high interest and storage costs) but, since some storage costs are likely to be related to the maximum storage capacity (i.e. storage facilities take time to construct and there is a large element of fixed costs within storage costs) the costs may increase more than proportionately to the increase in the required size of *average* buffer stock.

Our calculations show that the cost of even a partial stabilization scheme is likely to be larger than most earlier estimates would lead one to believe.

Assume that one wants to have a given probability of not exhausting the buffer stock in a period of N years. The stock required increases with N (for the particular specification employed in Chapters 20 and 29 it increases with the square root of N). Most earlier studies have implicitly either assumed that a high probability of running out of the stock is acceptable, or have been concerned with only very short-run stabilization programmes (small values of N). It appears, empirically, given the magnitude of the variations in quantity, for a reasonable level of confidence of not running out of the stock (say 10 per cent) and a reasonable number of years (16), the cost of running the buffer stock is significantly greater than estimated in some earlier studies, perhaps between twice and four times as much.

The problem is exacerbated by the difficulties in estimating the variance in supply after the introduction of the stabilization scheme. Further, it may take a long time for producers to learn how to respond optimally to the change in risk, so that the probability distribution of supply may gradually change over time.

3.4 Some alternative proposals

Our main conclusion is that price stabilization schemes have limited efficacy in stabilizing the real spendable income of producing countries and that most of the other benefits associated with the stabilization schemes are transfer benefits which, in many cases, seem to benefit the consuming countries at the expense of the producing countries. A number of alternative proposals have been suggested, and here we briefly summarize our conclusions about these alternatives.

There are two groups of alternative proposals: the first set of proposals is directly concerned with stabilizing income; the second set of proposals is directed at alleviating the consequences of variable income.

The income of the farmer is a function of (a) his inputs; (b) the price he pays for his inputs; (c) his outputs; and (d) the price he receives for his outputs. Price stabilization schemes affect only the price he receives for output, and hence only affect one aspect of his income. There have, to our knowledge, been no schemes actually implemented which stabilize income itself.

There have been a few attempts to deal directly with output variability (crop insurance). Certain kinds of insurance, against particular risks (hail), are provided by the market. But the supply of these insurance contracts is limited because of the familiar adverse selection and moral hazard effects[1] (Chapter 12).

We are not concerned here with crop insurance. It should be noted, however, that many stabilization schemes actually provide a combination of price insurance and output insurance. If the government, for instance, loans an individual a sum of money, allowing him to use the future crop as collateral then, if either the crop or the price is too low, below in value the amount which he is to repay, he forfeits his crop. It is as if the government owned the crop but has offered the farmer the right to repurchase the crop if he wishes for a fixed payment.[2]

The major alternative proposals for affecting the variability of producer's income with which we are concerned here involve some method of differentiating between the market price and the price received by the farmer.

The market price could be (partially) stabilized by a buffer stock. Then the benefits of a stabilized price are enjoyed by all those who transact in the market. Alternatively, the government could stabilize the price for some individuals, e.g. for producers who want the price to be stabilized for them; this is equivalent to making long-term contracts. This may, by removing a fraction of the demand and supply from the spot market, i.e. by making the spot market thinner, make that market more volatile but it need not, since the government could (and logically, for efficiency should) sell the contract crops in the spot market. On the other hand, as we have noted, stabilizing the price on the market may lead to inefficiencies, e.g. in the choice of the flexibility of the technology employed by different firms.

---

[1] That is, since farmers know their riskiness better than the insurance firm, individuals whose probability of a loss is greater are more prone to buy the insurance; this is known as the 'adverse selection problem'. Moreover, once the individual has insurance, he no longer has adequate incentives to avoid the risk; since his actions cannot be observed, the insurance contract cannot stipulate the actions he is to take. This problem is referred to in the insurance literature as the 'moral hazard problem'.

[2] This particular type of contract has peculiar incentive problems and is probably not the best contract for providing the output and price insurance. We do not, however, explore these contracts further in this book.

However, the most widely discussed proposal aimed at reducing income variability is the establishment of better futures markets. We discuss this in subsection 3.4.1. In subsection 3.4.2 we briefly present an alternative proposal aimed at directly stabilizing producers' income.

In subsections 3.4.3 and 3.4.4 we consider two alternative proposals which are concerned with reducing the fluctuations in *consumption* which a given degree of variability in income entails, i.e. in reducing the welfare losses associated with income variability.

3.4.1 *The establishment of better futures markets*

This is a proposal put forward by those who view the problem of price instability as one of market failure. Taking this view leads naturally to an attempt to identify and then remedy the source of the market failure. The absence of futures markets (stretching sufficiently far into the future) is an obvious market failure; it is therefore sometimes suggested that improving futures markets would provide an alternative way of alleviating the problems of price instability within a market framework.

It is our conclusion that, although the improvement of futures markets — extending them further into the future and making them more accessible to small farmers — would not eliminate all the risks presently borne by producers — it is not a substitute for a perfect insurance market — it might substantially reduce the risk-bearing required of farmers; such a policy would appear to be unambiguously better than a policy of attempting to stabilize prices directly.

The reason for this is that with futures markets farmers can *choose* the extent to which they wish to have their output price stabilized. If there were no supply variability (all price variability were due to the variability in output of other producers or of demand), then the farmer could sell his entire crop forward and face no risk. He might not decide to do so; if he decided not to, it would be evidence that he preferred to bear some risk.

There are, however, important limitations to the efficacy of futures markets, and we comment on these briefly. First, they only provide insurance, say at the time of planting, for the *price* of output, not for the value of output. Output itself remains risky. Second, because output itself is risky, they only provide partial insurance, since the number of units of output whose price is to be insured is not known at the time of planting. Third, the futures price varies, and in fact may vary even more than the spot price as a result of speculative activity; selling one's crop forward does not eliminate price variability, although it does reduce the risk borne by the producer himself. If futures markets extend at least as far as the longest gestation periods involved in the production process (e.g. for coffee, for at least the life of a coffee tree) then futures markets could (if supply were not variable) completely eliminate all *risk*; the farmer would know precisely what his income would be. His income, however, still might vary from year to year, and in the absence of good capital markets there would still be a cost associated with the variability in consumption which resulted. Finally, it should be pointed out that this approach ignores the reasons for the absence of adequate futures markets (discussed in Chapter 16, where it is shown that when information is costly such markets may either fail to exist, or if they exist, will not possess the optimality properties usually attributed to competitive markets).

Thus, although we do not believe that establishing better futures markets will solve all the problems with which we have been concerned here, we do believe that an attempt at establishing better futures markets, extending further into the future than such markets usually do at the present time, would be beneficial. Not only would it have substantial benefits in reducing risks borne by producers but it might also increase the efficiency with which resources are allocated, enabling farmers to make better production decisions and enabling more coordinated storage decisions.

3.4.2 *The income stabilization scheme*

The programme which we find the most likely to have the largest social benefits is the income stabilization scheme. There are well-known reasons why income insurance, at the individual level, is not feasible, for although it is obviously attractive to the farmer it removes the incentive to exert any effort. (This is referred to generically as the moral hazard problem.) The problem can, however, be avoided by stabilizing incomes. If the agency made the producer price inversely proportional to total output, then the only risk borne by the individual producer would arise from the imperfect correlation of his output with total output. The individual has the usual incentives to produce, since the amount that he receives is exactly proportional to the amount he produces (since he reasonably assumes he will have a negligible effect on total output).

Although this scheme solves the problem of moral hazard, and does provide fairly complete income insurance (if the random disturbances affecting crop output are highly correlated across farms within a region), it has one significant drawback: there would be incentives for arbitraging between the consumer (or world) price and the producer price, and perhaps over time as well. This would have to be prevented or the cost of operating such a scheme would, in effect, include a cost of subsidizing speculators and arbitrageurs. This, we suspect, is the main reason why such schemes have not developed within the private sector. The viability of the income insurance scheme would depend on the feasibility of preventing arbitrage. Even if it were difficult to prevent arbitrage, it might be possible to design some comprehensive scheme of partial insurance.

The advantage of this scheme is that it directly attacks the problem at hand: the variability of income. Commodity price stabilization schemes only affect price and therefore, as we have argued, might actually increase income variability and lower the welfare of producers.

The advantages of this scheme depend, to some extent, on whether the costs of income variability can be reduced, i.e. whether capital markets can be improved so that income variability does not lead to significant variability in consumption. The next two proposals are concerned with improvements in the capital market.

3.4.3 *The establishment of better borrowing facilities for producing countries*

These proposals are mainly directed at the macroeconomic stabilization and development objectives outlined in Chapter 2. The importance of these proposals depends on the extent to which such countries already have access to the international capital market (e.g. through IMF lending) and the total variability in export earnings (which, as we noted earlier, is likely to be smaller than the variability in the earnings from a single crop). Moreover, there are further problems in transferring the benefits of such a programme to the individual farmers. To do this requires a quite different kind of programme.

3.4.4 *The establishment of better credit markets within LDCs*

This would enable individual farmers to spread their income variations over a number of years. If interest rates were low, this would in fact be far more effective than price stabilization in stabilizing real spendable income. On the other hand, we are not very sanguine about the feasibility of establishing significantly better credit markets, since the main limit to their present scope is the high cost of operating such markets.

3.5 The empirical results

We have, by way of illustration, attempted to use our theoretical results as a basis of an evaluation of some of the costs and benefits of price stabilization programmes for selected commodities (cocoa, coffee, cotton, jute, rubber, and sugar) and an assessment of the distributional implications. There have been a few other attempts at determining the costs and benefits of price stabilization programmes (but to our knowledge, no real attempts to assess the risk benefits). To obtain results we have necessarily had to make a large number of assumptions but we have attempted to bias our choice of assumptions in favour of the price stabilization programme. In spite of this, our results seriously question the desirability of even modest additional price stabilization for most of the commodities examined.

First, as we noted above, a major efficiency gain from the price stabilization programme (completely ignored in all earlier estimates) is the reduction in risk borne by producers. (For reasons given earlier, our belief is that the risk-reduction benefit to consumers is likely to be negligible.) This is proportional to the reduction in the variation of *income* which results from the price stabilization. In our calculation, we have assumed that complete price stabilization is feasible; in fact, of course, we know it is not, and thus our estimates probably provide an overestimate of the risk benefit. These benefits, expressed as a percentage of revenues, turn out to be small; for five of the commodities examined, with no supply response, the risk benefits (averaged over the producing countries for each crop) were of the order of 1 to 3 per cent (multiplied by the coefficient of relative risk aversion, R, which might be between 1 and 2). The best prospect for stabilization, sugar, had a risk benefit of 12 per cent $\times$ R, but this result is seriously open to question, since it ignores the substantial restrictions on free trade known to be present.

The reason that these estimates are so small should be clear from our theoretical work where we have emphasized that it is reductions in income variability which are important; the reduction in income variability from the *complete* elimination of price variability is considerably smaller in most cases than the price variability itself; for instance, for Ghana, the price variability of cocoa (measured as the coefficient of variation) is 31 per cent, the reduction in income variability is 1 per cent; for Brazil, while the price variability of coffee is 15 per cent, the reduction in income variability is 2 per cent; and for sugar the price variability is 58 per cent, but the reduction in income variability is only 6 per cent.

It is also important to emphasize that aggregate estimates are a weighted average of the gains to individual countries; some countries may actually have a negative risk benefit, when price and quantity are negatively correlated, so that income variability is, at present, less than output variability (Mexico for cotton). The risk-reduction benefits are likely to be smaller for large producers, thus yielding a low value of the weighted average.

These estimates would increase proportionately if we assumed individuals were more risk averse than we have assumed, using a relative risk aversion of unity; but they would decrease if we assumed individual producers are diversified. Present data do not allow us to estimate the importance of these two effects. On the other hand, the fact that at the national level, income from the crop and total export revenue had a correlation coefficient exceeding 0.6 for less than 30 per cent of the countries and commodities examined suggests that the reduction in income variability may be significantly less than we have assumed, and consequently the risk benefit considerably smaller. The total remaining efficiency benefits (that is, excluding risk benefits), ignoring storage costs, are in the range 0-2 per cent for all crops except sugar, for which, with the previous proviso, the estimate is 4 per cent of revenue. The risk benefits are larger (assuming unit risk aversion) commodity by commodity than the other efficiency benefits which are usually the only benefits to be measured.

Although the risk benefit is the primary efficiency gain, there is a transfer from producers to consumers which is sufficiently large that producers may well be worse off. The magnitude of the transfer depends critically on two parameters, accurate estimates of which seem extremely hard to come by:

(i) The elasticity of demand — Behrman (1977, 1978) in his survey of demand estimates has noted the large variation in their values; we have used Behrman's median estimates, which are in reasonable accord with our own crude estimates, except for jute, where he provides the clearly unreasonable estimate of zero, and sugar, where he provides a range which encompasses our estimated value.

(ii) The magnitude of the variance in price; which is difficult to estimate at all accurately, i.e. the standard error associated with our estimated value is extremely large. There are large variations in the estimated value from one subperiod to the next.

In our conservative estimate, the transfer may be as large as 6 per cent for the case of sugar; in three cases, the magnitude of the transfer, though small, 1.5-3 per cent, is still greater than the risk benefit so that there is a reasonable chance that producers will actually be worse off. For two of the remaining commodities examined (jute and rubber), the net producer benefit was less than or equal to 2 per cent.

Finally, we come to the estimate of the costs. To estimate the cost of a stabilization programme, one must know: (a) the trend of demand and supply; (b) the magnitude of instability around trend; and (c) the extent of and method by which price stability is to be attained. One of the (perhaps not surprising) results of our study was that it will be extremely difficult to obtain accurate estimates of trend demand and supply and the magnitude of past price instability. Thus, although we have provided point estimates of these costs (in Chapter 20) which, with the exception of sugar, are of the order of magnitude of 1.2 to 2.4 per cent of annual average revenues, the standard error of these estimates is quite large. Consider coffee; assume, for instance, that the true value of the coefficient of variation of price is but one standard deviation larger than our point estimate, say, and that the true value of the elasticity of demand is 0.75 rather than 0.6, clearly within the range of estimated values. Then the cost will be more than *twice* our estimated cost. (On the other hand, if our estimate of the elasticity of demand is too high, say 0.45, and our estimate of price variability is also too high by one standard deviation, true costs will be approximately 40 per cent of the costs estimated.)

The implication of this, of course, is that if one wants a reasonably high probability of being able to stabilize prices (not having the buffer stock run out) then one will need a considerably larger stock of commodities in the buffer stock than the amounts we have estimated.

If we ignore the risk benefits and aim at achieving a 90 per cent chance of reducing the deviation of prices from trend to 50 per cent over a period of four years (a most modest objective, though not achieved in the most efficient way), then the benefit-cost ratio is less than 1 for all crops except sugar (for which it is 1.17).

If we include risk benefits (with unit relative risk aversion) and aim to reduce deviations to 50 per cent over a sixteen-year period with 90 per cent chance of success, the benefit-cost ratio just exceeds unity for cocoa (1.16), jute (1.05), rubber (1.02), and sugar (1.48).

The criterion we employed in the previous paragraph, whether the benefit-cost ratio for a particular stabilization policy is greater than unity, would, of course, be the relevant one if our only choice were to adopt the proposed scheme or keep the status quo. Probably a more relevant question is, what is the return from increasing the level of stabilization from that presently provided by the private market? Is there a significant scope for a public buffer stock scheme, in addition to that implicit in present private storage activities or for the subsidization of additional private storage? Again, we have only conducted rough calculations by way of illustration of the basic principles, but these calculations suggest that the optimal buffer stock (where the expected marginal benefits associated with further stabilization, i.e. a larger average buffer stock, equal the expected marginal costs) is likely to be very small; little if any augmentation of the level of stabilization presently provided by the market is likely to be required. We do, however, discuss the parameters which need careful measurement to decide whether to subsidize private storage in Chapter 30.

Finally, we should emphasize the tentative nature of all the empirical results reported. It is important to bear in mind that we have not made a detailed study of any of these markets; in any one of the markets examined there may be particular features which would need to be taken into account to assess the desirability of commodity price stabilization for that market. We are concerned here only with obtaining order-of-magnitude estimates for purposes of illustration. The fact that the same broad picture emerged from most of the commodities studied we found reassuring.

What *is* clear from our analysis is that previous studies have incorrectly calculated true costs and benefits, and that obtaining accurate estimates of the costs and benefits is likely to be extremely difficult. It is our view that further work, both of a theoretical and an empirical nature, investigating not only the buffer stock schemes but also alternative schemes (and in particular the income stabilization scheme proposed in subsection 3.4.2) would yield high returns.

It is our hope that the framework of analysis which we have provided will be helpful in these future research efforts.

Chapter 4

Statement of the Problem

The object of this chapter is to set the scene for the chapters which follow, to draw up a taxonomy of the causes of price variability, and to distinguish between the set of issues which we intend to discuss and a number of closely related (and often important) issues which we shall not examine.

This book is primarily concerned with the consequences of attempts to stabilize the prices of agricultural products which are subject to systematic variability as a result of systematic variability in either output or demand. We are not, as we have noted earlier, concerned with attempts to increase the price of agricultural products by restricting output or with any of a variety of other schemes designed to improve the plight of producers of agricultural commodities within less developed countries. Our analysis is confined to pure price stabilization schemes, especially those in which prices are stabilized by buffer stocks with no restrictions or taxes on supply or demand. Most (but not all) of our analysis is concerned with the impact of such stabilization schemes within a competitive market in equilibrium, but we shall have a little to say both about disequilibrium models (wage and price rigidities in Part VI) and about markets in which there are other distortions (Chapter 19).

We shall, moreover, assume that the demand and production functions within the sector do not change and, more generally, that the structure of the market remains unchanged as a result of a commodity price stabilization scheme, and, in particular, that the degree of competition and the set of markets and other institutions does not alter. Such an assumption is obviously suspect for any major change in one market, such as price stabilization, may well have far-reaching implications for the whole structure of the market, and indeed, of the economy as a whole. Individuals and firms may respond very differently to large organizational changes than to the incremental changes with which economists are usually concerned. These caveats must be borne in mind in reading the analysis of this book.

The remainder of this chapter is concerned with two sets of issues: the causes of price instability and the possible structural consequences of price stabilization. In the first part we develop a taxonomy which will help organize the questions addressed in our subsequent analysis. In both parts, we discuss a number of issues about which we shall have only a little to say later to distinguish them from our main concern.

4.1 The causes of price variability

It is important to understand the causes of price variability because it turns out that the effects of price stabilization schemes depend critically on the underlying source of price variability (variations in demand versus variations in supply). In particular, the welfare analysis of the benefits arising from price stabilization depend sensitively on the source of variability.

In the following discussion, we shall distinguish between two kinds of risks — *systematic* and *non-systematic*. The distinction, we believe, is important and although most of the subsequent analysis is necessarily restricted to the study of systematic risks, many of the more important risks are non-systematic. Moreover, it is difficult to design adequate insurance markets to cover these risks, while their presence makes the operation of buffer stock schemes much more difficult. Finally, for some kinds of non-systematic risks, there is no adequate welfare analysis.

In early discussions of risk, a great deal was made of the distinction between risk and uncertainty; the former was concerned with events like the occurrence of death or an illness — repeated events for which actuarial odds could easily be calculated — and most insurable risks fell within this category. With the widespread acceptance of the subjective approach to probability (see, for example, Savage 1954), this distinction no longer seemed very important. Individuals formed subjective probability judgements, and on the basis of that were willing to make explicit or implicit bets on the outcome, where an insurance contract was a particular type of bet.

While the blurring of the distinction between risk and uncertainty, or between systematic and non-systematic risk in our terminology, is attractive for the formulation of a consistent axiomatic treatment of risk (as in Savage), for our present purposes the distinction seems worth preserving for important practical reasons. A government agency running a buffer stock scheme may face serious difficulties when there is no consensus about the relevant probability distribution. There is likely to be widespread agreement about the probabilities of systematic supply and demand variation and thus, say, about how the scheme should be run, e.g. how large a stock is required. On the other hand, there are events such as the discovery of a synthetic substitute for a natural fibre which are not of a recurring kind; and accordingly, there are likely to be significant disagreements about the probability of their occurrence. It is then difficult to agree how to make adequate provision for such events in the design of the buffer stock scheme, and, indeed, even how to recognize some non-systematic risks when they have occurred. One broad class of such risks can be thought of as a change in the structure of the economy. It is important, but often difficult, to distinguish permanent or structural changes from 'normal' variation (e.g. it may be difficult to distinguish a permanent change in attitudes about the correct temperature at which a house should be maintained, thus giving rise to a change in the demand function, from a change in the demand function arising out of the normal temperature variations). The policies which would be appropriate in the two cases are obviously markedly different. The difficulty of making this distinction ought to be recognized in designing the policy for running a buffer stock.

Clearly, however, it will be more difficult to design a buffer stock scheme when there are important non-systematic risks than it would be if there were only systematic risks. With this caveat in mind, we proceed to a more detailed analysis of the causes of price variability.

Almost all of our analysis will be concerned with price variability in competitive markets, in which the price is determined by the intersection of demand and supply curves. Movements in prices can thus be attributed to shifts in either the demand curve or the supply curve, and we now consider the two sources of variability in turn.

4.1.1 Demand variability

4.1.1.1 Systematic demand variability. The demand for a commodity may vary over time in a systematic and predictable way; there are two primary reasons why this might occur:

(i) Income variability. Incomes of consumers vary, e.g., over the trade cycle, and this will lead to variations in the quantity of the commodity which will be demanded at any given price.

(ii) Variability in the price of other commodities. If there are systematic variations in the price of some other commodity, which is a close substitute or a close complement for the commodity in question, then there will be corresponding variations in the quantity of the commodity which will be purchased at any given price.

Note that while in the case of income variability or price variability of a substitute there are likely to be positive correlations between the prices of different commodities, in the case of price variability for a complement the prices will be negatively correlated. These correlations are important in determining the total finance required to run stabilization schemes which affect a number of related commodities.

Equally important, the benefits which accrue from stabilization are likely to be grossly mis-estimated if the sum of the values of the change in consumer surplus, commodity by commodity, are calculated ignoring these correlations. We provide the first systematic approach to the full impact of price stabilization on consumers in Chapter 9.

4.1.1.2 Non-systematic demand variability. Two major sources of non-systematic demand variability arise from changes in tastes and changes in technology.

(i) That changes in tastes for different commodities occur from time to time is well known, but predicting such changes and distinguishing permanent changes from passing fads is difficult. Moreover, the analysis of the welfare implications, both of the changes themselves and of any stabilization policies attempting to alleviate the consequences of such changes, raises difficult and subtle problems, not at present well understood. There is only one case in which it is clear how to proceed: when one can identify an underlying taste and the shift in demand as a consequence of new information about the commodity in question. Then the demand for the commodity can be thought of as a derived demand and the analysis is straightforward.

(ii) The demand for many commodities is not a final demand but a derived demand, e.g. the demand for oil, gas and coal are all derived demands for energy; a change in the technology for coal gasification would clearly lead to a change in the demand for coal. In that case, the preferences may be stable and the welfare gains, in terms of these underlying preferences, from any particular stabilization scheme may be analysed in a straightforward manner.

4.1.2 *Supply variability*

4.1.2.1 *Systematic supply variability.* As in the previous case various sources of systematic supply variability may be identified.

(i) Variability in rainfall and other production conditions. This is probably the major source of supply variability for agricultural commodities. The extent to which variations in supply affect the world price depends on the correlation of weather in different producing areas and the transport costs between these areas. Thus, crops such as cloves, the production of which is concentrated in a very small area, are likely to have much greater price variability than, say, wheat, which is produced in widely separated geographic areas.

Transport costs are important in determining the size of the market, and hence the extent to which supplies from different areas with different production conditions can even out total supply and hence price. If transport costs are low enough, then the whole world may make a unified market, though it does not follow that high costs always fragment the market. If consumers are geographically concentrated so that all supply must be transported to the same destination, then transport costs are mainly important in determining the net producer price, but if demand is dispersed, the market fragments into a number of smaller regions within each of which local supply conditions will be more important. Tariffs and taxes are similar to transport costs in fragmenting the market, while variations in the cost of transport will, in addition, induce variations in both demand and supply and thus contribute to price volatility.

(ii) Variability in prices of inputs. If the prices of the inputs in the production process vary systematically, there will be corresponding variations in the level of the supply schedule. Thus, for instance, a variation in the supply of coal may translate itself into a variation in the price of coal and thus in the price of steel. In an interconnected economy the repercussions of price variability in all but final outputs are felt elsewhere in the economy; this means, of course, that the benefits from price stabilization of these commodities may well be greater than the direct benefits accruing in the industry itself. We illustrate some of these repercussions in Chapter 25.

(iii) Variability in supply arising from variability in price expectations of output. One of the classic cases of price variability is the cobweb. The high price of corn this year leads to a large production of corn next year and hence to a low price, but this in turn leads to a low supply the following year and thus to a high price. Although undoubtedly oversimplified, it is clear that systematic variations in expectations can lead to systematic price volatility. What is not clear is whether, as individuals observe this pattern, they will continue to behave in this way. We need to know whether the persistence of this kind of price-expectational volatility implies a kind of irrationality (or inability to learn) on the part of producers.

In the conventional cobweb the price variability is completely endogenous to the market in that there exists an equilibrium with supplies and prices constant over time. If there is an exogenous systematic source of variability (such as the weather) then naïve expectations of the kind just discussed may exacerbate the consequent price variability, and it becomes more difficult for producers to learn how to forecast correctly and to eliminate endogenous instability. We discuss these issues further in Chapter 11.

4.1.2.2 *Non-systematic supply variability.* The sources of non-systematic supply variability parallel closely the sources of price volatility arising from demand except that changes in producers' tastes do not seem so important (though they might be for, e.g., milk supply if farmers grow to dislike the implied routine). The major source is undoubtedly technical change in the production of the commodity in question and/or for alternative commodities.

4.1.3 *Arbitrageurs and speculators*

Although producers and consumers are the two primary participants in agricultural markets, there are two other participants who may have a marked effect both on the degree of price variability and on the success of any commodity price stabilization scheme: arbitrageurs and the government. In this section we consider arbitrageurs and speculation, and in the next we consider the role of the government. Speculators are perhaps the least understood participants in the market. There is widespread populist feeling that they are a major cause of price instability. There has been extensive controversy about whether destabilizing speculation can be profitable. Apart possibly from some anomalies the basic argument that arbitrageurs make a profit by buying cheaply and selling dear means that they function to transfer resources from dates (locations) where they are relatively less valuable to those where they are relatively more valuable, and in so doing even out price differences. When they exacerbate the price fluctuations, they will make a loss.

This argument seems persuasive in a conventional partial equilibrium setting, in which the structure of information is assumed constant, but it is less convincing once we take account of the role of information. For instance, in the absence of information, the futures price for a non-storable commodity would be constant in a world in which the disturbances to the market were described each year by the same, independent distributions. However, if speculators could, by expending resources, find out about the weather (or any other determinant of output), then the price on the futures market would vary to reflect that information. The prices would vary even if no decision depended on the information conveyed by the future price, so that information had no productive value. Grossman and Stiglitz (1980) have analysed a variant of such a model and shown that in a model with perfect information (and considerable speculative activity) there may well be greater price volatility than in a world of no information.

If information can be acquired at some cost, then it follows that arbitrageurs cannot be perfectly successful in arbitraging prices, for if they were they would be unable to make a profit, i.e. to obtain a return on their time (or other resources) used in the process of arbitraging. Grossman and Stiglitz have formulated this more precisely and shown that with costly information there is an equilibrium 'degree of disequilibrium'.

A major effect of any governmental price stabilization programme may be to reduce price variability. If so, the incentives for arbitraging and for the private collection of information to allocate resources efficiently will be reduced. The net effect on price stability may therefore be much less than it would have been had the level of arbitrage activity remained constant.

Arbitrageurs impose, in addition, an important constraint on the behaviour of the stabilization policy, unless arbitraging activity is outlawed. If, for instance, in the absence of private arbitrage the expected price next period differs systematically from the price this period, there will be a strong incentive for speculation which may make it, if not impossible, at least very expensive, to run the stabilization programme in the manner desired. Effectively, the sequence of prices generated by any stabilization programme must be such that there is not a significant incentive for further speculation.

It is perhaps important to emphasize that it is not only speculators who are effectively engaged in intertemporal arbitrage, but any firm or individual storing commodities. Thus, if bread manufacturers keep stores of grain and these stores are not simply proportional to sales of bread but depend on their view of price movements, then they are effectively acting like speculators. Similarly, farmers often engage in a limited amount of speculative storage. The total expenditure (capital requirement) of price stabilization programmes may depend critically on the extent to which a public storage programme will serve as a substitute for a private storage programme.

4.1.4 *Government*

Changes in government action are probably not only a response to changed conditions in the market — induced by market volatility — but also a major cause of market volatility. Any change in taxation or regulation is likely to have an effect both on supply and demand and on market price. Further, policies which affect the level of national income will, indirectly, affect the demand for commodities. These changes are hard to anticipate and must thus be considered within the category of non-systematic risks.

4.2 Consequences of commodity price stabilization

The consequences of a commodity price stabilization scheme depend on the actions taken by consumers, producers, and speculators. Any major change such

Statement of the Problem 53

as a large buffer stock programme may have a significant effect on the actions of all the participants in the market and indeed on the structure of the market itself.

The simplest hypothesis is that farmers' production decisions are unchanged; consumers' purchases at each date are a function only of the price at that date, and there is no private arbitrage. Even in this simple case, the analysis of the incidence of a commodity price stabilization programme turns out to be quite complex, and Part IV is devoted to analysing this polar case which can also be thought of as the short-run impact of the scheme.

The next simplest hypothesis is that producers have a single production decision — either the choice of crops, or the level of inputs, or a choice of technique — while the assumptions concerning consumers and speculators remain unchanged. Part V is devoted to analysing the incidence of a commodity price stabilization programme under these conditions.

There are, however, a variety of additional responses which could play an important role in determining the over-all effects of a commodity price stabilization programme, some of which we discuss briefly in Part III. The programme may have an effect on speculators, on futures markets, on the demand for information, and on storage activities of farmers. We show that the presence of the alternative risk-reducing option open to agents may modify the impact of the price stabilization programme in quite complex and surprising ways.

Finally, there are three additional kinds of effects about which we will have little to say but which may be important.

The first is that a price stabilization scheme may have a significant effect on the shape of demand functions. Consider, for instance, the consequences of changing the variability of the price of oil and coal. Because the relative price of the two commodities is highly variable, consumers might have been induced to produce convertible boilers which could be used with either. This means that the demand functions for coal and oil both exhibit greater elasticity of demand than they otherwise would. This means too that if the government announces a price stabilization scheme, it may pay all individuals to purchase just coal, or just oil, boilers. The announcement of the price stabilization scheme then reduces the demand elasticity, which in turn increases the volatility of price in the face of variations in the quantities actually supplied to the market. Thus the size of the buffer stock required for a given degree of price stabilization may be greater than it would have been had consumers not adapted their consumption technology. This also means that there may well be an inefficiency introduced even if the operation of the stabilization scheme is not subsidized. For individuals will not take into account the extra storage and interest costs they induce by their choice of mode of consumption. This inefficiency is additional to the inefficiency which arises quite generally in the absence of insurance markets, and which we discuss in Chapter 15.

In addition to these effects on the elasticity of demand, there are further effects on the level of demand. Consider, again, the problem of stabilizing the price of, say, automobile fuel. The individual must decide on whether to purchase an automobile or to rely on public transport. Used-car markets are notoriously imperfect, so, as an extreme case, let us assume that used-car markets did not exist at all and that cars lasted for one period. The individual must make his decision about the purchase of the car before knowing the price of fuel, although he has a probability distribution over the prices. The benefit to be derived from owning an automobile depends, of course, on the use made of it, and this depends on the price of fuel (the marginal cost associated with using it). Accordingly, if there is a large price variability, and the individual is very risk averse, he may be inclined not to purchase the automobile; but with price stabilization, even if the mean price is increased slightly, he will purchase it. Thus, the reduction in risk for consumers shifts the demand curve to the right. Similar examples may be found for agricultural products: the large variability in the price of natural fibres (jute) may have provided part of the inducement for the search for and development of synthetic substitutes, and a larger part of the inducement to adopt such substitutes.

Stabilization programmes may also engender government policy responses, particularly when one group of participants is disadvantaged by the programme. Thus if consuming nations view stabilization as an attempt to establish a producer cartel, they may attempt to collude, so that the competitive market prior to stabilization is converted into one of bilateral monopoly. Moreover, governments of the consuming countries may react in a variety of other ways; they may for instance impose taxes and import duties. These will clearly affect the market equilibrium, including the price received by the producing countries.

In addition, the developed countries may respond (particularly if they believe that there is a cartel-type action involved) by reducing their direct aid. In all of these cases, the total impact of the proposed scheme on the developing country may be very different from that envisaged.

The final set of effects concerns the structure of the market itself. Here our remarks are somewhat more speculative. One of the interesting aspects of many commodity markets is that, in spite of the large number of producers, the middlemen are highly concentrated (e.g. grain milling and storage). This concentration does not seem explicable in terms of increasing returns to scale in production; the production units (silos, mills) are often small relative to the size of the market. How can we explain this? Does the prevalence of concentration within this sector — and the consequent imbalance of power between producers of grain and the purchasers — have anything to do with the widespread government intervention in this market? These are difficult questions and we only suggest a partial answer here.

The explanation we offer starts by observing the absence of adequate insurance (risk, stock) markets. The matter may be looked at in two different ways. It is common that the purchaser of the commodity also supplies credit; thus, if there is a bad year (in terms of profits) the credit is extended for another year. In effect, the firm is issuing a contingent contract. Thus, it faces a risk, but if the returns to different plots of land are imperfectly correlated, the risks will be pooled and the total risk, say, as measured by the coefficient of variation, will be smaller than that on any single plot. The risk-pooling effect means that the risk-adjusted required rate of return from a larger firm is smaller than for a smaller firm; there is, here, in effect, a natural monopoly — generated, not by technology, but by risk and the associated market imperfections. With a well-functioning stock market, this 'risk-pooling' on the part of the 'middleman' is not relevant; what is relevant is risk-spreading, i.e. the spreading of each risk among a large number of shareholders. Since the part of each risk borne by any individual is small, he treats it in an effectively risk-neutral manner. A similar argument arises — but even more strongly — if the middleman buys the commodities forward, thus providing price insurance.

What effect the existence of these monopolistic elements has on price stability and what effect price stabilization would have on these middlemen is a question for future research. It would appear that, if the above argument is correct, by reducing the insurance role of the middleman the sector might be made more competitive.

A natural question which arises at this point is why should these two functions — the purchase of commodities from farmers and the provision of insurance — be tied together? We have not a completely satisfactory explanation of this; there may be economies associated with monitoring; since the collateral on any loan is the crop, the lender has an incentive to monitor efforts which affect both the quality and quantity of output. Similarly for the firm which purchases the crop forward. Thus, it is at least conceivable that the stabilization of commodity prices will have a significant effect on the structure of the whole industry. This may be particularly important in LDCs where credit, land rental, and labour markets are more interconnected, with changes in one having wider repercussions on the market structure than in developed countries.

Important as all these considerations may well be, we shall have to leave them aside in our more formal analysis in the remainder of this book.

Part II

Fundamentals: Supply and Demand Under Risk

Introductory economics textbooks begin with the theory of supply and demand, presenting diagrams in which the quantity supplied or demanded is a simple function of the competitive price. At the next stage the student is shown how to derive these supply and demand schedules from individual profit or utility maximizing behaviour, thus placing these convenient analytical techniques on a rigorous theoretical base. It is then tempting to suppose that minor modifications would allow these same schedules to be used in the analysis of risk, and, indeed, most writers discussing risk and price stabilization have been so tempted. Unfortunately, life is not so simple, and we shall see just how misleading these simple extensions are.

In the following chapters we shall place the theory of demand and supply under risk on a rigorous analytical foundation and describe the resulting market equilibrium. Chapters 5, 6, and 7 are concerned with the analysis of producers' behaviour; Chapters 8 and 9 are concerned with consumers' behaviour under risk; and Chapters 10 and 11 develop the theory of market equilibrium.

The analysis of producers' behaviour begins with the theory of supply when producers are indifferent to income risk, that is, they are risk neutral, and shows that their behaviour will nevertheless be affected by the presence of risk.

Chapter 6 introduces some of the basic concepts employed in the analysis of risk: what is meant by risk aversion, by one farmer being more risk averse than another, and by one distribution being more risky than another. These basic concepts are then applied to analyse the behaviour of risk-averse farmers. It derives important comparative statics results concerning the behaviour of producers and shows how these depend on the specification of the utility and production functions. The chapter also examines the important simplifications of certainty-equivalence and mean-variance analysis and places them in context, and concludes with formulae for measuring the benefits of price stabilization. Chapter 7 provides the empirical counterpart to the theory of supply, and examines the evidence for the expected utility hypothesis and the magnitude of risk and risk aversion.

Chapter 8 derives the corresponding theory of demand and introduces the important concepts of duality, separability, and the indirect utility function, which simplify the derivation of the consumer benefits of price stabilization, the subject of Chapter 9.

The final two chapters are concerned with market equilibrium under risk.

Chapter 10 develops a theory of market equilibrium with risk on the hypothesis that producers hold rational expectations. That is, producers understand the way in which risk affects the outcome of their actions, and they use this knowledge in choosing their actions. Chapter 11 examines alternative theories of expectation formation, and distinguishes two different kinds of benefits which may flow from policies like price stabilization. Such policies may improve the quality of information available to decision-makers, who are led to make more rational decisions, and they may change the allocation of resources and hence the efficiency of equilibrium. If agents remain in rational expectations equilibrium before and after the policy change, then only the second kind of benefit is relevant, so the concept of rational expectations focuses attention on this kind of benefit.

This part of the book produces a logically self-contained theory of supply and demand under risk for a simple economy in which there is no choice between alternative crops, no futures or credit markets, and no storage. It lays the foundation for the subsequent parts in which these complications are introduced and analysed.

Chapter 5

Competitive Supply with Risk-Neutral Farmers

5.1 Introduction

In order to study the impact of commodity price stabilization we need a theory of why prices fluctuate and what effect risk has on farmers' decisions. The previous chapter discussed the various sources of price variability, while this and the following chapter analyses the farmer's choice of supply under risk and shows how his choice depends upon the source of the price variability. One popular method of describing the effect of risk on supply is to start from a theory which relates supply to the price of output, and then to argue that because risk makes production less attractive, the effect of risk can be captured by adjusting the return to production (the output price) downwards by a risk premium, this premium being the amount needed to compensate the farmer for undertaking the risk. Put another way, this approach would work in terms of a *certainty equivalent* price, that is, the perfectly certain price which would yield the same choices in the absence of risk as the farmer actually makes in the presence of risk. If such a price could be simply derived from the average price via the risk premium, then it would appear that the deterministic theory of supply could be simply translated into a theory of supply under risk.

We shall argue in the next two chapters that this is an unsatisfactory and potentially misleading approach to the study of risk, and needs to be replaced by a rigorous theory of behaviour under risk. One simple way to demonstrate this is to consider the behaviour of farmers who are risk neutral — that is, farmers who are indifferent between a risky return and a safe return yielding the same expected value. On the previous argument, for these farmers the risk premium should be zero, and hence we can ignore the effect of risk. We shall show in this chapter that even if farmers are risk neutral, risk nevertheless may have an important effect on their behaviour. In particular, the simple graphical methods of analysis which relate supply to price are quite misleading, so that the traditional Waugh-Oi-Massell analysis discussed in Chapter 2 rests on shaky foundations which need replacing.

The second objective of this chapter is to prepare for the fuller analysis of risk-taking when agents are not risk neutral, which we defer to the next chapter. We define precisely what is meant by the notion of a certainty equivalent price and assess the validity of this popular approach to the analysis of risk. We shall argue that it is important to distinguish between the *action certainty equivalent* price and the *utility certainty equivalent* price. The first is relevant to predicting the effects of risk on the level of supply, while the second is relevant for a welfare analysis of risk. We shall show that they may differ, and that they depend quite sensitively on the form and source of risk. In the next chapter, we shall further show that they also depend on attitudes to risk when farmers are not risk neutral, as assumed in the present chapter.

The first section of this chapter briefly reviews the theory of supply without risk, to provide both a bench-mark, and to introduce certain basic concepts which will be used repeatedly in what follows – concepts such as the production function, cost and profit functions, convexity and concavity. Readers already familiar with these may proceed directly to section 5.3 which presents the theory of supply for risk-neutral farmers.

5.2 Competitive supply without risk

Each farmer is assumed to have full information about his production possibilities, summarized by a production function relating inputs, $\mathbf{x}$, to output, q, and about the prices of inputs, $\mathbf{w}$, and output, p. It will be convenient to assume that the production function is differentiable and *concave*. Thus, if the production function is

$$q = f(\mathbf{x}), \quad \mathbf{x} = (x_1, x_2, \ldots, x_n) \tag{5.1}$$

where $\mathbf{x}$ is a vector of inputs (land, labour, fertilizer, seed, tractor services, etc.), then f is concave if for any pair of input bundles $\mathbf{x}^1$ and $\mathbf{x}^2$

$$f(\lambda \mathbf{x}^1 + (1-\lambda)\mathbf{x}^2) \geqslant \lambda f(\mathbf{x}^1) + (1-\lambda) f(\mathbf{x}^2), \quad 0 < \lambda < 1. \tag{5.2}$$

Figure 5.1 illustrates this property for the case of a single input, for which the inequality can be written $OB \geqslant OA$. Equation (5.2) is equivalent to the statement

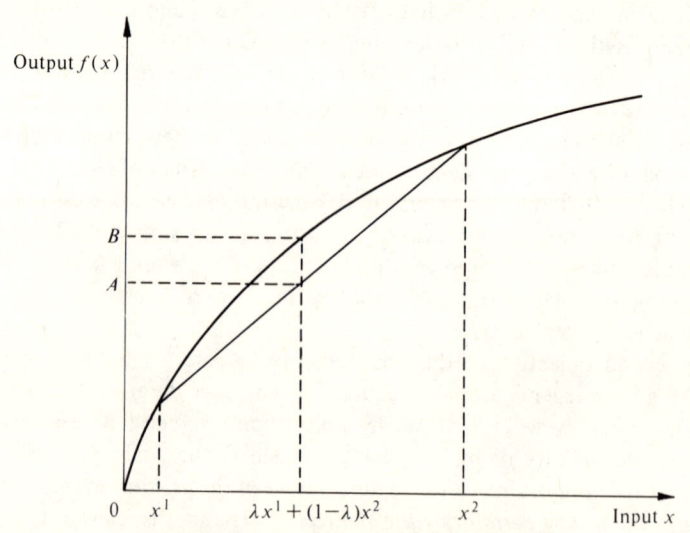

Fig. 5.1 Concave production function

that the chord joining points on the function lies below the function. Strict concavity requires a strict inequality. A *convex* function has the chord above the function, and the inequality reversed. The definition of concavity in equation (5.2) implies that

$$f(x) \leq f(\bar{x}) + \sum_i (x_i - \bar{x}_i) \frac{\partial f(\bar{x})}{\partial x_i} \tag{5.3}^1$$

and, if f is a twice continuously differentiable function of a single variable, it is concave if and only if

$$f'' \leq 0.$$

(For a vector function, the condition is that the matrix of second-order partial derivatives be negative semi-definite, while for convex functions the inequalities are reversed, or the matrix must be positive semi-definite.) These and other related properties of concave and convex functions will be used extensively in the rest of the book. Strict concavity holds if the inequality is strict and is the same as diminishing returns to scale, while concavity includes the case of constant returns to scale. Strict concavity is sufficient to ensure that the profit-maximizing choice of input levels is given by the first-order conditions, while for constant returns, input proportions are determined, but not their scale. Thus, if profits are Y

$$Y = pf(x) - \sum_i w_i x_i, \tag{5.4}$$

the profit-maximizing choice of inputs x_i is the solution to

$$p \frac{\partial f}{\partial x_i} = w_i, \quad i = 1, 2, \ldots, n \tag{5.5}$$

(assuming an interior solution). Equation (5.5) is the familiar result that the value marginal product of the ith input, x_i, is set equal to its price, w_i. Although this approach is the more fundamental, most textbooks use it as a stepping-stone to the derivation of cost curves. To do this, define a *cost-function*, $C(q, \mathbf{w})$ as the minimum cost needed to produce output q at input prices $\mathbf{w}$:

$$C(q, \mathbf{w}) = \min \sum w_i x_i \text{ subject to } f(x) \geq q. \tag{5.6}$$

(It can be shown that the cost function is *concave* in $\mathbf{w}$, using the same proof as proposition 1, Chapter 8.)

If the industry is competitive, the farmer will not be able to influence any prices $(p, \mathbf{w})$ and will maximize profits:

$$Y = pq - C(q, \mathbf{w}) \tag{5.7}$$

when output q is such that marginal cost is equal to price:

---

[1] Take $x^1 = x$, $x^2 = \bar{x}$ in equation (5.2) and let λ tend to zero.

$$p = \frac{\partial C(q, \mathbf{w})}{\partial q} \qquad (5.8)$$

provided that price is above average variable costs, otherwise higher profits are obtained at zero output. If there are diminishing returns everywhere this is guaranteed.

In most textbooks the average cost curve is typically shown as U-shaped, which corresponds to initially increasing returns to scale, perhaps due to indivisibility, followed by diminishing returns. In such cases the marginal cost will intersect the average cost at its lowest point. The distinction between variable or avoidable costs, and fixed or inescapable costs is obvious, but important. If price is below average variable cost, then profits would be increased by avoiding the costs altogether, that is, by closing down this line of production (and shifting the resources to some alternative use, which, in agriculture, usually means producing an alternative crop). Thus to summarize: the supply curve of a competitive firm is the portion of the marginal cost curve above average variable costs.

We can immediately deduce two important additional properties of the supply curve which make it useful in economic analysis. First, the supply of the whole industry is simply the horizontal sum of the individual supply curves and, second, the total cost of industry supply is the area under the supply curve. This follows from the derivation of the supply curve as the marginal cost curve, whose integral (the area below the curve) is clearly the total cost. This implies that profit, or producers' surplus, is the area between the price line and the supply curve, as Fig. 5.2 illustrates.

As drawn, the marginal cost curve is MEC, the supply curve is AEC, that portion above the average variable cost curve, and total costs are $OAECD$ (plus any inescapable, and hence irrelevant, costs).

Finally, we should draw attention to another feature of competitive, riskless markets. Even though the farmer may be interested in the utility of consumption,

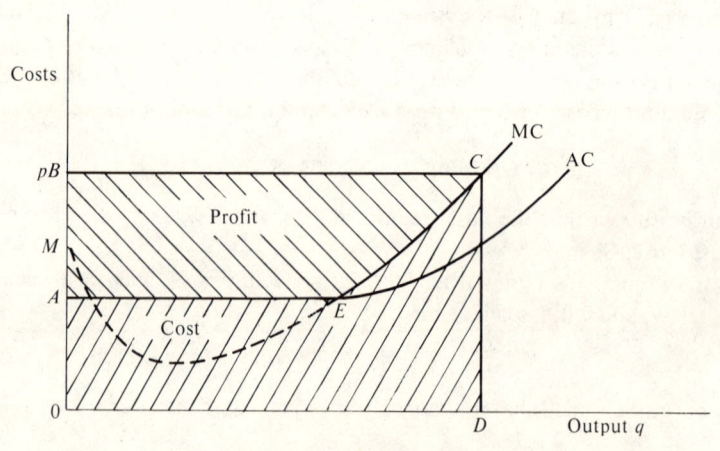

Fig. 5.2 Producer surplus

provided that all inputs and outputs can be traded on competitive markets, he can separate the two problems of making money (profits) and spending them. Even if he consumes the things he grows and some of the inputs he uses (especially his own time), he maximizes his utility by maximizing the cash value of his profits, since the more money he has, the more of every kind of consumption good he can buy. If, on the other hand, some inputs (such as entrepreneurial skill or effort) cannot be purchased on competitive markets, then farmers will not typically wish to maximize profits, but the utility of profits and effort. Thus, if effort is z, the farmer will choose x, z to maximize $U(Y, z)$, where U is his utility function. In this case traded input levels are determined as before:

$$\frac{\partial U}{\partial Y} \cdot \frac{\partial Y}{\partial x} = 0 \quad \text{or} \quad \frac{\partial Y}{\partial x} = 0$$

but effort, z, is found from

$$\frac{\partial U}{\partial Y} \cdot \frac{\partial Y}{\partial z} + \frac{\partial U}{\partial z} = 0.$$

The ratio $-U_z/U_Y$ (where subscripts denote partial derivatives) can be thought of as an implicit price for effort. For a further discussion of this point, see Scitovsky (1943).

To summarize, under riskless, perfect competition, both individual and aggregate supply can be expressed as a function of prices, and, in particular, a supply schedule can be drawn giving output as a function of output price, holding input prices constant. The area below this curve is total cost, and the area between the supply curve and the price is producer surplus, or profit. The farmer is interested in maximizing profits no matter what his consumption preferences are. None of these properties holds generally in the presence of supply risk.

5.3 Competitive supply with risk-neutral farmers

Agriculture is subject to all manner of risks. From the point of view of the individual farmer, these can be divided into two categories:

(i) Production risks: risks which affect his output and which arise because of variations in weather, the prevalence of pests and disease, and other natural causes, such as fire;

(ii) Price risks: risks which affect the prices he receives for the goods he produces or the inputs he plans to purchase (e.g. harvesting labour). Of these, output price risk appears to be more important for the farmer's decision-making and we shall henceforth ignore input price risk. As we noted earlier, price variability may be generated by supply variability or demand variability.

For the market as a whole, price and production variability are intimately connected: variations in output lead to variations in prices, and much of our subsequent analysis is concerned with the precise relationship between the two. For the moment, however, we consider a farmer who believes that the crop he is producing is subjected to a particular pattern of production and price risk, without enquiring how those expectations are formed, nor whether they are consistent or rational.

The farmer's profit Y is random:

$$\tilde{Y} = \tilde{p}\tilde{q} - wx \qquad (5.9)$$

where the tildes denote random variables. (We shall often omit the tilde when we are not concerned to stress the fact that the variable is random.) For simplicity suppose that there is a single input, whose price is not random, and that the farmer can produce only a single crop. In this special case, the farmer's only decision is the level of input (and hence the level of output). Although there was no ambiguity about what the correct objective of the farmer was in the riskless situation (he maximizes profit, Y), there is considerable controversy about the farmer's objective in the presence of risk.

The simplest hypothesis from an analytical point of view is that instead of maximizing profits farmers maximize expected (or average) profits, which we write as $E\tilde{Y}$. In certain circumstances, for example if farmers are wealthy, have widely diversified crops, and access to capital markets, or if they can hedge most of their risks (which we shall describe in greater detail in Chapter 13) this is a plausible objective.

A farmer who maximizes $E\tilde{Y}$ is said to be *risk neutral*; he neither seeks to avoid risk (he is not risk averse) nor does he seek after risk (he is not a risk lover, a gambler). Even though the individual is risk neutral, risk may have important effects on his behaviour. The farmer does *not* maximize

$$Eq \cdot Ep - wx = \bar{p}\bar{q} - wx.$$

(Bars over the variable will be used systematically to denote the expected or average value of that variable.) Unless price and output are uncorrelated, expected revenues are not just the product of mean output and mean price. If, as is likely, price and output are correlated, then expected profits are

$$E\tilde{Y} = \bar{p}\bar{q} + \text{Cov}(p, q) - wx \qquad (5.10)$$

where the covariance of p with q is defined as

$$\text{Cov}(p, q) = E(p - \bar{p})(q - \bar{q}) = Epq - \bar{p}\bar{q}.$$

If, for instance, there were a negative correlation between this particular farmer's output and the market price, were he to ignore the covariance term, he would overestimate the return to increasing his output.

It is sometimes convenient to refer to the *action certainty equivalent price* — the price which, if it prevailed on the market, and if there were no risk, would yield exactly the same supply response as does the random price. This is not the only useful certainty equivalent concept. It may be contrasted with the *utility certainty equivalent price*, the price which would generate the same level of expected utility in the absence of risk. The two are not in general equivalent, but they may be when the individual is risk neutral, as we shall see.

To calculate the certainty equivalent price we need to be somewhat more precise in our specification of the production variability, and the relationship between inputs and outputs. It is convenient to write the production function as

$$q = f(\mathbf{x}, \tilde{\theta}, \xi). \tag{5.11}$$

Output is a function of the inputs, $\mathbf{x}$, the state of nature which is described by the random variable $\tilde{\theta}$, e.g. weather, the incidence of pests and diseases, etc., and the choice of technique of production ξ, e.g. the timing of planting, harvesting, etc., all of which may have an important effect on the variability of output.

This is, however, too general for analytical and practical purposes. Two specifications have been used extensively in theoretical work and both are natural counterparts of alternative econometric specifications. For any given technique we have:

(i) *Multiplicative risk*

$$q = \tilde{\theta} f(x), \quad E\tilde{\theta} = 1, \quad \operatorname{Var} \tilde{\theta} = \sigma^2. \tag{5.12}$$

Rain at harvest times leads to spoilage which is a constant fraction of the crop, regardless of its size, or disease affects a fraction of the crop. If all farms within a particular area face the same risks, then total supply will also experience multiplicative risk:

$$\tilde{Q} = \tilde{\theta}\bar{Q}, \quad \bar{Q} = \Sigma f(x).$$

(Here average total supply is the sum of average individual outputs.) Econometrically such functions are estimated logarithmically, in which case it is typically assumed that θ is log normal: that is for $\log \theta$ to be normal.

(ii) *Additive risk*

$$q = f(x) + \tilde{\theta}, \quad E\tilde{\theta} = 0, \quad \operatorname{Var} \tilde{\theta} = \sigma^2. \tag{5.13}$$

Rain destroys a constant amount regardless of the size of the total crop; disease wipes out a limited area of the crop independent of the total area. This specification is attractive to econometricians wishing to estimate linear supply functions, but it is difficult to justify on theoretical grounds. It is difficult to see how to aggregate to obtain total supply without making total risk proportional to total output — in which case we are back with multiplicative risk. In our view, multiplicative risk seems a better approximation than additive risk, especially for a microeconomic theory of an individual farmer's decisions. Additive risk is at best a simplification used at the aggregate level for econometric estimation. Unfortunately, this simplification is bought at a price, for, as we shall show later, a number of results about the effect of commodity price stabilization schemes depend critically on which assumption is made.

Since price variability is affected by supply variability, we need a simple theory to model this dependence. In Chapter 10 the relationship is examined more carefully, but for the moment it will be enough to suppose that the price depends on two sources of variability

$$\tilde{p} = \bar{p} + \beta(\tilde{\theta} - \bar{\theta}) + \tilde{v}, \qquad E\tilde{v} = 0, E\tilde{v}\tilde{\theta} = 0. \tag{5.14}$$

The first source of risk is supply risk, and all remaining risk (that is, risk which is uncorrelated with supply risk) is placed in the residual term, $\tilde{v}$. For example, if the demand schedule is linear: $p = a - bQ$, supply risk is multiplicative, and if there is additional, independent, additive demand risk $\tilde{v}$, then the equation holds exactly, with $\beta = -b\bar{Q}$, where $-b$ is the slope of the inverse demand schedule. If supply risk is *multiplicative*, risk neutral producers maximize expected profit.

$$E\tilde{Y} = E\{\bar{p} + \beta(\tilde{\theta} - 1) + \tilde{v}\}\tilde{\theta} f(x) - wx, E\tilde{\theta} = 1,$$
$$= \hat{p} f(x) - wx,$$

where the certainty equivalent price is $\hat{p}$:

$$\hat{p} = \bar{p} + \beta\sigma^2 \tag{5.15}$$

or

$$\hat{p} = \bar{p} + \frac{\mathrm{Cov}(p, q)}{\bar{q}}.$$

(We have normalized θ to have mean unity, coefficient of variation σ.) It follows that

$$\hat{p} \gtreqless \bar{p} \text{ as } \beta \gtreqless 0, \quad \text{i.e. as } \mathrm{Cov}(p, q) \gtreqless 0.$$

It is clear that in this case the action certainty equivalent price and the utility certainty equivalent are identical. In particular, the certainty equivalent price exceeds or is less than the mean price as price is positively or negatively correlated with output.

If supply risk is *additive*, producers maximize

$$E\tilde{Y} = E\{\bar{p} + \beta\tilde{\theta} + \tilde{v}\}\{f(x) + \tilde{\theta}\} - wx, E\tilde{\theta} = 0$$
$$= \bar{p} f(x) + \beta\sigma^2 - wx. \tag{5.16}$$

In this case the action certainty equivalent price *is* the mean price though average profits are affected by risk and hence the utility certainty equivalent is greater or less than the mean price as $\beta \gtreqless 0$. The specification of risk evidently has an important bearing on the choice of supply.

We can obtain an expression for p in terms of observable parameters. In what follows σ_x is to be interpreted as the coefficient of variation of the variable x. With multiplicative supply risk we have, from equation (5.12)

$$\sigma_q = \sigma,$$

and from (5.14)

Competitive Supply with Risk-Neutral Farmers 67

$$\text{Var}(p) = \bar{p}^2 \sigma_p^2 = \text{Var}\,\nu + \beta^2 \sigma_q^2.$$

If $\beta < 0$, then this can be substituted into (5.15) and solved to give

$$\hat{p} = \bar{p}\left\{1 - \frac{\sigma_q}{\bar{p}}\sqrt{(\bar{p}^2\sigma_p^2 - \text{Var}\,\nu)}\right\}. \tag{5.17}$$

If, for instance, there is no pure demand risk, so $\text{Var}\,\nu = 0$, then

$$\hat{p} = \bar{p}(1 - \sigma_p \sigma_q).$$

In Chapter 10 we derive explicit expressions for the certainty equivalent price for particular demand functions. For example, if demand is stable and of constant elasticity ϵ, then equation (10.19) gives the action certainty equivalent price as approximately

$$\hat{p} = p(\bar{Q})\{1 + \tfrac{1}{2}(1 - \epsilon)\sigma_p^2\}, \tag{5.18}$$

where $p(\bar{Q})$ is the price when quantity is $\bar{Q}$.

5.3.1 Pitfalls in graphical analysis

In the first section we showed that in the absence of risk supply could be graphed as a function of price, independently of demand, to find the equilibrium output and level of profits. Many authors have been tempted to use similar graphical methods in the presence of risk. Even if we assume risk-neutral producers (the most favourable case) average supply is a function of the certainty equivalent price, which cannot be found independently of the demand schedule. In Fig. 5.3 inputs are chosen at the start of the year, and there is no demand risk.

The representative farmer will choose an expected level of supply $\bar{q}$ (corresponding to total supply $\bar{Q}$), such that the marginal cost of producing $\bar{Q}$ is equal

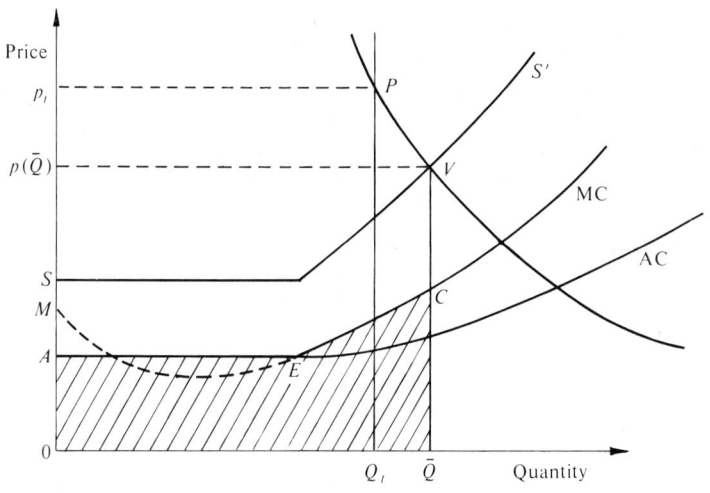

Fig. 5.3 Demand and supply with supply risk

to the action certainty equivalent price, or

$$\text{MC} = \hat{p}.$$

If the demand schedule has constant elasticity, this can be written, using equation (5.18), as

$$p(\bar{Q}) = \frac{\text{MC}}{1 - \tfrac{1}{2}(\epsilon - 1)\sigma_p^2} = (1 + m)\text{MC},$$

where

$$m = \frac{\tfrac{1}{2}(\epsilon - 1)\sigma_p^2}{1 - \tfrac{1}{2}(\epsilon - 1)\sigma_p^2}$$

and is graphed as SVS'. (The curves MC and AC are riskless, and are derived as for the riskless case of section 5.2.) SVS' is a long-run pseudo supply curve, derived by a 'mark up' m, equal to the ratio $VC/C\bar{Q}$ in Fig. 5.3 on MC. The average total supply will be $\bar{Q}$, where SVS' intersects the demand curve. The short-run supply curve will be vertical and fluctuate around $\bar{Q}$, assuming positions such as $Q_t P$ at date t, which leads to a market clearing price of p_t. Costs will be the area under the non-random MC curve, $OAEC\bar{Q}$, while revenue will be random, for example, $Op_t PQ_t$ at date t. Profit will be the difference between random revenue and non-random cost, and not the area between the price line and the (long-run pseudo) supply schedule SVS'.

To summarize, the concept of the certainty equivalent price is a useful one for describing how farmers make their decisions. But it is one to be used with caution, particularly when we are concerned with policies (such as commodity price stabilization schemes) which will affect the distribution of prices. Changes in certainty equivalent prices are in general not equal to (nor even proportional to) changes in mean prices. Different policies may have differential effects on mean prices and on certainty equivalent prices. Moreover, the certainty equivalent price for one farmer may be quite different from that for another farmer. Farmers in a region which is the primary source of a particular commodity (for example West African cocoa farmers) may have a high negative correlation between output and quantity (and hence a low certainty equivalent price), while farmers in a small region (Brazilian cocoa farmers) far away from the main supply region may face a nearly zero correlation between output and quantity. Then, for risk-neutral farmers, a change in the price distribution for the latter is only important in so far as the mean price is changed, whereas for the former, effects on the covariance are crucial, as we shall see later.

Chapter 6

Supply with Risk-Averse Farmers

6.1 Introduction

The previous chapter developed the theory of supply for a risk-neutral farmer and showed that even if the farmer was indifferent to risk, none the less his actions would in general be affected by the presence of risk. Since very few farmers are in fact indifferent to risk, we need to extend the analysis to deal with the case of risk-averse farmers. We start by discussing the concept and measurement of risk aversion, and then enquire into the precise meaning of risk. The remainder of the chapter applies these concepts to a variety of problems which will recur throughout the book. The eventual objective is to develop a method of analysing the effects of a change in the distribution of prices resulting from a commodity price stabilization scheme. This turns out to be a fairly difficult question, and it is helpful to break the problem down into a number of more manageable questions, some of which we discuss in the later sections of this chapter.

In section 6.4 we analyse the effect of changes in risk on the behaviour of producers. In the following section we examine the important special case of the mean-variance model, which has been widely employed because of its analytical simplicity. In this model the analysis of the effects of risk on farmer's behaviour is remarkably simple; unfortunately, as we shall argue, the conditions under which the model may reasonably be used are very restrictive. However, we also show that for many problems the impact of risk can be approximated by a Taylor series expansion in which only the mean and variances of the distribution appear, and we shall discuss when this approximation is legitimate.

While these two sections discuss the effect of changes of risk on the *behaviour* of producers, the final section is devoted to analysing the impact on the welfare of producers. It derives formulae which will be refined and applied later in assessing the costs and benefits of price stabilization. Of course, as this is an introductory chapter it necessarily simplifies, but it lays the foundation for the more comprehensive analysis to be developed later.

6.2 The meaning of risk aversion

Economists have for a long time modelled consumer behaviour on the assumption that the consumer's preferences between goods can be represented by an ordinal utility function defined over these goods. This is possible if the consumer has stable preferences and if he is rational, that is, consistent, in making choices. Given enough observations, a skilful econometrician would be able to derive this utility function by observing the consumer's choices at different prices and levels of money income, and then use it to predict the consumer's behaviour once his income and prices have been specified. (In Chapter 8 we summarize this theory and derive some of its implications.) If we also assume that the consumer is well informed about the consequences of his choices (which in any case is almost required if his preferences are to remain stable), and if we assume that the consumer is concerned with his own satisfaction, then we can draw certain welfare conclusions of the form 'if the consumer chooses A rather than B when both choices are feasible, then his welfare or satisfaction is higher with A than B'. If, further, we accept an individualist welfare ethic, then certain normative consequences follow, and the utility function can be used not only to describe behaviour, or for prediction, but also for welfare analysis and to evaluate social choices.

So much is basic in elementary welfare economics, and it is natural to extend this reasoning to choices involving risk. Most agents would prefer an action which has a sure return, Y, to another action which yields a risky return with the same expected value, and it seems reasonable that a rational agent should be able to compare alternative risky choices, balancing gains against risk, just as the rational consumer compares alternative baskets of goods. Indeed, under certain assumptions discussed in Chapter 8 agents will act as though they had a utility function, defined over the consequences of their choices, and will choose the action which maximizes the expected value, not of the outcome, but of the utility of the outcome. We thus postulate that individual behaviour in the face of risk can be described as if the individual

$$\text{maximizes } EU(\tilde{Y})$$

the expected value of the utility, U, of the risky outcome, $\tilde{Y}$. Essentially, agents need to know the consequences of their choices, to have beliefs about the probabilities of these consequences, and to be concerned only with the consequences (and not with the process by which they are brought about). Just how reasonable these assumptions are will be left until Chapter 7 when we examine some of the empirical evidence, but for the moment we shall explore some of the consequences of this approach. Since we are interested in the choices of producers, we shall suppose that they are primarily concerned with their money *income*, which they are free to spend on commodities whose prices are fixed. To keep the story simple we assume that the world comes to an end after the farmers have spent their income and enjoyed the consumption allowed. We shall discuss the strength of this assumption in Chapter 7 and the consequences of relaxing it in Chapter 14.

We shall proceed in our discussion as follows. First, we shall define what we mean by risk aversion and relate it to the properties of the utility function $U(Y)$. We shall then discuss a more precise quantification of risk aversion. Finally, we shall present several specific utility functions which have played a major role in the recent literature and which we will find useful in the subsequent analysis.

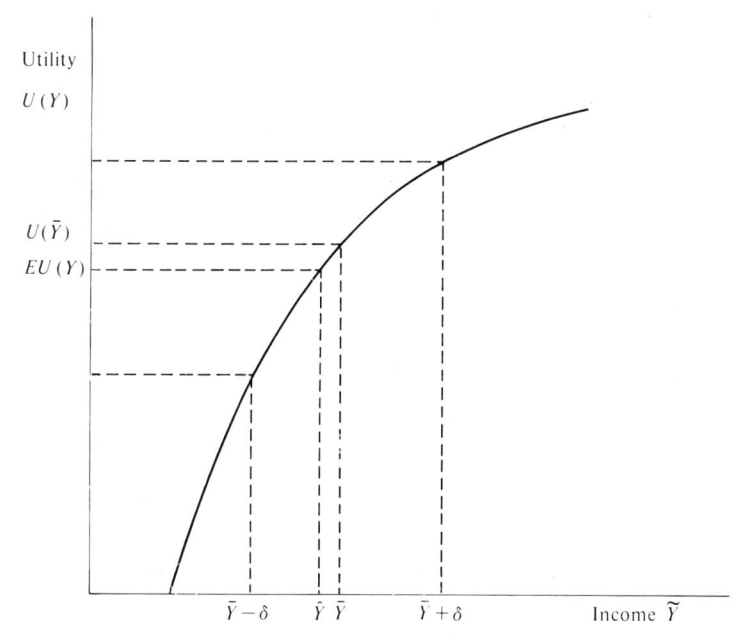

Fig. 6.1 The value of risky income

For a risk-averse individual, the utility function $U(Y)$ appears as in Fig. 6.1, where U is concave. To see that this does in fact correspond to our intuitive notions of risk aversion, calculate the expected utility associated with a random income

$$\tilde{Y} = \begin{cases} \bar{Y} + \delta & \text{with probability } \tfrac{1}{2} \\ \bar{Y} - \delta & \text{with probability } \tfrac{1}{2} \end{cases} \quad (6.1)$$

The expected utility is given by

$$EU(\tilde{Y}) = \tfrac{1}{2}\{U(\bar{Y} + \delta) + U(\bar{Y} - \delta)\},$$

i.e. is half-way between the two utility levels. But note from the diagram that with a concave utility function, this is less than $U(\bar{Y})$, the utility associated with the sure income of $\bar{Y}$.

The difference between the two is a measure of the cost of the risk in terms of the loss of expected utility. We can also measure this cost by asking how much of his sure income would he be willing to give up, and still prefer the sure income to the risky income. That is, what sure income is equivalent (in the utility that it yields) to the random income. In the diagram, $\hat{Y}$ gives the same utility, and is referred to as the *certainty equivalent* income. It can be defined formally by the equation

$$EU(\check{Y}) = U(\hat{Y}). \tag{6.2}$$

The difference between the mean income $\overline{Y}$, and its certainty equivalent is sometimes referred to as the *risk premium* (or the cost of the risk):

$$\rho = \overline{Y} - \hat{Y}. \tag{6.3}$$

The magnitude of the risk premium (the cost of the risk) can be related to the shape of the utility function and the probability distribution function of returns. We would expect that an increase in risk would increase the risk premium and so would an increase in risk aversion. There are simple representations for both of these. If, for instance, we increase δ, clearly this is an increase in riskiness. From Fig. 6.1 we immediately see that this does increase the size of the risk premium (it reduces the certainty equivalent income).

Similarly, greater risk aversion is associated with a more 'curved' utility function. In the limiting case of utility function which is a straight line ($U'' = 0$) there is no risk aversion (we call such an individual risk neutral and discussed his behaviour in the previous chapter). The risk premium is identically zero, regardless of the size of the risk.

These concepts have been made more precise in a series of papers (by Arrow, 1965; Pratt, 1964; Rothschild and Stiglitz, 1970, 1971; and Diamond and Stiglitz, 1974). Rather than repeat their detailed derivations, we shall simply summarize their results and attempt to provide an intuitive motivation for them.

6.2.1 Measuring risk aversion

Since greater risk aversion is associated with a more curved utility function, it is natural to relate risk aversion to the curvature of the utility function. One simple measure of this is the elasticity of marginal utility, or the *coefficient of relative risk aversion*, R, defined as

$$R(Y) = -\frac{YU''(Y)}{U'(Y)} \tag{6.4}$$

and evaluated at some chosen level of income, Y. As an elasticity it is dimensionless, and hence a very convenient way in which to describe risk aversion. The other simple measure is the *coefficient of absolute risk aversion*, A, defined as

$$A(Y) = -\frac{U''(Y)}{U'(Y)}. \tag{6.5}$$

It is not dimensionless and depends on the units in which income is measured. Therefore, if risk aversion is to be described by the numerical measure of the coefficient of absolute risk aversion, the income level must also be given to make sense of the value. Notice that the two measures are trivially related:

$$R(Y) = YA(Y). \tag{6.6}$$

To show that these measures are appropriate and useful, observe that $U(Y)$

can be expanded in a Taylor series. If $Y = \bar{Y} + h$, then

$$U(Y) = U(\bar{Y}) + hU'(\bar{Y}) + \frac{h^2}{2}U''(\bar{Y}) + r_3(h) \tag{6.7}$$

where r_3 is a remainder and r_3/h^2 tends to zero, as h tends to zero. If Y is now the random variable defined in equation (6.1), h is a random variable taking values $\pm\delta$ with equal probability, so the expected value $EU(Y)$ is found by taking the expectation of equation (6.7):

$$EU(\tilde{Y}) = U(\bar{Y}) + \tfrac{1}{2}\delta^2 U''(\bar{Y}) + Er_3(\delta). \tag{6.8}$$

The certainty equivalent income defined in equations (6.2) and (6.3) can likewise be expressed in a Taylor series:

$$U(\hat{Y}) \equiv U(\bar{Y} - \rho) = U(\bar{Y}) - \rho U'(\bar{Y}) + r_2(\rho), \tag{6.9}$$

where again r_2/ρ tends to zero with ρ. If δ is small, then the remainders can be ignored, and since by definition

$$EU(\tilde{Y}) = U(\hat{Y}),$$

it follows that the risk premium is approximately

$$\rho \approx -\tfrac{1}{2}\delta^2 \frac{U''(\bar{Y})}{U'(\bar{Y})} = \tfrac{1}{2}A \operatorname{Var} Y, \tag{6.10}$$

so the absolute size of the risk premium is approximately equal to one-half the variance times the coefficient of absolute risk aversion. However, it is more usual (and more useful) to express the risk premium as a fraction of mean income:

$$\frac{\rho}{\bar{Y}} \approx -\tfrac{1}{2}\frac{\delta^2}{\bar{Y}^2} \frac{\bar{Y}U''(\bar{Y})}{U'(\bar{Y})} = \tfrac{1}{2}R\sigma_Y^2, \tag{6.11}$$

where σ_Y is the coefficient of variation of income, and, like R, dimensionless. The relative risk premium is approximately equal to one-half the square of the coefficient of variation of income times the coefficient of relative risk aversion. In section 6.5, we shall ask how accurate these approximations are for more general distributions than the simple 2-point distribution of equation (6.1).

6.2.2 *Paramaterizing utility functions*

In the subsequent analysis, certain special utility functions are found to be extremely useful. These are:

(i) The utility function with constant relative risk aversion:

$$U(Y) = \frac{Y^{1-R}}{1-R}, \quad R \neq 1 \tag{6.12}$$

$$U' = Y^{-R}$$

$$\frac{-YU''}{U'} = R.$$

A special case of this class of utility functions is the logarithmic or Bernoullian utility function,

$$U(Y) = \log Y : R = 1$$

which has unit relative risk aversion. For this class of utility functions the degree of relative risk aversion is equal to the elasticity of marginal utility, and the functions are usually described as constant elasticity utility functions. For these functions the *proportional* risk premium is independent of the level of wealth, Y.

(ii) The utility function with constant absolute risk aversion:

$$U(Y) = -ke^{-AY} \qquad (6.13)$$

$$-U''/U' = A.$$

This class is often referred to as the exponential utility function. If the outcomes Y are normally distributed then the absolute risk premium is independent of the level of wealth — an implausible property which is nevertheless very useful in solving portfolio problems such as the choice of hedge in a futures market. Its properties are discussed more fully in section 6.5 and in Chapter 13.

(iii) The quadratic utility function:

$$U(Y) = -(a - bY)^2 \qquad (6.14)$$

$$-U''/U' = \frac{1}{a/b - Y}.$$

The quadratic utility function has several attractive features — it has linear marginal utility (useful in solving dynamic buffer stock problems, as in Chapter 30) and it allows expected utility to be expressed in terms of the mean and variance of income alone. However, it has the obvious limitation that utility decreases with income beyond a certain level, a/b.

All three types of utility functions are members of a more general class which satisfy the equation

$$A(Y) = -U''/U' = \frac{1}{\alpha + \beta Y}. \qquad (6.15)$$

Thus when $\alpha = 0$, $\beta = 1/R$ we have constant relative risk aversion; when $\beta = 0$, $\alpha = 1/A$, constant absolute risk aversion, and when $\beta = -1$, $\alpha = a/b$, the quadratic. Cass and Stiglitz (1970) describe the special properties of this wider class of functions.

The most important of these special properties as far as our later analysis is concerned is the linearity of asset demand functions with respect to wealth. Consider the case in which there is a risky asset yielding a return (per dollar invested) of $\tilde{r}$, and a safe asset with a return of s per dollar. Then if W_0 is the individual's initial wealth and Z is the amount invested in the risky asset, his wealth at the end of the period (when the risk has resolved) will be $\tilde{Y}$:

$$\tilde{Y} = \tilde{r}Z + s(W_0 - Z) + W_0. \tag{6.16}$$

The individual chooses Z to maximize expected utility, $EU(\tilde{Y})$, for which the first-order condition is

$$EU'(\tilde{Y})(\tilde{r} - s) = 0. \tag{6.17}$$

For the constant absolute risk aversion utility function of equation (6.13) this can be written as

$$kAe^{-A(1+s)W_0} \cdot E(e^{-A(\tilde{r}-s)Z}(\tilde{r} - s)) = 0.$$

This has a solution Z^*, which satisfies

$$Ee^{-A(\tilde{r}-s)Z^*}(\tilde{r} - s) = 0 \tag{6.18}$$

and which is independent of wealth, W_0, though it does depend on the distribution of $\tilde{r} - s$. Later on, we shall be particularly interested in the special case in which r is normally distributed. In this case Y, which is a linear function of r, is also normally distributed. Expected utility can now be written as

$$EU = -kEe^{-A\tilde{Y}} = -k\exp\{-A\bar{Y} + \tfrac{1}{2}A^2 E(\tilde{Y} - \bar{Y})^2\}. \tag{6.19}$$

(This result follows immediately from the definition of the moment-generating function of the normal distribution.) Consequently, maximizing expected utility of Y when Y is normally distributed is equivalent to maximizing

$$EY - \tfrac{1}{2}A \operatorname{Var} Y,$$

which is the maximand in the mean-variance model of asset demand discussed in section 6.5. In this particular case the solution Z^* must satisfy

$$Z^* = \frac{E(\tilde{r} - s)}{AE(\tilde{r} - s)(\tilde{r} - \bar{r})}. \tag{6.20}$$

Z is the dollar expenditure on the risky asset, and if its price is p per unit, then Z/p is the number of units purchased. Let X be the return per unit, so

$$r = X/p$$

$$\frac{Z^*}{p} = \frac{E(\tilde{X} - sp)}{AE(\tilde{X} - sp)(\tilde{X} - \bar{X})} = \frac{\bar{X} - sp}{AE(X - \bar{X})^2}. \tag{6.21}$$

Thus the demand functions for the asset are not only linear in wealth, they are also linear in price, p.

If the utility function exhibits constant relative risk aversion as in equation (6.12), then the solution to (6.17) is

$$Z^* = \alpha^* W_0$$

where α^* satisfies

$$EW_0^{-R}\{\alpha\tilde{r} + (1-\alpha)s + 1\}^{-R}(\tilde{r} - s) = 0. \tag{6.22}$$

For the quadratic utility function of equation (6.14) Z^* is given by

$$Z^* = \beta + \alpha W_0 \qquad (6.23)$$

where α and β solve

$$E[b(\tilde{r}-s)\beta + W_0 b\{\alpha(\tilde{r}-s) + (1+s)\} - a](\tilde{r}-s) = 0,$$

i.e.
$$\beta = \frac{a(\bar{r}-s)}{bE(\tilde{r}-s)^2}, \qquad \alpha = -\frac{E(\tilde{r}-s)(1+s)}{E(\tilde{r}-s)^2}. \qquad (6.24)$$

Thus, constant absolute risk aversion utility functions have a zero wealth elasticity of demand for the risky asset, constant relative risk aversion utility functions have a constant (positive) elasticity of demand, and quadratic utility functions have linear demand functions, with the demand for the risky asset decreasing with wealth.

It can be shown (see Stiglitz, 1970) that the only utility functions which always yield linear asset demand functions are those satisfying equation (6.15).

Although these parameterizations are extremely useful, it should be emphasized that they do have some special properties (such as, in the context of portfolio analysis, linearity of demand curves for assets as a function of wealth). In the context of poor countries, none of these utility functions adequately captures the large disutility associated with very low incomes (starvation). In such cases we would expect R to increase as income falls, or $dR/dY < 0$.

6.3 Measures of risk

One of the main objectives of this book is to analyse the effects of various stabilization schemes. Clearly, if we completely eliminated price or income instability, the new distribution of prices or income would be less variable than the old. However, for reasons which will become clearer, no stabilization scheme will ever *completely* eliminate risk. Accordingly, we are faced with the difficult task of comparing distributions, both of which are variable.

A natural solution to this problem which suggests itself is to look at some statistical measure of variability, like variance or the range of the distribution. Although this is a reasonable approach, and in many circumstances it may be the only practicable approach, there are certain limitations which need to be borne in mind. First, there are situations where the mean would remain the same, the variance be reduced, and yet expected utility be lowered. This can be seen diagrammatically in Fig. 6.2 where Y takes on three values, $Y_1 < Y_2 < Y_3$. The utility function is piecewise linear with a kink at $\hat{Y}$, where $Y_1 < \hat{Y} < Y_2$. In that case, any change in the distribution which keeps the mean, conditional on Y being greater than $\hat{Y}$, unchanged, leaves utility unaffected. In particular, there are many such changes which reduce variance. It is easy now to consider some further changes in the distribution which further reduce the variance, but which *lower* expected utility. Assume for instance we lower Y_1 a little and compensate

Supply with Risk-Averse Farmers 77

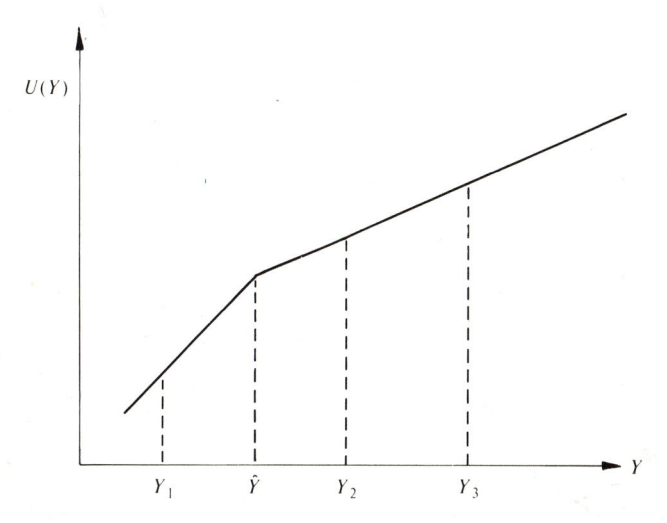

Fig. 6.2 Piecewise linear utility function

for it (to hold the mean constant) by a slightly increased Y_3, and also reduce the probability of either Y_1 or Y_3 occurring (to lower the variance). Clearly, this will make the individual worse off and lower expected utility.

Thus a reduction in variance, keeping mean constant, does not necessarily correspond to an increase in expected utility. Two questions naturally arise.

Are there circumstances in which it does? The answer is 'yes', but they are very restrictive: we must either impose restrictions on the utility function or on the probability distribution function: (a) the utility function must be quadratic, or (b) the distribution function of *incomes* must be fully described by its mean and variance. The second condition appears to offer quite a wide range of applications, but the appearance is deceptive, as we show in section 6.5.

The second question which we can ask is: is there a way of ranking distributions which is valid, say, for *all* risk-averse individuals? The answer is 'yes', but we obtain only a partial ordering, that is, we cannot rank all distributions.

Intuitively, if we have two distributions for incomes, denoted by their distribution functions F and G, we can say that F is more variable than G if (i) F could have been derived from G by simply adding noise (that is, by adding an uncorrelated, purely random, term). (ii) F could have been generated from G by taking some probability weight from the centre of the distribution and putting it into two tails, so as to keep the mean constant, as depicted in Fig. 6.3 which shows the density function. ($f(x)$ is the density function if $f(z)dz$ is the probability of x lying between z and $z + dz$. The distribution function is then

$$F(x) = \int_{-\infty}^{x} f(z)dz,$$

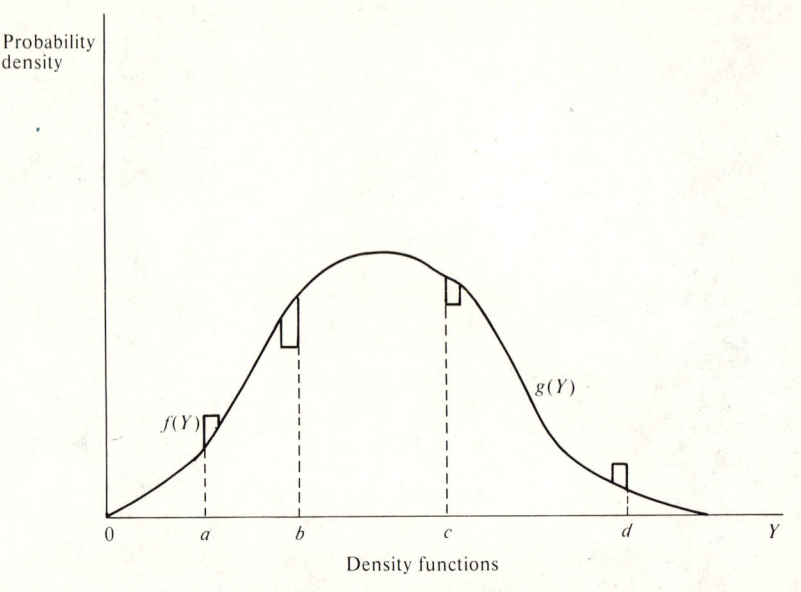

Fig. 6.3 Density functions

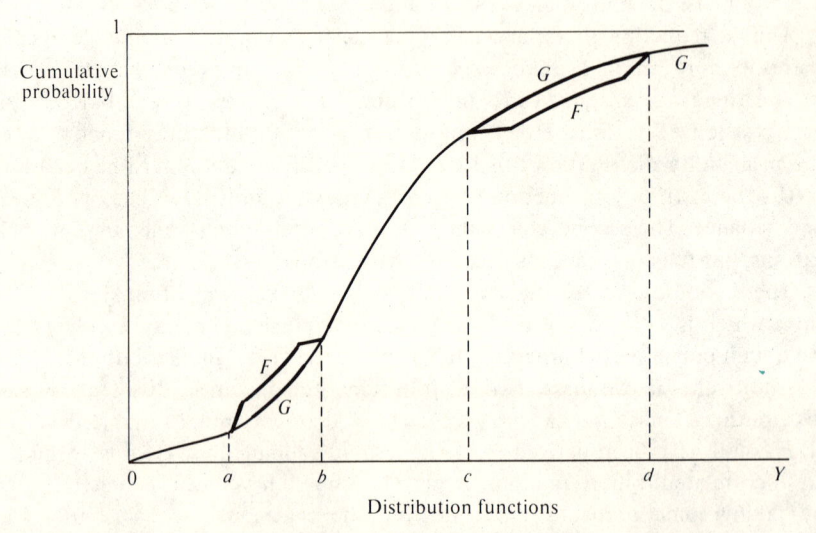

Fig. 6.4 Distribution functions

the probability that the variable is less than or equal to x.)

The resulting distribution function is depicted in Fig. 6.4. Note that it has the property that the distribution function F is initially above that for G (implying that there is a higher probability of very low values) and eventually it lies below G (this is clearly necessary if the two distributions are to have the same mean).

As a slight generalization to that, we can say that F is more variable than G if

$$\int_0^y F(Y)dY \geqslant \int_0^y G(Y)dY, \quad \text{for all } y \tag{6.25}$$

and

$$\int_0^\infty \{F(Y) - G(Y)\}dY = 0 \tag{6.26}$$

$$= [Y(F-G)]_0^\infty + \int_0^\infty Yg(Y)dY - \int_0^\infty Yf(Y)dY$$

(The second condition is simply that the two have the same mean, as the integration by parts confirms, since $[Y(F-G)]_0^\infty = 0$.)

Fortunately, as Rothschild and Stiglitz (1970) have shown, these different approaches are fully equivalent. If F could have been derived from G by simply adding noise, then equation (6.25) is always satisfied (and conversely), and all risk-averse individuals would prefer G to F (and conversely).

We have thus found a method of ranking distributions when the mean of the relevant variable is held constant. It is not, however, always apparent which is the appropriate variable whose mean is to be held constant. One of the important points we emphasize in Chapter 17 is that if we are comparing two price distributions it is not reasonable to hold the mean price constant, because this may not be feasible, but instead it is natural (and feasible) to hold constant the mean quantity sold. We have also found an unambiguous method of describing an increase in risk, for if we add a *mean-preserving spread* to a probability function g the resulting distribution f will be riskier. Moreover, just as a mean-preserving spread lowers expected utility for all concave utility functions, so that risk-averse individuals prefer the original distribution, as Figure 6.5 suggests, so mean-preserving spreads *increase* the expected value of convex functions as in Fig. 6.6. This is why the concept of a mean-preserving spread is so powerful in economics where many functions are known to be either convex or concave.

A closely related result which we shall make extensive use of is *Jensen's inequality*, which states that if $U(Y)$ is a concave function and $h(Y)$ is a convex function, then

$$EU(Y) \leqslant U(\bar{Y})$$

$$Eh(Y) \geqslant h(\bar{Y}).$$

These results follow directly from the definitions of concavity and convexity given in section 5.2 and are again intuitively clear from Figs. 6.5 and 6.6.

80 *Commodity Price Stabilization*

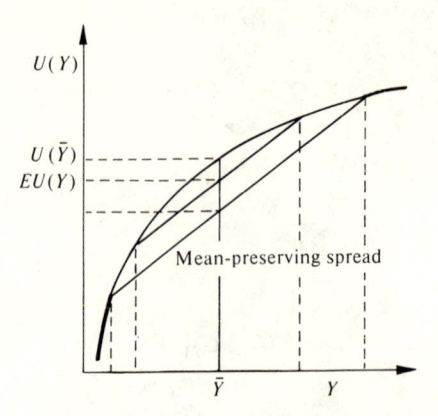

Fig. 6.5 Concave function

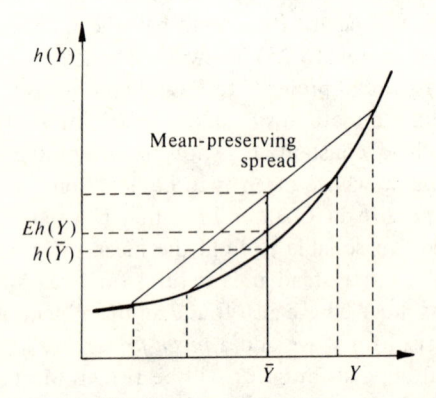

Fig. 6.6 Convex function

6.4* Comparative statics of risk analysis

The previous section gave a very general definition of an increase or reduction in risk which nevertheless yielded definite predictions under assumptions of convexity or concavity. In this section we shall see how far we can apply this approach to study the effect of a change in risk on the level of an individual farmer's supply and on his utility. We shall return to these questions more fully in Chapter 21; for the moment we shall restrict our attention to a very simple model.

Consider the case of multiplicative risk, in which the farmer produces a single crop. His revenue will be

$$\tilde{Y} = \bar{p}\tilde{\theta}f(x). \tag{6.27}$$

If the only input of the farmer is his own labour, x, and if his utility is separable

Supply with Risk-Averse Farmers 81

in income and leisure, then the farmer will maximize

$$EU\{\tilde{p}\tilde{\theta}f(x)\} - wx, \qquad (6.28)$$

where wx represents the disutility associated with labour. We shall make this assumption of separability repeatedly, since it greatly simplifies the analysis. It is equivalent to the assumption that income and leisure are on the borderline between being substitutes and complements. Since there is no clear empirical presumption either way, we thereby avoid having to deal with ambiguously signed cross-derivatives. The dedicated student can of course readily relax this assumption. For the moment, we also assume w is fixed (corresponding to constant marginal disutility of labour) but it is easy to show that this is not a critical assumption.

The utility maximizing farmer chooses x so that

$$EU'(\tilde{Y})\tilde{p}\tilde{\theta}f' = w. \qquad (6.29)$$

Equation (6.29) can be solved for the optimal level of the input (effort or labour), x.

We now ask three fairly standard questions:
1. What is the effect of a change in risk on the supply of effort?
2. What is the effect of a change in risk on the level of expected utility?
3. What comparative statics results can be deduced from market stability conditions?

6.4.1 *Effect of risk on effort*

Consider the effect of a mean-preserving spread, i.e. a change in the distribution of $\tilde{p}\tilde{\theta}$ (and it is only the product of these with which he is concerned) which leaves $E\tilde{p}\tilde{\theta}$ unchanged.

For simplicity, let us define a new random variable, $\tilde{r}$, and rewrite equation (6.29) as

$$EU'\{\tilde{r}f(x)\}\tilde{r} = w/f'(x), \quad \tilde{r} \equiv \tilde{p}\tilde{\theta}. \qquad (6.30)$$

Here $\tilde{r}$ is the random return to farming, which compounds the effect of price and output variability. Observe that $U'\{\tilde{r}f(x)\}\tilde{r}$ can be viewed as a function of the random variable $\tilde{r}$. We know from our earlier discussion and Figs. 6.5 and 6.6 that a mean-preserving spread of a variable reduces the expected value of every concave function of that variable and, conversely, increases the expected value of every convex function.

To see whether this function is convex or concave in r, differentiate $rU'\{rf(x)\}$ twice with respect to r, obtaining

$$\frac{dU'r}{dr} = U' + U''Y$$

$$= U'(1 - R)$$

$$r\frac{d^2U'r}{dr^2} = U''Y(1 - R) - U'R'Y.$$

$U'r$ is convex or concave as this is positive or negative. Figure 6.7 shows the effect of an increase in the expected marginal return to greater effort on the equilibrium supply of effort, namely, to increase it from x^* to x^{**}. Originally, expected net utility W reaches a maximum at M, with a corresponding supply of effort x^*, and zero expected net *marginal* return to effort. If this increases to some positive level (the slope at N is positive), then the maximum must shift to the right, to P, and effort must be increased. Conversely if the return falls. Thus we obtain the result that the expected *marginal* return to greater

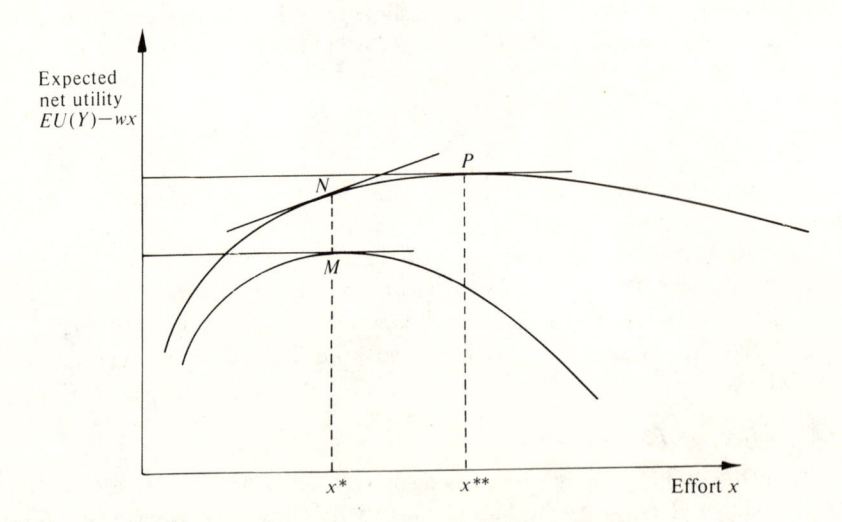

Fig. 6.7 Effect of increased risk on effort

effort is increased or decreased (and hence effort is increased or decreased for (6.30) to be satisfied again) as

$$R(1-R) + R'Y \lessgtr 0. \tag{6.31}$$

Certain special cases can now be identified:

(i) If $R' = 0$ (constant relative risk aversion) effort is increased or decreased as $R \gtreqless 1$. Individuals who are very risk averse increase their effort when risk is increased. They are worried, as it were, about the worst possible contingencies (e.g. starvation). When risk is increased, they have to work harder to avoid these extreme contingencies.

On the other hand, individuals who are less risk averse view the return to farming as lower; farming is a risky activity and risk is unattractive. Thus, they reduce their level of effort (output).

(ii) If, as seems likely, risk aversion is greater at low incomes, i.e. $R' < 0$, it becomes more important to avoid low outcomes and thus an increase in risk is more likely to lead to increased output.

6.4.2 Effect of risk on welfare

Although the effect on output is ambiguous, the maximized value of expected utility is always decreased by a mean-preserving spread. For, denoting a small increase in risk by $d\theta$, we obtain

$$\frac{d(EU - wx)}{d\theta} = \frac{\partial(EU - wx)}{\partial x}\frac{dx}{d\theta} + \frac{\partial EU}{\partial \theta}. \tag{6.32}$$

The first term is zero, because the individual is assumed to choose x to maximize his expected utility. The second term is negative, because U is a concave function of r, and a mean-preserving spread always decreases the expected value of a concave function of the random variable.

Notice that the effect of a change in risk on the level of utility and on the level of marginal utility may be markedly different. They may even be of opposite sign. This has an important implication for the use of certainty equivalents of the kind referred to earlier. As we noted above there are two distinct notions of certainty equivalent that we might use in this context. The *action certainty equivalent* value of the return is the certain value of $\tilde{r}$ which would lead the farmer to take precisely the same action (same level of effort) as the random $\tilde{r}$. The *utility certainty equivalent* value is the certain value of $\tilde{r}$ which would leave the farmer with the same level of expected utility. These are distinctly different numbers (and indeed one may exceed the mean value of r and the other be less than it) and can clearly be affected in different ways by different policies. It is therefore preferable to work with the original utility functions rather than attempting to summarize their salient features in simple measures of certainty equivalence.

6.4.3 Stability and comparative statics

Samuelson's classic text (1947) identified two main sources of meaningful theorems in economics. The first set of theorems proceeds from the assumptions of maximizing behaviour of individuals, and may be exemplified by the Slutsky symmetry condition for demand theory (discussed in Chapter 8). The second set of fruitful theorems in comparative statics may be derived from the stability conditions of market interaction, using what Samuelson refers to as the *correspondence principle*, and set out in his Chapter IX. He illustrates this principle by analysing the stability of a single market in a way directly relevant for our present concern. The first, and perhaps most important, point to make is that market stability is a property of the disequilibrium adjustment mechanism. He contrasts Walrasian stability, in which price responds positively to excess demand, with Marshallian stability, in which supply responds positively to the excess of the demand price over the marginal cost, and with cobweb stability. We shall discuss these alternative concepts of stability in Chapter 23, but our present concern is whether any of these notions of stability permit deductions

84 Commodity Price Stabilization

about comparative statics. As far as we know, very little work has been done applying the correspondence principle to risky markets, perhaps for good reasons. In a static riskless market, the relevant stability conditions are typically local and give information about the signs of various derivatives at the equilibrium point, which can then be used to derive comparative statics results about the directions of movement at this equilibrium point. In a risky market, the equilibrium typically depends on the shape of the various functions over the whole range of the probability distribution. Thus, for example, the supply of effort which solves equation (6.29) depends on the form of marginal utility over the whole range of values which income can take. Different distributions with the same mean (and variance) will give different results. Unless strong restrictions are placed on the functions (such as imposing constant relative risk aversion) little can be deduced about the local shape of these functions at equilibrium from the stability conditions, which depend on the average shapes of the functions over the range of the distribution.

To illustrate this problem we shall anticipate some of the stability analysis of Chapter 21. If there was no risk, straightforward implicit differentiation of equation (6.29) yields

$$\frac{pdx}{xdp} = \frac{1-R}{Rxf'/f - xf''/f'}. \tag{6.33}$$

If f has constant elasticity α, so that

$$f(x) = x^\alpha,$$

then

$$\frac{d\log x}{d\log p} = \frac{1-R}{R\alpha + 1 - \alpha}. \tag{6.34}$$

One appropriate measure of the elasticity of input in the presence of risk is to imagine the effect of a proportionate change of price in each state of the world, so that the new price distribution is

$$\lambda \tilde{p}.$$

The elasticity of input to changes in the whole level of prices is then

$$\frac{\lambda dx}{xd\lambda} = \frac{EU' \cdot \tilde{p}\tilde{\theta}f'(1-R)}{EU' \cdot p\theta f'(R\alpha + 1 - \alpha)} = \frac{1-\bar{R}}{\bar{R}\alpha + 1 - \alpha}, \tag{6.35}$$

where

$$\bar{R} = \frac{EU'\tilde{p}\tilde{\theta}f'R}{EU'\tilde{p}\tilde{\theta}f'}.$$

Thus the *effective* degree of relative risk aversion is a weighted average value. The market stability conditions will impose restrictions on the value of $\bar{R}$ if the market is to be stable, but unless R is assumed constant, this will not give useful information about the response of effort to risk, for example, which depends on R' as well: our knowledge of the sign of equation (6.31) will not be clarified by evidence on the average value of R.

6.5 Mean-variance analysis

It would obviously be convenient if we could describe attitudes to risk just in terms of the mean and variance of income, since these characteristics are simple to estimate and manipulate. The mean-variance model assumes that this is possible and has been extensively employed in the analysis of risk. Like most convenient models, it makes strong assumptions which prejudge the answers to various important questions and thus it is not suitable for proving general theorems. Provided its limitations are understood, it is very convenient for constructing examples and counter-examples, and we shall so use it in various places. Where possible, however, it is preferable to retain the more general utility framework, and appeal to general results on mean-preserving spreads on convex or concave functions. Even when it is necessary to approximate it is usually preferable to leave the Taylor series expansion until it is clear about which point to expand and how many terms to consider.

Given the simplicity and popularity of the mean-variance model it is worth discussing its main advantages and limitations in the analysis of risk. The first question to ask is under what assumptions on risk and the utility function is the mean-variance model valid? When, in other words, can we analyse the effects of risk on welfare and behaviour simply in terms of the mean and variance of income? Obviously, if the distribution of income is normal, this must be true, since the normal distribution is completely described by its mean and variance. If, therefore, the choices of the agent leave his income normally distributed, then all is well. This is particularly easy to see for utility functions with constant absolute risk aversion, for then (recalling the definition given in equation (6.13)) since

$$EU(Y) = -Ee^{-AY} \tag{6.36}$$

the expected utility can be found from the moment-generating function of the normal distribution; for if

$$Y = N(\bar{Y}, V^2)$$

(i.e. Y is normally distributed with mean $\bar{Y}$, variance V^2, then

$$-E \exp(-AY) = -\exp\{-A(\bar{Y} - \tfrac{1}{2}AV^2)\}$$

and the utility certainty equivalent, $\hat{Y}$ is thus

$$\hat{Y} = \bar{Y} - \tfrac{1}{2}AV^2. \tag{6.37}$$

One important class of choices which satisfy this condition are portfolio choices

86 Commodity Price Stabilization

in which the assets have jointly normally distributed returns. In the agricultural context if the income per acre from the i-th crop is $\tilde{r}_i$, and if the farmer allocates a fraction λ_i of each acre to crop i, then his total income per acre is

$$\tilde{Y} = \sum_{i=1}^{n} \lambda_i \tilde{r}_i \tag{6.38}$$

which has mean and variance

$$\bar{Y} = \sum \lambda_i \bar{r}_i$$

$$V^2 = \sum \lambda_i^2 \mathrm{Var}(r_i) + 2 \sum_{i \neq j} \lambda_i \lambda_j \mathrm{Cov}(r_i, r_j). \tag{6.39}$$

As the farmer varies his portfolio, that is, his farm plan, his income remains normally distributed, though its mean and standard deviation will depend on the choice of the fractions λ_i. Figure 6.8 plots the outcome of efficient portfolio choices (those which minimize V for given $\bar{Y}$), and the indifference curves associated with the utility function (that is, lines of constant expected utility).

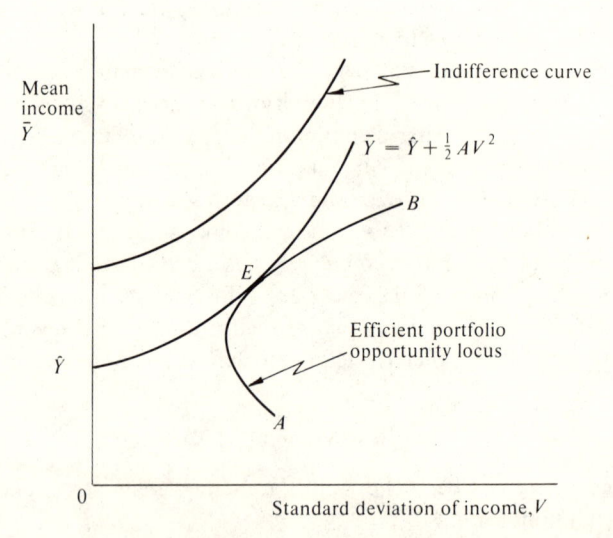

Fig. 6.8 Mean-variance portfolio choice

As shown the portfolio locus AEB is bowed to the left of the line AB, which merely requires that different crops are less than perfectly positively correlated. For example, if there were two crops of equal mean and variance, the portfolio mean would remain unchanged, but its variance would be

$$V^2 = \{\lambda^2 + 2\lambda(1-\lambda)\rho + (1-\lambda)^2\}v^2, \tag{6.40}$$

where v is the variance of one crop and ρ is the correlation coefficient of the returns. Minimizing the variance gives $\lambda = \frac{1}{2}$,

$$V^2 = \frac{1+\rho}{2} v^2 \qquad (6.41)$$

which is less than the variance of each crop separately (if $\rho < 1$) and possibly much less, if ρ is negative.

If, in addition to the risky crops, the farmer has a perfectly safe crop which always yields the same return, r_s, then the mean return from allocating a fraction λ to the safe crop and $1 - \lambda$ to a single risky crop with return $\bar{r}$, variance v^2, is

$$\bar{Y} = \lambda r_s + (1 - \lambda)\bar{r}$$

while the standard deviation is just

$$V = (1 - \lambda)v.$$

This means that the opportunity locus is a straight line DE when plotted in mean standard deviation space, as in Figure 6.9. The point E represents the risky crop, which could as well be a risky portfolio of crops. For example, if there are many

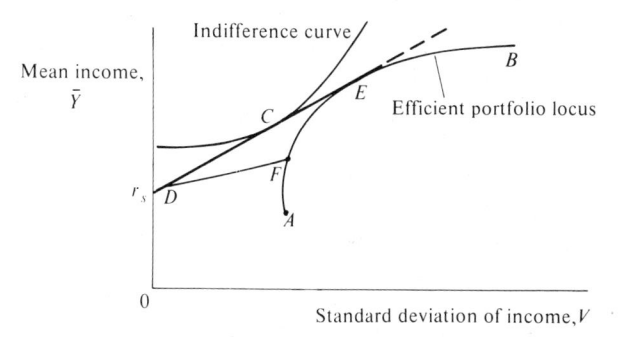

Fig. 6.9 Combination of risky and safe crops

risky crops with an opportunity locus AEB, then the point E is the tangent from D to the locus since any other point on the locus such as F, will yield less attractive final portfolio opportunities.

It follows that the farmer's decision can be made in two stages. First, given the returns on all the crops (including the safe crop), find the best crop pattern of risky crops as the point of tangency, E, from D to the locus of portfolio possibilities in Fig. 6.9. Second, decide on the amount of the risky crop pattern, which will be where the farmer's indifference curve touches DE at the point C. Only the second choice is affected by the farmer's attitude to risk so one can talk of *the* optimal crop plan for risky crops.

Now this portfolio separation theorem is very special and ceases to hold when the assumptions of mean-variance are relaxed. Nevertheless, the intuitive insight offered by mean-variance analysis — that it is the *covariance* of yields which are important determinants of the attractiveness of an asset or crop — is obviously a robust result which does not depend on the specific assumptions of mean-variance analysis.

The case of constant absolute risk aversion is special in a way which is obvious when its indifference curves are plotted in the mean-standard deviation Fig. 6.9 for all the indifference curves are vertical displacements. That is, the slope of the indifference curve depends only on the standard deviation and not on the mean of income. It follows that changes in wealth do not affect the choice of the risky portfolio at all — a most improbable implication. Nevertheless, this property is often very useful in the analysis of risk for essentially it sets the income effect to zero and concentrates attention on substitution effects, as risk changes. In several of our examples we shall find that while it would be almost impossible to solve for an equilibrium with general utility functions, the constant absolute risk aversion case, by separating out the risk and wealth effects, permits a simple solution. This is most apparent in solving for the equilibrium degree of speculation on the futures market, discussed in Chapter 13.

Mean-variance analysis will not work (except for the implausible case of quadratic utility functions discussed in subsection 6.2.2) where the probability distributions are non-normal or when the farmer's choice changes the *form* of the distribution of returns. The problem is that return is the product of price and quantity, less costs. Output cannot be normally distributed since that would imply some probability of negative output. Even if output were approximately normally distributed, and if this led to price being roughly normally distributed, their product would not be normal. One could cut through this problem by arguing that net returns *might* be roughly normally distributed to the extent that it would require considerable data to reject the hypothesis of normality. In many cases this is an adequate defence, but for some decisions the farmer will both be worried about extreme events (such as bankruptcy or starvation) and acutely aware that the risk is not symmetric or bell shaped. Indeed, his main decision problem might be to change the form of the distribution, to reduce the weight in the adverse tail. Most insurance schemes have this property and many actions can be thought of as insuring against adverse outcomes. For such decisions, mean-variance analysis may be seriously misleading.

There is one other special case which appears to offer the advantages of mean-variance analysis under a more plausible specification of risk and utility function, and that is the combination of constant relative risk aversion R, with a log-normal distribution of income (that is, the log of income is normally distributed).

6.5.1* *Properties of the log-normal distribution*

If a random variable X is log-normally distributed, with the mean of $\log X$ equal to μ, and the variance of $\log X$ equal to σ^2, then we write

$$X = \Lambda(\mu, \sigma^2) = e^Z, \tag{6.42}$$

where Z is a random variable normally distributed with mean μ, variance σ^2:

$$Z = N(\mu, \sigma^2).$$

Its properties are detailed in Aitcheson and Brown (1957), and the expected value of powers of X can readily be found from the moment generating function of Z, defined as

$$M_Z(t) = E \exp(tZ).$$

Thus, since Z is normal

$$EX^\beta = M_Z(\beta) = \exp(\beta\mu + \tfrac{1}{2}\sigma^2\beta^2). \tag{6.43}$$

In particular

$$EX = \exp(\mu + \tfrac{1}{2}\sigma^2)$$

$$\text{Var } X = \exp(2\mu + 2\sigma^2) - \exp(2\mu + \sigma^2).$$

If, therefore, income can be written

$$Y = \bar{Y}\Lambda(-\tfrac{1}{2}\sigma^2, \sigma^2),$$

then

$$EY = \bar{Y}$$

$$\text{Var } Y = \bar{Y}^2(\exp \sigma^2 - 1) \equiv \bar{Y}^2 \sigma_y^2 \tag{6.44}$$

But

$$\exp \sigma^2 = 1 + \sigma^2 + \sigma^4/2! + \ldots$$

so the coefficient of variation of Y, σ_y, is approximately σ.

Equation (6.43) allows us to calculate the utility certainty equivalent income, $\hat{Y}$, directly for

$$\frac{\hat{Y}^{1-R}}{1-R} = \frac{EY^{1-R}}{1-R} = \frac{\bar{Y}^{1-R}}{1-R} \exp\left\{-R(1-R)\frac{\sigma^2}{2}\right\}$$

or, from (6.44)

$$\hat{Y} = \bar{Y}(1 + \sigma_y^2)^{-R/2}. \tag{6.45}$$

This is an exact equation, to be compared to the approximate equation (6.11) above.

Log-normality is the natural assumption to make in many econometric specifications which assume constant elasticities and multiplicative risk, and it has the advantage that negative values are ruled out. Moreover, if output and price are log-normal, so will be revenue, while if output fluctuations *cause* the price fluctuations and demand is of constant elasticity, revenue will be log-normal, as required here. (These cases are discussed in more detail in section 6.6.) Unfortunately, we cannot use the previous portfolio analysis for crop choices in this case because the sum of two log-normal distributions is not log-normal.

Given the restricted conditions under which choices under risk can be accurately described in terms of means and variances alone, it is obviously important to ask whether it is possible to measure the impact of risk (and particularly changes in risk) *approximately* using just means and variances, and, if so under what conditions. The question is important for two reasons. In the first place, the concept of a mean-preserving spread is useful for qualitative analysis, but not for estimating the quantitative impact of changes in risk. Second, it is difficult enough to estimate the mean and variance of a probability distribution without having to investigate higher moments, and it would obviously simplify matters if these were not needed. The next section examines the conditions under which mean-variance analysis is approximately valid.

6.5.2 Quadratic approximations and Taylor series expansions

If the function $U(Y)$ is sufficiently differentiable then it can be expressed as a Taylor series:

$$U(Y) = U(\bar{Y}) + (Y - \bar{Y})U'(\bar{Y}) + \tfrac{1}{2}(Y - \bar{Y})^2 U''(\bar{Y}) \quad (6.46)$$

$$+ \ldots \frac{(Y - \bar{Y})^n}{n!} \{U^{(n)}(\bar{Y}) + \epsilon_n\}$$

where $\epsilon_n \to 0$ as $Y \to \bar{Y}$.

ϵ_n can be thought of as a remainder, or an error, which depends on Y and n. Take the expectation of both sides to obtain

$$EU(Y) = U(\bar{Y}) + \tfrac{1}{2}U''(\bar{Y})E(Y - \bar{Y})^2 + \eta_2 \quad (6.47)$$

$$\eta_2 = \tfrac{1}{2}E(Y - \bar{Y})^2 \epsilon_2(Y).$$

This says that expected utility can be approximately expressed as a function of the mean and variance of income. We wish to know under what conditions is this approximation valid, i.e. when is the error η_2 small relative to the second term. It is tempting to suppose that as the variance of Y tends to zero, the error tends to zero, but it is easy to show that this is not necessarily true. For example, consider the family of distributions of Y in which

$$Y = \begin{cases} \bar{Y} + \pi^{-1/3} & \text{with probability } \pi \\ \bar{Y} - \pi^{-1/3} & \text{with probability } \pi \\ \bar{Y} & \text{with probability } 1 - 2\pi. \end{cases}$$

Then

$$E(Y - \bar{Y})^2 = 2\pi^{1/3} \to 0 \quad \text{as} \quad \pi \to 0$$

$$E(Y - \bar{Y})^3 = 0$$

$$E(Y - \bar{Y})^4 = 2\pi^{-1/3} \to \infty \quad \text{as} \quad \pi \to 0.$$

Thus, as the variance goes to zero, the fourth (and higher even moments) become infinitely large. It is easy to see what goes wrong, for it is not enough for the variance of a probability distribution to tend to zero for $Y - \bar{Y}$ to tend to zero, and hence it is not possible to argue that $\epsilon_2 \to 0$. We need a stronger notion of convergence, and Samuelson (1967, 1970) introduces the concept of 'compact' probabilities, such that as some specified parameter goes to zero, all the distributions converge on the certain outcome. Thus if the distribution function of Y can be written

$$F(Y) = P\left(\frac{Y - \bar{Y}}{V}\right), \quad V^2 \equiv E(Y - \bar{Y})^2$$

for some given distribution function P, then as the variance of Y, V^2, tends to zero, the probability all piles up at $\bar{Y}$, and, assuming that P has finite moments, all the higher moments of Y will tend to zero. As Samuelson shows for such distributions, as the variance tends to zero, so the mean-variance approximation becomes progressively more accurate. In the counter example, as the variance went to zero, the form of the distribution was changing, and becoming *more* disperse, not less.

We shall therefore defend the use of Taylor series expansions on the grounds that they are valid for 'small risks', meaning not just that the variance is small, but the dispersion of the whole distribution is not 'too large'. However, it is usually advisable to delay taking approximations until as late as possible in the analysis to avoid the compounding of errors. For example, even when the quadratic approximation provides a good approximation to the level of expected utility, one must be careful in using mean-variance analysis for comparative statics analysis. That requires (for small variance) employing a quadratic approximation to the first-order condition, which may not be the same as the first-order condition derived from the quadratic approximation to the utility function.

As an illustration of the method of calculating expected values by Taylor series approximations consider

$$E\theta^\beta \quad \text{where} \quad \theta \equiv 1 + u, \quad Eu = 0, \quad Eu^2 = \sigma^2$$
$$\theta^\beta = (1 + u)^\beta \cong 1 + \beta u + \tfrac{1}{2}\beta(\beta - 1)u^2,$$

hence

$$E\theta^\beta \cong 1 + \tfrac{1}{2}\beta(\beta - 1)\sigma^2. \tag{6.48}$$

If in fact θ is log-normally distributed

$$\theta = \Lambda(-\tfrac{1}{2}s^2, s^2), \quad \sigma^2 = \exp s^2 - 1$$

then, from equation (6.43)

$$E\theta^\beta = \exp(-\tfrac{1}{2}\beta s^2 + \tfrac{1}{2}\beta^2 s^2)$$

$$E\theta^\beta = (1 + \sigma^2)^{\frac{1}{2}\beta(\beta-1)}. \tag{6.49}$$

For example, if $\beta = 3$, $\sigma = 0.3$, the error in the Taylor series approximation is 2 per cent, or 28 per cent of σ^2. If, however, $\beta = 1.5$, the error is only 1 per cent of σ^2. The accuracy of the approximation thus depends on the size of σ^2 and β.

6.6 Measuring the benefits of price and income stabilization

The most difficult part of the study of commodity price stabilization lies in measuring the responses by the various agents to the change in price instability. Farmers may change their allocation of inputs, their production techniques, their cropping plan, the amount of crop storage, and their dealings on futures markets. Consumers may also change their inventory policy, their dealings on futures markets, and, if they are intermediate producers, their production plans, though typically final consumers are not involved much in these activities. Much of the rest of the book is devoted to the study of these responses, but we can throw some immediate light on the central issue of the benefits of price stabilization if we are prepared to assume that there is *no* response to price stabilization. Obviously this is an extreme, and apparently unreasonable, assumption, but it can be defended, not only on the grounds that it is useful as a bench-mark. In the first place, it takes agents time to detect and measure changes in risk, for estimates of sample *variance* (to take one natural measure of risk) require large samples (or are themselves subject to wide sampling variation). Assuming no response is then equivalent to studying the short-run impact of the proposed stabilization scheme, to be compared with the long-run impact, after agents have fully adjusted to the new equilibrium. Second, we shall show that in some cases the long-run impact on producers is a simple fraction of the short-run impact. Finally, the short-run impact clarifies an important distinction between *transfer* benefits, which producers gain at the expense of consumers, or vice versa, and *efficiency* benefits, which represent net social gains. The long-run impact typically alters the transfer benefits, which are merely redistributive, without much affecting the efficiency benefits. For all these reasons, then, it is sensible to measure the producer benefits of stabilization schemes which change the variability of *incomes* (typically, by changing the variability of prices) without changing the level of inputs. Average output thus remains constant and we can ignore the (constant) disutility of effort. Moreover, we can apply some of the techniques developed in this chapter to obtain simple quantitative measures of the two types of producer benefits.

Suppose that initially a representative farmer has income $\tilde{Y}_0$ with mean $\bar{Y}$ and coefficient of variation σ_{y0}, and after stabilization this changes to $\tilde{Y}_1$ with mean $\bar{Y}_1$, coefficient of variation σ_{y1}. We wish to know what stabilization is worth to the farmer, that is, what sum of money, B, he would be willing to pay for the stabilization scheme to be introduced. This sum can be found by equating expected utility:

Supply with Risk-Averse Farmers

$$EU(\tilde{Y}_0) = EU(\tilde{Y}_1 - B). \quad (6.50)$$

Expand the left-hand side in a Taylor series:

$$\text{LHS} \cong U(\bar{Y}) + \tfrac{1}{2}E(\tilde{Y}_0 - \bar{Y})^2 U''(\bar{Y}) \quad (6.51)$$

and similar expand the right-hand side:

$$\text{RHS} \cong U(\bar{Y}) + (\Delta \bar{Y} - B)U'(\bar{Y}) + \tfrac{1}{2}E(\tilde{Y}_1 - \bar{Y} - B)^2 \cdot U''(\bar{Y}), \quad (6.52)$$

where Δ is the difference operator, so

$$\Delta \bar{Y} = \bar{Y}_1 - \bar{Y}_0.$$

Equating these two expansions and dividing by $\bar{Y}U'(\bar{Y})$ gives

$$\frac{B}{\bar{Y}} = \frac{\Delta \bar{Y}}{\bar{Y}} - \tfrac{1}{2}R\left\{\Delta\sigma_y^2 + \left(\frac{\Delta \bar{Y} - B}{\bar{Y}}\right)^2\right\}. \quad (6.53)$$

Evidently $(\Delta \bar{Y} - B)/\bar{Y}$ is of order σ_y^2 and its square can be ignored, given the accuracy of the approximation, so that

$$\frac{B}{\bar{Y}} = \frac{\Delta \bar{Y}}{\bar{Y}} - \tfrac{1}{2}R\Delta\sigma_y^2. \quad (6.54)$$

The first term is the *transfer* benefit, for the change in average income to the producer is matched by an equal change in average expenditure by consumers. The second term is the *efficiency* or *risk* benefit, the benefit from reducing costly risk to the farmer.

It is easy to quantify these benefits in particular cases. Suppose that the source of risk lies on the supply side, and that output is log-normally distributed. If demand is stable and has constant elasticity ϵ, so that

$$p = Q^{-1/\epsilon}, \quad Q = \bar{Q}\theta$$

with

$$\theta = \Lambda(-\tfrac{1}{2}\sigma^2, \sigma^2), \quad E\theta = 1, \text{ Var } \theta \simeq \sigma^2,$$

then income is also log-normally distributed

$$Y = pQ = \bar{Q}^{1-1/\epsilon}\theta^{1-1/\epsilon}.$$

Expected values of powers of θ can be found directly from equation (6.43), for

$$E\theta^\beta = \exp\tfrac{1}{2}\beta(\beta - 1)\sigma^2 \simeq 1 + \tfrac{1}{2}\beta(\beta - 1)\sigma^2 \quad (6.55)$$

(since $\exp x \cong 1 + x$).

Initially, the CVs of prices and incomes are

$$\sigma_p = \frac{\sigma}{\epsilon}, \quad \sigma_y = \left(1 - \frac{1}{\epsilon}\right)\sigma.$$

Suppose that stabilization reduces the CV of prices to a fraction $1 - z$ of its original value, so that z measures the degree of stabilization, with $z = 1$ corresponding to perfect price stability:

$$p = \bar{Q}^{-(1/\epsilon)}\theta^{-(1-z)/\epsilon}, \quad \sigma_p = \frac{(1-z)\sigma}{\epsilon},$$

then the CV of income will fall to

$$\sigma_y = \left(1 - \frac{1-z}{\epsilon}\right)\sigma.$$

The transfer benefit B_T is

$$B_T = \frac{\Delta \bar{Y}}{\bar{Y}} = \frac{\{E\theta^{1-(1-z)/\epsilon} - E\theta^{1-1/\epsilon}\}}{E\theta^{1-1/\epsilon}}.$$

Since the numerator is of order σ^2, and the denominator is $1 + k\sigma^2$, where k is of order 1 the error in assuming that the denominator is exactly 1 is of order σ^4 and can be ignored. Hence, using the approximation of equation (6.55)

$$B_T = \tfrac{1}{2}\frac{z}{\epsilon}\left(1 - \frac{2-z}{\epsilon}\right)\sigma^2. \tag{6.56}$$

Similarly, the risk benefit is

$$B_R = \tfrac{1}{2}R\frac{z}{\epsilon}\left(\frac{2-z}{\epsilon} - 2\right)\sigma^2 \tag{6.57}$$

so the total benefit is

$$B = \tfrac{1}{2}\frac{z}{\epsilon}\left\{1 - 2R - \frac{2-z}{\epsilon}(1 - R)\right\}\sigma^2, \quad 0 \leq z \leq 1. \tag{6.58}$$

Evidently each part of the total benefits can be either negative or positive, depending on the magnitude of risk aversion, R, the elasticity of demand, ϵ, and the degree of stabilization, z.

More generally, if there is additional multiplicative randomness in demand, so that supply and demand are respectively

$$Q = \bar{Q}\theta$$

$$Q^d = p^{-\epsilon}\phi, E\phi = 1,$$

and if θ and ϕ are jointly log-normally distributed, then so will be price and quantity. Suppose the correlation coefficient of $\log p$ on $\log Q$ is r (typically negative) and that stabilization of degree z lowers the coefficient of variation to $1 - z$ of its original value σ_{po}.

The square of the CV of income (itself log-normally distributed) is approximately equal to the variance of $\log pQ$:

$$\mathrm{Var}(\log p + \log Q) = \sigma^2 + 2r(1-z)\sigma\sigma_{po} + (1-z)^2\sigma_{po}^2,$$

so that the risk benefit is now

$$B_R = \tfrac{1}{2} Rz\{(2-z)\sigma_{po}^2 + 2r\sigma\sigma_{po}\}. \qquad (6.59)$$

The transfer benefit is found by evaluating

$$B_T = \frac{\Delta \bar{Y}}{\bar{Y}} = \frac{EX_1 X_2^{1-z} - EX_1 X_2}{EX_1 X_2}, \qquad (6.60)$$

where $X_1 = \theta, X_2 = (\phi/\theta)^{1/\epsilon}$ are jointly log-normally distributed. In the Appendix to Chapter 13 it is shown that

$$X_2 = \Lambda(\mu_2, \sigma_p^2); \quad \mu_2 = -\tfrac{1}{2}(\epsilon\sigma_p^2 + 2r\sigma\sigma_p),$$

while

$$X_1 = \Lambda(\mu_1, \sigma^2); \quad \mu_1 = -\tfrac{1}{2}\sigma^2.$$

Equation (13A11) demonstrates that

$$EX_1 X_2^{1-z} - EX_1 X_2 = -\tfrac{1}{2}z\{2\mu_2 + (2-z)\sigma_p^2 + 2r\sigma\sigma_p\}.$$

So, again approximating the denominator by unity, we obtain the same simple formula as before:

$$B_T = \tfrac{1}{2}z\{\epsilon - (2-z)\}\sigma_{po}^2. \qquad (6.61)$$

These formulae can be used to measure the short-run benefits of price stabilization as they are given in terms of the initial CV of output, σ, the initial CV of price, σ_{po}, the fractional reduction in the CV of price, $1-z$, the correlation between price and supply, r, the elasticity of demand, ϵ, and the degree of relative risk aversion, R. Table 6.1 gives as an example the results of a very simple regression exercise reported in more detail in Chapter 20.

Table 6.1 *Benefits of stabilizing the cocoa price by 50 per cent*

Country	Elasticity[a]	r[a]	σ %	σ_p %	Risk benefit %	Transfer benefit %
Ghana	0.5	−0.74	21	31	1.2R	−2.4
Brazil	−0.3	0.33	24	31	3.0R	−4.3

[a] As defined, price elasticity and the correlation coefficient have opposite signs.

It is interesting to note the difference between countries for the same crop, and the difference in sign of the two components of the benefit.

Chapter 7

Empirical Measurements of Producers' Attitudes to Risk

The theory developed in Chapter 6 assumed that farmers acted as though they were maximizing expected utility. How reasonable is this assumption? What does the available evidence have to say about attitudes to risk? How important is risk in agriculture? In this chapter we first consider the theoretical problems with the expected utility hypothesis, and then discuss the results of an important recent experiment which provides evidence of farmers' attitudes to risk. In section 7.4 we examine the non-experimental empirical evidence, and, finally, conclude with some evidence on the magnitude of agricultural risk.

7.1 Distinguishing among alternative hypotheses

Much of the qualitative analysis contained in this book does not depend critically on the assumption employed throughout the work that individuals maximize their expected utility. Our analysis emphasized three points:

(i) a change in the price distribution may well increase the variability of income faced by individual farmers;

(ii) this change in risk may cause changes in the production decisions of producers; and possibly in the consumption decisions of consumers, and

(iii) there are important general equilibrium consequences of these changes.

These results would be true under virtually any theory which argued that producers (and consumers) are concerned with the riskiness of their income. Moreover, the expected utility hypothesis is consistent with a wide range of behaviour, e.g. an increase in risk of one crop could lead to the farmer growing more or less of the crop.

But for policy purposes, we often need more than just a qualitative analysis. We would like to know: (a) how important is risk in agriculture; and in particular (b) how large is the response (and in which direction) to a change in risk.

To answer the second question, in particular, to know how farmers would respond to the kinds of changes in risk induced by a commodity price stabilization programme, we need to be able to infer that the individual's behaviour towards this new risk situation will be similar to his behaviour towards earlier risky situations which he has faced.

This postulate of *consistency* — that individuals behave systematically when faced with risky situations — is thus the basic hypothesis underlying our analysis. The consistency hypothesis underlies all of the theory of consumer behaviour. But on *a priori* grounds it has somewhat less force in this context than in others:

if a consumer chooses oranges instead of apples and then finds that he dislikes the taste of oranges, he learns immediately that he has been mistaken. With risky choices it is more difficult to learn from experience, since it is not clear whether the consumer made the wrong choice, or whether he was merely unlucky. This hypothesis has been subjected to testing in a variety of laboratory experiments, where individuals are confronted with different gambles. Inconsistencies in their behaviour were often noted.

Parts of the apparent inconsistencies may be explained by the lack of familiarity of the individuals with the kinds of choices being faced; alternatively, because the pay-offs in the experimental situations are usually trivial, individuals may not take the experimental situation seriously. With larger pay-offs, one might expect to find more consistent behaviour. This in fact turns out to be the case, as the study we report later in section 7.3 suggests.

The expected utility theory, of course, implies more than just consistency. More generally, we can write utility as a function of income in each of the states of nature:

$$U = U\{Y(\theta_1), Y(\theta_2), Y(\theta_3), \ldots\}$$

where

$$Y(\theta_i) = \text{income in state } i.$$

The expected utility theory postulates that the utility function can be written in a particular form:

$$U = \sum_i U\{Y(\theta_i)\}\pi_i$$

where π_i is the probability that state i occurs and

$$\sum \pi_i = 1.$$

There are a variety of alternative axiomatic foundations for the expected utility hypothesis (see, for instance, Savage, 1954; Arrow, 1970; Luce and Suppes, 1965). The critical hypothesis is the 'compounding' axiom, that an individual is indifferent between a lottery of lotteries and a single lottery yielding the same outcomes with the same probabilities. For instance, consider a lottery that yields

$1 with probability 0.25

$2 with probability 0.5

$4 with probability 0.25

Now, consider an alternative situation, where the outcome of the first lottery is that the individual gets one of two lotteries, either lottery A, which yields

$1 with probability 0.5,

or

$2 with probability 0.5,

or lottery B which yields

$2 with probability 0.5,

or

$4 with probability 0.5.

If lotteries A and B are equally likely (the individual has a 50 : 50 chance of drawing lottery A or lottery B), then the expected utility hypothesis postulates that the individual ought to be indifferent between the original lottery and the lottery of lotteries.

This hypothesis too has been subjected to testing, and systematic behaviour which is not consistent with it has been uncovered in experimental situations. Part of the problem is that most individuals are not very good at estimating (and compounding) probabilities, particularly in unfamiliar circumstances. It is difficult to distinguish between the hypotheses that individuals make choices which are consistent with the expected utility hypothesis, given their subjective probabilities, but that there are systematic biases in the manner in which those subjective probabilities are formulated, and the hypothesis that individual behaviour is not consistent with the expected utility hypothesis. There has been considerable work (see, for instance, Tversky 1969) suggesting that there are systematic biases in the way in which individuals form their subjective probability estimates. For example, individuals act as though they systematically overestimate low objective probabilities (such as the chance of winning at football pools, or the chance of an aircraft accident, or small chances in experimental situations).

Some proponents of the expected utility theory argue that the theory ought to be viewed as a normative theory, how rational individuals ought to behave in the face of risk. Others go further and suggest that when individuals are made aware of their inconsistencies with the expected utility theory, they change their behaviour; that is, when individuals know how to calculate probabilities, they will, in fact, behave consistently with the expected utility hypothesis. Again, the results reported below lend some substance to that view: when individuals are faced with *serious* choices, involving large stakes, their behaviour appears to be more in conformity with what a proponent of the expected utility hypothesis might hold.

Most of this book is concerned with situations where, at least in the long run, we can speak of 'objective' (relative frequency) probabilities. When individuals appear to use probabilities which are different from these objective probabilities, we say that they have miscalculated these probabilities.

This raises some interesting and not completely resolved issues in evaluating policy changes. There is a widespread view that the individual welfare ought to be evaluated using *ex ante* expected utility, i.e. using the individual's own probabilities. There is another view, which in this context we think is more persuasive, that it is the average *experience* of individuals which is relevant, i.e. the probabilities we ought to use are the relative frequencies of the different events. In this view, then, we can distinguish between the effects of policies assuming that agents act rationally, and the effects given their likely misperceptions (differences between objective and subjective probabilities). For example, as we shall argue in Chapter 11, a price stabilization programme may eventually reduce the average degree of misperception by farmers of the appropriate certainty equivalent price, although it is also quite possible that the introduction of the scheme initially worsens farmers' perceptions and decisions. Occasionally some policies have been justified primarily on grounds of misperceptions: that it improves matters (only) when agents act irrationally. Such arguments need, however, to be used with caution: the gains may be transient and reversed once agents learn to improve their decision-making skills; and it may be easier to provide the necessary information to improve decisions than to adopt the policy.

7.1.1 *Risk-taking in a multi-period context*

The analysis so far has assumed that individuals live for one period, or at least look at each decision as if it were in isolation. This is a convenient simplification, but when it comes to empirical verification of the model it is clearly unsatisfactory.

Farmers typically have to make choices each year (and, indeed, during the course of a crop year). In the static (one-period) model, there is no need to distinguish between income and wealth, but in a sequential problem the two are quite different. Economists usually argue that utility is produced by consumption, not income, and if an individual has substantial wealth, fluctuations in his income, especially if they are random from one year to the next, should not seriously reduce his ability to consume and hence generate utility. If individuals have few liquid assets, and if they cannot easily lend or borrow, or store goods from one period to the next, then their consumption would be constrained by their income, and it would be legitimate to define utility in terms of current income. If they can transfer income from one period to another, and if they rationally choose a lifetime consumption plan, then the problem becomes more difficult, and attitudes to risk will depend not only on the shape of the utility function, but on initial wealth, the rate of interest, the degree of independence of successive risks, and future income possibilities, as discussed in Chapter 14.

The empirical importance of this distinction between income and wealth will become apparent below. This completes our survey of the theory of behaviour under risk and the next step is to confront the theory with the empirical evidence.

Ideally, we would like to find the answers to a number of related questions:

(i) Do farmers make consistent choices between risky alternatives in a way which can be described as maximizing an expected utility function defined on the outcomes and the objective probabilities? In short, does the Expected Utility Hypothesis describe their choices satisfactorily?

(ii) Do farmers respond similarly and consistently to changes in income and wealth so that their choices can be described by maximizing an expected utility function defined over income, Y, and wealth, W of the form $U(W + Y)$? This is the Asset Integration Hypothesis, and it implies that individuals realize that their utility depends on their ability to obtain consumption goods, which in turn depends on *all* the factors which influence their purchasing power, and not just the immediate consequences of the next decision. Of course, if W is not affected by their current choices, and if the individual has a well-defined utility function $U(W + Y)$, then we can define another, current utility function, $V(Y)$, defined on current income, by the relation

$$V(Y) \equiv U(W + Y).$$

The empirical problem is that ideally we wish to find the functional form of U (assuming that such a function can be found which describes choices), but typically all that we observe are changes in Y, so that we are only able to measure the shape of $V(Y)$, or, equivalently, to find out about the shape of U in the neighbourhood of the given level of wealth, W.

(iii) Do different farmers behave similarly to risky prospects, so that we can usefully talk of a representative farmer?

(iv) Is there a reasonably simple functional form of the utility function which describes attitudes to risk?

7.2 Empirical evidence

The empirical attempts to measure risk aversion fall into two categories. The direct method, due to von Neumann and Morgenstern (1947) and extensively employed by behavioural psychologists, consists in confronting the subject with choices between sure things and risky alternatives, or between different risky alternatives. These choices may be hypothetical or actual. In the first case the subject is asked to conduct a thought experiment, of the form 'which of the two alternatives *would* you choose if you had to choose between them?' Dillon and Scandizzo (1978) have used this approach for near-subsistence farmers in northeast Brazil, and Lin, Dean, and Moore (1974) have tried it on wealthy Californian farmers. The attraction of the method is that it is relatively cheap to conduct the experiments and it appears to allow the exact shape of the utility function to be traced out, but it runs the risk that there is little incentive for the subject to think carefully about his answer, since nothing is at stake. The better alternative is to offer actual choices, preferably comparable in size to the gains and losses of that aspect of economic activity which is under investigation. The cost of experimenting on wealthy Californian farmers would be prodigious, but Binswanger (1978a, b) has conducted extensive experiments in rural India where wage rates are very low, so that the choices offered to the subjects involved relatively large gains at a low US$ cost. The cost of the experiment was roughly $2500 in prize money and $2500 in other costs, while to replicate it in the US would probably have cost over $200 000. Binswanger was also able to compare the results of offering hypothetical choices with actual choices, and concluded that *'evidence on risk aversion from pure interviews is unreliable, non-replicable and misleading*, even if one is interested only in a distribution of risk aversion rather than reliable individual measurement' (Binswanger, 1978b, p. 45, emphasis in original). Given this finding, and since there are no other suitable experimental studies, we shall merely summarize Binswanger's results and refer the interested reader to the original for the definitive discussion of the problem.

The other, or indirect, approach involves deducing attitudes to risk by observing actual decisions, and using these observations to estimate the parameters in an explanatory model of the farmer's behaviour. This method has the advantage that a large number of observations can be collected in the course of a more general investigation into the determinants of production, but it depends crucially on how well specified the model is. A recent example is provided by Moscardi and de Janvry (1977), and is discussed in section 7.4.

First, however, we examine Binswanger's evidence to see how far it supports the expected utility hypothesis adopted in the previous chapter, and what, if anything, it tells us about the degree of risk aversion of poor farmers.

7.3 Experimental determination of attitudes to risk

Binswanger's experiment was performed with over 300 individuals randomly selected from six villages in semi-arid rural India, and consisted in playing a sequence of games with real and high pay-offs. The subjects were offered a choice between the eight alternatives described in the upper part of Table 7.1, after which a coin was tossed and the outcome paid. The monthly unskilled wage rate in this region was 60–80 Rs. and the modal individual wealth was

Table 7.1 *Results of Binswanger's experiments*

Choice	O	A	B	C	E	F	D*	D	
Reward: heads	50	45	40	30	10	0	35	20	
tails	50	95	120	150	190	200	125	160	
Greatest value of partial risk aversion, P	∞	7.5	1.74	0.82	0.32	0	inefficient		
		Cumulative frequency of choice %					frequency %		N obs.
Game level									
0.50 Rs.	1.7	7.6	36.1	56.3	71.4	89.9	10.1		119
5 Rs.	0.9	9.4	35.0	71.8	83.8	92.3	7.7		117
50 Rs.	2.5	7.6	42.4	82.2	89.0	90.7	9.3		118
500 Rs.[a]	2.5	16.1	67.8	96.6	96.6	97.5	2.5		118

[a]Hypothetical game   Source: Binswanger (1978)

about 10 000 Rs. (roughly US$1200). The game was played seven or eight times over a period of six weeks, starting with five games at the 0.5 Rs. level (where the rewards are as shown in Table 7.1, divided by 100). The rewards were then increased by 10 (a perfectly certain outcome of 5 Rs.), then increased again by 10, and finally, hypothetical choices at the 500 Rs. level were asked.

The number of respondents making each choice can be deduced from the data in Table 7.1, and the local shape of the individual's utility function can be inferred within limits on the assumption that the choice made yields higher expected utility than any other alternative.

As we remarked above, the observations only give us information about the local shape of the function U defined in total wealth $W + Y$, or, equivalently, about the shape of the function V defined on current outcomes, Y, where

$$V(Y) \equiv U(W + Y) \tag{7.1}$$

is defined for a particular level of wealth. The shape of U or V can be described in a number of ways, such as by the coefficient of absolute risk aversion, A:

$$A \equiv -\frac{U_{ww}}{U_w} = -\frac{V_{yy}}{V_y}. \tag{7.2}$$

However, as the size of the bets increased, it was found that the respondents tended to choose slightly, but not very much less risky alternatives, which implies that for the modal individual, at the 0.50 Rs. level the value of the absolute risk aversion centres about 1, but falls rapidly to about 0.002 at the 500 Rs. level. In short, A is not stable as the proportional size of the outcomes increases.

A measure of risk aversion which was found to be relatively stable as the size of bets increased was what Menezes and Hanson (1970) term the coefficient of partial risk aversion, P (called the size-of-risk aversion by Zeckhauser and Keeler, 1970), which is defined on the current outcome, Y:

$$P \equiv -Y \frac{V_{yy}}{V_y}. \tag{7.3}$$

The coefficient of partial risk aversion is related to the coefficient of relative risk aversion, R, which is defined on total wealth, as follows:

$$P = \left(\frac{Y}{W+Y}\right) R \quad \text{where } R = -(W+Y)\frac{U_{ww}}{U_w}. \tag{7.4}$$

Clearly, if R is thought to be independent of wealth (and in particular, the proportionate size of the risky outcome) then P will decrease with wealth and increase with Y.

The greatest value of partial risk aversion, P, for which the individual would choose an outcome rather than the next less risky alternative is given in Table 7.1 and found by solving the equation

$$y_h^{1-P} + y_t^{1-P} = x_h^{1-P} + x_t^{1-P},$$

where (y_h, y_t) are the rewards under heads or tails of the alternative, and (x_h, x_t) are the rewards for the next less risky alternative. Thus choice A is indifferent to B at $P = 1.74$ because

$$45^{-.74} + 95^{-.74} \simeq 40^{-.74} + 120^{-.74}.$$

If P were slightly greater than 1.74, A would be preferred to B.

7.3.1 Interpreting the evidence

The first, and basic, question is how far the results of the experiment allow us to distinguish between the expected utility approach and alternative theories, of which the most popular are those based on security motives, recently reviewed by Anderson (1979). In all these approaches the individual is assumed to have an overridingly important objective, either to minimize the probability of experiencing a shortfall below some critical minimum income level, or to maximize the income level below which income will fall only a specified proportion of the time.

Binswanger finds that his evidence rejects all such theories which make testable predictions. On the other hand, his evidence is consistent with the hypothesis that individuals maximize expected utilities defined on outcomes. The weak form of the Expected Utility Hypothesis predicts choices reasonably well, and it is noticeable that as the choices become larger the proportion of inefficient choices (i.e. choices inconsistent with a concave utility function) decrease.

The answers to questions (iii) and (iv) are that most farmers make similar choices (B or C) at different game levels, so that one can attach some meaning to the representative farmer, and his attitude to income risk is quite well approximated by the constant partial risk aversion utility function, with risk aversion, P, lying between 1.74 and 0.32.

As the size of potential gain increases, so the median degree of partial risk aversion increases. Table 7.1 shows that when the rewards are comparable to a day's wages (at 0.5 Rs.) only 36 per cent of the sample had risk aversion greater than 0.82, while at the highest level (500 Rs.) the percentage rose to 68 per cent. Nevertheless, the partial risk aversion is remarkably stable given that rewards increase by a factor of 1000. It is, however, difficult to accept the Asset Integration Hypothesis, for if it were to hold, it would imply a utility function for a representative farmer with initial wealth W_0, of the approximate form

$$U(W + Y) = \frac{(W + Y - W_0)^{1-\rho}}{1 - \rho}. \tag{7.5}$$

If the same function were to apply to farmers with different wealth, then the coefficient of partial risk aversion should decrease rapidly with wealth:

$$P(W) = \frac{\rho Y}{Y + W - W_0}.$$

However, Binswanger found a very small decline in partial risk aversion with increasing wealth, and one must either reject the hypothesis that different individuals have a similar utility function, given by equation (7.5), or reject the Asset Integration Hypothesis. Binswanger (1978b) argues persuasively for rejecting the latter. In particular, one can reject the hypothesis of constant *relative* risk aversion, R, which would require $W_0 = 0$ in equation (7.5), since for a modal individual with wealth of about 10 000 Rs. relative risk aversion *falls* from about 1000 at the lowest game level to between 1 and 2 at the highest game level. It appears, then, as if decisions are compartmentalized, so that the decision is not seen in the context of the individual's over-all asset position. Only current outcomes seem relevant to current choices. Why might this be? One possible explanation is that different attitudes to income and wealth correspond to differences in short- and long-run attitudes to risk, which could arise for two different reasons.

(i) In the short run, the individual has a large variety of commitments; thus, what an individual could have done (the enjoyment he could have received) from \$$x$ if he allocates all of it simultaneously may be markedly different from what he can do (the enjoyment he receives) when he first commits $\frac{1}{2}x$, in the belief that that is all he will have, and *then* is told he has an additional amount of $\frac{1}{2}x$ to spend.

(ii) Individuals' *perceptions* about the value of money (in particular increments in wealth) depend on their actual level of wealth. An individual with a wealth of \$1000 is not likely to know how fast diminishing returns sets in, e.g. he may believe that he will be close to being satiated at a wealth of \$10 000. But an individual with a wealth of \$10 000 knows he is not satiated, but he could believe that satiation might set in at \$100 000.

An alternative explanation is that individuals exhibit *bounded rationality*: that is, they limit the amount of data they consider in making decisions in order to simplify the choice.

From the positive point of view, it is obviously convenient that choices appear to depend only on current income risk, for it is then relatively simple to predict responses to risk and changes in risk without enquiring into the wealth position of the individual. However, from a normative point of view the situation is less satisfactory, for it is hard to believe that a small reduction in income risk would, over a long period of time, raise the average welfare of the farmer as much as is suggested by a utility function with constant partial risk aversion.

In most of the rest of the book, we shall be concerned with attitudes to current income risk, and where it is convenient to explore the implications of a particular choice of utility function we shall variously assume constant absolute risk aversion (when the distinction between income and wealth is irrelevant), or constant partial risk aversion, which, from now on, we shall refer to as constant relative risk aversion defined on income, and use the symbol R. In short, in most of the book, we shall follow convention, supported by the evidence, of confining attention to income risk.

The other main conclusions are quickly summarized. Few individuals have risk aversion much above 2, even at very high game levels (where the SD of outcomes is more than one-third average annual incomes; and therefore higher than risks experienced in agriculture). The results contrast sharply with those of Dillon and Scandizzo (1978) in which more than half the farmers typically had risk aversion greater than 3. Binswanger found that the interview technique employed by Dillon and Scandizzo gave very unreliable results when employed on this sample, which suggests caution in accepting such results at face value. Binswanger also correlated risk attitudes against a variety of personal characteristics, but found few clear-cut relationships. Past luck made individuals less risk averse, while wealth and schooling tended to reduce risk aversion, as, to a lesser extent, did salaried employment. Progressive farmers were slightly less risk averse than the average, but age, sex, family composition, and amount of land rented had negligible effect. In all cases the estimated relationship was weak, in the sense that massive changes in these characteristics are needed to change risk aversion substantially.

While the experimental results are consistent with expected utility-maximizing behaviour, they are not consistent with security-based theories of behaviour in which the agent is primarily concerned with achieving a subsistence level of income and avoiding disaster.

To conclude, most individuals are risk averse, but not very risk averse, and react to fluctuations in income rather than consolidating such changes into lifetime wealth. The coefficient of partial risk aversion typically increases from about 0.5 for small fluctuations in income (SD of about one month's wage) to about 1.2 for large fluctuations (SD about 50 per cent of annual income).

7.4 Other empirical studies of attitudes to risk

Most agricultural economists would agree that farmers' attitudes to risk are quantitatively important determinants of their decision-making, especially in less developed countries where risks are relatively larger, incomes lower, and risk-spreading options fewer. Despite this recognition, there are relatively few empirical studies of attitudes to risk and very few indeed which are at all satisfactory. The reason is that it is more difficult to identify the effects of risk on decision taking than almost any other factor (such as changes in prices), and it is difficult enough to study even the most straightforward influences on decision-making. A change in the relative prices of crops is in principle an objective, observable influence (at least, in a world of certainty, or if these prices are quoted on futures markets), while risk is difficult to observe and quantify and remains largely subjective. It takes a large number of observations on a random variable to establish even such comparatively crude measures of its underlying distribution as its mean and variance with any precision, let alone the exact form of the distribution.

Given this difficulty in conducting empirical investigations, it is obviously desirable to collect, compare, and assess as many different attempts as possible to see if any strong pattern emerges, and to learn from experience how best to conduct future investigations. Unfortunately, it is often difficult to interpret the published results because too little of the supporting evidence has been made available. In particular, research workers seem unfamiliar with the desirability of presenting their results in a dimension-free way. In demand studies most economists appreciate the value of providing *elasticities* of demand, evaluated typically at the sample mean, rather than just slope *coefficients* whose values depend on the units in which price and quantity are measured. Most economists presenting evidence on attitudes to risk seem unaware of the fact that most summary measures, such as the coefficient of absolute risk aversion, are not dimensionless, and so cannot be interpreted without a figure for mean income. Only the coefficients of relative and partial risk aversion, defined in equations (7.3) and (7.4), among the common measures, are dimensionless elasticities. Even for these measures, however, it is important to see whether risk aversion varies with income, so it remains useful to present data on income levels and wealth.

In this section we examine two examples of studies which attempt to infer attitudes to risk from observed behaviour in the presence of risk. In the first, Moscardi and de Janvry (1977) postulated a safety-first objective, in which households maximize the income level below which income will fall only a specified proportion (presumably low) of the time. That is, farmers maximize

$$EY - K\sqrt{(\text{Var } Y)}, \tag{7.4}$$

where

$$Y = p\theta f(x) - \mathbf{w} \cdot \mathbf{x}, \quad E\theta = 1, \text{Var } \theta = \sigma^2, \tag{7.5}$$

and p is the output price, $\mathbf{x}$ is a vector of inputs, and $\mathbf{w}$ the vector of input prices. The solution to the problem is

$$1 - K\sigma = \frac{w_i x_i}{b_i pf(x)}; \quad b_i = \frac{x_i}{f}\frac{\partial f}{\partial x_i}, \tag{7.6}$$

where b_i is the imputed share of input i in average gross output, estimated by agronomists from observations on trial plots.

The results were a mean value of K of 1.12, standard error 0.61, and range between 0 and 2.0. Given Binswanger's rejection of safety-first rules, it is obviously interesting to ask how to interpret the data on the assumption that farmers maximize the expected utility of income

$$\underset{x}{\text{Max }} EU(Y) \tag{7.7}$$

which, given equation (7.5) yields

$$\frac{EU'(Y)\theta}{EU'(Y)} = \frac{w_i x_i}{b_i pf}. \tag{7.8}$$

If purchased inputs were negligible, or if riskless income matched the cost of these inputs, or if farmers were concerned with gross income and had constant (partial) relative risk aversion, R, then the left-hand side of equation (7.8) can be expressed as

$$\frac{E\theta^{1-R}}{E\theta^{-R}} \simeq 1 - R\sigma^2,$$

(where we assume that θ is log-normally distributed as $\Lambda(-\frac{1}{2}\sigma^2, \sigma^2)$ and use the expression of equation (6.43) to evaluate the expected values). If we knew the coefficient of variation of yield, σ, which the authors do not give, then we could estimate $R = K/\sigma$. Thus if, for example, $\sigma = 0.5$ (typical for wheat-growing areas in the US) then R would be about 2. Again, though, we are prevented from making full use of the data by the failure of the authors to present relevant information.

Moscardi and de Janvry actually used data on fertilizer inputs, a production function estimated from another, larger experiment, and collected additional socio-economic data from the forty-five farmers studied to relate risk attitudes to these socio-economic variables. As the authors point out, 'since risk aversion is measured as a residual ... it tends to include other sources of discrepancy ... such as, for example, imperfect market and agronomic information, restricted availability of financial capital and inputs, and high opportunity cost of family labour' (Moscardi and de Janvry, p. 711). To these sources of error one can add errors in specifying the production function and source of risk (as Cobb–Douglas and multiplicative), errors in the farmer's perception of the production function, errors in his perception of the relationship between price and output (discussed in more detail in 11.2.1), and the problem of identifying the sources of income risk (or income insurance). Since it is so hard for skilled econometricians to estimate the response to fertilizer, it is optimistic to assume that the *only* reason for under-supplying fertilizer is risk aversion (rather than, say, cautious learning behaviour).

In the second study, Schluter and Mount (1976) constructed a single time series of average yields and prices for six consecutive years for Surat District, India. Data from thirty-three unirrigated farms were then used to estimate the mean income and its mean absolute deviation (MAD) using the six-year data. A linear-programming (LP) model of the farm plan was built to find the trade-off between mean income and its MAD. The average MAD was 13 per cent, and the range was from 4 to 25 per cent. Income was defined as the gross value of farm output less purchased inputs, and if the randomness were roughly normal, then its coefficient of variation (CV) would be about 17 per cent, with a range from 5 to 32 per cent.

The LP model can be used to calculate the optimal farm plan for a representative farmer for differing levels of risk, and hence calculate the trade-off between mean income and its coefficient of variation (or more precisely, the mean absolute deviation.) Table 7.2 gives the mean income and coefficient of

Table 7.2 *Risk alternatives for representative unirrigated farm, India*

Income (Rs)	Coefficient of variation,[a] %	Relative risk aversion at which preferred
1530	11	3
1580	12	1.5
1630	14	1
1680	17	0.8
1730	20	0.5
1880	30	0.25
1950	40	0.05

[a] estimated as $\sqrt{(\pi/2)} \times$ MAD

Source: Schluter and Mount (1976)

variation (assumed to be $\sqrt{(\pi/2)} \times$ MAD) at different farm plans, the more risky involving more cash cropping and more fertilizer use. Since the table is for a representative farmer, and since actual farmers did not adopt risk-efficient farm plans (although they were typically within 5 per cent of the efficient frontier) it is difficult to deduce revealed attitudes to risk from the farm plans, since the data is not given in sufficient detail, but given that the average CV was 17 per cent, this corresponds to a coefficient of relative risk aversion of about 0.8.

The difficulty with this approach is that attitudes to risk are deduced from the frontier of an LP model, which will depend sensitively on the parameters of the model, the constraints imposed, and the magnitude of the risk. Many of the actual constraints facing farmers are too subtle to model in a simple LP, for example the seasonality of labour inputs and the extent to which they can be substituted, and one should therefore be cautious about deductions which depend on the shape of the estimated frontier.

7.5 The magnitude of income risk

The rough calculations of Chapter 6 showed that two factors influence decisions, the coefficient of risk aversion and the square of the coefficient of variation of income. How large is the CV of agricultural income? Although it is easy to measure the CV of agricultural yields, prices, and gross revenues, it is much harder to measure the relevant CV, which is that of income *net* of expenses, for the whole farm (and thus, typically, for a whole cropping pattern). Ideally, this should be measured from budget data over a run of years, but often this data is not available. Several writers have estimated the CV of net income from the underlying data on yield and price variability, the correlations between crop revenues, and a model which identifies the optimum farm plan for a given level of risk. In this section we give a few examples to suggest a range of plausible values; obviously the actual values will depend on a host of variables which vary from place to place. In Chapter 20 we provide more aggregative estimates of price, quantity, and revenue variability for some of the 'core' commodities for which buffer stocks have been proposed, while here we consider a wider range of agricultural activities.

Girao, Tomek, and Mount (1974) provide some evidence from the combined records of both the farm business and household for fifty southern Minnesota farmers for the seven years 1963-9. In many cases rather longer time series were available, and the results were split into two groups — those with dairy farms (and relatively stable incomes) and those without (Table 7.3).

Table 7.3 *Coefficient of variation of income of Minnesota farmers*

Number of farms with CV	Dairy	No dairy
< 0.3	16	3
0.3–0.4	4	6
0.4–0.5	2	6
> 0.5	1	12
Average income 1965-9	$9330	$12 786

Source: Girao, Tomek, and Mount (1974, Table 2).

Evidently the twenty-seven farms without a dairy enterprise experience very unstable incomes, with the median CV between 40 and 50 per cent.

Heady (1952), in his classic textbook, gives a great variety of data on yield and price variability, and some evidence on Iowa livestock enterprises for the period 1918-49. The CV of income varies from 14 per cent for dairy enterprises, to 39 per cent for feeder lambs, with most examples around 34 per cent. Other crops was often very much more variable. Thus the CV of wheat yields cited by Heady (p. 457) ranges from 9 per cent (Montgomery, Penn.) to 92 per cent for Baca, Col., estimated for the period 1926-48. Those counties with more than 60 per cent of the area under wheat averaged over 50 per cent. Other crops, such as rice, appear even riskier (p. 456) though they are often combined in a diversified cropping pattern.

In underdeveloped countries, Roumasset (1976) has calculated the mean and standard deviation of Philippines rice farm incomes from the underlying data, and finds for rain-fed rice using traditional methods a CV of 20 per cent, rising to over 50 per cent for modern techniques (which yield a higher mean income). The modern techniques are superior to traditional methods for relative risk aversion parameters of 4.5 or less. For irrigated rice traditional methods yield a CV of 25 per cent, while modern techniques yield much higher mean income (almost double) with a CV of between 33 and 42 per cent.

Finally, we have the estimates of Schluter and Mount (1976) already given, where the average coefficient of variation of unirrigated Indian farms was about 17 per cent.

To put these various estimates in perspective, we can use the concept of a risk premium, or proportional risk premium, defined in equation (6.11). If the coefficient of relative risk aversion, R, is taken to be 2.0, and a representative CV of income is 33 per cent, then the risk premium is 10 per cent of income. If, on the other hand, the CV is 50 per cent, then the premium rises to 25 per cent of income, showing that high risk can be very costly.

It is apparent, then, that the welfare losses with which we are concerned, arising out of the risks facing farmers, are significant, and that policies which change these risks may have significant welfare consequences.

Chapter 8

Theory of Consumer Demand

8.1 Introduction

In Chapter 6 we showed that it was misleading to measure producers' profits under risk as the area between the price line and the supply curve. The same problem arises in measuring consumer surplus, the counterpart of producer surplus on the demand side. As before, the solution is the same: to develop a microeconomic theory of consumer behaviour and to model risk explicitly.

The purpose of this chapter is briefly to summarize those aspects of the theory of consumer demand which we shall need in the rest of the book, and to develop measures of the benefits of price stabilization. Readers who are interested in extending our analysis are strongly recommended to read Gorman's survey article (1976) which demonstrates the analytical simplification which a judicious choice of variables and functional form can provide. The two basic ideas which simplify the study of consumer demand are those of *duality* and *separability*. We have already seen that the principle of duality allows one to choose the appropriate independent variable with which to work. In production theory one can choose to work with quantities of inputs and outputs, using a production function, or in terms of prices and a profit function. With production, the focus is typically on the input–output choice, but for consumers it is prices that are often more important. We shall therefore derive the properties of the indirect utility function which is defined over prices.

Assumptions about separability impose structure on the problem, and are of central importance in the study of risk. Assumptions about attitudes to risk have strong implications for the separability of indirect utility functions, and vice versa. (See Stiglitz, 1969.)

Moreover, if utility functions are chosen to be separable in certain variables, then these variables will not interact directly. In many cases it is reasonable to impose such conditions explicitly, more often it affords considerable simplification in the analysis, and sometimes it is completely inappropriate as it assumes the answer to the main question. If the object is to study the impact of variable wheat yields on the price of cotton, then it will prejudge the issue to assume that wheat and cotton enter separably. In short, it is important to think carefully about the appropriateness of separability assumptions before starting the analysis and choosing functional forms. Ideally one would choose appropriate variables and the appropriate separability assumptions to suit the problem in question. Unfortunately, there is a difference between assuming that the direct utility function is separable, and assuming that the indirect utility function is separable, and in such cases one of the simplifications

112 Commodity Price Stabilization

will typically have to be sacrificed. We shall return to this issue after deriving the duality results.

8.2* Duality, indirect utility functions, and the expenditure function

We start with the consumer's utility function, $U(\mathbf{q})$, defined over the vector of goods which he consumes, $\mathbf{q}$. This reflects his preferences, in the sense that if the consumer can freely choose between consumption bundles $\mathbf{q}^0$ and $\mathbf{q}^1$, and chooses, or reveals a preference for $\mathbf{q}^0$, then $U(\mathbf{q}^0) > U(\mathbf{q}^1)$. For most consumer theory, $U(\mathbf{q})$ can be thought of as an ordinal function, no more or less satisfactory than any monotonically increasing transform $\phi(U(\mathbf{q}))$, but this is not true if the consumer's choice under risk is to be described as one of maximizing expected utility as in the present context. In this case, $U(\mathbf{q})$ is defined up to an increasing linear transformation, i.e. if an individual's behaviour can be described *as if* he maximized $U(\mathbf{q})$, it could equally well be described as if he maximized $a + bU(\mathbf{q})$, $b > 0$. This amounts to requiring that $U(\mathbf{q})$ be a cardinal measure of satisfaction, while leaving the choice of origin and units of utility arbitrary. (It should be stressed that it is not necessary to represent choices as if the consumer had a cardinal utility function; merely convenient in that it allows the use of expected utilities. It is perfectly possible, though inconvenient, to define choices over outcomes and their probabilities without imposing additivity in the probabilities, see, e.g., Green, 1971, §13.3.)

Just as it is convenient to derive cost and profit functions from the production function, so it is useful to derive exactly parallel expenditure and indirect utility functions from the direct utility function. The same duality relationships also hold, and are most readily derived from the expenditure function, which is defined as the minimum expenditure needed to achieve a given level of utility U at prices $\mathbf{p}$:

$$g(\mathbf{p}, U) = \operatorname*{Min}_{\mathbf{q}} \mathbf{p} \cdot \mathbf{q} \text{ such that } U(\mathbf{q}) \geq U. \tag{8.1}$$

(The dot product of the two vectors $\mathbf{p}$ and $\mathbf{q}$, written $\mathbf{p} \cdot \mathbf{q}$ or, more loosely, as $\mathbf{pq}$, is defined as the scalar

$$\mathbf{p} \cdot \mathbf{q} \equiv \sum p_i q_i,$$

where p_i is the i-th component of the n-vector $\mathbf{p}$. In the present context it is just the cost of the bundle of goods represented by the vector $\mathbf{q}$.)

The indirect utility function gives the level of utility achievable with lump-sum income I and prices p:

$$V(\mathbf{p}, I) = \operatorname*{Max}_{\mathbf{q}} U(\mathbf{q}) \text{ such that } \mathbf{p} \cdot \mathbf{q} \leq I. \tag{8.2}$$

(Lump-sum income is income that does not depend on any of the consumer's current consumption choices. Wage income is best treated as a lump-sum income equal to the wage rate, w, times twenty-four hours per day, part of which is spent on the purchase of the n-th consumption good, leisure, whose price $p_n = w$. In most of the book neither lump-sum nor wage income will depend on the variables under study, except in Chapter 25, where it becomes important to be precise about the definition of income.)

The relationship between the expenditure function and the indirect utility function is that for all levels of utility, U

$$V(\mathbf{p}, g(\mathbf{p}, U)) \equiv U. \tag{8.3}$$

The following are important properties of these two functions:

1. *The expenditure function is concave in prices*

This is equivalent, by definition, to

$$g(\lambda \mathbf{p}^0 + (1-\lambda)\mathbf{p}^1, U) \geq \lambda g(\mathbf{p}^0, U) + (1-\lambda)g(\mathbf{p}^1, U), \quad 0 \leq \lambda \leq 1, \tag{8.4}$$

for any pair of price vectors, $\mathbf{p}^0$ and $\mathbf{p}^1$, and utility level U. Define the weighted average price

$$\mathbf{p}^\lambda \equiv \lambda \mathbf{p}^0 + (1-\lambda)\mathbf{p}^1, \quad 0 \leq \lambda \leq 1, \tag{8.5}$$

and suppose that the cost-minimizing choice of consumption which achieves U at any price $\mathbf{p}^i$ is $\mathbf{q}^i$, so that,

$$g(\mathbf{p}^i, U) = \mathbf{p}^i \cdot \mathbf{q}^i \leq \mathbf{p}^i \cdot \mathbf{q}^j, \quad j \neq i.$$

The inequality follows because any other consumption bundle $\mathbf{q}^j$ which achieves U must cost more at prices $\mathbf{p}^i$, or else it would have been chosen instead. Then

$$g(\mathbf{p}^\lambda, U) = \mathbf{p}^\lambda \cdot \mathbf{q}^\lambda = \lambda \mathbf{p}^0 \cdot \mathbf{q}^\lambda + (1-\lambda)\mathbf{p}^1 \cdot \mathbf{q}^\lambda,$$
$$\geq \lambda \mathbf{p}^0 \cdot \mathbf{q}^0 + (1-\lambda)\mathbf{p}^1 \cdot \mathbf{q}^1,$$

which is equivalent to equation (8.4), so the expenditure function is concave in prices. It follows that the average cost of achieving a given level of utility at random prices is less than the cost of achieving the same level of utility at prices stabilized at their mean (as another example of Jensen's inequality, see section 6.3).

2. *The indirect utility function is quasi-convex in prices and homogenous of degree zero*

A function $V(\mathbf{p}, I)$ is said to be quasi-convex in $\mathbf{p}$ for given I if for given U, the set of vectors satisfying

$$V(\mathbf{p}, I) \leq U$$

is convex. To prove quasi-convexity we need to show that

$$V(\mathbf{p}^i, I) \leq U \quad i = 0, 1$$

implies

$$V(\mathbf{p}^\lambda, I) \leq U$$

when $\mathbf{p}^\lambda$ is defined in equation (8.5). Suppose not, i.e.

$$V(\mathbf{p}^\lambda, I) = U(\mathbf{q}^\lambda) > U,$$

then

$$\mathbf{p}^\lambda \cdot \mathbf{q}^\lambda > \mathbf{p}^i \cdot \mathbf{q}^\lambda \quad i = 0, 1,$$

or else $\mathbf{q}^\lambda$ would have been chosen at prices $\mathbf{p}^i$. But this is impossible by the definition of $\mathbf{p}^\lambda$, hence V is quasi-convex in price. Homogeneity follows by noting that utility is unchanged by an equal proportional change in all prices and money income.

3. *Compensated demand* for good i is given by

$$q_i^c = \frac{\partial g}{\partial p_i} = q_i^c(\mathbf{p}, U). \tag{8.6}$$

This follows by noting first that the direct utility function is maximized at given prices, hence so is the Lagrangian

$$L = U(\mathbf{q}) + \lambda(I - \mathbf{p} \cdot \mathbf{q}),$$

whence

$$\frac{\partial U}{\partial q_j} = \lambda p_j. \tag{8.7}$$

Differentiate equation (8.1)

$$\frac{\partial g}{\partial p_i} = q_i + \sum_j p_j \frac{\partial q_j}{\partial p_i} = q_i + \frac{1}{\lambda} \sum_j \frac{\partial U}{\partial q_j} \cdot \frac{\partial q_j}{\partial p_i} \tag{8.8}$$

$$0 = \frac{dU}{dp_i} = \sum_j \frac{\partial U}{\partial q_j} \frac{\partial q_j}{\partial p_i}$$

and the second term of equation (8.8) vanishes, yielding the result.

The compensated demand schedule differs from the normal Marshallian or uncompensated demand schedule in that the consumer is kept at the same level of utility by money transfers as prices change, rather than holding money income constant and allowing utility to change. It is of central importance for welfare analysis, as the next result shows.

4. *The expenditure function is a direct measure of consumer surplus*
The consumer requires an amount of money equal to

$$CS = g(\mathbf{p}^1, U^0) - g(\mathbf{p}^0, U^0)$$

to compensate for moving from one set of prices $\mathbf{p}^0$ (and initial utility U^0) to another set of prices $\mathbf{p}^1$. This can be expressed as

The Theory of Consumer Demand   115

$$CS = \int_{\mathbf{p}^0}^{\mathbf{p}^1} \sum_i \frac{\partial g}{\partial p_i} dp_i = \int_{\mathbf{p}^0}^{\mathbf{p}^1} \sum_i q_i^c dp_i. \tag{8.9}$$

If only one price varies, p_i, say, then this measure of consumer surplus is the area under the *compensated* demand curve. If several prices vary, then in general there is no simple geometric equivalent and it can be very misleading to measure areas separately, holding all other prices constant.

5. *Roy's identity* gives the uncompensated or Marshallian demands

$$q_i = -\frac{\partial V/\partial p_i}{\partial V/\partial I}. \tag{8.10}$$

Differentiate equation (8.3) holding U constant:

$$0 = \frac{dU}{dp_i} = \frac{\partial V}{\partial p_i} + \frac{\partial V}{\partial I}\frac{\partial g}{\partial p_i}$$

$$= \frac{\partial V}{\partial p_i} + q_i \frac{\partial V}{\partial I}$$

using equation (8.6). This gives equation (8.10) by rearrangement, and since demand is now a function of *income* and price we have found the uncompensated demands. Naturally these coincide at the point where income is sufficient to yield the reference level of utility specified in the compensated demands. In general they differ elsewhere as the next result shows.

6. *Slutsky's theorem*

$$\frac{\partial q_i}{\partial p_j} + q_j \frac{\partial q_i}{\partial I} = \frac{\partial q_j}{\partial p_i} + q_i \frac{\partial q_j}{\partial I}. \tag{8.11}$$

This follows if the expenditure function is twice continuously differentiable, for if we define

$$S_{ij} \equiv \frac{\partial^2 g}{\partial p_i \partial p_j}$$

then, since the compensated and uncompensated demands coincide for a given level of utility, equation (8.6) gives

$$q_i^c = \frac{\partial g}{\partial p_i} = q_i\{\mathbf{p}, g(\mathbf{p}, U)\}$$

$$S_{ij} = \frac{\partial}{\partial p_j} q_i\{\mathbf{p}, g(\mathbf{p}, U)\} = \frac{\partial q_i}{\partial p_j} + \frac{\partial q_i}{\partial I} \cdot \frac{\partial g}{\partial p_j}$$

$$S_{ij} = \frac{\partial q_i^c}{\partial p_j} = \frac{\partial q_i}{\partial p_j} + \frac{\partial q_i}{\partial I} \cdot q_j, \tag{8.12}$$

then clearly the Slutsky symmetry condition is satisfied, for the order of differentiation does not matter:

$$S_{ij} = S_{ji}.$$

This result shows that the uncompensated and compensated demand schedules will only coincide if income effects are zero.

Finally, notice the duality between the direct and indirect utility functions which emerges very clearly in equations (8.7) and (8.10), especially when it is realized that λ in equation (8.7), being the shadow price of the income constraint, is the marginal utility of income, $\partial V/\partial I$.

8.3* Attitudes towards risk

The results of the previous section depended only on the ordinal properties of the consumer's utility function. In other words, the consumer's behaviour can be described *as if* he maximized a utility function $U(\mathbf{q})$, and any other cardinalization of the utility function $\phi(U(\mathbf{q}))$ with $\phi' > 0$ would do as well. However, as was remarked in the Introduction it is convenient to describe the consumer's choices under risk as though he maximized expected utility, in which case the precise cardinalization of the utility function does matter. In Chapter 6, we discussed how the producer's behaviour could be analysed in the presence of risk. There, we showed how if he were averse to risk, we could describe his behaviour as if he maximized a concave utility function of income $EU(Y)$.

For consumers we need to distinguish between attitudes towards income variability at fixed prices, and attitudes towards price variability at fixed incomes. For both it is convenient to use the indirect utility function $V(\mathbf{p}, I)$. It is natural to hypothesize that individuals are averse to variations in income at fixed prices, i.e. $V_{II} < 0$. In the limiting case, where individuals are neutral to income variability (at every set of prices), we require the indirect utility function to be of the form

$$V(\mathbf{p}, I) = v(\mathbf{p}) + w(\mathbf{p})I,$$

where v is homogenous of degree zero and w is homogenous of degree -1 in prices (see Stiglitz, 1969).

On the other hand, there appears to be no natural restriction to impose on consumers' attitudes towards price variability. We have already pointed out that the analysis of changes in price dispersion, keeping mean price constant, was in general of dubious value. But even if we consider a mean-preserving increase in price risk, under perfectly reasonable conditions consumers' welfare may increase, decrease, or remain unchanged depending on whether utility is convex, concave, or linear in that price. To see which holds, we need to ascertain the sign of V_{pp}. Recall that from Roy's identity (equation (8.10))

$$V_p = -qV_I.$$

Hence, differentiating with respect to I

$$V_{pI} = -\frac{qV_I}{I} \cdot \left(\frac{Idq}{qdI} + \frac{IV_{II}}{V_I}\right) = \frac{qV_I}{I} \cdot (R^c - \eta), \qquad (8.13)$$

where

$$\eta = \frac{d\log q}{d\log I}, \text{ the income elasticity of demand}$$

and

$$R^c = -\frac{IV_{II}}{V_I}, \text{ the consumer's relative risk aversion (to income variability).} \qquad (8.14)$$

Differentiate Roy's identity with respect to p:

$$V_{pp} = \frac{qV_I}{p}\left(-\frac{pdq}{qdp}\right) - qV_{Ip}$$

$$V_{pp} = \frac{qV_I}{p}\{\epsilon - \beta(R^c - \eta)\}, \qquad (8.15)$$

where

$$\epsilon = -\frac{d\log q}{d\log p}, \text{ the price elasticity of demand,}$$

and

$$\beta = \frac{pq}{I}, \text{ the expenditure share on the commodity.}$$

Although in general we would expect ϵ to be positive (as defined, i.e. demand schedules have a negative slope) and larger than $\beta(R^c - \eta)$, nevertheless this is not guaranteed, and indeed proposition 2 above only proved that V was quasi-convex in prices, not convex. Consequently, it is quite possible that consumers would prefer price variability to prices stabilized at their mean, and also possible that they would prefer price stability. However, they will prefer stable consumption to fluctuating consumption, since $U(q)$ is concave in q.

Finally, it turns out that for many of the issues we shall be interested in, what is crucial is the effect of price variations on the marginal utility of income, i.e. the sign of

$$V_{Ip} = \frac{qV_I}{I}(R^c - \eta)$$

which, as is apparent, may be either greater or less than zero. For homothetic indifference maps (whose slopes are constant along rays through the origin, i.e. the income elasticity of demand is unity, $\eta = 1$) whether the marginal utility of income increases as price increases depends simply on whether the aversion to variability of income (R^c) is greater than 1.

If $V_{Ip} = 0$, price has no effect on marginal utility, and hence the indirect utility function must be separable:

$$V(\mathbf{p}, I) = v(p_1, p_2, \ldots, p_n) + w(I, p_2, \ldots, p_n),$$

where $p = p_1$, and both v and w are homogenous of degree zero. If all other prices $p_2, \ldots, p_n$, are constant, this can be abbreviated to

$$V(\mathbf{p}, I) = v(\mathbf{p}) + w(I),$$

in which case, by Roy's identity, the demand schedule is

$$q = -v'/w'$$

and the income elasticity is

$$\eta = -\frac{w''I}{w'}$$

and for this to be unity,

$$w(I) = a \log I + b. \tag{8.16}$$

Similarly, if the price elasticity is to be unity

$$V = -\alpha \log p + w(I). \tag{8.17}$$

These special parameterizations will play a key role in much of the analysis to follow, and will be considered further in the next section. What is important, however, to remember is that even if the individual is very averse to variations in income, he may not be so averse to variations in prices: the two are quite distinct and should not be confused.

8.4 The specification of demand risk and utility functions

In an ideal world if consumers acted as though they maximized expected utility and had consistent expectations and preferences, it would be possible to estimate econometrically the cardinal utility function describing their behaviour and identify the nature of the underlying risk. In practice, data are sparse, of poor quality, and relate to time periods over which expectations are unlikely to be stable. Moreover, most data refer to aggregate consumption, and there are few utility functions which generate individual demands which can be aggregated to give a total demand of the same functional form. One of the few utility functions which does aggregate is the Stone-Geary utility function

$$U = \sum_i \beta_i \log(q_i - c_i); \sum \beta_i = 1, \tag{8.18}$$

where c_i is to be understood as the minimum acceptable level of consumption of good i. This gives demands

The Theory of Consumer Demand   119

$$q_i = c_i + \frac{\beta_i(I - \mathbf{p} \cdot \mathbf{c})}{p_i}, \qquad (8.19)$$

which has linear Engel curves (relating q_i to income I) and expenditures $p_i q_i$ are linear functions of income, hence the system is often referred to as the linear expenditure system. The indirect utility function corresponding to the linear expenditure system is

$$V(p, I) = \log(I - \mathbf{p} \cdot \mathbf{c}) - \sum \beta_i \log p_i - \sum \beta_i \log \beta_i. \qquad (8.20)$$

We have already encountered a special form of this function, for if $c = 0$, then relative risk aversion and all price and income elasticities are unity, and $V_{Ip} = 0$.

In general, one would not wish to make such restrictive assumptions, and so one should usually start with fairly general utility functions and impose appropriate, testable, empirical restrictions to explore their consequences – usually that elasticities are constant, or cross-elasticities are zero. This raises an important set of methodological questions, of which the most important is whether these empirical restrictions are consistent with any underlying utility function. We have already remarked that specific assumptions about attitudes to risk have strong implications for the structure of utility functions, and the converse is true, at least, once a particular cardinalization has been chosen (derived from, e.g., attitudes to income risk). For example, suppose we wished to impose the condition of constant income and price elasticities for two goods (in order to study the effect on one good of stabilizing another price). This suggests an indirect utility function which is some monotonic function of

$$V = v(\mathbf{p}_0) p_1^{1-\epsilon_1} p_2^{1-\epsilon_2} + \frac{1}{1-\eta} \left\{ \frac{I}{g(\mathbf{p}_0)} \right\}^{1-\eta} + w(\mathbf{p}_0), \qquad (8.21)$$

where $\mathbf{p}_0$ is a vector of all other prices, $v(\mathbf{p}_0)$ is homogenous of degree $\epsilon_1 + \epsilon_2 - 2$, g is homogenous of degree 1, and w is homogenous of degree 0. This form restricts the cross-elasticities of demand between the two goods, and if in addition the coefficient of relative risk aversion is to be constant, it must be equal to the income elasticity, η. Moreover, the aggregate demand function will not in general have constant income elasticity, making it difficult to argue that consumers in the aggregate behave as if they could be replaced by a single 'representative' consumer with a specific utility function.

We shall side-step all these problems by restricting our attention to small changes in prices or incomes so that it is reasonable to assume various parameters are locally constant without prejudging the general form of the utility function, and hence without necessarily imposing strong global restrictions on other parameters.

In order to estimate a demand system it is necessary to specify the form of demand risk. In Chapter 18 we shall demonstrate that different specifications lead to quite different predictions about the distributive impact of price stabilization, and so it is important to ask how reasonable the various alternatives are.

Since we are interested in studying the effects of the systematic variability in prices, we shall ignore non-systematic sources of variability, of which the most important are periodic changes in technology which affect the demand for goods. The invention of synthetic fabrics had an important effect on the demand for cotton, but is best viewed as a, perhaps intermittent, secular trend. Since invention occurs randomly, this secular trend will be random, making it very difficult to determine the level around which prices should be stabilized.

The two primary sources of systematic, or predictable, variability arise from variations in income (over the trade cycle) and variations in the prices of other commodities, perhaps caused by fluctuations in supply elsewhere.

The simplest econometric specification of a demand system is to assume constant elasticities:

$$Q_i = A p_i^{-\epsilon_i} I^{\eta_i} \prod_{j \neq i} p_j^{\epsilon_{ij}}, \qquad (8.22)$$

in which case the natural specification for demand risk is *multiplicative*, for either fluctuations in income or other prices will, on this specification, affect demand multiplicatively. The natural method for estimating this equation would be log-linear regression, and here too the errors are conveniently assumed multiplicative. (See Turnovsky (1976) for a defence of this assumption.)

The only serious alternative formulation is to suppose that risks are additive, which is consistent with a linear econometric specification. It is difficult to accept that demand is a linear function of income and prices, and that each of these has additive risk, as in

$$Q_i = \alpha_{i0} + \sum_{j \neq i} \alpha_{ij}(p_j + \tilde{u}_j) + \beta_i(I + \tilde{u}_i), \qquad (8.23)$$

except, perhaps, as a local approximation. Although different risk specifications can affect the distributions of the benefits of price stabilization, the real difference lies not between additive and multiplicative risk, but rather whether it is the demand or inverse demand curve which is affected. The formulation

$$p = \theta g(Q, I)$$

(multiplicative shifts in the inverse demand curve, shown in Fig. 8.1a) leads to a very different (and implausible) kind of demand shift from the multiplicative demand shift shown in Fig. 8.1b, and adopted here:

$$Q = \theta D(p, I).$$

(Additive shifts are vertical or horizontal displacements of the demand schedule, and it makes little obvious difference whether it is the demand or inverse demand which is shifted.)

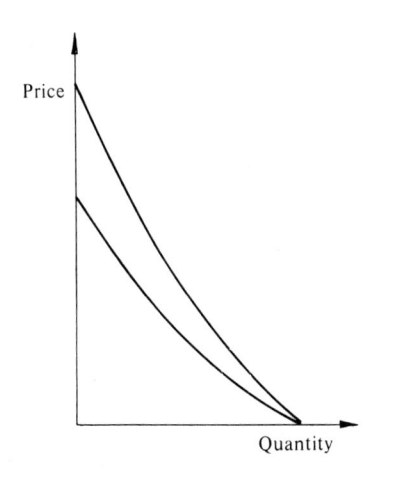

Fig. 8.1a Multiplicative inverse demand shifts

Fig. 8.1b Multiplicative demand shifts

Chapter 9*

Consumer Benefits of Price Stabilization

9.1 Introduction

The conventional measurement of the consumer benefits of price stabilization compares the Marshallian measure of consumer surplus (the area between the demand curve and the price) before and after the price is stabilized at its mean. This approach makes three errors.

(i) First, and least important, the Marshallian measure is only an approximation to the value of consumer surplus. In the first place, it only measures the cash value to the consumer accurately when the compensated and uncompensated demand curves coincide, as equation (8.9) showed. This requires a zero income elasticity of demand. Next, the value of the sum of money is only a good measure of value if the marginal utility of money remains constant, or $V_{Ip} = 0$ (see equation (8.13)). In some cases the two errors cancel (with logarithmic utility functions), but even when they do not the errors involved in using Marshallian measures are small, as Willig (1976) has shown.

(ii) The second, far more important error, is that it is rare for all other prices and incomes to be constant, especially in the context of risk analysis. If the demand *schedule* fluctuates, then this must be because of some more fundamental reason, such as some other price or income is varying. To use then a Marshallian measure as a means of calculating the benefits of, say, stabilizing this particular price, may be seriously misleading. To cite an example, suppose the demand for coffee fluctuates because the price of tea does. When the price of tea is low, the consumer substitutes tea for coffee, the demand for coffee drops, and the consumer is better off. However, the area under the coffee demand curve has fallen, and if used as a measure of the consumer's welfare would give exactly the wrong answer.

(iii) The third error lies in assuming that it is possible to stabilize a price at its mean. When dealing with price stabilization for producers we argued that in the short run inputs would remain fixed, in which case average supply would remain constant. We have already argued that unless demand schedules are linear, the average price will differ from the price of average supply. In the long run supply will adjust, and then, even with linear demand schedules, the price of average supply will change. The correct price around which to stabilize is the price at which average supply equals average demand.

We shall derive measures of the benefits of price stabilization for consumers which parallel those derived for producers in Chapter 6. However, since the formulae are more complex, we shall only calculate the benefits of completely stabilizing the price of the first commodity, leaving other prices and income random, and leave the derivation of the benefits of partial stabilization or of simultaneously stabilizing several prices to the reader.

9.2 Efficiency and transfer benefits

The cash value to the representative consumer of completely eliminating the randomness in the first price, p_1, is B, the solution to the equation

$$EV(\hat{p}_1, \tilde{p}_2, \ldots, \tilde{p}_n, \tilde{I}) = EV(\hat{p}_1, \tilde{p}_2, \ldots, \tilde{p}_n, \tilde{I} - B). \tag{9.1}$$

B is the amount of money which the consumer would give up in return for the price of the first commodity being stabilized at $\hat{p}_1$, leaving the average level of utility constant. The actual value of $\hat{p}_1$ will depend on the type of stabilization, but we shall assume that the mean output is held constant, so $\hat{p}_1$ is defined by the equation

$$\bar{q}_1 = ED_1(\tilde{p}_1, \tilde{p}_2, \ldots, \tilde{p}_n, \tilde{I}) = ED_1(\hat{p}_1, \tilde{p}_2, \ldots, \tilde{p}_n, \tilde{I}),$$

where D_1 is the demand for the first commodity, given by Roy's identity, equation (8.10). In general $\hat{p}_1$ will differ from the average price before stabilization, $\bar{p}_1$. Equation (9.1) can be solved, provided the coefficients of variations are small, by expanding each side in a Taylor series about $\bar{p}_1, \bar{I}$, as shown in the Appendix to this chapter, to yield:

$$B \cong -q_1(\bar{p})(\hat{p}_1 - \bar{p}_1) - \tfrac{1}{2}\bar{p}_1 q_1(\bar{p})\{\epsilon_1 \sigma_{p_1}^2 - 2 \sum_{i \neq 1} \epsilon_{i1}\rho(p_i, p_1)\sigma_{p_i}\sigma_{p_1} \tag{9.2}$$

$$+ 2(R - \eta_1)\rho(p_1, I)\sigma_{p_1}\sigma_I\},$$

where ϵ_1 is the own price elasticity of demand of good 1, defined to be positive for normal goods, ϵ_{ij} is the cross-price elasticity of demand defined to be positive for substitutes, σ_x is the coefficient of variation of x, and $\rho(x, y)$ is the correlation coefficient between variables x and y. All these terms are defined in the Appendix.

From now on, we shall drop the subscript 1, so that p and q are respectively the price and quantity of the first good. Although equation (9.2) is in a convenient form for calculating total consumer benefits, it does not distinguish between *transfer* benefits and the *efficiency* or *risk* benefits. As was pointed out in Chapter 6, the change in consumers' average expenditure is exactly matched by an equal and opposite change in the average revenue of producers (and/or the stabilizing authority), and as such it is a transfer and not a net social gain. The first term of equation (9.2) will be equal to the transfer benefit if supply is riskless, for then $q(\bar{p}) = q(\hat{p}) = \bar{q}$, which is constant, but otherwise it bears no simple relationship to any of the terms in the formula, for the simple reason that the formula was derived by expanding about mean price, $\bar{p}$, and not the price at mean quantity, $\hat{p} = p(\bar{q})$. The transfer benefit is

$$B_T = Epq - \hat{p}\bar{q}$$

or, writing $X(p) = pq(p)$, consumers' expenditure on the commodity,

$$B_T = EX(p) - X(\hat{p}). \tag{9.3}$$

The first term of equation (9.2) is, dropping subscripts,

$$(\bar{p} - \hat{p})q(\bar{p}) = X(\bar{p}) - \hat{p}q(\bar{p}). \tag{9.4}$$

Since we are interested in distinguishing between transfer and efficiency benefits, we shall use equation (9.3) to derive the transfer benefits, and obtain the efficiency benefits as the difference between the total benefits, given by equation (9.2), and the transfer benefits. The efficiency benefits will depend on the source of the instability, for this will affect the size and sign of the covariance terms. If the source lies in the variability of other prices, the crucial determinant will be the cross-price elasticities of demand, while if the source is fluctuations in income, income elasticities will be important. Not much more can be said without making specific assumptions, and to these we now turn.

9.3 Income variability alone

One of the more important sources of demand fluctuations for primary commodities arises from the trade cycle, that is, from the variability of income in the importing countries. Consider for simplicity the risk benefit when supply does not vary and when all cross-price elasticities are zero. The price variability induced by income variability is readily calculated. Since

$$q = q(p, I)$$

is fixed,

$$\frac{dp}{dI} = -\frac{\partial q/\partial I}{\partial q/\partial p} = \frac{p}{I}\frac{\eta}{\epsilon}$$

so that the coefficient of variation is

$$\sigma_p = \frac{\eta}{\epsilon}\sigma_I.$$

Since quantities are constant, the first term of equation (9.2), given by equation (9.4), reduces to the transfer benefit of equation (9.3). With no other sources of risk, all prices will be perfectly positively correlated with income fluctuations, so that equation (9.2) reduces to

$$B = B_T - \tfrac{1}{2}X(\bar{p})\{\epsilon\sigma_p^2 + 2(R^c - \eta)\sigma_p\sigma_I\}. \tag{9.5}$$

If we consider the special case of constant price and income elasticities discussed in section 8.4, equation (8.21):

$$q = p^{-\epsilon}I^\eta \quad I = \phi\bar{I}, \; E\phi = 1, \tag{9.6}$$

and if income risk is multiplicative, as in the natural specification, then

Consumer Benefits of Price Stabilization   125

$$B_T = \bar{q}(\bar{p} - \hat{p}) = X(\bar{p})\{E\phi^{\eta/\epsilon} - (E\phi^\eta)^{1/\epsilon}\}.$$

This can be evaluated using the methods of section 6.6 and is approximately

$$B_T = \tfrac{1}{2}X(\bar{p})\frac{\eta^2}{\epsilon^2}(1-\epsilon)\sigma_I^2 = \tfrac{1}{2}X(\bar{p})(1-\epsilon)\sigma_p^2. \tag{9.7}$$

The efficiency benefit is the second term of equation (9.5):

$$B_E = -\tfrac{1}{2}X(\bar{p})\frac{\epsilon}{\eta}(2R^c - \eta)\sigma_p^2. \tag{9.8}$$

For most agricultural commodities the income elasticity is small so that the efficiency benefit of price stabilization will usually be negative for consumers. The total benefit may also be negative, for

$$\frac{B}{X} = \tfrac{1}{2}\left(1 - \frac{2\epsilon R^c}{\eta}\right)\sigma_p^2. \tag{9.9}$$

(Notice that since the difference between $X(\bar{p})$, $X(\hat{p})$, and $EX(p)$ is of order of magnitude σ_p^2, it is not necessary to distinguish between them in equations such as (9.9).)

9.4 Supply variability alone

Again suppose that the cross-elasticities of demand are sufficiently small that supply risk does not spill over into other markets. With multiplicative supply risk and constant elasticity of demand the transfer benefit is

$$B_T = EX(q) - X(\bar{q}) \cong X(\bar{q})(E\theta^{1-1/\epsilon} - 1),$$

where
$$\sigma_\theta = \sigma_q = \epsilon\sigma_p$$

Hence

$$B_T \cong \tfrac{1}{2}X(\bar{p})(1-\epsilon)\sigma_p^2. \tag{9.10}$$

The total benefit is, from equation (9.2)

$$B = q(\bar{p})\hat{p}(E\theta^{-1/\epsilon} - 1) - \tfrac{1}{2}X\epsilon\sigma_p^2$$

$$B = \tfrac{1}{2}X\sigma_p^2, \tag{9.11}$$

so that the efficiency benefit is

$$B_E = B - B_T = \tfrac{1}{2}X\epsilon\sigma_p^2. \tag{9.12}$$

Here the efficiency benefit is unambiguously positive, as is the sum of the two terms. The same result can be derived directly from the indirect utility function by expanding about $\bar{q}$:

$$V(p) = V\{p(\bar{q})\} + (q-\bar{q})\frac{dV(\bar{q})}{dq} + \tfrac{1}{2}(q-\bar{q})^2\frac{d^2V}{dq^2}.$$

For constant elasticity demand curves

$$\frac{dV}{dq} = \frac{\partial V}{\partial p}\frac{dp}{dq} = \frac{\partial V}{\partial I}\frac{p}{\epsilon},$$

$$\frac{d^2V}{dq^2} \approx -\frac{\partial V}{\partial I}\frac{p}{q\epsilon^2}, \text{ if } \frac{\partial^2 V}{\partial p \partial I} \approx 0.$$

Hence the cash value of the total benefits from stabilization is approximately

$$B = \frac{V\{p(\bar{q})\} - EV(p)}{\partial V/\partial I} = \tfrac{1}{2}X\sigma_p^2. \tag{9.13}$$

9.5 Combining demand and supply variability

It would be convenient if the combined effect of income and supply variability were simply the sum of the two taken separately. We shall demonstrate that this is indeed the case under the assumptions made so far, that cross-price elasticities are zero, provided only that the income and supply variabilities are uncorrelated. In practice they are likely to be somewhat correlated for the following reason. Since the trade cycle has a period of between 4 and 8 years, this year's income is correlated with last year's income, which will be correlated with last year's price. Rational and myopic farmers alike will therefore adjust supply in the light of last year's price, introducing a correlation between income and supply. In our model, though, we are holding inputs constant, so this effect has been assumed away and the independence assumption seems reasonable.

If demands are independent, we have, by inverting the demand curve of equation (9.6):

$$p = q^{-1/\epsilon} I^{\eta/\epsilon}.$$

Hence if q and I are independent

$$\sigma_p^2 = \frac{1}{\epsilon^2}\sigma_q^2 + \left(\frac{\eta}{\epsilon}\right)^2 \sigma_I^2, \tag{9.14}$$

which is just the sum of the supply and income effects separately. If the correlation coefficient between price and income is ρ, then $\rho^2 = \lambda$ is the fraction of price variability caused by income variability:

$$\lambda \equiv \rho^2 = \frac{(\eta/\epsilon)^2 \sigma_I^2}{\sigma_p^2}. \tag{9.15}$$

Thus the terms in the braces of equation (9.2) are just the sum of the two impacts:

$$-\tfrac{1}{2}X\left\{\epsilon\sigma_p^2 + 2(R^c - \eta)\frac{\eta}{\epsilon}\sigma_I^2\right\}$$

$$= -\tfrac{1}{2}X\left\{\epsilon\,\frac{\sigma_q^2}{\epsilon^2} + (2R^c - \eta)\frac{\eta}{\epsilon}\sigma_I^2\right\} \qquad (9.16)$$

from equation (9.14).

The transfer benefit is

$$B_T = E pq - \hat{p}\bar{q}.$$

If $q = \bar{q}\theta$, $I = \bar{I}\phi$, where θ and ϕ are independent, then

$$B_T \cong X(\bar{p})\{E\theta^{1-1/\epsilon}\phi^{\eta/\epsilon} - (E\phi^\eta)^{1/\epsilon}\}$$

$$\cong \tfrac{1}{2}X(\bar{p})(1-\epsilon)\left\{\frac{1}{\epsilon^2}\sigma_q^2 + \left(\frac{\eta}{\epsilon}\right)^2\sigma_I^2\right\}$$

or, from equation (9.14)

$$B_T \cong \tfrac{1}{2}X(\bar{p})(1-\epsilon)\sigma_p^2 \qquad (9.17)$$

as before.

The total benefit is the sum of the two terms of equation (9.2). The first term is

$$(\bar{p} - \hat{p})q(\bar{p}) \approx X(\bar{p})\{E\theta^{-1/\epsilon}\phi^{\eta/\epsilon} - (E\phi^\eta)^{1/\epsilon}\}$$

$$= \tfrac{1}{2}X\left\{(1+\epsilon)\frac{\sigma_q^2}{\epsilon^2} + (1-\epsilon)\frac{\eta^2}{\epsilon^2}\sigma_I^2\right\}$$

$$= \tfrac{1}{2}X(1-\epsilon)\sigma_p^2 + X\epsilon\frac{\sigma_q^2}{\epsilon^2} = B_T + X\epsilon\frac{\sigma_q^2}{\epsilon^2}.$$

Thus

$$B = B_T + \tfrac{1}{2}X\left\{\epsilon\left(\frac{\sigma_q^2}{\epsilon^2}\right) - (2R^c - \eta)\frac{\eta}{\epsilon}\sigma_I^2\right\}.$$

Hence, from equation (9.15)

$$B_E = \tfrac{1}{2}X\left\{\epsilon(1-\lambda) - \lambda\frac{\epsilon}{\eta}(2R^c - \eta)\right\}\sigma_p^2$$

or

$$B_E = \tfrac{1}{2}X\epsilon\left(1 - \frac{2R^c\lambda}{\eta}\right)\sigma_p^2. \qquad (9.18)$$

Unless consumers have very low risk aversion, or unless most of the price variability originates on the supply side, the consumer risk benefit will be negative (though small).

Total consumer benefit is the sum of equations (9.17) and (9.18):

$$B = \tfrac{1}{2}X\left(1 - \frac{2R^c\lambda\epsilon}{\eta}\right)\sigma_p^2, \tag{9.19}$$

where $\lambda = \rho^2$, the squared correlation coefficient of price on income. It therefore seems justified to treat the various sources of risk additively, provided that they are independent for the simple reason that the formulae contain only terms which are linear in expenditure (and hence additive) or linear in variance (also additive). Therefore it suffices to consider the remaining sources of price variability in isolation.

Appendix: Derivation of formulae

The left-hand side of equation (9.1) yields the following Taylor expansion

$$V(\mathbf{p}, I) = V(\bar{\mathbf{p}}, \bar{I}) + \sum_i \frac{\partial V}{\partial p_i}(p_i - \bar{p}_i) + \frac{\partial V}{\partial I}(I - \bar{I}) \quad (9.\text{A}1)$$

$$+ \tfrac{1}{2} \left\{ \sum_i \sum_j \frac{\partial^2 V}{\partial p_i \partial p_j}(p_i - \bar{p}_i)(p_j - \bar{p}_j) + 2 \sum_i \frac{\partial^2 V}{\partial I \partial p_i}(p_i - \bar{p}_i)(I - \bar{I}) \right.$$

$$\left. + \frac{\partial^2 V}{\partial I^2}(I - \bar{I})^2 \right\}.$$

Similarly, the right-hand side yields

$$V(\hat{p}_1, \ldots, I - B) = V(\bar{\mathbf{p}}, \bar{I}) + \sum_i \frac{\partial V}{\partial p_i}(p_i - \bar{p}_i) + \frac{\partial V}{\partial I}(I - B - \bar{I}) \quad (9.\text{A}2)$$

$$+ \tfrac{1}{2} \left\{ \sum_i \sum_j \frac{\partial^2 V}{\partial p_i \partial p_j}(p_i - \bar{p}_i)(p_j - \bar{p}_j) \right.$$

$$\left. + 2 \sum_i \frac{\partial^2 V}{\partial I \partial p_i}(p_i - \bar{p}_i)(I - B - \bar{I}) + \frac{\partial^2 V}{\partial I^2}(I - B - \bar{I})^2 \right\},$$

where this time p_1 takes the non-random value $\hat{p}_1$. Take expectations of both equations, and note that $E(p_i - \bar{p}_i) = 0$, $E(I - \bar{I}) = 0$. Terms in B^2, $B(\hat{p}_1 - \bar{p}_1)$ and $(\hat{p}_1 - \bar{p}_1)^2$ can be ignored if $\hat{p}_1$ is sufficiently close to $\bar{p}_1$, since they are of order σ^4. Most of the cross-product terms cancel when the two expressions are equated, leaving

$$B \frac{\partial V}{\partial I} = -\tfrac{1}{2} \left\{ \frac{\partial^2 V}{\partial p_1^2} \text{Var}(p_1) + 2 \sum_{i \neq 1} \frac{\partial^2 V}{\partial p_i \partial p_1} \text{Cov}(p_i, p_1) \right. \quad (9.\text{A}3)$$

$$\left. + 2 \frac{\partial^2 V}{\partial I \partial p_1} \text{Cov}(I, p_1) \right\} + (\hat{p}_1 - \bar{p}_1) \frac{\partial V}{\partial p_1}.$$

The last term can be written, using Roy's identity, as

$$-(\hat{p}_1 - \bar{p}_1) q_1(\bar{\mathbf{p}}, \bar{I}) V_I$$

and is discussed in the text. The remaining coefficients in equation (9.A3) can be further approximated as follows. We have from equation (8.13):

$$\frac{\partial^2 V}{\partial p_i \partial I} = \frac{\beta_i}{p_i}(R^c - \eta_i) V_I$$

where β_i is the expenditure share for the ith good.
Similarly, from Roy's identity

$$\frac{\partial^2 V}{\partial p_i \partial p_j} = \frac{\partial V}{\partial I}\frac{q_i}{p_j}\left\{-\frac{p_j \partial q_i}{q_i \partial p_j} - \beta_j(R^c - \eta_j)\right\}.$$

If we are discussing price stabilization for a limited range of agricultural goods, β_j is small (less than 1 per cent for those agricultural consumption goods which UNCTAD is concerned to stabilize). It follows that to a first approximation the second term in the braces can be ignored, leading to the simplification

$$\frac{\partial^2 V}{\partial p_i \partial p_j} = -\frac{\partial V}{\partial I}\frac{\beta_i I \epsilon_{ij}}{p_i p_j}; \quad \epsilon_{ij} = \frac{p_j \partial q_i}{q_i \partial p_j}. \quad (9.A4)$$

Here ϵ_{ij} is the cross-price elasticity of demand, positive for substitutes, negative for complements, and zero for independent goods. The uncompensated elasticity can be as accurately replaced by the symmetric compensated elasticity. Substituting these terms in the first part of equation (9.A3) gives

$$-\frac{\beta_1 I}{2}\left\{\epsilon_1 \sigma_{p_1}^2 - 2\sum_{i \neq 1} \epsilon_{i1}\rho(p_i, p_1)\sigma_{p_1}\sigma_{p_i} + 2(R^c - \eta_1)\rho(p_i, I)\sigma_{p_1}\sigma_I\right\}V_I \quad (9.A5)$$

where

$$\rho(x, y) = \frac{\text{Cov}(x, y)}{\sqrt{\text{Var}(x)\,\text{Var}(y)}}$$

is the correlation coefficient between x and y.

Chapter 10

Market Equilibrium with Rational Expectations

10.1 Introduction

In the previous six chapters we have outlined the theory of producer and consumer behaviour in the presence of risk. We now turn to the analysis of market equilibrium.

As we shall see, a critical determinant of the nature of the market equilibrium is the formation of expectations on the part of producers; if they could sell their crops forward, and if they could purchase crop insurance, then they would not need to form these expectations (any more than any other participant in the economy would; that is, they could completely *hedge* all their production risks; they *might* decide to speculate, but their speculative activity is quite distinct from their production activities). But for virtually all farmers complete hedging is not possible, and thus they must rely to some extent on expectations in making their production decisions.

This chapter begins with a general discussion of the problem of expectations formation. We then introduce the concept of rational expectations equilibria, i.e. equilibria in which the probability distribution of prices and outputs which individuals believe corresponds to the frequency distribution of prices and output. It has been argued that the rational expectations equilibrium is the natural equilibrium concept to employ in the presence of risk, and section 10.3 examines this argument. We discuss the limits on the usefulness of the rational expectations equilibrium concept and explain why we have employed it so extensively throughout this book.

Finally, in section 10.4 we show how, with simple parameterizations of the demand functions and the probability distributions, the rational expectations equilibrium may be completely described and analysed.

The next chapter is devoted to the analysis of market equilibria in which individuals do not have rational expectations.

10.2 The nature of expectations

Farmers typically draw up a farm plan at the beginning of the crop year before they know the weather, the crop yields, and the prices at which they will sell the crops. In Chapter 6 we assumed that there was an exogenous distribution of prices, and that the farmer knew the joint probability distribution of his output and the price. Armed with this knowledge, he was able to determine the optimum farm plan, that is, the plan which yields the highest expected utility.

In fact, the price that eventually clears the market is not exogenous, but depends on supply and demand. If we are to describe market equilibrium we must explain first how the price distribution is generated, and how it depends on supply decisions, and second how farmers form expectations about prices and so decide on the level of supply. If supply depends on expectations, it is tempting to try to capture this relationship in an equation such as the following:

$$p_t^e = \phi(p_{t-1}, p_{t-2}, \ldots; q_{t-1}, q_{t-2}, \ldots; s_{t-1}, \ldots; z_{t-1}, \ldots). \qquad (10.1)$$

In this rather general formulation, the farmer forecasts the expected price at date t using his past observations on price, p, his own output, q, his perception of the states of the world, s (were prices high last year because of low supply or high demand?) and other relevant information, z (such as the level of exports of the commodity, the price of substitutes). In short, we imagine the farmer acting as a more or less sophisticated forecaster, given his prior beliefs about the way the economy works.

Before 1961 an econometrician attempting to model an agricultural market would have taken equation (10.1) and drastically simplified it to include only readily observed and obviously relevant variables such as past prices. We shall examine a typical example in the next chapter, but for the moment we are more concerned with whether this provides a satisfactory theoretical framework. In a seminal article in 1961, Muth argued convincingly that it does not. He observed that the behaviour of dynamic models was typically very sensitive to the specification of expectations, but these specifications were disturbingly *ad hoc*. Second, these naïve forecasting rules used information rather mechanically and therefore inefficiently. Many agencies, recognizing the importance of expectations, conduct regular surveys of expectations and intentions and publish them as leading economic indicators. These data show that averages of expectations in industry are typically more accurate than the forecasts of naïve models and as accurate as elaborate forecasting models. In other words, agents appear to use information more efficiently than these simple forecasting rules suggest.

The final objection is the most telling, for Muth pointed out that these forecasting rules did not explain how expectations were formed. Without such an explanation it is impossible to predict how expectations will adjust to a change in the amount of information or in the behaviour of the system. This is of central importance if we are interested in the introduction of price stabilization, for this will certainly affect the way the markets behave and the kind of information available to farmers.

Is there a more satisfactory theory of expectations which meets these objections and which is consistent with empirical evidence? Muth argued that there was and illustrated his argument in a simple model of agricultural supply and demand. He made two important simplifications — that supply and demand schedules were linear and that risk was additive, so that the certainty equivalent prices guiding supply decisions were equal to average prices. In Chapter 6 we argued that this was a very special case, and that in general the relationship between certainty equivalent prices and average prices depended on the sources of risk, the shape of the demand schedules, and the farmers' attitudes to risk. Moreover, the relationship between the certainty equivalent price and the average price would in general change if the economic environment changed. Since the main reason for developing a theory of expectations is to be able to deal with a change in the economic environment, it weakens the theory if we work in terms of an unchanged formula for the certainty equivalent price. For Muth's illustrative purposes, the simplification was well chosen to reveal the essence of his proposal, and his article is still an excellent introduction to the subject, but our concern is to develop a more general theory.

Instead of working in terms of a single certainty equivalent price this means that we should recognize that prices are uncertain and that farmers realize this. They therefore forecast a whole price distribution rather than a single-point estimate:

$$F^e(p_t) = \phi(p_{t-i}; q_{t-i}; s_{t-i}; z_{t-i}), \quad i = 1, 2, \ldots. \tag{10.2}$$

Here F^e is the *distribution function* of prices which the farmer expects, given his current information. Thus $F^e(p)$ is the probability that the price expected to rule at date t is no greater than p (with $F^e(0) = 0$, $F^e(\infty) = 1$). In Chapter 6 we showed how the choice of inputs could be systematically related to beliefs about the distribution of prices, as described by $F^e(p)$, and in particular to their variance and covariance with own production (and more subtle properties in the case of risk-averse producers). This choice of inputs, together with the underlying risk, generates a distribution of total output at date t, again represented by a distribution function:

$$G(Q_t) = \psi\{F^e(p_t)\}. \tag{10.3}$$

The demand for output may also be random, and depend on the state of nature, s. For the moment suppose that the commodity is not stocked, in which case demand is equal to current consumption, which will depend on the market clearing price, p_t, and possibly also s_t. The market clearing price today when supply is Q can thus be written

$$p_t = D_t(Q_t, s_t). \tag{10.4}$$

(If the commodity can be stocked, then part of the demand will be for addition to inventories, and will depend on expected future prices. A full analysis requires an intertemporal model of the kind set out in Part VII. As Muth shows, the notion of rational expectations equilibrium is not radically altered by such dynamic considerations.)

Finally, the distribution of supplies, $G(Q)$, together with the randomness in demand, will generate a distribution of market clearing prices, described by

$$F(p_t). \tag{10.5}$$

Figure 10.1 provides a simple geometric illustration for the case of non-random demand (and no storage) where the planned expected supply is $\bar{Q}$, distributed

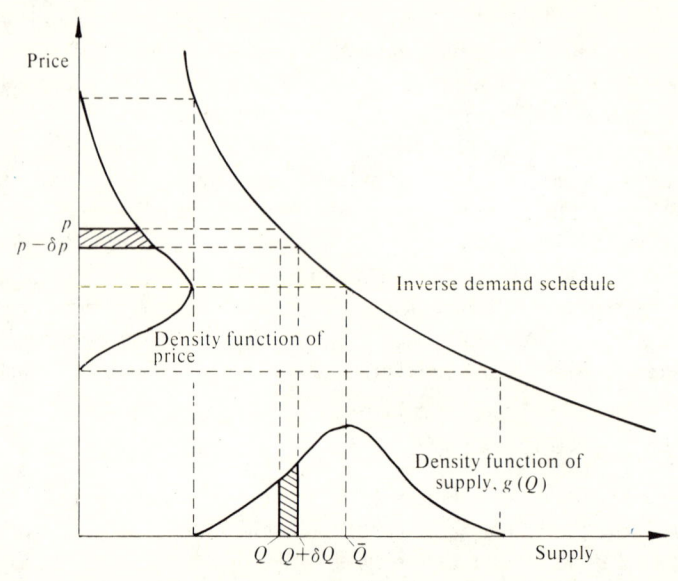

Fig. 10.1 Supply variability inducing price variability

as $G(Q)$. The density function of supplies, g, induces a density function of market clearing prices – the shaded areas are equal, and give the probability of supplies between Q and $Q + \delta Q$, prices between p and $p - \delta p$.

We have come full circle, for the actual distribution of prices will depend on the expected distribution of prices, and, of course, the structure of the system. It should now be clear that there is a natural description of expectations which meets the early objections of arbitrariness and informational inefficiency: a rational expectations equilibrium is a distribution of prices, $F^*(p)$, such that the actual price distribution is the same as the expected price distribution:

$$F^*(p) = F^e(p) = F(p).$$

The attraction of this concept is obvious, because it is the natural extension to a world of risk of the perfect foresight assumption so commonly used in traditional economic theory. If a unique rational expectations equilibrium exists (often a delicate question, though in our simple models such an equilibrium can be shown to exist) then it provides a logically consistent and satisfactory explanation of how expectations are related to information. It is the only specification of expectations which would not eventually be modified by observations, for if agents held different beliefs they would predict some outcomes as occurring more often than they would in fact, and others less often. Eventually, if the crop year were repeated often enough, they would collect enough observations to falsify their beliefs, and would, if rational, be forced to modify their expectations. To the extent that expectations were not rational, there would be scope for learning and the structure of the system would be changing. In practice, as we shall comment later, things are more complicated. In a non-stationary environment it may not be easy for a farmer to tell whether his expectations are 'rational'.

Another way to characterize a rational expectations equilibrium is to suppose that farmers have some theory about the way their economic environment works, and that this theory is consistent with observations. They observe that price is low when their own supply is large, and they postulate a downward sloping *aggregate* demand schedule, although they also realize that they would sell as much as they like at the prevailing market price – the demand schedule facing an individual farmer is flat. For example, suppose that the output of farmer i depends on his inputs x^i and the state of the weather, s; then he realizes that total supply Q will also depend on s:

$$Q = Q(s) = \sum_i f^i(x^i, s). \qquad (10.6)$$

The market price will also depend on s, for, from equation (10.4):

$$p = p(s) = D(Q(s), s). \qquad (10.7)$$

Farmer i holds rational expectations if he can calculate profit in each state, $Y^i(x^i, s)$, and knows the probability of the occurrence of that state, $\pi(s)$, say:

$$Y^i(x^i, s) = p(s)f^i(x^i, s) - w \cdot x^i. \qquad (10.8)$$

He then chooses $x^i = x^{i*}$ to yield the highest expected utility. For example, if farmers were risk neutral, x^{i*} would satisfy

$$Ep(s)\frac{\partial f^i}{\partial x^i}(x^{i*}, s) = \sum_s \pi(s)p(s)\frac{\partial f^i}{\partial x^i} = w. \qquad (10.9)$$

A rational expectations equilibrium is one in which the price used in equation (10.9) simultaneously satisfies

$$p(s) = D\left(\sum f^i(x^{i*}, s), s\right) \qquad (10.10)$$

when all farmers choose x^{i*} according to equation (10.9).

The obvious objection to make against the realism of rational expectations is that it supposes an unreasonable degree of rationality. Organization theorists such as Simon (1959) argue that the assumption of rationality leads to theories which are unable to explain observed phenomena. Muth's reply is that dynamic economic models do not assume enough rationality, and therefore do not do as well at predicting as expectations surveys reveal actually happens. Moreover, although we have set out a general and therefore quite demanding description of rational expectations, in many cases the relevant information *can* be summarized in a simple statistic, a certainty equivalent. For example, when choosing his inputs using equation (10.9), if multiplicative risk is assumed, all that is required is that the farmer forecast expected gross returns per hectare; if the farmer is risk neutral, he need only forecast average returns. In this case, the rational expectations hypothesis is that he makes on average an unbiased forecast. (In the final section of the chapter we show how in certain circumstances farmers can compress the relevant information into a certainty equivalent price and so simplify their decision problem.) To conclude, the rational expectations hypothesis does not assert that predictions are accurate, but only that they cannot be improved without additional information. The claim is that agents do not waste scarce and valuable information. If they did, and if expectations were not moderately rational, then there would be opportunities for profitable speculation.

10.3 The efficiency of rational expectations equilibria

In most of the rest of the book we assume the rational expectations hypothesis whenever characterizing a market equilibrium, and it is important to understand why. We do not believe that the economy is always in a rational expectations equilibrium, and, indeed, we specifically argue that if some policy such as price stabilization is introduced, then there will be a lapse of time during which agents will be collecting information about the new environment during which they are unlikely to forecast accurately. Thus, we shall distinguish between the *impact* effect of a policy and its long-run effect, when the system has moved to a new rational expectations equilibrium. Our defence of the hypothesis is that it allows us to draw a clear distinction between two effects which a policy may have. If the economy starts and finishes in a rational expectations equilibrium, then the policy, by changing the equilibrium, changes (and, one would hope, improves) the efficiency of resource allocation. If the economy is not in rational expectations equilibrium, then the policy may, by changing the information available to agents, move them closer to the rational expectations equilibrium. The second effect is properly counted as a benefit of improved information, and it may be achievable in other ways, for example, by directly improving the information available to farmers. Put another way, if the only advantage of price stabilization was to improve farmers' forecasts of prices, then it might be much cheaper to produce crop forecasting services. On the other hand, it may be that it is difficult or costly to provide this information, in which case a price stabilization scheme might be attractive because it reduces the need for such information.

Moreover, if we did not assume rational expectations, then we would be forced to make some rather *ad hoc* assumption about expectations. The impact of any policy would then consist of a 'true' efficiency gain (or loss) and gain (or loss) of more closely approaching the rational expectations equilibrium. The magnitude of the second effect would depend sensitively on two *ad hoc* assumptions about the initial and final expectations. Different economists, attracted by different assumptions about expectations, might disagree extensively about the desirability of a policy, yet not realize that their disagreement resulted from such arbitrary assumptions. If the two impacts are clearly distinguished, then it should be easier to resolve differences and identify the key determinants of policy success or failure. In the next chapter we shall demonstrate this distinction, and resolve a dispute which arises from this confusion.

Intuitively, a rational expectations equilibrium in a competitive economy would appear to be the best attainable equilibrium because it uses the available information about the future correctly, and, being competitive, does not allow producers to exploit their market power. If there were no uncertainty, rational expectations would correspond to perfect foresight, and the equilibrium would indeed be Pareto efficient. Unfortunately, however, with uncertainty this is no longer true (unless there is a complete set of insurance markets). Competitive rational expectations equilibria with incomplete markets can typically be improved by some form of intervention, as we show in two different contexts below. In Chapter 14 we discuss the nature of the bias in the choice of production technique under uncertainty, while in Chapter 23 we demonstrate the relative inefficiency of free trade in the presence of production risk.

Nevertheless, it must be admitted that the information required to improve the allocation of resources may be hard to come by; for the bias in the market allocation of resources depends on such features as the sign of the third derivative of the utility function, the source and nature of risk, and the heterogeneity of the population.

To conclude, the attraction of the rational expectations hypothesis is, first, that it can be applied to any dynamic system, and avoids the need for specific *ad hoc* assumptions about the formation of expectations. Second, it provides a natural bench-mark against which to measure deviations from rationality, or the potential gains from improved information and decision-making. Third, it allows us to draw the important distinction between changes in information which improve the efficiency of a given equilibrium, and movements between rational expectation equilibria (caused by, for example, a price stabilization programme). A similar and useful distinction is often made between movements towards the production possibility frontier (eliminating production inefficiency) and movements along the frontier (eliminating trade inefficiency).

10.4 Simple models of rational expectations with supply risk

In the case where the only source of disturbance to the market is supply variability, we can provide a fairly complete characterization of the rational expectations equilibrium. This will provide a basis for comparison of market equilibrium in which producers are 'ill informed' or 'irrational'. We have already illustrated the way in which supply variability is translated into price variability in Fig. 10.1, and note in passing that as shown the distribution of prices is skewed because the demand schedule is convex, so that the average price is above the price corresponding to average supply, $p(\bar{Q})$. This is another illustration of Jensen's inequality, discussed in section 6.3.

We can construct a rather simple model of supply risk to demonstrate the

138 Commodity Price Stabilization

way in which a farmer could form rational expectations. Assume supply risk is multiplicative

$$q(s) = \theta(s)f(x), \quad E\theta = 1, \text{Var } \theta = \sigma^2, \tag{10.11}$$

as in equation (5.12). If all farmers face the same, perfectly correlated risk and know the shape of the (static) demand curve, then a risk-neutral farmer would maximize:

$$EY = f(x)E\theta p(\theta \bar{Q}) - wx \tag{10.12}$$
$$= \hat{p}f(x) - wx$$

where

$$\hat{p} = E\theta p(\theta \bar{Q}). \tag{10.13}$$

Again, $\hat{p}$ is the action certainty equivalent price defined and discussed in Chapter 5, and $\bar{Q}$ is average total supply, which the farmer can either predict (if he knows total planted area and that other farmers are the same) or learn. Moreover, $\hat{p}$ is proportional to average gross return per acre, and so in principle is easy to observe.

It is easy to extend the model to allow farmers to experience diverse multiplicative risk. If farmer i faces supply risk θ_i then this can be treated as the sum of two orthogonal components, the general supply risk θ, and the farmer's individual risk ν_i:

$$\theta_i = \theta + \nu_i, \quad E\nu_i = 0, E\theta\nu_i = 0.$$

Then

$$Q = \sum \theta \bar{q}_i + \sum \nu_i \bar{q}_i \simeq \theta \bar{Q}$$

since the individual uncorrelated risks will approximately cancel by the law of large numbers.

If the demand schedule is linear, so that

$$p = a - bQ, \tag{10.14}$$

then the certainty equivalent price is

$$\hat{p}_i = E(\theta + \nu_i)(a - b\theta\bar{Q}) = a - b\bar{Q}(1 + \sigma^2) = \bar{p} - b\bar{Q}\sigma^2, \tag{10.15}$$

which is the same for all farmers, and the same expression as equation (5.15). Notice that with a *linear* demand function the average price is the price of average output

$$Ep = E(a - bQ) = p(EQ),$$

but as Fig. 10.1 showed this is not generally true. If $\bar{\epsilon}$ is the elasticity of demand evaluated at the average price, then equation (10.15) can be written

$$\hat{p} = \bar{p}\left(1 - \frac{\sigma^2}{\bar{\epsilon}}\right) = \bar{p}(1 - \bar{\epsilon}\sigma_p^2), \tag{10.16}$$

where σ_p is the coefficient of variation of prices.

The only information required by the risk-neutral farmer for planning purposes is the average price, $\bar{p}$, the coefficient of variation of price, σ_p, and the elasticity, $\bar{\epsilon}$. The first two are directly observable from past data, but the last must be inferred from a knowledge of both price and output. Linear regression of price on his own output will give him an appropriate estimate of $\bar{\epsilon}$. Thus, given a *theory* of the determination of price (in this case that the demand schedule is linear, and that there is zero correlation between supply and demand risk), the farmer can determine the certainty equivalent price which on average maximizes his profits. Rational expectations on this view means acting on a correct theory which describes the market environment. If the theory is correct, it will not be falsified by observation.

In the case of linear demand curves the certainty equivalent price, $E\theta p(\theta \bar{Q})$, takes a particularly simple form, but even so its relation to the average price depends on the magnitude of risk and the shape of the demand function (as measured by $\bar{\epsilon}$). It is no longer possible to derive a supply function independent of the nature of risk and the demand function. The situation is very similar to the problem of deriving a supply function for a monopolist. *If* the elasticity of the demand curve facing a monopolist is constant at ϵ, then marginal revenue is $p(1 - 1/\epsilon)$, a constant fraction of price. Equating marginal revenue to marginal cost, MC, gives the following pseudo supply-curve:

$$p = \frac{\epsilon}{\epsilon - 1}\text{MC}.$$

In the present case, since $\bar{p} = p(\bar{Q})$, average supply as a function of the price of average supply is given by

$$p(\bar{Q}) = \frac{\text{MC}}{1 - \bar{\epsilon}\sigma_p^2}, \tag{10.17}$$

where MC is the marginal cost as a function of average supply, $\bar{q}_i$.

The formula for the certainty equivalent price given in equation (10.16) was derived for the special case of linear demand, but it remains approximately correct for other demand specifications, provided risk remains multiplicative and on the supply side. For example, if demand has constant elasticity, ϵ, and if θ is log-normally distributed (the natural econometric specification for multiplicative risk, as discussed in section 6.5)

$$\theta = \Lambda(-\tfrac{1}{2}\sigma^2, \sigma^2),$$

so that

$$E\theta = 1, \text{Var } \theta = \exp\sigma^2 - 1 \simeq \sigma^2.$$

Then, from equation (10.13)

$$\hat{p} = Ep\theta = p(\bar{Q})E\theta^{1-1/\epsilon}. \qquad (10.18)$$

The properties of the log-normal distribution (set out in equation (6.43)) allow us to evaluate this expression as

$$p(\bar{Q}) \exp\left\{\tfrac{1}{2}\frac{1}{\epsilon}\left(\frac{1}{\epsilon}-1\right)\sigma^2\right\}.$$

Since

$$p = p(\bar{Q})\theta^{-1/\epsilon} = p(\bar{Q})\Lambda\left(\tfrac{1}{2}\frac{\sigma^2}{\epsilon}, \frac{\sigma^2}{\epsilon^2}\right)$$

the same technique gives the average price, $\bar{p}$

$$\bar{p} = p(\bar{Q}) \exp\left\{\tfrac{1}{2}(1+\epsilon)\frac{\sigma^2}{\epsilon^2}\right\}. \qquad (10.19)$$

Therefore

$$\hat{p} = \bar{p} \exp\left(-\frac{\sigma^2}{\epsilon}\right) \approx \bar{p}\left(1 - \frac{\sigma^2}{\epsilon}\right) = \bar{p}(1 - \epsilon\sigma_p^2). \qquad (10.20)$$

The first part of equation (10.20) is exact, the second an approximation for small σ, giving (approximately) the same result as equation (10.16). (The same result can also be obtained without assuming θ to be log-normally distributed, provided σ is small, by taking Taylor series expansions, as in subsection 6.5.2.)

If, on the other hand, supply risk is (implausibly) *additive*:

$$q = f(x) + \tilde{u}, \; E\tilde{u} = 0, \; E\tilde{u}^2 = \sigma^2, \qquad (10.21)$$

then expected profits are

$$EY = E\tilde{p}\{f(x) + \tilde{u}\} - wx$$
$$= \bar{p}f(x) - wx + E\tilde{p} \cdot \tilde{u}$$

so

$$\hat{p} = \bar{p} \qquad (10.22)$$

and the action certainty equivalent price is *equal* to the average price. (Note that the *utility* certainty equivalent price is *not* equal to the action certainty equivalent price, since $E\tilde{p}\tilde{u}$ is negative and risk therefore lowers average profits.) Thus whether risk is additive or multiplicative makes a difference to the calculation of the certainty equivalent price.

If the farmer is risk averse and maximizes an additively separable utility function as in equation (6.28):

$$EU\{p\theta f(x)\} - wx,$$

then the action certainty equivalent price, $\hat{p}$, is defined by the equation

$$\hat{p}U'(\hat{p}f) = Ep\theta U'(p\theta f). \tag{10.23}$$

If, as before, θ is log-normally distributed, demand is iso-elastic, and the utility function has constant relative risk aversion R (as in equation (6.12)), then

$$\hat{p} = \bar{p}\exp[-\{\epsilon + \tfrac{1}{2}R(\epsilon-1)^2\}\sigma_p^2], \tag{10.24}$$

which differs from equation (10.20) by the term in R. Provided the farmer knows his own attitude to risk he can calculate the appropriate certainty equivalent price without any additional information.

10.5 Concluding remarks

In this chapter we have defined the rational expectations equilibrium in the presence of risk, and in so doing have completed a logically consistent description of a competitive equilibrium in the presence of risk. We argue that the rational expectations equilibrium is the appropriate equilibrium concept to use in measuring the efficiency benefits of market intervention, as opposed to the informational benefits which might result if intervention improved the rationality of decision-making by making the market structure more transparent. In the next chapter we shall examine this distinction more carefully.

Chapter 11

Price Dynamics, Expectations, and Adjustments

11.1 Introduction

The previous chapter developed the theory of rational expectations according to which farmers use all the information potentially available to forecast the certainty equivalent price. We argued that the theory provides a natural benchmark against which to study the impact of price stabilization for the following reason. If farmers make naïve or biased forecasts, then price stabilization will probably reduce the forecasting error by reducing the variability of prices, and this should tend to improve allocative efficiency. Although these gains are important, they are more correctly described as returns to improved information, and might be achievable without price stabilization. The benefits attributable to stabilization alone are better measured by assuming that agents hold rational expectations before and after the introduction of the stabilization scheme.

We shall illustrate this distinction between the benefits of price stabilization and the benefits of improved information in the first part of this chapter, where we examine two models in which farmers form expectations incorrectly. Both models have been proposed as possible models of behaviour, and it is therefore interesting to contrast them with the predictions of the rational expectations model.

The analysis of these two simple models makes it clear not only that the nature of the market equilibrium depends critically on the nature of expectations, but also that the benefits which may accrue from a commodity price stabilization scheme will depend on the expectation formation process. Unfortunately, there is at the present time insufficient evidence to say that one particular expectation formation process is the appropriate one for the analysis of market equilibrium.

We are particularly interested in whether the rational expectations hypothesis may be taken as a 'reasonable' approximation to reality. Thus, section 11.2 discusses the empirical evidence for the rational expectations hypothesis. Our conclusion is that the evidence is ambiguous.

If expectations were systematically different from being 'rational' it would, of course, imply that there would be gains to be had by reducing the misperceptions, either by improving the quality of information or by reducing the need for information. It is the potential of commodity buffer stock schemes to reduce the need for information which is of particular concern for us here.

However, even if the market equilibrium is (approximately) consistent with rational expectations, it does not mean the economy is efficient. Rational expectations only guarantee a kind of consistency between individual *observations* and what they expect; it says nothing about whether they observe the right variables, whether they spend enough resources on information, etc. It is thus important to know something about what information is required, what sources of information are readily available and commonly used, and the efficiency with which markets generate, aggregate, and transmit information. A full discussion of these topics would take us beyond the scope of this book, but a beginning is contained in sections 11.3 and 11.4. (The discussion is continued, in a more complex model, in Chapter 16.)

11.2 Two models of incorrect expectations

In the first of these two simple examples, farmers fail to perceive the negative correlation between price and output and hence tend to oversupply. The example is interesting for several reasons. The model is structurally identical to a model of Hazell and Scandizzo (1975), in which they claimed that the rational expectations equilibrium was inefficient. We shall show in Chapter 14 that in general the rational expectations competitive equilibrium is indeed inefficient, but, ironically, in Hazell and Scandizzo's model the rational expectations equilibrium *is* efficient by their criterion of efficiency.

The model is also interesting in that it allows us to calculate the value of improved expectations, and show that the information changes the distribution of income, but that producers (who gain in this model) could over-compensate the consumers (who lose). In the second model, farmers use a popular econometric forecasting device of adaptive expectations. The model allows us to discuss the problem of testing the rational expectations hypothesis.

11.2.1 *Ignoring correlations*

In Hazell and Scandizzo's model producers are risk neutral and they take as the measure of social welfare the *expected net social surplus*, defined as the sum of expected profit plus consumers' surplus, the latter measured as the area under the demand curve. This Marshallian measure of consumers' surplus is suspect if demand is variable, as we argued in Chapter 2, and even if demand is stable, it is in general a crude measure of consumers' welfare, since it ignores their attitudes to risky prices. The one case in which it is an accurate measure of consumer welfare is if the marginal utility of consumers' income is independent of prices (and hence price instability), i.e. $V_{pI} = 0$ in equation (8.13). In short, the objective of maximizing expected net social surplus is reasonable if producers and consumers are risk neutral, which we shall show in Chapter 15 is a sufficient condition for the rational expectations equilibrium to be efficient. The reason is simple: inefficiency arises because the set of markets is incomplete (in this case, insurance markets are missing) and so different agents are not able to equate their marginal rates of substitution between different goods (or goods in different states of the world). In general, intervention will be able to improve the extent to which these marginal rates are brought into equality, and hence make all agents better off. However, if agents are risk neutral and hold rational expectations, then they would not wish to transact on risk markets even if they were present, hence they are inessential, and it makes no difference to efficiency if they are absent.

In the present model it is very easy to establish efficiency directly, as follows.

We use the model set out in equations (10.6)–(10.9), where total supply in state of the world, s, is

$$Q(s) = \sum_i f^i(x^i, s)$$

summing over the different farmers, indexed i. The price in state s is

$$p(s) = D\{Q(s), s\}$$

and net social surplus in state s when supply is y is the area under the demand schedule less the total cost of inputs, $\sum wx^i$. The expected net social surplus is thus

$$E \int_0^{Q(s)} D(y, s)dy - \sum wx^i.$$

This is maximized when the derivative with respect to x^i is zero for all i:

$$ED\{Q(s), s\} \frac{\partial Q(s)}{\partial x^i} = w$$

since the upper limit of integration depends on x^i. This equation reduces to

$$Ep(s) \frac{\partial f^i}{\partial x^i} = w,$$

which is identical to equation (10.9), the first-order condition for the rational expectations equilibrium. Therefore in this model the rational expectations equilibrium is efficient.

Suppose that there are two equally likely states of the world, so θ takes the values $1 - \sigma$ or $1 + \sigma$ with probability 1/2. There are n identical farmers with production functions

$$q = \theta\sqrt{(2bx)}, \qquad (11.1)$$

where x is input and q is output. Suppose there are an equal number, n, of consumers each with the same indirect utility function

$$V = \log I - a \log p,$$

where I is constant income, and p is the market clearing price. (It makes no difference to the general form of the solution if there is a different number of consumers.) In Chapter 8 we showed that this gives an aggregate demand function:

$$Q = \frac{naI}{p}. \tag{11.2}$$

It is convenient to choose units so that individual consumer income I is unity, as is w, the cost of the input x. If farmers are risk neutral and hold rational expectations, they will choose x to maximize expected profits

$$EY = Ep\theta\sqrt{(2bx)} - x, \tag{11.3}$$

whence

$$x = \tfrac{1}{2}b\hat{p}^2, \hat{p} \equiv Ep\theta, \tag{11.4}$$

where $\hat{p}$ is the (action) certainty equivalent price. Average output per farmer is

$$\bar{q} = b\hat{p}. \tag{11.5}$$

Total output must equal total demand, so

$$Q = nb\hat{p}\theta = \frac{naI}{p} \tag{11.6}$$

or, since $I = 1$,

$$p\theta = \frac{a}{b\hat{p}} = Ep\theta = \hat{p}. \tag{11.7}$$

(In this model unit elastic demand means that $p\theta$ and thus income are perfectly certain, and risk-averse farmers would choose exactly the same level of inputs. Compare equation (10.24) where the risk term vanishes if $\epsilon = 1$ as here.) Solving equation (11.7) gives

$$\hat{p} = \sqrt{\left(\frac{a}{b}\right)}, \quad \bar{Q} = n\sqrt{(ab)}, \quad p = \frac{1}{\theta}\sqrt{\left(\frac{a}{b}\right)}. \tag{11.8}$$

Average consumer welfare is

$$EV = -aE\log p$$

since income is unity, and $\log I = 0$, and since

$$E\log\theta = \tfrac{1}{2}\{\log(1-\sigma) + \log(1+\sigma)\}$$
$$EV = aE\log\theta + \tfrac{1}{2}a\log(b/a) = \tfrac{1}{2}a(\log(1-\sigma^2) + \log(b/a)). \tag{11.9}$$

Profits are constant in this special case of unit price elasticity:

$$EY = \tfrac{1}{2}a. \tag{11.10}$$

Compare this with the following model, due to Hazell and Scandizzo (1975). If farmers fail to perceive the relationship between price and their own output, they might observe the fluctuating market prices and try to forecast the future price. The unbiased forecast would then be the average price, $\bar{p}$, which they would adopt as the certainty equivalent price for making supply decisions. Total supply would then be given by putting $\hat{p} = \bar{p}$ in equation (11.6):

$$Q = \theta n b \bar{p}$$

and the market price would be similarly given by equation (11.7)

$$p = \frac{a}{\theta b \bar{p}}.$$

The average price is thus

$$\bar{p} = \frac{a}{b\bar{p}} \frac{1}{1-\sigma^2}$$

so

$$\bar{p} = \sqrt{\left(\frac{a}{b(1-\sigma^2)}\right)}. \qquad (11.11)$$

Average supply increases relative to the rational expectations supply to

$$\bar{Q} = n\sqrt{\left(\frac{ab}{1-\sigma^2}\right)} \qquad (11.12)$$

and prices are lower

$$p = \frac{1}{\theta}\sqrt{\left(\frac{a(1-\sigma^2)}{b}\right)} \qquad (11.13)$$

which makes consumers better off. Average consumer welfare is now

$$EV' = \tfrac{1}{2}a \log\left(\frac{b}{a}\right) > EV, \qquad (11.14)$$

and total average profits will be

$$EY' = \tfrac{1}{2}a\left(\frac{1-2\sigma^2}{1-\sigma^2}\right) < EY. \qquad (11.15)$$

The farmer is correct in forecasting the average price, but incorrect in failing to allow for the correlation between price and his own output. It might be thought that if he is acting competitively, his own output will not affect the market price, and to assume a relation is tantamount to the farmers implicitly colluding — which is obviously non-competitive. This argument is wrong, because the farmer can continue to believe that his own supply will make no difference to the price (if n is large), but observe that when the weather is good his output is high but the price is low, not because of *his* large output, but because the good weather increases total supply.

We can now calculate the net value of correct forecasting, after compensating those who lose once the rational expectations equilibrium is established (in this case, the consumers.) If the farmers are now correctly informed, they will gain an amount equal to equation (11.10) less equation (11.15) or

$$B = EY - EY' = \tfrac{1}{2}\frac{a\sigma^2}{1-\sigma^2}. \tag{11.16}$$

The amount of money required to compensate consumers, and maintain them at a level of utility EV' is C, bringing their income up to $1 + C$ where C is the solution to the equation

$$EV' = EV + \log(1 + C).$$

This can be solved using equations (11.14) and (11.9) to give

$$C = (1 - \sigma^2)^{-a/2} - 1 \cong \tfrac{1}{2}a\sigma^2\left\{1 + \tfrac{1}{2}\left(1 + \frac{a}{2}\right)\sigma^2\right\}, \tag{11.17}$$

where the approximation follows from the binomial expansion. The net value of information is thus

$$B - C \cong \frac{a(2-a)}{8(1-\sigma^2)}\sigma^4. \tag{11.18}$$

We can now compare the effect of price stabilization on the farmers holding naïve and rational price expectations. Suppose that the price can be perfectly stabilized (which, if it were to be done by a buffer stock, would require an infinitely large stock. For the moment we follow the implausible tradition that this is possible). In this special case of unit elastic demand the stabilized price would actually be the rational expectations certainty equivalent price, $\hat{p}$, since this is $p(\bar{Q})$. (In general, if the elasticity of demand ϵ is not unity $p(\bar{Q})$ will not be $\hat{p}$, as equation (10.19) shows.) With rational expectations average profits will therefore be unchanged by stabilization, but consumer welfare rises to

$$E\hat{V} = \tfrac{1}{2}a\log\left(\frac{b}{a}\right). \tag{11.19}$$

the same value as in equation (11.14). Therefore, the value of stabilization to the consumers is given by C in equation (11.17).

If, on the other hand, farmers naïvely use the forecast average price, then price stabilization changes the average price to $p(\bar{Q})$, which, in this special case, is equal to the original rational expectations certainty equivalent price, $\hat{p}$. Moreover, since farmers are risk neutral, the effect of price stabilization on farmers is exactly the same as informing them of the correct certainty equivalent price, so their profits will increase by B, given in equation (11.16).

Consumers originally enjoyed welfare EV' given in equation (11.14), and after stabilization enjoy welfare EV given in equation (11.19), which in this model are identical. Thus stabilizing a naïve equilibrium market only affects producers, while stabilizing a rational expectations equilibrium market only affects consumers (in this special unit elastic model).

The total benefit of stabilizing a naïve equilibrium market in B, which consists of two parts — the true or efficiency gains of stabilization, C, plus the gains from eliminating the losses due to incorrect forecasting, measured by $B - C$ in equation (11.18).

Lessons from the model. In this example improved forecasting has important distributional consequences, for it makes consumers worse off (relative to the naïve equilibrium) and producers better off. To say that the information is valuable is to say that producers could over-compensate customers. The example therefore illustrates a general principle, that information can, by changing the market prices, have far-reaching general equilibrium effects. In general, there is no guarantee that improved information will engender a potential Pareto improvement (i.e. one in which gainers could over-compensate losers) and Green (1978) gives an example in which improved information makes agents worse off.

The model also has the property that the informational benefits are small relative to the gains from stabilization: the ratio is approximately

$$\frac{B-C}{C} \simeq \frac{(2-a)\sigma^2}{4-(2-a)\sigma^2} \tag{11.20}$$

or about 2 per cent if σ is 30 per cent and a is unity. The main effect of improved information in this model is to change the distribution of income rather than to increase it significantly. It is very difficult to judge how robust this conclusion is, and it obviously depends on the extent to which farmers' decisions would be changed by better information, but the example reminds us that a change which is beneficial to one side of the market is typically harmful to the other, so that the net benefits may be quite small. The same happens with stabilization itself, which may generate quite large transfers relative to the net gains.

Finally, the example shows quite clearly how the gains from stabilization can be divided into the true efficiency gains, and gains from improved information.

11.2.2 *Adaptive expectations and the cobweb*

Suppose there is no risk in either supply or demand, but farmers forecast the price at harvest according to the following adaptive rule, suggested by Nerlove (1958):

$$p_t^e - p_{t-1}^e = \lambda(p_{t-1} - p_{t-1}^e). \tag{11.21}$$

Thus they compare last year's forecast, p_{t-1}^e with the actual market price, p_{t-1}, and adjust this year's forecast to reduce this discrepancy by some fraction λ. This expression can be written

$$p_t^e = \lambda p_{t-1} + (1-\lambda)p_{t-1}^e \tag{11.22}$$

or

Price Dynamics, Expectations, and Adjustments 149

$$p_t^e = \lambda \sum_{i=1}^{t} (1-\lambda)^{i-1} p_{t-i}, \qquad (11.23)$$

showing that the forecast is a geometric weighted average of past observed prices. If the supply schedule is linear (as in the previous model) in the forecast price, but the demand schedule is now linear

$$D_t = \alpha - a p_t \qquad (11.24)$$

$$S_t = \beta + b p_t^e \qquad (11.25)$$

$$D_t = S_t \qquad (11.26)$$

so

$$p_t = \frac{\alpha - \beta}{a} - \frac{b}{a} p_t^e, \qquad (11.27)$$

then elementary manipulation to eliminate p_t^e using equations (11.22) and (11.27) gives

$$p_t - \left\{ 1 - \frac{\lambda(a+b)}{a} \right\} p_{t-1} = \frac{\lambda(\alpha - \beta)}{a}. \qquad (11.28)$$

This first-order difference equation is easily solved, given the initial price p_0:

$$p_t = \bar{p} + \mu^t (p_0 - \bar{p}), \qquad (11.29)$$

where

$$\bar{p} = \frac{\alpha - \beta}{a+b}, \quad \mu = 1 - \frac{\lambda(a+b)}{a}. \qquad (11.30)$$

Provided that μ is less than unity in absolute value the market is stable and the price converges to its equilibrium value, $\bar{p}$, if disturbed. This stability condition requires

$$0 < \lambda < \frac{2a}{a+b}.$$

In the case of an extreme response, $\lambda = 1$, $p_t^e = p_{t-1}$, and last year's forecasting discrepancy is immediately eliminated. The system will be stable if $b < a$, that is, if the slope of the supply schedule is less steep than that of demand. Figure 11.1 shows why this model is often described as a cobweb.

(Note that, as is usual, the figure actually graphs the *inverse* supply and demand schedules, which give price as a function of quantity. The inverse supply schedule must be *less* steep than the inverse demand schedule. Normally there is no need to be so precise about the distinction, and we follow convention in loosely describing the inverse demand schedule as just the demand schedule.)

Even though production and demand are non-risky, prices will fluctuate

150   *Commodity Price Stabilization*

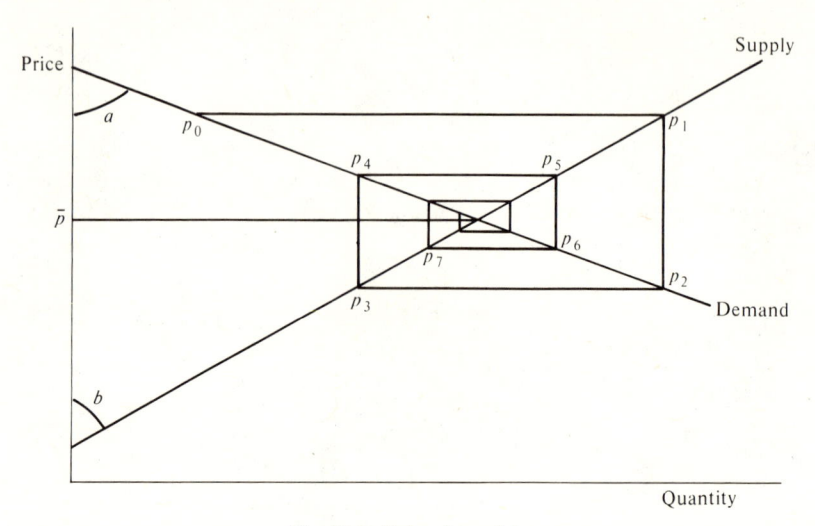

Fig. 11.1 Cobweb model

about the equilibrium price. Incorrect expectations thus give rise to endogenous price variability. A very smart farmer would correctly predict the actual market price if he knew the underlying structure of production and demand and knew the way in which other farmers forecast price, and would be able to benefit from this knowledge. However, he would not thereby escape the variability forced on him by the other farmers. Since smart farmers make more profits than naïve forecasters, they will presumably expand and prosper while the others may leave the industry. In this model, smart farmers will also cause the price to approach equilibrium more rapidly, consistent with the widely held view that profitable speculation is stabilizing. (This view is not undisputed, and it has been shown that if agents have market power, it may be profitable to destabilize the market — see, e.g., Hart, 1977; Newbery, 1978.) Smart farmers here speculate by producing more or less than their naïve colleagues as they predict a higher or lower price.

Now suppose that there is additive supply risk, so that

$$S_t = \beta + bp_t^e + \tilde{u}_t, E\tilde{u}_t = 0, E\tilde{u}^2 = \sigma^2.$$

The market clearing price will then satisfy

$$p_t - \bar{p} = -\frac{b}{a}(p_t^e - \bar{p}) - \frac{\tilde{u}_t}{a} \tag{11.31}$$

which, with the expectation equation (11.22), gives

$$p_t - \bar{p} = \mu(p_{t-1} - \bar{p}) - \frac{1}{a}\{\tilde{u}_t - (1-\lambda)\tilde{u}_{t-1}\}.$$

(The values of μ and $\bar{p}$ are the same as before, given in equation (11.30).) This equation can be solved:

$$p_t - \bar{p} = \mu^t(p_0 - \bar{p}) + \tilde{v}_t, \tag{11.32}$$

$$\tilde{v}_t = \frac{1}{a}\left\{-\tilde{u}_t + \mu^{t-1}(1-\lambda)\tilde{u}_0 + \frac{\lambda b}{a}\sum_{i=1}^{t-1}\mu^{i-1}\tilde{u}_{t-i}\right\}. \tag{11.33}$$

The certainty equivalent price used in supply decisions fluctuates for two, related reasons. The first is because of the non-risky cobweb effect, the second because of the gradual adjustment to risk. In the long run, if the cobweb is stable ($|\mu| < 1$), the fluctuations arising from the cobweb die away, but the risk-adjustment term, v_t, never vanishes. Moreover, if the disturbances, u_t, are independent, so that there is no serial correlation in risk, then equations (11.30) and (11.33) give:

$$E\tilde{v}_t = 0$$

$$\lim_{t \to \infty} \text{Var } \tilde{v}_t = \frac{\sigma^2}{a^2}\left\{1 + \frac{\lambda b^2}{(a+b)(2a - \lambda(a+b))}\right\} > \frac{\sigma^2}{a^2}, \tag{11.34}$$

which is the variance of prices in the long run. Compare the rational expectations model, in which the forecast price p_t^e remains constant, equal to $\bar{p}$, because if the weather is serially uncorrelated, there is no reason to use recent data to improve forecasts. If the weather was bad last year, there is no reason to assume it will be bad this year, which is implicitly what is happening in an adaptive expectations model. Equation (11.31) now becomes

$$p_t = \bar{p} - \frac{\tilde{u}_t}{a}$$

$$\text{Var } p_t = \frac{\sigma^2}{a^2} \tag{11.35}$$

and prices fluctuate less with rational expectations than adaptive expectations. In a certain world, if the cobweb is stable, last year's estimate is closer to the equilibrium than previous years' estimates, so it makes sense to attach more weight to the recent past. In a risky world attaching more weight to last year's estimate means attaching more weight to the irrelevant randomness of last year's outcome. This conflict can be seen as follows. The value of λ which gives the most rapid convergence to equilibrium in a certain world is $a/(a+b)$, since then $\mu = 0$, while it can be seen from equation (11.34) that the value which minimizes price instability in the long run is zero.

It follows that the value of price stabilization will depend critically on λ, for the larger is λ, the greater will be the steady-state price instability before price stabilization, and hence the greater will be the potential gain from price

152 Commodity Price Stabilization

stabilization — at least, if we ignore possible losses during the transition because of imperfect adaptation to the new price distribution. In this model the average price is the same whether expectations are adaptive or rational (because of linearity and additivity), and so consumers *prefer* a more unstable price. (The indirect utility function is convex in prices.) If producers become more rational they will gain at the expense of consumers, so, as in the last model, better information in the form of better forecasts makes some agents better off and others worse off.

11.3 Empirical tests of rational expectations

The cobweb model appears to provide an excellent opportunity for testing the hypothesis of rational expectations against naïve expectations, for equation (11.31) holds quite generally for any kind of expectation. If supply is subject to independent additive shocks, then the cobweb model makes the following price prediction:

$$E(p_t | p_{t-1}, p_{t-2} \ldots) = \bar{p} - \frac{b}{a}(p_t^e - \bar{p}). \qquad (11.36)$$

Unless expectations are rational, in which case $p_t^e = \bar{p}$, the predicted price moves in the opposite direction to that expected by the farmers. Most studies of expectations suggest that expected prices are positively correlated with actual prices:

$$p_t^e - \bar{p} = \beta(p_t - \bar{p}) + \bar{v}_t, \qquad (11.37)$$

where $0 < \beta < 1$ (see Theil, 1958), and as such are clearly inconsistent with the cobweb theory. Muth (1961, p. 333) shows that equation (11.37) is consistent with rational expectations, with the value of the estimated coefficient β given (in the limit) by

$$\hat{\beta} \to \frac{\operatorname{Var} p^e}{\operatorname{Var} p}.$$

The other standard piece of evidence for the cobweb model is the apparently regular cycles in the prices of various commodities. However, this is very weak evidence, for any dynamic system experiencing purely random shocks typically responds with cycles of a fairly stable period. In particular, Slutzky (1937) and Yule (1927) showed long ago that moving-average processes (such as those provided by storage, and holding cattle and pigs longer before slaughter) can lead to very regular cycles. Their period is, however, longer than that predicted by simple cobweb models. Coase and Fowler (1937) noted that the observed pig cycles were too long for the cobweb model, while Ezekiel's (1938) evidence for a cattle cycle also gives unreasonably long periods. A better test of cyclical regularity is provided by spectral analysis, but long time series are needed for reliably estimating cyclical periods. Larson (1967) claims to find a thirty-month cycle for the price of US eggs in the period 1955–65, corresponding to four

Price Dynamics, Expectations, and Adjustments 153

times the length of time required to produce a laying pullet from a fertile egg, but the number of observations is low and the period on the long side to be consistent with a cobweb. On the other hand, there was no evidence of any cycle in the futures price of eggs, suggesting that the futures price was an unbiased estimator of the future market price, not systematically influenced by movements in the spot price. Thus it could be argued that traders on the future market held rational expectations, while poultry producers (who made little use of the futures market) ignored these price forecasts in taking production decisions.

If the evidence of apparently regular fluctuations in prices is difficult to interpret, the question whether farmers correctly predict the correlation between price and output is even harder to answer. If farmers are moderately risk averse, as seems likely, then, as shown in Chapter 6, farmers will supply less than if they were risk neutral. If they fail to appreciate the negative correlation between output and price, they will over-supply. It will then be very difficult to deduce from the observed actions whether farmers are rational but risk averse, or non-rational and less risk averse. Attitudes to risk and information are both hard to observe and almost indistinguishable in such contexts.

The other problem with testing the rational expectations hypothesis is that, as was stated in the last chapter, it assumes that farmers use all the information *potentially* available. If the underlying structure (the number of farmers, the income and tastes of consumers, etc.) never changed, then eventually the farmers would be able to learn all the relevant information publicly available. In practice, there is no guarantee that the structure will remain unchanged over a long enough period to collect enough data, and much relevant information is not publicly available, but can be obtained at a cost, which may deter agents. Instead of assuming complete information, we should ask what information could farmers reasonably be expected to use in forming expectations, and to this question we now turn.

11.4 Learning and reasonable expectations

We showed in section 11.1 that the benefits of price stabilization could be subdivided into the benefits of improving the quality of information available to farmers (by reducing some of the price variability which tends to obscure the relevant information), and the benefits of stabilization alone which would be available even if farmers were well informed about the price distribution. We further showed that the distribution of these two types of benefits might be quite different, or, equivalently, that the distribution of the benefits of stabilizing a market in rational expectations equilibrium might be quite different from the distributive impact of stabilizing an imperfectly informed market.

There is therefore a presumption that the total benefits of price stabilization are likely to be greater, the less well informed is the market, and that the distribution of these benefits might depend quite sensitively on the extent to which decision-makers are informed about the underlying risk. A full analysis of price stabilization should therefore enquire how well informed the decision-makers are, how far the quality of information could be improved without a price stabilization programme, and then, finally, what remaining improvements in information would be made possible by price stabilization.

These are large questions on which little empirical evidence is available, and all we can reasonably do at this stage is to ask what kind of information the farmer needs, under what conditions he would be able to collect such information, and what information it is reasonable to suppose that he has. All these questions are somewhat open-ended, and the following section can only touch on some of the more obvious aspects, but we shall return to some of these issues in Chapter 16.

We can divide the problem facing the farmer into three parts:
1. What information should he gather?
2. How should he process this information, i.e. how should he use this information to obtain estimates of the price distribution?
3. Having obtained the estimated price distribution, how should he decide which crops to grow at what level of intensity?

Most of this book is concerned with the third question and only in this chapter and Chapter 16 do we discuss the first two questions at any length. They are, however, critical, and it is important to realize that they cannot really be separated from the third question. Only under special conditions can the problem of the choice of estimating procedure be separated from the use to which the estimate is to be put. We shall return to this point later.

For expositional purposes, however, the distinction is a useful one, and so we concentrate on the first two questions.

11.4.1 *Obtaining information*

At any date, a farmer could in principle collect data on the past prices of all commodities and, since in a general equilibrium system like a market economy almost all variables are potentially related to all other variables, it might seem that he would need all of this vast amount of information. The first question to ask is whether he can economize in the amount of information needed.

The concept of sufficient statistics. If there is a set of statistics which provides all the information which can be obtained about some random variable, say price, then we say it constitutes a set of *sufficient statistics* for price; that is, given an observation of the set of sufficient statistics, our estimate of the distribution of price is the same as it would be if we observed those statistics *plus* any additional statistics. For instance, if the demand schedule were known and unchanging, then knowing the aggregate supply would be a sufficient statistic for the price; knowing my own output in addition to the aggregate supply does not affect my beliefs about the price next period.

It is important to be able to identify sufficient statistics: for once we have obtained them, any further information is redundant. It may, however, not be easy to ascertain whether a set of statistics is sufficient or not. For example, in order to know whether aggregate output is a sufficient statistic for price, it is necessary to know something about the structure of the economy and about the various interactions. It might be that if output fell in one region, income would fall and affect aggregate demand more than if output fell in some other region. If so, then it would be necessary to know output by region, not just aggregate output. For aggregates to be sufficient statistics the economy has to be very homogeneous.

On the relevance of past prices. Indeed, not only is it difficult to identify sufficient statistics, it is often difficult to determine the relevance of particular pieces of information. For example, we could ask what information is likely to be conveyed in past prices.

The answer depends on the source of price variability, or, more precisely, on (a) whether the sources of price variability are systematically correlated over time; and (b) whether the variability in price induces systematic responses in subsequent periods on the part of producers or consumers.

Consider, for example, the model set out in subsection 11.2.2, in which demand is stable so that prices only fluctuate because of supply variations. If the source of supply risk is the weather, and if there is zero serial correlation between the weather in successive years, and no storage then there is no reason for supply and hence price to be correlated over time. The rational expectations forecast in equation (11.36) is just the average price, unchanging from year to year. If, however, a significant fraction of farmers failed to appreciate that the underlying risk was uncorrelated, they might use adaptive expectations in forecasting, and so induce serial correlation into the price series. A rational farmer would now use equation (11.36) to predict the future price, given the serial correlation in past prices. He could replace the term p_t^e with its value given in equation (11.23) to obtain his own forecasting equation:

$$E(p_t|p_{t-1},\ldots) = \bar{p} - \frac{b}{a}\left\{\lambda \sum_{i=1}^{t}(1-\lambda)^{i-1}p_{t-i} - \bar{p}\right\}. \quad (11.38)$$

These rational farmers would make forecasts negatively correlated with the naïve price expectations, and so would tend to eliminate the regular fluctuation. Alternatively, if the crop could be stored, it may pay agents to store the crop when its price is low and sell the next year. As Muth (1961) demonstrates, this will induce serial correlation.

Thus if some farmers are naïve, or if storage is profitable, there will be systematic responses which induce serial correlation and make past prices informative. However, for most kinds of systematic variability in supply and demand, it seems implausible that there will be significant serial correlation between the disturbances at different dates, except, perhaps, for demand variability induced by the business cycle. (Even here, there are those who claim that there is little serial correlation: see, e.g., Hall, 1978.)

On the other hand, for what we referred to as non-systematic risks, for instance with technological change or changes in consumer preferences — the shift in preferences of Americans towards red wine, in the early sixties, and then to white wines in the mid-seventies — there is likely to be significant serial correlation.

The difficulty facing any farmer is, of course, ascertaining whether the price at any particular date is low because of 'temporary' conditions or because of a permanent downward shift in the demand curve for the commodity in question, caused, say, by consumers shifting to an artificial substitute.

Other sources of information. Although past prices may have limited relevance, prices on futures markets may provide considerable information to the farmer. How they do this is one of the main subjects of Chapter 16. There are, of course, other sources of information available to the individual farmer. Market analysts or government agencies may publish forecasts of prices, satellite data may give advance estimates of total crop yields, and markets for intermediate products such as store cattle, day-old chicks, etc. may reveal changes in expected future prices for the final product. This brings us to the next question, which is how the farmer uses the information available to make a forecast of the price (or more accurately, the price distribution).

11.4.2 *Processing information*

We argued in section 10.4 that if the farmer was interested in choosing the optimum level of inputs, he would need to know the action certainty equivalent price rather than the average price. In Chapter 6 we showed that a farmer interested in choosing the optimum combination of different crops would be concerned not with the average price (or, more accurately, its return) but with its covariance with other crops. In other words, the determination of the certainty equivalent price depends both on the decision to be made and on the environment within which it is made. If for the moment we just consider the calculation of the certainty equivalent price for inputs of a single crop experiencing supply risk, then equation (10.24) can be written

$$\hat{p} \simeq \bar{p}[1 - \{\epsilon + \tfrac{1}{2}R(\epsilon - 1)^2\}\sigma_p^2],$$

showing that the farmer needs to estimate the elasticity of demand, ϵ, the average price, $\bar{p}$, the coefficient of variation of prices, σ_p, and his own coefficient of relative risk aversion, R. Most econometric studies have assumed that the farmer is only concerned with the average price, but the certainty equivalent price is only equal to the average price if producers are risk neutral, risk is additive, and demand is linear — convenient econometric assumptions but rather unreasonable restrictions. Accordingly, it is not just mean price (or mean expected price) which is relevant for determining their supply. Only in certain circumstances will the expected price and the certainty equivalent price be perfectly correlated so that one can be used as a surrogate for the other (indeed, only in certain circumstances can a certainty equivalent price even be defined) and even when they are, a change in the structure of the market, such as that resulting from a commodity price stabilization scheme, will change the relationship between the two.

The problem of correctly processing the price information would therefore appear very difficult. However, there is a danger that this concentration on estimating prices exaggerates the problem, for the farmer is interested in the distribution of returns rather than prices, and it may be easier to estimate these directly. For example, the inefficiencies in the first model of subsection 11.2.1 would disappear if farmers estimated average returns per acre.

11.5 The efficiency of expectations

Most of this book is concerned with the efficiency of market allocations for given information, assuming that farmers use the information rationally. There is, however, a prior question which needs at least to be asked if not adequately answered: is the competitive market efficient in providing the relevant information? Suppose that farmers need to estimate the elasticity of demand in order to calculate the appropriate certainty equivalent price. How would an intelligent central planner instruct farmers to behave if he were uncertain about the nature of demand and risk? The demand curve will be more accurately estimated if the data points are spread out, as Fig. 11.2 suggests.

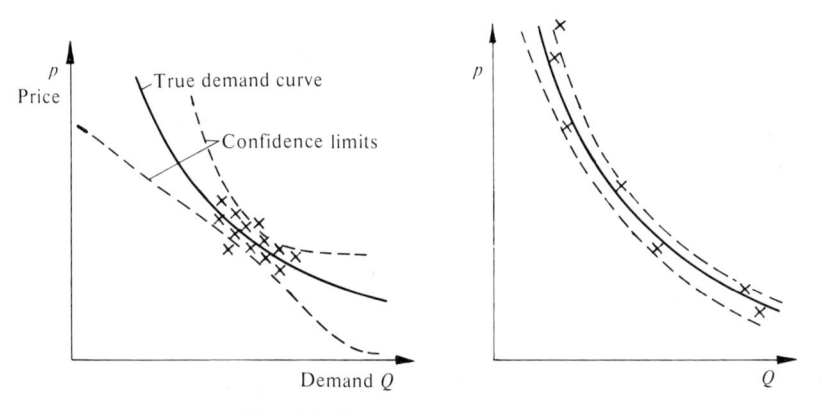

Fig. 11.2 Estimating demand curves

In Fig. 11.2 crosses represent observations, the continuous line is the true demand curve, and the dashed lines are confidence intervals for the estimated demand curve.

Thus the planner would deliberately destabilize the market in order to collect better information, the better to stabilize it in the future. A decentralized market would not do this, since destabilizing behaviour is individually costly, even if it is socially productive of better information. Information is thus a public good, and, as is well known, competitive markets tend to under-supply public goods, in this case by devoting insufficient resources to collecting extreme observations by destabilizing supplies.

This is, in fact, a critical aspect of the analysis of the optimality of market equilibrium. Even if the equilibrium is efficient in some sense given the state of information, it may be grossly inefficient in seeking out and disseminating information. This means that structural changes, such as a commodity price stabilization scheme, which reduces the information required by farmers to operate efficiently, may in fact be socially desirable; the private market may, in effect, supply too little stabilization because it fails to take into account the benefits associated with the reduction in the information requirements of farmers. We shall return to this important issue of the efficiency of the market in disseminating information in Chapter 16.

11.6 Conclusions

In the last chapter we studied market equilibrium under the strong hypothesis that farmers correctly used all potentially available information in calculating their optimum supply decision. In the first part of this chapter we analysed two alternative models of farmers' behaviour. In the first model, farmers correctly forecast the average price (as would an unbiased futures market) but failed to allow for the negative correlation between their output and the market clearing price; information which was potentially available from observations on past prices *and quantities*. In the second model, farmers adjusted their forecast of the future price in response to discrepancies between past forecasts and outcomes. Both models have been seriously proposed as plausible theories of behaviour, and both models demonstrate that price stabilization confers additional benefits in the form of improved decision-making, for the bias between the postulated forecast and the rational expectations forecast diminishes with a fall in price variability. In these models the rational expectations equilibrium was efficient, and hence any other method of forecasting results in losses which can be reduced by improved information, or by reducing the biases in the processing of information. In the first model, we showed that the size of the efficiency gains of improved forecasting were small relative to the changes in the distribution of income resulting from improved forecasting. The model also illustrated neatly how the gains from price stabilization could be decomposed into gains from improved information (which move the economy into a rational expectations equilibrium) plus gains from stabilizing a market in rational expectations equilibrium. Again, the former were small relative to the latter in the case studied. In general, of course, price stabilization will not completely eliminate informational inefficiencies, but there should still be gains if these inefficiencies are reduced.

The lesson of these models is that the distributive impact of price stabilization may be quite different if the market is using potentially available information efficiently than if it is not. It therefore becomes important to ask how farmers might collect and use such information, to see whether there is any presumption that they are or are not likely to be efficient. We argued that while it might be quite difficult to estimate the appropriate certainty equivalent *price* from past observations, if the problem was reformulated as one of estimating returns (i.e. price times output) then some of the difficulties would be overcome. This has obvious implications for the econometric modelling of supply responses.

Finally, we argued that any structural change in the market which altered the pattern of risk or the relationship between supply and price (such as that caused by a price stabilization scheme) might make it temporarily more difficult to estimate the appropriate certainty equivalent price or return. Although price stabilization may lead to a more efficient use of information in the long run, it might lead to greater inefficiency in the short run.

Part III

Market Equilibrium

Part II developed the analytical techniques needed for the analysis of market equilibrium in the presence of risk and laid the foundations for the welfare analysis of changes in risk. It showed that, while the analysis of market equilibrium requires an analysis of both supply and demand, the presence of risk makes their interrelationships more complicated than in simple static theory and the neat separation which prevails in conventional theory between demand and supply no longer obtains. A change in the demand function will lead to a change in the probability distribution of prices, which will, in turn, lead to a change in the supply decisions.

Nevertheless, the analysis was simplified in a number of important ways. First, it assumed that farmers had only to choose the scale of production, whereas they are typically confronted with more than one decision to make — which crops to grow, and how to grow them (whether to use fertilizers, irrigation, etc.), as well as the scale on which to grow them. Second, the market environment in which farmers typically operate is far more complex: there are futures markets, they can store commodities, they can borrow and lend, they may be able to purchase insurance, etc. Finally, they can decide to allocate resources to improve their forecast of future prices, they can attempt to acquire better information which will reduce the uncertainty which they face.

The other limitation of Part II was that it did not attempt (except in very special circumstances) to evaluate the efficiency with which the market allocated resources.

The object, then, of Part III is to extend our understanding of the effect of risk on the market equilibrium, to examine the various ways in which farmers can adjust and respond to risk, and to assess the efficiency with which the market allocates resources in the presence of risk. It is divided into five chapters. Chapter 12 presents an overview of the various methods by which farmers can share their risk with others in the community, and reduce them. Chapter 13 looks in considerable detail at one of the key markets available for reducing and transferring risk — the futures market. We demonstrate its central role in the analysis of commodity price stabilization by showing that it has superior risk-reducing properties to price stabilization schemes, although it may have different distributive impacts and induce a different supply response. Chapter 14 looks at the effect of storage and savings in the risk borne by the producer and examines how far such possibilities reduce the benefits

162 *Commodity Price Stabilization*

to be obtained from price stabilization and interact with the operation of government buffer stock programmes. We argue that the existence of futures markets, credit markets, and storage opportunities may significantly affect not only the benefits to be obtained from price stabilization, but also its impact on the market equilibrium.

The next chapter raises the central question of whether the competitive market will, in the absence of any government intervention, achieve a constrained efficient allocation of resources. If so, then this would seriously undermine the case for a government-run stabilization programme, since this would at best be an expensive method of redistributing income. However, we show that except in very special cases there is a presumption that the competitive market, even with rational expectations, is inefficient, and can be improved by taxes or subsidies.

Whereas Chapter 15 asks whether, given the best possible information, the market can achieve constrained efficiency, Chapter 16 asks whether the market is likely to gather and disseminate the required information. This is important as price stabilization might reduce the amount of information needed by individual producers, and hence improve at least one aspect of efficiency.

Although Part III contains some rather difficult chapters, we would argue that a proper analysis of the issues we raise is critical for a balanced assessment of price stabilization, and their neglect by other writers has seriously oversimplified their analysis.

Chapter 12

Sharing and Reducing Risk

In Chapter 6 we described the basic responses of a farmer to risk: how risk affected his level of utility, his level of effort (inputs), and his responsiveness to changes in expected price levels. There are, however, a number of other ways in which farmers respond to risk, and it is necessary to keep these in mind when considering the effects of a price stabilization programme. We can divide these responses into two groups:

(i) Actions which share or transfer the risk to someone for whom the bearing of the risk is less costly.

(ii) Actions which reduce the total amount of risk faced by the farmer.

These two types of responses to risk are discussed in the next two sections. Yet another way of responding to risk — obtaining more information — is discussed in Chapter 16.

The first half of this chapter gives a fairly non-technical account of these two types of response. In the first section we show that the total cost of risk-bearing can often be reduced by transferring it to others or sharing it among a larger number of agents, though there are two important limits on how far this can be done. It may be difficult to transfer the risks surrounding a decision to others without blunting the incentives for the decision-maker to act efficiently, and it may be difficult to share risks (by insurance) if the insurance agency is unable to discriminate between good and bad risks. Nevertheless, we identify a variety of mechanisms available for risk-sharing, and argue that their existence implies that the social cost of risk may be considerably less than if the risks were borne by farmers. To the extent that price stabilization schemes are introduced to reduce the risks facing farmers, if the existing risk-sharing possibilities are ignored there is a danger that the benefits of price stabilization will be overstated. We also argue that the distributional impact of price stabilization may be significantly modified by the presence of these alternative risk-sharing options.

In the second section we examine the ways in which the farmer can directly reduce the total risk by choosing less risky crops, less risky ways of producing given crops, or by growing more than one crop. These actions are important, for if the riskiness of any single crop is reduced by a price stabilization scheme, then the farmer will typically alter his risk-reducing decisions, and possibly increase the area allocated to the crop, or the riskiness of the production technique. These supply responses may substantially modify the impact of the stabilization programme, as demonstrated in a simple example, but it is not obvious whether calculations which ignore such supply responses under- or overestimate the total benefits (and costs) of stabilization. The moral of this section is that risk-reducing activities and programmes may interact in a complex and counter-intuitive fashion, and therefore need careful analysis.

12.1 Risk-sharing activities

We first assume that the risk itself cannot be altered, but it can be transferred to others or shared. There are two motives for sharing and transferring risk: first, a risk may be transferred from one individual to another more able or willing to bear it; second, by dividing risks among several individuals, not only is the risk faced by each reduced, but the aggregate cost of the risk is, in a sense, reduced.

We noted in our earlier discussion that the risk premium associated with any risk was proportional to the magnitude of the individual's risk aversion. If one individual is less risk averse than another, the cost of his bearing the risk will be less; to put it another way, there is a profitable exchange between the two individuals. The amount which one individual is willing to pay for the risk exceeds the amount which the other individual requires in compensation for giving up the risky prospect.

In the context of agriculture, landlords may be less risk averse than their tenants; there may exist speculators who are less risk averse than farmers; and large purchasers of agricultural commodities (middlemen) may be less risk averse than the primary producers themselves.

The differences in the amount required to compensate an individual for bearing risk may be attributed to several causes. First, there may simply be differences in risk aversion in general. Some individuals are born gamblers; others are naturally very cautious. Second, there may be differences in wealth, and risk aversion is likely to decline as wealth increases. (More precisely, the degree of absolute risk aversion, which is what is relevant here, is normally assumed to decline with wealth; what happens to relative risk aversion is more ambiguous.)

One individual may be more willing to bear a risk than another for a third reason: the particular risk may be negatively correlated with his income. To see this, consider a small risky prospect whose outcome is $\tilde{v}$. Assume that the individual has income from other sources denoted by $\tilde{Y}$. To see what price p_v would the individual be willing to pay for the risky prospect, i.e. for what value of p_v is

$$EU(\tilde{Y}) = EU(\tilde{Y} + \tilde{v} - p_v), \tag{12.1}$$

we take a Taylor series expansion about mean income, $\bar{Y}$, obtaining as before

$$EU(\tilde{Y}) \approx U(\bar{Y}) + \tfrac{1}{2} U''(\bar{Y}) E(\tilde{Y} - \bar{Y})^2$$

$$EU(\tilde{Y} + \tilde{v} - p_v) \approx U(\bar{Y}) + U'(\bar{Y})(\bar{v} - p_v) + \frac{U''(\bar{Y})}{2} \{E(\tilde{v} - \bar{v})^2 +$$

$$+ E(\tilde{Y} - \bar{Y})^2 + 2E(\tilde{v} - \bar{v})(\tilde{Y} - \bar{Y}) + (\bar{v} - p_v)^2\}.$$

Equating these expressions (and ignoring the term $(\bar{v} - p_v)^2$ which is, by assumption, small relative to the other terms)

$$p_v \approx \bar{v} - \tfrac{1}{2}A\{\text{Var}(\tilde{v}) + 2\,\text{Cov}(\tilde{v}, \tilde{Y})\} \qquad (12.2)$$

where $A \equiv -U''/U'$ is the coefficient of absolute risk aversion defined in Chapter 6. The greater the *negative* covariance, the more the individual is willing to pay for the risky prospect. Essentially, when the two are negatively correlated, the risky prospect acts like insurance; it pays large amounts when other income is small (and hence the marginal utility of income is high) and it pays small amounts when other income is high, and hence the additional income from the risky prospect would have had little value.

When output prices are high for farmers, input prices are high for intermediate producers. If, as one might suspect, profitability for producers of intermediate goods is negatively related to the level of input prices, prices and profits are negatively correlated, and hence such intermediate producers will be willing to bear at least some of the risk associated with price variability, i.e. they may be willing to buy the goods in the futures market, which, as we show in Chapter 13, effectively guarantees the price for the farmer and so reduces his risk. (This risk-saving advantage also provides a motive for vertical integration common in the processing, producing, and marketing of agricultural commodities.)

Similarly we noted earlier that the absolute size of the risk premium, ρ, for any individual was proportional to the variance of the risk:

$$\rho = \tfrac{1}{2}A\,\text{Var}(\tilde{Y}). \qquad (12.3)$$

Hence, if we divided the risk among two individuals, the variance is divided by two squared, and the size of the risk premium for each individual is divided by four. The total risk premium is thus divided in half. As the number of individuals, n, among whom the risk is divided becomes very large, the size of the aggregate risk premium goes to zero as $1/n$.

12.1.1 Limitations on risk-spreading and risk-sharing

The analysis would suggest that the most efficient organization of the economy would entail either that agricultural risks be transferred to those who are wealthier, or in any case find it less costly to bear these risks, or, at a minimum be shared among large numbers of individuals. The risk borne by the farmer himself ought to be negligible. This is clearly not the case, and we need to ask why. There are two primary reasons, both of which arise out of the costs of obtaining information:

1. *Moral hazard incentives.* Although in the beginning of our discussion we assumed that the distribution of output was fixed, in all realistic situations the output is affected by the input of the farmer. The input of the farmer, in turn, is affected by the incentives he faces, e.g. if he obtains no reward for adding additional inputs, he is unlikely to add them. Most risk-sharing arrangements

have a significant effect on the incentives which individuals face; for instance, if the landlord were risk neutral, our earlier analysis would have suggested that he ought to bear the entire risk, paying the worker a fixed wage (in competitive equilibrium, equal to his mean marginal product). But then the farmer's income would not be affected by, say, his weeding activity, and so he would not weed. This is the fundamental dilemma associated with insurance (risk-sharing and transferring) schemes.

Although there are important incentive effects associated with most risk-sharing/transferring schemes, these differ from scheme to scheme. In Chapter 3 we described briefly a risk-sharing scheme in which there were no deleterious incentive effects: the price the individual received was inversely related to the aggregate quantity produced in the region. The income of the farmer was thus proportional to the amount that he grew. If all farmers were identical and faced the same risk, this scheme would have no deleterious incentive effect and yet the farmer would face no risk. In general, since risks are not perfectly correlated, even within a region, the farmer would still face some risks under this scheme.

There are three responses to this conflict between the provision of insurance and incentives:

(i) In some cases, it may be possible to design risk-sharing arrangements which do not destroy incentives, as we have just described. But there are, as we noted in Chapter 3, important limitations on these schemes; for instance, for the particular scheme just described, we cannot allow intertemporal arbitrage to occur.

(ii) We may attempt to monitor inputs, since the incentive problem only arises when inputs are not observed. This may be costly, and it is in any case never possible to monitor all the inputs continuously.

(iii) Contractual arrangements may be devised which reflect a compromise between risk-sharing and incentives, providing neither perfect risk-sharing nor complete incentives.

Many contractual arrangements involve elements of more than one of these responses: sharecropping arrangements often stipulate certain (easily observed) inputs, provide cost-sharing arrangements for certain purchased inputs and provide sharing arrangements in which the worker has considerable incentives but still must bear a considerable proportion of the risk.

2. *Adverse selection problems.* The second problem arises from the fact that the risks faced by different individuals differ. Although those who could bear the risks better know this, they do not know who are the good risks and who are the bad risks. The problem was first discussed in the context of insurance; insurance companies observed that at any fixed premium, those who bought insurance were the worse risks. Since the insurance companies could not discriminate between good risks and bad risks, in any competitive equilibrium where the policies just broke even (on average), the good risks were (on average) subsidizing the bad risks; but the good risks might prefer to self-insure rather than pay this subsidy, and if so the insurance market would collapse.

12.1.2 *Mechanisms for risk-spreading*

We can now enquire into the institutional mechanisms by which risks are shared in agriculture. There are six primary methods of risk-sharing and risk-spreading:

(i) In simple agricultural communities, sharecropping arrangements represent a simple method by which the risk of agriculture is shared between the worker and the landlord.

(ii) A wage system can be thought of as a method of making the landlord bear the risk (the worker's wage is independent of the weather). This is efficient if the landlord is better able to bear the risk, e.g. because risk aversion decreases with wealth.

(iii) For many types of risks, insurance provides a method of shifting the risk from the individual to the insurance company. Crop insurance schemes are examples, but these have had only limited success, for both of the reasons we noted earlier — the difficulty of ascertaining whether the crop failure is due to lack of inputs (like fertilizers) or to exogenous circumstances which could not be overcome, and the difficulty of discriminating between good farmers and bad farmers (the adverse selection problem).

(iv) For many agricultural commodities, futures markets do provide an effective method of insuring not against quantity variations but against price fluctuations. The individual sells a part of his crop forward. If there were no uncertainty about his output, he could sell all of his crop in the futures market, and the uncertainty in income associated with price variability could be completely eliminated. (The farmer might not want to do this, since his expectations concerning future prices might differ from that of the market.) But if output is variable, the farmer cannot use futures markets to eliminate all risk. In Chapter 13 we show the extent to which the farmer can reduce his risk depends critically on the correlation coefficient between his output and market price.

Obviously, when the individual sells his output on the futures market, the risk in aggregate does not disappear. It is only transferred to speculators who are more able or willing to bear the risk.

(v) For farms owned by large corporations, the risk associated with the profits of the farm are shared among the large number of shareholders, and hence the effective risk borne by any single individual may be relatively small. This is typically the case with plantation crops like tea and rubber.

(vi) In almost all countries, there are a variety of government programmes, some directed at farmers, others more general, which act as effective risk-sharing devices. For instance, if a farmer faces a proportional income tax, with loss offset provisions, the government can be thought of as a silent partner to the individual sharing in the profits and losses of the enterprise.

In agriculture there is often a variety of price support programmes. These are often a way of effecting transfers from the non-agricultural to the agricultural sector, but there is usually a component of risk-sharing involved as well. Farmers receive higher than market prices when prices are low, and would (if these programmes were self-financing) receive lower than market prices when prices are high. Several of the macro-models discussed in Part VI illustrate this risk-sharing mechanism.

It is important to keep the existence of these programmes in mind, for, to the extent that they are effective, international price stabilization programmes may have little effect on the farmers directly, but simply substitute an international price stabilization scheme for a set of national schemes. Although this may in fact be desirable, the distribution of benefits as well as the total costs will depend critically on how governments respond with their domestic price support (and other risk-sharing) arrangements. Some of these issues are explored further in Chapter 19.

12.1.3 *Implications for the assessment of price stabilization schemes*

The existence of these various methods of sharing risk has important implications for the analysis of the effects of a price stabilization scheme and for an evaluation of the benefits which can be derived from such schemes.

First, since the risk is transferred from those who are less able to those who are more able to bear the risk, and since (by our earlier argument) the cost associated with a risk which is spread among a large number of individuals is much less than one which is concentrated upon a few, the existence of risk-sharing and risk-transferring possibilities in the economy implies that the social cost of risk may be considerably less than it would be if those risks were borne only by the farmers. Thus, in the subsequent analysis, where for analytical convenience we shall ignore the existence of these risk-sharing and risk-transferring mechanisms, we obtain, in effect, an overestimate of the benefits likely to accrue from such a scheme, since they overestimate the cost of the risks. In Chapter 13 we attempt to quantify the magnitude of this for one important risk-sharing mechanism, futures markets. The obvious way of offsetting this overestimate is to assume that agents are risk neutral, which should provide an underestimate. The true benefits will then lie somewhere between these two values.

Secondly, there are likely to be significant changes in the magnitude and nature of risk-sharing which will result from commodity price stabilization. These responses may greatly reduce the net benefits resulting from a price stabilization programme compared with the benefits which would result if there were no such response. For instance, we noted above that an international price stabilization scheme might simply serve as a substitute for a domestic price stabilization scheme, so that farmers themselves would be relatively little affected by the new programme. Successful price stabilization would reduce the demand for trading on futures markets and might thus eliminate a market which would have provided most of the benefits of price stabilization, as we shall show in Chapter 13.

Moreover, the changes in the risk-sharing are likely, in turn, to have an important effect on the supply decisions of farmers. For example, the presence of a futures market can change the supply response not only in magnitude, but also in direction. This is not surprising: with the availability of risk-sharing arrangements, individuals have additional instruments for responding to changes in risk and these instruments interact in an extremely complicated way. Even when the total impact of the change (say, on the variance of income) depends in a simple way on, say, the risk aversion of the individual, there may be no simple relationship between the effect of any particular instrument and the characteristics of the individual. For instance, in the context of much simpler portfolio problems which have been extensively discussed in the financial literature, it has been shown that if there is more than one risky asset, except in very special circumstances, it is not possible to derive simple theorems relating the demand for a safe asset to the wealth of the individual and his attitude to risk.

Finally, the existence of these various risk-sharing arrangements is important for another reason: the distribution of the benefits, as well as the total magnitude of the benefits which accrue as a result of a price stabilization may be very different from what they would have been in the absence of such risk-sharing arrangements.

For instance, in a sharecropping economy in which the tenant receives 50 per cent of the crop, and in which the landlord is risk neutral, price stabilization might have two effects:

(i) In the short run if the share arrangement remains unchanged, the benefit from eliminating income variability from a farm is approximately $A/8 \text{ Var } Y$, not $A/2 \text{ Var } Y$, where Var Y is the variance of income of the *farm*. The reason is that if the landlord is risk neutral, the only loss from the income variability is that borne by the tenant who receives one-half the income. The risk premium is related to the variance of *his income* and is thus reduced to one-quarter. Thus, a naïve calculation which ignores the possibility that risk is not borne by a *representative* agent, but the agent most willing to bear the risk, may greatly exaggerate the benefits from income stabilization.

(ii) In the long run, there may be changes in the tenancy arrangement. For instance, Stiglitz (1974) and Newbery and Stiglitz (1979a) have argued that sharecropping may reflect a compromise between, on the one hand, the need of the worker to shift the risk to the landlord who is more able to bear the risk, and, on the other hand, the need of the landlord to provide an incentive for the worker to work hard and so reduce the costs of monitoring and supervising the worker. If the riskiness of agriculture is reduced, it may allow the more extensive use of fixed-rent tenancies which provide more powerful incentives to increase output. Price stabilization may therefore generate additional efficiency gains which are very desirable.

12.2 Risk-reducing activities

To the extent that the farmer cannot pass on the risks which he faces to others, he may be able to take actions to reduce them directly. There are a number of dimensions to this: exactly which actions he takes will depend on the particular circumstances of the farmer.

12.2.1 The choice of technique

The farmer usually has available a number of techniques of production; these techniques will have different risk characteristics, e.g. one technique of production may yield a higher average return, but in certain circumstances, such as drought or early frost, yield a lower return. Some techniques using high-yield varieties may require large levels of purchased inputs of fertilizers, which imply that net income after paying for the purchased inputs will be lower in low-income states, but this may be compensated for by higher incomes in high-income states. Irrigation, on the other hand, typically reduces risk, as do many recent technical developments in farming practice. The variability in price may have an important effect on the choice of technique. For instance, if price is very negatively correlated with output or if price is positively correlated with output, then reducing price variability will reduce income variability. This may induce farmers to take riskier actions, which have a higher mean output. Conversely, if price is negatively correlated with output, but the correlation is not very high, reducing price variability increases income variability and may lead the farmer to take less risky actions (which reduce mean income).

12.2.2 Crop diversification

Not only may the farmer alter the techniques employed for growing a particular crop; he may change the mix of crops which he grows. If the return to different crops is imperfectly correlated, by diversifying his farm between the two crops he can reduce the total risk which he faces. For example, suppose that he has one hectare of land on which he can plant two different crops.[1] The return, per hectare, from crop 1 is $\tilde{r}_1$ and from crop 2 is $\tilde{r}_2$. The total expected return if he has one hectare and plants a fraction λ with the first crop and the remainder with the second is

$$\bar{r} = \lambda \bar{r}_1 + (1 - \lambda)\bar{r}_2. \tag{12.4}$$

The variance of his return is

$$E(\tilde{r} - \bar{r})^2 = \lambda^2 E(\tilde{r}_1 - \bar{r}_1)^2 + (1-\lambda)^2 E(\tilde{r}_2 - \bar{r}_2)^2 + 2\lambda(1-\lambda)\,\mathrm{Cov}(\tilde{r}_1, \tilde{r}_2). \tag{12.5}$$

Notice, for instance, that if the two crops have the same distribution of returns, but are independent, then his mean return is unaffected by the mix of crops, but the variance is

$$\lambda^2 E(\tilde{r}_1 - \bar{r}_1)^2 + (1-\lambda)^2 E(\tilde{r}_2 - \bar{r}_2)^2, \tag{12.6}$$

which is minimized when the land is divided equally between the two crops (because the variances are assumed equal), and reduces to half the variance of a single crop.

More generally, the farmer will be willing to sacrifice some mean return for a reduction in variance. The various possible patterns of return, characterized in

---

[1] This problem, as we noted in Chapter 6, is formally analogous to the traditional portfolio problem.

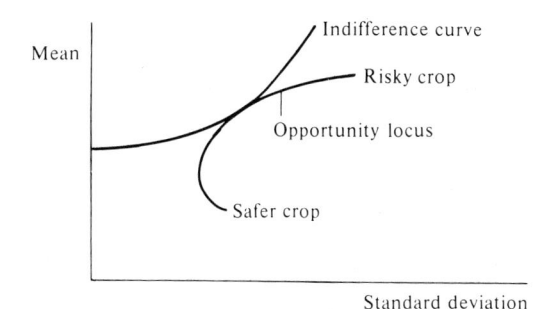

Fig. 12.1 Mean-variance choice of crop combination

mean-variance space, are depicted in Fig. 12.1. The choice of the individual will be determined by the tangency of the individual's indifference curve (again in mean-variance space) with the opportunity locus.

A price stabilization programme for a single crop will normally affect not only the variance of the return from growing the crop but also its mean. As a result, it may be difficult to predict not only the effect on the allocation to the stabilized crop, but also the effect on total farm income.

There are two reasons why mean income is affected.

First, as we noted earlier, a change in the distribution of prices which preserves the mean output changes the mean expenditure on the commodity, and thus the mean return to growing the crop.

Second, as a result of the change in the distribution of returns to growing the crop, there will be a supply response of producers; this secondary effect may alter the initial effect, not only quantitatively but also qualitatively. We postpone until Chapters 21 and 22 a detailed discussion of these long-run responses. Here, we note only a simple example illustrating the consequences of these long-run responses for a particular country.

Assume that the farmers within that country are growing two crops, one of which is relatively safe and the other is risky. The riskier crop has a higher mean return to compensate farmers for the additional risk which they bear. If a commodity price stabilization reduces the riskiness of the given crop, there is some presumption that there will be a switch into the risky crop. Initially, this will raise the mean income of the country. But as farmers switch into the risky crop, the return to growing the crop will fall. If the price stabilization scheme were able to reduce the risk of the crop to exactly the same level as that of the relatively safe one, one would expect that in equilibrium the mean returns would be the same. In the long run (if the supply elasticity of the relatively safe crop is very large) the mean national income of the country and the producers' welfare would actually be reduced, for the following reason. Initially, farmers could have specialized in the safe crop, but chose (and therefore preferred) to plant some of the risky crop. Now they are forced to produce only safe crops.

12.2.3* Implications

These effects on the behaviour of the farmer are important for our analysis, for they imply both that the aggregate level of costs and benefits will differ, perhaps significantly, from what they would have been had farmers not altered their behaviour, and that the distribution of the benefits will differ.

Much of Part V is devoted to elucidating how these long-run supply responses alter the short-run analysis, both qualitatively and quantitatively. Although we confine our attention to one particular choice facing the farmer — his level of input — it is important to realize that a similar analysis applies with respect to the other actions of farmers — choice of crop, choice of technique, amount of hedging on futures markets, etc.

Unfortunately, at this point it is not obvious whether calculations ignoring these supply responses will provide an under- or over-estimate of the total benefits and costs associated with a price stabilization scheme. Intuitively, one might have thought that there was some presumption that the conventional analysis would have provided an underestimate of the total gains. The gains to farmers, allowing them to change their actions in response to the new situation, must be at least as great as it would be if they were not allowed to adjust their actions. This intuitive argument is implicitly based on the assumption that nothing else changes, and hence ignores general equilibrium responses. In the example which follows, and later in Chapter 22, we shall demonstrate that the intuitive or partial equilibrium argument can be quite misleading. We shall show that while the long-run gain to farmers is usually less than the short-run gain, there are instances where a short-run gain is actually turned into a long-run loss (and vice versa).

At the same time, there is also an intuitive argument which suggests that there should be some presumption that the short-run calculations of the costs associated with a price stabilization scheme will provide an underestimate of the long-run costs. Because some of the costs of variability are absorbed by the public authority (if the stabilization programme is subsidized) producers will have insufficient incentives to minimize the costs of the variability in output. The following example shows this more precisely.

There are two equally likely states of nature. If the price of output were the same in each state, then demand would be higher in state 1 than state 2. In particular, if demand has constant elasticity, demand in state i is

$$Q_i^c = \theta_i p_i^{-\epsilon} \tag{12.7}$$

$$\theta_1 > \theta_2.$$

Prices will be stabilized if sales to consumers in each state satisfy

$$\frac{Q_1^c}{Q_2^c} = \frac{\theta_1}{\theta_2} \equiv 1 + u \tag{12.8}$$

where u is a measure of demand instability.

Farmers have a choice of technique trading off output in state 1 for output in state 2. All choices of technique have the same mean level of output, so

$$Q_1 + Q_2 = 2\bar{Q}. \tag{12.9}$$

Their production possibilities across states of nature are as shown in Fig. 12.2.

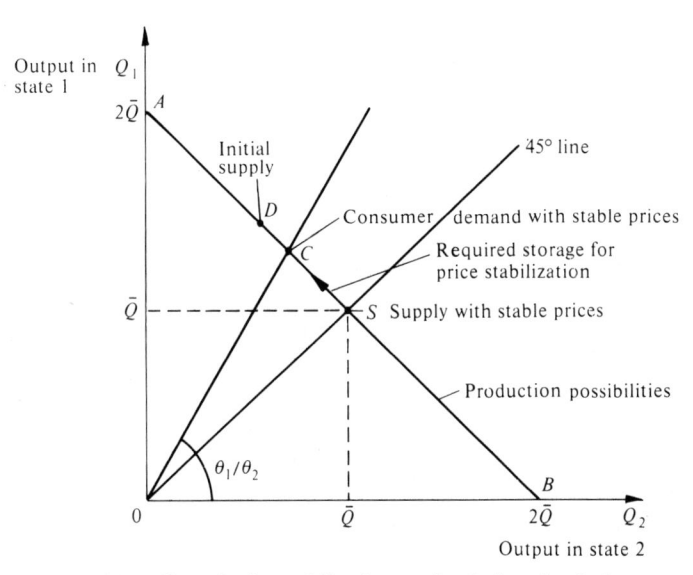

Fig. 12.2 Effect of price stabilization on the choice of technique

All farmers are identical, and they choose their production technique to maximize expected utility.

$$\text{Max } \tfrac{1}{2}U(Y_1) + \tfrac{1}{2}U(Y_2) \tag{12.10}$$

$$Y_i = p_i Q_i \tag{12.11}$$

subject to the production possibilities, equation (12.9). In equilibrium, therefore

$$p_1 U'(Y_1) = p_2 U'(Y_2). \tag{12.12}$$

In particular, if prices were stabilized, they would set $Q_1 = Q_2$ and produce at point S in Fig. 12.2, while consumers would demand a pattern of consumption given at point C, which satisfies equation (12.8). To achieve stability, goods would have to be transferred from state 2 to state 1, an amount equal to the projection of CS on the Q_2 axis.

In the absence of storage, prices will fluctuate and farmers will not choose to produce a stable supply at point S, but will choose Q_1 to satisfy equation (12.12). If their utility functions exhibit constant relative risk aversion R, then equation (12.12) can be written:

$$p_1 Y_1^{-R} = p_2 Y_2^{-R}, \qquad (12.13)$$

or, from equations (12.7) and (12.11),

$$(\theta_1^{1/\epsilon} Q_1^{-1/\epsilon})^{1-R} Q_1^{-R} = (\theta_2^{1/\epsilon} Q_2^{-1/\epsilon})^{1-R} Q_2^{-R},$$

or

$$\frac{Q_1}{Q_2} = \left(\frac{\theta_1}{\theta_2}\right)^k, \qquad (12.14)$$

where

$$k = \left(1 + \frac{R\epsilon}{1-R}\right)^{-1} \gtreqless 1 \quad \text{as} \quad R \gtreqless 1.$$

The equilibrium may thus correspond to a point such as D (to the left of C if $R > 1$, between C and S if $R < 1$). If the buffer authorities ignore the supply response to stabilization (that is, the change in the choice of technique which changes the relative supplies in the two states of the world) then they will estimate the required storage on the basis of moving from point D to point C. Clearly, this estimate could be a serious underestimate of the amount actually required (SC), and it might also be in the opposite direction, as shown here. Thus initially the buffer stock attempts to transfer output from state 1 to state 2, and, if successful in stabilizing the price, producers will shift to point S, and the buffer authority will be required to transfer goods from state 2 to state 1. The ratio of the required amount of storage to the estimated amount of storage will be

$$\frac{CS}{CD} \qquad (12.15)$$

which could be very large. Since if

$$\frac{Q_1}{Q_2} = \phi,$$

then from equation (12.9)

$$\frac{Q_1}{\bar{Q}} = \frac{2\phi}{1+\phi}. \qquad (12.16)$$

If demand instability is small, so u in equation (12.8) is small, then equation (12.15) can be written, using (12.16), as

$$\frac{Q_1^c - \bar{Q}}{Q_1 - Q_1^c} = \frac{\{2(1+u) - (2+u)\}/(2+u)}{\dfrac{2(1+u)^k}{1+(1+u)^k} - \dfrac{2(1+u)}{2+u}} \simeq \frac{1}{k-1}.$$

Thus, if $\epsilon = \frac{1}{4}$, $R = \frac{1}{2}$, $k = \frac{4}{5}$, and the required storage will be five times as large and in the opposite direction to that apparently required.

Obviously, this is an extreme example, in which farmers are assumed to have very substantial control over the responsiveness of their output to the weather (or whatever is the source of the risk). In general, they will have much less choice over the pattern of output over states of the world, but rather more choice over the level of inputs and hence average output. We study this other (and more important) supply response in Part V, but we should stress that all these models are necessarily highly speculative. The reason is that we have little direct information about how farmers would respond to a change in the price *distribution*; most of the empirical studies of agricultural supply responses have measured farmers' responses to price *levels*, not to the distribution of prices. For certain situations, we can infer their responses from knowledge (or guesses) about their attitudes towards risk and information about their supply responses in the absence of risk. However, as we shall show, these inferences only yield clear-cut answers on strong assumptions about the structure of the model, such as assuming that farmers have constant relative risk aversion and face constant elastic demand.

What this and later models show is that the economy (in this case, the farmers) may respond to changes in risk (caused by price stabilization) in a quite complex way, so that it is difficult to predict the long-run consequences. In the present example, the long-run response depends on the relationship between supply and farmer's income (and hence on the elasticity of demand), on the farmer's attitude to income risk, and on the choice open to the farmer to change the risk he faces.

12.2.4 *Other actions which affect the risk borne by producers*

There are two other sets of actions, besides those just discussed, which affect the risk borne by producers. The first is that individuals can borrow in bad years, balanced by savings in good years. They can, in other words, smooth their income over time. A close substitute to the use of the capital market is the use of storage. The implications of this are discussed in Chapter 14.

Secondly, farmers can attempt to acquire information which reduces the risk which they face. The means by which they can do this and the extent to which this reduces the risks faced by producers is discussed at greater length in Chapter 16.

12.3 Conclusions

The main justification for a price stabilization scheme is that it reduces the risks generated by fluctuating prices. To the extent that risk-bearing is costly, there is clearly an incentive for agents to seek ways of reducing the cost of risk, either by sharing it with others, transferring it to those better able to bear it, or by reducing it directly. It is therefore likely that institutions will have evolved to reduce the cost of risk, and the presence of the institutions will modify the impact of price stabilization. There is a simple argument which suggests that because the costs of risk have already been reduced, the benefit of further risk reduction will be lower, but this argument is not necessarily true. Price stabilization changes the nature of the risks that farmers face, and may change the market equilibrium in quite complex ways. Thus, it may reduce the problem of moral hazard or adverse selection and allow efficiency gains previously unobtainable. In this chapter we have concentrated on describing the various methods available for reducing the costs of risk, and argued that their presence may significantly modify the impact of price stabilization. In Chapter 13 we shall examine one particular institution, the futures market, to see how its presence affects the case for price stabilization.

Chapter 13*

Futures Markets and Risk Reduction

The response of economic agents to the presence of risk is to evolve methods of sharing and reducing this risk, in ways just described. The main theme of the previous chapter was that the presence of risk-sharing and risk-reducing institutions may significantly modify the impact of risk-reducing policies such as commodity price stabilization. Moreover, it is typically difficult to make any general prediction about the way such impacts are modified.

The root of the problem is that the economy does not have a complete set of markets, so that the existing markets must typically serve several different functions simultaneously, and none of them quite satisfactorily. In agriculture, markets induce producers to supply commodities which are then allocated among consumers. If this were all they had to do, and if they were competitive, they would be efficient. But they also share risk between consumers and producers, and this additional role modifies the efficiency with which the market allocates commodities. If a futures market is introduced, the risk-sharing role is now spread over two markets, and the operation of the spot market will be altered. The effect of price stabilization will thus depend on whether or not there is a futures market.

These general issues of market efficiency when markets are incomplete and so play several roles will be discussed in more detail in Chapter 15. In this chapter we are concerned with the way one particular institution, the futures market, modifies the impact of price stabilization.

In the past economists concerned with price stabilization have ignored the presence of futures markets, and, according to McKinnon (1967), this neglect is a fundamental reason why so many international commodity agreements have failed in the past. In his view futures markets dramatically modify the impact of price stabilization schemes so that it is seriously misleading to ignore their presence.

What we show in this chapter is that an unbiased futures market (that is, one in which the futures price is an unbiased estimator of the future cash price) provides unambiguously greater income risk insurance than perfect price stabilization. The reason is the standard revealed preference argument that an agent does better if he is free to choose the amount of price insurance as opposed to having a predetermined amount forced on him. The superior risk insurance properties of an unbiased futures market does not, however, mean that producers necessarily prefer futures markets to price stabilization, because in general price stabilization will change the average price (to the price of average output, which differs from the average price), and so generates different transfer effects and supply responses. Moreover, the result requires that futures markets be unbiased, which depends on the market structure.

178 *Commodity Price Stabilization*

We also examine the impact of price stabilization on the farmer's supply decision, and find that access to an unbiased futures market does indeed modify the impact of price stabilization on both supply and producer welfare. However, it is difficult to predict the direction in which both are modified without detailed knowledge of conditions of production and demand.

The chapter is organized as follows. We begin with a brief discussion of some of the general issues in the study of futures markets, and then address the main question of the risk-reducing role of futures markets as compared to price stabilization, assuming that average supply remains constant. In the last section we discuss the way in which the supply decision is affected by the presence of a futures market, and show how this complicates the analysis of price stabilization. Obviously our treatment of futures markets cannot be exhaustive, and the interested reader is directed to some of the excellent collections of readings available, such as Goss and Yamey (1976) or Peck (1977).

13.1 Futures markets and storage

Several writers have argued that it is important to distinguish between commodities like grain which have an annual harvest and for which stocks are held continuously, and commodities like live beef cattle or fresh eggs for which there are no inventories in the normal sense. Other commodities like potatoes have discontinuous inventories since it is too costly to store them from one year to the next. The claim is that futures markets only offer significant income risk insurance to producers for discontinuously stocked commodities. To see if this claim is valid, we first note that if stocks are continuously held, then the difference between the price at different dates must be just equal to the carrying costs less convenience yield. This convenience yield measures the advantage to the stockholder of the immediate availability of the commodity compared to holding cash and buying the commodity when required, and will be discussed in the next chapter. Stockholders can sell their entire stock forward on the futures market and so insure themselves against any fluctuation in the future price. Further, the futures market coordinates storage activities, for stockholders will continue to buy for storage and sell in the futures market until the futures price (reflecting expected future supplies) has been driven to the point at which no more storage is attractive. Moreover, the futures market ensures that storage is done at the lowest expected net cost.

If there were no uncertainty about future prices, and if the marginal carrying cost *less* marginal convenience yield on a unit of commodity held one period were c, we should expect prices at date t to satisfy

$$p_{t+1} = p_t + c_t. \qquad (13.1)$$

After the harvest the price would be low, and it would steadily rise through the year to just before the next harvest, when it should reach its peak as stocks are nearly exhausted. If the net cost c is not too sensitive to stock levels, then the pattern of relative prices over the year would be fairly stable. The futures market allows stockholders to insure themselves against price uncertainties, and arbitrage will ensure that

$$_0p^f_{t+1} = {_0}p^f_t + c, \qquad (13.2)$$

where $_ip^f_t$ is the futures price at date i for delivery at date t. Since the spot price at t is roughly equal[1] to the futures price for delivery at that date, $_tp^f_t$, any new information about future demand and supply which affects expectations about future prices, shifts all previous prices, including the current spot price, in sympathy. This is confirmed by the empirical evidence, which also reveals that cash and futures price are almost equally variable for continuously stocked commodities.

If it is impossible, or too expensive, to carry stocks, there is no reason for prices at successive dates to move in sympathy. In such cases the futures price is the best estimate of future cash prices, and is found to be more stable from year to year than the cash price. Table 13.1 reproduces data from Tomek and Gray (1970). Column (1) shows the variability from year to year of the futures price at the time of planting, and at the expiration of the futures contract (i.e. of the spot market after the harvest).[1] Column (2) gives the ratio of the variances, and provides a test that the futures price is less variable than the post-harvest price from year to year. It shows that for continuously stocked crops like corn and soybeans, there is no significant difference in variability, while for the discontinuously stocked Maine potatoes the futures price is significantly more stable. Finally, column (3) gives the uncertainty surrounding the post-harvest price at the start of the season, defined as

$$\text{SD}\left(\frac{p^f_t - p_t}{p^f_t}\right),$$

where p^f_t is the 30 April futures price and p_t is the futures price on the last day of the contract. Notice that this 'forecast error' is lower than the yearly variability of the futures price for the two continuously stocked commodities, but not for the discontinuously stocked commodity.

Tomek and Gray argue that futures markets only offer significant income risk insurance to producers for discontinuously stocked commodities, since they argue that the futures market is as risky as the spot market for continuously stocked commodities.

We shall argue that this does not necessarily follow as a consequence of the evidence in Table 13.1. For example, if there were no supply risk, the futures market could eliminate all income risk *for that particular year*. However, income

---

[1] The price of the futures contract in its delivery month *less* the spot price in that month is called the *maturity basis*. Arbitrage ensures that it is small, and the futures sellers option to choose grades and/or delivery location typically makes it slightly (but predictably) negative. Goss and Yamey (1976) quote the example of cotton between 1924 and 1939 where the range was from -0.17d/lb to -0.49d.

Table 13.1 *Variability of prices 1952-68*

	Coefficient of variation % Annual changes (1)	F ratio[a] (2)	CV of seasonal change, % (3)
December corn			
30 April	12.6	1.2	4.5
Last day	14.0		
November soybeans			
30 April	8.8	1.68	4.0
Last day	11.5		
November potatoes			
30 April	5.7	26.09	7.9
Last day	27.5		

Source: Tomek and Gray (1970).
[a] the 5% significance level for the difference in coefficients of variation is $F = 2.33$.

would still fluctuate from year to year, perhaps almost as much as if the farmer had not hedged in the futures market. If the farmer finances a large fraction of his crop costs by borrowing at fixed interest, then hedging within the year could still be very valuable.

There is another way to look at the distinction between the two types of commodity. Where commodities can be continuously stored, this activity itself will tend to stabilize the price (just like a buffer stock scheme). Historically, futures markets were first developed for such commodities and have as their main function the coordination of storage and the reduction of inventory price risks, as we shall show in the next chapter. For commodities which are not stocked continuously, futures markets can provide a similar kind of reduction in price variability (of the futures price) as storage did for the other crops. Thus storage and futures markets provide alternative methods of achieving the same result of reducing income variability. Futures and storage are also complementary, as futures markets coordinate the intertemporal price structure and share the risks of storage.

The main emphasis in this chapter will be on the role of futures markets in providing income insurance *within* a particular crop year, but futures markets may also stabilize prices (and, indirectly, incomes) *between* years by improving the informational efficiency of markets and reducing the importance of cobwebs and irrational expectations discussed in Chapter 11. Gray (1972) argues this case persuasively for potatoes, although the evidence of the onions market is mixed. Johnson (1973, in Peck, 1977, p. 329) argues that the onion market was as unstable before futures trading was suspended in 1958 as after. Powers (1970) compares price instability for beef and pork bellies for four years preceding the start of futures trading and four years afterwards and found a significant reduction in the variance of prices. There is a limit to this process though, for if too much of the instability is removed, then so are the opportunities for speculative profit and the futures market will decline. Larson (1967) attributes the decline in the once major egg futures market to increased producer concentration and reduced supply variability, which have reduced instabilities, and hence reduced the demand for futures. The butter market has apparently atrophied for similar reasons. If correct, these explanations are important for price stabilization, which would probably reduce and perhaps eliminate futures trading if prices were stabilized enough. It may then be academic to explore the extent to which the presence of a futures market modifies the impact of price stabilization. Instead the relevant comparison may be between the effect of a futures market and the effect of price stabilization with no futures market.

13.2 The risk-reducing role of futures markets

A futures market offers a farmer a guaranteed price for at least part of his crops, and hence can reduce some of the risks facing the farmer. If his output were certain, but the price were risky, he could completely eliminate income risk by selling his entire crop forward. (He may choose not to if he expects a higher price in the future; if so, then he would be *speculating* on a favourable price movement, and not *hedging* against price risk. We shall discuss his choice of forward sales in the next section, and sharpen the distinction between hedging and speculating.)

On the other hand, if there is substantial variability in his output, the variability in price may, if it is negatively correlated with output, provide income insurance and reduce the need for futures markets. For instance, if the demand function was stable and had unit price elasticity, and if all farmers faced the same risk, income would be perfectly certain and the futures market would offer no extra income insurance. Hence the extent to which the farmer will trade on the futures market and the benefit from so trading will depend on the correlation between price and output.

Consider, for example, an unbiased futures market in which the futures price p^f is equal to the expected cash price which will prevail in the market next period.

$$p^f = E\tilde{p} \equiv \bar{p}. \tag{13.3}$$

Let z be the amount of the commodity sold forward on the futures market by the representative farmer, and suppose that there is multiplicative supply risk so that his output is $\tilde{\theta}\bar{q}$. Then his income is

$$y = \tilde{p}\tilde{\theta}\bar{q} + (p^f - \tilde{p})z, \quad E\tilde{\theta} = 1. \tag{13.4}$$

The effect of selling the crop forward on the futures market on income variability may be seen diagramatically. There are three cases to consider. In the first case output and price are assumed to be positively correlated, so that when output is high, or θ is large, price is high. Then in the absence of futures markets, at a given level of input, the relationship between the state of nature, θ, and income is depicted in Fig. 13.1a. Because the price increases with θ, income increases rapidly with θ. If the individual sells a part of his crop forward, he receives in exchange for a variable income a certain income; thus his lowest income is increased, his highest income is reduced. If, as assumed, the futures price equalled the expected value of the spot price then mean income remains constant and so the riskiness of the individual's income would be unambiguously reduced (in the sense of Rothschild and Stiglitz (1970) discussed in Chapter 6). Figure 13.1b depicts the probability density function of his income before and after the sale of part of his crop on the futures market.

In the second case, price and output (θ) are negatively correlated, but not so negatively correlated that the price variability offsets the output variability. Hence, income variability is less than output variability. By selling some of his crop in the futures market the individual can increase his income in states in which the price is low, i.e. in which output and income are high, at the expense, of course, of reducing it in states where income and output are low. But because of the diminishing marginal utility, since the marginal utility in the high-income states is lower than in the low-income states, he would not wish to sell his crop forward but would wish to *buy* forward. This is shown in Figures 13.2a and 13.2b.

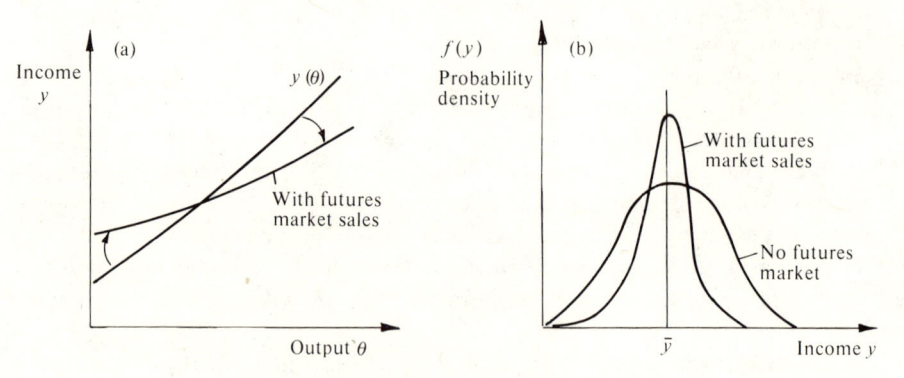

Fig. 13.1 Price and output positively correlated

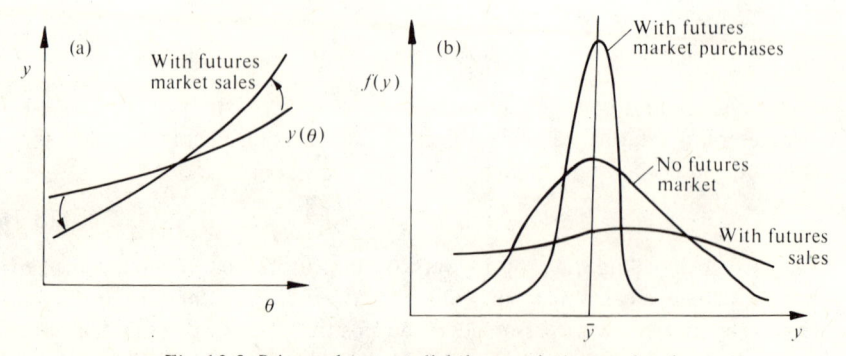

Fig. 13.2 Price and output slightly negatively correlated

The third case is that where prices and output are very negatively correlated, so negatively correlated that income decreases when output increases as shown in Fig. 13.3a. This case is an important one in the subsequent analysis. Note that selling the crop on the futures market increases income when *price* is low, i.e. when output is high but in which income is low. Thus, in this case, he will wish to engage in an actuarially fair forward sale.

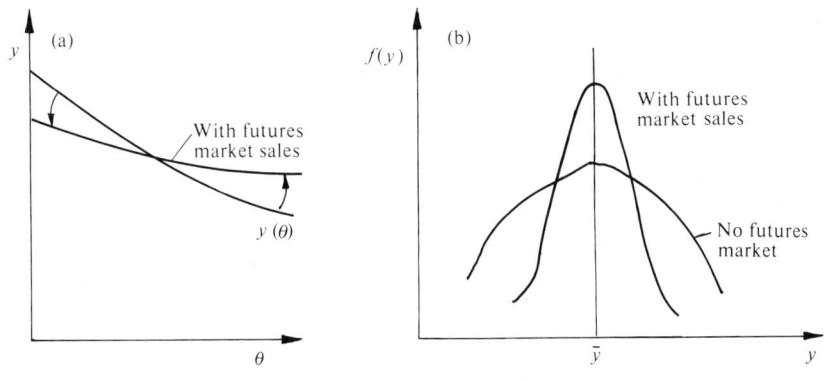

Fig. 13.3 Price and output very negatively correlated

13.3 Futures markets — hedging and speculation

Futures markets not only provide insurance against price fluctuations, but also provide opportunities for speculation. The insurance role, or hedging, typically involves taking opposite positions in the actuals and futures market. Thus a merchant who buys coffee now for storage can hedge by selling coffee futures, in which case he is 'long' in actuals and 'short' in futures. A farmer would likewise typically be a 'short hedger'. A 'long hedger' sells coffee for future delivery and buys coffee futures.

Speculation is usually contrasted as holding an uncovered position, such as selling forward without currently purchasing stocks, and instead planning to purchase in the actuals market when the time comes to make the delivery. Although much is made of this distinction, it is not very convenient for analytical purposes.

13.3.1 *Futures markets for commodities with no storage*

This will become clearer in the following model in which producers use the futures market to reduce income risk, but no one holds any stocks. The model is similar in spirit to that of McKinnon (1967) and assumes that consumers do not speculate in the futures market. If farmers and speculators have constant absolute risk aversion, and if prices and quantities are jointly normally distributed, we can employ the simple mean-variance analysis of the capital asset pricing model of Chapter 6. Alternatively, the results can be interpreted as second-order Taylor series approximations, which are accurate for the special case of constant absolute risk aversion. To that extent the measures of the benefits of introducing a futures market are as accurate as our estimate of the benefits of price stabilization derived in Chapter 6, but, as we stressed there, some of the other implications of constant absolute risk aversion and log-normality are unreasonably strong, and must be treated with caution. In particular, as we shall show, these assumptions give rise to linear demand schedules for forward sales (or purchases), which are clearly special but very useful because they permit simple aggregation and hence explicit solutions. In Chapter 16 we shall show that such aggregation properties have strong implications for the information-aggregating properties of futures markets.

We assume for the moment that farmers cannot vary their output, and examine the determination of equilibrium in the futures market and the extent to which the gains from price stabilization are modified by the presence of the futures market. In the last section we discuss the problems raised when producers can vary their supply.

If the farmer's average output is $\bar{q}$, and his forward sales are z, his income will be as given in equation (13.4):

$$y = \tilde{p}\tilde{\theta}\bar{q} - z(\tilde{p} - p^f), \tag{13.4}$$

where p^f is the price on the futures market. He chooses z to maximize expected utility, which, with constant absolute risk aversion, A, and joint-normality of p and $p\theta$ is, as section 6.5 shows, equivalent to maximizing:

$$W = Ey - \tfrac{1}{2}A \operatorname{Var} y \tag{13.5}$$

$$W = \bar{q}Ep\theta - z(\bar{p} - p^f) - \tfrac{1}{2}A\{\bar{q}^2 \operatorname{Var}(p\theta) - 2\bar{q}z \operatorname{Cov}(p, p\theta) + z^2 \operatorname{Var} p\}. \tag{13.6}$$

If z can be positive or negative (i.e. if forward purchases are also possible)

$$z = \frac{\bar{q} \cdot \operatorname{Cov}(p, p\theta)}{\operatorname{Var} p} - \frac{\bar{p} - p^f}{A \operatorname{Var} p}. \tag{13.7}$$

This formula can be interpreted by comparing it with the forward sales of a pure speculator who has no other sources of risky income, and who sells z' forward (or, more correctly, *buys* $-z'$ forward) to maximize

$$W' = z'(p^f - \bar{p}) - \tfrac{1}{2}A'z'^2 \operatorname{Var} p.$$

$$z' = -\frac{\bar{p} - p^f}{A' \operatorname{Var} p}. \tag{13.8}$$

In our very simple theory, a risk-averse speculator has no other risky income, and so can only be persuaded to take a long position (in which he *buys* futures from farmers which he will close out in the actuals market at a later date) if $p^f < \bar{p}$, that is, the futures price is a downward-biased estimate of its expiration value. The difference $\bar{p} - p^f$ is called *normal backwardation* and, in our theory, is simply a risk premium. It should be stressed that by ignoring other sources of risk and opportunities of risk-spreading our model is an over-simple description of a futures market.

The issue of market bias has attracted almost continuous attention since Keynes first advanced his theory of normal backwardation in an article in 1927, according to which the futures prices were downward-biased estimates of the final expiration values, the bias representing the risk premium for speculators. Since then considerable empirical effort has been devoted to trying to find this risk premium, with mixed success (see, for example, the selection of papers in Peck, 1977). Rather than summarize the findings here, it is enough to observe that for many markets the hypothesis of zero bias is reasonable, but for thin markets or markets which for institutional reasons are unattractive to speculators the risk premium may be positive. These issues may be explored further in the literature which shows the empirical and theoretical refinements necessary to test the hypothesis of zero bias.

We can now return to equation (13.7) and interpret the first term as the *hedging* component, and the second as the *speculative* component. The farmer can reduce or hedge his income risk by selling forward if price and income are positively correlated, but he can reduce the size of this hedge if he believes that $p^f < \bar{p}$, and to that extent he is speculating on a price risk.

If the coefficients of variation of quantity and price are σ, σ_p respectively, and if r is the correlation coefficient between price and quantity, the Appendix to this chapter demonstrates that the variances and covariances can be expressed in terms of these few parameters. In particular, equation (13.7) can be written

$$z = \bar{q}(1 + r\sigma/\sigma_p) - \frac{(\bar{p} - p^f)}{A\bar{p}^2\sigma_p^2}. \tag{13.9}$$

Thus if the only source of risk were demand risk, ($\sigma = 0$) were there no bias in the futures market (so that $p^f = \bar{p}$), the farmer would sell his entire crop forward. If the only source of risk is supply variability, $r = -1$, and $\sigma/\sigma_p = \epsilon$, the elasticity of demand, and with an unbiased futures price

$$z/\bar{q} = 1 - \epsilon. \tag{13.10}$$

If $\epsilon = 1$ the farmer is already perfectly hedged against income risk, and he would sell none of his crops forward.

13.3.2 *Equilibrium in the futures market*

For the futures market to be in equilibrium net sales must be zero, or, summing over farmers and speculators

$$0 = \Sigma z = \frac{\bar{Q} \operatorname{Cov}(p\theta, p)}{\operatorname{Var} p} - \frac{\bar{p} - p^f}{\operatorname{Var} p} \Sigma 1/A.$$

The bias in the market, or the normal backwardation, is

$$\bar{p} - p^f = \frac{\bar{Q}\operatorname{Cov}(p\theta, p)}{\Sigma 1/A}. \qquad (13.11)$$

(The advantage of assuming constant absolute risk aversion should be apparent for the linearity of demand schedules makes it simple to aggregate and solve for the price.) It follows from equation (13.8) and the equilibrium condition that the ith agent's speculative (long) position in the forward market is

$$\frac{\bar{p} - p^f}{A^i \operatorname{Var} p} = \frac{\bar{Q}(1 + r\sigma/\sigma_p)}{A^i \Sigma 1/A}, \qquad (13.12)$$

and the less risk-averse the agents the larger will be his speculative position. Agents who are risk neutral will eliminate the bias and share the speculative position between them; all other farmers will confine their activity to hedging.

Similarly, using (13.7) and the equilibrium condition, the total extent to which a farmer participates in the futures market in equilibrium can be written as

$$\frac{z}{\bar{q}^i} = \frac{\operatorname{Cov}(p, p\theta)}{\operatorname{Var} p}\left(1 - \frac{\bar{Q}}{\bar{q}^i A^i \Sigma 1/A}\right) = \beta(1 + r\sigma/\sigma_p), \qquad (13.13)$$

where

$$\beta \equiv 1 - \frac{\bar{Q}}{\bar{q}^i A^i \Sigma 1/A}$$

is a measure of the extent to which the farmer is more risk averse than average (the terms in A) and more exposed to risk (the term $\bar{q}^i/\bar{Q}$). If all farmers are identical and there are no speculators, $\beta = 0$, while if there is one risk-neutral agent, $\beta = 1$.

The variance of a farmer's income with optimal forward sales, y^f, is, from equations (13.4) and (13.13)

$$\operatorname{Var} y^f = \bar{q}^2\left\{\operatorname{Var}(p\theta) - \beta(2-\beta)\frac{\operatorname{Cov}^2(p, p\theta)}{\operatorname{Var} p}\right\}, \qquad (13.14)$$

so provided that the farmer is a net hedger ($\beta > 0$) his income risk is unambiguously reduced.

If r is the correlation coefficient between price and output the first term is (from the Appendix to this chapter)

$$\operatorname{Var}(p\theta) = \bar{p}^2\{\sigma_p^2 + 2r\sigma\sigma_p + \sigma^2 + (1 + r^2)\sigma^2\sigma_p^2\}. \qquad (13.15)$$

If the futures market is unbiased, i.e. if $\beta = 1$, his income risk is thus

$$\operatorname{Var} y^f = \bar{p}^2\bar{q}^2\sigma^2\{1 - r^2 + (1 + r^2)\sigma_p^2\}. \qquad (13.16)$$

For example, if the sole source of risk lies on the supply side so that $\sigma_p = \sigma/\epsilon$, $r = -1$, then the ratio of income risk with a futures market to that without is, using (13.15)

$$\frac{\operatorname{Var} y^f}{\operatorname{Var} y} = \frac{\sigma^2}{\frac{1}{2}(1-\epsilon)^2 + \sigma^2}. \tag{13.17}$$

For plausible values of ϵ, σ (e.g. 0.5, 0.2) this may be quite small (25 per cent). Moreover the futures market can completely eliminate risk which arises solely from demand fluctuations.

13.3.3 Comparisons with perfect price stabilization

Even if it were possible completely to stabilize the price the income risk would still be

$$\operatorname{Var} y^s = \bar{p}^2 \bar{q}^2 \sigma^2, \tag{13.18}$$

which exceeds the income risk remaining on an unbiased futures market unless the correlation between price and output is low enough, i.e. unless

$$r^2 < \frac{\sigma_p^2}{1 - \sigma_p^2} \tag{13.19}$$

(e.g. if $\sigma_p = 40\%$, $r^2 < 20\%$).

These reductions in income risk can be readily translated into measures of benefits, using the formulae of Chapter 6. Thus the benefit $\frac{1}{2}R\bar{y}(\Delta\sigma_y^2)$, to a farmer of making use of an unbiased futures market compared to the case where there is only a spot market is

$$B_{FM} = \tfrac{1}{2}\bar{R}\bar{y}(\sigma_p + r\sigma)^2, \quad \bar{R} \equiv A\bar{y}. \tag{13.20}$$

($\bar{R}$ is the coefficient of relative risk aversion at mean income, $\bar{y}$, and, unlike A, is dimensionless.) This formula is accurate given our special assumptions, and is otherwise a second-order Taylor series approximation. If B_R is the *risk* benefit of perfect price stabilization (in the absence of a futures market, and ignoring the transfer benefits), discussed in Chapter 6, then

$$B_{FM} = B_R + \tfrac{1}{2}\bar{R}\bar{y}\{r^2\sigma^2 - (1+r^2)\sigma^2\sigma_p^2\}. \tag{13.21}$$

In general, then, unbiased futures markets provide superior income risk insurance to price stabilization, because farmers are left free to choose the optimal hedge, instead of having essentially to hedge their entire crop. However, this does *not* imply that farmers will necessarily prefer to trade on futures markets to price stabilization, for the following reasons:

(i) The futures market may be biased, especially if it is thin or unbalanced (Gray, 1960). In such cases the gain to the farmer from the futures market is

$$B_{FM} = \tfrac{1}{2}\bar{R}\bar{y}\beta(2-\beta)(\sigma_p + r\sigma)^2, \tag{13.22}$$

which may be less than the risk benefit of price stabilization.

(ii) The farmer may *believe* that the futures market is biased, even if it is not, and this may discourage him from trading in it.

(iii) Price stabilization will typically change the price, generating an additional transfer benefit, since the price which equates average supply and demand will typically differ from the average price.

(iv) Both price stabilization and futures markets, by changing the farmer's risk, will in general induce a change in supply, and hence in average price (and income). The supply responses will typically differ.

(v) The transactions costs of using the futures market may make trading unattractive. These costs include the usual brokerage charges, and, in addition, the costs of having to use standard (typically large) contracts rather than the optimal amount. This last feature makes it unlikely that any but the larger farmers will be able to make use of the futures market.

Finally, it should be stressed that futures markets do not generate the arbitrage benefits (that is, the benefits of transferring goods from low-value to high-value states) which the storage associated with price stabilization can produce. Indeed, it is logical to see storage and futures markets as complementary, not competitive, activities, since futures markets both guide stockpiling decisions, and provide hedging facilities for stockholders.

This brings us to the question of the operation of the futures market for continuously stocked commodities like grain. It will be remembered from the introduction that for such commodities it appeared that the futures market offered little reduction in price variability. How can the results of this section be used to examine the force of this claim?

13.3.4 *Futures markets for continuously stocked commodities*

We implicitly assumed in the last section that the futures price stayed constant from year to year because the underlying forces of supply and demand were assumed not to change. In fact, these factors change in moderately predictable ways, and we shall suppose that at the start of the crop year, the futures price provides the best estimate of the cash price after the harvest in that particular year. The previous formulae continue to hold, but the coefficient of variation of price is now to be interpreted as the CV of differences between the futures and cash price (in an unbiased market), or, more generally, as a measure of the forecasting error:

$$(\sigma_p^e)^2 = E\left(\frac{p_t - p_t^f}{p_t^f}\right)^2. \tag{13.23}$$

It should be stressed that this is not the same as the CV of prices over time which will typically be much larger. Similarly, the correlation coefficient beween price and output is to be found by regressing the deviation in price $p_t - p_t^f$ on the deviation in output, $\theta_t - 1$. There may be large annual changes in, for example, total acreage planted, which are mainly responsible for the correlation between an individual's output and price. It is the latter which is relevant for his hedging decision.

Once these variables have been correctly specified, equation (13.16) with σ_p^e instead of σ, gives the variance in income about the mean for that year, but not the variance of income from year to year. If the annual changes in expected price level (measured by the futures price at the start of the crop year p_t^f) are uncorrelated with the weather variable, $\tilde{\theta}$, then income in year t will be

$$\tilde{y}_t = y_t^e(1 + \tilde{u}), \qquad (13.24)$$

$$y_t^e = \bar{q}E\tilde{p}_t\tilde{\theta}$$

$$= \bar{q}p_t^f(1 + r\sigma\sigma_p^e),$$

where $\tilde{u}$ is the uncertainty in income at the time of planting which can be hedged on futures markets, and variations in p_t^f are the variations which cannot be hedged. With no futures market equation (13.15) gives

$$\text{Var } u = \{\sigma^2 + 2r\sigma\sigma_p^e + (\sigma_p^e)^2 + (1 + r^2)(\sigma\sigma_p^e)^2\},$$

while with optimal hedging this is replaced by the formula of equation (13.16):

$$\text{Var } u^f = \sigma^2\{1 - r^2 + (1 + r^2)(\sigma_p^e)^2\}.$$

If the coefficient of variation of the initial futures price from year to year is V_p:

$$V_p = \left\{ \sum_{t=1}^{T} (p_t^f - Ep_t^f)^2/T \right\}^{\frac{1}{2}} / Ep_t^f$$

$$Ep_t^f = \sum_{t=1}^{T} p_t^f/T,$$

then the over-all variability of income, measured by its coefficient of variation, can be found from equation (13.24):

$$\tilde{y}_t = \bar{q}(1 + r\sigma\sigma_p^e)\tilde{p}_t^f(1 + \tilde{u}),$$

which, if $\tilde{u}$ and p_t^f are uncorrelated, is approximately

$$\text{CV}(y) = (V_p^2 + \text{Var } u)^{\frac{1}{2}}.$$

In Table 13.1 the first term is given in column (1), the second in column (3). For the two continuously stocked commodities corn and soybeans, Var u is respectively 13 and 20 per cent of V_p^2, while for the discontinuously stocked potatoes it is nearly double. Since the futures market only affects Var u (directly, at least), this implies that for these commodities, futures markets may not reduce income variability by a very large factor. Futures markets are thus relatively more important in markets where stocks have not already eliminated the predictable risks.

13.4 The supply response of introducing futures markets

Thus far we have assumed that supply is fixed, and the farmer merely chooses the size of his forward sales, z. Suppose that output is now a function of purchased inputs, x,

$$\tilde{y} = \tilde{p}(Q)\tilde{\theta} f(x) - wx - z(\tilde{p} - p^f) \tag{13.27}$$

The farmer will choose x so that

$$EU' \tilde{p} \tilde{\theta} f'(x) = wEU'.$$

With constant absolute risk aversion, A, equation (13.5) yields, on differentiating:

$$[E\tilde{p}\tilde{\theta} - A\{f \operatorname{Var} \tilde{p}\tilde{\theta} - z \operatorname{Cov}(\tilde{p}\tilde{\theta}, \tilde{p})\}]f'(x) = w. \tag{13.28}$$

If a futures market is introduced, his income risk will change, inducing a change in x, and a consequent change in $\bar{q}$. Price stabilization will induce further changes, and we shall examine these long-run effects in Chapter 19. For the moment we shall be content to illustrate the effect of introducing a futures market in a simple market with a linear demand schedule and only supply risk. (The linear demand schedule ensures that price and quantity are jointly normally distributed if supply is.) The demand schedule can be written as:

$$p = \bar{p}\left(1 - \frac{1}{\epsilon}\frac{Q - \bar{Q}}{\bar{Q}}\right), \tag{13.29}$$

where $\bar{p}$ is the mean price, $\bar{Q}$ is mean demand, and ϵ is the elasticity of demand at the mean price. Normalize so that $w = 1$, and suppose that

$$f(x) = \sqrt{(2\lambda x)}.$$

In this case, if $\hat{p}$ is the action certainty equivalent price, so that the farmer chooses x to maximize

$$\hat{p} f(x) - x, \tag{13.30}$$

then average supply is a linear function of $\hat{p}$:

$$\bar{q} = f(x) = \lambda \hat{p}. \tag{13.31}$$

In the absence of a futures market the certainty equivalent price is, from equation (13.28):

$$\hat{p}^0 = E\tilde{p}\tilde{\theta} - Af(x)\operatorname{Var}\tilde{p}\tilde{\theta}.$$

But, from equation (13.29)

$$\tilde{p}\tilde{\theta} = \bar{p}\left\{1 - \frac{1}{\epsilon}(\tilde{\theta} - 1)\right\}\tilde{\theta}$$

and if

$$R \equiv \bar{p}Af(x)$$

is the coefficient of relative risk aversion at $\bar{p}$, then, using equation (13.15):

$$\hat{p}^0 \cong \bar{p}\left\{1 - \left(\bar{R}\left(1 - \frac{1}{\epsilon}\right)^2 + \frac{1}{\epsilon}\right)\sigma^2\right\}. \quad (13.32)$$

In the presence of an unbiased futures market, the second term in equation (13.28) becomes (using equations (13.7) and (13.15)):

$$2A\sigma^4\bar{p}^2\bar{q}/\epsilon^2 = 2\bar{p}\bar{R}\sigma^4/\epsilon^2$$

so the action certainty equivalent price is, ignoring terms in σ^4:

$$\hat{p}^f = Ep\theta = \bar{p}(1 - \sigma^2/\epsilon) \quad (13.33)$$

At the same level of inputs $\hat{p}^f > \hat{p}^0$, inducing a higher level of inputs and average output. This drives down the average price, but in equilibrium *average output is higher with a futures market than without*. The comparison of farmers' welfare is somewhat tedious, as both income risk and average income change, and it is not necessarily true that farmers are better off with a futures market. Indeed

$$U^f \gtrless U^0 \quad \text{as} \quad \epsilon \lessgtr 1 \quad (13.34)$$

so farmers are only better off in this model if demand is inelastic.

It is also possible to calculate the effect of perfect price stabilization without a futures market for which the action certainty equivalent is:

$$\hat{p}^s = \bar{p}(1 - \bar{R}\sigma^2). \quad (13.35)$$

Average output is higher (or lower) with price stabilization than with a futures market as the coefficient of relative risk aversion $\bar{R}$ is less than (or greater than) $1/\epsilon$. This has the interesting (and surprising) implication that the more risk averse are producers, the more they would prefer futures markets to price stabilization. (When $\bar{R} = 1/\epsilon$, they prefer price stabilization but for $\bar{R}$ above a critical value $R_0 > 1/\epsilon$ they prefer a futures market).

It follows that if farmers hedge on futures markets, then it may be seriously misleading to calculate the benefits of price stabilization on the assumption that they do not, for the calculations may suggest that farmers gain from price stabilization, when in fact they would lose.

13.5 Conclusions

Unbiased futures markets provide superior income insurance to stabilizing the price over the period for which the futures market is open. This does not mean that futures markets are necessarily preferable to price stabilization, for in general they result in different levels of average produce income and different supply responses. If commodities are continuously stocked, then the main function of futures markets lies in coordinating and insuring stockholding activities. Such stockholding will typically be the prime source of price stabilization, with futures markets offering relatively smaller additional insurance. When commodities cannot be stocked, futures markets are a relatively good form of income insurance if output and price are strongly correlated. Such commodities are unsuitable for buffer stock price stabilization schemes, and if it were desired to further stabilize price, other methods would be needed, such as those suggested in section 3.4.

It might be thought that futures markets are not very important for income insurance as only large farmers are in a position to make use of them, but this would be a mistaken deduction. Merchants are unlikely to be willing to make forward contracts with small farmers unless they can hedge on futures markets, while government marketing boards in developing countries could similarly guarantee local producer prices and hedge the attendant risk on the main futures markets. Speculators are, however, rather suspicious of such activities, since they suspect that government-run marketing boards can manipulate prices and hence benefit from special inside information when trading in futures markets. The result may be a reluctance of speculators to make the market, resulting in a thin and biased futures market with lower benefits to the producers. Finally, it should be noted that futures markets only stabilize incomes over a relatively short time period, while producers may be more concerned about medium-run instabilities.

Futures markets have evolved standard contracts which specify the exact quality of the commodity, the month of delivery, the place (or places) at which delivery is to be made, and the quantity (normally quite large). Although this greatly reduces the transaction costs associated with dealing in the futures market, it is noticeable that most trading is confined to futures contracts which expire in six months or less, with markets becoming thinner for more distant contracts.

Presumably the advantages to be gained from more distant contracts diminish to the point where they no longer offset the costs of operating the markets, or, alternatively the costs of alternative institutional arrangements, such as long-term contracts or vertical integration, are lower. We shall not have much to say as to why the advantages decrease for more distant contracts, except to remark that there may not be much advantage in having futures markets covering a period longer than the period of production. For tree crops like tea, coffee, rubber, and sisal there exist alternative risk-sharing institutions, since these are frequently produced by plantations which are owned by companies whose shares are traded on stock-markets, but it should be stressed that these provide markets for future profits, rather than for future prices.

The thrust of these qualifications is to suggest that futures markets are not necessarily superior to price stabilization schemes, but they are a serious alternative and, where present, may significantly alter the impact of price stabilization.

Futures Markets and Risk Reduction 193

Appendix: Properties of joint normal distributions

If x and y are jointly normally distributed about the origin with SDs σ_1, σ_2, and correlation coefficient ρ, then write this

$$N(0, 0, \sigma_1^2, \sigma_2^2, \rho). \tag{13.A1}$$

The moment generating function (m.g.f.) is

$$M(t_1, t_2) = \exp\{\tfrac{1}{2}(\sigma_1^2 t_1^2 + 2\rho\sigma_1\sigma_2 t_1 t_2 + \sigma_2^2 t_2^2)\} \tag{13.A2}$$

and then

$$\mu_{rs} = Ex^r y^s = \text{coefficient of } \frac{t_1^r t_2^s}{r!s!}$$

in the expansion of the m.g.f. Therefore

$$\mu_{11} = \rho\sigma_1\sigma_2; \quad \mu_{22} = (1 + 2\rho^2)\sigma_1^2\sigma_2^2; \quad \mu_{12} = \mu_{21} = 0. \tag{13.A3}$$

To evaluate $Ep\theta$, $\text{Var}(p\theta)$, $\text{Cov}(p, p\theta)$, write

$$p = \bar{p}(1 + x), \quad \theta = 1 + y$$

$$Ep\theta = \bar{p}E(1 + x)(1 + y) = \bar{p}(1 + \mu_{11}) = \bar{p}(1 + \rho\sigma_1\sigma_2) \tag{13.A4}$$

$$\text{Var}(p\theta) = \bar{p}^2 E(1 + x + y + xy - 1 - \rho\sigma_1\sigma_2)^2.$$

$$\text{Var}(p\theta) = \bar{p}^2\{\sigma_1^2 + 2\rho\sigma_1\sigma_2 + \sigma_2^2 + (1 + \rho^2)\sigma_1^2\sigma_2^2\} \tag{13.A5}$$

$$\text{Cov}(p, p\theta) = \bar{p}^2 Ex(x + y + xy - \rho\sigma_1\sigma_2).$$

$$\text{Cov}(p, p\theta) = \bar{p}^2(\sigma_1^2 + \rho\sigma_1\sigma_2). \tag{13.A6}$$

Conditional Probabilities

If x, y are distributed as

$$N(\mu_1, \mu_2, \sigma_1^2, \sigma_2^2, \rho), \tag{13.A7}$$

then

$$y \mid x \text{ is } N\left\{\mu_2 + \rho\frac{\sigma_2}{\sigma_1}(x - \mu_1), \sigma_2^2(1 - \rho^2)\right\}, \tag{13.A8}$$

so

$$Ey \mid x = \mu_2 + \rho\frac{\sigma_2}{\sigma_1}(x - \mu_1). \tag{13.A9}$$

If

$$x = u$$

$$y = u + v$$

and
$$(u, v) \text{ is } N(\mu_1, \mu_2, \sigma_1^2, \sigma_2^2, 0),$$

then
$$(x, y) \text{ is } N(\mu_1, \mu_1 + \mu_2, \sigma_1^2, \sigma_1^2 + \sigma_2^2, \rho), \quad (13.\text{A}10)$$

where
$$\rho = \text{Corr}(u, u + v) = \frac{\sigma_1}{\sqrt{(\sigma_1^2 + \sigma_2^2)}}$$

Properties of joint log-normal distributions

If Z_1, Z_2, are jointly normally distributed:
$$N(\mu_1, \mu_2, \sigma_1^2, \sigma_2^2, r)$$
and if X_1, X_2, are lognormally distributed, with
$$X_i = \exp Z_i,$$
then
$$X_1 X_2^\beta \text{ is } \Lambda(\mu_1 + \beta\mu_2, \sigma_1^2 + 2r\beta\sigma_1\sigma_2 + \beta^2\sigma_2^2). \quad (13.\text{A}11)$$

In particular, if $X_1 = \theta$, $X_2 = (\phi/\theta)^{1/\epsilon}$, where
$$Q = \bar{Q}\theta \qquad \theta = \Lambda(-\tfrac{1}{2}\sigma^2, \sigma^2)$$
$$Q^d = p^{-\epsilon}\phi \qquad \phi = \Lambda(-\tfrac{1}{2}v^2, v^2)$$

and
$$\text{Corr}(\log \theta, \log \phi) = \rho,$$

then
$$X_2 = \Lambda\left\{\frac{1}{2\epsilon}(\sigma^2 - v^2), \frac{1}{\epsilon^2}(\sigma^2 - 2\rho\sigma v + v^2)\right\} \equiv \Lambda(\mu_2, \sigma_2^2) \quad (13.\text{A}12)$$

and
$$X_1 X_2 = \Lambda\left\{\mu_2 - \tfrac{1}{2}\sigma^2, \left(1 - \frac{1}{\epsilon}\right)^2\sigma^2 + 2\left(1 - \frac{1}{\epsilon}\right)\frac{1}{\epsilon}\rho\sigma v + \frac{v^2}{\epsilon^2}\right\}. \quad (13.\text{A}13)$$

Equate equations (13.A13) and (13.A11) with $\beta = 1$ together with (13.A12) to find
$$\mu_2 = -\tfrac{1}{2}(\epsilon\sigma_2^2 + 2\rho\sigma\sigma_2).$$

Chapter 14

Storage and Savings

If crops are stored when their price is low and sold when their price is high, then price fluctuations will be reduced in the same way as a buffer stock scheme would stabilize prices. This may or may not stabilize incomes and hence reduce income risk. If farmers save when their incomes are high and dis-save or borrow when incomes are low, their consumption risk will be reduced. Savings can be thought of as storing money when its value (marginal utility) is low, in contrast to storing goods when their value (price) is low, and is obviously a similar activity.

If commodities are stored this will also affect the operation of the futures market, as we saw in the last chapter. Moreover, if a buffer stock agency attempts to stabilize prices by operating a buffer stock scheme this may dramatically affect the profitability and hence the amount of private storage. In an extreme case the agency would have to take over the finance of all existing private storage as well as the additional storage which it planned to undertake. Obviously it is necessary to take account of storage activities in every study of commodity price stabilization, and the first part of this chapter will briefly survey some of the issues. Storage necessarily introduces a dynamic element into market equilibrium for prices and supplies in one year will now, through their effect on the size of the carry-forward, affect prices and consumption in subsequent years. A proper study of storage, and in particular the analysis of the optimum amount of storage, needs to take these complex dynamic factors into account, and will therefore be deferred until Part VII.

The possibility of averaging consumption by saving reduces consumption risk directly, and hence modifies the benefits to be achieved by price stabilization. We shall examine how far the benefits are reduced at the end of this chapter. First, we examine the effects of storage.

14.1 Storage

Commodities can be, and often are, stored by producers, consumers, middlemen, or merchants. They will presumably be stored if their convenience yield exceeds their carrying cost, and the agent with the comparative advantage in carrying stocks will be the one for whom this is the greatest.

Consider an agent with rational expectations choosing the amount of commodity to hold in store for one period, z, and the amount of income to save (or borrow), S. His income in period t is $\tilde{Y}_t$, random, the rate of interest on his bank balance is r, and his subjective discount factor is δ, so he chooses z and S to maximize utility over his planning horizon:

$$W = U\{Y_0 - (p_0 + c)z - S\} + \delta EU\{\tilde{Y}_1 + S(1 + r) + \tilde{p}_1 z\}, \qquad (14.1)$$

when p_t is the commodity price at date t, and c is the storage cost. Choosing savings S yields

$$\frac{\partial W}{\partial S} = -U'_0 + \delta(1+r)EU'_1 = 0, \quad (14.2)$$

while choosing z yields

$$\left. \begin{array}{r} \dfrac{\partial W}{\partial z} = -(p_0 + c)U'_0 + \delta EU'_1 \bar{p}_1 \leq 0 \\ \\ z \geq 0 \end{array} \right\} \text{complementary inequalities} \quad (14.3)$$

(Inequalities are complementary when strict inequality of one implies equality of the other, so the product of the two is always zero.) Agents will therefore wish to hold stocks if at $z = 0$ (substituting for U'_0 from equation (14.2))

$$p_0 + c < \frac{EU'\bar{p}_1}{(1+r)EU'}. \quad (14.4)$$

A risk-neutral agent would be willing to stockpile if at $z = 0$

$$p_0 + c < \frac{E\bar{p}_1}{1+r}, \quad (14.5)$$

so the *convenience yield* of storage can be defined as ρ

$$\rho = \frac{EU'p}{\bar{p}EU'} - 1 \quad (14.6)$$

(where we have omitted the subscript on price). It will be positive if U' and p are positively correlated. Consider first the case of price uncertainty arising from supply risk. Producers will thus enjoy positive convenience yield if the elasticity of demand is greater than one and price is negatively correlated with output. In such circumstances equation (13.10) shows that a farmer would like to hold negative futures in an unbiased futures market, that is, he would like to be able to deliver more than he grows at some future date, or, in other words to carry stocks forward.

Final consumers will enjoy a convenience yield if V_I, the marginal utility of income, I, and p are positively correlated, that is, if $V_{Ip} > 0$ where V is the indirect utility function. Equation (8.13) shows that V_{Ip} will be positive if the coefficient of relative risk aversion, R, is greater than the income elasticity of demand for the good, a most plausible condition for most agricultural goods.

Finally, intermediate producers (cocoa-grinders, chocolate-makers, cornstarch processors, etc.) will have a positive convenience yield since profit and input prices are negatively correlated; hence the marginal utility of profits will be positively correlated with price.

If supply is riskless but demand is risky producers will have negative convenience yield, while for consumers it will be positive unless prices vary because of income fluctuations. The same is true for intermediate producers when prices vary because demand for the final good varies.

The other determinant of the attractiveness of storage is the cost of storage, c. The capital cost of storage facilities is (at least initially) approximately proportional to the square of the linear dimension, while capacity is proportional to its cube, so that a 'two-thirds power law' will make carrying costs initially decrease with the amount stored, encouraging specialization. Further economies of scale arise from the operation of the law of large numbers, which allows large firms to operate with a smaller margin of spare capacity. Moreover, large stockpilers enjoy higher returns to improved information about risks than small producers, giving them a comparative advantage in forecasting the future price. It is perhaps not surprising that intermediate processors often are large relative to the market and do substantial storage.

If the convenience yield is sufficiently large, it may offset carrying costs, and thus eliminate any bias in futures markets, in contrast to the simple model of Chapter 13 which ignored convenience yields.

14.1.1 *The effect of storage on price stability*

Annual crops which can be stored, and which are continuously consumed, like corn, will of necessity be stocked throughout the year, and in conjunction with the futures markets, will even out fluctuations during the year so that the only remaining source of fluctuations is unanticipated news which affects expectations about the future. Without improving the flow of information it is difficult to see how price fluctuations could be further damped without distorting the allocative effects of the price changes. Like futures markets, then, storage of such crops will even out predictable fluctuations during that particular year. Stocks can be held from year to year, and can in principle stabilize prices between years, but it would be a mistake to exaggerate the importance or extent of such stabilization. We shall explore buffer stock policies to stabilize prices from year to year in Part VII, but it is easy to give a rough estimate of the importance of stockpiling.

For a risk-neutral stockholder, equation (14.5) gives the condition for a positive carry-forward. If prices are normally distributed about an unchanging mean, then the fraction of years in which positive stocks will be carried is approximately

$$\Pr\left(p + c \leqslant \frac{\bar{p}}{1+r}\right) \equiv \pi,$$

$$\pi = \Phi(-\gamma/\sigma_p), \quad \gamma = \frac{c}{\bar{p}} + \frac{r}{1+r}, \qquad (14.7)$$

where σ_p is the coefficient of variation of prices, $\Phi(x)$ is the normal distribution function, and γ is the total discounted proportionate carry-forward cost. Thus if $\gamma = 12$ per cent, $\sigma_p = 30$ per cent, stocks will be carried forward roughly one year in three and will only be carried forward more than one year 11 per cent of the time. On the other hand, using the data for the two storable crops given in Table 13.1 the CV of annual price changes is 14 per cent for corn and 11.5 per cent for soybeans. Total storage costs including interest, γ, are about 12 per cent for corn, so stocks will be carried forward for more than one year about once every twenty-five years. It thus seems reasonable as a first approximation to ignore subsequent years in estimating the size of stock to carry forward. In this case stocks will be withheld from the market in a good year until the current price is driven up and next year's price driven down enough to ensure equality in equation (14.5):

$$p_t + c = \frac{Ep}{1+r}.$$

For example, if demand is stable and linear, there will be no stockpiling if supplies today, Q_t, fall short of a critical level Q_c, which satisfies

$$p(Q_c) = Ep(Q)(1-\gamma).$$

If

$$p = a - bQ \qquad (14.8)$$

then

$$Q_c = \frac{a\gamma}{b} + \bar{Q}(1-\gamma), \qquad (14.9)$$

and the optimal carry forward, z, drives prices to satisfy equation (14.5) with equality:

$$a - b(Q_t - z) = \{a - b(\bar{Q} + z)\}(1-\gamma)$$

so

$$z = \frac{Q_t - Q_c}{2 - \gamma}, \quad \text{for } Q_t \geq Q_c. \qquad (14.10)$$

Thus roughly half the amount by which the harvest exceeds the critical level Q_c will be stored. The average carry-forward will thus be rather low, both because storage will be infrequent, and because z will typically be rather small. The average amount stored in a year in which there is storage is

$$E[z | Q_t \geq Q_c],$$

which, if Q is distributed normally with standard deviation $\sigma\bar{Q}$, is

$$\frac{1}{2-\gamma} \left[\frac{1}{\sqrt{(2\pi)}} \int_{Q_c}^{\infty} \frac{Q - \bar{Q}}{\sigma\bar{Q}} \exp\left\{-\tfrac{1}{2}\left(\frac{Q-\bar{Q}}{\sigma\bar{Q}}\right)^2\right\} \cdot dQ - (Q_c - \bar{Q}) \int_{Q_c}^{\infty} f(Q)dQ \right]$$

where $f(Q)$ is the normal density function. This can be integrated to give

$$\frac{\bar{z}}{\bar{Q}} = \frac{\sigma}{2-\gamma}\left[\frac{1}{\sqrt{(2\pi)}} e^{-\frac{1}{2}(\gamma/\sigma_p)^2} - \frac{\gamma}{\sigma_p}\{1 - \Phi(\gamma/\sigma_p)\}\right] \quad (14.11)$$

since, from equations (14.8) and (14.9),

$$\frac{Q_c - \bar{Q}}{\sigma \bar{Q}} = \frac{\gamma}{\sigma_p},$$

so the average carry-forward over a run of years will be this multiplied by the fraction π of equation (14.7). If $\sigma = 15$ per cent, $\sigma_p = 30$ per cent, $\gamma = 12$ per cent, then $\bar{z}/\bar{Q} = 1.8$ per cent, and the over-all average carry-forward will be less than 1 per cent of average supply.

These very crude estimates will be refined in Chapter 30 when we calculate the optimum storage rule, but it is difficult to escape the impression that transfers from one year to the next will typically be rather small. Does this mean that the private market performs an inadequate amount of storage? The efficiency of the competitive market is the proper subject of the next chapter, where we show that if all agents are risk neutral, competitive, and hold rational expectations, the market equilibrium will be Pareto efficient. The storage rule above was calculated on these assumptions, but can only be proven efficient given these unreasonably strong assumptions (or other, equally strong alternative assumptions). Nevertheless, as we shall see in Chapter 22 we cannot therefore conclude that too little storage is done – it could be excessive.

14.2 The effects of private storage on public buffer stocks

Suppose a stabilization authority is set up and instructed to reduce price variability by stockpiling when prices are low. In practice, if a commodity can be stored it is very likely that someone – producers, speculators, or consumers – will store when it is profitable. The amount of private storage will presumably depend on the price difference between the dates of buying and selling, Δp, and, if the buffer authority attempts to change Δp by storing δQ, it will thereby change the attractiveness of storage and lead to offsetting reductions in private storage. Putting it another way, in order to achieve a given change in Δp by storage, the buffer authority will have to store more, by the amount that the private sector releases. It is easy to write down a formula for this, but perhaps more useful to construct a model which allows the effect to be quantified. We do both. Suppose storage is $z(\Delta p)$, then

$$\Delta p = p(Q_1 + \delta Q + z(\Delta p)) - p(Q_2 - \delta Q - z). \quad (14.12)$$

Differentiate with respect to storage, δQ:

$$\frac{d\Delta p}{d\delta Q} = \sum_{i=1}^{2} \left\{ \frac{dp_i}{dQ_i}\left(1 + \frac{dz}{d\Delta p}\frac{d\Delta p}{d\delta Q}\right)\right\}$$

so

$$\frac{d\Delta p}{d\delta Q} = \frac{\sum \frac{dp_i}{dQ}}{1 - \frac{dz}{d\Delta p}\sum \frac{dp_i}{dQ}}. \qquad (14.13)$$

For example, if demand curves are linear, as in equation (14.8), and storage is proportional to the expected excess of next period's price over today's price,

$$z = \alpha \Delta p$$

then

$$\frac{d\Delta p}{d\delta Q} = \frac{-2b}{1 + 2\alpha b}, \qquad (14.14)$$

and the buffer authority must store $1 + 2\alpha b$ times as much as the private sector would to achieve the same price change. As a particular example, consider a model similar to that used to describe hedging in the presence of a futures market. Suppose there is no futures market, that the world lasts two periods, and that farmers have constant absolute risk aversion. There is multiplicative normally distributed supply risk, riskless linear demand, and inputs are fixed each year. Interest and storage charges are assumed zero. Consider the position after the first harvest, when θ_0, p_0 are known, when the farmers must choose storage z to maximize expected utility:

$$\underset{z}{\text{Max}}\; EY - \tfrac{1}{2}A\,\text{Var}\,Y$$

where

$$Y = p_0(\theta_0 \bar{q} - z) + \bar{p}(\bar{\theta}\bar{q} + z).$$

With manipulation similar to that employed in the hedging model the storage rule is found to be

$$\frac{z}{\bar{q}} = \frac{Ep - p_0}{A\bar{q}\,\text{Var}\,p} + \bar{e} - 1 \qquad (14.15)$$

where $\text{Var}\,p = \bar{p}^2\sigma^2/\bar{e}^2$ is the unstabilized price variance, and $\bar{e}$ is elasticity evaluated at the mean. For this model storage is proportional (at the margin) to the expected price difference, so (aggregating across farmers and using upper-case notation for aggregates)

$$\frac{dZ}{d\Delta p} = \frac{1}{A \operatorname{Var} p} \equiv \alpha \qquad (14.16)$$

and storage must be increased by a factor $1 + 2b/(A \operatorname{Var} p)$ to achieve the same degree of stabilization as in the absence of private storage.

The offsetting decisions by the private sector are the larger the less risk averse they are, and the smaller is the risk they face. The more successful is government action to reduce income variability, the harder it will be to make further improvements by storage.

14.3* Savings

Farmers have still another way to mitigate the effects of risk: they can save in periods in which their income is high against periods in which their income is low. The farmer is not concerned directly with variability in income, but with the variability in the standard of living which it induces. If he knew that every good year was always followed by a bad year, he could always save in the good year for the bad year. There would be no uncertainty associated with his standard of living, and the variability in his annual income would have no consequence. Even when the sequence of good and bad years is not so completely predictable, credit markets may, in certain circumstances, allow the farmer substantially to reduce fluctuations in his standard of living, even when he cannot directly reduce the instability of his income.

The problem facing the farmer is to plan his consumption pattern over time to reduce the costs of risk, or, more precisely, to maximize the expected utility of consumption. In the simplest specification consumption at date t, c_t, is chosen to maximize

$$E \sum_{t=0}^{T} \delta^t U(c_t) \qquad (14.17)$$

subject to

$$B_{t+1} = (B_t + \tilde{y}_t - c_t)(1 + r). \qquad (14.18)$$

This constraint assumes that the consumer can freely lend *and borrow* at the same rate of interest, r. The importance of this assumption of perfect capital markets is discussed below. In this specification utility at date t depends only on consumption at that date, and is discounted because of pure time preference. Bank balances at the start of period t, B_t, receive additions of random income, $\tilde{y}_t$, and deductions to finance consumption, and earn a rate of interest, r. Initial and final assets are given. The optimal choice of c_t, then satisfies

$$EU'(c_t) = \gamma EU'(c_{t+1}), \quad \gamma = \delta(1 + r), \qquad (14.19)$$

and the initial choice of consumption satisfies

$$U'(c_0) = \gamma E U'(c_1) = \ldots = \gamma^t E U'(c_t). \tag{14.20}$$

The similarity with the storage rule in equation (14.4) is obvious, since saving takes place until the value of consumption now (i.e. its marginal utility) is equal to the discounted expected value next year. Equation (14.20) is in general difficult to solve since it involves satisfying the asset equation (14.18), but we can obtain a feel for the effect of savings by considering some special cases. The most favourable case for the smoothing effect of savings would allow the farmer to average over the indefinite future, while the shorter the time horizon, the more current fluctuations in income must be absorbed by immediate changes in consumption. Let us examine a very simple case with an infinite time horizon, in which $\gamma = 1$ so that if income were constant there would be no saving. Any savings therefore arise because of income fluctuations, which we shall assume are independent over time about a constant mean, $\bar{y}$. If, in addition, one assumes a quadratic utility function, equation (14.19) simplifies considerably to

$$c_t = E c_{t+i}, \quad i = 1, 2, \ldots \tag{14.21}$$

At any date t, B_t and y_t will be known before c_t is chosen, and the amount carried forward will be worth next year

$$B_{t+1} = (1 + r)(B_t + y_t - c_t). \tag{14.22}$$

Next year's expected total income is then

$$\bar{y} + r B_{t+1}/(1 + r) = \bar{y} + r(B_t + y_t - c_t)$$

and, since on average consumption equals total income

$$c_t = E c_{t+1} = \bar{y} + r(B_t + y_t - c_t). \tag{14.23}$$

Let S_t be the sum available for saving or consuming:

$$S_t = B_t + y_t$$

then, solving equation (14.23)

$$c_t = r\beta S_t + \beta \bar{y}, \tag{14.24}$$

where

$$\beta = \frac{1}{1+r}.$$

Now, since

$$S_{t+1} = B_{t+1} + y_{t+1} = y_{t+1} + (1+r)(S_t - c_t)$$

from equation (14.22), substituting from equation (14.24) gives

$$S_{t+1} = S_t + (y_{t+1} - \bar{y}). \tag{14.25}$$

This gives an equation for S_t which can be solved

$$S_t = y_t + B_0 + \sum_{i=0}^{t-1} (y_i - \bar{y}),$$

whence, if $B_0 = 0$, gives, from (14.24)

$$c_t = \bar{y} + \beta r \sum_{i=0}^{t} (y_{t-i} - \bar{y}). \tag{14.26}$$

The cost of risk can be measured by an annual risk premium, ρ, which on the assumption that $\gamma = 1$, i.e. $\delta = \beta$, satisfies

$$\sum_t \beta^t U(Ec_t - \rho) = \sum_t \beta^t EU(c_t), \tag{14.27}$$

where $Ec_t = \bar{y}$. Each term can be expanded in a Taylor series, as in subsection 6.5.2, as follows:

$$U(\bar{y} - \rho) \cong U(\bar{y}) - \rho U'(\bar{y})$$
$$EU(c_t) \cong U(\bar{y}) - \tfrac{1}{2} A \, \text{Var}(c_t) \cdot U'(\bar{y}),$$

where A is the coefficient of absolute risk aversion. Equation (14.27) can now be solved, since $U'(\bar{y})$ cancels, to give

$$\rho = \frac{\tfrac{1}{2} A \Sigma \beta^t \, \text{Var} \, c_t}{\Sigma \beta^t}. \tag{14.28}$$

If, as we assumed, the y_t are independently distributed, then the variance of consumption can be found from equation (14.26):

$$\text{Var} \, c_t = r^2 \beta^2 t \, \text{Var} \, y \tag{14.29}$$

so

$$\rho = \tfrac{1}{2} r^2 \beta^2 A \, \text{Var} \, y \left\{ \frac{\Sigma t \beta^t}{\Sigma \beta^t} \right\} \tag{14.30}$$

or, evaluating the infinite sums,

$$\rho = \tfrac{1}{2} K A \, \text{Var} \, y$$

where

$$K = \frac{r^2 \beta^3}{1 - \beta} = \frac{r}{(1 + r)^2} \sim r.$$

With no saving, $c_t = y_t$, so equation (14.28) gives a risk premium of $\frac{1}{2}A \operatorname{Var} y$, so if for example, $r = 10$ per cent, $K = 0.083$, and the cost of risk is the same as it would be if the farmer could not save, but faced income risk whose coefficient of variation was only 29 per cent as large. Intuitively, the reason for the dramatic fall in the cost of risk is that any deviation of income from normal can be spread over the infinite future and will contribute each year a fraction equal to the rate of interest, r.

With a shorter time horizon, however, more of the income risk is concentrated into each year. If the time horizon is short (five years or less) we can ignore the rate of interest if it is not too large. Over T years total income will be

$$W = \sum_{i=1}^{T} y_i$$

and consumption will be

$$c = \frac{W}{T}$$

$$\operatorname{Var} c = \frac{1}{T^2} \operatorname{Var} W = \frac{1}{T}(\operatorname{Var} y) \tag{14.31}$$

and the cost of risk is reduced to fraction $1/T$ of its original value. Again, it is as though the coefficient of variation of income has been divided by $\sqrt{T}$.

14.3.1 *Asset integration and the perceived cost of risk*

The two extreme cases of an infinite and fairly short time horizon both suggest that quite dramatic reductions in risk appear possible if farmers can even out their consumption flows by lending and borrowing, provided the time horizon is not too short. Why, then, is income variability held to be so important?

The first explanation has already been discussed in Chapter 7, where the empirical evidence suggests that individuals act as though each risky decision were to be considered independently of all other decisions. This compartmentalization, or failure of the hypothesis of asset integration, is convenient for predictive purposes, but embarrassing for welfare evaluation. It may well be that individuals act in a myopic, sequential way (which is economical of information), but they may experience the outcome quite differently. In this case, farmers may worry about income risk in their choice of crops, but enjoy a standard of living which depends on the relative stability of their consumption stream. If, however, farmers are reluctant to borrow because they fail to perceive the averaging effects of successive years, then their perceptions, and consequent choices, will indeed affect their welfare, and they will not derive so much benefit from the ability to lend and save. If so, then price stabilization may compensate for this psychological obstacle to rationality.

A second, related explanation is that income does not (or farmers *believe* that it does not) fluctuate about a known mean, $\bar{y}$, but instead follows in part a *random walk*. A random variable, $\tilde{X}_t$, say, follows a random walk if, at each step it is equally probable that it will increase or decrease by one unit. The path of $\tilde{X}_t$ will then be that of a gambler's wealth when he stakes equally at each throw of the die, or that of a small speck of dust bombarded by gas molecules (Brownian motion), and it has the property that past history is no guide to the future. In the symmetric case the best estimate of X_{t+1} is X_t, and not

$$\frac{1}{t}\sum_{i=0}^{t} X_i,$$

as in the case of a stationary random variable.

In the case of the farmer's income, it is not implausible that the price follows something more like a random walk than a stationary process, at least in the medium run. Certainly, if prices are influenced by international, as opposed to national, costs of production, there is no reason for them to maintain a constant domestic purchasing power. The yield per hectare may also follow a random walk as new varieties are introduced and succumb to diseases. If current income is the best predictor of future income, then current consumption should be rapidly adjusted in line with income (if there are no adjustment costs) and consumption will be as variable as income. In such circumstances, price stabilization will be very difficult, for the same reason that the price around which to stabilize cannot be predicted. Consequently, the farmer may already have stabilized income as far as is feasible.

An alternative explanation is that income does fluctuate about a mean, but periodic structural changes (new varieties, devaluations, etc.) make it difficult for the farmer to identify the mean, or distinguish the trend. Again, in such cases, the buffer agency might find it equally difficult to stabilize prices.

A third possibility is that the farmer may not be able to lend or borrow to even out his consumption stream. He may be unwilling to lend because of the difficulty of recovering the loan (though he should be able to store money from period to period, although this may not be very satisfactory in periods of rapid inflation) and he may find it difficult to borrow, either because everyone's income is low when he wishes to borrow, or because lenders fear that borrowers will lack sufficient incentive to repay the debt. It may also be difficult for individuals to save in periods of high income if capital markets are poorly developed, as they often are in peasant agriculture. To see some of the implications of credit market constraints, consider an individual who lives two periods, and receives an income whose mean value is $\bar{y}$ in each period. For simplicity, assume a zero interest rate and zero time preference so that the individual would prefer to consume the same expected amount in each period. If he can freely lend and borrow he divides his expected wealth evenly over his life, and so sets

$$c_1 = \tfrac{1}{2}(y_1 + \bar{y}), \qquad \operatorname{Var} c_1 = \tfrac{1}{4}\operatorname{Var} y$$
$$c_2 = y_1 + y_2 - c_1, \qquad \operatorname{Var} c_2 = \tfrac{5}{4}\operatorname{Var} y.$$

The average variance of consumption without lending and borrowing would be $\operatorname{Var} y$, but it falls to $\tfrac{3}{4}\operatorname{Var} y$ with lending and borrowing. The benefit of being able to lend and borrow is thus approximately

$$\tfrac{1}{2}R\bar{y}\tfrac{1}{4}\sigma_y^2 = \tfrac{1}{8}R\bar{y}\sigma_y^2,$$

where, as usual, R is the coefficient of relative risk aversion and σ_y is the coefficient of variation of income in any period.

If the individual can lend (or, equivalently, costlessly store money or consumption goods) but not borrow, and lives two periods, then one-half of the time he is constrained. The average variance of his consumption is reduced by one-eighth, halving the gains from averaging to $1/16 R\bar{y}\sigma_y^2$.

Again, it can be shown that lengthening the time period reduces the consumption risk, and also reduces the effect of borrowing constraints. Over long periods of time the farmer would accumulate a stock of money which would allow him to even out his consumption flow with little recourse to the credit market, though if the opportunity cost of remaining sufficiently liquid is high, this may be a costly solution. The problem of optimum savings with no borrowing is fomally identical to the problem of optimal storage (where negative stocks are obviously infeasible) and is discussed in more detail in Chapter 30.

Finally, it should be stressed that if the farmer has a high level of already committed expenditures (on rent, food, educating his family, taxes, etc.) then income fluctuations will bear more heavily on discretionary consumption, and explain the apparently excessive concern farmers exhibit to current income risk.

Chapter 15

The Efficiency of Market Equilibrium

15.1 Introduction

In previous chapters we have described the rational expectations equilibrium and argued that it provides a useful bench-mark for the analysis of policies affecting risk. In a rational expectations equilibrium agents take into account all relevant information and there are no gains to be reaped from improving the use of existing information in decision-making. Although existing information is used efficiently, we have been careful not to say that the resulting equilibrium is optimal in any sense, except in the very special case of the model considered in subsection 10.1.1. There is, however, a long-standing presumption that competitive markets provide an efficient allocation of resources. Adam Smith's 'invisible hand' conjecture has been converted by Arrow (1951) and Debreu (1959) into one of the fundamental theorems of economics. The theorem establishes (under the restrictive conditions described below) that a competitive equilibrium is *Pareto optimal*. An allocation is Pareto optimal, or, using less emotive language, Pareto efficient if it is impossible to make anyone better off without making someone else worse off. Notice that nothing is said about the distribution of income, which could be such that a single person owned almost everything. To each distribution of initial resources there corresponds a Pareto-efficient allocation, and, comparing any two allocations, some individuals will be better off and others worse off in one allocation than in the other.

The important assumptions required to establish efficiency are that:

(i) The economy be perfectly competitive, in the sense that all individuals are price-takers; they believe that their actions have no effect on the prices in the market. For this to be a reasonable assumption, firms must be small. In agriculture this assumption is so obviously satisfied that agriculture has often been taken as the leading textbook example of competitive markets.

(ii) There are no externalities: the utility of each individual depends only on his own consumption and the production of each firm depends only on its own inputs. Although this is not always satisifed (diseases from one farmer's crops may affect other farmers' crops), this is not a major source of concern in the present context.

(iii) There is a complete set of futures and risk markets. This is an assumption which is clearly not satisfied. As we mentioned in Chapter 13, futures markets extend only a few months into the future and most risks cannot be insured, including important risks like crop failure. There may be good reasons for these markets to be imperfect, related to problems of moral hazard (the fact that the individual's crop is insured may lead him to take less care in his actions concerning crop failures) and of adverse selection[1] (those who buy the insurance are most likely to have a crop failure; the insurance company may be less informed than the individual farmer regarding the probability of crop failure for that particular farmer).

In this and the next chapter we shall examine the consequences of the last two assumptions: the absence of a complete set of markets and the absence of perfect information. We shall show that in fact the market does not provide an optimal allocation of resources (even in the limited sense of Pareto efficiency discussed above). In the present chapter we concentrate on finding the conditions under which a competitive agricultural economy with only limited risk-sharing arrangements provides an efficient allocation of resources. It is the fundamental question to ask before deciding on any market intervention such as setting up international buffer stocks to stabilize the price of agricultural commodities, for if the competitive market is efficient without government intervention, then such schemes will be at best a relatively inefficient vehicle for aid transfers to an arbitrarily defined group of recipients. (If the resource allocation is not efficient, it does not necessarily mean that a price stabilization programme would be desirable; to establish this requires further analysis, of the kind presented in Chapters 29 and 30.)

It is important in evaluating the performance of the market economy and assessing the desirability of various kinds of government intervention to make the appropriate comparisons. In particular, it is not reasonable to compare the allocation of resources with a complete set of markets and the market allocation of resources with an incomplete set. There are usually good economic reasons for the absence of a complete set of (risk and futures) markets in the shape of excessive transactions costs, broadly defined. Thus in evaluating the market economy, we ought to take these costs into account. In fact, however, we take a slightly different strategy. We can divide the question of the performance of the market economy into two separate sub-questions:

1. Does the economy provide the 'correct' set of markets? Should, for instance, the government establish a market for 'crop insurance' in situations where such markets do not exist?

2. Given the markets which do exist, are resources efficiently allocated, or are there some kinds of government interventions which would improve welfare?

In this book we are concerned about both questions. The question of whether a futures market for agricultural crops ought to be created is, of course, a question about whether the set of markets which presently exists is 'optimal'. Similarly, the question of the desirability of allowing speculative activity is a question about whether a market which does exist ought to be restricted or

---

[1] Heady (1952) attributed the failure of the all-purpose crop insurance in the US to adverse selection. The scheme, which was started in 1938, was based on average yields over broad and heterogeneous areas, and was unattractive to farmers of above-average quality land. Very specific, readily identified events like hail damage have long been commercially insurable.

eliminated. The results of Chapter 23 suggests that the answers to such questions may be quite unexpected.

Here we are concerned only with the second question as it arises in a particular context of agricultural production under risk. That is, we take the set of markets as given, and ask — given that there do not exist good insurance markets, or good credit markets — would a policy of government intervention be desirable for agricultural commodities? It is important to realize, however, that the two questions are intimately related. It may be better to attempt to change the market structure to improve credit and risk markets than to attempt to stabilize prices within the present structure.

We consider here an extreme case, where there is no credit market (so individuals cannot average out the effects of income fluctuations over time) and no market for insuring against output and price fluctuations. Each individual takes the price distribution as given, and chooses his technique of production optimally, given that price distribution. The equilibrium price distribution will, of course, be a consequence of all their decisions. If farmers act competitively, however, they take the price distribution as given. Nevertheless, in spite of such competitive behaviour, we shall show that in general their collective actions do not lead to an efficient allocation of resources. More precisely, we establish that, even if all individuals have rational expectations concerning the distribution of prices which will prevail on the market next period, the market allocation is, in general, not constrained Pareto efficient. In other words, if we constrain the government to work within the same set of markets, not allowing it either directly or surreptitiously to alter the set of available markets, it would make different production decisions. As a consequence, there exists a set of taxes/subsidies which would generate a Pareto improvement. There are some very special cases where the market equilibrium is constrained Pareto efficient; these, unfortunately, include some of the more commonly employed parameterizations (e.g. logarithmic utility function and multiplicative risk). Writers who make these assumptions for analytic convenience may not fully appreciate what strong implications these assumptions have for market efficiency.

A natural question to ask at this point is, why does the usual argument for the efficiency of the competitive economy not go through? As will be clear from the proofs we shall present, the absence of a complete set of markets is critical to our argument. With an incomplete set of markets, the marginal rate of substitution of different individuals between different states of nature will differ; farmers, in choosing their production technique, look only at the price distribution and their own marginal rates of substitution, which may differ markedly from those of other farmers and consumers. When they all do this, the equilibrium which results may not be Pareto efficient; there is some alternative choice of technique and redistribution of income which could make all individuals better off.

The point may be put another way: whenever there is an incomplete set of markets, a given market may also provide insurance, because if prices vary inversely with quantities, income will be less variable than output, provided the elasticity of demand is not too low. What is critical for our purposes is that production decisions of farmers may affect the extent to which the price system performs this role.

The allocation of goods depends on the price which clears the market, but the allocation of risk depends on the form of the whole price distribution, which is the outcome of a large number of competitive decisions, but which acts rather like a public good. It is well known that the competitive market is unlikely to supply the efficient amount of public goods, and here, too, we show that the market is unlikely to supply the efficient amount of risk.

The analysis of Arrow and Debreu provided *sufficient* conditions under which the market allocation was Pareto efficient. Our analysis can be viewed as attempting to assess to what extent the existence of a complete set of risk markets is *necessary* for the efficiency of the market. It is important to be clear in what sense competitive economies without a full set of markets are efficient. It is obvious (as Karl Borch (1968) has pointed out) that the economy will not in general attain a full Pareto-efficient allocation. But is it possible that the economy may be efficient in a more restricted sense?

This question was posed by Diamond (1967) who considered an economy in which the only possibilities of risk-sharing were through the stock-market. He provided a set of conditions under which the market allocation is constrained Pareto efficient, i.e. given the set of securities which are available on the market, value-maximizing competitive firms allocate resources efficiently. The notion of constrained Pareto efficiency we employ here is identical to that of Diamond. He made three critical assumptions: (a) firms had multiplicative risk, i.e. as they increased their investment, outputs in all states of nature increased proportionately; (b) there was a single homogeneous output; and (c) there were enough firms within any risk class that each of them believed their market value was proportional to their scale.

Several subsequent studies (Stiglitz (1972b, 1975), Drèze (1974), Hart (1975) cast doubt on the generality of Diamond's results. Hart, in particular, while providing a set of (restrictive) sufficient conditions under which the market equilibrium has certain efficiency properties, provides a number of interesting examples demonstrating that, when these conditions are not satisfied, the market equilibrium may not be constrained Pareto efficient. Our results extend Hart's in two important ways:

(i) Hart's analysis was limited to an exchange economy, and thus the inefficiencies which he noted were exchange inefficiencies; we are concerned with productive efficiency.

(ii) While Hart provided sufficient conditions for efficiency, we provide necessary and sufficient conditions; these conditions not only demonstrate that there is a strong presumption for the inefficiency of the market equilibrium, but provide considerable insight into the nature of the market failure. Moreover, they enable us to derive policies which lead to Pareto improvements in welfare and to estimate the magnitude of the welfare losses associated with non-intervention.

Moreover, most of Hart's examples (for given market structures) involve multiple equilibria; he shows that there may be two market allocations, one of which Pareto dominates the other. They are examples of what has been called elsewhere *structural inefficiencies* (Stiglitz (1972b)). By contrast, we are concerned here only with *marginal inefficiencies*, i.e. where the first order conditions corresponding to the (constrained) Pareto optimum appear to be clearly different from those equations describing the market equilibrium (cf. Stiglitz's (1975) analysis of the oil market).

Different choices of techniques have, in addition to the efficiency consequences we have been discussing so far, certain distributional consequences. Since we are only concerned to demonstrate inefficiency (we know there is no guarantee of distributional justice) we shall assume that the government can engage in (non-state-dependent) lump-sum redistributions between farmers and consumers (or among different groups of farmers), and thereby side-step issues of equity.

We present the argument in two parts. First, we consider a simple agricultural environment in which all farmers are identical (the risks which they face are perfectly correlated) and all consumers are identical. Second, we consider a slightly more complicated agricultural environment in which there are two groups of farmers with imperfectly correlated outputs.

In each case, we describe briefly the market equilibrium, then describe the *constrained* Pareto-optimal allocation of resources (and choice of technique): the constraint is that the government is only allowed to engage in lump-sum redistributions and to determine the choice of technique; it cannot establish markets not presently available.

We show that, even if all individuals have rational expectations (i.e. know perfectly the probability distribution of returns to agricultural production), the market equilibrium is a constrained Pareto optimum only under extremely restrictive conditions. In the absence of these conditions there always exists some policy which can improve everyone's welfare. Unfortunately, however, the direction of the bias may be towards too much or too little risk-taking, so that there is no simple rule (such as to subsidize risk-taking) which always improves the allocation.

This is probably the most difficult chapter in the book, and we do not expect that many readers will wish to follow all the intricacies of the mathematical arguments. We have accordingly summarized the results in the form of theorems, whose proofs can, if desired, be skipped and taken on trust. In addition, we have presented a diagrammatic illustration in subsection 15.4.2 and used this example to estimate the importance of the inefficiencies in section 15.6. Finally, we have summarized the main results in section 15.9.

15.2 A simple model with identical farmers and consumers

We examine these questions within the context of the simplest possible model. There are two groups within the population, farmers and consumers. All farmers are identical and all consumers are identical. We first describe the farmers' behaviour, then consumers', and finally market equilibrium. In the next section, we define and analyse the constrained Pareto optimum and compare it to the market equilibrium.

15.2.1 *Farmers*

All farmers are identical and must choose the value of the decision variable, ξ, at the start of the crop year, before the state of nature, θ (e.g. the weather), is known. Output, q is an increasing function of ξ and θ and concave in ξ:

$$q = f(\xi, \theta), \quad \frac{\partial f}{\partial \xi} \geq 0. \tag{15.1}$$

If there are N farmers, then aggregate output is

$$Q = Nq = Q(\xi, \theta). \tag{15.2}$$

Since all farmers are identical, we can represent the action taken by a single number (although in principle we should write down the action taken by each farmer).

Each farmer takes the *distribution* of prices as given (this is the natural generalization of the price-taking assumption of the conventional non-stochastic model). Later, we shall discuss how this price distribution is determined. As we shall see, it will depend on the actions taken by all other farmers, the state of nature, and the income of the consumers, I. If consumers do not have identical, homothetic indifference maps, it will also depend on the distribution of income as well; but since we assume that the income distribution remains invariant throughout the model, we shall simply write

$$p = p(\xi, \theta, I) = p(\xi, \theta).$$

The income of the farmer in state θ when he takes action ξ is thus

$$y = pf(\xi, \theta). \tag{15.3}$$

We assume the farmer has a concave utility function which depends both on his income and the action he takes

$$U = U(y, \xi)$$

$$U_y > 0, U_{yy} < 0, U_{\xi\xi} \leq 0$$

(the marginal utility of income is positive but diminishing and U is concave in ξ). He chooses ξ to maximize his expected utility at the start of the crop year before θ is known:

$$\max_{\{\xi\}} EU(y, \xi), \text{ given his expectations of } p(\theta, \xi^*, I) \tag{15.4}$$

so that he sets

$$E\{U_y p f_\xi + U_\xi\} = 0. \tag{15.5}$$

In the subsequent anlysis, we shall examine several special interpretations of this general model. In one interpretation, ξ is a choice of technique. In that case we postulate that ξ changes the probability distribution of outcomes, but does not directly affect utility, i.e.

$$U_\xi = 0. \tag{15.6}$$

A second important interpretation has ξ as the level of investment or the cost of purchased inputs such as fertilizer. Then, *net* income of the farmer is $y - \xi$ and we write

$$U = u(y - \xi). \tag{15.7}$$

In the third important interpretation ξ is the level of effort supplied by the individual. If the individual's utility function is separable between income and effort (an assumption defended in Chapter 6):

$$U = u(y) - z(\xi), \tag{15.8}$$

where $z(\xi)$ is the disutility of effort.

In each of these cases, the action taken by the individual farmer is a function of his *expectations* concerning the distribution of prices. If his expectations are rational, i.e. the expected price distribution corresponds to the actual price distribution, then, since the latter will depend on the actions taken by all other farmers his actions will depend on the actions taken by all other farmers. The precise relationship depends, however, on the properties of the demand functions of consumers, to which we now turn.

15.2.2 *Consumers*

Consumers make their consumption decisions after the state of nature and, hence, market prices are known. Their choices can therefore be described by an indirect utility function, which we represent as a function of the price of this particular good, p, and money income, I, the prices of all other goods being assumed constant. We assume, again for simplicity, that

(i) Consumers' income does not depend at all on producers' income or prices or θ, the state of nature (this makes sense if production and consumption occur in different locations, and consumers cannot or do not buy stock or speculate on the price of the agricultural commodity). The assumption is for simplicity, and can be relaxed, as in Stiglitz (1978), without changing the presumption of market inefficiency.

(ii) Producers do not consume the commodity which they produce at all (this again is a simplifying assumption, not crucial to the analysis).

(iii) The price of the given good does not have any significant effect on the price of other goods, an assumption which makes sense for a commodity which is a small part of consumers' budgets.

The representative consumer chooses his consumption of the commodity after its price is known, and thus his utility can be represented by the indirect utility function

$$V(p, I). \tag{15.9}$$

His demand, q^c, is derived from Roy's identity, given by equation (8.10):

$$q^c = -\frac{\partial V}{\partial p} \bigg/ \frac{\partial V}{\partial I}. \tag{15.10}$$

Aggregate demand, D, of the M identical consumers is just

$$D = Mq^c = D(p, I), \tag{15.11}$$

a function of price and the income of the representative consumer.

15.2.3 *Market equilibrium*

The rational expectations market equilibrium price distribution can now be defined, given the demand function (15.11): for each ξ and θ, there is a particular value of aggregate supply $Q(\xi, \theta)$ and the market clearing price is then the price which equates aggregate demand, D, to this supply:

$$Q(\xi, \theta) = D(p(\xi, \theta, I), I). \tag{15.12}$$

We described earlier the behaviour of farmers. Recalling equation (15.5) and now letting $p(\xi, \theta, I)$ be the solution to equation (15.12) (but suppressing the dependence of p on I for simplicity of notation), since all farmers are identical, a rational expectations market equilibrium is a value of ξ^* and a price function $p(\xi^*, \theta)$ for which

$$E\frac{\partial U\{p(\xi^*, \theta)f(\xi^*, \theta), \xi^*\}}{\partial y} pf_\xi(\xi^*, \theta) + E\frac{\partial U\{p(\xi^*, \theta)f(\xi^*, \theta), \xi^*\}}{\partial \xi} = 0, \tag{15.13}$$

and supply equals demand, so equation (15.12) is satisfied.

15.3 The inefficiency of market equilibrium

15.3.1 *Introduction*

We now wish to evaluate the market equilibrium described in the previous subsection. To do this, we need to compare the welfare of consumers and producers in the market equilibrium with that in some other feasible allocation. In making the comparison, however, we need to take into account the constraints on the set of markets. It is obvious that, except in certain special cases (to be detailed below), the marginal rate of substitution between income in different states of nature will differ for different individuals, so long as there are not markets which enable them to trade income in one state for income in another. Thus, were it costless to establish new markets, clearly there exists a resource allocation which is Pareto superior to the market equilibrium. But this is an unfair (and probably irrelevant) comparison. We wish to know, given the restrictions on the set of markets, whether there exists a Pareto superior allocation. The answer is that there almost always does. We proceed in our analysis in stages.

(i) First we show (in subsection 15.3.2) that, if the government could control the choice of technique directly and make compensating lump-sum redistributions which are fixed, independent of the state of nature (the reason for imposing the restriction should be obvious: otherwise, the government is, in effect, creating a new market – it could directly equate marginal rates of substitution across states of nature), then there exists a Pareto improvement under a very weak condition.

(ii) The next subsection is devoted to interpreting this condition. In particular, it is shown that a sufficient condition for the market to be a constrained Pareto optimum is that risk markets be redundant. The following subsection then shows the conditions under which risk markets will be redundant.

These results are not surprising: if risk markets are unnecessary, one would expect the market equilibrium to be Pareto efficient, and it is. That there exist some interesting conditions under which risk markets are redundant may, however, be somewhat surprising; more to the point, we show that the kinds of parameterizations which have been commonly employed in the analysis of risk because they simplify the analysis (e.g. logarithmic utility functions) satisfy the conditions which lead to the redundancy of risk markets and may therefore be very misleading.

(iii) The interesting question, as we point out, is whether there are other conditions in which the market attains a constrained Pareto optimum but not a full Pareto optimum. The answer is no, if one is not willing to restrict the set of technologies, i.e. one wishes for all utility functions and technologies for the economy to be a constrained Pareto optimum. However, if one imposes certain restrictions on the production functions, a slightly more general class of utility functions for which the market equilibrium is a constrained Pareto optimum (but not a full Pareto optimum) is derived.

15.3.2 *Constrained Pareto efficient allocations*

In this subsection, we assume the government controls directly ξ, the choice of technique, and can impose lump-sum transfers from consumers to producers. Suppose the lump-sum subsidy to each of the N producers is s, financed by a lump-sum tax on each of the M consumers of amount Ns/M, and that the government can choose the amount s.

The set of (constrained) Pareto optima is described by the solution to

$$\underset{(s,\xi)}{\text{Max }} L \equiv EV\left\{p(\theta,\xi,s), I - \frac{sN}{M}\right\} + \frac{\lambda N}{M} EU\{p(\theta,\xi,s)f(\xi,\theta,s) + s, \xi\} \quad (15.14)$$

for values of $\lambda \geq 0$. By changing λ we can trace out all points on the utility possibility frontier. This formulation assumes that the government has full power to redistribute income, so that the only remaining issue is the one under study of achieving an efficient allocation. Choosing s yields the first-order condition:

$$\frac{\partial L}{\partial s} = \frac{N}{M}(-EV_I + \lambda EU_y) + E\left(V_p + \frac{\lambda N}{M}U_y f\right)\frac{\partial p}{\partial s} = 0.$$

Using Roy's identity (equation (15.10), equation (15.12), and the fact that $Nf = Q$, total supply, and that $Q = Mq^c$, total demand, this can be rewritten:

$$E(\lambda U_y - V_I)\left(1 + \frac{Q}{N}\frac{\partial p}{\partial s}\right) = 0. \tag{15.15}$$

The term $\partial p/\partial s$ can be found by totally differentiating demand, which is fixed equal to the level of supply:

$$\frac{d}{ds}Q\left(p, I - \frac{Ns}{M}\right) = 0 = \frac{\partial Q}{\partial p}\frac{\partial p}{\partial s} - \frac{\partial Q}{\partial I} \cdot \frac{N}{M}.$$

or

$$\frac{Q}{N}\frac{\partial p}{\partial s} = \frac{Q\partial Q/\partial I}{M\partial Q/\partial p} = -\frac{\alpha\eta}{\epsilon}, \qquad \alpha \equiv \frac{pQ}{MI},$$

where α is the fraction of consumer income spent on the commodity, η is the income elasticity of demand, and ϵ is the price elasticity of demand. Equation (15.15) can be rewritten as

$$E(\lambda U_y - V_I)(1 - \alpha\eta/\epsilon) = 0. \tag{15.16}$$

Now choose ξ so that

$$\frac{\partial L}{\partial \xi} = E\left(V_p + \lambda\frac{N}{M}U_y f\right)\frac{\partial p}{\partial \xi} + \lambda\frac{N}{M}E\left(U_y p\frac{\partial f}{\partial \xi} + \frac{\partial U}{\partial \xi}\right) = 0. \tag{15.17}$$

From equation (15.5), in market equilibrium, the second term is zero. The first term can be simplified using Roy's identity and noting that

$$\frac{Q}{N}\frac{\partial p}{\partial \xi} = \frac{Q\partial p}{\partial Q} \cdot \frac{\partial f}{\partial \xi} = -\frac{pf_\xi}{\epsilon}.$$

We therefore have the fundamental result:

Theorem 1a.

The rational expectations equilibrium is constrained Pareto efficient only if

$$K(\xi) \equiv E(\lambda U_y - V_I)\frac{p}{\epsilon}\frac{\partial f}{\partial \xi} = 0. \tag{15.18}$$

If L is concave in s and ξ then equation (15.18) is both necessary and sufficient for a Pareto optimum. Hence, we immediately obtain:

Theorem 1b.
A sufficient condition for the market to be constrained Pareto optimal is that L be concave in s and ξ and, at the market allocation, ξ^m, $K(\xi^m) \equiv 0$.

If L is not concave in s and ξ, it is possible that $K(\xi^m) = 0$ would correspond to merely a local maximum, not the global maximum ξ^* at which $K(\xi^*) = 0$, or even that the market equilibrium would correspond to a local minimum. In either case the market allocation would not be Pareto optimal.

We shall show below that only in unusual circumstances will $K(\xi^m) = 0$ at the market equilibrium, and it follows that only in even more unusual circumstances will $K(\xi^m) = 0$ at the market equilibrium and the market not be a constrained Pareto optimum.

We should point out that concavity of U in s and ξ, of V in s, and of f in ξ is *not* sufficient to ensure the concavity of L, as can be seen by twice differentiating L. However, for the logarithmic indirect utility function which plays a central role in the following analysis concavity *is* ensured.

15.3.3 *Redundancy of risk markets and constrained efficiency*

In the previous subsection, we derived a simple condition which (together with the assumption of concavity) was both necessary and sufficient for the market equilibrium to be a constrained Pareto optimum. We need, however, to interpret this condition, to see in what circumstances it will be satisfied, in order to ascertain whether it is likely or not that the market equilibrium is a constrained Pareto optimum.

The condition (15.18) can be thought of as a generalization of the condition for full Pareto optimality that the marginal rate of substitution between different states of nature be the same for all individuals. What equation (15.18) requires is that some kind of weighted average marginal rate of substitution be the same.

That is, we can rewrite equation (15.18) as

$$K(\xi) \equiv E(\rho - 1) V_I Q \frac{\partial p}{\partial \xi} = 0, \qquad (15.19)$$

where

$$\rho = \frac{U_y(\theta)/U_y(\hat{\theta})}{V_I(\theta)/V_I(\hat{\theta})},$$

where ρ is the ratio of marginal rates of substitution and $\hat{\theta}$ is that state where the ratio of marginal utilities equals λ.

A special case of this arises when the marginal rates of substitution are the same state by state, i.e.

$$V_I = \lambda U_y, \text{ all } \theta,$$

for some value of λ. In that case, of course, if risk markets were opened up, there would be no trade on them. We say that in these cases risk markets are

redundant. We thus have as an immediate corollary of Theorem 1:
Theorem 2.

A sufficient condition for the constrained efficiency of the market equilibrium is the redundancy of risk markets. If risk markets are redundant, the market equilibrium is a full Pareto optimum.

We next ask three questions:

1. Are there restrictions on the utility functions which, for all production functions, ensure the redundancy of risk markets?

2. Are there weaker restrictions on the utility functions which, for all production functions, ensure the constrained efficiency of market equilibrium? If there are not, then, in a sense, the conditions for risk market dispensability are both necessary and sufficient for the constrained efficiency of the market.

3. Are there reasonable restrictions on the technology which, together with some weak restrictions on the utility functions, ensure the constrained Pareto efficiency of the market?

The first question is easy to answer: there is a set of (fairly restrictive) assumptions under which (in our simple model) risk markets are always redundant. These conditions are set out below in subsection 15.4.1.

The second question is more difficult to answer. The way we approach this question is to formulate a simple example in which we can see whether the critical condition, $K = 0$, is satisfied as we change the technology, for any arbitrarily specified set of utility functions. This will enable us to show that redundancy of risk markets is both necessary and sufficient for the market equilibrium to be a constrained Pareto optimum for all technologies.

The final question is the most difficult and sections 15.4 and 15.5 provide some insight into it.

15.4 Conditions for constrained Pareto efficiency

In the next subsection we provide a set of sufficient conditions and then, in subsection 15.4.2, a set of necessary conditions for the market to be a constrained Pareto optimum. Obviously, if the market equilibrium is fully Pareto optimal it must be constrained efficient, so the subsection 15.4.1 finds conditions which are sufficient for risk markets to be redundant, and which thus ensure the full optimality of the market equilibrium.

15.4.1 *Necessary and sufficient conditions for redundancy of risk markets*
Theorem 3a.

Sufficient conditions for the redundancy of risk markets are either that

(i) there is no risk,

or

(ii) producers are risk neutral and $V_{Ip} = 0$,

or

(iii) consumers have an indirect utility function of the form

$$V = -k\log p + b\phi(I), \tag{15.20}$$

which corresponds to a direct utility function defined on consumption q of the risky commodity and c of 'other goods':

$$\alpha \log q + (1-\alpha)\log c.$$

Proof.

(i) is trivial.

(ii) If $V_{Ip} = 0$, consumers' marginal utility of income, V_I, is constant in all states of nature, and if producers are risk neutral, their marginal utility is constant in all states of nature. Hence, the marginal rate of substitution between any two states of nature is unity for both producers and consumers, or ρ in equation (15.19) is unity, guaranteeing the redundancy of risk markets.

(iii) The logarithmic indirect utility function generates, by Roy's formula, demand curves which have unitary price elasticity. Hence farmers' income is constant. Hence, the marginal utility of farmers' income is the same in all states. Moreover, $V_{Ip} = 0$, so consumers' marginal utility of income is the same in all states. Hence the marginal rate of substitution between income in all states is unity and risk markets are redundant.

These conditions are, in fact, necessary as well. If risk markets are to be redundant, we require the ratio of the marginal utilities of income V_I/U_y, to be the same for all θ. As θ varies, so does Q, so this is equivalent to requiring

$$\frac{d\log U_y}{d\log Q} = \frac{d\log V_I}{d\log Q}. \tag{15.21}$$

But

$$\frac{d\log U_y}{d\log Q} = y\frac{U_{yy}}{U_y}\frac{d\log y}{d\log Q} = -R\frac{d\log pQ}{d\log Q} = -R\left(1 - \frac{1}{\epsilon}\right), \tag{15.22}$$

where again R is the coefficient of relative risk aversion of producers and ϵ is the price elasticity of demand by consumers.

Similarly, the right-hand side of equation (15.21) gives

$$\frac{d\log V_I}{d\log Q} = \frac{d\log V_I}{d\log p} \cdot \frac{d\log p}{d\log Q} \tag{15.23}$$

$$= -\frac{V_{Ip} p}{V_I} \frac{1}{\epsilon}.$$

In equation (8.13) we show that V_{Ip} can be evaluated as follows:

$$V_{pI} = -\frac{dQ}{dI}V_I - QV_{II} = \frac{V_I Q}{I}[-\eta + R^c]$$

so the right-hand side of equation (15.21) becomes

$$\frac{\alpha}{\epsilon}[\eta - R^c],$$

where η is the income elasticity of demand, R^c is the consumer's coefficient of relative risk aversion, and α is again the expenditure share on the commodity. Substituting this into (15.23) and equating to (15.22) gives the required condition

$$R(1-\epsilon) = \frac{-pV_{Ip}}{V_I} = \alpha(\eta - R^c). \qquad (15.24)$$

Equation (15.24) can also be written (if $\epsilon \neq 1$) as a condition relating producers' attitudes to risk to consumers' behavioural characteristics:

$$R = \frac{\alpha(\eta - R^c)}{1-\epsilon}. \qquad (15.24')$$

Equation (15.24) can be interpreted as a condition which *must* hold between producers' and consumers' attitudes, as measured by parameters R, R^c, η, ϵ and α if risk markets are to be redundant.

If producers are risk neutral, $R = 0$, so for (15.24) to be satisfied V_{Ip} must be zero. If (15.24) is to hold for all values of R, then ϵ must be unity *and* $V_{Ip} = 0$. But if $V_{Ip} = 0$ the indirect utility function is separable and must therefore have the special form

$$V = a(p) + b\phi(I),$$

so by Roy's identity, demand is

$$q^c = -\frac{a'}{b\phi'}.$$

If the elasticity of demand is unity, $a' = k/p$ for some constant k; hence

$$a = k \log p.$$

We have thus established (if there is risk):
Theorem 3b.

A necessary condition for risk-market redundancy with risk-neutral producers is that $V_{Ip} = 0$. If risk markets are to be redundant regardless of the risk aversion of producers, consumers must have a utility function of the form

$$V = k \log p + b\phi(I).$$

These results are important in identifying the special set of circumstances in which the market attains not only a constrained Pareto optimum, but a full Pareto optimum.

15.4.2 *Necessary conditions for constrained Pareto efficiency*

The sufficient conditions for the full Pareto efficiency of the market are, of course, very restrictive. We wish to know whether there are other conditions which will lead the market equilibrium to be constrained Pareto efficient. For particular values of the parameters, the market might happen to be constrained

Pareto efficient. But a small perturbation of any of the functions involved in the analysis — the consumer's utility function, the producer's utility function, the probability distribution of states, or the production function — might destroy the constrained efficiency of market equilibrium.

We establish here that the necessary conditions for the market equilibrium to be a constrained Pareto optimum for all technologies are exactly the same as the conditions for redundancy of risk markets. We establish this by looking at a special subset of technologies.

We assume there are two states of nature, which occur with probability π_1 and π_2 respectively ($\pi_1 + \pi_2 = 1$). Assume, moreover, that ξ does not directly affect utility; we are considering the choice of technique where the costs of alternative choices are the same. Finally, we assume $M = N = 1$. The farmer's expected utility is

$$EU \equiv u(y(q_1) + s)\pi_1 + u(y(q_2) + s)\pi_2, \qquad (15.25)$$

where

$$q_i = \text{output in state } i, \quad i = 1, 2$$

and

$$y(q_i) = p_i q_i, \text{ income of the farmer in state } i.$$

By differentiating the farmer's (expected) utility function,

$$dEU = \pi_1 \frac{\partial u_1}{\partial y_1} \frac{\partial y_1}{\partial q_1} dq_1 + \pi_2 \frac{\partial u_2}{\partial y_2} \frac{\partial y_2}{\partial q_2} dq_2 = 0$$

we obtain the farmer's *perceived* marginal rate of substitution between output in the two states (the farmer assumes prices will be unaffected by his decisions)

$$-\left.\frac{\partial q_2}{\partial q_1}\right|_{\overline{EU}} = \frac{u'_1 p_1 \pi_1}{u'_2 p_2 \pi_2} \qquad (15.26)$$

where $u'_1 = u'(y(q_1) + s)$, etc. (In this section subscripts refer to states of nature, and dashes refer to derivatives.) If there is a transformation curve, giving the maximal level of output in state 2 given the level of output in state 1,

$$q_2 = T(q_1) \qquad (15.27)$$

as shown in Fig. 15.1a, they choose the point along the transformation curve where the marginal rate of transformation equals the marginal rate of substitution.

$$\frac{u'_1 p_1 \pi_1}{u'_2 p_2 \pi_2} = -T'. \qquad (15.28)$$

However, the actual marginal rate of substitution, taking into account the effect of the changes in output on prices, is

(a)

q_2
Output in state 2

Market equilibrium

Producers' perceived indifference curve

Consumers' indifference curve

Producers' actual indifference curve

Transformation curve T

Output in state 1 q_1

(b)

q_2

Producers' indifference curve (actual and perceived)

Consumers' indifference curve

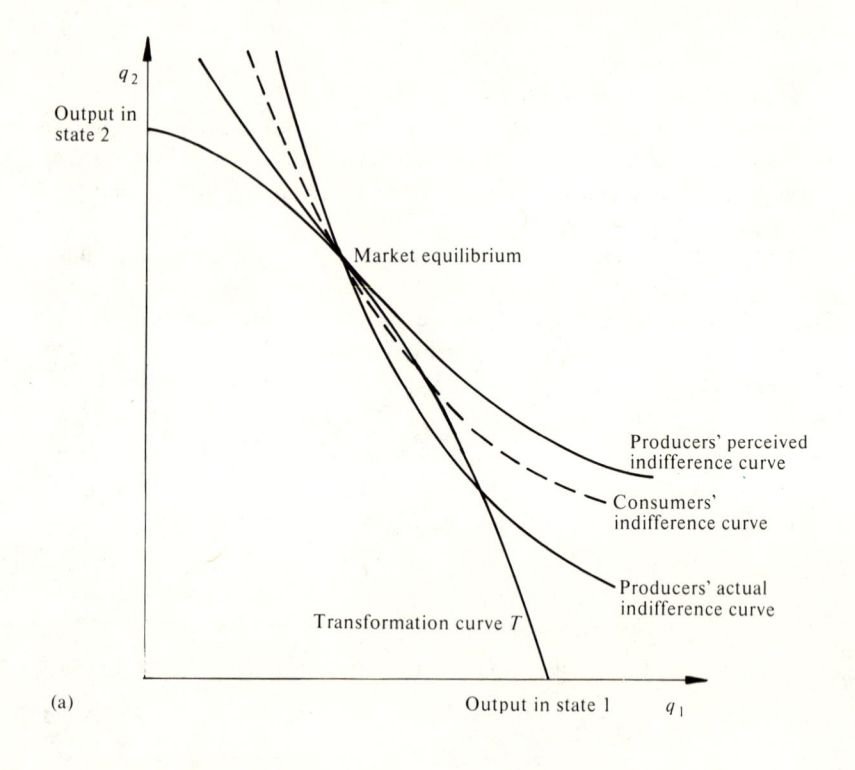

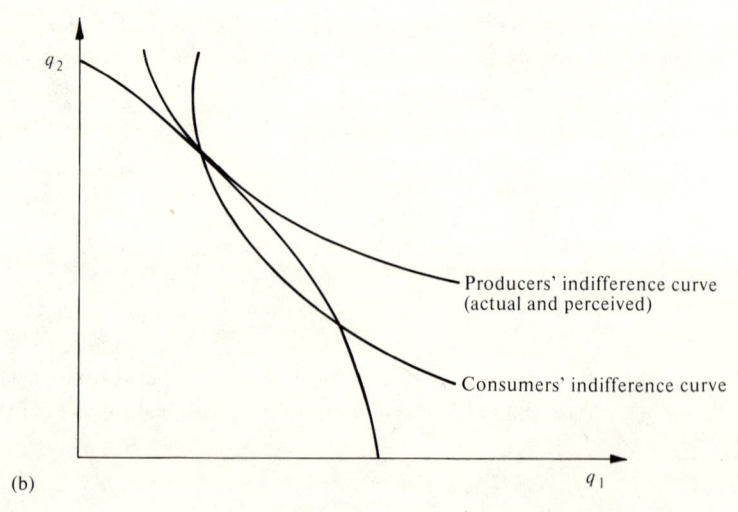

q_1

Fig. 15.1 Market equilibrium choice of technique

The Efficiency of Market Equilibrium 223

$$-\left.\frac{\partial q_2}{\partial q_1}\right|_{\overline{EU}} = \frac{u_1'y_1'\pi_1}{u_2'y_2'\pi_2} = \frac{u_1'p_1(1-1/\epsilon_1)\pi_1}{u_2'p_2(1-1/\epsilon_2)\pi_2};\qquad(15.29)$$

where (because of our normalization to $N = M = 1$, we can use q and Q interchangeably), ϵ_i is the elasticity of demand in state i;

$$\epsilon_i = -\frac{p_i dQ(p_i)}{Q(p_i)dp_i}.$$

When all the farmers change their production levels the relative prices change, which changes their incomes as shown here. If the elasticity of demand is constant (i.e. the same in both states) equations (15.28) and (15.29) are identical.

Similarly, the consumers' indifference curve in (q_1, q_2) space is

$$-\left.\frac{dq_2}{dq_1}\right|_{\overline{EV}} = \frac{\dfrac{\partial V(p_1, I)}{\partial p_1}\dfrac{dp_1}{dq_1}}{\dfrac{\partial V(p_2, I)}{\partial p_2}\dfrac{dp_2}{dq_2}} \cdot \frac{\pi_1}{\pi_2}$$

which, by Roy's identity, can be written as

$$-\left.\frac{dq_2}{dq_1}\right|_{\overline{EV}} = \frac{V_I(p_1, I)p_1\pi_1/\epsilon_1}{V_I(p_2, I)p_2\pi_2/\epsilon_2}.\qquad(15.30)$$

In Fig. 15.1, we have drawn the production possibilities schedule and depicted the point chosen by producers, as well as the consumers' indifference curve. Several possibilities emerge. In Fig. 15.1a, there exist choices of technique where (because the producers' perceived indifference curve does not coincide with his actual indifference curve) even without direct compensation a Pareto improvement is possible. On the other hand, Fig. 15.1b illustrates the possibility where consumers can be made better off — but only at the expense of making producers worse off. We then need to ask, is the gain to consumers sufficiently great that they could compensate producers? Since the indifference curves of producers and consumers are not tangent, the economy is obviously not Pareto efficient and there may be no point on the transformation curve at which both indifference curves are tangential.

As before, we are concerned with constrained efficiency, in which the government can decide the choice of techniques, that is, the point on the transformation frontier, and the lump-sum transfer to farmers, s. Again the objective is to maximize expected social welfare, as in equation (15.14), that is, to

$$\text{Maximize } W = E(V + \lambda u) = \sum_{i=1}^{2} \pi_i \{V(p_i, I-s) + \lambda u(y_i + s)\}\qquad(15.31)$$
$$s, q_1$$

224 Commodity Price Stabilization

subject to

$$y_i = p_i q_i, \quad i = 1, 2$$

and

$$q_2 = T(q_1).$$

Differentiating with respect to s again yields equation (15.16):

$$E(\lambda u' - V_I)(1 - \alpha \eta/\epsilon) = 0, \qquad (15.32)$$

where, again, α is the expenditure share on the good. In the special case where $\alpha\eta/\epsilon$ is constant, social optimality merely requires

$$\lambda E u' = E V_I$$

and the lump-sum transfers are made to bring λ, the relative social weight of consumers to producers, into equality with the ratio of expected marginal utilities. However, in the general case, the indirect distributional effects of the lump-sum transfers working through changes in prices need to be taken into account. To see if the market is a constrained Pareto optimum let the social weight be

$$\lambda \equiv \left. \frac{EV_I(1 - \alpha\eta/\epsilon)}{Eu'(1 - \alpha\eta/\epsilon)} \right|_{s=0, q_1 = q_1^m} \qquad (15.33)$$

(where q_1^m represents the market choice of technique). This choice of λ ensures that at the competitive equilibrium no redistribution is desired, so that all we are concerned with is whether the competitive equilibrium will make the constrained efficient choice of technique.

The optimum choice of technique, q_1, can be found by differentiating equation (15.31) with respect to q_1, or directly from equation (15.18) by replacing f_ξ by dq_i/dq_1, i.e. 1 in state 1 and T' in state 2, to give

$$\lambda \left(\pi_1 u_1' \frac{p_1}{\epsilon_1} + \pi_2 u_2' T' \frac{p_2}{\epsilon_2} \right) = \pi_1 V_I(p_1) \frac{p_1}{\epsilon_1} + \pi_2 V_I(p_2) T' \frac{p_2}{\epsilon_2}, \qquad (15.34)$$

suppressing the dependence of V on I. Replace λ by its value given in equation (15.33) and T' from the first-order condition of equation (15.28) to obtain as a necessary condition for constrained Pareto efficiency that

$$u_1' \left(\frac{1}{\epsilon_1} - \frac{1}{\epsilon_2} \right) = \frac{Eu'(1 - \alpha\eta/\epsilon)}{EV_I(1 - \alpha\eta/\epsilon)} \cdot V_I(p_1) \left\{ \frac{1}{\epsilon_1} - \frac{1}{\epsilon_2} \frac{u_1'/u_2'}{V_I(p_1)/V_I(p_2)} \right\}. \qquad (15.35)$$

If equation (15.35) is to be satisfied identically for *all* technologies, it must be satisfied identically for all values of q_1, q_2, and π_1. Define

$$\psi_i = u_i'(1 - \alpha_i \eta_i/\epsilon_i) \qquad (15.36a)$$

$$\chi_i = V_I(p_i, I)(1 - \alpha_i \eta_i/\epsilon_i). \qquad (15.36b)$$

Equation (15.35) can be rewritten as

$$\left(\frac{1}{\epsilon_1} - \frac{1}{\epsilon_2}\right) = \frac{E\psi}{E\chi}\left(\frac{1}{\epsilon_1}\frac{\chi_1}{\psi_1} - \frac{1}{\epsilon_2}\frac{\chi_2}{\psi_2}\right) = \frac{\pi_1\psi_1 + (1-\pi_1)\psi_2}{\pi_1\chi_1 + (1-\pi_1)\chi_2}\left(\frac{1}{\epsilon_1}\frac{\chi_1}{\psi_1} - \frac{1}{\epsilon_2}\frac{\chi_2}{\psi_2}\right), \tag{15.37}$$

which can be rearranged to give

$$\left(\frac{\chi_2}{\chi_1} - \frac{\psi_2}{\psi_1}\right)\left(\frac{1-\pi_1}{\pi_1} + \frac{\psi_1 \epsilon_1}{\psi_2 \epsilon_2}\right) = 0. \tag{15.38}$$

If this is to hold for all values of π_1, then

$$\frac{\chi_2}{\chi_1} = \frac{\psi_2}{\psi_1}, \quad \text{or} \quad \frac{u_2'}{V_I(p_2)} = \frac{u_1'}{V_I(p_1)}, \tag{15.39}$$

and the ratio of the marginal utilities is the same state by state. But this is precisely the condition we identified before as the necessary condition for risk-market redundancy (equation (15.21)).

We summarize our analysis in:

Theorem 4a.

A necessary condition for the constrained Pareto optimality of the market equilibrium for all technologies and for all attitudes towards risk by farmers is that risk markets be redundant.

Theorem 4b.

Only for those particular combinations of utility functions of farmers and consumers satisfying equation (15.24') will the economy be a constrained Pareto optimum for all technologies.

The remainder of this chapter is devoted to clarifying further the kinds of conditions under which the market equilibrium is a constrained Pareto optimum. These entail restricting the set of admissible technologies.

15.5 Restrictions on technology which ensure efficiency

The previous section established that, without restrictions on the technology, the necessary and sufficient conditions for the efficiency of the market equilibrium were precisely the conditions for the redundancy of risk markets. If we impose conditions on the set of technologies, then we can obtain constrained efficiency under conditions which are weaker, but only slightly so.

15.5.1 *Multiplicative risk*

In this and the next subsection, we consider two special cases of the technology. In the first case the production function exhibits multiplicative risk

$$f(\theta, \xi) = g(\theta)h(\xi). \tag{15.40}$$

In Diamond's (1967) study of the stock-market, the assumption of multiplicative risk played a critical role. When there is multiplicative risk, the ratio of outputs in different states is fixed; it is as if the firm produced a particular composite commodity. If the firm is a price-taker in that particular composite commodity, then, in the single commodity world, perhaps not surprisingly, the market equilibrium is a constrained Pareto optimum. It was difficult, within the single commodity world, to assess precisely the role played by the assumption of multiplicative risk. With multiplicative risk, a firm can act as a price-taker; it can assume its market value is simply proportional to its scale. (Whether it is reasonable for it to assume this is, of course, another matter.) But in the absence of multiplicative risk, a change in scale changes the ratio of outputs in different states. It is not clear what should be meant by price-taking competitive behaviour. How is the individual (or firm) to evaluate the consequences of changing the scale of operation? Thus, the Diamond analysis was confined to a very narrow set of choices, only those in which the ratio of outputs in different states is fixed.

In our model, individuals take as given the prices in each state of nature, but when the aggregate level of input in one crop changes, it will change the price distribution, and hence will have an effect on the nature of the risks faced by any one firm. There is thus a difference between private multiplicative risk (which we may still have) and social risk (which in our model is no longer multiplicative) in contrast to the single commodity model, where these are identical. Thus, only in special cases will the market with multiplicative risk still be a constrained Pareto optimum. In particular, we have:

Theorem 6.

Sufficient conditions for the competitive equilibrium to be a constrained Pareto optimum are that

(i) producers face multiplicative risk, and

(ii) consumers' preferences can be represented by the indirect utility function

$$V = \phi(I(a + bp)^{-1/b}) \qquad (15.41)$$

where ϕ is any monotonically increasing function.

Proof.

The demand functions implied by equation (15.41) are

$$q = \frac{I}{a + bp},$$

whence

$$1 - \alpha \eta / \epsilon = 1 - 1/b, \text{ constant.}$$

Equation (15.16) can therefore be written

$$\lambda E U_y = E V_I. \qquad (15.42)$$

Multiplicative risk and the demand function implies that

$$\frac{p f_\xi}{\epsilon} = \frac{I}{b} \frac{h_\xi}{h}, \text{ independent of } \theta$$

and so equation (15.42) implies that $K = 0$ in equation (15.18) and the competitive equilibrium is constrained efficient.

Not only is this a sufficient condition, but it is also necessary in the sense described in the next two theorems.

Theorem 7.

If individuals have homothetic indifference maps and firms have multiplicative risk, then, if for all specifications of the probability distribution of returns and producers' utility functions the market equilibrium is to be a constrained Pareto optimum, the consumers' utility function must be of the form of equation (15.41).

Theorem 8.

If consumers' utility function is of the form of equation (15.41) (which includes the constant demand elasticity as a special case), then, a necessary condition for constrained efficiency is that either risk markets be (locally) redundant or that there be multiplicative risk.

15.5.2 *Costless choice of techniques*

If the farmer's utility is unaffected by the choice of technique, then in competitive equilibrium equation (15.5) reduces to

$$EU_y p f_\xi = 0. \tag{15.43}$$

If, in addition, the elasticity of demand is constant, then equation (15.18) can be written

$$K(\xi) = \frac{1}{\epsilon} E(\lambda U_y p f_\xi - V_I p f_\xi) = -\frac{1}{\epsilon} E\left(\frac{V_I}{U_y} \cdot U_y p f_\xi\right).$$

Using equation (15.43)

$$-\epsilon K(\xi) = E\left(\frac{V_I}{U_y} - E\frac{V_I}{U_y}\right)(U_y p f_\xi - E U_y p f_\xi), \tag{15.44}$$

which is to say that the covariance between the ratio of the marginal utilities of income and $U_y p f_\xi$ must be zero. This will be true for all distributions if and only if there is risk market redundancy. For small variances, the right-hand side of equation (15.44) can be approximated by a Taylor series expansion:

$$E \frac{d}{d\theta}\left(\frac{V_I}{U_y}\right) \cdot \frac{d}{d\theta}(U_y p f_\xi)(\theta - 1)^2$$

$$= \frac{d}{d\theta}\left(\frac{V_I}{U_y}\right)\left\{(1-R)(1 - 1/\epsilon)\frac{f_\theta}{f} + \frac{f}{f_\xi}\frac{d}{d\theta}\left(\frac{f_\xi}{f}\right)\right\} U_y p f_\xi \sigma^2.$$

Since the approximation improves the smaller are the terms, the expression is zero if the term in braces is zero. This result is summarized in:

Theorem 9.

Sufficient conditions for competitive equilibrium to be constrained efficient are

either that risk markets are redundant;
or (i) costless choice of technique,

$$U_\xi = 0$$

and (ii) multiplicative risk,

$$\frac{d}{d\theta}(f_\xi/f) = 0$$

and (iii) constant elasticity of demand,
and (iv) *either* $R = 1$, *or* $\epsilon = 1$.

These are also necessary conditions if the competitive equilibrium is to be constrained efficient for all probability distributions of θ.

It may be helpful to see what goes wrong in the case where $V_{Ip} = 0$, i.e. consumers' marginal utility is the same in all states, but price elasticities are not unitary.

Then $K(\xi) = 0$ if and only if

$$EV_I pf_\xi = V_I \cdot Epf_\xi = 0, \tag{15.45}$$

i.e. farmers maximize the value of their output. But farmers will do this if and only if they are risk neutral or there is no risk, i.e. consumers have unitary price elasticity.

15.6 The magnitude of the distortions

In previous sections we have established conditions required for the market equilibrium to be a constrained Pareto optimum. We would like to be able to assess the magnitude and direction by which the optimal value of ξ differs from the market equilibrium value. To do this, rewrite the first-order condition for constrained Pareto optimality, equation (15.17)

$$-E(\lambda U_y - V_I)\frac{p}{\epsilon}f_\xi + \lambda E(U_y pf_\xi + U_\xi) = 0$$

or, defining

$$X(\xi) = U_y pf_\xi + U_\xi$$

the optimal choice of ξ, ξ^o, must satisfy

$$EX(\xi^o) = \frac{1}{\lambda}K(\xi^o). \tag{15.46}$$

The left-hand side of equation (15.46) can be expanded about the market choice of technique, ξ^m, to find the direction and magnitude of the bias away from the constrained efficient allocation:

$$\xi^o - \xi^m \approx \frac{K(\xi^m)}{\lambda EX'(\xi^m)}. \tag{15.47}$$

The Efficiency of Market Equilibrium   229

In order to interpret this result, it is necessary to decide how best to parameterize the choice of technique, ξ. One natural method is to let ξ measure the standard deviation (or perhaps the CV) of output, in which case, equation (15.47) will measure the extent to which the farmers choose insufficiently risky production, and the right-hand side will typically depend on the degree of risk aversion and the extent to which mean output increases as more risky techniques are employed. Rather than derive various measures of the bias, it might be more useful to illustrate the method for the two-state example of subsection 15.4.2. Moreover, the fundamental issue is how large is the loss of welfare resulting from the market failing to achieve a constrained Pareto optimum relative to the likely welfare gains to be derived from specific policy intervention (such as price stabilization).

Consider the special case in which there are equally probably states of the world, and the production trade-off between output in the two states of the world is linear:

$$q_2 = T(q_1) = a - bq_1, \quad b > 1. \tag{15.48}$$

Suppose also that the choice of technique does not affect farmers' welfare ($U_\xi = 0$) and that consumers have an indirect utility of the form

$$V(p, I) = \frac{(p^{-\alpha} I)^{1-R^c}}{1 - R^c} \tag{15.49}$$

so that price and income elasticities are unity and their coefficient of relative risk aversion is R^c. Suppose, finally, that the distribution of income is satisfactory at the competitive equilibrium (i.e. we are only interested in efficiency).

In this simple model, farmers experience no risk and their welfare is independent of the state of world and the level of output, since (with equal numbers of consumers and farmers)

$$y_i = p_i q_i = \alpha I, \quad i = 1, 2.$$

The competitive equilibrium choice of q_1, q_2 is given by equation (15.28):

$$-T' = \frac{u'_1 p_1 \pi_1}{u'_2 p_2 \pi_2} = \frac{p_1}{p_2} = \frac{q_2}{q_1},$$

since $\pi_1 = \pi_2 = \frac{1}{2}$, $u'_1 = u'_2$, and $p_1 q_1 = p_2 q_2$. Since from equation (15.48), $T' = -b$, this can be solved to give

$$q_1^m = \frac{a}{2b}, \quad q_2^m = \frac{a}{2}, \quad \bar{q}^m = \frac{a(1+b)}{4b}, \quad \sigma^m = \frac{b-1}{b+1}, \tag{15.50}$$

where $\bar{q}^m$, σ^m are respectively mean output and its coefficient of variation at the market equilibrium. This allows the coefficients a and b to be interpreted, for

$$a = 2\bar{q}^m(1 + \sigma^m), \quad b = \frac{1 + \sigma^m}{1 - \sigma^m}.$$

230   Commodity Price Stabilization

The constrained efficient solution is given by equation (15.30), where $\epsilon_i = 1$:

$$-T' = \frac{V_I(p_1)p_1}{V_I(p_2)p_2} = \left(\frac{p_1}{p_2}\right)^{1-\alpha(1-R^c)} = \left(\frac{q_2}{q_1}\right)^{1-\gamma} = b, \qquad (15.51)$$

where $\gamma = \alpha(1 - R^c)$. Hence if $\nu = 1/(1 - \gamma)$, the optimal allocation is

$$q_1^o = \frac{a}{b + b^\nu}, \quad q_2^o = \frac{ab^\nu}{b + b^\nu}, \quad \bar{q}_2^o = \frac{a(1 + b^\nu)}{2(b + b^\nu)}, \quad o^o = \frac{b^\nu - 1}{b^\nu + 1}.$$

If $R^c > 1$, $\gamma < 0$, and the optimal choice of technique involves less risk than the market choice, while if consumers are not very risk averse ($R^c < 1$) the market supplies too little risk. The optimum and competitive equilibria are shown in Fig. 15.2 for the case $R^c < 1$.

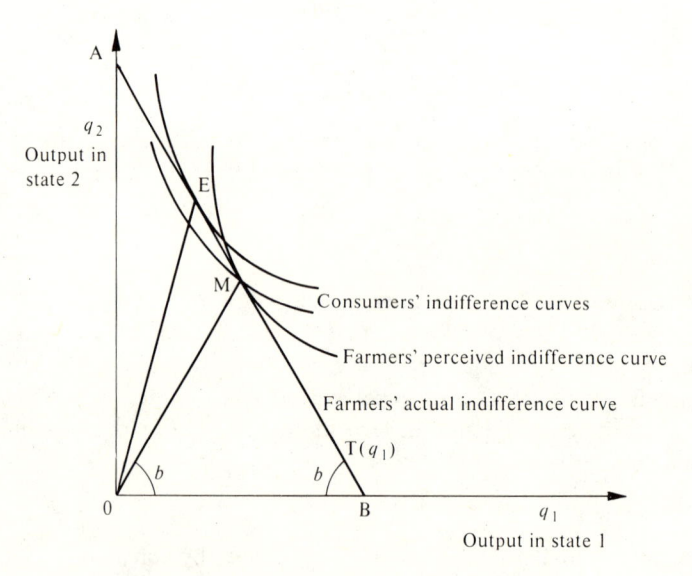

Fig. 15.2 The difference between market and efficient choice of technique

Since farmers enjoy the same income for any output (unit price elasticity) their welfare is constant along the transformation frontier AB. Consumers would, however, rather be at E than M, and the inefficiency of competitive equilibrium can be measured by the lump-sum tax on consumers' income which, if paid at E would make them no better off than at M. The benefit of moving from M to E (equal to this lump sum) can be found by expanding consumers' welfare in a Taylor series, and, as a fraction of consumer expenditure on the commodity is approximately

$$B \simeq \frac{\Delta \bar{q}}{\bar{q}} - \frac{(1-\gamma)}{2}\Delta\sigma^2, \quad \Delta\bar{q} \equiv E q^o - E q^m$$

$$\Delta\sigma^2 = (\sigma^o)^2 - (\sigma^m)^2.$$

These terms can also be evaluated by Taylor series expansions, assuming b is near 1, so σ is small:

$$\frac{\Delta \bar{q}}{\bar{q}} \simeq \frac{\gamma}{1-\gamma}\sigma^2; \quad \Delta\sigma^2 \simeq \left\{\left(\frac{1}{1-\gamma}\right)^2 - 1\right\}\sigma^2 \qquad (15.53)$$

where σ is the competitive CV of output. Altogether, the proportional benefit from eliminating inefficiency is approximately

$$B \approx \frac{\gamma^2}{2(1-\gamma)}\sigma^2. \qquad (15.54)$$

Although this expression is of the same order of σ as the benefits of price stabilization, it should be remembered that $\gamma = \alpha(1 - R_c)$ is small, since the expenditure share, α, for most commodities is very small. It may be objected that had the model been different so that all the benefits of moving to the constrained optimum accrued to producers, then the benefits would probably have been greater, but this argument is not convincing. The assumption that the government can engage in lump-sum redistributions (i.e. that we are only concerned with efficiency) makes the two benefits comparable. Moreover, in general, we would expect the transformation possibilities represented by T to exhibit diminishing returns, whereas we have assumed linearity. This will further depress the benefits of moving to the optimum.

15.7 Optimal corrective tax policy

The allocation described in subsection 15.3.2 could be attained if the government could directly control ξ, the choice of technique. One interpretation of our finding is that the fundamental decentralization theorem does not hold in the absence of a complete set of risk markets, for it is not possible to achieve the constrained efficient allocation on competitive markets using only lump-sum taxes. Since direct control is evidently impractical, it is necessary to enquire whether there are tax policies which allow the constrained optimum to be decentralized. This in turn will depend on the range of taxes which it is feasible to impose. This question of feasibility raises subtle questions.

For example, if the government levies an *ad valorem* tax on producers, its tax revenue will depend on the state of the world, and we must ask whether its budget is to be balanced in *each* state of the world or only on average. In the former case, the lump-sum transfer will vary with the state of the world, while in the latter case purchasing power will vary. It can, however, be shown that regardless of the restrictions on feasible tax policies it is in general possible to make Pareto improvements.

Let us consider the simplest case in which the government budget must balance state by state, and taxes can either be at constant *ad valorem* rates or lump sum. Then the problem of supporting the constrained optimum can be written

232 Commodity Price Stabilization

$$\underset{s,\,\tau}{\text{Max}}\; EV\left(p, I - \frac{sN}{M}\right) + \lambda EU\{p(1-\tau)f + L + s, \xi\}, \quad L = \tau p f(\xi^*).$$

That this can be done is demonstrated in:
Theorem 10.

A constant *ad valorem* tax rate (the proceeds of which are distributed as lump-sum payments to producers) of

$$\tau^* = \frac{E(\lambda U_y - V_I)pf_\xi/\epsilon}{\lambda EU_y pf_\xi} \tag{15.55}$$

supports the constrained Pareto optimum.
Proof.

Farmers will set

$$EU_y p(1 - \tau^*)f_\xi + EU_\xi = 0. \tag{15.56}$$

Substituting for the tax rate τ^*, this implies

$$E(U_y pf_\xi + U_\xi) - \frac{1}{\lambda} E(\lambda U_y - V_I)pf_\xi/\epsilon = 0$$

which is the condition for constrained Pareto optimality of equation (15.17).

15.7.1 Conclusions on market efficiency with identical producers

The previous subsections have shown just how restrictive are the conditions required for the competitive equilibrium to be a constrained Pareto optimum. Unless consumers have a logarithmic direct utility function (corresponding to equation (15.20), and with unit price, income, and marginal utility elasticities) then except for some special constellations of farmers' utility functions, technology, or the distribution of θ, the market will be (constrained) inefficient. The next section shows that even these special conditions are insufficient to ensure efficiency if farmers do not have perfectly correlated returns.

15.8 Imperfectly correlated output risk

We shall now show that if farmers do not have perfectly correlated outputs, then, even under the stringent conditions in which the market allocation is a constrained Pareto optimum with perfect correlation, the market allocation is unlikely to be a constrained Pareto optimum. We prove that,

Theorem 11a.

A sufficient condition for constrained Pareto optimality with imperfectly correlated returns is the redundancy of risk markets.

Theorem 11b.

Necessary and sufficient conditions for redundancy of risk markets for all technologies are that all farmers be risk neutral and $V_{Ip} = 0$.

Theorem 11c.

If the economy is to be a constrained Pareto optimum for all technologies all farmers must be risk neutral and $V_{Ip} = 0$.

The first theorem is obvious: if risk markets are redundant, the economy in fact attains a first best optimum. Sufficiency in the second theorem is also fairly trivial. If the marginal rates of substitution between any two states are the same for all individuals, clearly risk markets will be redundant; and they will be the same if the marginal utility of income of all individuals is constant. But if all farmers are risk neutral, and $V_{Ip} = 0$, clearly, the marginal utility of all producers and all consumers is constant.

Necessity is only slightly more difficult to establish. If risk markets are to be redundant, the marginal rates of substitution between income in different states of nature must be the same for all farmers, i.e. letting $U^j(y^j)$ represent the utility of the jth farmer as a function of his income y^j, we require that U_y^j/U_y^k be constant. Differentiating logarithmically with respect to aggregate output, Q, we obtain

$$R^j \left(\frac{d \log q^j}{d \log Q} - \frac{1}{\epsilon} \right) = R^k \left(\frac{d \log q^k}{d \log Q} - \frac{1}{\epsilon} \right) \tag{15.57}$$

where q^j is the output of the jth farmer, R^j is his relative risk aversion, and $d \log q^j / d \log Q$ measures the correlation between the jth farmer's output and aggregate output. In the previous discussion, this was assumed to be unity. However, in the more general case with imperfect correlation this can take on any value; hence, if equation (15.57) is to hold for all technologies, clearly $R^j = R^k = 0$, all farmers must be risk neutral. Moreover, if their marginal rate of substitution between income in different states is unity, so must the consumer's be, if risk markets are to be redundant. But this implies $V_{Ip} = 0$.

Theorem 11c is the most difficult to prove. To do this we first state a characterization theorem for the constrained Pareto optimality of markets with many producers which is the analogue to Theorem 1. (The proof is exactly parallel to that of Theorem 1.)

Theorem 12.

A necessary condition for the rational expectations equilibrium to be a constrained Pareto optimum is that

$$K^i(\xi^i) \equiv E \left(\sum_k \lambda^k \beta^k U_y^k - V_I \right) \frac{p}{\epsilon} f_\xi^i = 0, \quad \text{all } i \tag{15.58}$$

where

$f^i(\theta, \xi^i) = i$th farmer's production function,

λ^k = Lagrange multiplier associated with kth farmer's utility,

$\beta^k = \dfrac{q^k}{Q}$, share of kth farmer's output in aggregate output, $\left(\sum_k \beta^k = 1 \right)$.

Defining ρ^k as in equation (15.19), we can rewrite equation (15.58) as

$$K^i(\xi^i) = E\left(1 - \sum_k \rho^k \beta^k\right)\frac{p}{\epsilon} V_I f_\xi^i = 0. \qquad (15.59)$$

This says that a necessary condition for the constrained Pareto optimality of the market is that a particular weighted average of marginal rates of substitution of producers and consumers be the same.

Since, from Theorem 3b, we already know that if the market is to be a constrained Pareto optimum for all perfectly correlated technologies, either farmers must be risk neutral and $V_{Ip} = 0$ or consumers must have logarithmic utility functions, to establish Theorem 11c all we need to do is to show that, for the logarithmic utility function, if returns are not perfectly correlated, for some technologies equation (15.59) is not satisfied. Consider the case where there are two symmetric groups of farmers with N farmers of each type and N consumers; the production functions of the two groups are identical except for the effect of risk, which we assume is multiplicative and symmetrically distributed:

$$Q^i = Nf^i(\theta^i, \xi^i) = N\theta^i h(\xi^i), \qquad i = j, k. \qquad (15.60)$$

Given this symmetry in production, it is natural to assume symmetry in social weight, $\lambda^j = \lambda^k = \lambda$. The optimal lump-sum subsidy to the ith producer is derived as in subsection 15.3.2. Since consumers have utility functions:

$$V(p, I) = \log I - \alpha \log p,$$

V_I is constant, and income and price elasticities are unity, $\epsilon = \eta = 1$. The counterpart to equation (15.16) is therefore

$$E(\lambda U_y^i - V_I) + \alpha E(V_I - \lambda \beta^j U_y^j - \lambda \beta^k U_y^k) = 0, \qquad i = j, k \qquad (15.61)$$

which, because of our symmetry assumptions, can be simplified to

$$V_I = \lambda E\left(\frac{1 - 2\alpha\beta^i}{1 - \alpha}\right) U_y^i \qquad i = j, k, \qquad (15.62)$$

since V_I is constant for the logarithmic utility function.

From equation (15.60), since $\bar{Q}^i = Nh(\xi^i) = \frac{1}{2}\bar{Q}$,

$$f_\xi^i = \frac{Q^i}{N}\frac{h'(\xi^i)}{h(\xi^i)} = 2\beta^i h'(\xi^i) \cdot \frac{Q}{\bar{Q}}. \qquad (15.63)$$

Substitute this in equation (15.58), which, together with the fact that for the logarithmic utility function pQ/ϵ is constant, gives

$$V_I E\beta^i = \lambda E(\beta^j U_y^j + \beta^k U_y^k)\beta^i, \qquad i = j, k. \qquad (15.64)$$

By symmetry

$$E(\beta^j)^2 U_y^j = E(\beta^k)^2 U_y^k = E(1 - \beta^j)^2 U_y^k$$

$$E\beta^j = \tfrac{1}{2},$$

so equation (15.64) can be written

$$\tfrac{1}{2}V_I = \lambda E\{(\beta^j)^2 U^j_y - (1-\beta^j)^2 U^k_y + \beta^k U^k_y\} = \lambda E\beta^j U^j_y. \qquad (15.65)$$

If β^j is constant, then equation (15.62) implies (15.64) and efficiency is ensured, but β^j will only be constant if the outputs of the two groups of farmers are perfectly positively correlated, in which case the example collapses into the earlier case of a single group of farmers. If β is not constant, then equations (15.62) and (15.65) together require

$$E(\beta^i - \tfrac{1}{2})U^i_y = 0.$$

But β^i and y^i are positively correlated (unless β^i is constant), so, unless $U^i_{yy} = 0$ (farmers are risk neutral)

$$E(\beta^i - \tfrac{1}{2})U^i_y < 0.$$

It is easily checked that given the form of the indirect utility function total welfare is concave in the control variable, which completes the proof of Theorem 11c.

15.9 Conclusions

This chapter has shown that even when individuals have rational expectations — they have fully absorbed all the information which is available on the market and they use it efficiently in making their production decisions — the market equilibrium is, in general, not even constrained Pareto efficient. Specific biases have been identified in the context of some simple models, but in more general situations the exact nature of the inefficiency may be hard to ascertain. The force of our argument is that there is no presumption that market equilibria are efficient; indeed, there is a strong presumption that the market equilibrium is not a constrained Pareto optimum.

In a sense, these results should not be surprising: when there is not a complete set of markets, farmers will not have the right prices to use in making their production decisions. We showed, in the diagrammatic expositon of sub-section 15.4.2, how, in making their decisions, farmers paid attention only to their own marginal rates of substitution across states of nature. In general, these will differ from those of consumers because there is no market to bring them into equality, and hence the market allocation will not be Pareto efficient.

There is another way of looking at these results which may prove instructive. In a world of complete markets, insurance markets allocate risk and goods markets allocate goods, but in the absence of insurance markets, the remaining goods markets have to serve both functions. For example, if the source of the variability lies on the supply side, and if demand is not too inelastic, the negative correlation between price and output means that the output market transfers some of the risk facing producers to consumers, and producers' income variability will be less than their output variability. In a rational expectations equilibrium each farmer correctly forecasts the distribution of prices and chooses the level and riskiness of output to maximize his expected utility. Together, these output decisions generate a distribution of total supply which in turn generates the price distribution. No one farmer can influence the price distribution, but each one is affected by it, and, collectively, their actions reproduce it. The price distribution is therefore a public good, or collective consumption good, and its form affects the level and distribution of income risk. However, we already know that the competitive market will in general fail to induce the optimum level of supply of public goods, so it should come as no surprise that the output market does not in general induce the optimum level of income risk.

If an omniscient planner were to decide on the choice of technique he would take account of the effect of supply on the price distribution and hence on the distribution of risk. Insurance markets in this context transform a public good (the whole price distribution) into a set of private goods (one price for output in each state of the world.) Notice that the one-commodity world popular in early risk analysis is very special, because income and output risk are the same, and there is no public good element of a collectively produced price distribution.

There were basically two cases where the market allocation was efficient. In the first, consumers had unitary price elasticity and all farmers were identical. This meant that farmers faced no income risk. They thus maximize their expected income. This coincides with what consumers would like farmers to maximize, since price is proportional to the marginal utility of consumption of the given commodity.

In the second case, farmers are risk neutral and again maximize expected income. As before, this would coincide with consumers' objectives if price were proportional to the marginal utility of consumption of the commodity. However, this time the marginal utility to consumers of increasing output and hence consumption, Q, in some state of nature is

$$U_Q = pV_I$$

and this is proportional to price p if V_I does not vary with p, i.e. $V_{Ip} = 0$, so that consumers are price risk neutral.

When there is more than one type of farmer, i.e. when the output of different farms is not perfectly correlated, these simple relationships between output and income which we have assumed above will not prevail. Even with unitary price elasticity, farmers will still face income risk, and hence will not maximize the value of their output, so that even if consumers' marginal utility of consumption were proportional to price, as with the logarithmic utility function, consumers' interests will not be maximized by farmers. The only general condition which ensures optimality is that consumers are price risk neutral and farmers are income risk neutral.

Some readers have found the following alternative interpretation of the inefficiency of the market allocation instructive. Except under unusual conditions (described in the text), the absence of a full set of risk markets implies that the marginal rate of substitution between income in different states of nature differs between consumers and producers. Consider a production decision which increases output in one state and decreases it in another. The market allocation is made, as we have emphasized, with producers assuming the price distribution is given. Now, by increasing output in one state and decreasing it in a second, the price will decrease in one state and increase in the other; if the elasticity of demand is less than unity, producers will be worse off in the first, better off in the second, while consumers will be better off in the first, worse off in the second. It is clear that such a marginal change can reduce the difference between consumers' and producers' marginal rates of substitution between the two states; thus, this production decision can serve as a partial substitute for the risk market which is absent.

For production decisions which entail, say, decreasing the level of output of the crop in all states of nature (as with the multiplicative production function) similar arguments hold. If the elasticity of demand is less than unity, producers will have a higher income in all states of nature, but a higher level of effort. The increase in income will (if the elasticity of demand is small enough) more than compensate for the increase in effort. The decrease in output will generate an increase in price which will make consumers worse off in every state of nature, but the marginal rate of substitution between different states of nature will change, and, in particular, so will the 'average' difference between the marginal rate of substitution of consumers and producers. Again, the production decision is serving as a partial substitute for the absent risk markets.

The important point is that it is only in very special circumstances that the market allocation will attain even the weak sense of optimality implicit in our notion of constrained Pareto efficiency. In the absence of these circumstances, there exists some tax policy which would generate a Pareto improvement over existing market allocations. The difficulty, however, is that when different farmers face different distributions of output, each would have to be faced with a different tax, and that the tax would depend sensitively on the specific form of production and utility functions. Although the competitive market fails the minimal test of efficiency, we are pessimistic about the ability of public policy to improve matters, since the required intervention appears to depend on more accurate information than that currently available.

Chapter 16

Information and Market Equilibrium

16.1 Introduction

In Chapter 12 we noted that there were three ways in which farmers could respond to risks: (a) they could attempt to share the risk with others; (b) they could attempt to alter the risk; or (c) they could attempt to acquire information which reduced the risk.

In this chapter we shall briefly discuss the last of these three methods. It is important for the measurement of the returns to price stabilization for three reasons. First, as we remarked earlier, there is a widespread belief that competitive markets will be efficient and in particular will provide the appropriate amount of commodity storage. If this view were correct, then there would be a prima facie case against governmental price stabilization schemes, which would at best merely displace the required storage activity from the private to the public sector. Chapter 15 shows that in the absence of a complete set of risk markets there was no longer a presumption that the market would be efficient. We have already remarked in section 11.4 that there are reasons to suppose that a competitive market is not efficient either in the amount or kind of information collected or in its dissemination. As a result of this additional source of inefficiency, the market will not necessarily supply the efficient amount of stabilization. If the private sector is inefficient in the collection and dissemination of information, then it can be argued that the government ought to provide information directly or provide incentives for the private sector to collect and disseminate information, and/or it ought to take actions which reduce the need for information, e.g. by reducing the variability in price.

Second, even if we were only interested in *describing* the effects of a commodity price stabilization programme without making any welfare judgements, we would need to take some account of the effect of the programme on the acquisition of information, and the effect of this on the supply behaviour of farmers.

Third, even were the markets efficient in the incentives provided for obtaining and disseminating information, the welfare analysis of a commodity price stabilization programme would require an analysis of the risks actually borne by farmers; and these risks in turn depend critically on the information available to the individual.

Throughout this chapter, our analysis is qualitative; we do not attempt to quantify the magnitude of the various information effects. The arguments we present, however, do suggest to us that the market may provide insufficient stabilization, so that the social gain from further stabilization beyond the level provided by the private market might well exceed the private gains.

This chapter is divided into three parts. In the next section, we return to the discussion of section 11.4 concerning the mechanisms by which farmers obtain information, focusing on the role of futures markets in conveying information. In section 16.3, we discuss the implications of our analysis of the futures market for the efficiency of the economy. In section 16.4, we attempt to draw together the results of Chapter 11 and the first two sections of this chapter in assessing the implications of our analysis for commodity price stabilization.

16.2* Futures markets

In Chapter 11 we discussed a variety of mechanisms by which individuals acquired information about the prices which were likely to prevail when they came to sell their output. In particular, we noted that although economists frequently assume that the farmers base expectations of future prices on past prices, the rationale for doing this was somewhat questionable (if the exogenous shocks, which gave rise to variability, were in fact uncorrelated over time).

Past prices are, of course, not the only prices which may convey information about the price which will prevail at harvest time: prices on futures markets may also convey information. This informational role is quite distinct from the risk-sharing role of futures markets discussed in Chapter 13.

Why (and in what circumstances) does the price on the futures market convey information? To examine this, let us begin with a simple example: assume there is a large group of speculators who have *perfect*·information about the demand function which will prevail next period. (The demand for some crop may depend on the price of some other crop, and these speculators have been able to obtain information about the price of the other crop.) Assume supply is non-stochastic. Then the speculators will know precisely the spot price which will prevail at harvest time. Thus, the only possible equilibrium price in the futures market is that spot price. The futures market price thus conveys the information of the speculators perfectly to the uninformed farmers.

The ability of the futures market to convey information is actually greater than we have just suggested. For suppose that each speculator has some information about demand, but demand is still not known perfectly. It is still the case that futures price will convey all the information from the informed speculators to the uninformed farmers; for the futures price will move monotonically with the information received.

For example, if each speculator specializes in collecting information about the demand of one group of consumers (in a particular industry, or region) and if his information is useful (that is, it modifies his evaluation of demand given the publicly available information, including the futures price), then he will trade in the futures market until the price has moved in the direction indicated by his special information. In these circumstances if supply is non-stochastic and with the usual linearity assumptions of Chapter 13, it can be shown that farmers can (with rational expectations) infer perfectly the information available to the informed speculators (see Bray, 1979).

There is another, equally important function which the futures market may perform: it may aggregate the information possessed by different farmers. Suppose that each farmer only knows the size of his own crop (perhaps imperfectly). This information will affect the farmers' demands for futures (as described in Chapter 13) and the market equilibrium futures price will clearly be a function of the information of each of the farmers. In some sense, then, the futures market aggregates the information.

There are two related issues concerning the behaviour of such markets:

(i) Does the market convey *all* the information from those who have it, the informed, to the uninformed? Is the market informationally efficient?

Though there has been considerable discussion concerning this question, the answer should be obvious: since the 'dimensionality' of information is far greater than the dimensionality of the price system, it is impossible for prices to convey *all* the information. Heuristically, by creating more markets, more information might be conveyed, but given the limited number of markets actually in existence, it is apparent that prices cannot convey all available information. One can, of course, construct simple models in which there is only a single piece of information (e.g. the mean return on a security); then the price could convey *all* the information, if there were no other disturbance to the market (e.g. variations in supply). But these models are clearly very special.

(ii) Even if the market does not convey all the information, it might be able to convey certain critical information, e.g. by aggregating the information possessed by different farmers, it might be able to convey information about the aggregate output.

Let us consider a special model due to Grossman and Stiglitz (1976) in which this aggregation is perfect. Suppose that a large number of separate farmers can each estimate the size of his own crop, q_i, before the harvest, but do not know the size of the total harvest, Q, and hence cannot deduce the market clearing price, p. Suppose that output depends on the weather, θ, and special local conditions, ϵ_i, with

$$q_i = \bar{q}_i(\tilde{\theta} + \tilde{\epsilon}_i), \tag{16.1}$$

where (ϵ_i, ϵ_j) are uncorrelated, and θ, ϵ, are independent normal random variables $N(1, \sigma^2)$, $N(0, \gamma^2)$. Since q_i and θ are correlated normal random variables, q_i and Q will be jointly normally distributed, and the conditional distribution of Q given q_i is normally distributed with mean

$$E(Q|q_i) = \bar{Q} + \frac{\text{Cov}(Q, q_i)}{\text{Var } q_i}(q_i - \bar{q}_i) \equiv \alpha_i + \beta_i q_i/\bar{q}_i \tag{16.2}$$

and variance

$$\text{Var}(Q|q_i) = \text{Var } Q - \frac{\text{Cov}^2(Q, q_i)}{\text{Var } q_i} \equiv V_i^2 \tag{16.3}$$

where

$$\alpha_i = \bar{Q}\left(1 - \frac{\bar{q}_i}{\bar{Q}} \frac{\gamma^2}{\sigma^2 + \gamma^2}\right)$$

$$\beta_i = \bar{Q} \frac{\sigma^2 + (\bar{q}_i/\bar{Q})\gamma^2}{\sigma^2 + \gamma^2}$$

$$V_i^2 = \text{Var } Q - \bar{Q}^2 \frac{\{\sigma^2 + (\bar{q}_i/\bar{Q})\gamma^2\}^2}{\sigma^2 + \gamma^2}.$$

(For the derivation of these formulae see Appendix to Chapter 13.)

If there are a large number of individually small farmers, then $\bar{q}_i/\bar{Q}$ will be negligible and can be ignored, so that α_i, β_i, and V_i^2 will be the same for all farmers. If in addition the demand schedule after the harvest is linear

$$p = a - bQ, \tag{16.4}$$

then the conditional distribution of the post-harvest price p given the farmer's observation on his own output, q_i, is also normal:

$$E(p|q_i) = a - b(\alpha + \beta q_i/\bar{q}_i) \tag{16.5}$$

$$\text{Var}(p|q_i) = b^2 V_i^2 \cong \frac{b^2\sigma^2\gamma^2\bar{Q}^2}{\sigma^2 + \gamma^2} < \text{Var } p. \tag{16.6}$$

Although the farmer's knowledge of q_i reduces the variance of price and improves his estimate of its mean, the post-harvest price is still risky. Since farmers differ in their expectations there is an incentive to set up a futures market. If farmers have constant absolute risk aversion A_i, then the model of Chapter 13 can be used to derive the size of the forward sale, z_i, as a function of the futures price, p^f:

$$z_i = q_i - \frac{E(p|q_i) - p^f}{A_i \text{Var}(p|q_i)}. \tag{16.7}$$

Equilibrium in the futures market requires the net forward trade to be zero, or

$$0 = Q - \sum_i \left\{\frac{a - b\alpha - b\beta(q_i/\bar{q}_i) - p^f}{A_i b^2 V^2}\right\}. \tag{16.8}$$

If $A_i\bar{q}_i$ is the same for all farmers and equal to $A\bar{q}$ (or, equivalently, if risk is additive and risk aversion is the same for all farmers), then

$$Q\left(1 + \frac{\beta}{bV^2 A\bar{q}}\right) = \frac{a - b\alpha - p^f}{b^2 V^2} \sum_i \frac{1}{A_i} \tag{16.9}$$

and the futures price perfectly predicts the size of the harvest, and hence the post-harvest spot price:

$$p = a - bQ = c - dp^f \tag{16.10}$$

where c and d are constants to be found from equations (16.9) and (16.10).

In this case the futures market has perfectly aggregated all the information about individual output (known perfectly to the separate farmers) to give a perfectly certain predictor for total output and the market clearing price. Once the farmers realize that it is possible to predict perfectly the futures price (once they learn or calculate the values of the parameters c and d in equation (16.10)), then there will be no remaining uncertainty about the post-harvest price, hence no income risk and no reason to hedge on the futures market. Indeed, as soon as any farmer deduces the form of equation (16.10), he will risklessly arbitrage the future price into line with the spot price, and in so doing will invalidate the reasoning upon which the predictor was derived. Put another way, if farmers are identical, then equation (16.7) cannot be the rational expectations equilibrium, since farmers will form expectations based on the futures price and their own output. The futures price gives a perfect prediction provided it is ignored in making that prediction, but if it is used then the market will collapse, and it will no longer provide the required prediction.

In this limiting case, then, there is no market equilibrium. We can, however, easily generalize the model. Let us assume that the farmer observes his crop imperfectly, i.e. what he observes at the beginning of the period is an imperfect predictor of his harvest. Then, the market still aggregates the information perfectly, but now an equilibrium exists. The argument is simple. We assume that the futures prices perfectly convey the *aggregate* information. We derive producers' demand functions for futures, where each producer's demand will be a function of his own information (his own observation), and each producer recognizes the relationship between the futures price and the aggregate information. Because of the uncertainty in his output even with this information, his demand function for futures depends on his own information, unlike the previous case. We can then show that the futures price will be a perfect aggregator: it will be a linear function of expected aggregate output. But then the futures price will perfectly convey information about expected aggregate output, as originally hypothesized.

Thus, although the market does not convey all the information, i.e. each individual's information, it does convey aggregate information and, for certain purposes such as predicting the future spot price, this may be all that is relevant.

However, this result is also very special. For in deriving the result, because of the assumption of constant absolute risk aversion, the distribution of output among different farmers with different attitudes towards risk made no difference. But in more general models, this will not be the case. Assume, for instance, that some farmers, when they believe that they are likely to have a large crop, decide to speculate heavily on the futures market. In other words, their willingness to bear more risk increases with their perceived wealth, so that they wish, say, to sell less of their crop forward. Other farmers, however, behave in just the opposite way. If so, it would be impossible to distinguish between two situations, in one of which the price on the futures market might be high because all individuals have a small crop, and so the expected spot price is high, and in the other some farmers have a large crop which induces them to sell less on the futures market. These two situations may correspond to very different levels of total supply and hence market clearing price.

Thus, although the market may convey and aggregate information, it does it far from perfectly, except in very special circumstances.

16.3 Implications

These results are important for at least two reasons. First, there is a widespread view that futures markets are efficient in aggregating and transmitting information, that the futures price provides an unbiased estimate of the future spot price, p, that is

$$p^f = Ep. \qquad (16.11)$$

If equation (16.11) is satisfied, then the market is said to be efficient, in a very restricted sense: there are no profits to be made by simply looking at the futures price. A 'chartist' — someone who plots the history of prices to infer future prices — could not expect to make any profits.

However, even if the futures market provides an unbiased estimate of the future spot price, it may not be an efficient estimator in the econometric sense because the variance of the estimate may be very large. The notion of efficiency must therefore be interpreted rather carefully. We shall return to this theme below.

Thus, although we would argue that the price on the futures market provides a signal concerning the future spot price, it does not necessarily convey all the available information; there is still scope for further information to be provided, e.g. by the government. The efficient market hypothesis is valid only under stringent conditions.

Second, even when the market is efficient in transmitting information it may not provide the correct incentives for the acquisition of information. Indeed, we would argue that there is a trade-off between the two: if the market were perfectly efficient in transmitting information, those who acquired the information would be unable to obtain any return from doing so.

Even when there is some incentive for collecting information the incentives are far from perfect. So long as some information is conveyed by the futures price, not all the benefits of collecting information are appropriated by the individual who has spent the resources to acquire (or produce) it.

There are also incorrect incentives with respect to the kind of information acquired. There is an incentive for individuals to attempt to acquire information which is not already contained in the price system. If everyone does this, the price system may be less informative than it could have been, had the resources been devoted to collecting information been better allocated. There is a bias towards collecting information of purely private value rather than of social value.

16.4 Information and commodity price stabilization

The analysis of this chapter and the results of Chapter 11 have several important implications for the desirability of price stabilization schemes.

First, we noted that if information is costly, then farmers will be imperfectly informed and markets will be imperfectly arbitraged. Moreover, we noted that information is a public good, and like most public goods there is a presumption that the market will provide an under-supply of information.

If farmers had perfect (or close to perfect) information, then the assumption of rational expectations might provide a good approximation to reality, but given significant imperfections of information, the assumption of rational expectations loses some of its force. Indeed, there is considerable evidence that farmers' behaviour cannot be well described by the rational expectations hypothesis. (We employ the assumption of rational expectations extensively in our analysis, but primarily as an analytical bench-mark against which we can evaluate alternative schemes.)

In these circumstances, there is a distinct role for government intervention, both in improving the information available to farmers and in reducing the need for information. If it were costless to supply information, the government could simply resort to supplying information to farmers, and, having corrected this market distortion, the private market would provide the efficient amount of commodity storage (ignoring the considerations of imperfect risk markets noted in Chapter 15). But information is costly to collect, and thus there is an argument for the government both to supply information and to attempt to reduce the need for information, in particular, by reducing the variability in returns. In addition, the government might attempt to improve the mechanisms by which the private market provides information; for instance, it may be that a 'more orderly' futures market conveys more information to farmers, and the government may thus attempt to regulate the actions of speculators in futures markets. Note, however, that what farmers are concerned with is not price variability itself, but, as we have said, variability in returns; ideally, if the government could ensure that prices varied inversely with quantity, so farmers faced no risk, then they would require no information either about the distribution of output or prices. They would simply need to know the *certain* return to growing each crop. On the other hand, since farmers are likely to be well informed about the distribution of their output, even if they are not about the distribution of prices and its correlation with output, a price stabilization scheme might improve their information (eliminating the inefficiencies, for instance associated with the cobweb) even though it increased the risks faced by farmers.

We shall not have anything further to say about the aspects of commodity price stabilization which we have discussed in this chapter (and Chapter 11); but the fact that we have not attempted to quantify the

Information and Market Equilibrium 245

benefits of improved information is not to say that we view them either as unimportant or uninteresting. At the very least, they provide an important part of the rationale for governmental intervention. But a full treatment of these issues would take us beyond the scope of this book.

Part IV

Price Stabilization with No Supply Response

Part IV is devoted to developing and applying a method for estimating the benefits of a commodity price stabilization programme under the assumption that average supply does not change with the introduction of the programme. There are several reasons for making this assumption. In the first place, it allows us to examine other important problems without unnecessarily complicating the analysis. Second, we shall show in Part V that under reasonable empirical assumptions, the long-run impact of stabilization, allowing for any supply responses, can be derived quite simply from the short-run impact, when supply does not change. Third, the main consequences of supply responses are redistributive and do not greatly affect the efficiency benefits of stabilization. Finally, it is quite probable that average supply will not change in the short run, after the introduction of price stabilization, since it may take farmers some time to learn and adapt to the new distribution of returns. As such, Part IV can be interpreted as examining the short-run impact of price stabilization.

Perfect price stabilization is infeasible, at least if average supply is to be equal to average demand, and it is therefore necessary to develop a theory of partial or incomplete price stabilization. Chapter 17 is addressed to this problem and develops a theoretical framework for analysis based on the concept of a mean-quantity-preserving decrease in price dispersion as a feasible small improvement in price stabilization. The chapter demonstrates the importance of the distinction between transfer and efficiency benefits, and shows that while the distributional consequences of price stabilization are very sensitive to the specification of demand functions and risk, the latter are not and can thus be estimated with greater confidence. In Chapter 18 the determinants of the distributional impact of price stabilization are examined in greater detail, to demonstrate the importance of econometric specification in the empirical measurement of the welfare gains and losses resulting from price stabilization.

The book has so far assumed that markets are competitive, but in practice international trade is subject to a variety of distortionary interventions such as tariffs, quotas, and domestic price support schemes. Chapter 19 therefore asks whether the presence of market distortions modifies the case for price stabilization and shows how to analyse their impact, at least in simple cases.

Finally, Chapter 20 applies the theory to estimating the benefits of price stabilization. The purpose of this chapter is twofold — to demonstrate the applicability of the theory and to give order-of-magnitude estimates of the possible benefits, and so examine the quantitative importance of price stabilization. While we think the estimates are interesting, we would not claim that they are definitive, and they could obviously be improved by better estimating procedures and by taking proper account of the existence of the other risk-sharing institutions described in Part III. We also provide order-of-magnitude estimates of the benefits of alternative ways of stabilizing producer income which, if feasible, look considerably more attractive than conventional price stabilization schemes.

Chapter 17

The Theory of Partial Price Stabilization

We have argued at some length in Chapters 6 and 8 that the conventional measurements based on Marshallian surplus measurements are suspect and incomplete, and should be replaced by explicit models of behaviour under risk. In those two chapters we derived simple formulae for the benefits of risk reduction using Taylor series approximations. We believe that this approach is a significant improvement on the Marshallian method and is the best operational approach currently available, but its advantages will only be realized if it is carefully used. The formulae are derived making explicit assumptions about functional forms for production functions and demand schedules, and about the specification and source of risk. This is, of course, true of any econometric work, although it is often argued that the exact functional form is not particularly critical for the application in question, at least, when the objective is to test some economic hypothesis or forecast some variable. We shall argue that when it comes to the measurement of the distributional aspects of price stabilization, the specification is critical and largely predetermines the outcome. On the other hand, if the intention is merely to estimate the total benefits of price stabilization, regardless of their distribution, then we shall show that the choice of model specification is less critical. Both questions are important: the distributional impact is clearly critical for international negotiations about the design of any stabilization scheme, while the magnitude of the total benefits places obvious constraints on the amount it is worth spending on the operation of any stabilization scheme.

It is therefore important to decide which question is being asked, and, if the distributional impact is important, it is important to make an informed choice of econometric specification. This chapter sets out the analytical framework for the analysis of price stabilization, distinguishes between the various benefits, and discusses their distributional impact. It then shows how to calculate the total benefits of price stabilization, ignoring these distributional impacts. The next chapter deals with these distributional impacts and contrasts the implications of alternative specifications.

17.1 The definition of price stabilization

A price stabilization scheme is any programme that leads to a reduction in the dispersion of price. Although most empirical studies use statistics such as the coefficient of variation to measure price instability, we argued in Chapter 6 that such measures were analytically unsatisfactory. It was argued that it is more satisfactory to restrict attention to changes in risk which would be generated by a sequence of *mean-preserving spreads*, and it is very natural to apply this technique to the analysis of price stabilization schemes. The first issue to resolve is the choice of variable whose mean is to be preserved. Most writers have implicitly used a mean-price-preserving decrease in price variability but we have argued that this is inappropriate, because in general the average price will change even if average supply does not, and it may be infeasible to change supply in such a way as to maintain the average price. We argued in Chapter 6 that the appropriate mean to preserve is mean supply, rather than mean price, and we shall analyse stabilization schemes on this assumption. A mean-quantity-preserving decrease in price dispersion is feasible, easy to interpret, and is effected by transferring (by storage, which we assume occurs without wastage) a unit of output from a date at which price is low to a date when it is high. Thus, if $p_i = p_i(Q^c)$ is the price at date i when consumption is Q^c, and if

$$p_1 > p_2$$

the price distribution generated by

$$Q_i^c = \begin{cases} Q_i^c & i \neq 1, 2 \\ Q_1^c + \delta Q & i = 1 \\ Q_2^c - \delta Q & i = 2 \end{cases} \quad (17.1)$$

is less disperse than the original distribution, provided δQ is small enough (and assuming demand at i is independent of price at j, which is reasonable since we are attempting to measure the impact of storage on an otherwise undisturbed market. Demand for storage, as opposed to consumption, will obviously depend on prices at different dates).

Fig. 17.1 illustrates the effect of a mean-output-preserving transfer on the price distribution. The curves show the effect on the probability density function, which is to shift some weight from Q_2 to $Q_2 - \delta Q$, and from Q_1 to $Q_1 + \delta Q$.

It is easy to show that theorems analogous to those proved by Rothschild and Stiglitz (1970, 1971) and Diamond and Stiglitz (1974) for mean-quantity-preserving and mean-utility-preserving spreads also hold for mean-quantity-preserving spreads in *price* distributions. In particular, we say that one price distribution $F_1(p)$ is less disperse than another price distribution $F_2(p)$ (which we write as $F_1 < F_2$) if the same average *quantity* is demanded under each price distribution so that

$$\int_0^\infty Q^c(p) dF_1(p) = \int_0^\infty Q^c(p) dF_2(p),$$

but

$$\int_0^{\hat{p}} Q^c(p) dF_1(p) \leq \int_0^{\hat{p}} Q^c(p) dF_2(p) \quad \text{for all } 0 \leq \hat{p} \leq \infty$$

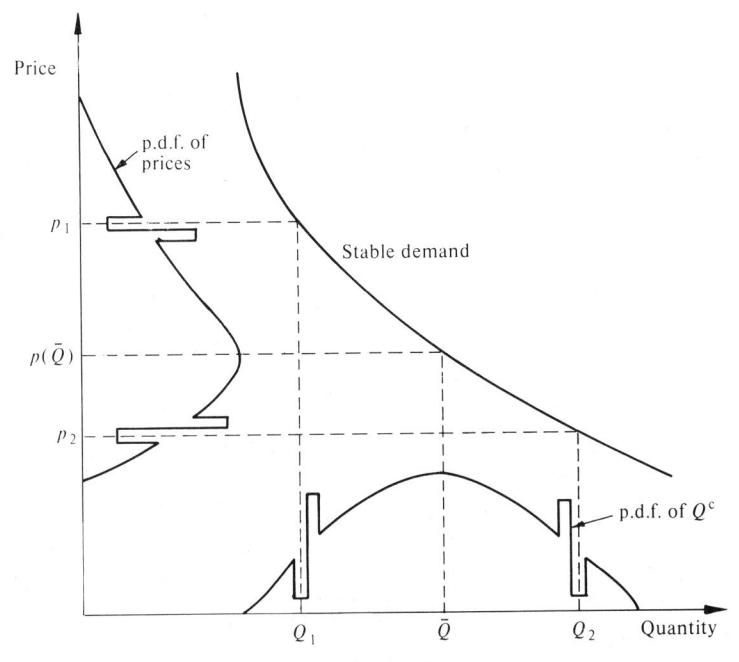

Fig. 17.1 Mean-quantity-preserving decrease in price variability

so that there is unambiguously less consumption at low price dates with F_1 than with F_2.

The results which will be most useful were briefly stated in section 6.3 and are summarized here as theorems whose proofs can be found in the original articles:

Theorem 1:

Mean-quantity-preserving spreads define a *partial ordering* of probability distributions. That is, if

$$F_1 \geqslant F_2 \quad \text{and} \quad F_2 \geqslant F_3 \quad \text{then} \quad F_1 \geqslant F_3.$$

This implies that a sequence of storage transfers which rearrange the pattern of consumption and are all of the form of equation (17.1) will always induce a mean-quantity-preserving reduction in price variability. Moreover, the converse is also true:

Theorem 2:

If $F_1 \geqslant F_2$, then there exists a (possibly infinite) sequence of storage transfers, each of which satisfies equation (17.1) which will generate F_2 from F_1.

Theorem 3.

F_1 is less disperse than F_2 if and only if every risk-averse consumer would prefer the distribution of consumption associated with F_1 to that associated with F_2: i.e. if $U(Q^c)$ is concave

$$F_1 < F_2 \text{ if and only if } \int_0^\infty U(Q^c)dF_1 < \int_0^\infty U(Q^c)dF_2 \text{ for all concave } U.$$

This result is obviously useful for welfare analysis, but it only holds when there is a one-to-one relationship between price and consumption, Q^c, that is, when the demand schedule is stable. It is not relevant for price variability induced by demand variability. Theorem 2 is, however, quite general and very useful, because it allows us to analyse *any* mean-output-preserving reduction in price variability by means of a sequence of simple storage transfers of the form of equation (17.1). Two important provisos must, however, be kept in mind. The first is that we are assuming costless storage, although in practice storage costs are significant and drastically limit the extent to which stabilizing prices is desirable. The second is that it is only possible to make transfers forward in time, from an earlier date to a later date. To achieve the same result as a transfer from a later to an earlier date requires an adequate initial stock which is drawn down at the earlier date and restored later. Thus the statement that we can analyse a reduction in price variability by a sequence of transfers implies that the initial stock is adequate for this sequence to remain feasible. If storage costs are non-zero, then it will not pay to maintain stocks sufficient to always ensure this. However, we shall defer the question of optimal stocking rules with transaction costs to Chapter 30.

17.2 The welfare effect of stabilization

The central question for the study of price stabilization is the effect on the welfare of the three interested parties: consumers, producers, and the storage agency. In this chapter we assume that input decisions are fixed and do not respond to changes in the price distribution. The long-run impacts of price stabilization when supply has time to adjust fully to the equilibrium price distribution are discussed in Part V. Consider, then, an agent who receives income Y_t at date t. For the moment we need not enquire whether he is a consumer, producer, or a storage agency, but suppose that he enjoys utility $U(Y_t)$. What is the effect on his utility of transferring δQ from date 2 to date 1? As a result of the transfer the amount produced, Q^s, remains unchanged, but the amount consumed, Q^c, is altered, and as a result the price changes. The impact on the agent's total utility is

$$\delta W = \frac{dU(Y_1)}{dQ^c}\delta Q - \frac{dU(Y_2)}{dQ^c}\delta Q$$

or more briefly

$$\delta W = \Delta \left[\frac{dU}{dY} \cdot \frac{dY}{dQ^c}\right] \delta Q, \qquad (17.2)$$

when Δ is the difference operator, giving the difference in the value in square brackets between dates 1 and 2. This expression can be broken into two parts, for

$$\Delta[xy] \equiv x_1 y_1 - x_2 y_2 = \frac{y_1 + y_2}{2}(x_1 - x_2) + \frac{x_1 + x_2}{2}(y_1 - y_2),$$

i.e.

$$\Delta[xy] = \Delta[x] \cdot Ey + \Delta[y] \cdot Ex.$$

Therefore

$$\delta W = \Delta\left[\frac{dY}{dQ^c}\right] \cdot EU' \cdot \delta Q + \Delta[U'] \cdot E\frac{dY}{dQ^c} \delta Q. \qquad (17.3)$$

The first term is the utility value of the change in income while the second is the value of transferring income between dates at which its value (marginal utility) differs. This second term will be zero if the marginal utility of income is the same at every date, that is, if the agent is risk neutral.

17.2.1 The welfare effects on the three participants

The easiest impact to measure is that on the buffer agency, which we shall assume is risk neutral. Buffer stock income at date t is

$$Y_t^b = p_t(Q_t^c - Q_t^s). \qquad (17.4)$$

Hence, from equation (17.2), since supply Q^s does not change:

$$\delta Y^b = \Delta\left[\frac{dY^b}{dQ^c}\right] \delta Q,$$

or using (17.4)

$$\delta Y^b = \Delta[p]\delta Q + \Delta\left[(Q^c - Q^s)\frac{dp}{dQ}\right] \delta Q. \qquad (17.5)$$

If we consider introducing a little stabilization starting from a position of no intervention, then $Q^c = Q^s$, and the second term is zero. On the other hand, if prices are already perfectly stabilized, and we consider the effect of a little destabilization, the first term will be zero (since $p_1 = p_2$), but the second will typically be non-zero, as $Q^c \neq Q^s$. Thus our methodology allows us to ask whether agents initially gain from introducing stabilization, and whether they continue to do so as stabilization is carried to its (typically infeasible) extreme. As we shall see, the direction sometimes reverses, suggesting either that a given agent would prefer an intermediate level of stabilization, or one of the two extreme positions (which will then need to be compared).

Now consider producers. For the moment assume that farmers do no storage, so that sales at each date are Q_t^s, and revenue Y_t is

$$Y_t = p_t Q_t^s.$$

254   Commodity Price Stabilization

Again, the transfer δQ makes no difference to Q^s, but does alter price, so that the value of stabilization, B, i.e. the amount the individual would pay (or that is required to be paid in compensation) for a small mean-quantity-preserving reduction in price dispersion, is, from equation (17.3)

$$B = \frac{\delta U}{EU'} = \Delta\left[Q^s \frac{dp}{dQ^c}\right]\delta Q - \frac{\Delta[U']}{EU'} \cdot E\left(\frac{p}{\epsilon}\right)\delta Q, \qquad (17.6)$$

where ϵ is the elasticity of demand.

The remaining participants are consumers, whose welfare is best measured by the indirect utility function $V(p, I)$, as explained in Chapter 8, where I is consumer income. As before:

$$\delta V = \Delta\left[\frac{dV}{dQ^c}\right]\delta Q = \Delta\left[\frac{\partial V}{\partial p}\frac{dp}{dQ^c}\right]\delta Q.$$

By Roy's identity

$$\frac{\partial V}{\partial p} = -V_I Q_c,$$

where V_I is the marginal utility of income, $\partial V/\partial I$, so the value of stabilization to consumers, B^c, i.e. the amount consumers would pay for the reduction in price variability, is, from equation (17.3):

$$B^c = \frac{\delta V}{EV_I} = \Delta\left[-Q^c \frac{dp}{dQ^c}\right]\delta Q + \frac{\Delta[V_I]}{EV_I} E\left(\frac{p}{\epsilon}\right)\delta Q. \qquad (17.7)$$

All three expressions give the cash value of the welfare effect of the price stabilizing transfer, since they are deflated by the marginal utility of income, and to that extent they are comparable. Notice, first of all, that if we ignore the terms involving changes in marginal utilities, ($\Delta U'$ and ΔV_I), then the sum of all three benefits is simply the sum of equations (17.5-17.7):

$$\delta Y^s = \delta Y^b + B + B^c = \Delta[p]\delta Q. \qquad (17.8)$$

Thus, if we could ignore the effects of stabilization on marginal utilities of income, and, if we could ignore distributional questions, the benefits of price stabilization are simply the benefits of arbitrage, that is, of moving consumption from dates of low value (low price) to dates of high value. If this can be achieved costlessly then it is worth completely arbitraging away any price variability. Later, in Chapter 30, we use this principle to characterize the optimum degree of price stabilization when storage is not costless, though continuing to assume away distributional considerations.

17.2.2 Efficiency and distributional effects

There is another way of expressing the benefits of stabilization which will be useful. The sum of the changes in producer and buffer stock income is

$$\delta Y^b + \delta Y = \Delta\left[p + Q^c \frac{dp}{dQ^c}\right]\delta Q = \delta X^c,$$

where $X^c = pQ^c$ is consumers' expenditure on the commodity. If we notionally aggregate buffer profits with producers then the increase in producers' income is matched by an equal increase in consumers' expenditure. However, consumer benefits are, from equation (17.7):

$$B^c = -\delta X^c + \Delta[p]\delta Q + \frac{\Delta V_I}{EV_I} E\left(\frac{p}{\epsilon}\right)\delta Q. \tag{17.9}$$

The benefits are the sum of the *transfer benefit* (equal in magnitude but of opposite sign to that enjoyed by the producer and the buffer agency), the *arbitrage benefit* $\Delta[p]\delta Q$, which is the benefit of transferring consumption from low to high value dates, and the *real income-averaging benefit*. The sum of the last two is an *efficiency benefit*, and is a net social benefit, while the transfer benefit is merely a redistribution between participants. Even when supply adjusts in response to price stabilization, it remains true that the efficiency benefits are net gains, with the transfer benefits, now potentially larger as both supply and price change, being merely redistributional.

If we assume agents are risk neutral, so that the real income averaging benefits are zero, then the effect of stabilization is to transfer income from producers to consumers (or vice versa), and to generate efficiency gains in the form of arbitrage benefits for consumers. Put another way, even though everyone is income risk neutral, they are not commodity risk neutral — there are gains to smoothing out the consumption of goods. It is important to bear in mind the distinction between redistribution and efficiency in the next chapter where we examine each of the agents in turn. We shall show that the magnitude and direction of redistribution depends on the specification of risk, the shape of the demand schedules, and the source of variability. Moreover, the magnitude of the transfer is comparable in size to the efficiency gains, so anyone studying the total impact of stabilization on producers should be aware of the importance of the specification of the model.

The efficiency gains, however, are less sensitive to specification, though they obviously depend on the extent of price stabilization. In the remainder of this chapter we consider the magnitude of these efficiency benefits, ignoring for the moment the costs of operating the price stabilization scheme.

17.3 The total efficiency benefits of price stabilization

If we are prepared to ignore the effects of price stabilization on the distribution of income between producers and consumers, and on the marginal utilities of incomes, then equation (17.8) gave the total social benefit as

$$\delta Y^s = \Delta[p]\delta Q.$$

The conventional defence in cost-benefit analysis for ignoring distributional considerations is that these could be compensated if it were thought important. Presumably the argument in this context is that side payments in the form of aid would be associated with proposals for price stabilization to secure the consent of parties who would otherwise be harmed by the proposed scheme. In the present case additional assumptions are needed before this equation is satisfactory, for it ignores risk benefits. Essentially this reduces to the requirement that agents are risk neutral or that there is no appreciable change in risk. In some cases this might be a reasonable approximation, though we shall show in the next chapter that in many cases it is unreasonable. If, however, we are prepared to make this assumption, and if, in addition, we consider the case of supply risk, in which the demand schedule does not vary, then we have made all the assumptions required for traditional Marshallian surplus analysis.

The simplest way to quantify the effects of partial price stabilization is to calculate the benefits of completely stabilizing both the initial and final price distributions, giving the benefits of moving between the two as the difference. We therefore ask how to calculate the benefits of total stabilization. The Marshallian assumption is that the total surplus associated with selling output Q at price $p(Q)$ is

$$S(Q) = \int_{Q_0}^{Q} p(q)dq - C(\bar{Q}) + S(Q_0) \qquad (17.10)$$

where Q_0 is a reference level of output designed to avoid improper integrals, and where $C(\bar{Q})$ is the cost of production (incurred before the harvest, and hence only a function of expected output). In the present case these costs are held constant, and can be ignored in comparing changes in benefits. The total benefit of price stabilization holding mean output constant at $\bar{Q}$ is thus

$$B = S(\bar{Q}) - ES(Q) = E \int_{Q}^{\bar{Q}} p(q)dq. \qquad (17.11)$$

A second order Taylor series expansion of $ES(Q)$ about $\bar{Q}$ gives

$$B \cong -\tfrac{1}{2} E(Q - \bar{Q})^2 \frac{d^2S}{dQ^2} = \tfrac{1}{2} \frac{X}{\epsilon} \sigma^2, \qquad (17.12)$$

where $X = p(\bar{Q})\bar{Q}$ is stabilized expenditure, σ is the coefficient of variation of output, and ϵ is the elasticity of demand at mean output, $\bar{Q}$. This follows by noting that, holding input costs constant

$$\frac{d^2S}{dQ^2} = \frac{dp}{dQ} = -\frac{p}{Q\epsilon}.$$

Of course, this result is an approximation, whose accuracy can be checked once the form of $S(Q)$ has been specified. For linear demand schedules

$$p = a - bQ$$

$$S(Q) = aQ - \tfrac{1}{2}bQ^2$$

and equation (17.12) is exact if ϵ is evaluated at $\bar{Q}$. For constant elasticity demand with log-normal supply risk (the natural econometric specification) we can use the results of equations (6.43–6.45) for the log-normal distribution:

$$Q = \theta \bar{Q}, \quad \theta = \Lambda(-\tfrac{1}{2}\sigma^2, \sigma^2) \quad \text{so} \quad E\theta = 1.$$

From equation (17.11)

$$B = E \int_{Q}^{\bar{Q}} q^{-1/\epsilon} dq = \frac{1}{1 - 1/\epsilon}(\bar{Q}^{1-1/\epsilon} - \bar{Q}^{1-1/\epsilon} E\theta^{1-1/\epsilon})$$

which, from equation (6.43) gives

$$B = \frac{X\left[\exp\left\{\tfrac{1}{2}\tfrac{1}{\epsilon}\left(\tfrac{1}{\epsilon}-1\right)\sigma^2\right\}-1\right]}{\tfrac{1}{\epsilon}-1} \cong \frac{1}{2}\frac{X}{\epsilon}\sigma^2.$$

(The proportionate error is approximately

$$\tfrac{1}{4}\tfrac{1}{\epsilon}\left(\tfrac{1}{\epsilon}-1\right)\sigma^2,$$

which, for agricultural commodities will typically be less than 2 per cent.) This suggests that the specification of demand is not very critical for the calculation of total Marshallian surplus.

At this point it might be asked how this Marshallian surplus analysis is related to the formula of equation (17.8). The answer is that they are exactly equivalent, for consider the benefits of completely stabilizing the price distribution when the distribution function of supply is $F(Q)$, and density function $F'(Q)$. Consider a sequence of storage transfers δQ from a date when supply is $\underline{Q}$ to a date when it is $\bar{Q}$, starting with the lowest possible output, $\underline{Q}$. The effect of making this transfer is to reduce the probability of consumption at $\underline{Q}$ and increase the probability of consumption at $\underline{Q} + \delta Q$ by the same amount. The probability weight at $\underline{Q}$ is $F'(\underline{Q})$, so that at $\underline{Q} + \delta Q$ it becomes $F'(\underline{Q} + \delta Q) + F'(\underline{Q})\delta Q$. This in turn is duly transferred to state Q, increasing the probability of consumption at state $\underline{Q} + 2\delta Q$. The probability weight eventually accumulated in state Q at the moment when it is to be transferred is then the sum of all these rightward shifts in probability

$$\int_{0}^{Q} F'(q) dq = F(Q)$$

and the transfer benefit is

$$\Delta[p]\delta Q = F(Q)(p(Q) - p(\bar{Q})).$$

The same procedure of notionally negative transfers from states above $\bar{Q}$ gives the total benefit as

$$B = \int_0^{\bar{Q}} F(Q)\{p(Q) - p(\bar{Q})\}dQ + \int_{\bar{Q}}^{\infty} \{1 - F(Q)\}\{p(\bar{Q}) - p(Q)\}dQ. \quad (17.13)$$

Integrating by parts gives the required result

$$B = S(\bar{Q}) - \int_0^{\infty} S(Q)F'(Q)dQ$$

which is identical to equation (17.11).

The approximate benefit of reducing the coefficient of variation of *prices* from σ_p to σ'_p is thus

$$B = \tfrac{1}{2}X\epsilon(\sigma_p^2 - \sigma_p'^2). \qquad (17.14)$$

17.4 Stabilizing variable demand

A slightly different approach suggests itself when demand variability is the source of the price instability. When consumers are risk neutral equation (17.9) identifies the arbitrage or efficiency benefits of consumers with the total social benefit. We can therefore use the approximate Taylor series results of Chapter 9 to measure the total social benefits of complete price stabilization. If income variability is the source of price instability, and if risk aversion is zero equation (9.8) gives the social benefit as

$$B = B_E = \tfrac{1}{2}X\epsilon\sigma_p^2, \qquad (17.15)$$

where again σ_p is the CV of prices. It is interesting to see that the same formula emerges, despite the varying sources of risk, confirming the robustness of estimates of the total benefits of price stabilization which ignore risk and distributional considerations. In the next chapter we show how unrobust estimates of the distribution impact are, or, equivalently, how important correct specification is if these are to be identified with any reliability.

Chapter 18*

Determinants of the Distributional Impact of Price Stabilization

The last chapter developed a theoretical framework for the analysis of partial price stabilization and drew the important distinction between distributional or transfer effects and efficiency gains. Only the second are unambiguously net gains to society, and their magnitude was shown to be relatively insensitive to the specification of risk, the shape of demand schedules, and the source of the price variability. In this chapter we show that the gains to producers or consumers taken separately are highly sensitive to these factors, since they consist of the sum of efficiency and transfer benefits, and the transfer benefits are very sensitive to the specification. Any international negotiated stabilization scheme will have to pay close attention to the distributional impact, and our analysis shows how far the choice of econometric specification prejudges the answers which will be extracted from the available data. It points to the importance of distinguishing between alternative specifications, as well as identifying the parameters which are needed for the calculation of these benefits.

We shall continue to assume that only the buffer authority does any storage. In Chapter 14 we showed that if a buffer authority attempted further to stabilize prices in a market in which producers undertook storage on their own account, then the amount of storage needed to achieve a given reduction in price dispersion would be a multiple of the amount needed in the absence of private storage. While this obviously affects the costs of operating a buffer scheme, and hence the desirability of further price stabilization, it is tangential to our present concern of examining the importance of alternative model specifications, and so we shall ignore private storage.

The chapter is organized as follows. The first section examines the benefits of price stabilization to risk-neutral producers, first under supply risk, then under demand risk. The next section extends this to risk-averse producers while the third section examines consumers. In each section we examine the impact of introducing a small amount of price stabilization into a market with no storage, then the effect of slightly destabilizing the price in an otherwise completely stabilized market, and finally compare complete price stabilization with no stabilization in order to see how the benefits of price stabilization vary with the degree of stabilization. For some specifications this shows that one set of agents will prefer an intermediate level of price stabilization to either extreme.

The method of analysis is set out in the last chapter, and we continue to assume that

$$p_1 > p_2$$

and that a mean-quantity-preserving increase in price stability is achieved by transferring δQ (by storage) from date 2 (hence raising p_2) to date 1 (lowering p_1). Notice that if supply is risky, this transfer stabilizes the quantity consumed, but if supply is constant and demand is risky, the transfer destabilizes the quantity consumed. In this chapter, stabilization means *price* stabilization, which is not necessarily the same as consumption stabilization.

18.1 The benefits to risk-neutral producers

Suppose initially that producers are risk neutral. (We consider risk-averse producers in the next section.) Since we assume no producer storage, producer benefits are just the change in expected revenue, and are given by the first term of equation (17.6)

$$\delta Y = \Delta \left[Q^s \frac{dp}{dQ^c} \right] \delta Q = -\Delta \left[\frac{Q^s}{Q^c} \frac{p}{\epsilon} \right] \delta Q, \qquad (18.1)$$

where again $\Delta[x] = x_1 - x_2$.

This simple formula provides the basis of our analysis of partial stabilization schemes, and the rest of this section is devoted to analysing special cases.

18.1.1 *Stabilizing price with supply variability*

Suppose first that all price variability arises because of fluctuations in supply caused by weather, pests, or disease. Consider first

18.1.1.1 *Effects of a little price stabilization* If there is no stockpiling, $Q_t^s = Q_t^c$, and

$$\delta Y = -\Delta \left(\frac{p}{\epsilon} \right) \delta Q. \qquad (18.2)$$

With constant elasticity demand curves, a little stabilization always lowers expected revenue.

Notice that this is true regardless of the source of variability, provided that the variations do not change the elasticity of demand. This is actually quite a severe restriction on the form of demand variability allowed, as we shall see when we consider demand variability later. On the other hand, if the elasticity of demand differs in the two states, then the effect depends simply on whether the elasticity increases in proportion to the price. To be precise, when demand is stable, so that the concept of demand elasticity is well defined, then

$$\delta Y \gtrless 0 \quad \text{as} \quad \frac{d}{dp}\left(\frac{p}{\epsilon}\right) \lessgtr 0,$$

i.e. as

$$\frac{pd\epsilon}{\epsilon dp} \gtrless 1. \qquad (18.3)$$

It follows that if demand is less elastic at high prices (as has been argued for grain, where human consumption is less elastic than animal feed consumption, for which grain is used if the price is low enough) then a little stabilization lowers expected revenue.

In the special case of linear demand schedules it is possible to establish sharp results, for then

$$\Delta \left[Q^s \frac{dp}{dQ^c} \right] = \frac{dp}{dQ} \Delta [Q^s] > 0 \qquad (18.4)$$

since both dp/dQ^c and ΔQ^s are negative.

With linear demand curves, a little stabilization always increases revenue.

18.1.1.2 Effects of slight destabilization. The crucial simplification which allowed us to obtain fairly general results in the preceding cases was that, with no stabilization, $Q^s = Q^c$. With perfect stabilization, and when supply is the sole source of variability, the crucial simplification changes to $Q_i^c = \bar{Q}$. Consumption is the same at all dates, and so the price derivative is the same at all dates. Therefore

$$\delta Y = -\frac{p(\bar{Q})}{\epsilon \bar{Q}} \Delta [Q^s] \delta Q > 0. \qquad (18.5)$$

Hence a slight amount of destabilization from perfect price stability always lowers revenue, regardless of the nature of the stochastic disturbance to supply and the shape of the demand function. This suggests that producer benefits as a function of the degree of stabilization appear U-shaped, as shown in Fig. 18.1 (which will also be shown to apply to some kinds of demand risk).

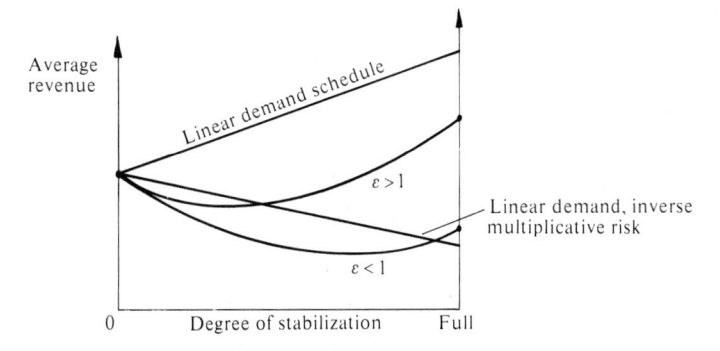

Fig. 18.1 The effect of stabilization on producer revenue for constant elastic demand with supply risk or multiplicative demand risk

In general stabilization has a markedly different impact on the unstabilized market, so that it becomes important to compare no stabilization with complete stabilization.

18.1.1.3 *Total stabilization versus no stabilization.* The comparison of expected income of producers in a regime of complete stabilization with that of no stabilization when the mean output of producers is constant at $\bar{Q}$ turns out to be a simple matter. In the case of *supply variability* we simply compare expected revenue $EY(Q) = Ep(Q)Q$ with $Y(\bar{Q}) = \bar{Q}p(\bar{Q})$. If Y is a concave function of Q, as in Fig. 18.2, then Jensen's inequality (see section 6.3) implies that stabilization raises income, and vice versa if Y is convex. Revenue $Y(Q)$ is concave or convex as d^2Y/dQ^2 is negative or positive; hence total stabilization raises or lowers expected revenue as

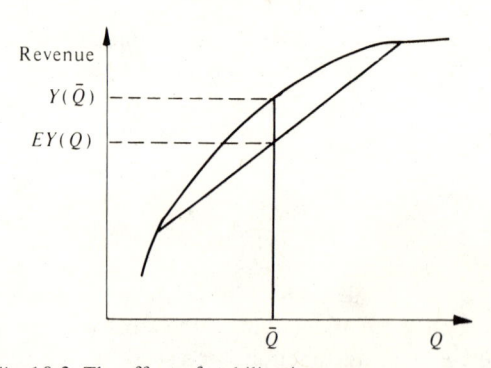

$$\frac{pd\epsilon}{\epsilon dp} \gtreqless 1 - \epsilon. \qquad (18.6)$$

Fig. 18.2 The effect of stabilization on average revenue

With a constant elasticity demand curve, the effect of total stabilization depends simply on whether the elasticity of demand is greater or less than unity; under the normal presumption of an elasticity less than unity, stabilization lowers expected income. In the special case of linear demand, however, total stabilization raises income, just as does partial stabilization. These results are illustrated in Fig. 18.1.

18.1.2 Stabilizing price with variable demand

Demand may vary because the price of other commodities varies or because consumer incomes vary. If supply is stable, price stabilization requires that the quantity consumed be destabilized. It is more difficult to analyse as it becomes necessary to describe the way in which the whole demand schedule varies with risk, and even if we confine attention to additive and multiplicative shifts, there are still four cases to examine, depending whether the demand or inverse demand schedule is shifted. The four cases are:

(i) *Additive demand shifts*

$$Q = D(p) + \tilde{\theta}, \quad E\tilde{\theta} = 0, \quad \Delta[\theta] > 0 \qquad (18.7)$$

which shift the demand curve vertically, or the inverse demand curve horizontallly.

This is the natural specification for linear demand schedules, which can be estimated by linear regression.

(ii) *Multiplicative demand shifts*

$$Q = \tilde{\theta}D(p), \quad E\tilde{\theta} = 1, \quad \Delta[\theta] > 0. \tag{18.8}$$

These are typically estimated by log-linear regression, and are most suitable for constant elasticity demand functions.

(iii) *Additive inverse demand shifts*

$$p = g(Q) + \tilde{\theta}, \quad E\tilde{\theta} = 0, \quad \Delta[\theta] > 0 \tag{18.9}$$

which shift the inverse demand curve vertically, and are identical to additive demand shifts for linear demand schedules.

(iv) *Multiplicative inverse demand shifts*

$$p = \tilde{\theta}g(Q), \quad E\tilde{\theta} = 1, \quad \Delta[\theta] > 0. \tag{18.10}$$

This is a very implausible type of demand variability, as can be seen by contrasting it with multiplicative demand risk for the linear demand schedule. It rotates the schedule in the opposite direction and can thus be expected to have quite different effects.

The one simplification allowed by demand risk is that supply is constant at $\bar{Q}$, so that equation (18.1) simplifies to

$$\delta Y = \bar{Q}\Delta\left(\frac{dp}{dQ}\right)\delta Q. \tag{18.11}$$

The crucial question is what happens to dp/dQ at constant $\bar{Q}$ (for a little price stabilization) or at constant price, $\hat{p}$ (for a little price destabilization from perfect stability). Fig. 18.3 illustrates the principle for additive demand risk.

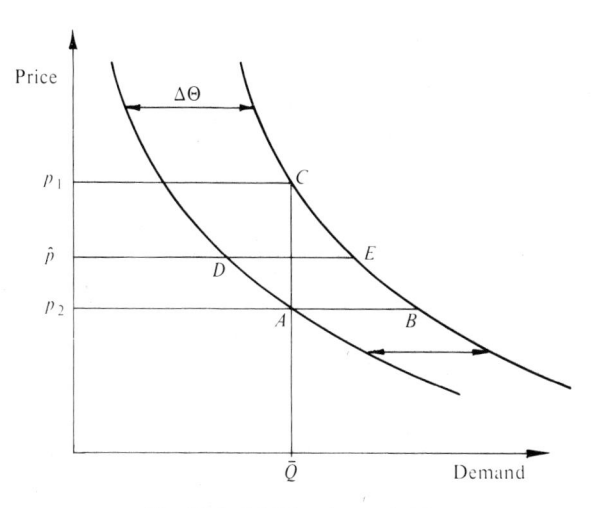

Fig. 18.3 Additive demand risk

18.1.2.1 Additive risk.

Since the curves are horizontally parallel, slopes at A and B are the same, so for convex demand curves the slope at C is more negative than at A and $\Delta[dp/dQ]$ is negative at constant $\bar{Q}$, that is, for a little price stabilization. However, at constant $\bar{p}$, the slopes at D and E are the same, and so there is no change to producer revenue from a little price destabilization.

A similar diagram and arguments show that if the *inverse* demand curve has additive risk (so that the slope at A and C are the same) a little price stabilization has no effect, and if the schedule is convex then a little destabilization from complete price stability lowers producer revenue. There is no change in the direction of benefit going from little price stabilization to full stabilization, so it follows that complete price stabilization raises producer revenue with inverse additive risk, and lowers it with direct additive risk, for convex demand schedules (and vice versa for improbable concave demand schedules). The linear demand is a boundary case in two senses, since the two forms of additive risk are equivalent, and it is a boundary between convex and concave curves. Figure 18.4 summarizes the results, and demonstrates the importance of risk specification.

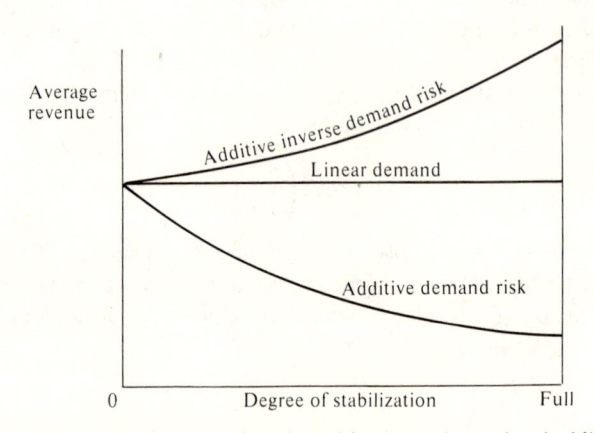

Fig. 18.4 The effect of price stabilization with convex demand and additive risk

18.1.2.2 Multiplicative demand risk.

Let us consider the central case of multiplicative demand risk, which we argued in Chapter 8 was the natural econometric specification, and which we shall use in the later empirical estimates reported in Chapter 20. Multiplicative demand risk has another appealing property, for a small amount of price stabilization has exactly the same effect as it does with only supply risk. Writing

$$p = f(Q/\theta)$$

$$\frac{dp}{dQ} = \frac{f'}{\theta} = -\frac{p}{\epsilon Q} \qquad (18.12)$$

so, as with supply risk

$$\delta Y = -\Delta[p/\epsilon]\delta Q \geq 0$$

as

$$\frac{pd\epsilon}{\epsilon dp} \geq 1. \tag{18.13}$$

In particular, with constant elastic demand curves and multiplicative demand risk a little price stabilization lowers expected revenue.

Notice that, unlike multiplicative inverse demand risk considered below, expected revenue is not necessarily lowered, though it is under normal assumptions about the shape of demand. Indeed, for linear demand schedules expected revenue is raised.

At full price stabilization equation (18.12) gives

$$\delta Y = -\frac{\bar{p}\bar{Q}}{\epsilon(\bar{p})}\Delta\left[\frac{1}{Q^c}\right] = -\frac{\bar{p}\bar{Q}}{D(\bar{p})\epsilon(\bar{p})}\Delta\frac{1}{\theta} > 0 \tag{18.14}$$

which, since $\Delta[\theta] > 0$, is positive for any shape demand schedule, a little price destabilization always lowers revenue. Given the similarity with supply risk, it is not surprising that the benefits of stabilization have the U-shaped form shown in Fig. 18.1. It remains to compare full stabilization with no stabilization. This is somewhat trickier to analyse than supply variability since the buffer stock has to destabilize sales to offset the fluctuations in the demand curve, even though supply remains fixed. Since supply is fixed at $\bar{Q}$, average revenue increases if the stabilized price $\hat{p}$ is above the average price before stabilization, $\bar{p}$. In the case of multiplicative risk $\hat{p}$ must satisfy

$$\bar{Q} = E\theta D(\hat{p}) \quad \text{or} \quad \hat{p} = D^{-1}(\bar{Q}),$$

from which it follows that

$$\hat{p} = p(E\theta) > \bar{p} = Ep(\theta)$$

if p is concave in θ, and vice versa if p is convex. Now since

$$D(p(\theta)) = \bar{Q}/\theta \tag{18.15}$$

$$\frac{dp}{d\theta} = -\frac{1}{D'} \cdot \frac{\bar{Q}}{\theta^2} = \frac{p}{\epsilon\theta}$$

and concavity requires

$$\frac{d^2p}{d\theta^2} = \frac{p}{\theta^2\epsilon^2}\left\{1 - \epsilon - \frac{pd\epsilon}{\epsilon dp}\right\} < 0$$

so price stabilization raises or lowers producer revenue as

$$\frac{pd\epsilon}{\epsilon dp} \geq 1 - \epsilon. \tag{18.16}$$

If elasticity is constant, then the graph of average revenue is exactly the same as Fig. 18.1, and, indeed, equations (18.13) and (18.16) are identical to equations (18.3) and (18.6), confirming the identity of supply risk and multiplicative demand risk. Likewise for linear demand schedules stabilization raises average revenue.

18.1.2.3 *Multiplicative inverse risk.* For completeness we summarize the results for the implausible case of equation (18.10). For a little price stabilization equation (18.11) gives

$$\delta Y = \bar{Q} g'(\bar{Q}) \Delta[\theta] < 0$$

and a little price stabilization always lowers revenue, even for linear demand schedules. Similarly, a little price destabilization lowers revenue if

$$\frac{Qd\epsilon}{\epsilon dQ} < -1.$$

Complete price stabilization raises or lowers average revenue as

$$\frac{Qd\epsilon}{\epsilon dQ} \gtreqless 1 - 1/\epsilon$$

so again the graph of average revenue against the degree of price stabilization appears as in Fig. 18.1, except for linear demand schedules, where stabilization *lowers* average revenue.

To summarize briefly, if demand schedules are inelastic, price stabilization lowers average revenue except for additive inverse demand risk. Figures (18.1) and (18.4) present the results graphically.

18.1.3 *Including buffer profits*

If we add buffer profits to producer revenue, then the combined gain is equal to the transfer loss by consumers, and is a convenient summary statistic of the magnitude of redistribution. Adding the two gives

$$\delta X^c = \Delta \left[\frac{d}{dQ^c} (pQ^c) \right] \delta Q. \qquad (18.17)$$

With constant elasticity demand functions and variable supply *or* multiplicative demand (and inverse demand) risk

$$\delta X^c = (1 - 1/\epsilon) \Delta[p] \delta Q \qquad (18.18)$$

and so a little bit of price stabilization increases or decreases revenue as the elasticity is greater or less than unity. For the linear demand schedule $p = a - bQ^c$, and either supply or multiplicative demand risk

$$\delta X^c = -2b\Delta[Q^c]\delta Q = 2\Delta[p]\delta Q > 0.$$

In both cases, the transfer tends to zero at full stabilization. Adding buffer profits thus makes a considerable difference, as Fig. 18.5 shows. The dotted

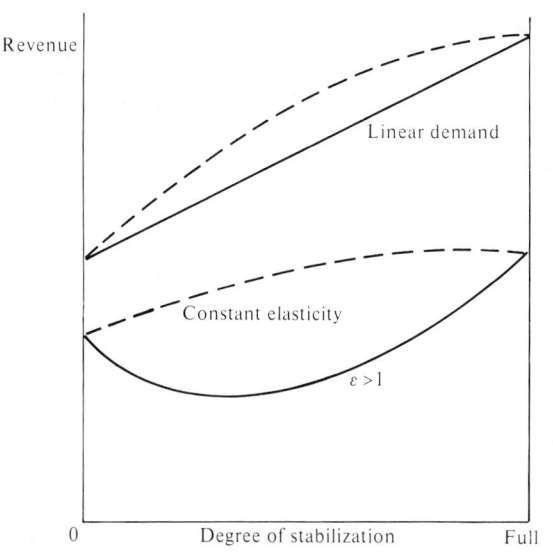

Fig. 18.5 Effects of including buffer profits

line shows the combined buffer and producer revenue, the continuous line shows the producer revenue alone. Notice that since on average the buffer stock makes zero profits at both zero and perfect stabilization the lines meet at the end points.

With additive demand risk the curves in Fig. 18.5 are similarly bowed upwards.

18.2 Price stabilization with risk-averse producers

The preceding sections studied the effect of price stabilization on the mean income of producers and ignored changes in the riskiness of their income. As such it is incomplete unless producers are risk neutral, or unless they obtained only an infinitesimal fraction of their total income from the stabilized crop. However, the farmers we wish to study are heavily dependent on these crops and are risk averse.

For such farmers the effects of price stabilization programmes can be decomposed into two parts, the risk reduction effect (the effect of the reduction in variability of income resulting from the reduction in the variability of price) keeping mean income constant, and the effect on mean income, which we have already measured. Both effects were distinguished in equation (17.6), which we repeat for the constant elastic case:

$$B = \Delta \left[Q^s \frac{dp}{dQ^c} \right] \delta Q - \frac{\Delta [U'] \bar{p}}{EU'} \frac{1}{\epsilon} \delta Q, \qquad (18.19)$$

Whether the risk benefit, that is the second term of equation (18.19), is positive or negative depends on whether a reduction in price variability increases or decreases income variability; if the source of variability is supply, then if the elasticity of demand is less than unity, dates at which there is low supply are dates of high income. Increasing consumption (by transferring resources from high-supply dates) lowers income at those dates. Conversely, if the elasticity of demand is greater than unity, dates at which there is high supply are dates of high income. Thus, with supply variability, whether a small price stabilization programme reduces or increases income variability depends on whether the elasticity of demand exceeds or is less than unity.

Similarly, if demand is the source of variability, lowering the price at high-price dates and increasing it at low-price dates must reduce income variability. Hence, for a farmer growing a single crop, a small price stabilization programme reduces income variability if demand fluctuations are the sole source of price variability.[1]

On the other hand, the effect is exactly reversed at complete stabilization. With perfect stabilization of prices, income variability is equal to the variability of supply. A little destabilization which increases the quantity consumed in a high-output state will lower price, and hence lower income, and conversely for a low-output state. Hence a little destabilization always reduces the variability of income if the source of variability is on the supply side and conversely if the source is on the demand side.

The magnitude of the risk benefit can be calculated by expanding $\Delta U'$ using the mean value theorem (that is, by expanding in a Taylor series of one term). If demand is non-risky, income is a function of supply, Q:

$$\Delta U'\{Y(Q)\} = U''(\hat{Y}) \cdot p(\hat{Q})(1 - 1/\epsilon)\Delta Q.$$

If the coefficient of relative risk aversion at $\hat{Y}$ is R:

$$R = -\frac{\hat{Y}U''(\hat{Y})}{U'(Y)}$$

then

$$\Delta U' = \frac{-RU'(\hat{Y})}{\hat{Q}}(1 - 1/\epsilon)\Delta Q. \qquad (18.20)$$

If the elasticity of demand is constant, and if Q_1 and Q_2 are suitably chosen so that $\hat{Q} = \bar{Q}$, it follows from equations (18.19) and (18.20) that the total impact on producers for a little stabilization will be measured by

$$B = -\left\{R\left(1 - \frac{1}{\epsilon}\right) + \frac{1}{\epsilon}\right\}\Delta[p]\delta Q = \frac{\Delta[p]}{\epsilon}\{R(1-\epsilon) - 1\}\delta Q > 0 \quad (18.21)$$

$$\text{if } R > \frac{1}{1-\epsilon} \quad \text{and} \quad \epsilon < 1.$$

---

[1] If the elasticity of demand is unity, then there is no effect on income variability.

Determinants of the Distributional Impact of Price Stabilization

The first term is the risk effect, negative unless $\epsilon < 1$, and the second term is the transfer effect (always negative). With pure supply risk and constant elastic demand, a little stabilization only increases welfare if the degree of relative risk aversion is greater than $1/(1 - \epsilon)$ and $\epsilon < 1$. If risk aversion is low or demand is elastic, the net effect on producers will be negative, even allowing for the benefits of risk reduction.

If, on the other hand, supply is non-risky

$$\frac{\Delta[U']}{EU'} = -\frac{R}{\bar{p}}\Delta[p]$$

and the risk benefit is always positive. With constant elastic demand and multiplicative demand risk the total impact will be

$$B = \frac{1}{\epsilon}(R - 1)\Delta[p]\delta Q \qquad (18.22)$$

where again the first term is the risk benefit. Whether producers benefit depends simply on whether $R \gtreqless 1$.

Similarly, with supply risk, a little destabilization from perfect stability increases or decreases the welfare of producers as relative risk aversion is greater than or less than unity:

$$B = \frac{\bar{p}(R-1)}{\epsilon \bar{Q}} \Delta[Q^s]\delta Q. \qquad (18.23)$$

With demand risk, a little price destabilization has no risk effect, since utility is constant at complete stabilization; hence the only effect is the transfer effect.

18.3 The consumer benefits of price stabilization

The total effect on consumers was shown to be the sum of a transfer effect, an arbitrage effect, and a risk benefit. Equation (17.7) in the constant elasticity case becomes

$$B^c = \Delta\left[-Q^c \frac{dp}{dQ^c}\right]\delta Q + \frac{\Delta[V_I]}{EV_I}\frac{\bar{p}}{\epsilon}\delta Q \qquad (18.24)$$

which can be rewritten as

$$B^c = -\delta X^c + \Delta[p]\delta Q + \frac{\Delta[V_I]}{EV_I}\frac{\bar{p}}{\epsilon}\delta Q \qquad (18.25)$$

showing the three effects. Again we consider the importance of specifying the source of the price variability.

18.3.1 *Stabilizing price with variable supply*
If the source of risk is on the supply side, then

$$\Delta\left[\frac{\partial V}{\partial I}\right] \cong \frac{\partial^2 V}{\partial p \partial I}\Delta[p] \cong 0$$

since consumers' expenditure on the stabilized commodities is such a small fraction of income. (See equation (8.13) for the value of $\partial^2 V/\partial p \partial I$.) In this case the benefits are easily calculated. The arbitrage effect is always positive, and the total effect of a little stabilization is, with constant elastic demand

$$B^c = \Delta[p/\epsilon]\delta Q = \frac{1}{\epsilon}\Delta[p]\delta Q > 0; \qquad (18.26)$$

while with linear demand

$$B^c = -\frac{dp}{dQ}\Delta[Q^c]\delta Q = -\Delta[p]\delta Q < 0. \qquad (18.27)$$

More generally, a little price stabilization benefits or harms consumers as

$$Q\frac{d\epsilon}{dQ} \gtreqless -1. \qquad (18.28)$$

A little destabilization from perfect price stability has no effect.

18.3.2 Stabilizing price with variable demand

If the source of risk lies in fluctuations of consumers' income, then (if $V_{Ip} \approx 0$)

$$\Delta\left[\frac{\partial V}{\partial I}\right] \approx -R\frac{\partial V}{\partial I}\frac{\Delta[I]}{I} < 0$$

where here (and throughout this subsection) R is the coefficient of relative risk aversion of consumers. If supply is fixed, then from Roy's identity:

$$\frac{\Delta I}{I} = \frac{\epsilon}{\eta}\frac{\Delta p}{p} > 0$$

where η is the income elasticity of demand $d\log Q/d\log I$. With constant elastic demand curves $Q = p^{-\epsilon}I^{\eta}$ equation (18.24) gives

$$B^c = \frac{\delta V}{EV_I} = \frac{1}{\epsilon}\Delta[p]\delta Q - \frac{R}{\eta}\Delta[p]\delta Q,$$

or

$$B^c = \frac{\eta - R\epsilon}{\epsilon\eta}\Delta[p]\delta Q \qquad (18.29)$$

which is of ambiguous sign. On the other hand with linear demand schedules and constant income elasticity

$$Q^c = \bar{Q}\left\{1 + \epsilon\left(\frac{\bar{p}-p}{\bar{p}}\right)\right\}\left(\frac{I}{\bar{I}}\right)^{\eta} \qquad (18.30)$$

$$B^c = -\left(1 + \frac{R}{\eta}\right)\Delta[p]\delta Q < 0 \qquad (18.31)$$

and consumers unambiguously lose from a little price stabilization. At perfect price stability with constant elastic demand the consumer benefit is

$$\frac{\delta V}{EV_I} = -\frac{\bar{p}R}{\epsilon}\frac{\Delta[I]}{\bar{I}}\delta Q < 0 \qquad (18.32)$$

and a little price destabilization raises consumer welfare. With linear demand schedules the benefit is

$$\frac{\delta V}{EV_I} = -\frac{dp}{dQ^c}\Delta[Q^c]\delta Q - \frac{R\bar{p}}{\epsilon}\frac{\Delta[I]}{\bar{I}}\delta Q$$

which, from equation (18.30) is

$$\frac{\delta V}{EV_I} = \frac{\bar{p}}{\epsilon}(\eta - R)\frac{\Delta[I]}{\bar{I}} \gtreqless 0 \quad \text{as} \quad \eta \gtreqless R, \qquad (18.33)$$

so slight destabilization lowers consumer welfare if $\eta > R$.

18.4 Conclusions

The distribution of benefits between consumers and producers has been shown to be sensitive to the degree of price stabilization, the allocation of buffer profits (i.e. whether producers or consumers stockpile commodities,) the shape of demand schedules, and the nature and source of risk. It is thus important in empirical work to test alternative econometric specifications and to appreciate the magnitude of the possible errors of functional mis-specification (over and above the errors revealed by the *t*-statistics on parameter estimates).

Chapter 19

Effects of Market Distortion

19.1 Introduction

In some commodities, notably foodstuffs, international trade is subject to a variety of distortionary interventions such as tariffs, import quotas, domestic subsidies, and various non-price restrictions, notably health and sanitary regulations. These typically emerge when local producers find themselves in competition with imports, and are quantitatively important for sugar, cereals, and, to a lesser extent, meat and dairy products. Their presence raises two, quite distinct questions: (a) what are the costs of their presence, or the benefits of removing distortions? and (b) does their presence strengthen or weaken the case for price stabilization?

The first question admits a very simple answer if Marshallian surplus analysis can be used. The presence of trade distortions implies that domestic consumer prices in different countries will differ from the world price. Consider the resulting equilibrium once the harvest is in and each country's supply is known. In the absence of distortions, there would be a world market clearing price, p^0, as shown in Fig. 19.1, which illustrates the equilibrium for a world of two countries. The distortions result in domestic prices p_i. If we ignore the distribution of income between consumers and producers, and between countries, then the cost of the distortion is the loss in potential consumer surplus, shown as the shaded triangle OAC in the figure, itself the sum of the two triangles OAB and OBC. If demand schedules are linear and non-stochastic:

$$D_i = d_i - a_i p_i \tag{19.1}$$

then this loss is, by simple geometry,

$$L = \tfrac{1}{2} \sum_i a_i (p_i - p^0)^2.$$

If we measure the degree of distortion by the divergence between domestic and world market clearing prices, then the greater the degree of distortion, the greater the loss according to this measure.

Needless to say, this Marshallian approach can be quite misleading. It ignores the distribution of losses, and if some countries gain from the distortions they may be unimpressed with the argument that the world would gain from their elimination. The changes which would flow from trade liberalization would include supply responses which might substantially alter the magnitude and distribution of benefits. But, more important, as we shall consider in detail in

Effects of Market Distortion 273

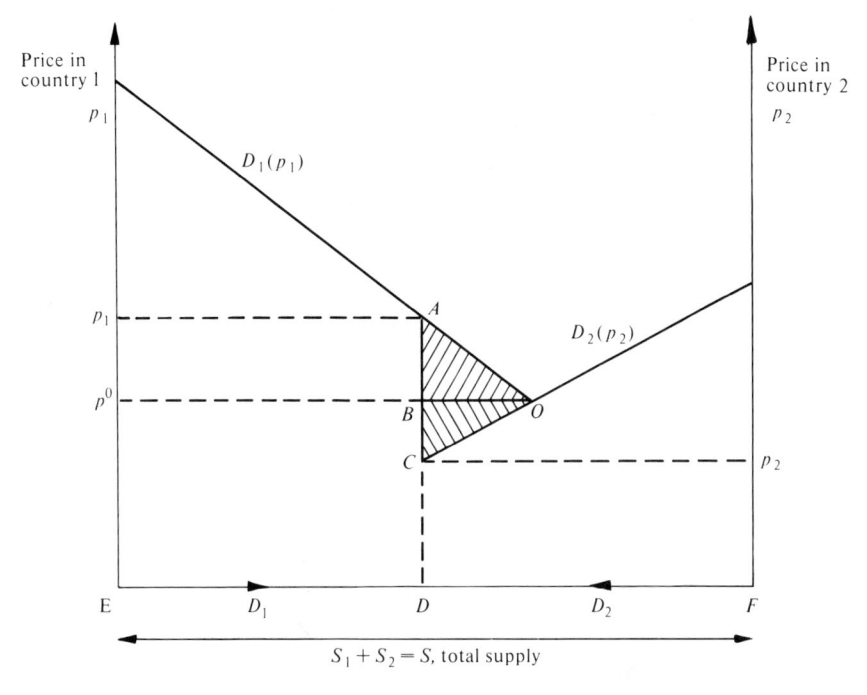

Fig. 19.1 Effect of distortions on world trade

Chapters 23 and 24, it ignores the change in risk which would follow from trade liberalization. If countries have diverse risk, then free trade acts rather like price stabilization in smoothing out individual fluctuations. Such price stabilization may not be attractive to producers. In Part V, where we study supply responses, we shall see that it is possible for producers to be made worse off by price stabilization, and for them to so reduce their supply that consumers are also made worse off. In such cases trade liberalization might make everyone worse off, as we show in Chapter 23. The case for dismantling distortions is thus more complex than it seems at first sight, as we shall see when we discuss trade policy in Chapter 24.

It is, however, important to realize that international trade, by reducing price instability in particular countries, has very similar effects to a buffer stock scheme and may be a cheaper substitute.

This chapter is concerned with the second question. On the assumption that it is difficult to negotiate multilateral reductions in trade restrictions, does the presence of trade distortions strengthen or weaken the case for price stabilization? To the extent that domestic price support programmes and sliding-scale tariffs are designed to stabilize domestic prices, distortions may already have reaped many of the potential benefits of price stabilization, and hence weaken the case for additional buffer stock schemes. However, there are several, admittedly casual, arguments which suggest that distortions may strengthen the case for price stabilization, though little theoretical work has been done to make these arguments precise.

Price stabilization may generate larger benefits in the presence of trade distortions than in their absence for four quite different reasons:

(i) It is often argued that world and domestic prices are more volatile in the presence of trade restrictions than in their absence, and less use is made of the risk-sharing aspects of international trade. If stabilization is desirable under free trade then the greater instability under restricted trade makes it even more desirable. Between 1972 and 1974 the US wholesale grain price more than tripled, while in the EEC it rose by 20 per cent, and in the USSR it apparently remained unchanged. Johnson (1975) argues that the international market could have absorbed the modest world production shortfalls with only modest price increases, but because the shortfalls were only shared by part of the world market the price instability was severe.

At this point, it should be stressed that the link between trade restrictions, market fragmentation, and price volatility is not simple, and many types of trade policy may actually reduce price volatility, as we show in the next section. Another apparent source of market fragmentation is when much of the trade is sold on long-term fixed-price contracts, with a smaller fraction sold on the spot market. The crucial determinant of the volatility of the spot market is then the extent to which consumption decisions are guided by the spot market or the long-term contract price. If consumers are willing to resell on the spot market when the spot price is high, and buy when the price is low, then the long-term contract is equivalent to hedging on a futures market, with all trade effectively passing through the spot market. In such cases the actual volume of spot trade is a poor guide to the effective volume which determines the price and its volatility. While perhaps not so important for agricultural commodities (except for bilateral trade), such contracts are pervasive for many minerals.

(ii) It has been argued that private speculators are less willing to stockpile and reduce price fluctuations in the presence of market distortions (FAO, 1975; Gray, 1960).

The argument is that in such markets speculators have to forecast the actions of governments who have taken responsibility for regulating the markets. There is an important and unresolved question as to how speculators would react to the presence of agents with considerable market power, such as governments fixing tariffs or exchange rates to benefit the domestic economy. A similar issue arises in foreign exchange markets when Central Banks engage in 'managed' or 'dirty' floating. Speculators may believe that this market power will be used to manipulate the market in such a way as to generate profits for the intervening authority at the expense of the speculators (cf. Hart, 1977). If so, the speculators will be less willing to undertake stabilizing speculation, and there will be insufficient stabilization, and additional price stabilization is needed, which would not be required in a competitive market. This second argument is mainly

Effects of Market Distortion 275

about who will have to do the stabilization, or how much stabilization is needed, rather than about the benefits of the stabilization.

(iii) If the total world consumption of commodities subject to distortion is increased, then there is an additional gain (equal to a reduction in the excess burden of the distortion) equal (roughly) to the increase in supply multiplied by the difference between consumer and producer price. This benefit is an important component in cost-benefit analysis (see e.g. Boadway, 1974, or Harberger, 1971). The argument is then that price stabilization induces a positive supply response which then generates extra efficiency gains (over and above those realized on competitive markets). Whether in fact price stabilization will lead to increased supply will be discussed in Part V, where it will be seen that the answer is by no means obvious.

(iv) It has been cogently argued (FAO, 1975) that if price stabilization is achieved by creating buffer stocks, then this will provide an impetus to highly desirable trade liberalization. The argument here is that restricted trade and the resulting price volatility make both the availability and cost of supplies so uncertain to importing countries that they create farm support programmes to ensure supplies, and impose further restrictions to make them viable. If the world price were stabilized and supplies guaranteed, then these restrictive measures would be unnecessary and might be dismantled. Even where the original intervention was inefficient its true cost may remain obscure until the price is stabilized. Once the cost is evident, the source of the inefficiency might be removed.

This last argument may well be the most important, but it requires a theory of the choice of trade policy before it is possible to say how institutional change may affect the structure of trade distortion. In Chapter 24 we go some way towards a theory of the choice of trade policy under risk, which suggests that countries may actually increase protection if world prices are successfully stabilized, but this ignores the other reasons for trade policy, specifically market power. Buffer stocks by making world demand more elastic may reduce market power and hence lower the optimum tariff.

On the face of it these arguments seem quite persuasive, but in the absence of any formal model it is difficult to see whether the arguments are generally true, true under restrictive assumptions, or, indeed, false. In this chapter we build a very simple model which can be used to investigate the first argument, and which could be extended to analyse the third, supply response argument. A detailed analysis of supply responses must await Part V, however.

We find that *linear* trade policies (in which there is a linear relationship between domestic and world prices, as with tariffs) do not affect the benefits of price stabilization significantly, but *non-linear* policies do. In particular, if countries use quotas rather than tariffs, then even if they do not change with price stabilization, there may be additional benefits over and above the benefits conventionally calculated (assuming no distortions). The reason is that with linear policies the average degree of distortion does not change as the variability of prices changes, but with non-linear policies it may be reduced.

Thus the competitive measure of stabilization benefits will tend to overestimate the gains to the extent that it ignores existing domestic policies which partly stabilize income, but underestimate gains to the extent that it ignores quotas and other quantitative restrictions (at least those which bind less than half the time, as we show below).

In this chapter we examine the simplest model of trade distortions, and ignore distributional issues, supply responses, attitudes to risk, in order to direct attention at the non-linearity of policies. The model itself has linear supply and demand schedules, for the same reason that the model of the futures market made assumptions which generated a linear demand for forward sales — it allows demand to be aggregated across consumers and hence it allows an explicit solution for the prices. We shall also assume that it is possible to stabilize perfectly the world price, since it is easier to calculate the consequences of so doing. It would be a relatively simple matter to modify the analysis to consider the effect of reducing the variability of world prices by some fractional amount, but since we are not concerned with the distribution of benefits this would not alter the thrust of our conclusions. We also ignore any private storage activity. Although the detailed results obviously depend on these simplifying assumptions, the essential insight into the importance of the nature of the distortional policies appears quite robust, which is our defence for making these simplifying assumptions. The next subsection examines linear trade distortions, and the following subsection contrasts the effect of non-linear distortions.

19.2 A simple linear model of distorted trade

Sarris and Taylor (1978) construct a simple model of price stabilization under restricted trade to see how far the conventional welfare analysis is affected by distortions. We shall use their model, though for rather different purposes. Suppose that in every country i, demand is linear and non-stochastic, while supply experiences additive risk:

$$D_i = d_i - a_i p_i \tag{19.1}$$

$$S_i = b_i + \tilde{\theta}_i, \quad E\tilde{\theta}_i = 0, \quad E\tilde{\theta}_i^2 = \sigma_i^2. \tag{19.2}$$

Here p_i is the domestic price in country i and $\tilde{\theta}_i$ is the randomness in supply. Sarris and Taylor assume that the $\tilde{\theta}_i$ are homoscedastic and independent across countries and time, which they claim is a reasonable assumption for the major grains, the subject of their concern. As we remarked above, the assumptions of linearity and additive risk are strong, but enormously simplify the determination of equilibrium in a multi-country trading world, since they generate linear excess demand equations. The supply side is not explicitly modelled, but is consistent with expected profit-maximizing behaviour of risk-neutral producers holding rational expectations, provided the average producer price does not change upon price stabilization. (We showed in Chapter 6 that the certainty equivalent price was the average price for additive risk and linear demand.) The assumed absence of any supply response means that the model is silent on the third category of welfare gains, which must await the analysis of Part V. We can, however, make a few remarks about the likely direction of this supply response (and hence of the welfare gains) after the model has been analysed. The advantages of ignoring supply responses are obvious, as production costs remain constant in each country and can be ignored.

Restrictions on trade are modelled as follows. Domestic excess demand is

$$Z_i = c_i - a_i p_i - \tilde{\theta}_i, \quad c_i \equiv d_i - b_i, \tag{19.3}$$

but this is modified to give a demand for imports

$$M_i = c'_i - a'_i p - \alpha_i \tilde{\theta}_i \tag{19.4}$$

where p is the world price, and α_i measures the degree to which domestic fluctuations are transmitted abroad. Equating (19.3) and (19.4) gives the relation between the domestic and world price

$$p_i = \left(\frac{a'_i}{a_i}\right) p + \frac{1}{a_i} \{c_i - c'_i - (1 - \alpha_i) \tilde{\theta}_i\} \equiv \left(\frac{a'_i}{a_i}\right) p + \bar{u}_i. \tag{19.5}$$

A pure tariff-cum-export subsidy has $a'_i/a_i = 1 + \tau_i$, $c'_i = c_i$, $\alpha_i = 1$, but most distortions do not fit easily into this framework since they are typically non-linear. Thus an import quota which always binds has $a'_i = 0$, $\alpha_i = 0$, but if it only binds some of the time p_i will be a non-linear function of p and θ_i. Likewise for a country which fluctuates between surplus and deficit, and which has an import tariff with no corresponding export subsidy, the relationships will again be non-linear. Since non-linearities are more difficult to handle we shall continue with the Sarris-Taylor linear model and then explore non-linear distortions in subsection 19.2.2.

The linearity of the excess demands of equation (19.4) makes it easy to solve for the world price, since world excess demand must be zero each year:

$$p = \frac{\sum c'_j - \sum \alpha_j \theta_j}{\sum a'_j}. \tag{19.6}$$

(The θ_j are realizations of the random variables $\tilde{\theta}_j$.) The variability of world prices measured by the coefficient of variation is

$$\sigma_p = \frac{\sqrt{\{\sum (\alpha_j \sigma_j)^2\}}}{\sum c'_j}. \tag{19.7}$$

Unless countries are very successful in exporting instability ($\alpha_j > 1$) or in lowering

c', restrictions will lead to stabler world prices. This is a consequence of the linear distortion assumption. The claim that distortions lead to more unstable world prices is thus an implicit claim that distortions are non-linear. Moreover, it it is not even clear that linear distortions will even reduce the volume of trade in this model. The average volume of exports of those countries which on average export is

$$\sum_m \bar{M}_i = \sum_m (c'_i - P \cdot a'_i), \quad P = \sum c'_j / \sum a'_j,$$

where m is the set of countries for which $\bar{M}_i$ is positive, and P is the average world price. Whether this rises or falls depends on the relative changes of a_i and c_i.

The distribution of benefits between producers and consumers is strongly influenced by the linearity assumptions, but the sum of the net benefits is less sensitive to linearity, and provides the simplest measure of the total benefits of stabilization. Denote stabilized prices by a hat, then the effect of international price stabilization which perfectly stabilizes the world price, p, is, from equation (19.5):

$$\hat{p}_i = \left(\frac{a'_i}{a_i}\right)\bar{p} + \tilde{u}_i \tag{19.9}$$

where

$$\tilde{u}_i = \{c_i - c'_i - (1 - \alpha_i)\bar{\theta}_i\}/a_i.$$

Unless $\alpha_i = 1$, domestic prices will not be perfectly stabilized. The total gain is the sum of increased consumer surplus, B_c, increased profits, B_p, and reduced import costs, B_m:

$$B_c = \tfrac{1}{2}(p_i - \hat{p}_i)\{D(p_i) + D(\hat{p}_i)\}$$
$$B_p = (\hat{p}_i - p_i)S_i$$
$$B_m = pM_i(p) - \hat{p}M_i(\hat{p}).$$

The linearity of equations (19.5) and (19.6) means that the mean prices do not change with stabilization, so that the expected benefits are easily calculated in terms of variances:

$$EB_c = -\tfrac{1}{2}a_i(\operatorname{Var} p_i - \operatorname{Var} \hat{p}_i)$$
$$= \frac{a'_i}{a_i}\{-\tfrac{1}{2}a'_i \operatorname{Var} p + (1 - \alpha_i)\operatorname{Cov}(p, \theta_i)\}$$
$$EB_p = -\frac{a'_i}{a_i}\operatorname{Cov}(p, \theta_i)$$

$$EB_m = -\{a'_i \operatorname{Var} p + \alpha_i \operatorname{Cov}(p, \theta_i)\}$$

where from equation (19.6)

$$\text{Cov}(p, \theta_i) = -\frac{a_i \sigma_i^2}{\sum a_j'}$$

and Var p is found from equation (19.6):

$$\text{Var}\, p = \frac{\sum (\alpha_j \sigma_j)^2}{\left(\sum a_j'\right)^2}.$$

The total average benefit from costless world price stabilization is for country i:

$$B_i' = \left\{ \left(1 + \frac{a_i'}{a_i}\right)(\alpha_i \sigma_i)^2 - \frac{a_i'}{\sum a_j'}\left(1 + \frac{a_i'}{2a_i}\right)\sum_j (\alpha_j \sigma_j)^2 \right\} \Big/ \sum a_j'. \quad (19.10)$$

19.2.1 Linear trade policies

A trade policy is a set of instruments such as quotas, tariffs, acreage allotments, etc. which generate a relationship between the domestic price p_i, the world price p, and other relevant variables (such as domestic supply). A linear trade policy is one for which the relationship between the domestic and world price is linear and independent of the state of the world, which requires $\alpha_i = 1$ in equation (19.5). A pure tariff-cum-export subsidy is the simplest example of a linear trade policy. A non-linear trade policy is any other policy.

If we set

$$\frac{a_i'}{a_i} = 1 + \tau_i, \quad (19.11)$$

then the total world benefit of stabilizing the world price is the sum of equation (19.10):

$$B' = \frac{1}{2 \sum a_j'} \left\{ \left(1 - \frac{\sum a_j' \tau_j}{\sum a_j'}\right) \sum \sigma_i^2 + 2 \sum \tau_i \sigma_i^2 \right\}. \quad (19.12)$$

If τ_i is uncorrelated with a_i and σ_i across countries, then this becomes

$$B' = \frac{\sum \sigma_i^2}{2 \sum a_j}. \quad (19.13)$$

In the absence of distortions, the benefit to country i of costless world price stabilization is:

$$B_i = \left(2\sigma_i^2 - \frac{3a_i}{2\sum a_j}\sum \sigma_j^2\right)\bigg/\sum a_j \tag{19.14}$$

and the total world benefit is:

$$B = \frac{\sum \sigma_i^2}{2\sum a_j}, \tag{19.15}$$

which is the same as the benefits under uncorrelated linear trade distortions. One particular case in which distortions have no effect is the case of a uniform tariff-cum-export subsidy, in which domestic prices will be exactly as they would have been with no distortion. On the other hand, the distribution of benefits of stabilization could be quite different if different countries have different tariff rates. The reason that tariffs do not affect the gains from stabilization is that the average degree of distortion (measured by the difference between the domestic and world market clearing price) depends on the tariff rate and not the degree of price instability, so it does not change with stabilization. This is not true with non-linear trade policies like quotas.

19.2.2 Non-linear trade policy

Most trade policies are non-linear, since, for example, it is unusual to subsidize exports in surplus years as much as imports are taxed in deficit years, though a country may operate on a linear part of the relationship, as, for example, if it always imported goods and imposed a constant tariff. An example of non-linear policy is a quota, which, if set at a fixed level $\bar{q}_i$ implies the following import demand equation (compare equations (19.3) and (19.4)):

$$M_i = \begin{cases} c_i - a_i p - \theta_i, & \text{if } \theta_i \geq k_i(p) \\ \bar{q}_i & \theta_i \leq k_i(p) \end{cases} \tag{19.16}$$

where

$$k_i(p) = c_i - \bar{q}_i - a_i p \tag{19.17}$$

is the level of domestic supply risk below which the import quota binds. The domestic price is then

$$p_i = \begin{cases} p, & \theta_i \geq k_i(p) \\ \dfrac{1}{a_i}(c_i - \theta_i - \bar{q}_i), & \theta_i \leq k_i(p) \end{cases} \tag{19.18}$$

which is a non-linear function of p.

It is obviously difficult to solve for the international price when a large number of countries have stochastic non-linear excess demand functions, but we can gain some qualitative insight by examining the effect of a quota on a single small country. A country is small in this context if $\text{Cov}(\tilde{p}, \tilde{\theta}_i)$ is sufficiently small to be ignored, so that the actions of the country are assumed not to affect the world price.

Moreover, since $\tilde{\theta}_i$ is uncorrelated with $\tilde{\theta}_j$, $\tilde{\theta}_i$ will therefore be uncorrelated with the world price $\tilde{p}$. In the absence of international price stabilization, $k_i(\tilde{p})$ is a random variable, and the probability of the quota restricting trade is

$$\pi_i(\tilde{p}) = \Pr\{\tilde{\theta}_i < k_i(\tilde{p})\} = G\{k_i(\tilde{p})\},$$

where $G(\theta_i)$ is the distribution function of θ_i, while if the world price is perfectly stabilized at $\bar{p}$, then the probability becomes

$$\pi_i(\bar{p}) = \Pr\{\tilde{\theta}_i < k_i(\bar{p})\}.$$

If the probability density function of θ_i is $g(\theta_i) = dG/d\theta_i$, symmetric about its mean of zero, and unimodal, as shown in Fig. 19.2, then $\pi_i(\bar{p})$ is the shaded area.

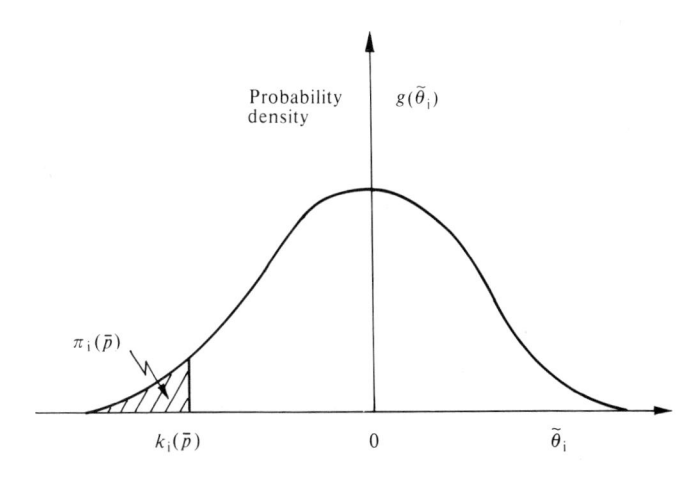

Fig. 19.2 Probability of quota binding

We wish to know whether the proportion of the time that the quota binds increases with price stabilization; i.e. if

$$\pi_i(\bar{p}) > E\pi_i(\tilde{p}),$$

which will be the case if π_i is a concave function of p. Since p is a linear function of k_i from equation (19.17), this is equivalent to

$$\frac{d^2\pi_i}{dp^2} = a_i^2 \frac{d^2\pi_i}{dk_i^2} = a_i^2 \frac{dg_i(k_i)}{dk_i} < 0$$

or g must be increasing over a range of values near $k_i(\bar{p})$. This is equivalent to requiring $k_i(\bar{p}) < 0$, as in Fig. 19.2, or the quota must bind less than half the time. If $k_i(\bar{p}) > 0$, and the quota binds more than half the time, then price stabilization will reduce the proportion of the time it binds.

Obviously, the more often the quota binds, the greater will be the disparity between the domestic and world price, and hence the greater will be the degree of distortion and the total cost of distortion (ignoring, as mentioned before, the distribution of the cost and the costs of risk aversion).

Summarizing, we can say that price stabilization which does not change the mean world price leads to a reduction in the degree of distortion caused by a quota, provided that the quota binds less than half the time after stabilization. If, however, the quota then binds more than half the time, price stabilization will have increased the degree of distortion. In quite plausible circumstances, then, price stabilization will generate some additional efficiency gains by reducing the average level of distortion in the world economy.

Moreover, the change in average distortion has other effects as well. The average domestic price is an increasing function of the degree of distortion as measured by the probability π_i, because the quota raises the domestic price relative to the no-quota case. For a small country whose supply risk is independent of world risk, price stabilization has no effect on average profits in the absence of a quota (assuming as before no change in the mean world price) but with a quota average profits fall, since the average domestic price will fall with stabilization. (We continue to assume that the quota binds less than half the time after stabilization.) This fall in average profits may lead producers to reduce supply. Since the quota encourages inefficiently high domestic supply, this fall in supply will improve world efficiency, and generate a world welfare gain equal, roughly, to the fall in supply times the average excess of domestic over world price. This factor will augment the efficiency gains due to the fall in average distortion. If we continue to trace through the effects of the quota, we note that the average demand for imports rises with stabilization, since the quota restricts imports less often, compared with the no-quota situation. This will tend to raise the world price, and to offset the fall in supply. Given assumptions about the distribution of θ_i, p, and the production function it would be possible to identify each of these effects and find their over-all size and direction.

19.3 Conclusions

The benefits of a price stabilization scheme depend critically on what happens to the prices facing consumers and producers within each country. An international price stabilization scheme affects international price variability, but its effect on domestic prices is mediated through the trade and price policies of each country. We argued in the introductory chapters, and again in Chapters 12-14, that the benefits of international price stabilization might be overstated if the existing risk-reducing and risk-sharing activities of agents were ignored,

Effects of Market Distortion 283

and, in particular, if the domestic price stabilization programmes were ignored. In this chapter, we have argued that trade policies typically cause distortions and inefficiencies, and that international price stabilization may reduce the magnitude of these distortions and generate additional benefits. The crucial determinant of these extra efficiency benefits was whether trade policies were non-linear, where a linear trade policy is one for which the relationship between the domestic and world price is linear and independent of domestic risk. In practice, most trade policies are non-linear, and we showed that the distortions caused by a quota which binds less than half the time would be reduced by international price stabilization.

There are, however, several caveats which should be borne in mind. First, we ignored supply responses, which might generate further efficiency gains, but which, if perverse, as Chapter 22 shows is quite possible, could offset the gains. Second, we ignored risk benefits and implicitly assumed that all agents were risk neutral. In Chapters 23 and 24 we show that trade policy, and particularly quotas, may improve efficiency by reducing domestic risk. Finally, we have ignored the other risk-sharing and risk-reducing activities which one would expect to find. In Part III we showed that their presence might significantly modify the benefits of international price stabilizaion, and one would expect them to modify the impact of changes in the degree of price distortion.

Nevertheless, we found some support for the view that international price stabilization might reduce the degree of price distortion and hence generate additional welfare benefits.

Chapter 20

Estimates of the Benefits of Price Stabilization

20.1 Introduction

The last three chapters have brought us to a point where we can produce rough estimates of the benefits of price stabilization under various simplifying assumptions. Most of our qualifications to the conventional approach suggest that simple estimates will tend to overestimate the benefits and underestimate the costs. If we ignore these qualifications we shall be presenting an optimistic case for price stabilization. If, on these assumptions, price stabilization looks very attractive, then it will be worth taking the qualifications into account to refine the estimate; but if price stabilization looks only marginally attractive then it must be doubtful whether it would in fact be worth while setting up an international scheme.

This chapter can thus be thought of as a quick cost–benefit analysis of the value of careful empirical research on price stabilization, or, less ambitiously, as a quantitative illustration of some of the theoretical arguments developed so far. The calculations ignore any risk-reducing or risk-sharing activities which producers may engage in, such as hedging on futures markets, averaging via credit markets, or diversifying their farm plan. It will ignore trade distortions (which might, as we have just seen, improve the case for price stabilization), and it will only consider the short-run impact of price stabilization during which supply does not respond. In the long run when farmers learn how the stabilization schemes affect their returns they may adjust supply and modify the impact, as we show in Part V below. However, there are three good reasons for concentrating on the short-run impact. In the first place, the 'short run' may last many years, for as we stressed in Chapter 11, it takes a large number of observations on a random variable (like revenue per acre) to test the hypothesis that its variance has changed. Since price stabilization will not be perfect, and since its effect on income stability is in any case indirect, producers will have to learn the effect of stabilization by observation, and this will be a slow process. Second, the main consequence of any supply response is to change the distribution of benefits, rather than the over-all level. Chapter 18 showed that the distribution of benefits was in any case sensitive to the form and location of risk, the degree of stabilization, and the nature of demand, so that it would in any case be rather difficult to reach any precise conclusions about the distributive impact. Finally, as we show in Chapter 21, in certain circumstances, the long-run impact on producers at least, is a simple fraction of the short-run impact, which thus serves as the logical bench-mark in calculations.

We shall estimate the impact costs and benefits for six representative primary commodities. As part of its proposed Integrated Programme for Commodities the United Nations Conference on Trade and Development (UNCTAD) proposed establishing stockpiles for ten 'core' commodities: cocoa, coffee, cotton, rubber, sugar, jute, tea, sisal, copper, and tin. Of these the first five accounted for over one-third of agricultural exports from LDCs in 1976. We shall therefore examine these five commodities, together with jute (as a representative hard fibre), for the period 1951-75 as experienced by fourteen developing countries for whom these commodities are most important.

On our simplifying assumptions there appears to be a case for reducing the price variability by a small amount for all these commodities, though the amount of stabilization required appears low. If prices were to be perfectly stabilized, producers would in most cases lose and consumers gain (ignoring the costs of stabilization). The transfer benefits are comparable in size to the risk benefits, and, except for sugar, the total benefits are rather small. We are hesitant to say that they are large for sugar, since the world sugar market is so distorted that our competitive assumption is least appropriate.

The chapter is divided into three main parts. The first part discusses the problem of measuring variability, the second presents the evidence on instability, and the final section estimates the benefits.

20.2 Measurement problems

In the last fifteen years many writers have attempted to measure the extent and consequences of export instability, and, using essentially the same data, have reached widely differing conclusions, particularly as to whether instability has increased or not. An important part of the explanation of this disagreement is that the authors have employed almost as many different measures of instability as the number of studies. (See, for example, the survey of Wilson, 1977.) Gelb (1979), in an important methodological contribution, has argued that too little attention has been paid to the choice of the measure of instability and that the natural *method* of measuring instability is by using spectral analysis. We shall not follow that approach here, but draw upon his findings in constructing a suitable measure, and criticizing alternatives.

The first point to make is that it is conceptually difficult to measure the instability of a time series without specifying the purpose for which the measure is to be used. Since we are interested in measuring the benefits to be derived from price stabilization, the logical approach is to choose an instability measure which is proportional to the harm caused by the instability, so that changes in instability can be equated with changes in welfare.

In the algebraic formulae for the cost of risk we find that the square of the coefficient of variation (CV^2) is a good approximation, whether we are discussing prices, revenues, or supplies, provided that the instabilities are not too large. The reason is that if the CV is less than 30 per cent, the error in estimating costs by expanding in Taylor series only to the second term is typically less than the square of 30 or 9 per cent. (See the discussion in Chapter 6.) We shall argue that this is well within the accuracy of our empirical parameter estimates.

The most popular alternative measure of instability encountered in empirical studies is the mean absolute percentage deviation

$$\text{MAPD} = \frac{100}{T} \sum_{t=1}^{T} \left| \frac{x_t - \bar{x}}{\bar{x}} \right| \equiv m$$

where $\bar{x}$ is the mean of the series (or an appropriate trend, such as the five-year moving average). This measure, as well as many others, can be converted into the CV if the form of the distribution of the prices is known, and may well be a more robust measure of a stability. For example, if the series x_t is normally distributed about $\bar{x}$, with CV σ,

$$\sigma = \sqrt{\left(\frac{\pi}{2}\right)} m \cong \frac{5}{4} m.$$

If x_t is log-normally distributed, however, the ratio of σ/m would be appreciably higher, at about 1.9. In House of Lords (1977, Table 3.1) m and σ are given for the thirteen major primary commodities for the period 1950–75. The average value of σ/m is 1.33, SD 0.19, which is not significantly different from 1.25.

Since our formulae all use the coefficient of variation it seems sensible to measure the coefficient of variation directly.

If the weight to be attached to large deviations is one dimension of choice, the other is the period over which to measure the fluctuation. Very short period fluctuations are of little consequence, since these will be automatically buffered by consumers and producers, especially for annual crops which can, and must, be stored for a period of months, while very long period changes can be gradually accommodated. This leaves the medium period fluctuations as the most costly — those with a period of five years. Gelb's work suggests that most instability measures which use rather short time series (of ten to fifteen years) employ methods of filtering and trend removal which emphasize the high-frequency components, and measure the important medium-frequency fluctuations very imprecisely. It is therefore very difficult to detect changes in instability, and estimates of the degree of instability are to be interpreted as having a fairly broad confidence interval. Thus in Lawson (1974) only two countries out of forty-five possess instability differing at the 5 per cent level from that of any other country over 1950–9.

The implications of this simple observation are far-reaching. First, consider the various tests of the effect of commodity control schemes on price stability. In the first place, since few international agreements have lasted more than a few years, it is very difficult to test the hypothesis that they have been successful in stabilizing prices. Second, it suggests that in estimating the required size of a buffer fund a period of a decade may be too short, particularly if the estimate is based on a non-stochastic simulations of past history.

In our empirical work we have therefore used relatively long time series of twenty-five years rather than a decade and have tried different methods of filtering and trend removal. We have also used annual data rather than monthly (or even daily) data, since this eliminates very high-frequency fluctuations. UNCTAD has occasionally published instability measures based on the CV of monthly data, which dramatizes the degree of instability in commodity prices, but which poorly measures the important medium-frequency components. The basic data are the constant US$ price series published by the World Bank, defined as the average daily spot price for the year, deflated by the index of manufactured goods import prices into LDCs. They are thus a measure of LDCs' purchasing power and correct for some of the distortions due to inflation, although ideally we would like an index of the individual farmer's purchasing power. The simplest method of trend removal is to eliminate exponential time trends, and measure the variability of the residuals, as in column (1) of Table 20.1. The next step is to filter the series by first differencing, as in column (2). A more satisfactory filter is to take deviations from a centred five-year moving average as in column (4). The five-year moving average is used by IMF as the basis of the formula used in their Compensatory Financing Fund as the best estimator of the long-run equilibrium price in any year, their equivalent of the 'fair and equitable' price often referred to in international commodity agreements.

Table 20.1 *Measures of price instability 1951–75*
Coefficients of variation per cent

	p (1)	Δp (2)	Residuals (3)	MA5 (4)
Cocoa	31	32	27	22
Coffee	26	16	15	14
Cotton	30	21	15	9
Jute	20	22	16	15
Rubber	40	27	20	19
Sugar	58	60	33	34
Average	34	30	21	19

Data: World Bank (1977b).
Key: (1) CV of detrended real prices p_t; (2) SD of $p_t - p_{t-1}$ deflated by mean p_t; (3) SD of residuals of regressing p_t on p_{t-1}, deflated by mean p_t; (4) SD of $(p_t - M_t)/M_t$, where M_t is 5-year moving average.

The final measure, given in column (3), is a crude attempt to measure the uncertainty about the forecast price, p_t^e, defined by the equation

$$p_t^e = a + bp_{t-1}.$$

The forecast errors were found by regressing p_t on p_{t-1} and strong evidence of first-order auto-correlation was found, with the coefficient b taking values between 0.5 and 0.85. In Chapter 13 we argued that this forecast error is a better measure of the amount of instability affecting decision-makers which might be reduced by hedging on futures markets or by buffer stocks.

The deflated price series does not in fact trend strongly, except for rubber, which decreased at 4 per cent p.a. and coffee, which decreased at $2\frac{1}{2}$ per cent p.a. over the period 1951-75.

It is clear from Table 20.1 that the deviations about the five-year moving average are less than the deviations about trend, suggesting that the latter is picking up long-period fluctuations which buffer stock schemes are not well designed to influence.

Table 20.2 gives more evidence on this and other issues, this time for a specific country and longer time period.

Table 20.2 *Instability facing Nigerian cocoa producers*
Coefficients of variation per cent

1	Export unit value	MA5	1900-74	23
2	Export unit value	MA7	1900-74	26
3	Export unit value	MA2/MA7	1900-74	22
4	Producer's price	MA5	1923-64	18
5	Producer's real price	MA5	1923-64	19
6	Producer's real income	MA5	1923-64	25

Source: Helleiner (1966, Tables II-B-1, IV-A-9)

Rows (1) and (2) shows that the choice of time period over which to average, whether five or seven years, is not crucial. Moreover, extending the length of the time series makes little difference beyond twenty years (three consecutive periods of twenty years give figures of 23 per cent, 25 per cent, and 19 per cent for five-year moving averages). Moreover, the choice of export unit value, EUV (i.e. annual export revenue divided by annual export volume) rather than average price makes little difference to the instability of price (though it may do for *income*). This is convenient, as EUV data must be computed by country, while price data is more readily available.

Row (3) calculates the deviation of the two-year moving average from a seven-year moving average, and gives a rough estimate of the remaining instability after averaging prices over two years. Although the figure appears similar to row (2), the social net benefit of so averaging is proportional to the change in *squared* CV, and the reduction in the cost of instability is 33 per cent.

The next row calculates the instability of the price facing the producer (strictly, the price paid at the marketing board at the port of shipment, and hence excluding the transport costs to the buying post). Since our theory is based squarely on the prices facing the decision-maker (producer or consumer) this is a better measure of the relevant instability. Although the instability appears lower on this measure than using export unit value data the difference between row (4) and (1) is not significant at the 5 per cent level using an F test.

Estimates of the Benefits of Price Stabilization 289

Row (5) shows the effect of deflating by the Nigerian consumer price index, showing that the method of trend removal effectively corrects for at least moderate inflation (the index stood at 325 in 1964 relative to 100 in 1923).

Finally, and central to our concern, row (6) given the variability of real producer income. Unfortunately, this is not the variability of a single producer's income, which is what we ideally need, but for the country as a whole. It is significantly greater than the variability of real price at the 10 per cent level, but not at the 5 per cent level.

Thus, to conclude, price variability can be adequately measured using proportional deviations from five-year moving averages over a time period of twenty-five years, using annual data. Shorter time periods are unsatisfactory, longer periods appear unnecessary. Ideally, the data would be the real prices facing the relevant decision-maker, but in practice different price series appear to give similar results, and the most accessible source is world price data from the World Bank's tables. Income variability, must, however, be measured at a disaggregated level, since the experience of different countries will depend on the correlation between their output and the world price which will depend on their importance in world supply.

20.2.1 *The instability facing individual countries*

Most studies of commodity price instability have focused on price instability alone, and as such have not needed to enquire how the instability affects individual countries. Our view is that as far as producers are concerned the costs of commodity instability are better measured by income variability, which will also depend on supply variability. Moreover, the impact of stabilization schemes depends quite sensitively on the location of the source of the instability, which may vary from country to country.

We have selected fourteen developing countries which were either large exporters of the chosen commodities, or for which the commodities were major exports, and for which it was possible to obtain data for the period 1951–75. These countries are listed in Table 20.3. The main omissions from our study are Indonesia, for which the data are poor, and the small Latin American countries, for which Colombia stands as a proxy.

Between them these fourteen countries provide a wide range of interesting cases. However, before turning to their detailed experience there are some provisos to bear in mind.

First, all the data refer to export volumes, price, and revenues deflated by an index of manufacturing imports. They therefore measure the instability as it affects the countries' ability to import manufactured goods, and not directly their instability in real income, nor the instability of the actual producer's income. This may be particularly important for commodities like sugar and cotton for which exports may be a small fraction of total production for some countries like Brazil. Secondly, most of the commodities are storable, and part of the fluctuations in exports may reflect speculative stocking activities. Again,

Table 20.3 Shares in total exports of six commodities for selected countries, 1970–3 average (percentages)

Cocoa		Coffee		Cotton		Jute		Rubber		Sugar	
Ghana	32	Brazil	31	Egypt	14	Thailand	19	Malaysia	53	Brazil	11
Nigeria	22	Colombia	15	Sudan	7	Bangladesh	69	Nigeria	4		
Ivory Coast	13	Ivory Coast	5	Brazil	6			Thailand	10	Philippines	8
Brazil	9	Mexico	3	Mexico	5			Sri Lanka	6	Mauritius	3

Sources: UNCTAD (1975); Jute, for 1970–2, World Bank (1977b)

Table 20.4 *Instabilities by country and commodity 1951-75*

Crop/country	CV (percentages)				Corr (p, Q) (5)	Corr (Q, Q_w) (6)
	Q (1)	pQ (2)	p (3)	Q_w (4)		
Cocoa from						
Ghana	21	22	31	36	−0.7	0.3
Nigeria	21	19	31	22	−0.7	0.6
Ivory Coast[a]	12	40	31	21		0.2
Brazil	24	46	31	23	0.3	−0.3
Coffee from						
Colombia	8	17	15	10	−0.1	−0.1
Ivory Coast	20	27	15	9	−0	−0.1
Mexico	14	23	15	9	0.3	−0.5
Brazil	13	15	15	11	−0.4	0.1
Cotton from						
Egypt	14	20	26	22	−0.6	0.6
Mexico	30	25	26	21	−0.6	0.5
Sudan	33	40	26	21	−0.3	0.5
Brazil	49	56	26	21	−0.1	0.3
Jute from						
Bangladesh	8	22	21	14	−0.0	−0.1
Thailand[a]	42	54	20	14	0.4	−0.2
Rubber from						
Malaysia[a]	7	22	16	16	0.8	0.3
Nigeria	29	37	20	9	0.2	−0.5
Thailand	8	26	20	8	0.7	0.2
Sri Lanka	11	24	20	8	0.1	0.1
Sugar[b] from						
Mauritius	12	63	58	38	0.2	−0.2
Philippines	12	63	58	41	0.1	−0.2
Brazil	72	78	58	42	−0.3	0.1

Sources: IMF (1977), World Bank (1977b), FAO *Trade Yearbook* (various years).
Notes: [a] Estimated for period 1958-75; [b] same 'world' sugar prices series used for all countries.
Key: Q, detrended export volume; p, detrended deflated price; Q_w, detrended export volume of rest of world; corr(p, Q), corr(Q, Q_w) are correlation coefficients of p and Q, Q and Q_w.

this may weaken the relationship between the reported income instability and that facing the producers. Thirdly, the series for Malaysian rubber, Ivory Coast cocoa, and Thailand jute show zero exports for the first few years and a rapid but erratic growth thereafter. Finding deviations about trend is particularly difficult in such cases, and reported instabilities should be treated with caution. Also, the world sugar market is so fragmented and subject to special purchasing agreements that a proper study of sugar price stabilization would need to take these features specifically into account. The estimates below are therefore to be treated with great caution as they ignore market imperfections.

Finally, the data have been detrended by regression of the logarithm of the

292 Commodity Price Stabilization

relevant variable on time rather than by measuring deviations from a moving average. The reason was to simplify the regressions of log price on log quantity, but the effect is to overstate the degree of instability, as Table 20.1 shows.

Table 20.4 summarizes the results of the analysis and measures the magnitude of the various instabilities. Columns (1)–(4) give the CV of detrended export volume, revenue, price, and the volume of the rest of the world's exports. The same figures for the raw data present a similar but less coherent picture. Column (5) gives the correlation coefficient between price and quantity, and thus provides an explanation of the relationship between income, price, and supply instability. Column (6) similarly measures the extent to which the country's supply correlates with the rest of the world's supply, and similarly throws light on relationships between the country's supply and the world price (affected by total supply).

20.2.2 Summary

Five of the six crops have current income instabilities (measured by the coefficient of variation of the detrended series) of about 25 per cent for representative well-placed countries, though the less well-placed countries do substantially worse. These measurements, summarized in Table 20.5, clearly single out sugar as he most generally unstable crop, though for some countries it is closely followed by jute and cotton. The most dramatic effects of price stabilization would be felt for sugar, followed some way behind by jute, rubber, and cocoa. Stabilizing cotton prices appears to have a small effect on incomes, but possibly a worthwhile macro-stabilizing effect, as the correlation coefficient between total exports and cotton revenue (detrended) was 0.8 for Egypt and Sudan.

Table 20.5 *Income instability Percentages*

Crop	Current instability			Price stabilized, CV of income	
	(price)	(income)			
		(A)	(B)	(A)	(B)
Cocoa	31	20	46	20	24
Coffee	15	20	27	12	20
Cotton	26	25	56	23	50
Jute	20	22	54	8	42
Rubber	20	25	37	10	29
Sugar	58	63	78	12	72

Source: Table 20.4.
Key: (A) representative/average of well-placed countries, (B) worst case.

20.3 The benefits of price stabilization

The simplest measure of the benefits of price stabilization, and the one least susceptible to specification errors, is the Marshallian measure of total benefits of section 17.3 which ignores the distribution of benefits. Table 20.6 presents estimates of the returns to completely eliminating price instability. The benefits of a partial price stabilization of degree z (i.e. a programme which reduces the CV of prices to a fraction $1 - z$) can be found by multiplying by $z(2 - z)$, as shown in Chapter 6. The formula (from equation (17.15)) gives the ratio of benefits to total expenditure on the commodity:

$$\frac{B}{X} = \tfrac{1}{2}\epsilon\sigma_p^2, \qquad (20.2)$$

where ϵ is the elasticity of demand. The elasticities used in Table 20.6 are a compromise between the median world price elasticities given in Behrman (1977, 1978) and our own estimates from regression analysis. Notice how sensitive the resulting benefits are to the method of measuring the price instability, with deviations from a five-year moving average giving only about one-quarter of the benefits measured by conventional log-linear trend removal. Notice also how small the benefits are (except for sugar, for which the figures are most suspect), although it should be remembered that they ignore the risk benefits, which we show in subsection 20.3.2 are of comparable magnitude (for moderate coefficients of risk aversion).

The next step is to compare these net efficiency benefits with the costs of stabilizing prices.

Table 20.6 *Net efficiency benefits of total price stabilization*

	Price elasticity ϵ (1)	$100\,\sigma_p^2$ (2)	$100\,\sigma_p^2$ (MA) (3)	B/X % (4)	B/X (MA) % (5)
Cocoa	0.4	9.6	4.8	1.9	1.0
Coffee	0.6	6.8	2.0	2.0	0.6
Cotton	0.4	9.0	0.8	1.8	0.2
Jute	0.5	4.0	2.3	1.0	0.6
Rubber	0.8	16.0	3.6	6.4	1.4
Sugar	0.7	33.6	11.6	14.3	4.1
Average				4.6	1.3

Notes: (1) Estimates from Newbery and Stiglitz (1977; (2) From col. (1) of Table 20.1 — CV of detrended prices; (3) From col. (4) of Table 20.1 — variation from moving average; (4) $\tfrac{1}{2}$col. (1) × col. (2); (5) $\tfrac{1}{2}$col. (1) × col. (3).

20.3.1 The costs of price stabilization

We have not yet developed a theory of the optimal method of achieving a given reduction in price variability, and must therefore seek a short-cut to give a crude estimate of the costs involved. These will presumably depend on the costs of storage and the amount on average in store, which in turn will depend on the planned reduction in price variability and the elasticity of demand. If the buffer buys when the price is low and sells when the price is high, then successive additions and withdrawals will make the stock size follow a random walk, in a way described in Chapter 29. If the average absolute value of the change of stock is σ_s, then equation (29.6) shows that the initial stock must be

$$S_0 = k(\beta)\sqrt{(n)}\sigma_s \qquad (20.3)$$

for the buffer to have a probability of exhausting the stock of less than β per cent before n years has elapsed, where $k(\beta)$ is the β per cent point of the cumulative normal distribution. Thus if $n = 10$ years, $\beta = 10$ per cent, then $S_0/\sigma_s \cong 4$. If the aim is to achieve a fraction z of complete stabilization

$$\sigma_s = z\epsilon\sigma_p.$$

The average cost of operating the stockpile will be $(r + c)S_0$ per annum, where r is the rate of interest and c is the storage cost as a fraction of the price. Thus the average cost to achieve this level of price stability will be

$$z\epsilon\sigma_p(r + c)k\sqrt{n}.$$

The fractional benefits of price stabilization will be

$$\tfrac{1}{2}z(2 - z)\epsilon\sigma_p^2 \qquad (20.4)$$

so the ratio of benefits to costs will be

$$\frac{B}{C} = \frac{(1 - \tfrac{1}{2}z)\sigma_p}{k\sqrt{(n)}(r + c)}. \qquad (20.5)$$

This shows clearly that the marginal net benefit of increasing price stability falls with the degree of stabilization. In Table 20.7 this ratio is calculated for $n = 4$ years, $\beta = 10$ per cent, $k\sqrt{n} = 2.5$, $z = \tfrac{1}{2}$, and $r = 5$ per cent. Column (3) suggests that some stabilization is cost effective (if the trend *can* be forecast) (since at $z = 0$, $k\sqrt{n} = 1$, the benefit-cost ratio is greater than unity). However, for the modest degree of price stabilization involved in holding stocks equal to two and a half times the SD of annual stock changes, only sugar has a benefit–cost ratio above 1 (column (4) is given as a *percentage*). Cocoa and rubber look the next most attractive candidates, followed by coffee.

20.3.2 The distributive and risk-reducing effects of price stabilization

The distributive effects of price stabilization are sensitive to many imperfectly measured parameters, as Chapter 19 showed. Here we calculate the benefits of complete price stabilization (to avoid the sensitivity of the results to the actual

Table 20.7 *Storage costs and returns*
Percentages

	Storage costs c (% of price) (1)	$\dfrac{\sigma_p}{MA}$ (2)	$\dfrac{\sigma_p}{r+c}$ (3)	Benefit cost ratio $n = 4$ years (4)
Cocoa	2.5	22	2.9	88
Coffee	1.4	14	2.2	66
Cotton	1.2	9	1.5	44
Jute	4.9	15	1.5	45
Rubber	2.4	19	2.6	77
Sugar	4.7	34	3.5	105

Notes: (1) from UNCTAD TD/B/C 1/198; (2) = col. 4 of Table 20.1; (3) $r = 5\%$; (4) calculated from Eqn. (20.5), $z = 0.5$, $k\sqrt{n} = 2.5$, as a percentage.

design of the method of stabilization). They are calculated using the detrended figures of Table 20.5, which tend to overestimate the instability, so they are an optimistic measure for two reasons.

20.3.2.1 *Producers.* The risk benefit of perfectly stabilizing prices as a proportion of revenue from the product is from equation (6.54)

$$B_R = \tfrac{1}{2}R\Delta\sigma_y^2, \qquad (20.6)$$

when R is the coefficient of relative risk aversion, and $\Delta\sigma_y^2$ is the fall in the squared coefficient of variation. This will be the initial income variability less the supply variability if the latter does not change with price stabilization, and can be calculated directly or from equation (6.57). The transfer benefit of perfectly stabilizing prices is found from equation (6.61) with $z = 1$. It is given by

$$B_T = \tfrac{1}{2}(\epsilon - 1)\sigma_p^2. \qquad (20.7)$$

The risk benefit will vary from country to country, but the transfer benefit is evaluated for the world as a whole. The results of the calculations are given in Table 20.8, where the coefficient of relative risk aversion is taken as unity (for which the supply response will also be zero). If producers have higher risk aversion then the risk benefits will be proportionately increased.

Table 20.8 shows that the transfers are comparable in size to the risk benefits, and, on the assumptions (constant elastic demand and multiplicative risk), unfavourable to producers. Unless producers have greater than unit relative risk aversion, the net benefits are negative for the first three crops, and only substantial for sugar (for which the figures are most suspect).

20.3.2.2 *Consumers.* The consumer benefits are equal to the net efficiency benefits plus the transfer from producers, plus the income risk term. This last item is probably best estimated direct from the covariance between price and income in equation (9.A6), which, as a proportion of revenue is

Table 20.8 Producer benefits of complete price stabilization
Percentages

Crop/Country (1)	Share of world exports, % (1)	Risk benefit $\frac{1}{2}\Delta\sigma_y^2$ (2)	Transfer benefit (3)	Net producer benefit (4)
Cocoa from				
Ghana	32	0		
Nigeria	22	−0.5		
Ivory Coast	13	7		
Brazil	9	7		
weighted average	76	2.1	−2.9	−0.8
Coffee from				
Colombia	15	1		
Ivory Coast	5	2		
Mexico	3	1.5		
Brazil	31	0.5		
weighted average	54	0.7	−1.4	−0.7
Cotton from				
Egypt	14	1		
Mexico	7	−1.5		
Sudan	6	2.5		
Brazil	5	3.5		
weighted average	32	1.2	−2.7	−1.5
Jute from				
Bangladesh	69	2		
Thailand	19	6		
weighted average	88	2.9	−1.0	1.9
Rubber from				
Malaysia	53	2		
Nigeria	4	3.5		
Thailand	10	3		
Sri Lanka	6	2		
weighted average	73	2.3	−1.6	0.7
Sugar from				
Mauritius	3	19		
Philippines	8	19		
Brazil	11	4.5		
weighted average	22	11.8	−6.1	5.7

Key: Benefits measured as percentage of average revenue from crop assuming risk aversion $R = 1$ (col. (4) = col. (3) + col. (2)).

Source: Tables 20.4, 20.6.

$$B_{\text{res}} = -R^c \rho \sigma_p \sigma_I, \tag{20.8}$$

where R^c is the consumers' risk aversion, ρ is the correlation between price and income and σ_p, σ_I are CV of price and income. The value of this residual risk term should properly be measured country by country using consumer income and consumer price variability, but in Table 20.9 the coefficient of variation of OECD GDP of 3.1 per cent is used, together with the world price variability of Table 20.1, column (1). Column (2) of Table 20.9 shows that when relevant the price variability facing consumers is much less than that of world prices, presumably because of averaging, mark-ups, and domestic price policies. The residual benefit is thus probably overestimated by column (4), but even so, the figures are so small that they could be ignored.

Table 20.9 *Consumers' residual stabilization benefit*
Percentages

	Expenditure as % of income (1)	Consumer price CV s_p (2)	Corr(p, I) ρ (3)	Residual benefit $-\rho\sigma_p\sigma_i$ (4)
Cocoa	0.1	4.3	−14	0.1
Coffee	0.3	5.7	40	−0.2
Cotton	0.2	n.a.	37	−0.3
Jute	0.0	n.a.	11	−0.1
Rubber	0.1	n.a.	35	−0.2
Sugar	0.4	6.0	−35	0.6

Notes: (1) ratio of commodity export value to OECD consumer expenditure (1975); (2) CV of UK retail prices 1960–74, detrended; (3) correlation coefficient between world price and OECD GDP deviations; (4) is the consumers' residual benefit, assuming $R^c = 1$.

20.4 Alternatives to buffer stocks

Buffer stocks are an expensive and indirect method of stabilizing incomes which typically involve transfers between consumers and producers as well as income insurance — in the present case these transfers appear to be at the expense of the producers. It would seem more logical to offer some insurance directly and thus avoid the physical costs of storage.

The alternative is for the IMF, or, perhaps preferably, some other body to provide income stability directly. Given an estimate of the trend production of a given commodity by a given country and an estimate of world price trends it would be possible to determine the trend path of income. The country would then be paid a price p_t in year t such that $p_t Q_t = E p_t Q_t$ trend income. No stocks need be carried, only adequate funds to provide for fluctuations in revenues and receipts. The main problems would be of insulating producers from the world market price, of choosing an appropriate numeraire in which to index income, of ensuring that the benefits were passed back to the producers, and of estimating the trend sufficiently well to provide income stability at the level of the individual producer. This last consideration means that it is necessary to forecast changes in planted area and numbers of producers, though it might be possible to make retrospective adjusting payments when this information is known. If this were successfully achieved the benefits averaged over the chosen countries by crop would be as shown in Table 20.10. The costs in real terms should be small and could be borne by the producers.

At this point it should be asked why, if there is a cheap and desirable form of contract available, it is not already offered by entrepreneurs. There are at least three possible answers. It may already be available through the stock-market (for plantations), or through the friendly local bank (for other crops); or, if not available, it may be that the problem of ensuring that individual farmers do not purchase from other farmers when the price is low (and conversely when the price is high) make it only viable at the level of a whole country with marketing boards controlling the sales of the entire crop. Given that marketing boards are subject to government regulation and might manipulate the price or supply at the expense of the insuring body, and moreover that the scale of the operation would be large, no individual enterprise would have the resources or the inclination to undertake the insurance. Hence, obviously, the need for some international organization, which would also be better placed to monitor illegal direct sales. Finally, it is of course possible that no one has seriously thought out the possible advantages of such a scheme. Discussions over commodity stabilization have been so confused as to whether it is prices that need to be stabilized, or whether average price should be raised, or disadvantageous trends reversed, that little serious thought has been given to this proposal.

Table 20.10 *Risk benefits from successful income stabilization*

Crop	$\tfrac{1}{2}\sigma_y^2\%$
Cocoa	6
Coffee	1.5
Cotton	5.5
Jute	5
Rubber	3
Sugar	25

Source and Key: as for Table 20.8.

20.5 Conclusions

Most estimates of the net benefits of price stabilization are based on shaky theoretical foundations, and many are unduly optimistic as to the precision with which price trends and measures of instability can be estimated. Our theoretical and empirical work suggests that the benefits of price stabilization are comparatively small compared with the likely costs of operating the buffer stock and that they are not necessarily distributed in favour of the producers. Further, these benefits are small when compared with forecasting errors, and also when compared to the confidence intervals surrounding the parameters from which they are derived, which suggests both that the costs of stabilization have been underestimated (since we have not estimated the costs of error in forecasting the trend) and the confidence which can be placed on our finding that the benefits are positive for some crops is also small. Moreover, the benefits to consumers of successful producer price stabilization appear to be almost entirely transfer benefits at the expense of the producers, and the pure arbitrage benefits are extremely small, at least for those commodities which are directly consumed — the foodstuffs.

Given all these qualifications, it appears as though sugar and jute are the main contenders for price stabilization, followed by cocoa and cotton. Rubber and coffee look less attractive for buffering, perhaps because sufficient buffering already takes place leaving little scope for extending this activity. Indeed, if an international body undertook to buffer these commodities it might find that it had to accept the stocks currently held by private stockists and government agencies (mainly in Brazil).

Our main finding is that price stabilization is comparatively ineffective at stabilizing incomes and that direct income stabilization appears very much more attractive.

Part V

Supply Responses to Stabilization

Any price stabilization scheme changes the probability distribution of prices facing producers. The short run is, by definition, the period during which producers do not alter their capacity decisions, or, in the agricultural context, their planned supply, and Part IV was devoted to the analysis of the short-run impact of price stabilization. In the long run, supply can be adjusted and a position of long-run equilibrium will prevail when no producer wishes to make any further adjustments, given the final price distribution which prevails — itself the outcome of the method of stabilization and the ensuing supply response. In this part we explore some of the consequences of this supply response to see how far they modify or reverse the impact effects.

How long the short run is depends critically on the form of the stabilization scheme. At one extreme the scheme might involve announcing intervention prices before the start of the crop season, which, if they were significantly different from the past, or if they were perceived as significantly changing producer risk, might have a substantial and immediate effect. If, on the other hand, dispersed producers had to deduce the effects of some new international scheme by observing local market prices, it might take many years' observations before they were able to detect confidently any change. The question is important because the impact effects can be identified with greater precision than the long-run effects, for reasons that become clear in Fig. V.1. The impact effect of a stabilization scheme on producers' welfare can be traced through a unidirectional causal chain in the top part of the diagram. Stabilization affects producer sales and hence the price distribution. This, depending on the shape of the demand schedule (and especially its elasticity, ϵ) affects the producer's income risk, and, given the utility function, his welfare. The long-run impact breaks this uni-causal chain, and introduces more complex feedbacks. Supply decisions depend upon both prices and the distribution of *marginal* utility. If the stabilization scheme is to maintain equilibrium in the market, average supply and demand must be equal, so changes in supply will have to generate appropriate changes in demand.

The complexity of these interactions raises important methodological questions. Chapter 15 demonstrated that in general we cannot expect rational expectations competitive equilibria to be even relatively efficient, so there is little point in developing a perfectly general treatment since there are no generally valid results. In such cases modelling is useful for its insights, for showing how different factors influence the outcomes and, it is hoped, for distinguishing the

302 *Commodity Price Stabilization*

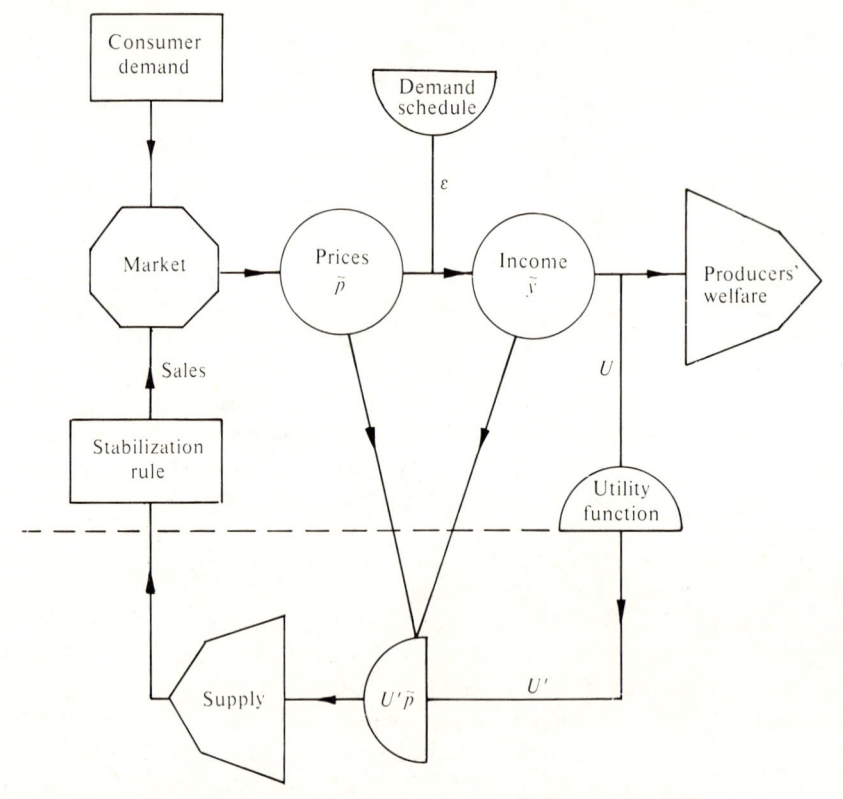

Fig. V.1 Factors influencing the impact of price stabilization

important from the less important factors. To give useful insights, models must be simple, but no single, simple model will be able to address all the issues. Many models will be needed before it becomes clear how best to examine each question, and the models described in this part are proposed both as a first attempt at such an enterprise and to stimulate further attempts. (The same is also true of Part VI, which explores the even more complex field of macroeconomics.)

The philosophy of modelling

Models can be distinguished by the way they treat key assumptions and by their methods of analysis. The key assumptions of the first model in Chapter 21 are that all income risk is ultimately generated by the production risk of the single crop, and producers must decide how much 'effort' to supply. Effort has increasing marginal cost and can be thought of as other, riskless, opportunities forgone. The crucial simplification is to assume a specific simple form for the utility function, which is additively separable in revenue and effort and has constant relative risk aversion to revenue fluctuations. For such a utility function the

Introduction 303

elasticity of supply is a simple function of the coefficients of the production and utility functions, and the long-run impact is a simple multiple of the short-run impact.

The next model, set out in Chapter 22, explores the importance of this assumption and simplifies in a different direction, this time assuming that there are only two states of the world: good weather or bad. This allows a simple geometric analysis and throws a different perspective on the algebra of the first model. The second model demonstrates that constant relative risk aversion is special and shows how the results change for different specifications. This is important as the specifications of these functions depend on the relationship between total producer income and crop gross revenue, and on the interpretation of 'effort'.

The last model in Chapter 23 is the simplest model which allows for a choice between alternative crops, one of which is risky, and which examines trade between areas with imperfectly correlated risk. It thus provides a different model for the opportunity cost of growing the risky crop, and for the risk facing the particular producer (or consumer). The last model is amazingly rich in its implications and bears on much wider issues than just the long-run consequences of price stabilization, for it discusses the efficiency of free trade and the nature of optimal trade policy.

Chapter 21*

The Simple Theory of Supply Response to Price Stabilization

This chapter analyses the effects of a commodity price stabilization scheme within a simple long-run equilibrium model in which producers adjust their output in response to changes in risk. The basic model is the simple rational expectations equilibrium model presented in Chapters 10 and 15. The price stabilization scheme changes the expected marginal utility of production, which induces a change in the level of output. An equilibrium price stabilization programme is one in which average consumption continues to be equal to average output, where average output is itself a function of the price stabilization scheme. We show that with constant relative risk aversion, although the supply reponses may reduce the level of welfare gains associated with an equilibrium price stabilization, they never eliminate them or reverse their direction.

The chapter is divided into six main sections. Section 21.1 presents the basic model of producer behaviour. Section 21.2 introduces two new concepts: *equilibrium* price stabilization schemes and *homothetic* price stabilization schemes. Section 21.3 presents a set of general formulae relating the long-run to the short-run effects of a price stabilization scheme on welfare and effort, and shows how these formulae simplify for the case of constant relative risk aversion. It also compares briefly the long-run and short-run effects on consumers. Section 21.4 applies these results to derive formulae for various specific stabilization schemes, section 21.5 looks at the distributional impact of stabilization when producers differ in their attitude to risk, and section 21.6 briefly discusses demand induced variability. We conclude with some caveats about the generality of these results.

21.1 A model of supply under price risk

Farmers grow only a single crop. All farmers face identical, multiplicative production risk and have access to the same production possibilities, so that output per farmer, q, is a linear stochastic function of input of effort, x:

$$\tilde{q} = \tilde{\theta}x, \quad E\tilde{\theta} = 1, \qquad (21.1)$$

where $\tilde{\theta}$ is the random effect of weather, and the source of the randomness in prices. (A comparison of this model with that of section 6.4 shows that there is little difference between diminishing returns to effort and increasing marginal disutility of effort, so we choose the simplest formulation.) Total output $\tilde{Q}$ is thus

$$\tilde{Q} = \tilde{\theta}\bar{Q}, \quad \bar{Q} = \sum x, \qquad (21.2)$$

where $\bar{Q}$ is average output, the sum of individual farmer's average output, x. Price is a stable function of the random total output, $p(\tilde{Q})$, and is hence random. His welfare depends both on his income and the effort he has expended, x:

$$U = U(\tilde{y}, x) \tag{21.3}$$

$$\tilde{y} = p(\tilde{\theta}\bar{Q})\tilde{\theta}x. \tag{21.4}$$

The farmer chooses how much effort to supply before the weather is known and aims to maximize expected utility, EU, which, for simplicity, is assumed to be additively separable:

$$EU(\tilde{y}, x) = Eu(\tilde{y}) - v(x), \tag{21.5}$$

where $u'' < 0$, i.e. the farmer is risk averse, and $v'' > 0$, i.e. increasing marginal disutility of effort.

21.1.1 Equilibrium without price stabilization

Equation (21.4) implies that, for the individual farmer, income risk is also multiplicative with the random factor $\tilde{p}\tilde{\theta}$, but obviously for society this is not true. The individual farmer maximizes expected utility taking the price distribution as given, but he is aware that p depends on θ, and that good weather with high personal production will be associated with low prices. In short, farmers are assumed to hold rational expectations. The reason for this assumption is that we are interested in the long-run supply response to stabilization, once farmers have learnt how the price distribution has changed. In the short run it is probably more appropriate to assume that supply does not respond as we did in Part IV. There are, of course, other possibilities as well, as we discussed in Chapter 11. In particular, individuals can form expectations on the basis of some naïve rule relating forecasted price to past observed price. Turnovsky (1974) has analysed one variant of such a model. There are two effects associated with any change in the price distribution: the supply response, with which we are concerned here, and in addition, the average inefficiency resulting from forecasting error may change. The models of Chapter 11 illustrated these points.

The farmer chooses input x, yielding average welfare W:

$$W = \underset{x}{\text{Max}} \ [Eu\{p^e(\tilde{\theta})\tilde{\theta}x\} - v(x)], \tag{21.6}$$

where $p^e(\theta)$ is the expected price when the state is θ, a stable function of the random demand.

The choice of x satisfies

$$Eu'(\tilde{y}^e)p^e(\tilde{\theta})\tilde{\theta} = v'(x), \quad \tilde{y}^e = p^e(\tilde{\theta})\tilde{\theta}x. \tag{21.7}$$

This can be solved to find the farmer's supply of effort as a function of the price distribution. We write the ith farmer's input as

$$x_i = x_i\{p^e(\tilde{\theta})\}. \tag{21.8}$$

From (21.2), we obtain that the actual price in state θ is

$$p(\theta) = p\left(\theta \sum_i x_i\right). \tag{21.10}$$

A rational expectations equilibrium is one in which

$$p(\theta) = p\left[\theta \sum x_i\{p^e(\theta)\}\right] \tag{21.10}$$

when

$$p^e(\theta) \equiv p(\theta) \tag{21.11}$$

for *all* individuals, i.e. all individual expectations coincide precisely with the realization. (Rational expectations equilibrium can be shown to exist in our model under reasonable assumptions. However, in more general models, there are some non-trivial existence problems.)

21.1.2 *The stability of equilibrium*

In Chapter 6 we remarked that the stability of market equilibrium can only be analysed once the disequilibrium adjustment process has been specified. Even in riskless markets there are at least three possible adjustment processes, which Samuelson (1947, ch. IX) labelled as Walrasian (prices adjust to excess demand), Marshallian (supplies respond to profitable demand), or cobweb (supplies respond to lagged prices). In Chapter 11 we discussed a simple model of learning in the presence of risk, which suggested that adjustment processes are considerably more complex than in riskless markets. Two adjustments are now necessary instead of one, for expectations have to adjust as well as supplies. Since it is difficult to be very definite about the way in which expectations adjust we shall analyse stability under two different extreme assumptions: presumably the truth will be somewhere between the two. The optimistic extreme is to assume that the Walrasian adjustment process works, so that prices are adjusted in the 'right direction'. The difficulty with this Walrasian process is that, with risky prices, the whole distribution must somehow be adjusted, and it is not clear how this is to be interpreted. Moreover, since it is unclear why (and how) the price (or price distribution) should be so conveniently adjusted, one could expect the resulting condition to be a very minimal stability condition. The alternative, pessimistic extreme is to look for conditions which guarantee stability even if agents adapt their expectations immediately, as in the single lag cobweb model. In general, with slower adaptation, the stability conditions will be less stringent than those suggested by this criterion.

The first problem is to identify the relevant measure of the elasticity of supply in the presence of risk. It would be convenient if the elasticity corresponds to the natural measure of elasticity in the riskless case, and fortunately that is the case. If there were no risk, the supply elasticity can be found by

The Simple Theory of Supply Response to Price Stabilization 307

totally differentiating equation (21.7)

$$\frac{d\log Q}{d\log p} = \frac{yu''/u' + 1}{xv''/v' - yu''/u'} \equiv \zeta \tag{21.12}$$

$$\zeta = \frac{1 - R}{\gamma + R}, \tag{21.13}$$

where ζ is the elasticity of supply, R is the coefficient of relative risk aversion, and γ is the elasticity of the marginal disutility of effort:

$$\gamma = \frac{d\log v'}{d\log x} = \frac{xv''}{v'}. \tag{21.14}$$

(Cf. equation (6.35), where the *output* elasticity is α times the input elasticity. With separable utility, there is little difference between diminishing returns to effort or increasing disutility of effort.)

Our optimistic stability condition would have prices adjusted towards equilibrium in response to disequilibrium, according to some such process as

$$\frac{dp}{dt} = \phi(D - S), \quad \phi' > 0, \quad \phi(0) = 0. \tag{21.15}$$

If the elasticity of demand is ϵ (as a positive number), then stability requires that at the equilibrium price p^*

$$\frac{d\phi}{dp} = \phi' \cdot \frac{Q(p^*)}{p^*}(-\epsilon - \zeta) < 0$$

or

$$\zeta > -\epsilon. \tag{21.16}$$

With risk, it becomes necessary to shift the whole price distribution in response to disequilibrium. One natural way to do this is to shift the distribution by a scale factor, λ, so that the new distribution is $\lambda p(\theta)$. It is easy to show that with constant relative risk aversion

$$\frac{\lambda dEQ}{EQd\lambda} = \frac{\lambda dx}{xd\lambda} = \frac{1 - R}{\gamma + R} = \zeta, \tag{21.17}$$

suggesting that this is a natural way to define the elasticity of supply with risk. Rather than pursue this course, we can address the stability question directly, using our more stringent cobweb stability criterion. We ask, how would each producer respond in his choice of inputs, x, if all other producers increased inputs to μx^*, $\mu > 1$, thus changing the price distribution to $p(\mu \bar{Q}^*)$. Would the change in price distribution lead to a reduction in inputs towards the former level, x^*, or not? The equilibrium will be stable if

$$\left|\frac{\mu dx}{xd\mu}\right| < 1 \tag{21.18}$$

where the absolute value imposes the condition that the inputs should not overshoot by an amplified amount. To evaluate this, observe that for a constant elasticity of demand

$$p(\mu \dot{Q}) = \mu^{-1/\epsilon} p(\theta) = \lambda p(\theta)$$

for $\lambda = \mu^{-1/\epsilon}$. Then, either by differentiating the first-order condition of equation (21.7) with respect to μ, or using equation (21.17) directly we obtain

$$\left| \frac{\mu dx}{dx\mu} \right| = \left| -\frac{1}{\epsilon} \frac{\lambda dx}{x d\lambda} \right| = \left| -\frac{\zeta}{\epsilon} \right| < 1 \qquad (21.19)$$

and the stability condition can now be written as

$$0 > \zeta > -\epsilon$$

or

$$0 < \zeta < \epsilon.$$

For values of ζ such that

$$\zeta > \epsilon > 0$$

the system is unstable by the cobweb criterion, though not by the less stringent condition (21.16). It follows that if expectations are adjusted slowly enough the market will be stable for all positive values of ζ. Conversely, the market will never be stable if $\zeta < -\epsilon$ so that the supply curve slopes down less steeply than demand.

21.2 A general characterization of stabilization schemes

A stabilization scheme changes the probability distribution of prices corresponding to a given output so that we have

$$\tilde{p} = p(\tilde{\theta}, \bar{Q}, z), \qquad (21.20)$$

where z is some parameterization of a family of stabilization schemes, $\bar{Q}$ is average output, and θ describes the underlying source of risk (which here is scalar, since there is only uniform supply risk). For example, the simplest linear buffer stock rule would be to purchase all production but to sell a more stable, weighted average of $\bar{Q}$ and Q, to consumers:

$$Q^c = z\bar{Q} + (1-z)Q = \bar{Q}\phi(z), \quad 0 \leq z \leq 1 \qquad (21.21)$$

$$\phi(z) \equiv z + (1-z)\theta.$$

Then $z = 0$ corresponds to no stabilization, $z = 1$ to perfect stabilization. The consumer price would then be

$$p = p\{\bar{Q}\phi(z)\} = p(\bar{Q}, \tilde{\theta}, z).$$

A *homothetic stabilization scheme* is one which allows the price to be expressed as a product of a riskless and a risky term:

$$p = g(\bar{Q}, z)h(\hat{\theta}, z). \qquad (21.22)$$

This implies that the percentage change of price resulting from a change in average output is independent of the state of the weather, that is, the value of the random variable $\hat{\theta}$. The linear stocking rule above gives a homothetic stabilization scheme if the elasticity of demand is constant.

When the elasticity of demand is constant

$$g(\bar{Q}) = \bar{Q}^{-1/\epsilon}$$

and

$$\log p = -\frac{1}{\epsilon} \log \bar{Q} + \log h(\theta, z).$$

The total impact of a change in the degree of stabilization, z, on prices is then

$$\frac{1}{p}\frac{dp}{dz} = -\frac{1}{\epsilon}\frac{1}{\bar{Q}}\frac{d\bar{Q}}{dz} + \frac{1}{p}\frac{\partial p}{\partial z}. \qquad (21.23)$$

The proposed formulation of the price stabilization for supply risk has

$$h(\theta, z) = \phi^{-1/\epsilon} \equiv \{z + (1-z)\theta\}^{-1/\epsilon}.$$

More generally, provided risk is multiplicative and demand of constant elasticity, it is always possible to design a homothetic stabilization scheme no matter what the source of the risk, or the objective of the buffer (to stabilize prices or producer incomes.)

Again as in equation (21.10) equilibrium, for a given z, requires that

$$\tilde{p}(\bar{Q}, \theta, z) = p\left[\hat{\theta} \sum x\{\tilde{p}(\bar{Q}, \theta, z)\}\right] \qquad (21.24)$$

when

$$\bar{Q} = \sum x\{\tilde{p}(\bar{Q}, \hat{\theta}, z)\}.$$

Thus, *equilibrium* price stabilization schemes have the property that

$$\frac{d\bar{Q}}{dz} = \sum \frac{\partial x}{\partial \tilde{p}} \frac{\partial \tilde{p}}{\partial \bar{Q}} \frac{d\bar{Q}}{dz} + \sum \frac{\partial x}{\partial \tilde{p}} \frac{d\tilde{p}}{dz}, \qquad (21.25)$$

where the term $\partial x/\partial \tilde{p}$ is to be read as the change in effort resulting from the change in the price distribution, and the term $\partial \tilde{p}/\partial \bar{Q}$ is to be read as the change in the price distribution resulting from a change in mean output.

Once the particular stabilization scheme has been specified, equation (21.7) can be solved to give the equilibrium supply of effort (and hence average output) as a function of the level of stabilization z

310 *Commodity Price Stabilization*

$$x = x\{\tilde{p}(\bar{Q}, \tilde{\theta}, z)\}. \qquad (21.26)$$

Equilibrium price stabilization schemes are those which take into account their own effect on the level of output, and the effect on the change in output on the price which will prevail in each state of nature.

21.3 The effects of equilibrium homothetic price stabilization schemes

In this section, we ask what are the short-run and long-run equilibrium effects of a change in the degree of stabilization on the level of effort and welfare.

The short-run effects ignore the change in output and are straightforward:

$$\frac{\partial W}{\partial z} = Eu'\tilde{\theta}\frac{\partial \tilde{p}}{\partial z}x + \frac{\partial E\{u - v(x)\}}{\partial x}\frac{\partial x}{\partial z} \qquad (21.27)$$

$$= Eu'\tilde{\theta}\frac{\partial \tilde{p}}{\partial z}x$$

using the envelope theorem (that $\partial W/\partial x = 0$). From (21.7) we obtain

$$\frac{\partial \log x}{\partial z} = \frac{E\left\{u''(\tilde{y})\tilde{\theta}x\frac{\partial \tilde{p}}{\partial z}\tilde{p}\tilde{\theta} + u'\tilde{\theta}\frac{\partial \tilde{p}}{\partial z}\right\}}{v''x - Eu'' \cdot \tilde{y}\tilde{p}\tilde{\theta}} \qquad (21.28)$$

$$\frac{1}{x}\frac{\partial x}{\partial z} = \frac{Eu'\tilde{\theta}\frac{\partial \tilde{p}}{\partial z}(1-R)}{v''x - Eu''\tilde{y}\tilde{p}\tilde{\theta}}$$

$$= \frac{Eu'\tilde{\theta}\frac{\partial \tilde{p}}{\partial z}(1-R)}{Eu'\tilde{p}\tilde{\theta}} \cdot \frac{1}{\gamma + \bar{R}},$$

where

$$\bar{R} = \frac{Eu'\tilde{p}\tilde{\theta}R}{Eu'\tilde{p}\tilde{\theta}}.$$

We thus obtain the important result that if *relative risk aversion is constant*

$$\frac{\partial x}{\partial z} = \frac{\varsigma}{v'}\frac{\partial W}{\partial z}, \qquad (21.29)$$

where ς is the elasticity of supply of equation (21.17).

The response of effort is proportional to the effect on welfare with the proportionality factor being the elasticity of supply with respect to price divided by the marginal disutility of effort.

Moreover, we obtain the result that the short-run impact on welfare and that on output are of the same or opposite sign as relative risk aversion is less than or greater than unity.

The immediate implication of this is that the long-run equilibrium effect can be ignored if and only if the stabilization programme has no effect on welfare.

We now calculate the long-run impact:

$$\frac{dW}{dz} = Eu'\tilde{\theta}\frac{d\tilde{p}}{dz}x \qquad (21.30)$$

and

$$\frac{d\log x}{dz} = \frac{Eu'\tilde{\theta}\frac{d\tilde{p}}{dz}(1-R)}{v''x - Eu''\tilde{y}\tilde{p}\tilde{\theta}} \qquad (21.31)$$

where

$$\frac{d\tilde{p}}{dz} = \frac{\partial\tilde{p}}{\partial z} + \frac{\partial\tilde{p}}{\partial \bar{Q}}\frac{d\bar{Q}}{dz}. \qquad (21.32)$$

Hence for a homothetic price stabilization scheme, with constant elasticity demand (equation (21.23) above) and with identical farmers

$$\frac{d\tilde{p}}{dz} = \frac{\partial\tilde{p}}{\partial z} - \frac{\tilde{p}}{\epsilon}\frac{1}{\bar{Q}}\frac{d\bar{Q}}{dz} \qquad (21.33)$$

$$= \frac{\partial\tilde{p}}{\partial z} - \frac{\tilde{p}}{\epsilon}\frac{d\log x}{dz}.$$

Then substituting (21.33) into (21.31) and rearranging.

$$\frac{d\log x}{dz} = \frac{Eu'\tilde{\theta}\frac{\partial\tilde{p}}{\partial z}(1-R)}{v''x - Eu''\tilde{y}\tilde{p}\tilde{\theta}} \bigg/ \left[1 + \frac{1}{\epsilon}\left\{\frac{Eu'\tilde{\theta}(1-R)\tilde{p}}{v''x - Eu''\tilde{p}\tilde{\theta}\tilde{y}}\right\}\right]. \qquad (21.34)$$

In the case of constant relative risk aversion we obtain from equation (21.17)

$$\frac{d\log x}{dz} = \frac{\partial\log x}{\partial z}\frac{1}{1 + \frac{\zeta}{\epsilon}} \qquad (21.35)$$

since

$$Eu'\tilde{\theta}\tilde{p}(1-R) = (1-R)Eu'\tilde{\theta}\tilde{p} = v'(1-R)$$

by the first-order condition, equation (21.7).

Thus

$$\left|\frac{d\log x}{dz}\right| \gtreqless \left|\frac{\partial\log x}{\partial z}\right| \text{ as } R \gtreqless 1. \qquad (21.36)$$

The absolute value of the long-run change in output is greater or smaller than the short-run change as relative risk aversion is greater or less than one (the algebraic value is always decreased).

Substituting (21.29) into (21.35), we obtain

$$\frac{dx}{dz} = \frac{\partial W}{\partial z} \frac{\zeta}{v'} \frac{1}{1 + \zeta/\epsilon}. \tag{21.37}$$

To obtain the long-term impact on welfare, we obtain, substituting (21.33) into (21.30):

$$\frac{dW}{dz} = \frac{\partial W}{\partial z} - (Eu'\hat{\theta}\tilde{p}) - \frac{1}{\epsilon}\frac{d\log x}{dz}.$$

Making use of the first-order condition, we have for all utility functions

$$\frac{dW}{dz} = \frac{\partial W}{\partial z} - \frac{v'}{\epsilon}\frac{dx}{dz}. \tag{21.38}$$

In the special case of constant relative risk aversion, we have, using equation (21.37)

$$\frac{dW}{dz} = \frac{\epsilon}{\epsilon + \zeta}\frac{\partial W}{\partial z}. \tag{21.39}$$

Summarizing, we can say that if farmers have constant relative risk aversion the long-run equilibrium welfare gains are smaller or greater than the impact welfare gains as ζ, the supply elasticity, is positive or negative, but so long as the stability condition (21.16) is satisfied, the direction of the short- and long-run welfare gains are the same. In the next chapter we show that this result depends crucially on the assumption of constant relative risk aversion.

21.3.1 *The effect on consumers*

The relationship between the impact and long-run effects on consumers is particularly simple in the case of stable consumer demand. Let $V(p, I)$ be the level of consumers' utility when the price is p. Then

$$\frac{dEV(\tilde{p}, I)}{dz} = \frac{\partial EV(\tilde{p}, I)}{\partial z} + \frac{\partial EV(\tilde{p}, I)}{\partial \bar{Q}}\frac{d\bar{Q}}{dz}. \tag{21.40}$$

The first term is the short-run impact effect, the second is a transfer term resulting from the change in the average supply. If producers and consumers are weighted equally, this will cancel out. A mean-quantity-preserving change in price dispersion is thus all that is needed to value the impact on total welfare in this special case (though it is inadequate to investigate the distributional impact).

Roy's identity can again be used to evaluate equation (21.40) for homothetic stabilization schemes with constant elasticity demand curves:

The Simple Theory of Supply Response to Price Stabilization

$$\frac{dEV}{dz} = -V_I \left\{ E\tilde{Q}^c \frac{\partial \tilde{p}}{\partial z} - \frac{1}{\epsilon} E(\tilde{Q}^c \tilde{p}) \frac{1}{\bar{Q}} \frac{d\bar{Q}}{dz} \right\} \quad (21.41)$$

provided that $V_{Ip} = 0$, or the marginal utility of income is roughly constant.

If the source of price variability is supply variability, then a small stabilization scheme has the property that

$$Q^c \approx Q$$

so

$$E\tilde{Q}^c \frac{\partial \tilde{p}}{\partial z} = E\tilde{Q} \frac{\partial \tilde{p}}{\partial z} = \text{change in revenue of producers.}$$

If the elasticity of demand is constant, this is unambiguously negative.

The sign of $d\bar{Q}/dz$, however, depends on the value of ζ (which in turn depends on the value of R, the degree of risk aversion). Thus, the short-run and long-run equilibrium effects on consumers are not only of different magnitudes, but may be of opposite signs, particularly if there are large supply responses.

21.4 The evaluation of particular schemes

It is straightforward to evaluate a variety of stabilization schemes, depending on the source of the risk and the objective of the scheme. As an example, consider the price stabilization scheme of equation (21.21).

$$\frac{\partial p}{\partial z} = \frac{p(\theta - 1)}{\epsilon \phi}, \quad \phi \equiv z + (1 - z)\theta,$$

so from (21.27)

$$\frac{\partial W}{\partial z} = \frac{x}{\epsilon} Eu'\theta p(\theta - 1)/\phi, \quad x = Eq = \bar{q}. \quad (21.42)$$

21.4.1 A small degree of stabilization

At $z = 0$, $\phi = \theta$, and a Taylor series expansion of the right-hand side of equation (21.42) about $\theta = 1$ gives, for the case of constant elasticity ϵ, and constant risk aversion, R, the short-run impact as:

$$B = \frac{1}{u'} \frac{\partial W}{\partial z} = \frac{p(\bar{Q})\bar{q}}{\epsilon} \{(1-R)(1 - 1/\epsilon) - 1\} \sigma^2$$

$$B = -\frac{p(\bar{Q})\bar{q}}{\epsilon} \{R(1 - 1/\epsilon) + 1/\epsilon\} \sigma^2, \quad (21.43)$$

where $\sigma^2 = E(\theta - 1)^2$, the variance of θ. (That is, σ is the coefficient of variation of output.) Equation (21.43) is the same as equation (18.21) derived using the general method of mean-quantity-preserving reductions in price dispersion. If all producers are alike, the second term of equation (21.41) can be derived from equation (21.37):

$$\frac{1}{\bar{Q}}\frac{d\bar{Q}}{dz} = \frac{d\log x}{dz} = \frac{1}{xv'}\frac{\zeta}{1+\zeta/\epsilon}\frac{\partial W}{\partial z}.$$

Using equation (21.43) this becomes:

$$\frac{1}{\bar{Q}}\frac{d\bar{Q}}{dz} = -\frac{\zeta}{\epsilon+\zeta}\{R(1-1/\epsilon)+1/\epsilon\}\sigma^2. \tag{21.44}$$

The supply response to a small amount of stabilization is thus likely to be negative, which explains why the long-run effect on producers is not so disadvantageous as the immediate impact.

The immediate impact on consumers is the first term in equation (21.40) whch is positive

$$B^c = \frac{1}{V_I}\frac{\partial EV}{\partial z} = -\frac{1}{\epsilon}EpQ^c(\theta-1)/\theta = \bar{p}\bar{Q}\frac{\sigma^2}{\epsilon^2} = \bar{X}\sigma_p^2, \tag{21.45}$$

where X is expenditure and σ_p is the coefficient of variation of prices.

The long-run impact can be found from equations (21.41), (21.44), and (21.45) taking $EpQ^c = \bar{X}$ is

$$B^c = \frac{\bar{X}}{\epsilon+\zeta}\{\epsilon+\zeta R(\epsilon-1)\}\sigma_p^2 \tag{21.46}$$

which is positive or negative as $R(\epsilon-1) \gtreqless \epsilon/\zeta$.

The change in average buffer profits Y^b is found as follows. If

$$Y^b = Ep(Q^c - Q) = z\bar{Q}Ep(1-\theta)$$

$$\frac{1}{\bar{Q}}\frac{dY^b}{dz} = Ep(1-\theta) + z\left\{E(1-\theta)\frac{\partial p}{\partial z} + E(1-\theta)\frac{\partial p}{\partial \bar{Q}}\frac{d\bar{Q}}{dz}\right\}. \tag{21.47}$$

At $z = 0$ this reduces to

$$\frac{dY^b}{dz} = \bar{Q}p(\bar{Q})\frac{\sigma^2}{\epsilon} = \frac{\partial Y^b}{\partial z}.$$

If these profits are attributed to producers equation (21.43) is replaced by

$$\frac{1}{u'}\frac{\partial W}{\partial z} = \frac{p(\bar{Q})\bar{q}}{\epsilon^2}(1-R)(\epsilon-1)\sigma^2, \tag{21.48}$$

which could easily be of the opposite sign to that excluding profits.

21.4.2 Small departures from complete stabilization

At $z = 1, \phi = 1, p = p(\bar{Q})$ and the short-run impacts are approximately

$$\frac{1}{u'}\frac{\partial W}{\partial z} = \frac{p(\bar{Q})\bar{q}}{\epsilon}(1-R)\sigma^2 > 0 \quad \text{if} \quad \zeta > 0 \tag{21.49}$$

$$\frac{\partial EV}{\partial z} = 0.$$

The Simple Theory of Supply Response to Price Stabilization   315

The supply response is

$$\frac{1}{\bar{Q}}\frac{d\bar{Q}}{dz} = \frac{\zeta}{\epsilon + \zeta}(1-R)\sigma^2 > 0$$

since ζ has the same sign as $1 - R$, so the long-run impact on consumers is

$$\frac{(1-R)\zeta\epsilon}{\zeta+\epsilon}\bar{X}\sigma_p^2 > 0. \tag{21.50}$$

At complete stabilization the welfare impact and supply response are thus typically in the opposite direction to those produced by a small amount of stabilization. The effect on buffer income is found from equation (21.47) setting $p = p(\bar{Q})$, constant, and $z = 1$:

$$\frac{dY^b}{dz} = -\bar{Q}p(\bar{Q})\frac{\sigma^2}{\epsilon} = \frac{\partial Y^b}{\partial z} < 0,$$

which, if attributed to producers, gives a short-run impact of

$$\frac{1}{u'}\frac{\partial W}{\partial z} = -\frac{p(\bar{Q})\bar{q}}{\epsilon}R\sigma^2 < 0 \tag{21.51}$$

exactly reversing the direction of the short-run impact if $\zeta > 0$.

21.5 The distributional impacts of stabilization with diverse producers

Land holdings are typically very unequally distributed among farmers, and it may therefore be very misleading to characterize the supply response to stabilization schemes in terms of a representative farmer. It is important to know whether farmers with different characteristics (like risk aversion) are affected differently by stabilization. Equations (21.30) and (21.32) give

$$\frac{dW}{dz} = \frac{\partial W}{\partial z} - \frac{1}{\epsilon}\frac{\bar{q}}{\bar{Q}}\frac{d\bar{Q}}{dz}Eu'\theta p.$$

Suppose most farmers are alike, and dominate in determining the supply response, but a few are different. Let asterisks denote the dominant producers, and consider a small degree of stabilization when the scheme is as in equation (21.21). It follows from (21.39) and (21.43)

$$\frac{1}{\bar{y}^*u'^*}\cdot\frac{dW^*}{dz} = -\left(\frac{1}{\epsilon+\zeta}\right)\left\{R^*\left(1-\frac{1}{\epsilon}\right)+\frac{1}{\epsilon}\right\}\sigma^2. \tag{21.52}$$

Taking the change in over-all output as given by (21.44) in terms of R^* and combining this with (21.30) and (21.32) the impact on the small group is

$$\frac{1}{\bar{y}u'}\cdot\frac{dW}{dz} = -\left(\frac{1}{\epsilon+\zeta}\right)\left[\left(1-\frac{1}{\epsilon}\right)\left\{R+\frac{\zeta}{\epsilon}(R-R^*)\right\}+\frac{1}{\epsilon}\right]\sigma^2. \tag{21.53}$$

It is evidently possible for more risk-averse farmers to be affected in the opposite

21.6 Demand-induced variability

The analysis follows closely along the lines of the previous section except now we have to specify the nature of the stochastic variations in the demand functions and the form of the stabilization scheme. As an example, suppose that in addition to the supply risk of the previous section the demand function is

$$Q^c = \dot\psi p^{-\epsilon}, \quad E\dot\psi = 1,$$

where $\dot\psi$ is a random factor (perhaps generated by variations in other prices, or in income). A stabilization scheme which sells

$$Q^c = \bar{Q}\theta^{1-z}\psi^z$$

so that

$$p = (\psi/\theta)^{(1-z)/\epsilon}\bar{Q}^{-1/\epsilon}$$

is homothetic and as z varies from 0 to 1 gradually introduces complete price stabilization. The previous general formulae stand, except that

$$\frac{\partial p}{\partial z} = \frac{p}{\epsilon}\log(\theta/\psi),$$

so that, for example, using equation (21.27)

$$\frac{\partial W}{\partial z} = \frac{x}{\epsilon}Eu'\hat{\theta}\hat{p}\log(\hat{\theta}/\hat{\psi}).$$

Obviously the correlation between θ and ψ will affect the outcome. If $\theta \equiv 1$ so that there is only variability in demand,

$$\frac{1}{\bar{y}\bar{u}'}\frac{\partial W}{\partial z} = -(1-R)(1-z)\frac{\sigma^2}{\epsilon^2}$$

where $\sigma^2 = \text{Var }\psi$. This can also be expressed in terms of the remaining price variability, σ_p (the coefficient of variation)

$$\frac{1}{\bar{y}\bar{u}'}\frac{\partial W}{\partial z} = -\frac{1-R}{1-z}\sigma_p^2. \qquad (21.54)$$

Income stabilization schemes can likewise be analysed. Thus, if demand and supply variability are as before, the buffer sells

$$Q^c = \bar{Q}\theta^{1+z(\epsilon-1)}\psi^z$$

and farmer's income is then

$$y = p\theta x = xp(\bar{Q})\{\theta^{(1-1/\epsilon)}\psi^{(1/\epsilon)}\}^{1-z}.$$

21.7 Concluding remarks

This chapter has developed a general method of converting short-run impact analysis into long-run full equilibrium analysis. The long-run incidence of a commodity price stabilization scheme may be markedly different from the short-run incidence.

The direction of change in output and welfare is the same or different as relative risk aversion is less than or greater than unity. The magnitude of the long-run effect on average output is always algebraically smaller than the short-run equilibrium effect. The short-run and long-run effect on the welfare of producers is of the same sign: the magnitude of the long-run effect is a simple multiple of the short-run effect: the multiple is greater or less than one depending on whether relative risk aversion is greater or less than unity. If the elasticity of demand is very low, the long-run effect is much smaller than the short-run effect. On the other hand, the long-run welfare gains of consumers may be of opposite signs to that of the short-run gains.

Perhaps the most important result is that changes in output can be viewed as pure transfer effects. Thus the analysis of the mean-quantity-preserving price stabilization schemes (Part IV) is all that is required for an analysis of the 'net' welfare gains associated with a small change in the degree of stabilization.

Many of the results of this chapter depended critically, however, on the assumption of constant relative risk aversion, the assumption that all farmers were identical and grew only one crop, and the assumption that the number of farmers growing that crop was fixed. These assumptions, as we indicated in the introduction to Part V, are critical. In the next chapter, we explore the importance of these assumptions more carefully.

Chapter 22

Risk Aversion and Supply Response: A Geometrical Analysis

22.1 Introduction

The last chapter demonstrated the considerable simplification made possible by assuming constant relative risk aversion. This amounts to assuming a specific relation between marginal and total utility in Fig. V.1 of the Introduction to Part V, and, as a consequence, the effect of a change in the price distribution on utility and marginal utility are proportional. Marginal utility affects supply, total utility affects welfare, so supply responses produce a simple proportional modification to welfare changes in this formulation. In general, however, price stabilization might affect total and marginal utility quite differently, so that the supply response might even reverse the direction of the immediate impact. In this chapter we simplify the model of the previous chapter further by assuming that there are only two equally probable states of the world, so that the price can only take one of two values. This enables us to examine the model geometrically to see first, why the long-run effects of price stabilization are in the same direction as the impact effect with constant relative risk aversion, and, second, under what conditions this ceases to be true.

We also use the model to investigate another important earlier result, which suggested that the net welfare effect of price stabilization was always positive. In Chapter 18 we showed that if mean supply remained constant, and if the marginal utilities of incomes of producers and consumers also remained constant, then the beneficiaries of price stabilization could afford to compensate the losers. Ignoring the costs, price stabilization was a potential Pareto improvement.

There has been a long-standing controversy concerning whether it is profitable for firms to randomize their prices, and indeed whether consumers might be better off as a result of randomization of prices. Waugh (1944) pointed out that consumers would prefer to buy at random prices rather than at prices stabilized at the arithmetic mean. Oi (1961) showed that competitive producers would earn higher profits by selling at varying prices than by selling at prices stabilized at their arithmetic mean. However, as Samuelson (1972a, p. 488) forcefully argued, where competitive *laissez-faire* leads to stability, 'no bootstrap operation of manufactured price instability can accomplish the wonderful promises of the Waugh and Oi prospectuses, namely to make both producers and consumers better off'. The argument is that any competitive equilibrium is Pareto efficient, so any movement away from one equilibrium to another must make some agents worse off.

Another way of putting the argument is to observe that it will not in general be feasible to keep the mean price constant for mean sales will in general change as prices are destabilized, as will mean supply. Although profits and utility are convex in prices, production functions and utility are conventionally assumed concave in quantities, demonstrating the infeasibility of making both parties better off by destabilization.

The argument, however, rests on two assumptions — that the economy is competitive and that there is no exogenous source of instability. Newbery (1978) showed that in the presence of imperfect competition it might be possible to make everyone better off by destabilizing prices, and this chapter shows that if there is an exogenous source of instability in a competitive economy, it may make both producers and consumers worse off to stabilize prices, or, more dramatically, it may make both parties better off to further destabilize prices.

In this chapter we establish two important results: (a) the long-run impact may differ not only quantitatively but qualitatively from the short-run impact: producers may be better (worse) off in the short run, but worse off (better off) in the long run; and (b) a commodity price stabilization scheme may make both consumers and producers worse off.

The first result is somewhat surprising; normally, we expect impact and long-run results to differ in magnitude, but not in direction. The intuitive reason for the conventional view may be put as follows: assume stabilizing commodity prices improves the welfare of producers in the short run. This will lead them to produce more (since the 'certainty equivalent' return to farming is greater). But they will never increase output so much as to decrease price levels to the point that utility was the same as it was prior to commodity price stabilization; for were they to do so, the certainty equivalent return to farming would be the same as it was prior to stabilization, in which case inputs (effort) would be the same and therefore, output would be the same.

What is wrong with this argument is that it assumes that there is a simple relationship between expected *marginal* utility (which determines the level of effort) and expected *total* utility; in the case of constant relative risk aversion, there is a simple (proportional) relationship, and it is this which accounts for the simple results obtained in the previous chapter. But if relative risk aversion is not constant (and there is no reason to assume that it is) then the two may move in quite different ways.

The second result has a simple interpretation. Price stabilization may increase income instability; since prices and output are negatively correlated, if the elasticity of demand is not too low, income variability is less than output variability. Thus, under not implausible conditions, price stabilization makes producers worse off in the short run; if there is constant relative risk aversion (weaker conditions will suffice) then effort and aggregate output (in all states of nature) will be reduced. This will modify the quantitative effect on producers' welfare, but they will still be worse off in the long run. In addition, consumers will be worse off as a result of the lowering of output; they will be better off as a result of the reduction in the variability of sales. In general the net effect is ambiguous, but there are conditions in which the net effect is unambiguously negative.

As we observe later, these perversities are not (necessarily) related to a failure of the usual stability conditions to hold. They can obtain for quite 'reasonable' values of the parameters.

22.2 The model

Since our object is to examine the special features of the earlier results, we use essentially the same model as in the last chapter. Output per farmer in state i is q_i, where there are two equally likely states of the world, $i = 1, 2$:

$$q_i = \theta_i x \quad i = 1, 2 \tag{22.1}$$

$$\theta_1 < \theta_2, \quad \frac{\theta_1 + \theta_2}{2} = 1.$$

There is no demand variability, so without price stabilization

$$p_1 > p_2.$$

As before, there are constant returns to effort but diminishing separable disutility of effort (indistinguishable from diminishing returns to effort) so the farmer's expected utility is

$$W = EU = \tfrac{1}{2}u(p_1\theta_1 x) + \tfrac{1}{2}u(p_2\theta_2 x) - v(x). \tag{22.2}$$

Again, an equilibrium price stabilization scheme must ensure that average supply equals average demand:

$$D(p_1) + D(p_2) = 2\bar{Q} \tag{22.3}$$

$$\bar{Q} = nEq = nx \tag{22.4}$$

where n is the number of farmers. Each farmer chooses effort, x, to maximize expected utility, yielding first-order conditions

$$Eu'p\theta = \tfrac{1}{2}(u'_1 p_1 \theta_1 + u'_2 p_2 \theta_2) = v' \tag{22.5}$$

where u'_i is marginal utility of income, y_i, in state i:

$$u'_i \equiv u'(y_i), \quad y_i \equiv p_i \theta_i x.$$

22.3 Outline of the diagrammatic approach

The basic ideas of static general equilibrium can be conveniently illustrated for the two-good case by drawing production possibilities and indifference curves in quantity space. In the present model we have two goods — output in each state of the world — but it is more convenient to work in price space, (p_1, p_2), for then any price stabilization scheme is just a new pair of prices (p_1^*, p_2^*) which lies closer to the 45° line than the original set of prices.

It is easy to draw indifference curves describing consumer preferences in price space, using the indirect utility function $V(p, I)$, for the consumers' expected utility is constant for price pairs (p_1, p_2) such that

$$EV = \tfrac{1}{2}(V(p_1, I) + V(p_2, I)) = \bar{V}, \text{ constant}.$$

In contrast to a normal indifference map, welfare falls with higher prices. In the *short run*, defined as the period during which effort (and average supply) does not change, producers' welfare is also just a function of prices, given by equation (22.2). A price stabilization scheme is feasible in the short run if average demand equals average supply, that is if it lies on the *short-run feasibility locus*, defined as the set of prices for which equation (22.3) holds, assuming that the change in the price distribution has no effect on effort. In the Figures such curves are labelled SR, to distinguish them from the *long-run feasibility locus* (labelled LR), defined as the set of prices for which average demand equals average supply taking account of the fact that, as the price distribution changes, effort, and hence average output, changes. The long-run equilibrium level of effort is given by equation (22.5), and the locus of prices which yields a constant level of effort can also be drawn in the price space, and is labelled $\bar{x}$. Whether effort increases or decreases with higher prices depends on whether risk aversion is less than or greater than unity, as reflected in the supply elasticity of equation (21.17). Changes in effort affect the feasibility locus, but they do not (to a first-order approximation) affect the producers' welfare, by the envelope theorem. (That is, a small change in effort leaves his welfare unchanged at the optimum, by the first-order condition of equation (22.5).) Hence it is not necessary to distinguish between a short- and long-run indifference curve for producers.

Since we restrict attention to supply instabilities and assume unchanged consumer demand functions, any price stabilization scheme will buy when prices are low and sell when prices are high. However, such storage is not costless if only because of interest charges on the stockpile. In Chapters 29 and 30 we shall consider the optimum stocking rule when storage is costly, but here it is enough to consider two extreme possibilities, with the truth lying somewhere in between. The first, and conventional, assumption is that storage is costless, with the buffer profits reallocated to the producers, as in the last chapter. This may be defensible if the question is whether to introduce some stabilization, starting from no storage. Evidently, the answer will be biased in favour of stabilization, particularly as producers typically lose in the absence of such compensation. The second alternative, which is simpler, is to assume that storage activities exhibit constant returns to scale, that stock owners are risk neutral, and the storage industry is in competitive rational expectations equilibrium. In such cases, the returns to storage will just cover storage costs, and there will be no buffer profit to consider. This assumption is the natural one to make if the question is whether the market supplies an inadequate or excessive amount of price stabilization.

Whether buffer profits are allocated to producers, or dissipated in storage costs will affect the location of the representative producer's indifference curve, labelled $\bar{U}$, the locus of constant effort, and the long-run feasibility locus. However, given the assumption about buffer profits, the entire impact of price stabilization is described by the relative positions of the various loci. Fig. 22.1 illustrates this for the model analysed in the previous chapter in equations (21.43–46), except that the coefficient of relative risk aversion is assumed

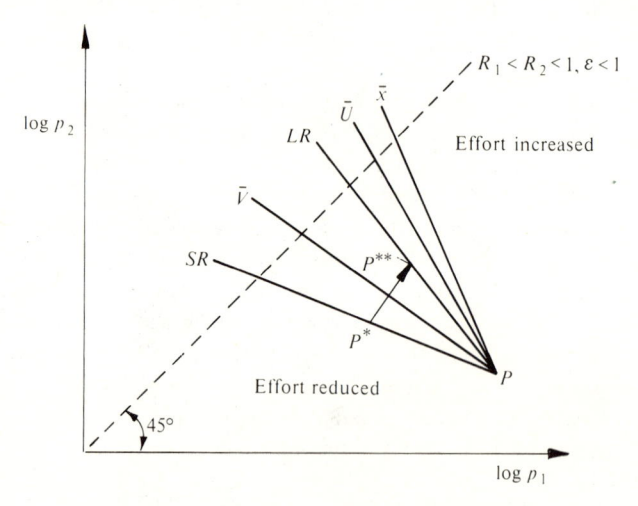

Fig. 22.1 Disadvantageous price stabilization

slightly lower in the high price (high income) state 1. Stabilization moves the economy from its initial position P to P^* in the short run, and eventually to the long-run equilibrium position P^{**}. Demand is inelastic, and producers are not very risk averse, so stabilization in the short run has a beneficial risk benefit, but insufficient to offset the adverse transfer effect (cf. equation 18.21). In the Figure this follows because SR is less steep than $\bar{U}$, so the producer is made worse off by the move from P to P^*. As drawn, P^* is below the constant effort locus, labelled $\bar{x}$, and, since farmers are not very risk averse ($R < 1$), effort falls with lower prices, supply is reduced, prices rise, and the long-run equilibrium at P^{**} is one which is less adverse for farmers.

Consumers, on the other hand, are initially made better off by the lower average prices (the beneficial transfer effect of moving to P^*) but are harmed by the fall in supply, and finish up worse off at P^{**} (i.e. facing higher prices and hence lower welfare). As drawn, Fig. 22.1 illustrates a case in which a competitive supply of price stabilization would make both producers and consumers worse off in the long run than having no storage (or less storage).

We shall show that essentially any configuration of the curves can occur under not implausible conditions. If we confine our attention to producers and ignore buffer profits, if any, then Fig. 22.2a illustrates a case which is more favourable to farmers. Farmers are more risk averse ($R > 1$) so in the short run stabilization benefits them if demand is inelastic. Stabilization also reduces their effort, since they are now less worried about low income states, and so supply falls, prices rise, and in the long run they are even better off. Here the supply response magnifies the short-run impact, whilst in Fig. 22.1 it diminished it.

Thus the relative positions of $\bar{x}$ and SR, together with the direction of the supply response (whether higher prices increase or reduce effort), determine whether the long-run feasibility locus is above or below the short run locus. Once the relative slopes of SR, LR and $\bar{U}$ have been found, the consequences of price stabilization can be read off. Fig. 22.2b shows that not only can the supply response magnify the short-run impact, but it may reverse it. As shown, the

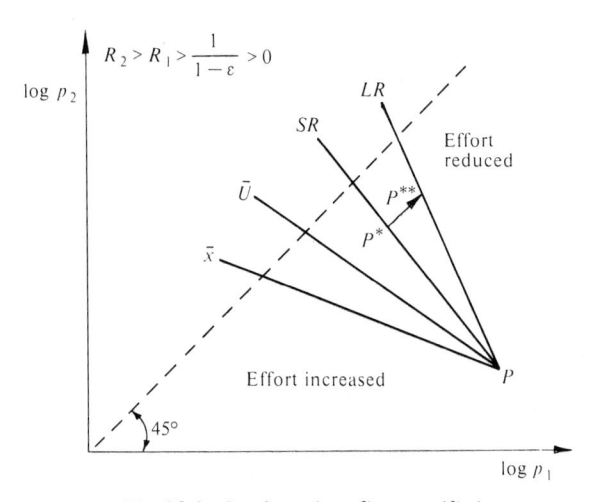

Fig. 22.2a Producer benefits magnified

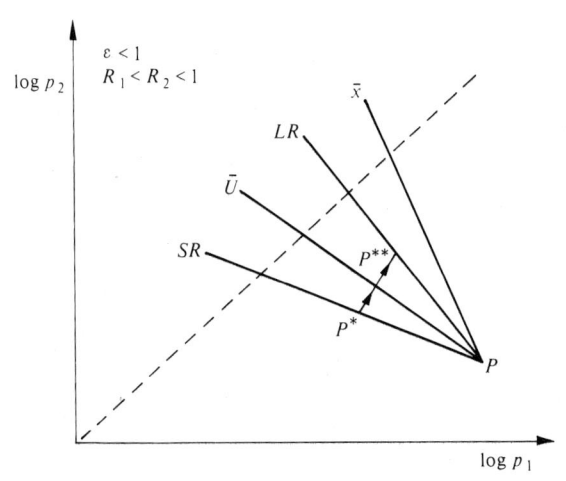

Fig. 22.2b Producer benefits reversed

324   *Commodity Price Stabilization*

initial impact is adverse, but farmers respond by reducing effort, which raises prices, and this rise in prices can be sufficient to reverse the short-run impact. In the last chapter this was impossible because with constant relative risk aversion the farmer's indifference curve coincides with the constant effort locus. However, since this restrictive assumption is dropped, cases such as Fig. 22.2b become possible. (As an exercise, the reader might wish to confirm that if $\bar{U}$ and $\bar{x}$ coincide, Fig. 22.2b is impossible.)

Just as price stabilization may make producers better off or worse off in the short run and/or long run, so may it make consumers better off or worse off. The only constraint limiting what may happen is that the resulting equilibria must be stable if they are to persist long enough to warrant attention. Which outcome actually occurs depends on the detailed calculation of the relative slopes of the various loci, to which we now turn. Since we are initially mainly concerned with the effect on producers, we shall ignore the allocation of buffer revenue.

22.3.1 *The producer's indifference curve*

The locus of values of p_1 and p_2 which generate the same expected utility as the original pair can be found from equation (22.2), ignoring any changes in effort (since, by the envelope theorem, these will not affect utility near the equilibrium point). This locus is an indifference curve in price space, and its elasticity at any point is found by implicitly differentiating equation (22.2) with respect to p_1:

$$\xi_{\bar{u}} \equiv \left(\frac{-d\log p_2}{d\log p_1}\right)_{\bar{u}} = \frac{u_1' p_1 \theta_1}{u_2' p_2 \theta_2} = \frac{u_1' y_1}{u_2' y_2} > 0. \qquad (22.6)$$

(Notice that on logarithmic graphs, the elasticity of a curve is simply its slope, and that at any point, comparing elasticities is the same as comparing slopes.)

22.3.2 *The iso-effort locus*

The locus of price pairs which generate the same supply of effort, $\bar{x}$, is found by differentiating equation (22.5), and its elasticity is

$$\xi_{\bar{x}} \equiv \left(\frac{-d\log p_2}{d\log p_1}\right)_{\bar{x}} = \frac{u_1' p_1 \theta_1 (1-R_1)}{u_2' p_2 \theta_2 (1-R_2)} = \left(\frac{1-R_1}{1-R_2}\right)\xi_{\bar{u}}, \qquad (22.7)$$

where R_i is the coefficient of relative risk aversion in state i:

$$R_i \equiv -y_i u''(y_i)/y_i, \quad y_i = p_i \theta_i \bar{x}.$$

This shows that the curve of constant expected utility and constant effort coincide if we assume constant relative risk aversion, and this coincidence explains the results of the last chapter, as we shall see.

22.3.3 The short-run feasibility locus
The set of price pairs which equate supply and demand in the short run, with effort held constant describe a short-run equilibrium stabilization scheme, and the locus is described by equation (22.3). Its elasticity is

$$\xi_{SR} \equiv \left(\frac{-d \log p_2}{d \log p_1}\right)_{\bar{Q}} = \frac{\epsilon_1 D(p_1)}{\epsilon_2 D(p_2)} > 0, \tag{22.8}$$

where ϵ_i is the price elasticity of demand in state i:

$$\epsilon_i \equiv -\frac{d \log D(p_i)}{d \log p_i}, \quad i = 1, 2.$$

Initially, then, in the absence of any price stabilization,

$$\xi_{SR} = \frac{\epsilon_1 \theta_1}{\epsilon_2 \theta_2}.$$

22.3.4 The long-run feasibility locus
In the long run the stabilization scheme scheme must take account of the supply response, and hence recognize that the right-hand side of equation (22.3) is a function of prices:

$$\bar{Q} = nx(p_1, p_2)$$

where the relationship satisfies equation (22.5). Its elasticity is

$$\xi_{LR} \equiv -\frac{d \log p_2}{d \log p_1} = \frac{\epsilon_1 D(p_1) + \bar{Q}\chi_1}{\epsilon_2 D(p_2) + \bar{Q}\chi_2}, \tag{22.9}$$

where the χ_i are partial supply elasticities, found from equation (22.5):

$$\chi_i \equiv 2 \frac{\partial \log x}{\partial \log p_i} = \frac{u'_i p_i \theta_i (1 - R_i)}{Eu'p\theta R + xv''}, \quad i = 1, 2, \tag{22.10}$$

which has the same sign as $1 - R_i$. Effort thus increases with p_i if and only if $R_i < 1$. Notice that

$$\xi_{\bar{x}} = \frac{\chi_1}{\chi_2} \tag{22.11}$$

so that the long-run elasticity is made up of the terms which appear in the short-run elasticity and the effort elasticity. Equation (22.9) can be rewritten as

$$\xi_{LR} = \lambda \xi_{\bar{x}} + (1 - \lambda)\xi_{SR} \tag{22.12}$$

where

$$\lambda = \frac{\bar{Q}\chi_2}{\epsilon_2 D(p_2) + \bar{Q}\chi_2}.$$

Thus if χ_2 is positive, i.e. $R < 1$, ξ_{LR} lies between the short-run feasibility locus and the iso-effort locus, as in Fig. 22.1; otherwise it may not, as in Fig. 22.2a.

Making use of the first-order condition of equation (22.5) we can write

$$\chi_i = (1 - R_i) \frac{u'_i p_i \theta_i / Eu' p\theta}{\bar{R} + \gamma}$$

where, as in equation (21.14)

$$\gamma \equiv \frac{d \log v'}{d \log x} = \frac{xv''}{v'} > 0,$$

is the elasticity of the marginal utility of effort, and $\bar{R}$ is a weighted average of risk aversion:

$$\bar{R} \equiv \frac{Eu' p\theta R}{Eu' p\theta}.$$

If we measure the elasticity of supply as the proportional increase in average output to the same proportional change of prices in all states, then

$$\zeta \equiv \frac{d \log \bar{Q}}{d \log p} = \tfrac{1}{2}(\chi_1 + \chi_2) = \frac{1 - \bar{R}}{\bar{R} + \gamma}. \tag{22.13}$$

The other property of the long-run elasticity ξ_{LR} is that both numerator and denominator are required to be positive for the system to be stable in the Walrasian sense, itself the weakest condition (see Samuelson, 1947, p. 264). The counterpart to equation (21.16), which requires the sum of the demand and supply elasticities to be positive, is

$$\epsilon_i D(p_i) + \bar{Q}\chi_i > 0. \tag{22.14}$$

22.4 Effect on producers

We continue to ignore buffer profits and inquire into the relative slopes of the *short-run* feasibility loci and the producer's indifference curve.

22.4.1 *The short-run impact on producers*

In the short run the effects of stabilization are to move prices along the short-run locus of equation (22.3). Whether this makes producers better or worse off depends on whether this locus is steeper or flatter than the indifference curve, i.e. whether

$$\xi_{SR} \gtreqless \xi_{\bar{u}}$$

i.e.

$$\frac{\epsilon_1 \theta_1}{\epsilon_2 \theta_2} \gtreqless \frac{u'_1 p_1 \theta_1}{u'_2 p_2 \theta_2}.$$

This can be seen in Fig. 22.2a, which shows the case in which producers are better off at P^* than the initial point P. (Higher sales prices *raise* producer welfare.)

The producer is better off if and only if

$$u_2'p_2/\epsilon_2 > u_1'p_1/\epsilon_1. \tag{22.15}$$

The expression $\epsilon/u'p$ appears repeatedly in the following analysis, and it is convenient to define a new function of output, q:

$$\beta(q) \equiv \frac{\epsilon\{p(q)\}}{p(q)u'\{qp(q)\}}, \quad q = \theta x.$$

Then

$$\frac{d\log\beta}{d\log q} = \frac{d\log\epsilon}{d\log p}\frac{d\log p}{d\log q} - \frac{d\log p}{d\log q} - \frac{d\log u'}{d\log y}\frac{d\log y}{d\log q}$$

$$q\beta' = \frac{1}{pu'}\left\{R(\epsilon-1) + 1 - \frac{d\log\epsilon}{d\log p}\right\}. \tag{22.16}$$

From equations (22.15) and (22.16) it follows that, since $\theta_2 > \theta_1$, producers are better or worse off in the short run as

$$\beta_2 \lessgtr \beta_1, \quad \text{i.e.} \quad \beta' \lessgtr 0,$$

i.e. if

$$R(1-\epsilon) \gtrless 1 - \frac{p}{\epsilon}\frac{d\epsilon}{dp}. \tag{22.17}$$

Thus whether or not producers are better off in the short run depends on three factors: the degree of relative risk aversion, the elasticity of demand (whether it is greater or less than unity), and the rate of change of the elasticity of demand. Whilst this last is zero for constant elastic demand schedules, for linear demand

$$\frac{p}{\epsilon}\frac{d\epsilon}{dp} = 1 + \epsilon,$$

considerably weakening the conditions for producers to be better off. As we remarked in Chapter 17, there are two effects of price stabilization — to change the mean income and its variability. If, for example, the elasticity of demand is constant, then price stabilization benefits producers if $R(1-\epsilon) > 1$. If the demand elasticity is unity, price stabilization has no effect on mean income, but always increases its variability. If demand is elastic, mean income is lowered and variability is increased, unambiguously lowering welfare.

22.4.2 *Long-run impact on producers*

In the long run the stabilization scheme must take account of supply responses, and if relative risk aversion is constant this is particularly simple, as the indifference curve coincides with the locus of constant effort. If $R < 1$, then equation (22.10) implies a positive response of effort to prices, and the long-run feasibility locus must lie between the short-run locus and the constant effort (and utility) locus, as equation (22.12) shows. The effect on welfare must be to reduce but not reverse the magnitude of the short-run effect. If $R > 1$, then effort responds inversely to price, and the long-run feasibility locus is on the other side of the short-run locus, as in Fig. 22.2a, and the effect is to magnify but again, not reverse, the direction of the short-run locus. If relative risk aversion is not constant, then the long-run effect may be in the opposite direction to the short-run effect, as in Fig. 22.2b. We now inquire under what conditions each possibility will occur. As before, we calculate relative slopes (elasticities) at the no stabilization point, P, ignoring buffer profits. From equations (22.8) and (22.9)

$$\xi_{LR} - \xi_{SR} = \left\{ \frac{\epsilon_1}{p_1 u_1'} - \frac{\epsilon_2}{p_2 u_2'} - v(R_1 - R_2) \right\} \frac{u_1' p_1 \theta_1}{\theta_2 \epsilon_2 + \chi_2} \qquad (22.18)$$

where

$$v = 1/\{(\bar{R} + \gamma) E u' p \theta\}.$$

From equation (22.18), producers' welfare is increased in the long run if

$$v(R_2 - R_1) - (\beta_2 - \beta_1) > 0, \qquad (22.19)$$

since the term outside the braces must be positive from equation (22.14). Since $q_2 > q_1$, a sufficient condition for the inequality in equation (22.19) to be satisfied is that

$$v \frac{dR}{dy} \cdot \frac{dy}{dq} - \beta' > 0$$

or, using (22.16), producers are better or worse off as a result of stabilization as

$$R(\epsilon - 1) + 1 - \frac{d \log \epsilon}{d \log p} \lessgtr \frac{R\kappa}{R + \gamma} \left(1 - \frac{1}{\epsilon} \right), \quad \kappa \equiv \frac{R' y}{R}, \qquad (22.20)$$

where κ is the elasticity of relative risk aversion. Thus five parameters determine the outcome: the elasticity of demand and its rate of change, relative risk aversion and its rate of change, and the elasticity of the disutility of effort, γ. Comparing equations (22.17) and (22.20) the short- and long-run effects can clearly go in opposite directions only if $R' \neq 0$, i.e., if relative risk aversion is changing. For the short-run impact to be favourable while the long run is unfavourable to producers, $\beta' < 0$ and $(1 - 1/\epsilon)R' < 0$, i.e., if $\epsilon < 1$, then $R' > 0$, i.e. relative risk aversion is increasing sufficiently fast. Similarly, if the short-run impact is to be harmful and the long-run impact beneficial, as in Fig. 22.2b, then $\beta' > 0$ and $(1 - 1/\epsilon)R' > 0$. If, as seems reasonable, R falls as income rises, the most likely case for the long-run impact to be a reversal of the short-run impact is when $\epsilon < 1$ and

$$\frac{-ydR}{Rdy} > \frac{\epsilon}{1-\epsilon}(1+\gamma/R)\left\{1 - R(1-\epsilon) - \frac{p}{\epsilon}\frac{d\epsilon}{dp}\right\} > 0 \qquad (22.21)$$

which is not an unduly restrictive condition. All that is required is for the coefficient of risk aversion to be sufficiently sensitive to changes in income, which is quite plausible near subsistence levels.

It should be stressed that, unlike many 'perversities' in economies, this reversal has nothing to do with the failure of any stability conditions. For example, in Fig. 22.2b, if $\epsilon < 1$ and $1 > R_2 > R_1$, the effort response to a price rise is positive and the system is stable by any conventional comparative static criterion. Initially the buffer agency sets prices at P^* and utility falls. However, prices are too low to induce the same supply of effort as P^* is below the effort locus, hence prices must rise to reduce demand and increase supply, until at P^{**} demand equals supply (on average). In moving from P^* to P^{**} the indifference curve has been crossed, and so the necessary rise in prices has eventually improved welfare, despite the adverse initial effect.

22.5 Consumers' welfare and Pareto optimality of the market equilibrium

So far, we have only studied the effects of price stabilization on producers, both in the short run and in the long. This is natural if our primary concern is with the welfare of producers. But from a global point of view, we need to consider also the welfare of consumers. This may easily be done using the diagrammatic techniques already employed.

We represent the consumer's welfare by his indirect utility function $V(p, I)$, where I is consumer income, assumed independent of prices and the state of the world, θ, so that his expected utility is just

$$EV(p, I) = \tfrac{1}{2}V(p_1, I) + \tfrac{1}{2}V(p_2, I)$$

and his indifference curve in (p_1, p_2) space has an elasticity (with an absolute value) of

$$\xi_{\bar{V}} = \frac{p_1 V_{p_1}}{p_2 V_{p_2}} = \frac{D(p_1)p_1 V_I(p_1, I)}{D(p_2)p_2 V_I(p_2, I)} \qquad (22.22)$$

(using Roy's identity that $V_p = -D(p)V_I$). Consumers are made better off by stabilization in the long run if

$$\xi_V > \xi_{LR}$$

(remembering that consumers prefer *lower* prices). Using equations (22.22) and (22.9), this is equivalent to

$$\frac{p_1\theta_1 V_1'}{p_2\theta_2 V_2'} > \frac{p_1\theta_1 u_1'\{\beta_1 + \nu(1-R_1)\}}{p_2\theta_2 u_2'\{\beta_2 + \nu(1-R_2)\}} \qquad (22.23)$$

where β and ν are as defined in equations (22.16), (22.18) and V'_i is the marginal utility of consumer income in state i:

$$V'_i \equiv V_I(p_i, I).$$

A sufficient condition for inequality (22.23) to be satisfied is

$$\frac{d}{dq}\left[\frac{u'}{V_I}\{\beta + \nu(1-R)\}\right] > 0$$

which, given the stability condition (22.14), is equivalent to

$$-R\left(1-\frac{1}{\epsilon}\right) + \frac{1}{\epsilon}\frac{pV_{Ip}}{V_I} + \left\{\frac{q\beta' - \nu R'y\left(1-\frac{1}{\epsilon}\right)}{\beta + \nu(1-R)}\right\} > 0.$$

The term in braces is the transfer term, and, with the opposite sign, is the condition for producers to be better off, in equation (22.20). This equation can be expanded to give as a condition for consumers to be made better off or worse off by stabilization

$$\frac{pV_{Ip}}{V_I} + \frac{1 - \dfrac{d\log \epsilon}{d\log p}}{1 + \dfrac{1-R}{\epsilon(R+\gamma)}} - \frac{R(\epsilon-1)(1-R+\kappa)}{(R+\gamma)\epsilon + 1 - R} \gtrless 0. \qquad (22.24)$$

Finally, approximation techniques can be applied to the stability condition of equation (22.14) to find constraints on the parameters which allow a viable (stable) equilibrium to exist:

$$\epsilon > \frac{R-1}{R+\gamma} \qquad (22.25)$$

which is automatically satisfied if $R < 1$.

Bearing in mind that we are assuming that buffer receipts are entirely exhausted in operating the stabilization scheme, we can now ask if the competitive market supplies unambiguously inadequate or excessive price stabilization; that is, whether (more) stabilization makes both consumers and producers better off or worse off. Since the equations contain a large number of unfamiliar parameters it may be helpful to relate these to more familiar assumptions. Remember that from equation (8.13) that if α is the consumer's expenditure share on the commodity

$$\frac{pV_{Ip}}{V_I} = \alpha(R^c - \eta)$$

where R^c is consumer's relative risk aversion and η is the income elasticity of demand. Moreover, for

Constant relative risk aversion	$\kappa = 0$
Constant absolute risk aversion, $A: R = Ay$	$\kappa = 1$
Constant elasticity of demand	$\dfrac{d \log \epsilon}{d \log p} = 0$
Linear demand schedule	$\dfrac{d \log \epsilon}{d \log p} = 1 + \epsilon$
Constant marginal utility of income	$\dfrac{p V_{Ip}}{V_I} = 0.$

In general, we could expect pV_{Ip}/V_I to be small, as it is weighted by consumers' expenditure share on the commodity, which would typically be small for a single commodity, except possibly essential food grains, in which case it would typically be positive. If producers are near subsistence one might expect κ to be negative. We can now examine a number of special cases.

(a) The easiest case to analyse is that in which $\gamma = \infty$, $\nu = 0$, or the producer is completely unwilling to vary his effort and supply is totally inelastic. In this case the short- and long-run impacts are identical. Equations (22.20), (22.24), and (22.25) now show that both groups are better or worse off as

$$\frac{d \log \epsilon}{d \log p} + \alpha(\eta - R^c) \lessgtr 1, \qquad (22.26)$$

$$\frac{d \log \epsilon}{d \log p} + R(1 - \epsilon) \gtrless 1. \qquad (22.27)$$

Not surprisingly, when there is no producer response, whether consumers are made better or worse off depends only on the properties of the consumer's utility function. If demand is of constant elasticity less than unity, and producers are sufficiently risk averse, $R > 1/(1 - \epsilon)$, then the market supplies inadequate stabilization, while if demand is linear, and

$$R > \frac{\epsilon}{\epsilon - 1} > 0,$$

$$\alpha(R^c - \eta) < \epsilon,$$

then the market supplies excessive stabilization.

(b) $V_{Ip} = 0$ and $d \log \epsilon / d \log p = 0$, i.e. constant elasticity of demand and constant marginal utility. In this case both groups are better or worse off as

$$1 - \frac{R(1-R)(\epsilon - 1)}{\epsilon(R + \gamma)} \gtrless \frac{\kappa R(\epsilon - 1)}{\epsilon(R + \gamma)} \gtrless 1 + R(\epsilon - 1). \qquad (22.28)$$

Given the stability condition of (22.25), since κ can in principle take any value, positive or negative, these inequalities can be satisfied if

$$R(\epsilon - 1) \leq 0.$$

Thus there is inadequate stabilization if $\epsilon < 1$, and κ takes a suitable negative value, i.e. risk aversion increases as income falls, which is empirically reasonable. Correspondingly, for there to be excessive stabilization, demand must be elastic, $\epsilon > 1$, in which case κ must be sufficiently positive (relative risk aversion must be increasing with income), as it would if producers had constant absolute risk aversion. For example, if farmers have constant absolute risk aversion, so that $\kappa = 1$, then stabilization is excessive if $\epsilon = 4$, $\gamma = 0$, $R < 2/3$. We can summarize this last finding as follows.

Proposition. For costly price stabilization to be Pareto inferior to no stabilization with constant elasticity demand and constant marginal utility of consumer income, demand must be elastic and relative risk aversion must be increasing.

22.6* The allocation of buffer profits

The analysis so far has assumed that the revenue earned by the buffer authority in arbitrage has been just enough to cover its operating costs, as would be the case in a rational expectations competitive equilibrium with constant storage costs and risk-neutral speculators. The less realistic but more popular alternative assumption is that stabilization is costless, in which case, if the buffer profits are returned to the farmers as lump-sum transfers, their income in state i will be

$$y_i = p_i\{\theta_i(x - x^*) + D(p_i)\}, \quad i = 1, 2, \tag{22.29}$$

where x^* is the supply of effort of the representative farmer, equal to x in equilibrium. Evidently, this transfer, by providing an additional state dependent source of income, will change the producer's indifference curve and supply response, and hence alter the previous conditions. Rather than repeat the whole analysis, it suffices to ask under what conditions price stabilization is Pareto inferior to no stabilization in the long run, for, in this case, given that such stabilization is costly, it will certainly be undesirable.

From equation (22.29) we have in equilibrium, when $x = x^*$

$$\frac{dy_i}{dp_i} = D(p_i)(1 - \epsilon_i)$$

so, from equation (22.2), the farmer's indifference curve has elasticity

$$\xi_{\bar{u}}^* = \frac{(1-\epsilon_1)u_1'y_1}{(1-\epsilon_2)u_2'y_2} = \frac{1-\epsilon_1}{1-\epsilon_2}\xi_{\bar{u}}, \tag{22.30}$$

where the starred elasticity includes buffer profits, unstarred not. The elasticity of the long-run feasibility locus has the same form as before, in equation (22.9), but the partial supply elasticities χ_i have changed:

Risk Aversion and Supply Response: A Geometrical Analysis

$$\chi_i^* \equiv 2\frac{d\log x}{d\log p_i} = \frac{u_i'p_i\theta_i\{1 + R_i(\epsilon_i - 1)\}}{\gamma Eu'p\theta}. \tag{22.31}$$

For both groups to be made worse off in the long run we require

$$\xi_{\bar{u}}^* > \xi_{LR}^* > \xi_{\bar{V}}^*$$

Producers will be made worse off if

$$\frac{d}{dq}\left[\frac{\epsilon}{1-\epsilon}\left\{\frac{\epsilon}{u'p} + \frac{1 + (\epsilon - 1)R}{\gamma Eu'p\theta}\right\}\right] > 0 \tag{22.32}$$

(cf. equation (22.20)), or

$$-R(1-\epsilon)^2 + 1 - \epsilon + \frac{d\log\epsilon}{d\log p}\left(1 - \frac{1}{\gamma}\right) + \frac{R\kappa}{\gamma} + \frac{R\kappa(1-\epsilon)^3}{\epsilon} > 0. \tag{22.33}$$

Likewise, consumers will be made worse off if

$$\frac{d}{dq}\left[\frac{u'}{V_I}\left\{\gamma Eu'p\theta\left(\frac{\epsilon}{pu'}\right) + 1 - R(1-\epsilon)\right\}\right] < 0. \tag{22.34}$$

(cf. equation (22.20)), or

$$\gamma\left(1 + \frac{pV_{Ip}}{V_I} - \frac{d\log\epsilon}{d\log p}\right) + \frac{1 - R(1-\epsilon)}{\epsilon}\left(R(1-\epsilon) + \frac{pV_{Ip}}{V_I}\right) + $$

$$+ \frac{R}{\epsilon}\left\{\kappa(1-\epsilon)^2 - \frac{d\log\epsilon}{d\log p}\right\} < 0. \tag{22.35}$$

Thus if $\gamma = \infty$, and demand is linear, stabilization is Pareto inferior if

$$R < \frac{2}{(1-\epsilon)^2}.$$

$$\frac{pV_{Ip}}{V_I} = \alpha(R^c - \eta) < \epsilon.$$

If, on the other hand, demand is constant elastic, and consumers are price risk neutral ($V_{Ip} = 0$), then from equation (22.35) and the stability condition (22.25)

$$(1-\kappa)R(1-\epsilon)^2 > 1 + \epsilon\gamma > R(1-\epsilon) \tag{22.36}$$

while from (22.33)

$$R(1-\epsilon)^2\left\{\frac{\kappa(1-\epsilon)}{\gamma\epsilon} - 1\right\} + 1 - \epsilon > 0. \tag{22.37}$$

In contrast to the costly buffer case, κ must be negative. Thus, if $\epsilon = 4$, $\gamma = 1/8$, $R = 2/3$, then $\kappa < -1/4$.

Again, if the inequalities are reversed, it is possible to identify cases in which some (costless) price stabilization is Pareto improving. Exactly what happens depends on the signs and magnitudes of the six parameters, describing attitudes to risk $(R, pV_{Ip}/V_I, \kappa)$, demand $(\epsilon, d\log\epsilon/d\log p)$, and supply (γ). The reason for the complexity of the results should be apparent. A number of distinct effects can be identified.

(a) In the short run, when producers do not adjust their production levels, there are two effects, a risk effect and a mean income effect. Both these may be of either sign. Since price and quantity are inversely related, a reduction in the variability of prices will actually increase the variability in income of farmers, unless the elasticity of demand is very low. This increase in the variability of income will lower producers' welfare. It will reduce it more the greater is their risk aversion. If the elasticity of demand is low, price stabilization will reduce the variability of farmers' income.

Mean expenditure by consumers on the given commodity may increase or decrease, again depending on the structure of demand. If the individual has a unit elastic demand curve, then mean expenditure will be unaffected. With a constant elasticity demand curve, expenditure is a convex or concave function of quantity consumed depending on whether the elasticity of demand is greater or less than unity, and thus, mean income of farmers increases or decreases as the elasticity of demand is greater or less than unity.

(b) In the long run, producers will adjust their effort, and this will affect the prices they receive. The magnitude of this response depends on the effect of price stabilization on the mean value of the marginal return to effort, and this need not move in the same direction as the mean value of utility. Whether it does or not depends on the whole shape of the utility function as well as on the shape of consumers' demand functions (which determine the effect of the change in effort on prices).

22.7 Concluding remarks

Although there is little doubt that producers in less developed countries face considerable risk from the fluctuations in the agricultural prices which they receive, there is considerable controversy concerning whether any of the various proposals for stabilizing these prices would be desirable.

On the one hand, there is a widespread belief that since agricultural markets are competitive they provide an efficient level of storage activity (and hence an efficient level of price stabilization). We have shown that this belief is not well founded: we have identified conditions under which either increasing or reducing the degree of stabilization could make everyone better off.

On the other hand, we have also shown that the widespread belief in the desirability of stable prices may also not be well founded, when there are exogenous sources of risk and when there are incomplete or absent risk markets. In particular, it is possible that the stabilization of commodity prices may lead both producers and consumers to be worse off. An implication of this result is that under these circumstances further destabilization of prices would make both consumers and producers better off. Alternatively, there are conditions under which stabilization may make both groups better off. In still other cases, one group gains at the expense of the other.

Chapter 23

Pareto-inferior Trade and Price Stabilization

23.1 Introduction

Most of our analysis so far has dealt with farmers in a single country choosing the level of supply of a single crop. In practice, most farmers can choose between a variety of crops, and the same crop is grown in a variety of countries. If, as is typically the case, the weather in different parts of the world varies, then the over-all variability in world production will be less than the variability in any one country or climatic region. Free trade in commodities would lower the price variability associated with supply or demand variability within each country. Free trade between sufficiently diverse producers would be very similar in its effects to setting up buffer stocks to stabilize prices.

In this chapter we examine trade as an alternative method of stabilizing prices in a model which allows us to explore some of the general equilibrium effects so far neglected — the choice of crops and the interaction between different producers. In Chapter 15 we showed that unless different producers experienced perfectly correlated output risk, then the rational expectations competitive equilibrium was not efficient. In the last chapter we showed that a sufficiently strong adverse supply response to price stabilization would make both producers and consumers worse off. This chapter pushes these results even further and establishes a result which seems remarkable in the present context of international trade in agricultural commodities.

As we noted in Chapter 19, international trade in agricultural commodities is severely restricted by quotas, tariffs, farm support programmes, the Common Agricultural Policy of the EEC, and a whole host of non-tariff barriers. One of the basic tenets of liberal economics is that everyone could be made better off as a result of reducing restrictions on trade. Even though some groups in the population may be made initially worse off, those who gain as a result of trade liberalization can more than afford to compensate those who suffer. We show that in a competitive but risky economy, free trade may be Pareto inferior to no trade, and under fairly general conditions a restriction in trade from the free trade position will constitute a Pareto improvement.

In the next chapter we investigate the appropriate trade policy response to this finding. One result consistent with traditional beliefs is that there exists some form of liberalization from the no-trade situation which constitutes a Pareto improvement. Dasgupta and Stiglitz (1976) have already noted that tariffs and quotas are not equivalent in the presence of uncertainty, and have shown that if the objective of trade policy is to raise a given revenue, then tariffs are preferable to quotas if the revenue requirement is small, but not necessarily if the requirement is large.

Pareto-inferior Trade and Price Stabilization   337

We extend the analysis of the comparison of quotas and tariffs by establishing in our model, that tariffs are preferable to quotas near the no-trade equilibrium, but quotas are preferable to tariffs near the free trade equilibrium.

The basic idea behind our model is simple. There are two countries (regions) both of which grow a risky agricultural crop and a safe crop. The output in the two regions is negatively correlated. The results can easily be extended to cases where the correlation is zero or even positive, so long as the correlation is not perfect, as discussed in Chapter 15.

In the absence of trade, price rises whenever output falls. If demand functions have unitary price elasticity the price variations provide perfect income insurance for the farmer. But with the opening of trade, because of the negative correlation between output in the two regions, price variations no longer offset output variations in each country and so the riskiness of growing the crop faced by each farmer is increased. This induces farmers to shift production away from the risky crop, raising its average price. However, in the special model we examine, where consumers have unit price elasticity and thus constant expenditure on both crops, the mean income of the farmers remains constant with the opening of trade. Since its riskiness increases, it follows that farmers' welfare necessarily decreases, as shown in Fig. 23.1.

Whereas, before trade was opened, consumers bore all the risk, with free trade they bear none, and, other things being equal, this would make them better off. However, the change in the pattern of supply, and the rise in the average price of the risky crop, make them worse off. Near autarky, the risk benefit dominates

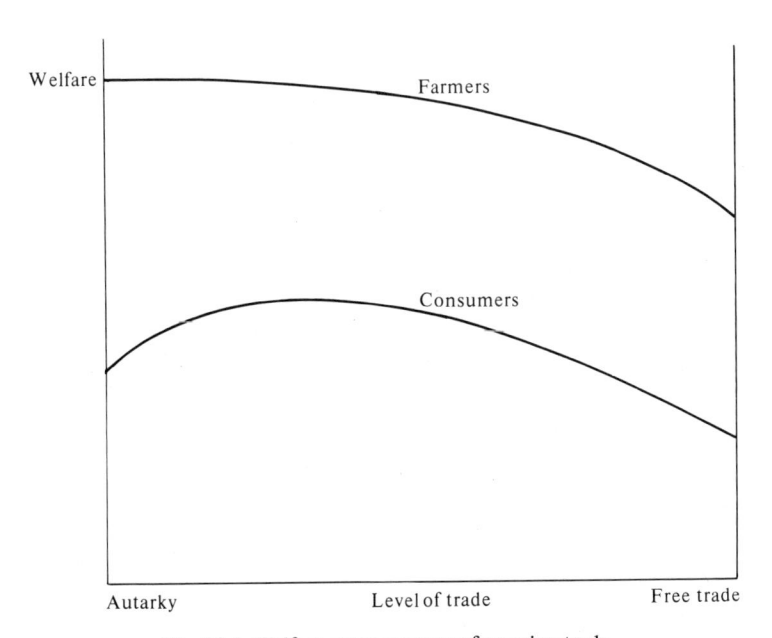

Fig. 23.1 Welfare consequences of opening trade

this allocation effect, as shown in Fig. 23.1, but near free trade the opposite is the case. If the change in supplies and prices is sufficiently large (which it will be if producers are sufficiently risk averse) and if the consumer risk benefits are sufficiently small (i.e. if consumers are not very risk averse) then consumers will be made worse off by opening trade. Since producers are necessarily worse off (in this model) it follows that free trade is Pareto inferior to autarky.

The reconciliation of our results with the standard theorems of welfare economics in which free trade is Pareto efficient is straightforward; the conventional argument requires not only that markets be competitive (as we assume), but also complete. In our model there must be a complete set of insurance markets enabling farmers to purchase both price and output insurance. For a variety of reasons, such as moral hazard and adverse selection, the set of markets is not complete. Essentially what happens in our example is that while autarky provides farmers with income insurance, when a new market is opened (in this case international trade markets in the risky commodity) the commodity market no longer provides implicit insurance, and it is as though insurance markets were closed. If there is a complete set of markets then each market provides one, and only one, marketing service, but if there is not a complete set then some markets may be providing several services, allocating both goods and risk. Institutional change may change the number of services provided by a particular market, and in our example such changes can make everyone worse off. Welfare analysis which assumes that each market serves only one function can be seriously misleading in these cases.

The model we shall analyse in this and the next chapter has been deliberately made as simple as possible to make the main points as clear as possible. In particular, we choose very special functional forms — unit price elasticity — for consumer demand which allow us to employ the concept of mean preserving changes in risk, and which thus allow a very intuitive explanation of our results. It will become clear from our model that any other specification would greatly complicate the analysis, since changes in trade will in general lead to changes in both mean income and its risk. In Chapter 15 we have already demonstrated the inefficiency of competitive (i.e. free trade) equilibria for a more general model, and to that extent the general results derived in the present chapter are robust, and would continue to apply in more general models. In fact, only two assumptions are critical for our results. First, there must be some agents who, on average, are net sellers of the risky good (in our model, the farmers) and others who are net buyers (consumers). Since these individuals must engage in trade, their welfare is affected by the price distribution. Second, neither producers nor consumers can buy insurance for the risks (the variability of output of the risky crop and of its price) which they face. Then changes in the level of trade change the price distribution and the risks that individuals face. If they could perfectly insure, then there would be no change in risk, and hence no adverse consequences. However, we would argue that it is more realistic to assume that individuals cannot perfectly insure themselves, and that therefore risk, and changes in risk, do matter. In section 23.5 we defend the robustness of our results at greater length.

The chapter is divided into three main sections. In the next section we present the model, analyse the no-trade and the free trade equilibria and compare the results. Three critical parameters which determine whether free trade is Pareto inferior are identified: the risk aversion of consumers, the risk aversion of producers and the size of risk. The greater the risk aversion of producers and the smaller the risk aversion of consumers the more likely is free trade to be Pareto inferior to autarky.

In section 23.3 we show that the model, which is the simplest one in which two countries and two crops can be examined, may none the less have multiple equilibria, some stable and some unstable. Section 23.4 shows how the results are affected by assuming that both the countries are relatively small producers of the safe crop, so its price is unaffected by their actions. This has a significant effect on the results and suggests that in this context partial equilibrium analysis may be very misleading. The last section examines the robustness of the results, summarizes the findings, and raises the questions to be dealt with in the following chapter.

23.2 Comparison of autarky and free trade

23.2.1 *The model*

A region has n identical farmers, each owning one unit of land. A typical farmer allocates a fraction x of his land to growing a risky crop, which we denote by subscript r, and the remainder, $1 - x$, to the safe crop, denoted by subscript s. Output per hectare of the risky crop is $\tilde{\theta}$, a random variable, with mean unity and variance σ^2. The output per hectare of the safe crop is always unity. (These are just normalizations.) The prices of the crops are established in competitive markets after the harvest where each of the m consumers has an indirect utility function:

$$V = V(I, p, q). \qquad (23.1)$$

Here I is income, which is constant and independent of risk and of farmers' income, p is the price of the risky crop, and q of the safe crop. For most of the analysis we shall assume that the utility function takes a special form:

$$V = \frac{(Ip^{-a}q^{-b})^{1-\rho}}{1-\rho}, \quad \rho \neq 1, \qquad (23.2a)$$

or

$$V = \log I - a \log p - b \log q, \quad \text{for } \rho = 1, \qquad (23.2b)$$

where ρ is the coefficient of relative risk aversion. These both yield aggregate demand functions for the two commodities which have unitary price and income elasticities:

$$Q_r = \frac{amI}{p} \tag{23.3a}$$

$$Q_s = \frac{bmI}{q} \tag{23.3b}$$

where Q_i is aggregate demand for commodity i, and mI is aggregate consumer income. This specification of the utility function is chosen for several reasons: it greatly simplifies the calculations, it is the utility function for which consumer surplus calculations employed in conventional welfare analyses are valid (see, e.g., Samuelson, 1942), and it implies that there will be no income redistribution effects in the policy changes which we shall consider, and thus this specification enables a simple separation out of the efficiency and distributional consequences of trade policy. Indeed, since consumer expenditure on each crop is constant, the farmers' mean income will also remain constant in moving from autarky to free trade, allowing us to evaluate this as a mean income preserving increase in risk. No other utility function has this advantageous property. Moreover, demand functions with unitary price elasticity play a critical borderline role in the analysis of risk with more than one commodity; if the elasticity of substitution between the two commodities is less than unity, the induced price variability results in farmers treating the safe commodity as if it were riskier than the risky commodity (see Stiglitz (1972a)). Finally, the utility function exhibits constant (income) risk aversion, ρ, and in the special case of unitary risk aversion of equation (23.2b)

$$V_{Ip} = V_{Iq} = 0,$$

so changes in prices do not affect the marginal utility of income. In the final section, we show that these apparently very special assumptions are not essential for our results, but are chosen mainly for simplicity.

If all farmers act alike then market clearing prices are

$$\bar{p} = \frac{ay}{x\bar{\theta}}, \quad q = \frac{by}{1-x} \tag{23.4}$$

where $y = mI/n$, consumers' expenditure per farmer.

23.2.2 Farmers' allocation of land

As before, we assume that farmers must choose their farm plan (the choice of x) before they know the state of the world, but they do so holding rational expectations about the relationship between the state of the world, θ, and the prices which will prevail after the harvest. They thus choose x to maximize the expected utility of profits:

$$EU(\pi), \quad U' > 0, \quad U'' < 0, \tag{23.5}$$

where

are the profits. Thus the expected utility-maximizing choice of x is given by the solution to

$$\tilde{\pi} = x\tilde{p}\tilde{\theta} + q(1-x) \tag{23.6}$$

$$EU'(\tilde{\pi})(\tilde{p}\tilde{\theta} - q) = 0 \tag{23.7}$$

or, if the variance of $\tilde{p}$ and $\tilde{\theta}$ is small, the condition is approximately

$$E\tilde{p}\tilde{\theta} - q + \frac{U''}{U'} xE(\tilde{p}\tilde{\theta} - \overline{p}\overline{\theta})^2 = 0. \tag{23.8}$$

Define $A = -U''/U'$ as the coefficient of absolute risk aversion so that, if $\text{Var}(\tilde{p}\tilde{\theta}) > 0$

$$x = \frac{E\tilde{p}\tilde{\theta} - q}{A\,\text{Var}(\tilde{p}\tilde{\theta})}. \tag{23.9}$$

In the present case, however, equation (23.4) yields in equilibrium

$$\tilde{p} = \left(\frac{ay}{x^*}\right)\frac{1}{\tilde{\theta}}$$

where x^* is the equilibrium value of x, so the crop whose output is risky yields a perfectly safe return. If farmers are to grow both crops the returns must be identical

$$\tilde{p}\tilde{\theta} = q$$

or

$$\frac{ay}{x} = \frac{by}{1-x},$$

so

$$x^* = \frac{a}{a+b}, \quad q = (a+b)y.$$

Producers' profits are given by

$$\pi = q,$$

so producers' welfare is simply

$$U\{(a+b)y\}.$$

The representative consumer's average welfare in the logarithmic case is

$$EV = V_0 + aE\log\tilde{\theta}$$

where V_0 is the utility without risk:

$$V_0 = \log I - (a+b)\log\{(a+b)y\}.$$

The money value of the loss from the randomness in θ is found by expanding $aE\log\theta$ and is approximately $\frac{1}{2}a\sigma^2$, or one-half of the share of the risky crop in expenditure times its squared coefficient of variation in output. In the case of constant relative risk aversion not equalling unity

$$EV = E\frac{\tilde{\theta}^{a(1-\rho)}V_0}{1-\rho},$$

where in this case

$$V_0 = I^{1-\rho}\{(a+b)y\}^{-(a+b)(1-\rho)} = \{I^{(1-a-b)(1-\rho)}\}\left\{\frac{n}{m(a+b)}\right\}^{(a+b)(1-\rho)}.$$

The loss from risk is approximately

$$\tfrac{1}{2}a\{1-a(1-\rho)\}\sigma^2$$

which agrees with the logarithmic case for $\rho = 1$.

Note that the unit-elasticity consumer demands transfer all the risk from farmers to consumers. Fluctuations in the supply of the risky crop affect only its price and not that of the safe crop, so that one can really distinguish between a safe and a risky crop. Except in this special case, production risk for one commodity will spill over to generate price risk for other commodities, as Stiglitz (1972c, p. 343) demonstrates.

23.2.3 *Autarky versus free trade*

Now suppose that, to the east on the other side of a mountain range there is another region, identical to the one described above in every respect save one — the weather. (This assumption rules out the conventional reasons for trade and allows us to concentrate on the risk aspect alone. Regions have a comparative advantage in weather alone in this model. Obviously, this heavily qualifies any policy conclusions which might be drawn from the study, in ways which we discuss in the final section.) When it rains in the West, it is dry in the East, and vice versa. The output of the risky crop is perfectly negatively correlated between the two regions. Formally, let

$$\tilde{\theta}^E + \tilde{\theta}^W = 2.$$

Initially there is no trade between East and West, but there is a pass through the mountains which permits virtually costless exchange. If it is opened there will be competitive free trade; if not, the regions will remain autarkic. Is free trade desirable?

First, we establish Lemma 1. *If trade is allowed, there will be trade.* For assume not. Then the allocations will be identical to that described in the previous section; hence in every state the price of the risky crop must differ (except for the improbable event that $\theta^E = 1$ exactly). Hence in every state there will be trade. *There exists no autarkic equilibrium if trade is allowed.*

Consider now the feasible symmetric equilibrium with free trade, in which each region plants the same fraction x of the risky crop and $1-x$ of the safe crop, yielding total supplies

$$\tilde{Q}_r = nx\tilde{\theta} + nx(2-\tilde{\theta}) = 2nx, \quad 0 \leq \tilde{\theta} \leq 1,$$

and

$$\tilde{Q}_s = 2n(1-x).$$

Prices will be perfectly stabilized at

$$\hat{p} = \frac{ay}{x}, \quad q = \frac{by}{1-x}.$$

Hence each farmer's total profits are now

$$\tilde{\pi} = \hat{p}x\tilde{\theta} + (1-x)q,$$

or

$$\tilde{\pi} = (a\tilde{\theta} + b)y$$

and farmers' income is now risky, though its mean value is unchanged.

Farmers' equilibrium allocation is given by the solution to equation (23.7):

$$EU'\{y(a\tilde{\theta} + b)\}\left(\frac{a\tilde{\theta}y}{x} - \frac{by}{1-x}\right) = 0. \tag{23.10}$$

Let us denote the equilibrium value of x, p, q, etc. with trade by $\{x^t, p^t, q^t\}$ and in autarky by $\{x^*, p^*, q^*\}$. Proposition 1 compares the allocations of the two equilibria in the two situations:

Proposition 1.

If farmers are risk averse

$$x^t < x^*,$$
$$q^t < q^*.$$

Proof.

We know that

$$\hat{p} = \frac{ay}{x}.$$

Hence if $x^t = x^*$, the return to farming the risky crop with trade constitutes a mean-preserving spread in the return compared with what it was under autarky. If the farmer is risk averse he will need a higher expected return to compensate for the risk so that

$$E\hat{p}\tilde{\theta} > q.$$

Hence, if the symmetric free trade equilibrium is stable, since at x^t, returns to the risky crop exceed those to the safe crop, x must increase when income risk is eliminated. Hence

$$x^* > x^t.$$

For small σ^2 a quantitative estimate of the adjustment can be made. From equation (23.9), x^t is the value of x for which

$$x = \frac{\dfrac{ay}{x} - \dfrac{by}{1-x}}{A \dfrac{a^2 y^2}{x^2} \sigma^2}$$

or

$$x^t = \frac{a(1 - Aay\sigma^2)}{a + b - Aa^2 y\sigma^2} \approx \frac{a}{a+b}\left(1 - \frac{Aaby\sigma^2}{a+b}\right). \qquad (23.11)$$

Define a coefficient of relative risk aversion for farmers, R, evaluated at a reference level of profits, $\hat{\pi}$:

$$R = -\frac{U''\hat{\pi}}{U'} = A\hat{\pi} = A(a+b)y \qquad (23.12)$$

$$x^t \approx \frac{a}{a+b}\left(1 - \frac{abR\sigma^2}{(a+b)^2}\right)$$

(where A is absolute risk aversion of equation (23.9)).

Thus the fall in land allocated to the risky crop is

$$\Delta x \equiv x^* - x^t = \frac{ab}{(a+b)^2} R\sigma^2. \qquad (23.13)$$

The greater the risk aversion of farmers, the larger the risk, and the larger the share of the risky crop in consumption the larger is the change in the allocation of crops.

More generally, we can easily establish:

Proposition 2.

(a) The more risk averse are farmers the greater is Δx (Diamond and Stiglitz, 1974).

(b) The greater the riskiness of θ (in the sense of Rothschild and Stiglitz, 1970), the greater is Δx, at least provide the range of $\tilde{\theta}$ is not too great. The second part follows from the concavity of the expression in equation (23.10), using a similar argument to that set out in subsection 6.4.1: if

$$M \equiv U'\{(a\tilde{\theta} + b)y\}\left(\frac{a}{x}\tilde{\theta} - \frac{b}{1-x}\right),$$

then

$$\frac{\partial M}{\partial \theta} \equiv aU'\left\{\frac{1}{x} - \frac{R}{a\theta+b}\left(\frac{a}{x}\theta - \frac{b}{1-x}\right)\right\}$$

$$\frac{\partial^2 M}{\partial \theta^2} = \frac{Ra^2U'}{a\theta+b}\left\{-\frac{2}{x} + \left(1 + R - \frac{R'\pi}{R}\right)\left(\frac{a\theta}{x} - \frac{b}{1-x}\right)\bigg/(a\theta+b)\right\}.$$

If the range of $\tilde{\theta}$ is small, $(a\tilde{\theta}/x) - (b/1-x)$ will be small, so $\partial^2 M/\partial \theta^2 < 0$.

23.2.4 Welfare analysis

In free trade equilibrium the mean income of farmers is unchanged but risk has increased. Hence

Proposition 3.

Farmers are always made worse off as a result of the opening of trade.

A quantative estimate of their welfare loss is provided by a Taylor series approximation:

$$\frac{\Delta U}{U'} = \frac{U\{(a+b)y\} - EU\{(a\tilde{\theta}+b)y\}}{U'} \simeq \frac{a^2Ry}{2(a+b)}\sigma^2. \qquad (23.14)$$

Free trade means that consumers now face no risk, which, other things being equal, always makes them better off. However, in return, there is a change in x which always makes them worse off. To see this, note that consumer welfare as a function of x is

$$V = V\left\{I\left(\frac{ay}{x}\right)^{-a}\left(\frac{by}{1-x}\right)^{-b}Z(\theta)\right\}$$

where $Z(\theta) > 0$ measures the consumers' exposure to risk. ($Z(\theta) = \theta^a$ in autarky, 1 in free trade equilibrium.) The choice of x which maximizes consumer welfare in any state is independent of θ, and is given by

$$x = \frac{a}{a+b} = x^*, \qquad (23.15)$$

the farmer's choice under autarky. Any other choice makes the consumer worse off. In Fig. 23.1 as the degree of trade increases consumers are initially made better off (risk decreases rapidly for them, but is still insignificant for farmers, so they do not change x much). However, near free trade, there is little subsequent advantage in reducing consumer risk, but the farmers are increasingly encouraged to switch out of the risky crop and so worsen the consumers' allocation. The change in consumer welfare between free trade and autarky thus depends on the size of the resource shift, Δx, which depends, from Proposition 2, on

(i) the size of the risk, σ,
(ii) the size of the share of the risky crop in consumption, a, and
(iii) the degree of farmers' risk aversion, R,

as well as on the benefits the consumer gains from reducing the risk he faces,

which, for given x, depends on
   (iv) the degree of consumer risk aversion, ρ,
   (v) the share of the risky crop in consumption, a, and
   (vi) the size of the risk.

It thus seems that if the consumer risk benefits are small, (ρ is small) and the allocative effects Δx are large (because R is large), then the consumer is worse off with free trade. Conversely, if the risk benefits are large (high ρ) and the allocative effects small (farmers are not very risk averse) then consumers will be better off. The effect of opening trade on welfare is shown in Fig. 23.1 for one configuration of parameter values (R, a, ρ, σ), while the importance of attitudes to risk in determining whether free trade is Pareto inferior to autarky is shown in Fig. 23.2. The frontier $R = f(\rho)$ delimits the range of values of R, ρ for which

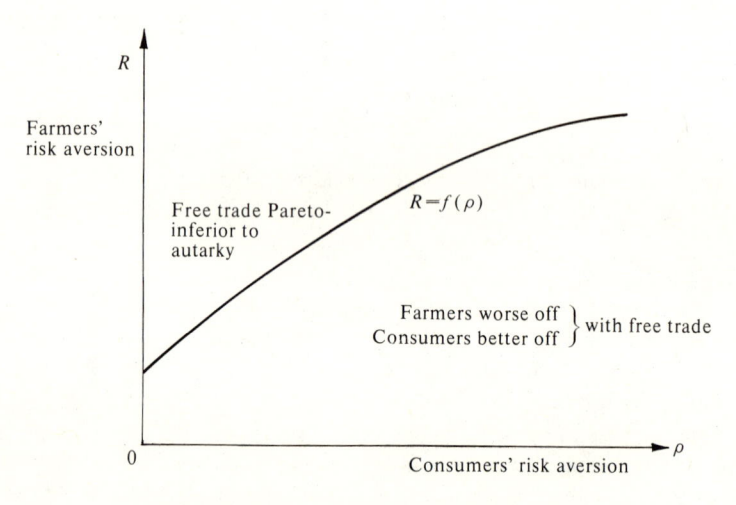

Fig. 23.2 Determinants of inferiority of free trade

free trade is Pareto inferior, and corresponds to consumers being just indifferent to free trade and autarky (since farmers are always worse off). Its general shape corresponds to the heuristic argument given above, and its detailed shape can be found as follows. First, fix a, b and the form of the distribution of risk θ, and then see for which values of R, ρ, consumers are indifferent between free trade and autarky. Under autarky,

$$(1-\rho)EV^* = E\{(x^*)^a(1-x^*)^b \theta^a\}^{1-\rho} \qquad (23.16a)$$

while under free trade

$$(1-\rho)V^t = \{(x^t)^a(1-x^t)^b\}^{1-\rho}. \qquad (23.16b)$$

Equating these gives

$$\{E\tilde{\theta}^{a(1-\rho)}\}^{1/a(1-\rho)} = \left(\frac{x^t}{x^*}\right)\left\{\frac{1-x^t}{1-x^*}\right\}^{b/a}. \tag{23.17}$$

It is immediate that the LHS of (23.17) is a monotonically decreasing function of ρ, with

$$\lim_{\rho \to \infty} \{E\tilde{\theta}^{a(1-\rho)}\}^{1/(1-\rho)a} = \theta_{\min} < 1,$$

$$\lim_{\rho \to 0} \{E\tilde{\theta}^{a(1-\rho)}\}^{1/(1-\rho)a} = \{E\theta^a\}^{1/a} < 1.$$

Since $x^* = a/(a+b)$, the RHS is a single peaked function of x^t with the maximum attained at $x^t = x^*$, as noted above in equation (23.15). Hence, using Proposition 2, the right-hand side is a monotonically decreasing function of R. Hence

Proposition 4.

For a given risk and demand parameters (a, b), there exists a critical function $f(\rho)$, $f' > 0$ such that if $R > f(\rho)$ free trade is Pareto inferior to autarky. Moreover,

$$\lim_{\rho \to 0} f(\rho) > 0.$$

The last part of the proposition follows because the value of the LHS of equation (23.17) has a value less than unity when $\rho = 0$, as shown above. (This is because even if consumers are income risk neutral, they are averse to fluctuations in the quantity of the risky good they consume.) Thus the RHS of equation (23.17) must have a value less than unity, which requires farmers to be sufficiently risk averse to reduce their supply of the risky crop under free trade. The results of the proposition show that the Pareto inferior frontier, $f(\rho)$, is as shown in Fig. 23.2.

The exact location of the curve f depends obviously on a, b and the magnitude of risk. We have not yet been able to obtain a general characterization of how each affects the boundary curve. For instance, an increase in risk decreases both the left- and right-hand sides of equation (23.17) (the re-allocation effect is larger, but the reduction in risk borne by consumers is also larger).

23.3 Multiple equilibria and stability

The previous section compared the free trade symmetric equilibrium and the no-trade equilibrium. In fact, however, our simple model is somewhat more complicated than the previous analysis has suggested, for there may be multiple equilibria. The reason is that the symmetric equilibrium shares the risk equally bewteen the producers, but an asymmetric equilibrium may exist in which one country dominates in the production of the risky crop, and hence dominates in the determination of its price. In so doing its farmers will be provided with insurance sufficient to persuade them to produce as much as required, while the other country's farmers now face a more risky price, and hence are only willing to undertake a small amount of risky production.

If there is more than one equilibrium, it is likely that only some of them will be stable – indeed, there is a presumption that neighbouring equilibria will be alternately stable and unstable. Obviously, there is little point in characterizing the welfare properties of unstable equilibria, since these are unlikely to persist, and so it is important to check the stability properties of the various possible equilibria.

This may be done as follows. Label the countries 1 and 2 (rather than East and West) and suppose that they allocate proportions x_1 and x_2 of their land to the risky crop respectively. Then, the supply of risky crop from country 2 affects the price distribution facing country 1, and, taking x_2 as given, there is an expected utility-maximizing choice x_1 for country 1 which depends on x_2, or $x_1 = g(x_2)$. These choices are *reaction functions*, and describe the reaction of one country's farmers to the choices of the other, and they can be graphed as in Fig. 23.3. If one country takes the other's choice as given (the normal Nash assumption) then there is a natural concept of stability illustrated by the arrowed paths in Fig. 23.3. Thus, if the initial configuration (x_1, x_2) is at the asymmetric equilibrium A, a slight mistake in planning might lead to a choice B in one year. If so, then while this is an equilibrium for country 1 (as shown), it is not for country 2. The following year the choice will be C, farther away from the initial equilibrium, and eventually the system will settle at the stable symmetric equilibrium S. The various equilibria are where the reaction functions cross, plus possibly corner equilibria where one country specializes. From the Figure it should be clear that stability (in this Nash dynamic sense) depends on the relative slopes of the reaction functions. The critical condition for (local) stability is that deviations from equilibrium are self-correcting, or

$$\frac{d}{dx_1}|g(g(x_1))| < 1 \quad \text{or} \quad \left|\frac{dx_1}{dx_2}\right|\left|\frac{dx_2}{dx_1}\right| < 1.$$

To apply this condition, we need to find the reaction functions, and since they are symmetric, we need only find $x_1 = g(x_2)$, for then $x_2 = g(x_1)$, given by

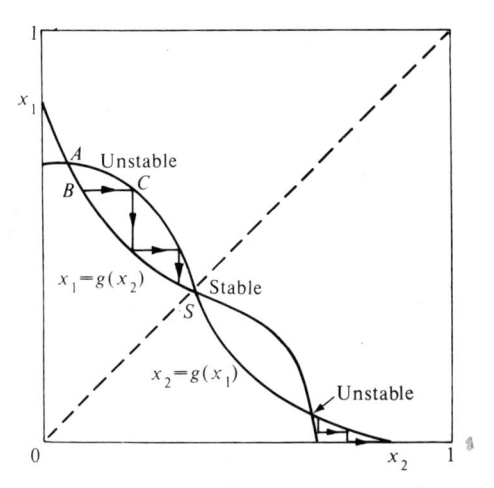

Fig. 23.3 Five equilibria, symmetric stable

the same function. For an interior solution (i.e. $0 < x_i < 1$), given x_2 the equilibrium choice of x_1 is the solution to

$$EU'\{\tilde{\pi}_1(x_1, x_2)\}(\tilde{p}\theta - q) = 0 \tag{23.19a}$$

where

$$p = \frac{2ay}{x_1\theta + x_2(2-\theta)} \tag{23.19b}$$

$$q = \frac{2by}{1 - x_1 + 1 - x_2} \tag{23.19c}$$

$$\pi_1 = px_1\theta + q(1 - x_1).$$

For a boundary solution at $x_1 = 1$ we require

$$EU'\{\pi_1(1, x_2)\}(p\theta - q) \geq 0 \tag{23.20a}$$

while for a boundary solution at $x_1 = 0$ we require

$$EU'\{\pi_1(0, x_2)\}(p\theta - q) \leq 0. \tag{23.20b}$$

We would like to know when the symmetric equilibrium is stable, when it is unique, and which equilibria are stable when there are multiple equilibria. Thus, in Fig. 23.3 the symmetric equilibrium is stable while in Fig. 23.4 the symmetric equilibrium is unstable and the corner equilibria are stable. Unfortunately, the reaction functions are difficult to characterize, since they are defined by first-order conditions of functions of unspecified shape (the utility functions), and this has precluded their complete characterization. In Appendix

2 to this chapter we show that a sufficient condition for the stability of the symmetric equilibrium is that the farmers' risk aversion be not too high, so that in Fig. 23.2 the region in which free trade is Pareto inferior *and* the symmetric equilibrium we examined is also stable is restricted to points above the frontier $R = f(\rho)$ and below a critical value R^*. In short, it is still possible to find stable free-trade equilibria which are Pareto inferior to autarky, and the relevance of the analysis of section 23.2 is confirmed. We also show that certain boundary equilibria can be ruled out. Altogether, the results of Appendix 1 can be summarized as follows.

23.3.1 *Boundary equilibria*

(i) If farmers are less than infinitely risk averse, then there cannot exist an equilibrium in which one of the two countries specializes in the safe crop, but there may exist an equilibrium in which one of the two countries specializes in the risky crop.

(ii) If farmers are infinitely risk averse, there is always an equilibrium with one country specializing in one crop, and it may also have the other country specializing in the other crop.

23.3.2 *Stability*

(i) If farmers are not too risk averse the symmetric equilibrium is stable.

(ii) If farmers are infinitely risk averse the symmetric equilibrium is always unstable, but the boundary equilibria are stable.

The proofs of these propositions (which are tedious) are relegated to the Appendices. If, however, farmers are risk neutral, it is easy to establish uniqueness and stability, as the example below shows. The propositions, together with the critical function $R = f(\rho)$ of Fig. 23.2 imply that there are some sets of attitudes to risk and forms of risk for which the symmetric free-trade equilibrium is stable but Pareto inferior to autarky.

We conjecture, but have only established for the case in which farmers are solely concerned with the mean and variance of income, that the symmetric equilibrium is stable when unique, but unstable with multiple equilibria.

23.3.3* *Example: Risk-neutral farmers*

For risk-neutral farmers the expected return from the two crops must be the same. Thus we require

$$q = E\tilde{p}\tilde{\theta} = E\tilde{p}(2 - \tilde{\theta}). \tag{23.21}$$

Solving for x_1 as a function of x_2 gives from equation (23.19b) and (23.19c)

$$\frac{2by}{2 - x_1 - x_2} = E\frac{2ay\tilde{\theta}}{x_1\tilde{\theta} + x_2(2 - \tilde{\theta})}. \tag{23.22}$$

Thus

$$\left.\frac{dx_1}{dx_2}\right|_{x_1=x_2} = \frac{E\tilde{\theta}^2 - 2 - \dfrac{bx^2}{a(1-x)^2}}{E\tilde{\theta}^2 + \dfrac{bx^2}{a(1-x)^2}}. \qquad (23.23)$$

At $x_1 = x_2 = x$ equation (23.22) simplifies to give

$$\frac{b}{1-x} = \frac{a}{x}$$

and equation (23.23) can then be solved:

$$\left.\frac{dx_1}{dx_2}\right|_{x_1=x_2} = -1 + \frac{2\sigma^2}{\dfrac{a}{b} + 1 + \sigma^2} > -1$$

and by symmetry,

$$\left.\frac{dx_1}{dx_2}\right|_{x_1=x_2} = \left.\frac{dx_2}{dx_1}\right|_{x_2=x_1}.$$

Hence, the symmetric equilibrium is stable. We can also establish for this case that this is the *unique* equilibrium, since equilibrium requires (from the second part of equation (23.21)):

$$2E\frac{(1-\tilde{\theta})}{x_1\tilde{\theta} + x_2(2-\tilde{\theta})} = 0.$$

But if $E\tilde{\theta} = 1$, this can only be true if $x_1\tilde{\theta} + x_2(2-\tilde{\theta})$ is independent of $\tilde{\theta}$ (i.e. $x_1 = x_2$).

23.3.4* Stability of symmetric equilibrium for infinitely risk-averse farmers

Infinite risk aversion is equivalent to

$$U = \text{Min } \pi = \underset{\theta}{\text{Min }} \tilde{\theta}\tilde{p}x + q(1-x).$$

An interior solution requires Min $\tilde{p}\tilde{\theta} = q$, and the reaction function for country 1 is

$$\frac{1-\gamma}{x_1(1-\gamma) + x_2(1-\gamma)} = \frac{c}{2-x_1-x_2},$$

where

$$1 - \gamma = \text{Min } \tilde{\theta}, \quad c = b/a.$$

Hence

$$x_1 = \frac{2}{1+c} - \left\{1 + \frac{2c\gamma}{(1+c)(1-\gamma)}\right\} x_2$$

and

$$\left|\frac{dx_1}{dx_2}\right| > 1,$$

so the symmetric equilibrium is unstable. Fig. 23.4 illustrates, and Appendix 1 categorizes, the three different boundary equilibria which can result.

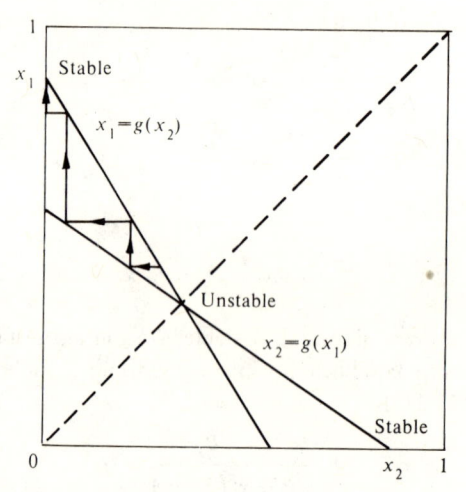

Fig. 23.4 Three equilibria, symmetric unstable

23.4 Partial versus general equilibrium analysis

Our simple model illustrates another general principle: it is often thought that general equilibrium analysis will modify the quantitative conclusions of partial equilibrium analysis, but that it will not (if the equilibrium is stable) reverse the qualitative results. Our model provides a striking example of such a reversal.

Partial equilibrium analysis assumes that other things remain equal when studying a change, such as the opening up of trade. In this case the natural partial equilibrium assumption would be that the price of the safe crop remains unchanged as a result of opening up trade. A defence of this assumption might be that the safe crop is widely traded on world markets, and the regions under study are small relative to this world market, so that prices remain constant. This means that the opening of trade must make farmers better off, because they can still obtain $\pi = q$ simply by planting the safe crop. But in equilibrium it will always pay them to grow some of the risky crop provided they are not infinitely risk averse. Hence, the rise in the mean price of the risky crop must be large enough to compensate for the increase in its riskiness.

It is thus immediate that $x^t < x^*$, the allocation to the risky crop is smaller under free trade than autarky. But now the resource allocation shift effect on consumers is much larger because q fails to fall as resources get shifted towards the safe crop. Thus, for instance, for infinitely risk-averse producers

$$\frac{\theta_{\min} ay}{x^t} = q$$

or

$$x^t = \frac{\theta_{\min} ay}{q},$$

while with no trade

$$x^* = \frac{ay}{q}$$

$$EV^t/EV^* = \theta_{\min}^{a(1-\rho)}/E\theta^{-a(1-\rho)}$$

as opposed to our earlier analysis, where

$$x^t = \frac{\theta_{\min} a}{a\theta_{\min} + b}$$

so

$$\frac{EV^t}{EV^*} = \frac{\theta_{\min}^{a(1-\rho)}}{E\theta^{-a(1-\rho)}} \left\{ \left(\frac{a+b}{a\theta_{\min}+b} \right)^{(1-\rho)(a+b)} \right\}.$$

Notice that since

$$\frac{a\theta_{\min}+b}{a+b} < 1,$$

EV^t/EV^* with q variable is greater than with q fixed, i.e. if consumers were worse off with q variable, they are even worse off with q fixed.

Thus consumers are more likely to be made worse off, while producers are made better off as a result of the opening of trade.

23.5 Robustness of the analysis

The model we have developed in this chapter is, admittedly, quite special. The model was chosen as the simplest one which would illustrate the basic point at issue: the opening of trade would increase the income variability facing farmers, thus lowering their welfare; at the same time, although it reduced the risk faced by consumers, it led farmers to reallocate their resources (make alternative production decisions) which could also lower the welfare of consumers. The assumptions made were far from pathological – indeed the constant price and income elasticity demand function employed in the analysis is perhaps the most commonly employed parameterization for consumers' behaviour. None the less, it is worth asking, how robust are our results? Could they be generalized?

We have considered a number of modifications of the model. These lead us to the conclusion that the model is in fact very robust. Changing any of the assumptions obviously changes the precise conditions under which a Pareto-inferior trade equilibrium will result, but the possibility remains. More generally, the possibility that (a) producers will be worse off; (b) the gains to consumers will not be enough to compensate the producers; and (c) there exists some form of trade intervention such as those considered in the next chapter which would be a Pareto improvement, remain.

In this section, we discuss briefly a few of the directions in which the model might be extended. We show (heuristically) how these modifications to the model will alter the conclusions.

23.5.1 *Alternative specifications of consumers' demand curves*

The major reason that the unit price elasticity assumption is employed is that it avoids the confusion between *transfer* and *risk* effects (which we discussed at greater length in Chapter 17). With unit price elasticity, the mean income of farmers is the same regardless of what action they undertake. It also has the convenient property that, before trade, there is no income risk. We need to distinguish two cases.

(i) If the price elasticity is not too small, income variability before trade is still smaller than income variability after trade. However, mean income is, in general, affected by the opening of trade. Whether mean income is increased or decreased depends on the concavity or convexity of the revenue function as a function of output. Either is possible. If the demand functions for each of the crops are independent, but of constant elasticity, then whether mean revenue is increased or decreased depends simply on whether the price elasticity is greater or less than unity.

There are now two possibilities: the opening up of trade has increased the variability of the returns to growing the risky crop, but it may also have increased the mean return. If it increases the mean return enough, then it induces the farmer to shift resources into the risky crop. In this case, the results of this chapter may not apply.

But unless this transfer effect is quite large, if farmers are sufficiently risk averse, they will shift out of the risky crop, precisely in the manner described. Moreover, if the price elasticity is sufficiently greater than that for the safe crop (the precise condition is easy to derive) the income of farmers will be reduced and as a result farmers are made unambiguously worse off.

The analysis of the effect on consumers follows along the lines of the earlier analysis: there is a risk reduction effect and an allocation effect, working in opposite directions.

(ii) If the price elasticity is very small (less than one-half), then pre-trade income variability is greater than post-trade income variability, in which case the opening of trade may be Pareto superior (even without direct compensation schemes).

23.5.2 *Alternative specifications of risk*
We assumed that the two regions had perfectly negatively correlated crops. The results, however, remain valid so long as the correlation is not perfect. For any positive degree of correlation (less than perfect), farmers' mean income will (with the unitary price elasticity assumption) remain unchanged, while the opening of trade will induce some degree of income variability. Note that the case of perfect correlation (which has received extensive discussion within the trade literature) is an extreme and special case, as we showed in Chapter 15.

23.5.3 *Alternative specifications of producers' utility functions*
Throughout, we assumed that producers only consumed the numeraire good; the relative price of the agricultural goods did not affect their welfare, except in so far as it affected their income.

We could easily extend the model to allow producers to consume the goods which they produce. All that is critical for our analysis is that, for all values of the price, they remain producers, i.e. they continue to sell the agricultural goods (which, given our assumption that they have no other sources of income, will remain the case provided variations in the output of the risky agricultural good are not too large). The reason that introducing producers' consumption complicates the analysis is that net sales (to pure consumers) are then not just equal to (or in general a simple function of) the gross output. If, however, we assume the producers also have a logarithmic utility function (or an ordinal transformation of a logarithmic utility function), the analysis is completely unaffected: producers' expenditures on each of the crops are a constant fraction of gross income, and although the details of the calculations need to be modified, all the qualitative properties remain unchanged.

23.5.4 *Two factors and comparative advantage*
Specialists in traditional trade theory have, on a number of occasions, expressed an unease with our analysis on the grounds that it appears to ignore the principle of comparative advantage which underlies conventional trade theory. Note that this is not quite correct. Although there is no long-run comparative advantage, each of the countries having precisely the same endowments and tastes, every period there is a significant comparative advantage, depending simply on the weather.

We can, however, easily incorporate elements of traditional comparative advantage theory within our framework. Although we leave the formal development of such a synthesis to another occasion, let us briefly show how it may be done. Assume, for simplicity, that there are two factors, say capital and labour. Assume that the safe crop is labour intensive. For simplicity, let us assume that the two countries have the same factor endowments. Clearly, there is again no 'long-run' comparative advantage. We can ask, however, what happens as a result of the opening up of trade. Our previous analysis applies almost identically, except now farms do not face a straight-line production possibilities schedule, but face a concave production possibilities schedule. It is still true, however, that the opening up of trade will lead to an increase in the production of the safe crop, and this in turn implies that the opening up of trade will lead to an increase in the return of the factor which is intensive in the safe crop (in this case labour). Assume now that the two countries have slightly different factor endowments. There will now be two effects: in the absence of risk, the opening up of trade will lead to the equalization of factor prices, a decrease in the price of labour in one country and an increase in its price in the other. Now, however, there is an additional risk effect: regardless of the riskless or static comparative advantage effects, there will be shift towards the production of the safe crop (more, presumably, in the country which has a comparative advantage in its production). This effect may outweigh the first effect, so that, still, the price of labour in both countries rises; it is even possible that factor price differentials widen.

What is, of course, crucial for our analysis is the absence of a complete set of risk markets. And although there may be disagreements about the precise reason that such markets are not much in evidence, the fact of the matter is that they are not: the assumption, employed throughout our analysis, that there are no risk markets, would appear to be a far better approximation to reality than the contrary assumption, conventionally employed, that such markets are perfect.

23.6 Concluding remarks

There is an argument, popular with economists, that if markets are competitive and agents well informed, then government intervention will lead to inefficiency.

This argument has been used both to argue against restrictions on trade and against the establishment of international buffer stocks. At the moment, many LDCs are pressing for the establishment of international buffer stocks for certain core primary commodities. However, most commodity markets are very competitive, forward markets exist to disseminate information quickly through the market, and private agents can stockpile if it is privately profitable. Therefore, it is argued that international buffer stocks, if they are to stabilize prices further, will have to go beyond the efficient level. At best, the scheme will provide an inefficient mechanism for a concealed aid transfer, and would be better replaced by an international credit agency (such as the IMF) and direct aid transfers.

Our analysis questions the premises of this reasoning. We show that there is no presumption that free markets will be Pareto optimal. But our analysis is not simply negative. We provide a framework which enables, in any situation, a detailed evaluation to be made of whether trade liberalization or a commodity buffer stock will be a Pareto improvement. Our analysis suggests that, under quite plausible conditions, it is desirable for the government not to introduce a buffer stock or engage in free trade in order to stabilize prices. The obvious question which this raises is: what is the appropriate policy in such cases? The next chapter examines this question.

Appendix 1* Conditions for boundary equilibria

Proposition 1.

Provided farmers are not infinitely risk averse, there cannot be an equilibrium in which one country (say country 2) specializes in the safe crop.

Proof.

At $x_2 = 0$, for an interior solution for x_1,

$$\theta p = \frac{2ay}{x_1} = \frac{2by}{1 - x_1 + 1} = q. \quad (23.\text{A1})$$

For $x_2 = 0$ to be an equilibrium

$$EU'(\pi_2)\{p(2-\theta) - q\} = U'(q)\{Ep(2-\theta) - q\} \leq 0. \quad (23.\text{A2})$$

(This is where the assumption that producers are not infinitely risk averse is used. Compare Proposition 2 below.) But we know from (23.A1)

$$Ep\theta = q$$

so we require (substituting)

$$\frac{4ayU'}{x_1} E\left(\frac{1-\theta}{\theta}\right) \leq 0 \quad (23.\text{A3})$$

which is impossible.

It is trivial to show that if $x_2 = 0$, x_1 cannot equal 1. Hence, there cannot be equilibrium in which one country specializes in the safe crop.

Proposition 2.

If farmers are infinitely risk averse, there is always an equilibrium in which one country specializes in one crop. There are three possible cases to consider

(i) Assume $x_2 = 0$. For an interior solution for x_1, (23.A1) must hold, so $a < b$ and

$$x_1 = \frac{2a}{a+b}.$$

For $x_2 = 0$ to be an equilibrium, since

$$U(\pi_2) = q + x_2\{\min \check{p}(2 - \tilde{\theta}) - q\},$$

$$\min p(2 - \theta) = y(a+b) \min\left(\frac{2-\theta}{\theta}\right) < q = \frac{2by}{2 - x_1} = y(a+b),$$

which it is provided $\sigma^2 > 0$. Thus

$$(x_1, x_2) = \left(\frac{2a}{a+b}, 0\right) \quad (23.\text{A4})$$

is an equilibrium.

(ii) Assume $x_2 = 1$. For an interior solution for x_1,

Pareto-inferior Trade and Price Stabilization

$$\min\left(\frac{2ay\theta}{2-\theta+x_1\theta}\right) = \frac{2ay\theta_{\min}}{2-(1-x_1)\theta_{\min}} = \frac{2by}{1-x_1} = q,$$

i.e.

$$x_1 = \frac{a\theta_{\min} - b(2-\theta_{\min})}{(a+b)\theta_{\min}}.$$

For this to be an equilibrium we require

$$0 < x_1 < 1,$$

i.e.

$$\theta_{\min} > \frac{2b}{a+b} \qquad (23.\text{A}5)$$

and

$$\min p(2-\theta) = \min\left\{\frac{2ay(2-\theta)}{2-\theta+x_1\theta}\right\} = \frac{2ay\theta_{\min}}{\theta_{\min}+x_1(2-\theta_{\min})} > \frac{2by}{1-x_1} = q$$

which it will, provided

$$\theta_{\min} + x_1(2-\theta_{\min}) < 2 - \theta_{\min} + x_1\theta_{\min}$$

or

$$x_1 < 1.$$

(iii) Finally, assume $x_2 = 1$ and $x_1 = 0$. Then we require

$$\min\left(\frac{2ay\theta}{2-\theta}\right) = \frac{2ay\theta_{\min}}{2-\theta_{\min}} < 2by$$

and

$$\min 2by < 2ay,$$

i.e.

$$b < a \qquad (23.\text{A}6)$$

and

$$\theta_{\min} < \frac{2b}{a+b}. \qquad (23.\text{A}7)$$

Since at least one of the set of inequalities (23.A4)-(23.A7) must hold, there must be a boundary equilibrium.

Appendix 2* Stability Analysis

From equation (23.19), at the symmetric equilibrium (where $p = \hat{p}$)

$$\frac{dp}{dx_1} = -\frac{p\theta}{2x}; \quad \frac{dp}{dx_2} = -\frac{p(2-\theta)}{2x}$$

$$\frac{dq}{dx_1} = \frac{dq}{dx_2} = \frac{q}{2(1-x)},$$

whence

$$\frac{d}{dx_1}(p\theta - q) = -\tfrac{1}{2}\left(\frac{p\theta^2}{x} + \frac{q}{1-x}\right)$$

$$\frac{d}{dx_2}(p\theta - q) = -\tfrac{1}{2}\left\{\frac{p\theta(2-\theta)}{x} + \frac{q}{1-x}\right\} = -\frac{d}{dx_1}(p\theta - q) - \left(\frac{p\theta}{x} + \frac{q}{1-x}\right).$$

Since

$$\pi_1 = p\theta x_1 + q(1 - x_1),$$

$$\frac{d\pi_1}{dx_1} = \tfrac{1}{2}\{p\theta(2-\theta) - q\} = -\frac{d\pi_1}{dx_2}.$$

Consider equation (23.19a):

$$EU'(\pi_1)(p\theta - q) \equiv \phi = 0 \tag{23.A8}$$

$$-\frac{dx_1}{dx_2} = \frac{\partial\phi/\partial x_2}{\partial\phi/\partial x_1} = \frac{EU'\dfrac{\partial}{\partial x_2}(p\theta-q) + EU''(p\theta-q)\dfrac{\partial \pi_1}{\partial x_2}}{EU'\dfrac{\partial}{\partial x_1}(p\theta-q) + EU''(p\theta-q)\dfrac{\partial \pi_1}{\partial x_1}}$$

$$= -1 + \frac{2EU'\left(\dfrac{p\theta}{x} + \dfrac{q}{1-x}\right)}{EU'\left(\dfrac{p\theta^2}{x} + \dfrac{q}{1-x}\right) - EU''(p\theta-q)\{p\theta(2-\theta) - q\}}.$$

The second term is positive, and stability requires it to be less than 2, i.e.

$$EU'\left(\frac{p\theta}{x} + \frac{q}{1-x}\right) < EU'\left(\frac{p\theta^2}{x} + \frac{q}{1-x}\right) - EU''(p\theta-q)\{p\theta(2-\theta) - q\}$$

or, since p is non-stochastic in the symmetric equilibrium,

$$\frac{p}{x}EU'\theta(1-\theta) < -EU''(p\theta-q)\{p\theta(2-\theta) - q\}. \tag{23.A9}$$

Pareto-inferior Trade and Price Stabilization

This is trivially satisfied if $U'' = 0$, i.e. producers are risk neutral, since

$$E\theta(1-\theta) = -\sigma^2 < 0.$$

If producers have constant absolute risk aversion $A = -U''/U'$, then the condition reduces to

$$\frac{p}{x}EU'\theta(1-\theta) < AEU'(p\theta - q)\{p\theta(2-\theta) - q\}$$

or, substituting for $x = ay/p$

$$EU'[\theta(\theta-1) + k(\theta - q/p)\{\theta(2-\theta) - q/p\}] > 0, \quad k \equiv Aay. \quad (23.A10)$$

If $k\sigma$ is small, U' in equation (23.A8) can be expanded in a Taylor series around the no-risk level of profits $\bar{\pi}$:

$$\pi = \bar{\pi} + px(\theta - 1)$$

so

$$U'(\pi) \simeq U'(\bar{\pi}) + px(\theta - 1)U''(\bar{\pi}) = U'(\bar{\pi})\{1 - k(\theta - 1)\}. \quad (23.A11)$$

Equation (23.A8) now becomes

$$E\{1 - k(\theta - 1)\}(\theta - q/p) = 0$$

or

$$1 - q/p = k\sigma^2.$$

Hence the stability condition (23.A10) becomes, substituting from (23.A11),

$$U'(\bar{\pi})E(1 - ku)\{u(u + 1) + k(u + k\sigma^2)(-u^2 + k\sigma^2)\} > 0 \quad (23.A12)$$

where $u = \theta - 1$, $Eu = 0$, $Eu^2 = \sigma^2$. In particular, if u is normally distributed, then

$$Eu^3 = 0, \quad Eu^4 = 3\sigma^4$$

and equation (23.A12) becomes

$$EU'(\bar{\pi})\sigma^2\{(1 - k) + 2k^2\sigma^2\} > 0$$

or

$$k(1 - 2k\sigma^2) < 1. \quad (23.A13)$$

Thus if producers have low enough risk aversion this will be satisfied. Although it may also be satisfied for large values of k, this cannot be confirmed without checking the validity of the approximation (23.A11), which assumed small $k\sigma$.

Chapter 24

Trade Policy

24.1 Introduction

In the last chapter we remarked that tariffs and quotas are not equivalent in the presence of risk, and we established that free trade could be Pareto inferior to no trade. Fortunately, we are not forced to choose between these two extremes, and in this chapter we investigate the appropriate trade policy for the model of risky trade of the last chapter. We establish four remarkable results:

1. In the symmetric free trade equilibrium, some trade restriction is always Pareto improving, provided that producers are sufficiently risk averse.
2. In the no-trade equilibrium, allowing some trade will be a Pareto improvement.
3. Near the symmetric free trade equilibrium, quotas are preferable to tariffs, again, provided that producers are sufficiently risk averse.
4. Near the no-trade equilibrium, tariffs are preferable to quotas.

The intuition behind these results is simple. In the free trade equilibrium, producers bear all the risk. A slight trade restriction (with revenues, if any, redistributed to producers) leaves producers' mean income unchanged, but reduces risk, and thus makes them better off. The reduced risk induces them to increase the supply of the risky crop, which makes consumers better off. Consumers now bear some risk, but for small trade restrictions it has a negligible cost. Since quotas are most effective in states where output is very high or very low (and hence producers' income is very high or low) they are more effective at reducing producers' risks than tariffs. Similar arguments apply at the no trade equilibrium.

24.1.1 *Symmetric trade policies*

The first two results are almost self evident from Fig. 23.1, but to derive them formally we consider the effect of identical trade policies by each country so that symmetry is not disturbed. Suppose that when a policy instrument is set at level z, in state $\tilde{\theta}$ (so that production of the risky crop is $x\tilde{\theta}$) the level of imports is $xt(\tilde{\theta}, z)$, and the import or world price is $p^w(\tilde{\theta}, z)$. Symmetry then requires that

$$t(\tilde{\theta}, z) = -t(2 - \tilde{\theta}, z) \qquad (24.1)$$

$$p^w(\tilde{\theta}, z) = p^w(2 - \tilde{\theta}, z)$$

so that imports are matched by exports, and the world price p^w only depends on the level and not the direction of trade. For example, with import quotas set at Tx:

$$t(\bar{\theta}, T) = \begin{cases} T & \theta \leq 1 - T \\ 1 - \theta & 1 - T \leq \theta \leq 1 + T. \\ -T & \theta \geq 1 + T \end{cases} \quad (24.1')$$

The corresponding distribution of domestic prices (in the symmetric case) will be

$$p(\bar{\theta}, x^*, z) = \frac{ay}{x^*\{\theta + t(\theta, z)\}}. \quad (24.2')$$

In our example of quotas, the domestic price will be

$$p = \begin{cases} \dfrac{ay/x^*}{\theta + T} & \theta \leq 1 - T \\ ay/x^* & 1 - T \leq \theta \leq 1 + T. \\ \dfrac{ay/x^*}{\theta - T} & \theta \geq 1 + T \end{cases} \quad (24.2'')$$

With quotas, either there is free trade (in the central range of values of θ) or trade is set equal to the level of the quota in the importing country, and domestic prices then clear the market given the constrained supply. The natural assumption about the world price is that it is equal to the domestic price in the exporting country, given the constrained level of exports.

The corresponding trade policy with tariffs is to impose a duty at rate τ on imports, and a tax on exports at the same rate. Tariffs operate quite differently from quotas, for over the middle range of values of θ prices in each country will differ by less than the height of the tariff barrier and no trade will occur. If trade does take place, it will move domestic prices to within 2τ of each other and leave the world price at the free trade level. In the event of positive trade occurring, the form of the function $t(\theta, \tau)$ can be found from the equation of the domestic price differences:

$$p^E - p^W = \frac{ay}{x}\left\{\frac{1}{\theta + t(\theta, \tau)} - \frac{1}{2 - \theta - t(\theta, \tau)}\right\} = 2\tau.$$

There will be no trade for $\hat{\theta} \leq \theta \leq 2 - \hat{\theta}$, where $\hat{\theta}$ is the value of θ for which $t = 0$ in this equation, namely

$$1 - \hat{\theta} = \frac{-k + \sqrt{(k^2 + 4)}}{2}, \quad k = \frac{ay}{x\tau}.$$

The value of $t(\theta, \tau)$ is then

Commodity Price Stabilization

$$t(\theta, \tau) = \begin{cases} \hat{\theta} - \theta & \theta \leqslant \hat{\theta} \\ 0 & \hat{\theta} \leqslant \theta \leqslant 2 - \hat{\theta}. \\ -\hat{\theta} + (2 - \theta) & \theta \geqslant 2 - \hat{\theta} \end{cases} \quad (24.1'')$$

In the absence of uncertainty such tariffs and quotas would have identical effects, but it is clear that in the presence of uncertainty they have quite different effects on the distribution of prices, profits, and consumption levels. The difference between the (domestic) price distributions under quotas and tariffs is shown in Fig. 24.1.

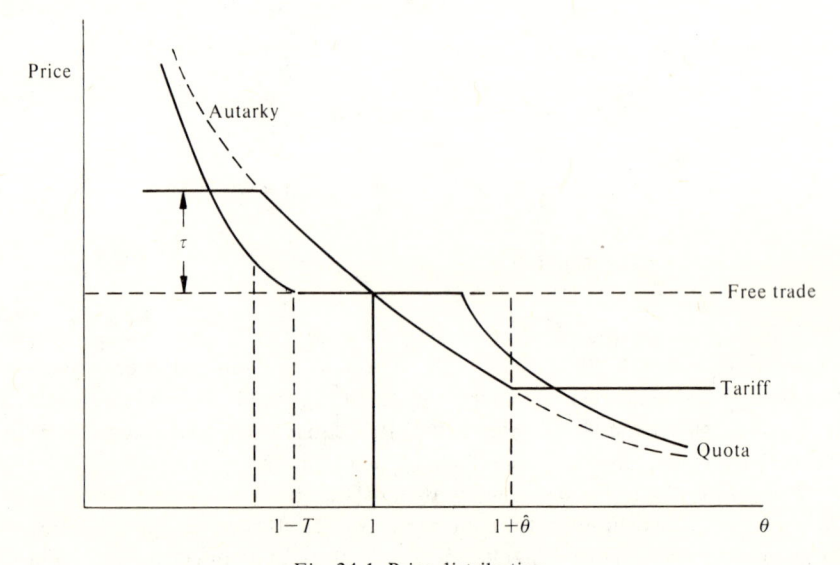

Fig. 24.1 Price distribution

Corresponding to these prices, the distribution of consumption is shown in Fig. 24.2.

Before we can calculate the level of producer profits we have to decide what happens to the revenue collected from the trade policy (the import duties or proceeds from auctioning the import licences). The spirit of the model requires these to be distributed to producers as lump-sum transfers, for then they will not disturb the amounts that consumers spend on the safe and risky commodities. Producer profits will now be:

$$\tilde{\pi} = \bar{p}x\tilde{\theta} + q(1-x) + L(\tilde{\theta}, z), \quad (24.3)$$

where $L(\tilde{\theta}, z)$ is the lump-sum transfer to producers when imports are $xt(\tilde{\theta}, z)$. In equilibrium producers must receive the amount spent by consumers on the safe and risky crops, less the balance-of-trade deficit from importing the risky crop:

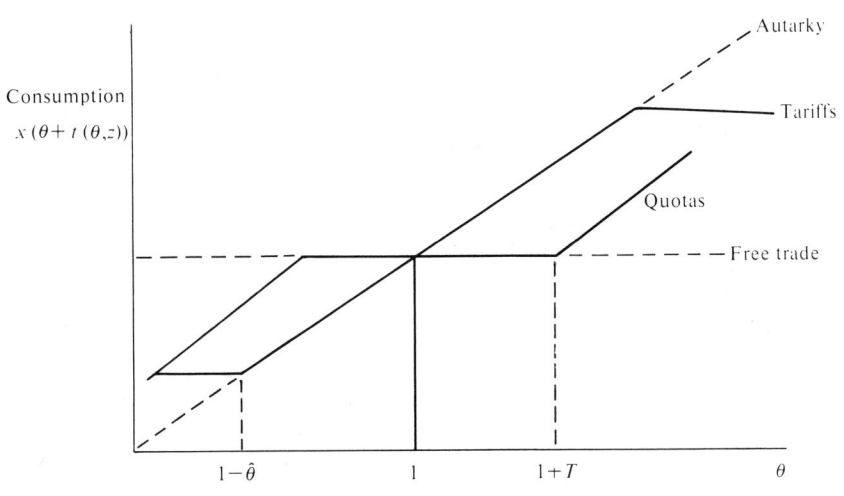

Fig. 24.2 Consumption distribution

$$\pi^*(\tilde{\theta}, z) = (a+b)y - D(\tilde{\theta}, z), \qquad (24.4)$$

where

$$D(\tilde{\theta}, z) = p^w(\tilde{\theta}, z)x^*t(\tilde{\theta}, z) = -D(2-\tilde{\theta}, z).$$

The distribution of producer profits will also be quite different under tariffs and quotas, as Fig. 24.3 shows.

Since balance-of-payments equilibrium over time requires

$$ED(\tilde{\theta}, z) = 0, \quad \text{all } z,$$

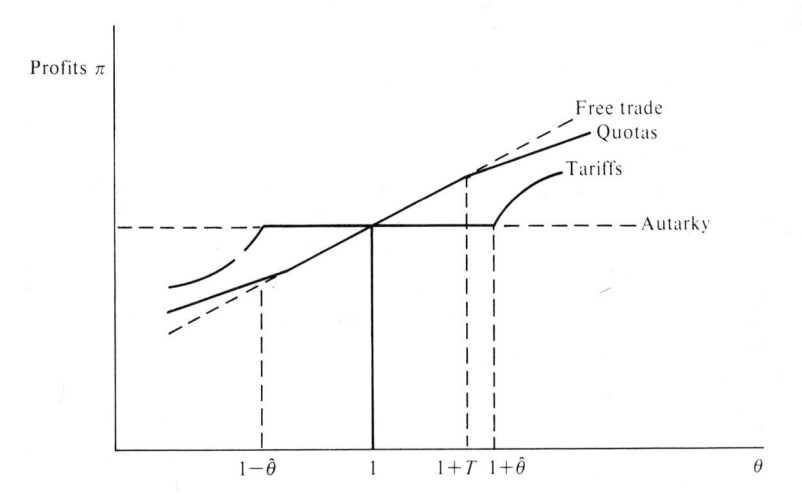

Fig. 24.3 Profit distribution

opening trade represents a mean-preserving spread in farmers' profits compared to autarky and so they must be worse off.

Let us now calculate the effects more precisely. The effect of a small change in policy can be found by differentiating totally with respect to z. We follow the convention that $z = 0$ corresponds to autarky, an increase in z represents a liberalization of trade. The effect of this on *producers* is, from equations (24.3) and (24.4)

$$\frac{dEU(\pi)}{dz} = \frac{dx}{dz} \cdot \frac{\partial EU(\pi)}{\partial x} - EU'(\pi^*)\frac{\partial D(\bar{\theta}, z)}{\partial z}. \tag{24.5}$$

The first term is zero by the envelope theorem, while the second can be written

$$\frac{dEU(\pi)}{dz} = -\int_0^1 \left[U'\{\pi^*(\theta, z)\}\frac{\partial D(\theta, z)}{\partial z} + U'\{\pi^*(2-\theta, z)\}\frac{\partial D(2-\theta, z)}{\partial z} \right] dF(\theta),$$

where $F(\theta)$ is the distribution function of θ, and we have used the symmetry of F about the mean $\theta = 1$. From equation (24.4) this can be written

$$\frac{dEU(\pi)}{dz} = -\int_0^1 [U'\{\pi^*(\theta, z)\} - U'\{\pi^*(2-\theta, z)\}] \frac{\partial D(\theta, z)}{\partial z} dF(\theta). \tag{24.6}$$

The term in square brackets can be expanded using the mean value theorem and the expression for π^* of equation (24.4), to give, for some intermediate value of λ:

$$\frac{dEU}{dz} = \begin{cases} 0 \text{ if } t = 0 \\ \\ 2\int_0^1 D(\theta, z) U''\{(a+b)y + \lambda D(\theta, z)\} \frac{\partial D(\theta, z)}{\partial z} dF(\theta); \quad -1 < \lambda < 1. \end{cases}$$

The second alternative is negative if

$$U'' < 0, \quad t > 0 \text{ for } \theta \leq 1, \text{ and } \frac{dt}{dz} \geq 0.$$

Thus, an infinitesimal liberalization has no effect on producers, but any finite liberalization makes them worse off if they are risk averse, as shown in Fig. 23.1.

The effect on *consumers* is likewise

$$\frac{dEV}{dz} = \frac{\partial EV}{\partial z} + \frac{\partial EV}{\partial x}\frac{dx}{dz}$$

$$= EV_p \frac{\partial p}{\partial z} + E\left(V_p \frac{\partial p}{\partial x} + V_q \frac{\partial q}{\partial x}\right)\frac{dx}{dz}. \tag{24.7}$$

Since

$$p = \frac{ay}{x(\theta + t(\theta, z))}, \quad q = \frac{by}{1-x}$$

$$\frac{\partial p}{\partial z} = -\frac{p}{(\theta + t)} \frac{dt}{dz} \tag{24.8a}$$

$$\frac{\partial p}{\partial x} = -\frac{p}{x} \tag{24.8b}$$

$$\frac{\partial q}{\partial x} = \frac{q}{1-x} \tag{24.8c}$$

and, from Roy's identity, if we assume for convenience the same number of producers as consumers:

$$V_p = -V_I x(\theta + t) \tag{24.8d}$$

$$V_q = -V_I(1-x). \tag{24.8e}$$

Hence

$$\frac{dEV}{dz} = EV_I \left[\tilde{p}x \frac{dt}{dz} + \{\tilde{p}(\tilde{\theta} + t) - q\} \frac{dx}{dz} \right]. \tag{24.9}$$

Finally, notice that if the effect of the policy is to increase trade (or not reduce it) in every state of nature (for fixed x), and be symmetric,

$$\frac{dt(\tilde{\theta}, z)}{dz} = -\frac{dt(2 - \tilde{\theta}, z)}{dz} \geq 0 \quad \text{for} \quad 0 \leq \theta \leq 1.$$

In other words, dt/dz is negatively correlated with θ. We can now examine special cases.

24.2 Effect of allowing a small amount of trade

Starting from a position of autarky, producers have riskless income, so the effect on producers of increasing trade at $t = 0$ is zero, as we have already noted. The effect on *consumers*, since $p\theta = q$ under autarky, is, at $t = 0$

$$ayEV_I \cdot \frac{1}{\theta} \frac{dt}{dz} = a(1-\rho) \frac{ayV_0}{I} E\theta^{a(1-\rho)-1} \frac{dt}{dz} > 0, \tag{24.10}$$

where

$$V_0 = \left(\frac{1}{a+b}\right)^{(1-\rho)(a+b)} I^{(1-\rho)(1-a-b)},$$

provided the direct utility function is concave in the risky product, that is,

368 Commodity Price Stabilization

provided
$$a(1-\rho) < 1.$$

The effect of trade liberalization from the consumers' point of view is that of a mean-quantity-preserving decrease in the riskiness of consumption, which, if consumers are risk averse, that is, utility is concave in the risky good, is beneficial.

24.3 Effects of a small restriction on free trade

Free trade corresponds to the trade policy
$$t(z, \tilde{\theta}) = 1 - \tilde{\theta},$$

and the effect of restricting trade is of reducing z, which we have already shown to be positive, in equation (24.6). A small reduction in trade thus improves producer welfare. Put another way, a symmetric trade restriction is a mean-preserving reduction in risk for producers.

For consumers, who face no risk in free trade,
$$\left.\frac{dEV}{dz}\right|_{t=1-\tilde{\theta}} = V_I E \left\{ \hat{p}x \frac{dt}{dz} + (\hat{p}-q)\frac{dx}{dz} \right\}$$

which, since $p = \hat{p} > q$, and since $E dt/dz = 0$ by symmetry, gives
$$\frac{dEV}{dz} = (\hat{p}-q)V_I \frac{dx}{dz}.$$

This has the same sign as dx/dz, since, for risk-averse farmers, $\hat{p}$ must exceed q to induce them to plant the risky crop. In general we would expect protection to increase the allocation to the protected sector, in which case dx/dz would be negative, and consumers would be made better off by the trade reduction.

We thus need to consider what happens to the first-order conditions of the producers' maximization problems at a fixed value of x. If $EU'\{p(\tilde{\theta}, z, x^*)\tilde{\theta} - q\}$ decreases with z then, if the economy is stable, an increase in z will induce a decrease in x.[1]

---

[1] Stability is not always ensured by the second-order conditions. For stability in a closed economy, we require

$$EU''(p\theta - q)^2 + EU''\left\{\frac{\partial p}{\partial x}x\theta + (1-x)\frac{\partial q}{\partial x}\right\}(p\theta - q)$$
$$+ EU'\left(\frac{\partial p}{\partial x}\theta - \frac{\partial q}{\partial x}\right) < 0.$$

The second-order condition only ensures the negativity of the first term. However, using (24.8), we can rewrite this as

$$-EU'\left(\frac{p\theta}{x} + \frac{q}{1-x}\right) < 0$$

The sign of dx/dz will therefore be the sign of

$$\frac{\partial}{\partial z} EU'\{\pi^*(\theta, z)\}(p\theta - q) \qquad (24.9)$$

where π^* is given by equation (24.4). This can be evaluated, and the argument in Newbery and Stiglitz (1981) shows that dx/dz is negative provided the coefficient of relative risk aversion, R, is sufficiently great, and in particular, exceeds $1 + b/a$.

24.3.1 Quotas versus tariffs

Quotas and tariffs are well known to be equivalent in the absence of uncertainty, but with uncertainty they have very different implications as we have already noted.

We would like to make statements like 'a tariff is preferable to an 'equivalent' quota if —— is true' but to do this, we have to define 'equivalent'. Any such comparison involves a certain degree of arbitrariness. One approach would be to analyse the optimal policy, which would involve mixtures of tariffs, quotas, and perhaps other forms of trade restrictions. Here, we take a somewhat simpler approach. We focus on trade policies which yield zero revenue, i.e. the quota is given on a pro-rata basis to producers, and the tariff is matched by a lump sum transfer to producers so that the government gets no revenue from the price distortion. The simplest comparison is between trade policies having the same effect on trade, i.e. letting $xt(\theta, z)$ be the amount of trade occurring when output is $x\theta$ for trade policy z, then we compare policies for which

$$E|t(\theta, z)x|$$

is the same.

Starting initially at no trade, it is immediate that all small trade policies in which revenues are redistributed back to producers are equivalent from the point of view of producers; all have zero effect on his welfare and on his action. For consumers, however, there is a difference, which can best be seen by examining the effect on expected utility using the direct utility function. Since for all such programmes, x^* is the same, all such programmes represent mean-preserving changes in the distribution of the consumption of the risky crop, Q_r. Utility is a concave function of Q_r. We noted earlier that tariffs lead to less trade in states of nature near the mean (since in those states, the quota is not binding, the solution is equivalent to free trade for those states). Thus, there is more trade in states of nature far from the mean, i.e. more exports in high θ states and more imports in low θ states. Thus Q_r is less disperse with tariffs as shown in Fig. 24.2. We have thus established for trade restrictions which allow only a small amount of trade, tariffs are Pareto superior to quotas.

---

which is guaranteed by the first-order condition. However, in an open economy, stability is a more complicated matter, as we saw in Section 23.3.

At the other extreme, at free trade, consumers' ranking of trade policies is based simply on their effect on x, since the risk effect, at given x, is zero.

Clearly, producers have the same mean income under each trade policy, but quotas change the price only in the tails of the distribution as shown in Fig. 24.3; thus, quotas result in a less disperse distribution of profits, and hence producers' utility is higher with quotas than with tariffs.

The effect on their actions follows immediately upon observing that at any given x the distribution of returns to the risky crop is more disperse with the tariff than the quota. The mean return is unchanged, the 'switch' from a quota to a tariff is a mean-preserving increase in risk; hence, x is reduced, and consumers are worse off.

Hence, we have established that near the free trade equilibrium a quota has a greater allocative effect, a greater improvement on producer welfare, and a greater improvement on consumer welfare than does the tariff of corresponding restrictiveness on trade.

24.4 Financial markets

In this chapter and the last we have investigated the consequences of free trade in commodities when there is no securities market. We now wish to consider how these results are affected by the availability of various financial instruments. First, we note that in the central case of consumers having logarithmic utility functions, there is no scope for future markets in the no-trade situation (since price is not variable in the free trade situation there is never scope for a futures market there); for then $V_{Ip} = 0$, the marginal utility of income is the same independent of the state of nature, and hence market equilibrium requires that if a small futures market would be introduced, it be actuarially fair. But for producers, profits are constant, and they too would require an actuarially fair futures market. Hence the only equilibrium is one where there is no trade on the futures market.

The consequences of opening up ownership shares in farms is more serious. (We must ignore all the problems of moral hazard, which are fundamental to an understanding of why such markets might not exist.) If farmers could purchase shares in each others' farms, then incomes of farmers would be constant; producers would thus be indifferent between the opening of trade and autarky, but consumers would be unambiguously better off. Thus, the standard result that free trade is preferable to no trade is restored if there is a complete set of securities markets.

But an essential part of the argument so far is that trade is costless. With costly trade, the possibility that opening trade will at least lower the welfare of producers is restored. With free trade in securities markets, farmers' income is completely smoothed, but the opening of trade leads to farmers' net income being lower by the expenditure on transport costs. Thus farmers are unambiguously worse off as a result of the opening of trade.

24.5 Conclusions

It is important to remember that the model examined in this and the previous chapter generated trade without comparative advantage (except in the tautological sense that, at any particular date, one country had a larger supply of the risky crop than the other). The direction of trade varies from year to year, and does not depend on factor endowments or tastes, but simply on the outcome of some random variable. Obviously, once the existence of genuine comparative advantage is acknowledged, autarky becomes a very unattractive alternative. Nevertheless, our results about trade policy towards risky products near a competitive free trade equilibrium appear quite robust. If one views the current situation to be 'closer' to free trade than autarky, then our model provides some explanation for the seemingly prevalent agitation for the use of quotas rather than tariffs. Moreover, this agitation is likely to increase as transport costs fall and previously isolated regions are increasingly exposed to the rigours of international trade. We believe our analysis provides the first economically rational defence of quotas in a competitive trading environment, although it does not follow that quotas are in fact desirable. If, on the other hand, trade is severely impeded, as it seems to be for many commodities, then the analysis tentatively suggests that quotas should be dismantled, and, if necessary or expedient, replaced by tariffs.

The other interpretation of our results is that in certain circumstances (diverse supply risk, unit elastic demand) the competitive market may supply excessive amounts of intertemporal arbitrage. In these cases, not only should the authorities not set up a buffer stock to stabilize prices, but they should actively restrict the arbitrage activities of speculators (as opposed to taxing them.) Again, though, this result needs qualification, for we showed in Chapters 15 and 22 how sensitive the direction of intervention was to the exact specification of demand and supply, and in the last chapter how important it was that all offsetting adjustments fell on the alternative safe crop.

Part VI

Macroeconomic Repercussions

In the first part of this book we concentrated on the effects of price instability in the context of an economy in which the only market imperfection was the absence of a complete set of risk markets. This meant that even if individuals had rational expectations the market equilibrium would not, in general, have the optimality properties we usually associate with competitive market equilibrium. Although this meant that there might be a prima facie case for some kind of government intervention, the directions of bias were difficult to ascertain and the magnitudes of potential gain from intervention were rather small.

Perhaps not surprisingly most of the official discussion of price stabilization schemes has been conducted at quite a different level; it has been concerned with issues like the effect of price instability on the level of national income, balance-of-payments deficits, investment, and growth; that is, it has been concerned with the effect of price stabilization on various macroeconomic aggregates. The models we have formulated so far do not adequately capture these kinds of effects. The result is that our estimates of the economic benefits and costs associated with price stabilization are incomplete.

The problem is that while the first part of the book makes assumptions (of rational expectations, unchanging information, and perfect competition) which allow us to develop conceptually well-defined models, the corresponding macroeconomic models, and, indeed, macroeconomic theory, is not so well formulated. The reason is that in macroeconomics the emphasis is on the way in which the economy responds to a disturbance in some market, and, in particular, the way in which this disturbance is transmitted to other markets. In macroeconomics it is recognized that agents must choose their actions on the basis of incomplete and changing information and that these choices will affect the flow of information in the economy, and hence affect subsequent choices. Suffice it to say that it is difficult to describe this process satisfactorily and even more difficult to characterize the final outcome of an initial disturbance. Faced with this difficulty, macroeconomists have been forced to simplify drastically the main components of the transmission mechanism. The usual assumption is that prices respond more slowly than quantities to any disturbance, so that they can be considered approximately constant. This seems reasonable once it is recognized that most goods and services are not sufficiently homogenous to be traded on competitive auction markets, but must have their prices set by the seller (or buyer, in the case of labour). Moreover, most goods are sufficiently durable in the short run that temporary fluctuations in demand or supply can be accommodated by stock changes, so, faced with a change in demand, most suppliers initially react by changing supply rather than price while they accumulate information about the new demand situation relevant for future price-setting.

Macroeconomics has been largely developed to study advanced industrial economies for which this price *rigidity* seems a reasonable assumption, so comparatively little attention has been paid to the macroeconomic response to price *changes*, particularly in less developed primary-producing countries. Moreover, with some notable exceptions, the main concern has been with the transmission mechanisms at work inside a particular economy, and less with those between economies. In the following chapters we shall construct a variety of fairly simple macro-models which attempt to fill this gap, and to cast light on some of the macroeconomic consequences of price instability. Of necessity, these models are in a more preliminary state than those of the earlier chapters and their purpose is rather different. First, earlier empirical studies of instability lack any clearly stated theoretical base, and so are even more *ad hoc* than most macroeconometric studies. Our models are forced to identify key links in the transmission mechanism which can be separately tested, thus providing a more discriminating empirical test of the consequences of instability. Second, they are constructed to provide quick, crude estimates of the magnitude of repercussions, and so help in deciding whether it is worth attempting to improve the modelling of particular components, or whether the main problems lie elsewhere. Finally, they provide the first few examples of what we hope will become a longer catalogue of comparable models. Subsequent models should be easier to develop, and it should be easier to identify their critical assumptions, by seeing where their predictions differ from our early models. Our models, then, are hardly ready for a macro cost–benefit analysis of stabilization policies, but may increase the very low degree of precision with which these issues are currently discussed.

The key component in all these macro-models is the mechanism by which a disturbance in the primary commodity market is transmitted to the rest of the economy (or to the rest of the world). We have already constructed a two-commodity, two-country model which demonstrates that these linkages may be important from a welfare point of view, but here the emphasis is less on an accurate welfare measurement and more on the crudely measured size of response to the disturbance. Ideally, the model should encompass both aspects, but a welfare analysis of many interacting sectors is difficult without very restrictive assumptions, and a welfare analysis of unemployment is even more difficult. The first model provides a bridge from our earlier microeconomic welfare analysis to a macroeconomic analysis with price rigidities. The model demonstrates the importance of price rigidities in the transmission mechanism and shows that welfare need not be reduced by price rigidity. The first model confines its attention to the impact of commodity price instability on an isolated economy, but it is extended to deal with a succession of phenomena.

Firstly, we observe that the instability in the price of the export good will lead, in an economy with flexible wages and prices, to instability in the prices of other goods. Thus, the costs of price instability are borne not only by those in the export industry, but are shared, in part, by all sectors of the economy. Moreover, the variation in incomes in the export industry may not provide a good estimate of the costs of instability; for the price of the domestically produced (non-traded) goods which they consume will be positively correlated with their income, and hence the variation in real wages may be significantly smaller than the variations in nominal wages. In our rather special model it turns out that the partial equilibrium effect, looking only at the cost to workers in the export sector, but ignoring the variations in domestic prices, provides an overestimate of the total cost of price variation, even though we ignore the impact on other sectors; but in general there will be no simple relationship between the partial and total impact.

The model is then modified to allow for wage rigidity in the non-traded good sector, so that fluctuations in demand lead to fluctuations in employment. In this model, if money wages are inflexible downwards and if monetary policy is permissive, then price fluctuations generate inflation at a rate which depends on the degree of price instability. Perhaps more interesting, there is a trade-off between the average rate of inflation and the level of unemployment. In all these variants, the main transmission mechanism is fluctuations in demand for the non-traded good, but in Chapter 26 we discuss briefly a model in which fluctuations in export earnings are translated into fluctuations in investment and national income. Whereas fluctuations mediated through price changes of the non-traded good are relatively mild, fluctuations induced in the level of investment, and, via a Keynsian multiplier, in total demand seem much larger.

In Chapter 27 we examine a different transmission mechanism, in which the government stabilizes producer income by trading through a marketing board, at the cost of destabilizing its public expenditure, and hence destabilizing total income. Such problems are potentially serious for countries like Zambia, in which government revenue and foreign exchange are so heavily dependent on a single export commodity (copper), but they can be reduced by compensatory foreign borrowing.

Chapter 27 deals with one of the main controversial empirical issues — the relationship between export instability and growth in LDCs. Recent empirical findings suggest that instability does not reduce investment, and may stimulate it, reversing the claim that instability is harmful. This view is scrutinized, and the simple permanent income explanation is shown to require other market imperfections before it can be sustained. An alternative theory of the labour market and investment behaviour suggests that instability can increase investment. Finally, in the last chapter of this section, we examine Kaldor's (1976) claim that world instability can only be understood by focusing on the interaction between primary producers and industrial economies. We argue that this international transmission mechanism may be important in explaining infrequent, large deviations of prices and output. We construct a model in which either changes in primary supplies or industrial demand can precipitate a recession, though with different implications for LDCs. We are, however, sceptical that Kaldor's solution of much greater commodity buffer stocks will solve the problem, which we argue is either soluble by other means, or sufficiently infrequent for this remedy to be prohibitively expensive.

Chapter 25

Export-led Price Instability

The importance of the export sector in LDCs has long been recognized, though there is less agreement about the relationship between export instability and the development of the economy. We begin our study with a static model in which export instability leads to fluctuations in domestic demand for non-traded goods, but has no effect on the rate of investment. Instability is therefore costly, since there are no offsetting benefits in the form of possibly higher investment, as recent writers, notably Knudsen and Parnes (1975) have argued. (We consider these benefits briefly in Chapter 27.) Moreover, the costs of instability are not confined to the export sector, but spill over into the rest of the economy. On the other hand, spreading the effects of instability more widely reduces the real income risk facing producers, for as their money incomes fall, so does the demand and hence the price of non-traded goods, mitigating the fall in real incomes.

The first model assumes perfectly flexible wages and prices and hence full employment, and as such provides a reference point for the analysis of a more plausible model in which the urban money wage is less than completely flexible. Since the non-traded capital stock is assumed foreign owned, inflexible wages with fluctuating demand imply more variable profits, and so more of the variability can be exported than if wages are perfectly flexible. (We assume that the supply of foreign capital is unaffected by the variability of returns, which may not be plausible in the long run, though foreign companies are well placed to diversify their risks and act risk-neutrally.) This is an important stabilizing feature of many LDCs, and in the present model it can reduce the costs of instability below the level associated with a completely flexible wage. However, the costs of instability increase with the degree of labour market rigidity beyond a certain critical point at which unemployment first emerges.

25.1 The model

There are three commodities: the export crop, denoted by a subscript x, the imported good, which can be consumed or invested, denoted by a subscript o, and a non-traded consumption good, denoted by a subscript c. Their prices are thus respectively p_x, p_o, and p_c. The total available labour force of N men is allocated at the beginning of the year either to the agricultural sector or to the urban sector. There are constant returns in both sectors, but while agriculture requires labour only, the non-traded good requires both capital, K, as well as labour. We choose units for measuring output so that

$$X = N_x \qquad (25.1)$$

(output of export crop is equal to the labour force employed), while

$$C = \min(N_c, K/v) \tag{25.2}$$

is the output of consumption goods, v is the capital–output ratio, assumed constant, and

$$N_u = N - N_c - N_x \geq 0 \tag{25.3}$$

is the number of individuals unemployed. The export sector is competitive, and its price fluctuates randomly, so that the wage there is also random

$$w_x = \tilde{p}_x. \tag{25.4}$$

The capital is owned by foreigners. The return to capital, r, fluctuates as the urban wage and the price of consumption goods fluctuate:

$$\tilde{r} p_o K = \tilde{p}_c C - \tilde{w}_c N_c. \tag{25.5}$$

We assume that all workers have the same utility function:

$$U = \log(2 - l) + \beta \log c + (1 - \beta) \log m - \log\{\beta^\beta (1 - \beta)^{1-\beta}\} \tag{25.6}$$

where l is the worker's supply of labour, c and m his consumption of the consumption good and the imported good. Faced with wages and prices w, p_c, p_o, he will choose to supply one unit of labour, independently of wages or prices. His indirect utility function is

$$V(w, p_c, p_o) = \log w - \beta \log p_c - (1 - \beta) \log p_o. \tag{25.7}$$

(Strictly speaking, if lump-sum income is I, the full indirect utility functions is

$$V(w, p_c, p_o, I) = 2 \log\left(1 + \frac{I}{2w}\right) + \log w - \beta \log p_c - (1 - \beta) \log p_o, \tag{25.7a}$$

where w is now the price of leisure, consumed in amount $2 - l$. Lump-sum income is here zero, hence utility is given by equation (25.7). Roy's identity applies to the full indirect utility function.) This particular form of the utility function is chosen because it generates unit price elastic demands which can be perfectly aggregated across individuals of differing incomes. If total wage income in the economy is Y, demands are

$$C = \frac{\beta Y}{p_c}, \quad M = \frac{(1-\beta)Y}{p_o} \tag{25.8}$$

$$Y = w_x N_x + w_c N_c. \tag{25.9}$$

It is easily checked that the balance of payments is always in equilibrium, for the current account surplus exactly equals the deficit on the capital account

$$p_x X - p_o M = w_x N_x - (1 - \beta) Y$$
$$= Y - w_c N_c - Y + p_c C$$

$$= rp_o K.$$

If there were no price uncertainty, then wages would be equated in both sectors and investment would continue to flow in until the rate of profit had been driven down to its supply price $\bar{r}$. In equilibrium from equation (25.4)

$$w_x = w_c = p_x$$

where p_x (and p_o) are determined on world markets and are hence exogenous. With full employment of capital and labour, equation (25.2) gives consumption output as

$$C = \frac{K}{v} = N_c = N - N_x.$$

Equation (25.5) yields the price of the non-traded good,

$$p_c = w_c + \bar{r} p_o v$$

or, in equilibrium

$$p_c = p_x + \pi \qquad (25.10)$$

(where $\pi = \bar{r} p_o v$ is the average profit per unit of C), while equations (25.8) and (25.9) determine employment there:

$$p_c N_c = \beta w_c N \qquad (25.11)$$

or

$$\frac{N_c}{N} = \frac{\beta p_x}{p_x + \pi} < \beta < 1. \qquad (25.12)$$

The impact of export price fluctuations depends critically on whether the economy has perfectly flexible prices so that it can always maintain full employment, or whether price rigidities reduce its flexibility. The following two models contrast the impacts in the two cases. In both cases we assume that capitalists are risk neutral, and so only worry about the average rate of profit.

25.2 Perfect wage and price flexibility

The allocation of labour is made before the export price is known and so is non-random. We assume that wages in the C-sector adjust to those in the export sector, although, given the fixed coefficients there, an alternative contract would be a guaranteed wage in return for guaranteed employment. Since capitalists are assumed risk neutral, we can take the expected value of equations (25.10) and (25.11) to find the allocation of labour:

$$\frac{N_c}{N} = \frac{\beta \bar{p}_x}{\bar{p}_x + \pi}, \quad \frac{N_x}{N} = \frac{(1-\beta)\bar{p}_x + \pi}{\bar{p}_x + \pi} \qquad (25.13)$$

$$\bar{p}_c = \frac{\beta N}{N_c}\bar{p}_x = (\bar{p}_x + \pi)\frac{\bar{p}_x}{\bar{p}_x}.$$

Expected values are indicated by a bar. Note that the allocation of labour depends just on the average price of exports, not on its variance. This is a result of some of our special assumptions (in particular the risk neutrality of capitalists and the special form of the demand functions) and would not be true generally. Prices and incomes are variable, and an individual's utility is from equation (25.7)

$$V = \log \tilde{p}_x - \beta \log\left(\frac{\beta N}{N_c}\tilde{p}_x\right) - (1-\beta)\log p_o$$

which, if $p_o = 1$, can be written

$$V = (1-\beta)\log \tilde{p}_x - \beta \log(\beta N/N_c). \tag{25.14}$$

The total money cost of this price instability can be measured by the lump-sum tax L/N per capita which equates utility with stable prices to utility with varying prices: from equation (25.7a) and (27.14) this is

$$2\log\left(1 - \frac{L}{2N\bar{p}_x}\right) + (1-\beta)\log \bar{p}_x = (1-\beta)E\log \tilde{p}_x$$

or, the total loss L is approximately

$$L \cong \tfrac{1}{2}(1-\beta)\bar{Y}\sigma_p^2, \tag{25.15}$$

where σ_p^2 is the coefficient of variation of export prices and $\bar{Y}$ is average net national income, calculated from equation (25.9). A naïve estimate of the cost of risk would have confined attention to the agricultural workers alone and estimated the loss at

$$L' = \tfrac{1}{2}\bar{w}N_x\sigma_w^2 = \tfrac{1}{2}\frac{N_x}{N}\bar{Y}\sigma_p^2. \tag{25.16}$$

Equation (25.13) shows that

$$N_x \geqslant (1-\beta)N \quad \text{as} \quad \pi \geqslant 0$$

so that the naïve estimate overstates the true loss. The reason is that the variability of non-traded goods prices reduces the real income variability of farm workers by transferring some of it to other workers and some of it abroad to the capitalists. It should be evident that the log-linear form of the utility function is highly special in preserving near equality in the two measures of the cost of risk. More general utility functions will in general amplify and possibly change the sign of the difference between L and L' by making prices p_c more or less sensitive to fluctuating incomes.

25.3 Price rigidities and unemployment

In the previous model perfect wage flexibility ensured that the economy remained in full employment despite fluctuation in incomes and demand. The distinctive feature of macroeconomic models, as we have noted, is the recognition that prices respond at finite speeds to disturbances and so cannot continuously ensure that markets are in equilibrium with supplies equal to demands. The simplest way to model this important feature of the economy is to assume that wages in the urban sector cannot fall below some specified level, w_m, whose determination we discuss below. Excess demand in the labour market is, however, likely to induce wages to rise above this minimum, and we shall suppose that when demand is strong wages rise to the market clearing level. This asymmetry in the working of the labour market is both plausible and provides a simple theory of inflation, for if *money* wages are inflexible downwards, then real wages must adjust by increases in the price level. We shall take up this simple theory of inflation in the next section; for the moment we assume that urban money wages can fall back to the minimum, resistance level w_m.

Wages in agriculture are assumed perfectly flexible, and workers must choose at the start of the year whether to work in agriculture or be available for employment in the urban sector. Apart from the working of the labour market, all the previous assumptions are retained. The urban production function gives rise to the supply schedule shown in Fig. 25.1, and the price of output cannot fall below the average variable cost, or the minimum wage, w_m. When demand is high, there is full employment and market clearing prices. If demand is sufficiently low, urban unemployment appears and the price falls to w_m. It will simplify matters if we assume that export prices are equally likely to be high,

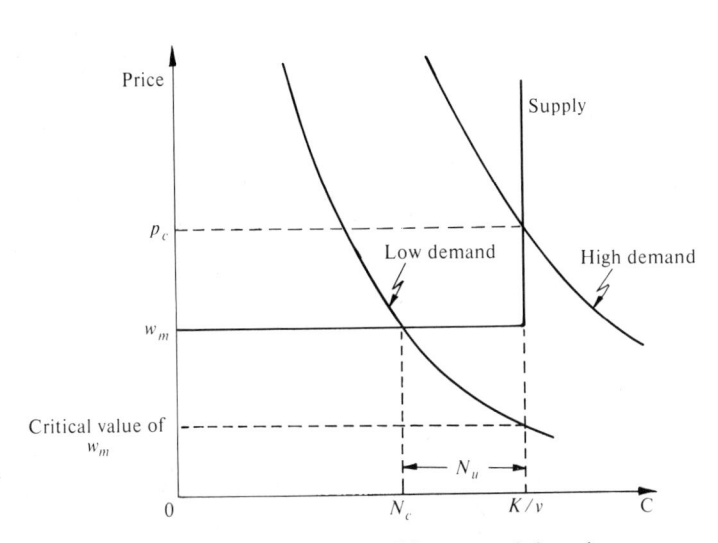

Fig. 25.1 Supply and demand for non-traded goods

$p_x = \bar{p}(1+\sigma)$, or low, $\bar{p}(1-\sigma)$. There are two possibilities: either the minimum wage is set low enough (below the critical value in Fig. 25.1) so that urban unemployment never appears, or it is set above this level, with consequent unemployment, N_u, as shown. We consider these two possibilities in order.

25.3.1 Minimum wage below critical level: full employment

Demand for the non-traded good is given by equations (25.8) and (25.9):

$$p_c C = \beta(w_x N_x + w_c N_c).$$

Since there is full employment $C = N_c = K/v$, and so

$$p_c = \beta p_x \frac{N_x}{N_c} + \beta w_c.$$

The average rate of profit must be equal to $\bar{r}$, so

$$\frac{\bar{r} p_o K}{C} = \bar{r} p_o v \equiv \pi = E(p_c - w_c) = \beta \bar{p} \frac{N_x}{N_c} - (1-\beta) E w_c \qquad (25.17)$$

where, as before, π is the average profit per unit of C. Once the average wage $\bar{w}$ in the C-sector is specified, this can be solved for the distribution of labour, N_x/N_c; and the prices p_c:

$$\frac{N_x}{N_c} = \frac{\pi + (1-\beta)\bar{w}}{\beta \bar{p}}; \quad \bar{w} \equiv E w_c$$

and

$$\tilde{p}_c = \{\pi + (1-\beta)\bar{w}\}\frac{\tilde{p}_x}{\bar{p}} + \beta \tilde{w}_c. \qquad (25.18)$$

Equilibrium in the labour market requires that the expected utility of working in each sector be the same, or, in this full employment model

$$E \log \tilde{w}_c = E \log \tilde{p}_x.$$

If w_c takes either a high value, w_h, or a minimum value, w_m, then this reduces to

$$w_h w_m = \bar{p}^2(1-\sigma^2). \qquad (25.19)$$

An alternative way of writing this would be

$$w_h = \bar{w}(1+\lambda\sigma),$$
$$w_m = \bar{w}(1-\lambda\sigma), \quad 0 \leq \lambda \leq 1,$$

where $\bar{w}$ is the average wage and λ is a measure of the extent to which wage fluctuations elsewhere are passed on to the C-sector. The average wage, $\bar{w}$, depends on λ, for, substituting in equation (25.19):

$$\bar{w} = \bar{p}\sqrt{\left(\frac{1-\sigma^2}{1-\lambda^2\sigma^2}\right)} \cong \bar{p}\{1 - \tfrac{1}{2}(1-\lambda^2)\sigma^2\} \leq \bar{p}.$$

The average wage in the C-sector is thus less than that in the export sector if $\lambda < 1$.

The specification is now complete, for once w_m, or, equivalently, λ is fixed, then so is $\bar{w}$, and hence the allocation of labour, the demand for capital, and the prices in each of the two states. We shall refer to the case $\lambda < 1$ as one of wage rigidity, meaning that wages are less than perfectly flexible, rather than that they never change.

Because workers on both sectors have the same average utility we can study the welfare impact of wage rigidity by looking at its effect on export workers, in which case the only effect is through changes in p_c. The extra utility generated by wage rigidity is then

$$\beta(E \log \tilde{p}_c - E \log \tilde{p}_c |_{\text{rigid}}). \tag{25.20}$$

In the absence of rigidities equation (25.10) gives

$$\tilde{p}_c = \tilde{p}_x\left(1 + \frac{\pi}{\bar{p}}\right), \quad E\tilde{p}_c = \pi + \bar{p}$$

$$E \log \tilde{p}_c = \tfrac{1}{2} \log\{\bar{p}^2(1-\sigma^2)(1+\pi/\bar{p})^2\}$$

In the presence of rigidities, provided there is no unemployment, equation (25.18) gives:

$$E \log \tilde{p}_c |_{\text{rigid}} = \tfrac{1}{2}\log\left\{\bar{p}^2(1-\sigma^2)\right\}\left[\left\{\frac{\pi + (1-\beta)\bar{w}}{\bar{p}} + \frac{\beta w_h}{\bar{p}(1+\sigma)}\right\}\left\{\frac{\pi + (1-\beta)\bar{w}}{\bar{p}} + \frac{\beta w_m}{\bar{p}(1-\sigma)}\right\}\right] \tag{25.21}$$

and

$$E\tilde{p}_c |_{\text{rigid}} = \pi + \bar{w} < \pi + \bar{p} \quad \text{if } \lambda < 1.$$

Note that if $\lambda = 1$, then $\bar{w} = \bar{p}$, $w_h = \bar{p}(1+\sigma)$, $w_m = \bar{p}(1-\sigma)$, and there is no change in p_c, and hence no change in utility, as expected. If $\lambda < 1$, then the average p_c falls, but so does its variance, and so it is not immediately clear what happens to $E \log \tilde{p}_c$, which is a concave function of p_c. However, from equation (25.19):

$$\bar{w} = \tfrac{1}{2}\left(w_m + \frac{\bar{p}^2(1-\sigma^2)}{w_m}\right)$$

and

$$\frac{w_h}{1+\sigma} = \frac{\bar{p}^2(1-\sigma)}{w_m},$$

so equation (25.21) can be expressed as a function of w_m. Differentiating:

$$\frac{d}{dw_m}(E\log \tilde{p}_c \,|\, \text{rigid}) = \left(1 - \left(\frac{1-\sigma}{1-\lambda\sigma}\right)^2 \phi(w_m)\right)$$

for some positive function ϕ, and hence as w_m rises, equation (25.21) decreases, and utility, given by equation (25.20), increases. The money value of wage rigidity as a proportion of reference GNP, Y, can be found from equation (25.20):

$$\frac{B}{Y} \cong \tfrac{1}{2}\beta \log\left\{\frac{\pi + \bar{p}}{\pi + (1-\beta)\bar{w} + \beta w_h/(1+\sigma)} \cdot \frac{\pi + \bar{p}}{\pi + (1-\beta)\bar{w} + \beta w_m/(1-\sigma)}\right\}, \quad (25.22)$$

which is zero if wages are not rigid, and positive and increasing in w_m (or λ) if wages are rigid, provided the minimum wage does not exceed the critical level at which unemployment first occurs, w_m^c, calculated in the Appendix to this chapter.

The reason for this benefit is that wage rigidity reduces the wage variability in the urban sector, which reduces the cost of labour in C-good production and hence reduces its average price. Put another way, wage rigidities transfer some of the income variability abroad as more variable profits, which can be better borne by the less risk-averse capitalists. Provided there is never unemployment, there are no offsetting costs.

25.3.2 Minimum wage above critical level: periodic unemployment

Demand for non-traded goods is again given by equations (25.8) and (25.9):

$$p_c C = \beta(w_x N_x + w_c N_c).$$

When demand is low, price just covers the (variable) marginal cost of production: $p_c = w_m$ (provided demand is low enough relative to w_m) and for the value of the demand for the C-sector, $\beta(w_m N_c + w_x N_x)$, to equal the value at output, $w_m N_c$,

$$w_m N_c = \frac{\beta}{1-\beta} \bar{p}(1-\sigma)N_x, \quad (25.23)$$

while when demand is high, $N_c = C = K/v$, and the demand equals supply condition becomes

$$p_c N_c^* = \beta(p_x N_x + w_h N_c^*)$$

or

$$p_c = \beta\left\{\bar{p}(1+\sigma)\frac{N_x}{N_c^*} + w_h\right\}, \quad (25.24)$$

where N_c^* is the full employment level of output. Again, the average rate of profit must be $\bar{r}$, but this time there will only be positive profits in the high price state, so the counterpart to equation (25.17) is

$$\pi = E(p_c - w_h) = \tfrac{1}{2}\left\{\beta\bar{p}(1+\sigma)\frac{N_x}{N_c^*} - (1-\beta)w_h\right\}. \tag{25.25}$$

Once w_h has been fixed, this determines the allocation of labour and the demand for capital. Equilibrium in the labour market (which determines w_h) requires that the expected utility of working in each sector is the same.

In order to calculate expected utility in the C-sector, we need to specify the income of unemployed workers and how they are rationed when wages are fixed above the market clearing level. Consider the simplest case in which work is shared equally with workers going on short time. In the presence of unemployment, labour supplied will be $l < 1$, and the associated utility is, from equation (25.6)

$$V(w, p_c, p_o, l) = \log(2 - l) + \log(wl) - \beta \log p_c - (1-\beta) \log p_o.$$

Equating expected utilities in the two sectors gives, since product prices are the same

$$\tfrac{1}{2}\left\{\log\left(2 - \frac{N_c}{N_c^*}\right) + \log\left(w_m \frac{N_c}{N_c^*}\right) + \log w_h\right\} = E \log w_x = \tfrac{1}{2}\log \bar{p}^2(1-\sigma^2),$$

where $N_c^* \equiv N - N_x$, the level of employment in the C-sector when demand is high. Hence

$$\frac{N_c}{N_c^*}\left(2 - \frac{N_c}{N_c^*}\right) w_m w_h = \bar{p}^2(1-\sigma^2) \tag{25.26}$$

or, if u is the sectoral unemployment rate in slump years:

$$u \equiv 1 - \frac{N_c}{N_c^*},$$

then

$$(1 - u^2) w_m w_h = \bar{p}^2(1-\sigma^2) \tag{25.27}$$

which reduces to equation (25.19) if $u = 0$ as expected.

Equations (25.23), (25.25), and (25.26) give three equations for the three unknowns, N_c, N_c^*, and w_h. Substitute equation (25.23) into (25.25) to give

$$w_h = \left(\frac{1+\sigma}{1-\sigma}\right)(1-u)w_m - \frac{2\pi}{1-\beta}. \tag{25.28}$$

This can be substituted into (25.27) to give

$$(1+u)\left(w_h^2 + \frac{2\pi w_h}{1-\beta}\right) = \bar{p}^2(1+\sigma)^2. \tag{25.29}$$

There are several methods of solving for the equilibrium. The logical approach would be, given w_m, to find the implied level of unemployment u, and hence, from (25.28) a value for w_h. This approach gives a cubic equation in u which can be solved approximately for small values of u by taking a Taylor expansion. In this case

$$u \cong 1 - \left\{\frac{\bar{p}(1-\sigma)}{w_m}\right\}^2 - \frac{2\pi}{(1-\beta)w_m}\frac{(1-\sigma)}{(1+\sigma)}. \tag{25.30}$$

A formally equivalent approach which is much simpler would start from w_h, solve for u from (25.29), and then find the implied value of w_m from equation (25.28):

$$u = \frac{\bar{p}^2(1+\sigma)^2}{w_h^2 + \dfrac{2\pi w_h}{1-\beta}} - 1. \tag{25.31}$$

Either way, there are limits on the value which w_m can take, since if it is below the critical value shown in Fig. 25.1, then the assumption of zero profits in the low price state does not hold, the equations must be modified, and there will be no unemployment. If w_m is set too high, then full employment will not be possible in the high-price state, and again the equations must be modified. These limits are calculated in the Appendix.

The extra loss in utility caused by wage rigidities is again the difference in

$$\beta E \log \tilde{p}_c$$

since workers in different sectors have the same average utility, and the only difference wage rigidities make to the export workers is through its effect on the price p_c. In the absence of rigidities $E \log \tilde{p}_c$ is given by equation (25.21):

$$E \log \tilde{p}_c = \tfrac{1}{2} \log\{\bar{p}^2(1-\sigma^2)(1+\pi/\bar{p})^2\}.$$

In the presence of rigidities the price of C is given by equation (25.24) in the high-price state and is equal to w_m in the low-price state so

$$E \log \tilde{p}_c |_{\text{rigid}} = \tfrac{1}{2}\log\left\{w_m w_h \left(1 + \frac{2\pi}{w_c}\right)\right\}$$

which, from equation (25.27) can be written

$$E \log \tilde{p}_c = \tfrac{1}{2}\log\left\{\bar{p}^2 \frac{(1-\sigma^2)}{1-u^2}\left(1 + \frac{2\pi}{w_h}\right)\right\}.$$

The *extra* loss in money terms as a fraction of average GNP caused by wage rigidities is then

$$\frac{L}{Y} \cong \beta(E \log \tilde{p}_c|_{\text{rigid}} - E \log \tilde{p}_c) = \tfrac{1}{2}\beta\left\{\log\left(1+\frac{2\pi}{w}\right) - \log(1+\pi/\bar{p})^2 - \log(1-u^2)\right\}, \tag{25.32}$$

where u and w_h are related by equation (25.29), and both are functions of the underlying source of rigidity, w_m.

In particular, if the profit term is negligible, then equation (25.32) gives the appealing result that

$$\frac{L}{Y} \cong -\tfrac{1}{2}\beta \log(1-u^2) \cong \tfrac{1}{2}\beta u^2.$$

This formula is, however, rather misleading, for we showed that if the minimum wage was below the critical level but above the competitive level, then the economy benefited through a lower price for the non-traded good. This benefit continues and to some extent offsets the loss due to unemployment. The Appendix shows that if the loss is correctly measured as in equation (25.32), then it increases with w_m, or equivalently, the benefit of wage rigidity falls for w_m above the critical level. The graph of welfare against w_m is as shown in Fig. 25.2.

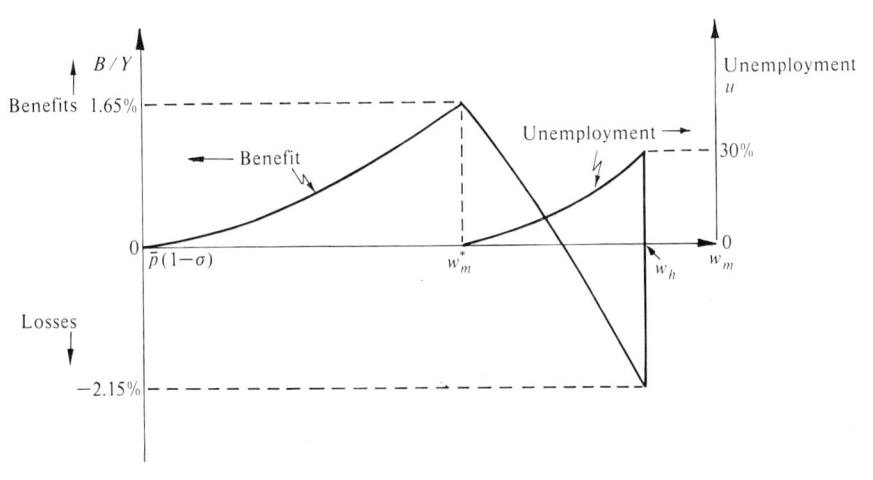

Fig. 25.2 Benefits of wage rigidity

For example, if $\bar{p} = 1$, $\pi = \tfrac{1}{4}$, $\sigma = \tfrac{1}{2} = \beta$, and $w_h = 1$, then $u = \tfrac{1}{8}$ from (25.31) and $w_m = 16/21$. The rough estimate of u in equation (25.30) for $w_m = 16/21$ is 13 per cent instead of $12\tfrac{1}{2}$ per cent. The rough estimate of the proportionate loss is $\tfrac{1}{2}\beta u^2 = 0.39$ of 1 per cent, while the accurate estimate of the loss is -0.63 of 1 per cent, or the effect of wage rigidity is to *raise* welfare.

The Appendix shows how to calculate the feasible range of values for w_m such that there is unemployment but only in the low-price state. In this example as w_m increases from 0.69 to 0.91 the level of urban unemployment in slump years rises from zero to 30 per cent, while the urban wage level in high-price years falls from 1.081 to 0.91 (at which point it meets the minimum level, w_m). The loss due to rigidities rises from -1.65 per cent (i.e. a *gain* of 1.65 per cent of GNP) to 2.15 per cent at $u = 30$ per cent.

The allocation of labour and the size of the capital stock are readily calculated. For the flexible economy from equation (25.13)

$$\frac{N_x}{N} = \frac{1 - \beta + \pi/\bar{p}}{1 + \pi/\bar{p}},$$

$$K = vN_c = \frac{N\beta v}{1 + \pi/\bar{p}}$$

while for the rigid economy equation (25.23) gives

$$(N - N_x)(1 - u) = \frac{\beta}{1 - \beta} \frac{\bar{p}}{w_m}(1 - \sigma)N_x$$

or

$$\frac{N_x}{N} = \frac{1}{1 + \dfrac{\beta}{1-\beta} \dfrac{\bar{p}}{w_m} \dfrac{(1-\sigma)}{(1-u)}}$$

and

$$K = vN(1 - N_x/N).$$

In the example the flexible economy has 60 per cent of the labour force in the export sector, while in the rigid economy as the minimum wage rises from 0.69 to 0.91 so the proportion of labour in the export sector falls from 58 to 56 per cent.

25.3.3 Fixing the minimum wage

The model provides a rationale for setting an urban minimum wage, since wage inflexibility provides workers with income insurance which benefits the rest of the economy. We have shown that the optimum level at which to fix it in this simple economy with only two levels of demand is w_m^*, the critical level at which unemployment is on the point of occurring. If export prices are a continuously distributed random variable, then one would conjecture that the welfare maximizing level of the minimum wage might be set above the level which guaranteed continuous full employment.

25.4 A simple model of inflation

The previous model assumed that the urban money wage would fall back to w_m whenever demand fell. It is easy to modify the model to generate a simple theory of inflation if urban workers resist any fall in their money wages. If the government is prepared to devalue in order to reduce the real urban wage to its former level, then all domestic prices will rise by the amount of the devaluation, and the economy behaves exactly as in the previous model in real terms, but with a proportionate rise in prices $\rho = \frac{1}{2}(w_c/w_m - 1)$ whenever world export prices fall. The price level will then follow a simple random walk with drift ρ per period and the average rate of inflation is ρ. If the average rate of urban unemployment is $\bar{u}$

$$\bar{u} = \tfrac{1}{2}u = \tfrac{1}{2}(1 - vN_c/K),$$

then equation (25.28) gives a relationship between the average rate of inflation and the average rate of urban unemployment:

$$\rho = \tfrac{1}{2}\left(\frac{w_c}{w_m} - 1\right) = \frac{\sigma}{1-\sigma} - \left(\frac{1+\sigma}{1-\sigma}\right)\bar{u} - \left(\frac{\pi}{1-\beta}\right)\frac{1}{w_m(\bar{u})}$$

where w_m is monotonically increasing in $\bar{u}$ as shown in Fig. 25.2. In other words, the relationship between the rate of inflation and the level of unemployment is similar to the Phillips curve, and the higher is the instability of export prices, the higher will be the average rate of inflation. Using the previous numbers, the rate of inflation falls from 28 per cent p.a. at zero unemployment, to 8.7 per cent p.a. at $\bar{u} = 10$ per cent, and zero inflation at the maximum level of urban unemployment, $\bar{u} = 15$ per cent where $w = w_m$, as shown in Fig. 25.3.

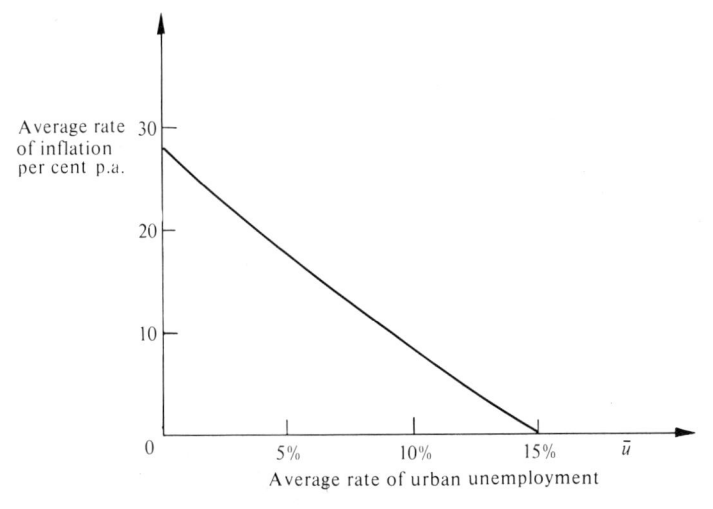

Fig. 25.3 Trade-off between urban unemployment and inflation

25.5 Lessons from the models

The flexible wage model demonstrated that some of the risks in the export sector could be shared with the rest of the economy and hence reduced. When money incomes rose in the export sector, so did demand for the non-traded goods, and hence so did price, tending to reduce fluctuations in real income and consumption. Although wages were destabilized in the rest of the economy, the resulting fluctuations in prices more than compensated for this extra risk in the special case we considered.

If wages in the non-traded goods sector were less than completely flexible the economy responded rather differently to fluctuations in the export sector. Wage inflexibility responded rather differently to fluctuations in the export sector. Wage inflexibility has several consequences: on the one hand it tends to reduce the variability of urban wage income, but, on the other hand, if wages are too inflexible, periodic urban unemployment occurs, which tends to increase real income variability. The price variability of non-traded goods depends on total demand variability. If urban income is less variable then non-traded goods price variations provide *less* real income insurance to the economy, but urban workers are willing to work for lower average wages which lowers the average price of non-trade goods. In short, the general equilibrium effects of wage rigidities are a complex mixture of effects on price variability and levels and income instability and its distribution. The rigid wages model demonstrates that some rigidity could be beneficial in reducing the average price of non-traded goods and shifting some income variability abroad in the form of greater profit variability. Beyond a certain point the costs of unemployment outweighed these benefits. In the model the costs of unemployment were minimized by sharing the fall in labour demand equally over all workers in the form of short time. If wage rigidities lead instead to some workers becoming wholly unemployed, then the welfare costs would be much greater. Correspondingly, the benefits of price stabilization will depend sensitively on the extent and nature of the unemployment induced by price instability.

If money wages are inflexible downward, but exchange rates, prices, and real wages are flexible, then the model exhibits inflation which increases with the variability of export prices. If, in addition, urban real wages are not completely flexible, then the model exhibits a classic Phillips-type trade-off between inflation and urban unemployment.

Appendix: The feasible range for the minimum wage for periodic unemployment

The highest level at which w_m can be set without jeopardizing full employment in high-price years is such that $w_h = w_m$. Solving equation (25.28) gives

$$u = \frac{2}{1+\sigma}\left\{\sigma - \frac{\pi(1-\sigma)}{w_m(1-\beta)}\right\} \tag{25.A1}$$

while equation (25.27) gives

$$u^2 = 1 - \frac{\bar{p}^2(1-\sigma^2)}{w_m^2}. \tag{25.A2}$$

Together these give a quadratic expression for w_m, and hence for u.

The lowest level at which w_m exerts any influence on the level of employment can be found by setting $u = 0$ in equations (25.27) and (25.28) to give

$$\left(\frac{1+\sigma}{1-\sigma}\right)w_m^2 - \left(\frac{2\pi}{1-\beta}\right)w_m - \bar{p}^2(1-\sigma^2) = 0.$$

If w_m is below this, but above $\bar{p}(1-\sigma)$, the wage in the export sector in the low-price year, then there will be no unemployment, but price risk will be greater. Between the minimum and maximum levels of w_m, L is a decreasing function of w_h or an increasing function of w_m:

$$\frac{1}{Y}\frac{dL}{dw_h} = \tfrac{1}{2}\beta\left\{\frac{-2\pi}{w_h^2 + 2\pi w_h} + \frac{2u}{1-u^2}\frac{du}{dw_h}\right\}$$

from equation (25.32) while

$$\left(2w_h + \frac{2\pi}{1-\beta}\right) = -\frac{\bar{p}^2(1+\sigma)^2}{(1+u)^2}\frac{du}{dw_h}$$

so $du/dw_h < 0$ and hence $dL/dw_h < 0$.

Chapter 26

Balance-of-payments Policy

The preceding chapter analysed the consequences of price instability for an economy in which the government took only a passive role. Most governments have not been idle bystanders; they have attempted both to mitigate the effects of price instability on the farmers by operating internal price stabilization schemes (usually through marketing boards) and on the national economy by engaging in macro-stabilization policies. To the extent that they have been successful, the major disadvantages which we have ascribed to price instability – or the risks borne by farmers, the induced unemployment, and the induced instability of domestic prices – will not be realized. The costs of price instability are of a quite different kind: the country will experience variations in its balance of payments and/or the government will experience variations in its deficit and surplus. If the economy had adequate foreign exchange reserves (and/or if speculators were confident about the long-term stability of the currency) these fluctuations might have minimal effects. But typically LDCs have small foreign exchange reserves and speculators are not confident about the long-term stability of the currency. The consequence is that it is in general impossible for the government to pursue an independent price and employment stabilization policy. Indeed, one might argue that a more accurate description is provided by the hypothesis that government expenditure is determined by the magnitude of the balance-of-payments surplus.

To see the implications of this, we consider an extremely simple macroeconomic model in which export prices take on only two values, a high value and a low value; the government stabilizes producer prices at a level somewhat below the low export price, using the difference to finance public expenditure. Typically, it is not direct government employment which varies with the government revenue, but public investment. We shall assume that all investment is publicly financed (or, equivalently, that private investment is constant). We also assume that all wages and prices are rigid so that adjustments occur through variations in output and employment. We therefore have the standard national income model

$$Y = C + \bar{I} + I_g + \bar{G}, \qquad (26.1)$$

where I_g is public investment, $\bar{I}$ is (constant) private investment, and $\bar{G}$ is (constant) current public expenditure. If tax revenues are T

$$T = (\tilde{p} - \hat{p})X, \qquad (26.2)$$

the difference between export receipts $\tilde{p}X$ and stabilized producer revenue, $\hat{p}X$, then it is reasonable to assume that consumption is given by a relationship:

$$C = C_0 + (1-s)(Y-T), \qquad (26.3)$$

where s is the short-run marginal propensity to save out of disposable income. Let the short-run marginal propensity to import goods in category j be m_j ($j = c$ for consumption, i for investment, g for government expenditure), and suppose that these marginal propensities are constant (and, for notational convenience equal to the average propensities). If public investment is constrained to maintain a balanced trade account, then exports will equal imports, or

$$pX = m_c C + m_i(\bar{I} + I_g) + m_g \bar{G} \equiv M_0 + m_i I_g + m_c(1-s)(Y-T) \quad (26.4)$$

where

$$M_0 = m_c C_0 + m_i \bar{I} + m_g \bar{G}$$

is a constant. (Differences between average and marginal import propensities can be absorbed into M_0.) Hence public investment is constrained to be

$$I_g = \frac{pX - m_c(1-s)(Y-T) - M_0}{m_i}. \qquad (26.5)$$

Equations (26.2), (26.3), and (26.5) can be substituted in equation (26.1) to give

$$Y = C_0 + \bar{I} + \bar{G} - M_0/m_i + (1-s)\left(1 - \frac{m_c}{m_i}\right) Y$$

$$+ X\left\{ \frac{\tilde{p}}{m_i} - (\tilde{p} - \hat{p})(1-s)\left(1 - \frac{m_c}{m_i}\right) \right\}$$

or

$$Y = Y_0 + (\alpha \tilde{p} - \gamma \hat{p}) X \qquad (26.6)$$

where

$$\alpha = 1 + \frac{1 - m_i}{m_c + s(m_i - m_c)}, \quad \gamma = 1 - \frac{m_i}{m_c + s(m_i - m_c)}.$$

If the sole source of instability arises from price fluctuations, so that X is constant, then the variance of income is α^2 times the variance of export revenue, which, since α is greater than one, amplifies the disturbance, possibly substantially. Thus, if $m_c = 0.2$, $m_i = 0.6$, $s = 0.5$, the variance of income is four times that of export earnings. Evidently the benefits of stabilizing export revenue would be very large in such an economy (if the production of exports is also risky, then the formulae in the Appendix to Chapter 13 can be used to show that the variance of income is in general less than α^2 times the variance in export revenue).

If, on the other hand, the balance of trade need not be instantaneously balanced, then the government can choose a level of investment which is some compromise between its desired level of investment I_g^* (assumed constant) and that required for trade balance, $\tilde{I}_g$, given by equation (26.5). Actual public investment might then be

$$I_g = (1-\beta)I_g^* + \beta\tilde{I}_g \qquad (26.7)$$

where β represents the weight attached to the short-run objective of balance-of-trade equilibrium, $1-\beta$ that attached to long-run objectives. Substituting equation (26.7) in equation (26.1) gives, after similar manipulations, a value for α in equation (26.6) of

$$\alpha = \frac{\beta\{1 + m_c(1-s)\} - m_i(1-s)}{\beta m_c + s(m_i - \beta m_c)}.$$

With the right choice of β it is possible completely to stabilize GNP at the expense of fluctuating balance-of-trade deficits (though our simple model abstracts from time lags which would in practice complicate such fine tuning).

It would appear that if an international agency were to extend a line of credit to the country, allowing it to borrow on the basis of shortfalls in export revenue, the country would benefit from internal price stabilization without the consequence of fluctuating public expenditure. This is exactly what the IMF's Compensatory Financing Facility and the Stabex programme of the EEC are designed to achieve.

However, there are problems with these schemes, for it is typically difficult to distinguish fluctuations from structural shifts or changes in trends. While the international agency may adopt a rather generous attitude to extending credit, other creditors may be less optimistic and reduce their credit by (in an extreme case) the amount extended by the agency. In short, the desirability of international credit facilities can only be properly assessed if the response of other sources of credit is taken into account. If 'adequate' private credit was initially forthcoming, there is some presumption that there will be offsetting reductions in private credit when international credit is increased.

Chapter 27

Export Instability and Growth

Before the publication of MacBean's (1966) study of export instability the consensus view was that export instability was both harmful and particularly severe in LDCs, and the macro-models constructed so far concur in finding instability costly. MacBean argued that there was little empirical evidence either that export instability was linked to instability in domestic income or that export instability impeded growth. More recently, Knudsen and Parnes (1975) have conducted a more thorough empirical test of a permanent income theory of consumption and investment for LDCs. According to this theory, consumption is based on permanent, or long-run trend income, and is unaffected by transient fluctuations in incomes, such as those caused by fluctuating commodity revenues. Income instability is, however, argued to reduce the average proportion of income consumed, and hence to increase aggregate savings. If the rate of investment is constrained by the level of savings, as is usually argued to be the case for LDCs, then this will result in higher investment and growth (Knudsen and Parnes, p. 119). Far from hindering growth, instability will encourage investment. Moreover, since investment goods are typically imported, fluctuations in investment are not transmitted to the domestic economy, and since consumption does not fluctuate much with export receipts, there is little link between export instability and income instability. Their empirical tests confirm that

(i) the propensity to consume decreases with higher levels of income instability;

(ii) that investment is not harmed by instability, but positively correlated with it;

(iii) that instability is positively correlated with the growth of both GNP and GNP per capita;

(iv) that there is no relation between domestic and export instability.

Of course, these results are to be interpreted as rejections of the null hypothesis of adverse relationship between instability and investment and growth, rather than confirmation of a causal link from instability to investment and growth. Indeed, it seems quite plausible that causation runs the other way, with high average rates of growth inducing periodic imbalances and bottlenecks which are resolved through fluctuations in exports. Further, the welfare implications of the positive relationship between instability and growth are more complex than these studies suggest, since they involve an assessment of the costs of risk (in the form of fluctuating consumption) and the benefits (or costs) of changing the intertemporal pattern of consumption away from the present towards the future.

If markets are competitive and investors rational and risk averse, then increases in income risk *may* (but need not) increase savings, but *will* reduce welfare. This can be seen in a simple two-period model in which individuals invest a fraction s of first-period income to maximize the expected present value of utility:

$$\underset{s}{\text{Max}} \, U\{(1-s)Y_0\} + \frac{1}{1+\delta} EU\{\tilde{Y}_1 + s(1+r)Y_0\}.$$

Here Y_i is income in period i, r is the (certain) rate of return, and δ is the rate of pure time preference. In equilibrium

$$U'\{(1-s)Y_0\} = \frac{1+r}{1+\delta} EU'\{\tilde{Y}_1 + s(1+r)Y_0\}. \quad (27.1)$$

If $U'(C)$ is convex, then a mean-preserving increase in the riskiness of Y_1 will increase the right-hand side of (27.1), and so increase the attractiveness of saving. Thus if the third derivative of utility is positive (that is, if the coefficient of relative risk aversion is not increasing too fast) then increased income risk increases savings, as hypothesized, but, since utility is concave in consumption, increased risk will lower expected utility.

Thus, to argue that income risk is not harmful, it is necessary to argue both that investment is increased and that investment is too low. This is indeed often held to be the case, for it is argued that the rate of investment is too low because of labour market imperfections. The shadow wage rate is argued to be below the market wage rate because the latter exceeds the marginal product of labour in alternative employment (usually agriculture), and hence the social rate of return to investment exceeds the private rate. If, as assumed, investment is constrained by the level of savings, then increasing the rate of savings is advantageous, and generates an additional net social benefit equal to the difference between the accounting prices of investment and consumption, which Little and Mirrlees (1974) argue could be large.

It is plausible that the relationship between instability and investment varies between countries, and even that the direction of causation may differ. At the moment there is a shortage of adequately specified theoretical models of this relationship which can be used to generate empirically refutable propositions, and which might serve to distinguish between different linkages. The following model is extremely simple, but is a natural extension of the model of Chapter 25, and shows how sensitive the results are to the workings of the labour market.

Suppose that all investment goods are imported at constant prices (of unity), that agricultural export revenues $\tilde{X}$ fluctuate (because prices and/or supplies fluctuate), and that the urban sector produces import substitute goods. The fraction of income spent on these goods, β, increases as tariff rates are raised, but, for any given level of tariffs, the domestic price p is limited by the foreign price plus tariff. Profits, π, are equal to revenue, $p\tilde{C}$, less wage costs, wN:

$$\pi = p\tilde{C} - wN \quad (27.2)$$

and a fraction s of profits are invested, $(1-s)$ consumed. Total disposable income is therefore

$$\check{X} + wN + (1-s)\pi$$

and a fraction β is spent on the import substitute goods:

$$p\check{C} = \beta\{\check{X} + (1-s)p\check{C} + swN\}. \tag{27.3}$$

This implies that profits are

$$\check{\pi} = p\check{C} - wN = \frac{\beta\check{X} - (1-\beta)wN}{1 - \beta + s\beta}. \tag{27.4}$$

If wages are fixed, then profits will fluctuate more than export revenue, and the average rate of profit will depend on the wage level. If the level of protection is sufficiently high, workers will be able to raise the wage level above the supply price of labour without reducing average profit below an acceptable level (essentially at the expense of rural workers). Suppose for simplicity that export revenue can either be high, $\check{X} = \bar{X}(1 + \sigma)$, or low, $\check{X} = \bar{X}(1 - \sigma)$, and that workers succeed in raising wages to the point at which profits fall to zero in bad years. (If they increased wages further, there would be a positive danger of bankruptcy, which firms would resist.) Then

$$wN = \frac{\beta\bar{X}(1-\sigma)}{1-\beta}. \tag{27.5}$$

The rate of investment, I, in this model depends on the level of profit which, given the determination of the wage bill, makes

$$I = s\pi = \frac{s\beta}{1-\beta+s\beta}\{\check{X} - \bar{X}(1-\sigma)\} \tag{27.6}$$

$$EI = \frac{s\beta\bar{X}\sigma}{1-\beta+s\beta}. \tag{27.7}$$

Thus the greater the instability of export revenue, the higher the rate of investment and rate of growth of the urban economy. If β is constant, then the urban economy will grow at the same rate as exports, while if tariffs increase so that β steadily rises, the urban economy will grow faster than export revenue, wage rates will rise, and so will the price of import substitutes — implications which are consistent with the empirical evidence.

It might be thought that the result depends critically on both the assumption that urban wages are inflexible and that they do not depend on the level of rural wages in the export sector. It is true that the crucial relationship is between the average level of urban wages and the variability of export revenue, and that it is not immediately clear what determines this relationship. Suppose, for example, that we modify the model of Chapter 25 so that urban wages are less flexible than rural wages, but their level adjusts so that on average the utility levels of urban and rural workers are the same. For example, if the urban wage is related to the rural wage as follows:

$$\tilde{w} = \bar{w}\left\{\frac{\lambda \tilde{X} + (1-\lambda)\bar{X}}{\bar{X}}\right\} = \bar{w}(1 \pm \lambda\sigma), \qquad (27.8)$$

then the coefficient of variation or urban wages will be only a fraction λ of that of rural wages. With logarithmic utility functions (as in Chapter 25), full employment, and only two states of the world, equating expected utility requires

$$E\log \tilde{w} = E\log(\tilde{X}/N_x) \qquad (27.9)$$

whence

$$\bar{w} = \bar{w}_x \sqrt{\left(\frac{1-\sigma^2}{1-\lambda^2\sigma^2}\right)} \cong \{1 - \tfrac{1}{2}(1-\lambda^2)\sigma^2\}\bar{w}_x, \qquad (27.10)$$

and the average urban wage, $\bar{w}$, is a decreasing function of σ and an increasing function of λ. Average profits again increase with σ:

$$EI = \frac{s\bar{X}}{1-\beta+s\beta}\left\{\beta + (1-\beta)\frac{N_c}{N_x}\sqrt{\left(\frac{1-\sigma^2}{1-\lambda^2\sigma^2}\right)}\right\}. \qquad (27.11)$$

If, on the other hand, labour is supplied elastically to both the urban and export sectors from a riskless subsistence sector where earnings are c, then equating expected utility when the urban wage is given by equation (27.8) gives:

$$E\log \tilde{w} = \log c$$

or

$$\bar{w} = \frac{c}{\sqrt{(1-\lambda^2\sigma^2)}} \cong c(1 + \tfrac{1}{2}\lambda^2\sigma^2).$$

In this case average urban wages increase with export variability and the average rate of investment is adversely affected by export instability.

Thus, although it is possible that investment be increased by price instability, it is clearly not always the case, and it is not even clear whether there is a presumption that it would, without more detailed knowledge of the determination of urban wages and profits.

Chapter 28

International Instability

All the macro-models constructed so far have focused on one single country and ignored its relations with the rest of the world. This is justifiable if the country is small in the sense that the source of its instability is not closely correlated with the level of world trade or income, and this appears to be the case for most primary producers in normal years. However, periodically, all primary product prices move together, usually dramatically, as in the Depression of 1930, again in 1951, and more recently in 1973-6. Several economists, notably Kaldor (1976), have argued that economies do not adjust smoothly to these periodic large price changes. Instead of behaving as in competitive theory, with price changes signalling appropriate substitutions between commodities while maintaining full employment, adjustments take place through changes in the levels of output and employment. If primary product prices fall dramatically, primary producers suffer a fall in export receipts, and reduce their demand for manufactured goods, precipitating a recession in the developed countries. However, when prices rise dramatically, the developed countries move into trade deficit, which induces governments to deflate in order to restore balance-of-payments equilibrium.

The main difficulty in constructing a formal model of this adjustment process, as with all macro-modelling, lies in specifying responses to disequilibrium. The following model abstracts from undoubtedly important time lags, which will complicate the cyclical responses, but seems the simplest consistent with the view that adjustments to changing terms of trade occur via changes in levels of employment.

Suppose that all prices except prices of primary products are fixed and that the world contains two kinds of countries, primary producers and industrialized countries. Total income in the industrialized countries is Y, the quantity of primary exports is $\tilde{Q}$, and price $\tilde{p}$, where

$$Q = ap^{-\epsilon}Y^{\eta}, \tag{28.1}$$

is the demand for primary products. The export revenue of primary producers, X, is equal to imports by industrialized countries. Imports by primary producers, M, do not fully adjust to fluctuations in export receipts:

$$\tilde{M} = \beta \tilde{X} + (1-\beta)\bar{X} \tag{28.2}$$

where a bar denotes the average value of the variable. The industrialized countries have the following income identity

$$Y = C + M + G \tag{28.3}$$

where G is government expenditure and we have ignored investment, assumed constant. Disposable income in the industrialized countries is $Y - X$, and consumption is a function of both current income and permanent (or long-run average) income:

$$\check{C} = (1-s)(\check{Y} - \check{X}) + s(\bar{Y} - \bar{X}). \tag{28.4}$$

The government adjusts its expenditure in response to deviations in the level of production $\bar{Y} - \check{Y}$, and to balance-of-payments deficits, $X - M$:

$$\check{G} = \gamma(\bar{Y} - \check{Y}) + \delta(\check{M} - \check{X}). \tag{28.5}$$

Together these equations imply that

$$\check{Y} - \bar{Y} = k(\bar{X} - \check{X}); \quad k = \frac{(1+\delta)(1-\beta) - s}{\gamma + s} \tag{28.6}$$

where

$$\check{X} = \check{p}\check{Q} = (a\check{Y}^\eta)^{1-1/\epsilon}. \tag{28.7}$$

The effect on Y of a fluctuation in Q can be found by differentiating equation (28.6):

$$\frac{dY}{dQ} = \frac{k(1-\epsilon)X/Q}{\epsilon + \eta kX/Y}. \tag{28.8}$$

The interesting feature of this model is that if the governments of all industrialized countries coordinated their fiscal policy, by choosing δ such that

$$\delta = \frac{s}{1-\beta} - 1,$$

then $k = 0$, and income would be perfectly stable in industrialized countries. Since, however, there is no supra-national agency with the power to so choose δ, it is quite likely that Y will fluctuate in response to fluctuating primary supplies.

It is not even clear what sign k will have, though it is more likely to be positive if government reactions to balance-of-payment deficits are strong (high δ). The recent oil price rise which led to a rise in X and a fall in Y is consistent with this view. If we take a value of s of 0.5 (corresponding to the short-run consumption function estimates for the UK in Davidson et al., 1978) and a similar figure for β, then k will be positive if δ is positive.

Given the relative magnitudes of Y and X, δ is likely to be larger than γ, and if $\delta = 0.5$, $\gamma = 0.2$, then $k = 0.36$. If units are chosen so that $p = 1$ when $Q = \bar{Q}$, then the coefficient a is the normal ratio of primary imports to industrial GNP, now rather small. If $\eta = 0.7$ (the income elasticity of demand for primary products), $\epsilon = 0.2$ (the price elasticity), and a is as high as 0.1, then

$$\frac{dY}{dQ} = 1.26.$$

The effective price elasticity facing primary producers evaluated at the mean is

$$-\frac{p\,dQ}{Q\,dp} = \epsilon + \frac{(1-\epsilon)ak}{1+\eta ak} \cong 0.3.$$

Thus a 20 per cent shortfall in supplies would lead to a 66 per cent price rise and a fall in industrial GNP of $2\frac{1}{2}$ per cent. Notice that the larger is the price elasticity, ϵ, the smaller is the resulting fluctuation in industrial output, so price flexibility reduces adjustment problems. Moreover, the change in price is smaller (if $k>0$) than it would have been if industrial output had remained unchanged, so some of the price risk is shifted on to the industrialized countries.

A positive value of k and a low value of ϵ means that shortfalls lead both to a fall in industrial GNP and a rise in primary export prices and receipts, which is consistent with the recent grain and oil price rises, but not with the Depression, nor with the view that industrial output is positively correlated with prices. Cooper and Lawrence (1975) found that the real prices of agricultural raw materials responded positively to changes in industrial production in the OECD area. The same model is consistent with this explanation if instead of supplies Q varying, with prices responding, industrial demand Y varies with Q constant. In this case

$$X = ap^{1-\epsilon}Y^{\eta}$$

and

$$\frac{Y}{p}\frac{dp}{dY} = -\frac{1+k\eta X/Y}{k(1-\epsilon)X/Y}.$$

If k is negative, then prices and industrial GNP will move together. This is consistent with less governmental concern with the balance of payments (low δ) and higher values of β and s, corresponding to permanent income behaviour in the industrial countries, and a high propensity to import in primary-producing countries. All these assumptions seem reasonable in normal times. This simple model is thus capable of explaining responses to supply shocks and demand fluctuations, particularly as the parameters δ and β are likely to depend on the source of the disturbance.

One final model will be useful to demonstrate the effect of primary products of trade on industrial fluctuations. Suppose that for the usual trade cycle reasons investment fluctuates, so that we now need explicitly to include investment in the income identity of industrialized countries:

$$Y = C + I + M$$

and

$$C = C_0 + (1-s)(Y-X)$$

$$I = I_0 + b\sin wt.$$

(Investment thus exhibits regular cycles of length $2\pi/w$ years)

$$M = \beta X + (1-\beta)\bar{X}.$$

If primary supplies are constant, and the normal ratio of primary imports to industrial GNP is again a, then, combining these equations with equation (28.7) yields

$$Y = \bar{Y} + \frac{a(s+\beta-1)}{s}(Y^{\eta/\epsilon} - \bar{Y}^{\eta/\epsilon}) + \frac{b}{s}\sin wt. \qquad (28.9)$$

If deviations of income from normal are small, then this equation can be approximately solved by expanding the bracketed term to yield

$$\frac{Y-\bar{Y}}{\bar{Y}} = \frac{mb}{s\bar{Y}}\sin wt; \quad m = \frac{1}{1 - \dfrac{a\eta}{\epsilon s}(s+\beta-1)}. \qquad (28.10)$$

Fluctuations are larger than in a closed economy (with $a = 0$), and smaller the larger is the price elasticity, ϵ. Primary export revenues will fluctuate proportionately η/ϵ times as much as industrial GNP, with recessions synchronized but much deeper. Lewis (1978) argues that LDCs are particularly badly placed because their balance-of-payments problems occur in slumps, rather than in booms, as in industrialized countries, and that these deficits are particularly hard to finance as they are synchronized with general depression, with attendant difficulties in short-term borrowing.

All these macro-models can be extended to include time lags and to allow both for fluctuations in supply, Q, and demand, Y. The effect is likely to be the superposition of several cycles of different periods together with a random component. Such models exhibit small, frequent fluctuations when the different cycles are out of phase with each other and the supply shocks, with occasional large fluctuations when cycles and shocks coincide. If this analysis is correct, and it corresponds moderately well with the historic record, then the policy implications are not necessarily favourable to stabilizing commodity prices by buffer stocks. Infrequent (once in twenty years) large fluctuations in prices would require large buffer stocks held for long periods, and would be very costly. Most of the macro-models have other policy variables which, if chosen appropriately, with the necessary inter-government co-operation, would eliminate, or reduce the severity of, large fluctuations in income. There is some irony in noting that Keynesian theory has encouraged governments to take an increasingly active role in domestic demand management, but has provided the temptation to export instabilities to the world market in which there is no supranational demand management. It is a moot point whether inter-government negotiations mitigate instabilities or merely increase the degree of synchrony between national economies, worsening instability.

Part VII

Dynamic Considerations

The objective of a commodity price stabilization scheme is to transfer output from dates at which it has a low market valuation (a low price) to dates at which it has a high market valuation. The gain in doing so is, of course, simply the difference in the valuations at the two dates. There is, however, a cost which we have ignored in most of the discussion so far: the costs of storage (including interest costs). If these are large, it may not pay to store the commodity, even with quite large variations in price.

A second deficiency in the analysis so far is that we have not taken adequate account of the stochastic structure of the problem of price stabilization: if every good year were followed by a bad year (or, as in the Bible, seven years of plenty were followed by seven years of famine), our results would be immediately applicable. The buffer stock would simply store some of the crop from the good year to the following bad year. The length of time which the crop would be in storage would be known precisely. In such circumstances complete price stabilization is feasible.

In practice, however, there is a large stochastic element in supply, so that there may be a run of good years, followed by only a single bad year, or by several bad years. If we were required to have sufficient stocks to cover all possible sequences of good and bad years, we would have to have enormous stocks because it is possible (although not likely) that we could have an extremely long run of bad years. Even if we start with large initial stocks, if the stock manager buys and sells so as to stabilize the price perfectly, then eventually, but certainly, he will either exhaust his stock or run out of storage capacity and at that date he will be unable to continue maintaining the chosen price. Perfect price stabilization is thus impossible.

This raises a number of important questions.

(i) What are the consequences of different storage rules? A storage rule specifies the amount to be taken into or out of storage as a function of certain variables, e.g. the size of the buffer stock, the size of the harvest, etc. In particular, with each buffer stock rule, there will be associated a probability distribution of the amount in storage. We are particularly interested in (a) the probability that the buffer stock runs out of stock; (b) the probability that the capacity of the buffer stock be exceeded; (c) the average (discounted) value of the costs of maintaining the buffer stock; (d) the consequences of the buffer stock rule for price variability; and (e) the magnitude and distribution of the benefits from the buffer stock.

(ii) Since each buffer stock rule will have different consequences, if we specify an objective function (a way of weighing the benefits and costs accruing to different groups at different times) we can determine the optimal storage rule.

What does this rule look like? How does it differ in form, costs, and consequences from other rules (such as the popular rule of attempting to keep prices within a given band width)? How does the optimum rule depend on the degree of instability and the cost of storage?

(iii) What is the nature of the storage which will occur in a market economy, and what effect will the presence of private storage have on the operations of the buffer stock scheme?

(iv) How can the optimum storage rule be implemented in a competitive market economy?

(v) What other market intervention, if any, is desirable?

The main conclusions of our analysis are:

1. Not only is perfect price stability not feasible, but under the optimum storage rule only modest reductions in instability are warranted.

2. The optimum storage rule is very different in form from the conventional storage rule, which is to attempt to keep prices within a predetermined bandwith. This rule is infeasible in the long run and it is particularly vulnerable to speculative attacks. Moreover, the maximum value of welfare gains (from choosing the band-width storage capacity, etc. optimally) is significantly smaller than with the optimal rule.

3. If the buffer agency is not concerned with the cost of income risk nor the distribution of costs and benefits, then, as Gustafson showed over twenty years ago, the optimum storage rule is identical to the activities of risk-neutral competitive private store operators holding rational expectations. In such cases the optimum rule can be decentralized by leaving storage to the competitive market and providing good forecasting services, and risk-sharing facilities (to ensure risk neutrality). In these circumstances, public storage would replace private storage on a one-for-one basis. There would be no gain in price stability by a public buffer stock unless public storage was taken to the point that there was *no* private storage or unless all private storage facilities were filled to capacity.

If, however, producers are not risk neutral, or the agency is concerned about the distribution of stabilization benefits, then the optimum storage rule will differ from the competitive market equilibrium supply of storage, and market intervention will be needed to increase social welfare. Some apparently attractive modes of intervention are, however, vulnerable to offsetting actions by private storage. Nevertheless, the concept of a *competitive storage rule* (the storage which would be undertaken by a rational expectations risk-neutral competitive market) remains a natural bench-mark from which to start in the calculation of the social optimum, and is useful in providing insight into the form of the rule and the costs (or price) of additional reductions in price instability. It also acts as a strong reminder that the rule has to be implemented within a competitive economy. The logical approach would seem to be first to

Introduction 405

determine whether the competitive market supplies too little or too much storage, then to subsidize or tax private storage activity (and possibly complement it by additional public storage).

Our analysis is divided into two chapters. Chapter 29 presents an elementary discussion of the nature of buffer stocks, and shows how each buffer stock rule gives rise to a stochastic process (for, say, the size of the buffer stock). It shows how for some simple rules one can calculate the probability distribution of the stock running out within any time interval.

It then discusses how one might choose among alternative buffer stock rules, and in particular, it defines the notion of the optimal buffer stock scheme. The fundamental equivalency theorem between competitive equilibrium storage and optimal storage is established, and some of the implications of competitive storage are then derived.

The final section of the chapter illustrates the nature of buffer stocks with some simple examples where a complete characterization of the stochastic processes generated by the buffer stock rule is possible.

Chapter 30 is devoted to the further analysis of optimal commodity stockpiling rules. The level of mathematics required, though elementary, is rather tedious, and the reader not interested in the details may turn to the final section of the chapter where the results are summarized.

Chapter 29

Buffer Stocks

The analysis of the consequences of alternative buffer stock rules, their costs and benefits, and the derivation of optimal storage rules turns out to be a fairly difficult matter. In particular, it appears extremely difficult to obtain general analytical solutions, or to use analytical techniques to obtain general qualitative characteristics of alternative rules.

On the other hand, although analytical techniques are difficult, numerical techniques (with high-speed computers) allow the numerical solution (or approximate solutions) to many of the questions at issue. One must, of course, first formulate the problem in a meaningful way; but, as we have emphasized elsewhere, any model formulation requires some simplification of reality, and one must be sure that one is not simplifying away the essence of the problem. Thus, one needs to test the robustness of the model, to obtain some feeling for what are the critical parameters determining the nature of the outcomes.

The objective of this chapter is to develop the basic ideas underlying the dynamic analysis of buffer stocks. The analysis is intended to be simple and intuitive, to help the reader understand the basic issues at hand, and to present a framework from which further work may be developed.

We start our enquiry in this chapter by examining the consequences of various simple buffer stock rules, and show that they can be best appreciated as generating stochastic processes, with various implications. We contrast two approaches to the choice of stock rules — the first specifies the rule and chooses appropriate values for its parameters, such as the required initial stock. The second asks directly the form of the optimum rule. The remainder of this chapter discusses some of the implications of the optimum rule, and then studies some simple examples of storage rules to gain a feel for the likely size of buffer stocks and for the form of the stochastic processes implied. The next chapter discusses the solution of the optimum stock rule.

29.1 Buffer stocks as stochastic processes

The simplest buffer stock scheme is described by the following elements:
  (i) There is a stock S_{t-1} carried forward from the previous period.
  (ii) To this is added a random supply, $\tilde{h}_t$ (for harvest).
  (iii) Thus, at any date there is available, either for current consumption or for storage, an amount x_t:

$$x_t = h_t + S_{t-1} = C_t + S_t \qquad (29.1)$$

where C_t is current consumption. (This specification assumes no losses in storage. More generally, $S_t = \alpha(x_t - C_t)$ where α is the fraction of initial stocks remaining at the start of the next harvest.)

In this simplest formulation we do not distinguish between consumers and producers (the economy is centrally planned), and we assume that planned supply does not change from year to year, so that, assuming weather etc. to be serially uncorrelated, harvests $\bar{h}_t$ will be serially uncorrelated. Given these provisos so that we can ignore income distribution, the state of the economy at date t is completely described by x_t. (If we were concerned with income distribution, then we should be interested in producers' revenue, which would depend on h_t as well as x_t (unless all storage was done by producers). A buffer stock rule says, for each value of x_t, what the level of storage and consumption should be:

$$S_t = f(x_t), \qquad (29.2)$$

$$C_t = g(x_t) = x_t - f(x_t). \qquad (29.3)$$

For a buffer stock rule to be feasible

$$f(x_t) \geq 0 \qquad (29.4)$$

since stocks cannot become negative. If there is a limit on storage capacity of K, then additionally

$$f(x_t) \leq K. \qquad (29.5)$$

Any buffer stock rule thus gives rise, for any sequence of harvests h_t and initial stock S_0, to a sequence of stock levels and consumption levels. Since the harvests are stochastic, the stock levels and consumption levels are described by a stochastic process. Consider, as an example, the simple rule

$$C_t = \bar{h} \quad \text{if } x_t > \bar{h}$$
$$= x_t \quad \text{if } x_t \leq \bar{h}.$$

In this case, if there is no maximal capacity K,

$$S_t = S_{t-1} + h_t - \bar{h} \quad \text{if } x_t > \bar{h}$$
$$= 0 \qquad \qquad \text{otherwise}$$

and the buffer stock rule generates a particularly simple stochastic process for S_t: S_t is a random walk with a reflecting barrier at 0.

If there were a capacity constraint at K then this rule (appropriately modified) would generate a random walk with reflecting barriers at 0 and K, as shown in Fig. 29.1. Associated with the consumption level would be a price, which, if demand were stationary, as we shall assume, would be stabilized only so long as $C_t = \bar{h}$. This immediately demonstrates the important point that with any finite initial stock, no matter how large, if consumption is set equal to

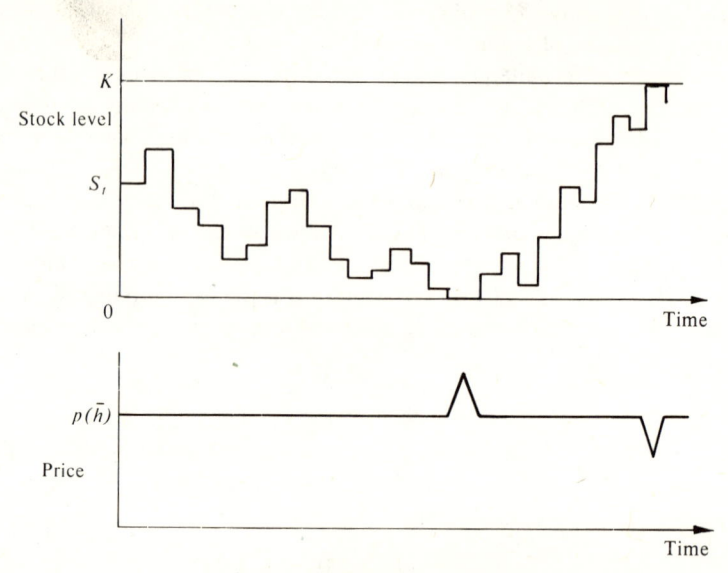

Fig. 29.1 Stock levels and price

average supply, then with probability 1 there will occur a sufficiently long run of bad years that the stock will be eventually exhausted. The gambling analogy is that with equal wagers on the fall of a fair coin, a gambler will eventually be ruined for any finite initial wealth. If the consumption level were set low enough (e.g. below Min h) then exhaustion can be avoided but at the cost of ever-increasing stocks which will eventually reach the capacity constraint.

Of course, the larger the initial stock, the longer it will be before we are likely to run out, but the greater will be the cost of maintaining this larger stock. If successive harvests have a CV of σ, and if the discrete random walk is approximated by a continuous diffusion process, then the probability distribution of the stock level at date t before it hits a boundary is normal, $N(S_0, \sigma^2 t)$. The probability of running out of stock (if K is sufficiently large) before date t is then

$$\beta = F(-S_0/\sigma\sqrt{t}) \tag{29.6}$$

where F is the distribution function of $N(0, 1)$. Doubling the initial stock increases the time before this reaches a given probability by two squared, or four. We used this simple property of the random walk to gain rough estimates of storage costs in Chapter 20, by specifying β and t to calculate the required initial (and average) stock S_0.

The price band rule can similarly be specified once the nature of demand has been specified. Thus if demand schedule is nonstochastic, $C = d(p)$, and if the price has upper and lower bands set at p^u, p^l, then the stock rule is

$$f(x, h) = \begin{cases} x - d(p^l), & h > d(p^l) \\ x - h, & d(p^u) \leqslant h \leqslant d(p^l) \\ x - d(p^u), & h < d(p^u), \quad x > d(p^u) \\ 0, & \text{otherwise.} \end{cases}$$

Notice in this case that the stock rule depends not just on x, but also on h, which makes no sense if the sole object is to stabilize consumption, but which can be defended if the distribution of income is felt to be important. It reduces to the previous rule if $p^l = p^u$, and can be thought of as a possibly cheaper method of eliminating the more costly extreme fluctuations at the expense of permitting mild fluctuations.

29.2 The choice of stock rule

Two distinct approaches to the choice of stock rule can be discerned. The first, and more popular, consists in specifying the form of the rule and then choosing its parameters to best meet a stated objective. Thus the width of the price band and the size of the initial stock might be specified to minimize the cost of achieving a given level of price stabilization over some period with a given probability of avoiding exhaustion. This approach has the attraction that, if the rule and the objective are simple, then the calculation of the appropriate parameters is simple. We shall consider some examples below as part of an exercise designed to give some feel for the effects of various rules. Even where the rule or objective is not simple, computer simulation provides a relatively simple method of solution. Thus Reutlinger (1976) simulates the effect of following a storage rule which attempts to keep consumption of wheat (and hence price) within a specified band width, using as data 300 simulations of 30 years of random-number-generated data. Behrman (1977, 1978) likewise simulates the operations of buffer stocks designed to keep 13 commodity prices from fluctuating outside a range of 15 per cent on either side of the trend for the last 25 years. The simpler case of finding a level of stocks required to reduce the probability of large production shortfalls to some chosen level has been examined by a long list of investigators, surveyed in Stein and Smith (1977, p. 28).

The limitation of this approach is obvious — there is no guarantee that the specific rule chosen is an efficient method of achieving the stated objective at minimum cost. The alternative, but harder approach is to first specify the objective, model supply and demand, and then determine the optimum rule. This approach was first developed by Gustafson (1958) and then virtually forgotten until the recent reawakening of interest in international buffer stocks. Important recent contributions have been made by Danin, Sumner and Johnson (1975), Schechtman (1977), Goreux (1978), and Gardner (1979).

Under conventional simplifications (whose strength does not appear to have been adequately recognized), the problem is easy to formulate. Suppose we are solely concerned with optimizing the consumption flow from a serially uncorrelated sequence of harvests, as in equations (29.1)–(29.4). The objective is then to

$$\text{Max } E \sum_{t=0}^{T} \delta^t U(C_t, M_t - \gamma S_t) \tag{29.7}$$

where M_t is money expenditure on all other goods (whose prices remain constant), including the annual storage costs, γ per unit stored, and δ is the pure time preference discount factor. The choice variables are the amounts carried over, S_t, and expenditure on other goods, subject to the constraints

$$S_t \geq 0, \quad x_0, S_T \quad \text{given},$$

$$\sum_{t=0}^{T} \beta^t M_t = W_0, \quad \text{given}, \tag{29.7a}$$

where $\beta = 1/(1 + r)$, the discount factor when the money rate of interest is r, and W_0 is the present value of wealth and future money income receipts. We are assuming that the economy can freely lend *and borrow* at the same interest rate. The maximization problem can be written

$$\mathcal{L} = U(x_0 - S_0, M_0 - \gamma S_0) + \delta E U(\bar{h}_1 + S_0 - S_1, M_1 - \gamma S_1) +$$

$$+ E \sum_{t=2}^{T} \delta^t U(C_t, M_t - \gamma S_t) + \mu \left(W_0 - \sum_{t=0}^{T} \beta^t M_t \right) \tag{29.8}$$

Differentiate with respect to M_0, M_1:

$$U_M(C_0) = \mu = \frac{\delta}{\beta} E U_M(C_1) \tag{29.9}$$

where

$$U_M(C_t) \equiv \frac{\partial U(C_t, M_t - \gamma S_t)}{\partial M_t}$$

and

$$U_C(C_t) \equiv \frac{\partial U(C_t, M_t - \gamma S_t)}{\partial C_t}.$$

Differentiate with respect to S_0,

$$\left. \begin{array}{c} -U_C(C_0) - \gamma U_M(C_0) + \delta E U_C(C_1) \leq 0 \\ S_0 \geq 0 \end{array} \right\} \text{complementary inequalities} \tag{29.10}$$

In a competitive market economy if the price of the commodity after the harvest at t is p_t, then

$$p_t = \frac{U_C(C_t)}{U_M(C_t)} \qquad (29.11)$$

so equation (29.10) can be written, after substituting from (29.9) as

$$\left. \begin{array}{l} p_0 + \gamma \geqslant \dfrac{1}{1+r} \dfrac{Ep_1 U_M(C_1)}{EU_M(C_1)} \\[2mm] S_0 \geqslant 0 \end{array} \right\} \text{complementarily.} \qquad (29.12)$$

If the marginal utility of expenditure on other goods, U_M, is uncorrelated with the price of the commodity, or, equivalently, if the consumer is price risk neutral, then equation (29.12) can be written as

$$\left. \begin{array}{l} p_0 + \gamma \geqslant \dfrac{Ep_1}{1+r} \\[2mm] S_0 \geqslant 0 \end{array} \right\} \text{complementarily}$$

or, in words, storage is desirable if the spot price plus storage cost is less than the expected discounted future price, and optimal storage will drive the spot price plus storage cost up to this level. But this is just the market equilibrium condition for competitive risk neutral storage operators with rational expectations. In this sense *the competitive market will supply the socially optimal level of storage, if consumers are price risk neutral.*

Equation (29.12) holds for successive dates, as the harvest becomes known, and in expectation into the future; i.e.

$$\left. \begin{array}{l} Ep_t + \gamma \geqslant \dfrac{Ep_{t+1}}{1+r} \\[2mm] S_t \geqslant 0 \end{array} \right\} \text{complementarily.} \qquad (29.13)$$

We shall call the rule which generates this sequence of relationships the *competitive storage rule* and discuss its solution below. However, it is important to realize how restrictive are the conditions under which the competitive rule is socially optimal. We have ignored the distribution of income, tacitly assumed that consumers can provide producers with income insurance (by aggregating them), ignored supply responses, assumed perfect intertemporal transfers of other goods, whose relative prices do not change with the price of the stored commodity, and required risk-neutral store operators. If these conditions (or other, similarly restrictive, conditions) do not hold, then the analysis of Chapter 15 suggests that the private market will not supply the socially optimal level of storage. The problem can be reformulated, but the attractive simplicity of equation (29.13) vanishes. For example, if producers cannot store or lend and borrow, and if they have a social weight λ, while consumers store and have access to a perfect capital market, the problem can be rewritten

$$\text{Max}\, E \sum_{t=0}^{T} \delta^t \{V(p_t, I_t) + \lambda U(p_t, h_t)\} \qquad (29.14)$$

where

$$I_t = M_t + p_t(C_t - h_t) - \gamma S_t$$

and the constraints are given by equation (29.7a). I_t is spendable net income, including profits from operating the buffer stock, and V is the consumer's indirect utility function. Social utility still depends on consumption, but if we wrote

$$W = V + \lambda U$$

$$\frac{\partial W}{\partial C} = \{V_p + V_I(C - h) + h\lambda U'\}\frac{\partial p}{\partial C} + p V_I$$

$$\frac{1}{V_I}\frac{\partial W}{\partial C} = p + \frac{\lambda U' - V_I}{V_I} h \frac{\partial p}{\partial C}$$

instead of the social marginal utility of consumption being just proportional to price.

Despite these limitations, the competitive storage rule is the natural benchmark, for two reasons. It is typically difficult to solve equations such as (29.14), and probably easier to enquire whether the competitive market under- or over-supplies storage, and then devise compensating policies. Second, it is not sufficient to solve for the centrally planned optimum if the economy is a private market economy, for this begs the question of implementing the solution. Ideally the economy and the feasible policy measures should be modelled and optimal levels for these measures chosen. Such problems are typically very intractable. The advantage of starting from the competitive storage rule and possibly adding policies such as subsidizing storage, is that they are at least feasible equilibria for a market economy.

29.2.1 Implications of the competitive storage rule

The competitive storage rule is found by solving equation (29.13) recursively. Given the specified terminal carry-forward stock S_T, Ep_T is computed, then Ep_{T-1}, etc. back to p_0. If the expected present discounted value of the terminal stock, $E\beta^T p_T S_T$, tends to zero as the horizon increases, then the influence of the terminal stock can be ignored for sufficiently long time horizons. If demand is non-stochastic (as modelled, with stationary utility and no other risk) then the optimum stock rule is a function $f(x)$ such that

$$p\{x - f(x)\} + \gamma = \frac{1}{1+r} Ep[\bar{h} + f(x) - f\{\bar{h} + f(x)\}] \quad (29.15)$$

for $f(x) \geqslant 0$, and zero otherwise, where $p(C)$ is the market clearing price for consumption C. We defer the problem of solving for $f(x)$ to the next chapter, but note first that if h is stationary, then the stock rule is a function of x (harvest plus carry-over) alone. The price band model is therefore not a competitive storage rule, nor is it ever optimal to keep the expected price constant with positive storage and/or interest costs.

The next implication is stronger. If prices are sufficiently dispersed and the government attempts perfectly to stabilize price at a level which equates average supply to demand, then it is bound to be subjected to a speculative attack in which the private sector purchases the entire public stockpile. The argument, due to Salant (1979), goes as follows. By 'sufficiently disperse' prices, we mean that, if $F(h)$ is the probability distribution function for h, then

$$\int_0^{\bar{h}} p(h)dF + \{1 - F(\bar{h})\}p(\bar{h}) > (1+r)\{p(\bar{h}) + \gamma\}. \quad (29.16)$$

This means that if the government guarantees to purchase for stock whatever is needed to keep the price at the stabilized level, $p(\bar{h})$ (at which average supply, $\bar{h}$, equals consumption), then in the absence of any stocks, public or private, it must be profitable to buy stocks now at price $p(\bar{h})$ in the expectation of gain if there is a shortfall in the harvest tomorrow. This is actually quite a stringent condition, for suppose harvests are roughly normally distributed and that demand is linear, so that in the absence of stockpiling its CV would be σ_p. Then equation (29.16) is equivalent to

$$\sigma_p > \sqrt{(2\pi)}(r + c), \quad c \equiv \frac{(1+r)\gamma}{\bar{p}}$$

$$\sim 2.5(r + c)$$

which is only satisfied by cocoa, rubber, and sugar, given our estimates of Table 20.7.

However, if the condition is satisfied, then the result is immediate, for if the government places a lower bound on the price, then there is a critical public stock level S^* below which it is profitable for the private sector to carry stocks, defined by the equality

$$\int_0^{\bar{h}-S^*} p(h)dF + \{1 - F(\bar{h} - S^*)\}p(\bar{h}) = (1+r)\{p(\bar{h}) + \gamma\}. \quad (29.17)$$

If equation (29.16) holds, then there must be a solution in $S^* > 0$ for equation (29.17). The private sector holds no stocks until public stocks first fall to S^*, at which point it is profitable for the private sector to buy all the public stocks, for at any public stock level above S^*, the stocks are sufficient to avoid most of the profitable next period price rises, while below S^* the government will fail to prevent prices rising next period sufficiently often to make speculative storage profitable.

The final step in the argument is to note that since the public stockpile follows an unbiased random walk, it must, with probability 1, eventually fall below this critical level S^*.

Buffer programmes which differ substantially from the competitive storage rule run the risk of such speculative attacks which would abruptly end the programme. This may rule out one potentially very attractive stabilization rule discussed at the end of Chapter 20. According to this rule, the government pays producers a price $\hat{p}$ where

$$\hat{p}_t = \frac{\bar{Y}}{Q_t},$$

where $\bar{Y}$ is trend revenue for the region and Q_t is the actual production at date t. This scheme stabilizes individual producer's income to the extent that his output risk correlates with regional output, but it apparently avoids the usual insurance problems of adverse selection and moral hazard. The first and most obvious problem is that the consumer price would typically differ from the producer price, and hence provide strong incentives for black markets to develop. The second problem is that it might be vulnerable to private storage by producers.

Assume, for instance, that there are only two states of nature, a good harvest with output $1 + \sigma$ and a bad harvest with output $1 - \sigma$. If there is a large harvest this year, the expected (proportional) increase in price is approximately

$$\frac{\frac{1}{2}\left(\frac{1}{1+\sigma} + \frac{1}{1-\sigma}\right) - \frac{1}{1+\sigma}}{\frac{1}{1+\sigma}} = \frac{1}{1-\sigma} - 1 = \frac{\sigma}{1-\sigma}$$

which, for large σ, will exceed the rate of interest and private storage costs by a considerable amount. This provides a strong incentive for private storage (speculation).

Thus, the extent to which the buffer stock agency is constrained by private speculation in determining producer prices (assuming that it can separate that policy from the policy for consumer prices) is determined by the magnitude of the storage (interest) costs which they face and, in particular, by the extent to which they exceed those facing the buffer stock agency (net of any subsidy which the agency might receive).

29.2.2 *Some simple examples of stock rules*

Since the solution of the optimum stock rule is difficult we defer discussion to the next chapter and discuss first some simpler examples which are designed to bring out the stochastic nature of the problem and the influence of the objective on the choice of stock rule.

Suppose that there are only two equally likely states of the world, corresponding to good or bad harvests:

$$h = 1 \pm \sigma.$$

We suppose that the objective is as before to even out consumption over time, but we shall consider three different utility functions. The first is the standard iso-elastic or constant relative risk aversion utility function

$$U(C) = \begin{cases} \dfrac{C^{1-R}}{1-R}, & R \neq 1, \\ \log C, & R = 1 \end{cases}$$

where R is the coefficient of relative risk aversion.

In the second, we are particularly concerned with famine, and the objective of the buffer stock is to avoid starvation:

$$U(C) = \begin{cases} C, & C < 1 - \tfrac{1}{2}\sigma \equiv \hat{C} \\ \hat{C}, & C \geq \hat{C}. \end{cases}$$

In this utility function, the marginal utility of consumption is very high up to some critical level, $\hat{C}$ (below the mean output), and zero thereafter. In the last, we are particularly concerned about satiation (or flooding the market), i.e. the objective of the buffer stock is to keep some of the output off the market in years of plenty.

$$U(C) = \begin{cases} C, & C < 1 + \sigma/2 \equiv \hat{C} \\ \hat{C}, & C \geq \hat{C}. \end{cases}$$

In this utility function, the marginal utility of consumption is also zero beyond some critical level, but this is in excess of the mean output. As we have depicted the last two utility functions, they have the same shape, except the kink in the utility function occurs, in the first, at a level of output below the mean, while in the second it occurs at a level of output beyond the mean. We shall refer to them as the 'famine' and 'flood' utility functions respectively; the famine utility function is illustrated in Fig. 29.2.

Corresponding to these three different objectives there are three naturally associated stock rules, which would be optimal in the absence of storage costs:

(i) In good years it puts in the same number of units into storage that it takes out in bad years (subject, of course, to the constraints noted above).

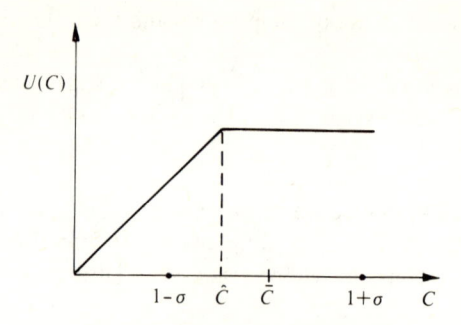

Fig. 29.2 Famine utility function

(ii) In good years, it puts into storage the excess above $\hat{C}$, until capacity is reached; in bad years it takes out enough to ensure $\hat{C}$. (The famine rule.)

(iii) (The flood rule.) This is the same as the famine rule except that the definition of $\hat{C}$ has changed.

Let us consider each of these rules in turn.

29.2.3 *The pure random walk model*

With the iso-elastic utility function the natural target is to stabilize consumption at unity, so the natural operation of the first storage rule is for the buffer stock to store the excess output (σ units) in good years and take out σ units in bad years in an attempt to maintain consumption constant. We define a 'storage unit' as σ units of output. We then ask, what, in steady state, is the probability distribution of the size (in storage units) of the buffer stock of capacity K, where K is an integer (for reasons which will become clear below).

Let π_V be the probability that the stock contains exactly V units. The period before there must have been either $V-1$ or $V+1$ (unless $V=0$ or K) and these prior states are equally likely (since additions and subtractions to the stock are equally likely). Therefore

$$\pi_0 = \tfrac{1}{2}(\pi_0 + \pi_1) \quad \text{or} \quad \pi_1 = \pi_0$$
$$\pi_1 = \tfrac{1}{2}(\pi_2 + \pi_0) \quad \text{or} \quad \pi_2 = \pi_1$$
$$\pi_V = \tfrac{1}{2}(\pi_{V+1} + \pi_{V-1}) = \pi_{V+1}.$$

Thus if the storage capacity is exactly K units, there are $K+1$ possible levels of stock: $0, 1, 2, \ldots, K$, and so

$$\pi_V = \frac{1}{K+1}.$$

(If K is not an integer, the number of possible stock levels will be much larger, and the problem more complex.) There is a *uniform* distribution of amounts in storage. Prices are successfully stabilized $K/(K+1)$ of the time, but $\tfrac{1}{2}/(K+1)$ they rise to the unstabilized high price and $\tfrac{1}{2}/(K+1)$ they fall to the unstabilized low price. From the point of view of consumers, the expected utility which is generated by such a rule (ignoring discounting) in steady state is

$$\bar{U} = \frac{K}{K+1} U(1) + \frac{U(1-\sigma) + U(1+\sigma)}{2(K+1)}.$$

Thus for the iso-elasticity utility function the value of the risk reduction is approximately

$$B = \frac{R\sigma^2 K}{2(K+1)}.$$

For both the famine and flood utility functions, the value of the risk reduction achieved by rule (i) is just

$$B = \frac{\sigma K}{4(K+1)}.$$

For all three utility functions the marginal gain of increasing capacity is proportional to $(1/K + 1)^2$, i.e. there is sharply diminishing returns to increasing capacity.

Since the distribution is uniform the average buffer stock size is $K/2$ stock units of $(K/2)\sigma$ units of output. Thus, if s is the storage cost per period per unit of storage (including interest) and ξ the cost of maintaining a storage capacity of a unit, total (expected) costs would be (per period)

$$\left[\frac{sK}{2} + \xi K\right] \sigma.$$

Notice that this is linear in K. The net benefits of operating the stock rule are

$$G = B - \tfrac{1}{2}(s + 2\xi)K\sigma$$

which are maximized when

$$\frac{dB}{dK} = \tfrac{1}{2}(s + 2\xi)\sigma.$$

Thus the optimal size of the buffer stock for the iso-elastic case following this rule is approximately

$$K^* \approx \sqrt{\left(\frac{R\sigma}{s + 2\xi}\right)} - 1.$$

If $R = 1$, $\sigma = 0.5$, $s + 2\xi = 0.1$, then $K = 1.23$, $K\sigma = 0.6$, and the optimal stock capacity has just over half a year's output. If K is restricted to be integer valued then it is necessary to calculate the net benefits. For the iso-elastic function

$$G(K) = \frac{\sigma K}{2} \left\{\frac{R\sigma}{K+1} - (s + 2\xi)\right\}$$

418 Commodity Price Stabilization

with $G(1) = 3.75$ per cent, $G(2) = 3.33$ per cent, and $K = 1$ is better, so that prices are stabilized on average half the time. Although the buffer stock does not do a very good job of stabilizing consumption, it does not pay to have a very large stock – its average value is just three months' average output.

With the other two functions

$$K^* = \sqrt{\left\{\frac{1}{2(s+2\xi)}\right\} - 1}$$

which, with the same parameters as above gives the same value of K^* and $G(K)$.

29.2.4 Famine stock rule

With the famine utility function there is no point in consuming in excess of $\hat{C}$, and it is logical to store this (at least, if we ignore storage costs). Therefore, consider the rule which puts the entire surplus ($3\sigma/2$ units) into store in good years and takes out $\sigma/2$ in bad years (bringing consumption up to $\hat{C}$). Define a unit of storage as $\sigma/2$ units of output, then each year with probability 1/2 storage increases by 3 units and/or reaches full capacity, or falls by one unit. Thus level zero can be reached (with equal chance) from level 0 or 1; level 1 only from level 2; level 2 only from level 3; level 3 from level 0 or 4 etc., and hence

$$\pi_0 = \tfrac{1}{2}(\pi_0 + \pi_1)$$
$$\pi_1 = \tfrac{1}{2}\pi_2$$
$$\pi_2 = \tfrac{1}{2}\pi_3$$
$$\pi_3 = \tfrac{1}{2}(\pi_0 + \pi_4).$$

The solution is

$$\pi_0 = \pi_1$$
$$\pi_2 = 2\pi_1 = 2\pi_0$$
$$\pi_3 = 2\pi_2 = 4\pi_0$$
$$\pi_n = 2\pi_{n-1} - \pi_{n-4}, \quad n > 3,$$

where

$$\sum_{i=0}^{K} \pi_i = 1.$$

The probabilities are solved for capacity levels $K = 2, 3, 4, 5$ in Table 29.1, which also gives the average stock size in stock units ($= \tfrac{1}{2}\sigma$ output units)

$$\bar{S} = \sum_{V=1}^{K} V\pi_V.$$

It can be seen that marginal costs increase as capacity is increased.

Table 29.1 Probabilities of stock levels

K	π_0	π_1	π_2	π_3	π_4	π_5	Average stock size (stock units)
1	$\frac{1}{2}$	$\frac{1}{2}$					$\frac{1}{2}$
2	$\frac{1}{4}$	$\frac{1}{4}$	$\frac{1}{2}$				$1\frac{1}{4}$
3	$\frac{1}{8}$	$\frac{1}{8}$	$\frac{2}{8}$	$\frac{4}{8}$			$2\frac{1}{8}$
4	$\frac{1}{15}$	$\frac{1}{15}$	$\frac{2}{15}$	$\frac{4}{15}$	$\frac{7}{15}$		3
5	$\frac{1}{28}$	$\frac{1}{28}$	$\frac{2}{28}$	$\frac{4}{28}$	$\frac{7}{28}$	$\frac{13}{28}$	$3\frac{13}{14}$

With the famine utility function the expected gain from the buffer rule is

$$\frac{\sigma}{4}(1-\pi_0)$$

and the costs are

$$\frac{\sigma}{2}(s\bar{S} + \xi K).$$

Marginal costs and benefits of increasing K are shown in Table 29.2, which demonstrates the sharply diminishing returns.

Table 29.2 Marginal costs and benefits of capacity expansion

Increasing K from	Marginal benefit $\frac{1}{2}\sigma$	Marginal cost $\frac{1}{2}\sigma$
1 to 2	0.125	$\xi + \frac{3}{4}s$
2 to 3	0.0625	$\xi + \frac{7}{8}s$
3 to 4	0.0292	$\xi + \frac{7}{8}s$
4 to 5	0.0155	$\xi + \frac{13}{14}s$

If $\xi = 2$ per cent, $s = 8$ per cent, it is only worth setting $K = 2$ so the average stock is $5\sigma/8$ units of output, but if $\xi = 1$ per cent, $s = 4$ per cent, then $K = 3$,

420 *Commodity Price Stabilization*

and the average stock is just over σ. It is also interesting to note that in both cases the best famine stock rule gives higher net benefits than the best simple random walk stock rule, showing the importance of storage costs in determining the appropriate rule.

The evaluation of the benefits with the iso-elastic utility function, and the case of the flood stock rule are left as exercises for the reader.

29.3 Conclusions

Under simplifying assumptions such as those used in this chapter it is relatively easy to characterize the stochastic process followed by the buffer stock and to evaluate the costs and benefits. We find that even for large risk and low storage costs the average buffer stock is small, and that the buffer rule which would be optimal if costs are ignored often looks relatively unattractive compared with alternatives once the costs are included.

Chapter 30

Optimal Commodity Stockpiling Rules

30.1 Introduction

If the distribution of income between producers and consumers if of no concern, and if both are risk neutral, the competitive storage equilibrium achieves the optimum amount of price stabilization. We argued in the last chapter that the competitive storage rule is the natural bench-mark from which to calculate the optimal rule. It is characterized by the condition that storage today continues until the present price, p_t, plus storage cost, γ per unit stored, has been driven up to equality with the present discounted value of the expected future price, or, if present prices are high, stocks are sold now until the price plus storage cost has been driven down to this level, or until stocks, S_t, are exhausted. Mathematically

$$\left.\begin{array}{c} p_t + \gamma \geqslant \beta E p_{t+1} \\ \\ S_t \geqslant 0 \end{array}\right\} \text{ complementarily, } \quad \beta \equiv \frac{1}{1+r} \qquad (30.1)$$

and β is the discount factor. Solving this rule is difficult because the expected price next year depends on planned carry-overs next year, which depend on expected prices the year after, etc. To find the storage rule now we need to know the storage rules to be followed hereafter. To solve the problem we need to start with a terminal date at which the carry-forward is specified, and hence known, and work backwards. This is the standard method of solution of stochastic programming problems such as this, but with a long time horizon is computationally demanding. If, however, the time horizon is allowed to lengthen and if the expected present discounted value of terminal stocks, i.e. $\beta^T S_T E p_T$, tends to zero, then the influence of the future on the present also tends to zero, and we can instead of looking for a particular solution, look for a stationary stock rule, which specifies the carry-forward as a function of total available supply only, and not the date.

In the notation of the last chapter, if S_t is stocks carried forward in year t, h_t is the harvest, and x_t is total supply:

$$x_t = h_t + S_{t-1} = C_t + S_t \qquad (30.2)$$

and we seek a function $f(x)$ such that for all x_t

$$S_t = f(x_t) \geqslant 0. \qquad (30.3)$$

If demand is non-stochastic, this function must solve equation (30.1), and since

$$C_t = x_t - f(x_t)$$

this implies

$$p\{x_t - f(x_t)\} + \gamma \geq \beta Ep[\tilde{h}_{t+1} + f(x_t) - f\{\tilde{h}_{t+1} + f(x_t)\}]$$

$$f(x_t) \geq 0.$$

complementary inequalities

(30.4)

The problem in solving this arises from the right-hand side, in the term $f\{h + f(x)\}$. One key feature of the rule is, however, immediate.

1. *The optimum storage rule is non-linear.* This follows because stocks must be non-negative, so $f(x) = 0$ below some critical value of x_0, for which

$$p(x_0) + \gamma = \beta Ep\{\tilde{h} - f(\tilde{h})\}. \qquad (30.5)$$

The next few results are not so obvious and for rigorous proofs the reader is referred to Schectman (1977) (who also gives the proofs of the existence and optimality of the competitive rule. Gustafson (1958) and Samuelson (1971) also give such proofs).

2. *The stock function $f(x)$ is continuous and monotonically increasing.*

3. *In a stationary world with bounded harvests stocks are bounded.* If the maximum possible harvest is h_m, then there is a unique number x_m such that

$$x_m = h_m + f(x_m) \qquad (30.6)$$

and for all $x > x_m \, (> h_m)$

$$f(x) < x - h_m.$$

The stock function thus looks as in Fig. 30.1. It follows that if by some unforeseen event supply ever rises above some level x_m, say to x^*, the stock level must

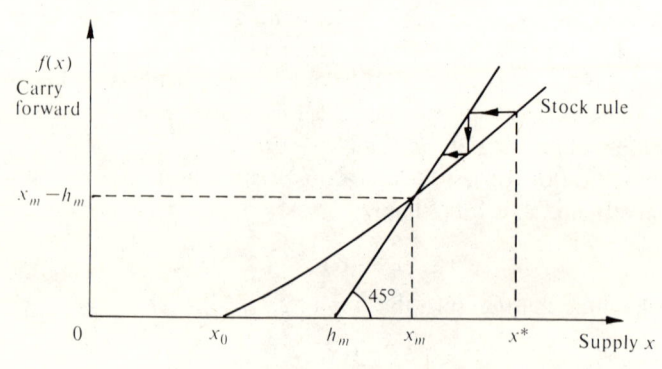

Fig. 30.1 Storage rule

steadily decrease, for even a sequence of bumper harvests h_m will lead to a successive decrease in supply and hence stocks, as shown by the arrowed line in Fig. 30.1.

4. *The buffer stock breaks even on average if marginal storage costs are constant*, and makes a loss if the marginal cost is below the average cost (if, for example, there are overheads). This follows from equation (30.1), where γ is to be interpreted as marginal storage costs.

30.2 Approximate solutions

From now on we shall work with a linear demand schedule to simplify the algebra, although it is entirely feasible, as Gustafson (1958) shows, to work with any non-stochastic schedule. Choose units so that the average harvest is unity and the elasticity of demand at the mean pre-stabilized price $\bar{p}$ is ϵ, so the inverse demand schedule is

$$p = \bar{p}\left\{1 - \frac{1}{\epsilon}(C-1)\right\} \quad E\tilde{h} = 1. \qquad (30.7)$$

Equation (30.4) can now be written

$$\bar{p}(1-\beta)\left(1+\frac{1}{\epsilon}\right) + \gamma \geqslant \frac{\bar{p}}{\epsilon}\{x - f(x) - \beta E[h + f(x) - f\{h + f(x)\}]\} \quad \left.\begin{array}{l}\\\\\end{array}\right\} \text{complementary inequalities}$$

$$x \geqslant x_0.$$

where x_0 is defined by equation (30.5).

Or, rewriting

$$f(x) \begin{cases} = \dfrac{1}{1+\beta}[x - a + \beta Ef\{\tilde{h} + f(x)\}], & x \geqslant x_0 \\ = 0, & x \leqslant x_0. \end{cases} \qquad (30.8)$$

where a is a constant:

$$a \equiv 1 + \epsilon(1 - \beta + \gamma/\bar{p}) \cong 1 + \epsilon c$$

and c is the total annual storage cost including interest, as a fraction of the average price, $\bar{p}$.

There are at least three methods of solving equation (30.8) (or its non-linear counterpart). The first is to choose a time horizon of say five years, specify a zero terminal carry-forward, and solve for the optimum five-year rule. For the parameters appropriate to commodity stockpiling (given in Chapter 20) this is a very close approximation to the stationary solution. Gustafson shows the steps involved; Goreux (1978) has used a similar method. Quite lengthy, but computer programmable, computations are needed. Gardner (1979) provides a reasonably elementary discussion of this approach.

The second is to expand $f(x)$ as a Taylor series in $x - x_0$, and solve by equating coefficients, as in Newbery and Stiglitz (1977, Appendix F). This requires a simple specification of the distribution of h to be algebraically feasible (e.g. a rectangular distribution), but allows several terms to be approximated using a pocket calculator in about twenty minutes (cf. Goreux's calculations cost about $60 of computer time).

The third, and most attractive method, gives only a piecewise linear approximation to the optimum rule, but, provided the variability is not too great, Gustafson has shown that it provides a very good approximation to the optimum rule (and is the natural first approximation to use for calculating the optimum). The technique is to replace the random variable $\hat{h}$ on the right-hand side of equation (30.8) with its expected value, to find the form of $f(x)$, then using this approximation, to calculate x_0 from equation (30.5). Gustafson's calculations show that the general shape of $f(x)$ is approximated quite accurately by this assumption, but its horizontal location does depend on the variability of output. The first step finds the shape, the second locates the position.

The Appendix to this Chapter demonstrates that if the demand schedule is linear, then the approximation to the optimum stock rule, which we shall call $\phi(x)$, is piecewise linear, as shown in Fig. 30.2.

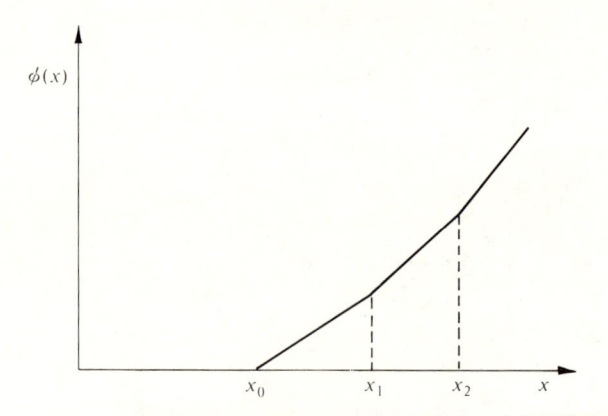

Fig. 30.2 Linear approximation to storage rule

The Appendix also shows how to compute the function $\phi(x)$. As an example of the accuracy of this method, we may use Gustafson's data for US grain for which he has computed the exact solution. His basic case assumes

$\sigma = 10.29\%$ CV of output
$\epsilon = 0.5275$ elasticity at mean price
$\gamma/\bar{p} = 0.064$ storage cost
$\beta = 0.95$ discount factor

This gives a value for a of 1.0603, which can be used as a first approximation to x_0, assuming no variability in output. If it is assumed that output is normally distributed then equation (30.A14) gives a revised estimate of 1.05367. Actually, output is skewed to the left but, nevertheless, the estimate of x_0 is accurate to the fourth decimal place. With the revised estimate of x_0 the storage function is

$$\phi(x) = \begin{cases} 0.5128\,(x - 1.0537), & 1.1713 \geqslant x \geqslant 1.0537 \\ 0.6836\,(x - 1.1713) + 0.0603, & 1.3433 \geqslant x \geqslant 1.1713 \\ 0.7689\,(x - 1.3433) + 0.1779, & 1.5670 \geqslant x \geqslant 1.3433 \\ 0.8200\,(x - 1.5670) + 0.3499 & 1.8398 \geqslant x \geqslant 1.5670 \end{cases}$$

This linearized approximation is accurate to within 1 per cent over the whole range, and yet is remarkably simple to compute.

Gustafson's sensitivity analysis shows that the shape of the function is insensitive to small changes in β, and relatively large changes in c, ϵ, and σ. The location of x_0 is, however, sensitive to c and ϵ, as is to be expected from the definition of $a \cong 1 + \epsilon c$. If the demand schedule has constant elasticity the slope of $f(x)$ is slightly reduced and x_0 lowered; the latter being the more important effect.

The Appendix also shows that in special cases the optimum stock rule is exactly linear over the range $[x_0, x_m]$, where x_m is defined in equation (30.6) and is the maximum supply. For example, if the harvest has a four point distribution $h = 1 \pm u$, $1 \pm 2u$, all equally likely, then if the parameters lie in a suitable range the stock rule is

$$f(x) = \alpha(x - x_0). \tag{30.9}$$

The Appendix shows that equation (30.8) now becomes, for $x \geqslant x_0$

$$(1 + \beta)\alpha(x - x_0) = x - a + \frac{\alpha\beta}{2}\left\{1 + \frac{3u}{2} + \alpha(x - x_0) - x_0\right\}$$

which allows α, x_0 to be solved by equating coefficients:

$$\alpha = \frac{1 + \beta - \sqrt{(1 + \beta^2)}}{\beta}$$

$$x_0 = \frac{a - \dfrac{\alpha\beta}{2}\left(1 + \dfrac{3u}{2}\right)}{1 - \alpha\beta/2}$$

Thus if $a = 1.05$, $\beta = 0.95$, $u = 0.05$ (so $\sigma = 7.9$ per cent) then $\alpha = 0.6$, $x_0 = 1.04$, $x_m = 1.19$.

The effect of the storage rule is to alter the relationship between supply and demand, and hence price, as shown in Fig. 30.3.

The non-linearity in the supply-price relationship occurs at the point at which storage first occurs, and its effect is to more than double the elasticity at x_0. Note that supply is the harvest plus last year's stock, so that the relationship between production and price is now stochastic.

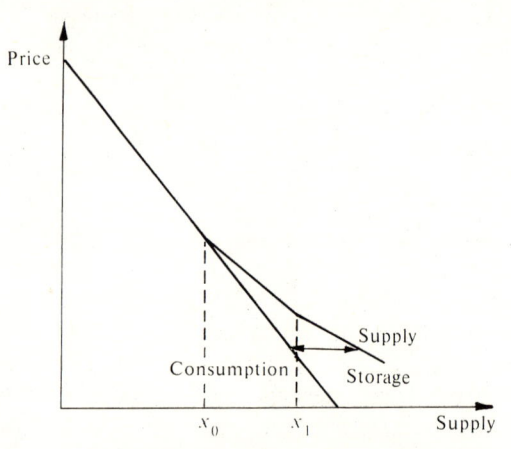

Fig. 30.3 Price as a function of supply

30.2.1 Average stock size

The average stock carried is

$$\bar{S} = Ef(x) = Ef\{h + f(x_{-1})\}. \tag{30.10}$$

Since h and $f(x_{-1})$ are uncorrelated, this can be written as

$$\bar{S} = Ef(h + \bar{S}).$$

The linear approximation $\phi(x)$ and the method of equation (30.A14) then gives for h normally distributed with density function Φ

$$(1+\beta)\bar{S} = \frac{\sigma}{\sqrt{(2\pi)}} \exp\left\{-\tfrac{1}{2}\left(\frac{x_0 - \bar{S} - 1}{\sigma}\right)^2\right\} - (x_0 - \bar{S} - 1)\left\{1 - \Phi\left(\frac{x_0 - \bar{S} - 1}{\sigma}\right)\right\} \tag{30.12}$$

which can be solved numerically by iteration, starting with $\bar{S} = 0$ on the right hand side. For example, using Gustafson's data ($\sigma = 0.103$, $x_0 = 1.054$), then $\bar{S} = 1$ per cent, and average stocks are very low.

If, on the other hand, $\epsilon = 0.5$, $\sigma = 0.2$, $\beta = 0.95$, $\gamma/\bar{p} = 0.03$, $a = 1.04$ (as more representative of tropical commodities), then $x_0 = 1.01$ and $\bar{S} = 5.2$ per cent. (Several iterations of the approximation formulae are required for $\bar{S}$.) The average cost of operating this stock will be 0.4 of 1 per cent of average crop revenue.

30.2.2 The degree of price stabilization

In Fig. 30.3 price is shown as a function of supply, which is equal to the current harvest plus the stock carried forward from last year. Both stocks and the harvest are random variables, and, given the simplifying assumption that the harvest is a stationary random variable, they are independent. (If the area planted depended on the forecast price, stocks would depress this forecast, and reduce the harvest, making stocks and harvests negatively correlated. It is straightforward but tedious to modify the analysis to take account of this supply response). Total supply is thus distributed as the sum of the two independent random variables of harvest and stock, and the effect of the buffer stock policy is to increase average supply by $\bar{S}$. The probability density function of supply will have the same general shape as that of the harvest, except that it will be 'stretched' to the right, though remaining anchored at the same left hand point, Min h. If the stock is small, then the supply distribution can be approximated by $h + \bar{S}$. To see what this might imply, suppose, as a not unreasonable approximation, that $x_0 = 1 + \bar{S}$, then the mean supply will occur at x_0 in Fig. 30.3, and the effect on the price distribution is easily described. The median price will fall from $p(1)$ (the unstabilized mean price, $\bar{p}$, given linear demand) to $p(x_0)$, but the lower half of the price distribution will be contracted by the more elastic gross demand (= consumption plus storage) schedule. The effect is roughly to reduce the SD of this part of the price distribution to a fraction $\beta/1 + \beta$ (considering just the first segment of the approximation $\phi(x)$.) If supplies were normally distributed, then prices will now be distributed approximately as

$$N_+\left(\bar{p}\left\{1 - \frac{\bar{S}}{\epsilon}\right\}, \left(\frac{\bar{p}\sigma}{\epsilon}\right)^2\right) \qquad p \geq \bar{p}(1 - \bar{S}/\epsilon)$$

$$N_-\left(\bar{p}\left\{1 - \frac{\bar{S}}{\epsilon}\right\}, \left(\frac{\bar{p}\beta\sigma}{(1 + \beta)\epsilon}\right)^2\right) \qquad p \leq \bar{p}(1 - \bar{S}/\epsilon).$$

(30.13)

The new mean price will be

$$\bar{p}\left(1 - \frac{\bar{S}}{\epsilon} + \frac{1}{2\epsilon\sqrt{(2\pi)}} \frac{1}{1 + \beta}\right) \sim \bar{p}\left\{1 - \frac{1}{\epsilon}(\bar{S} - 0.1\sigma)\right\} \qquad (30.14)$$

which could be greater or smaller than $\bar{p}$. If $\epsilon = 0.7$, $\sigma = 0.2$, $\beta = 0.95$, $a = 1.0665$, $\bar{S} = 4.1$ per cent, so that $x_0 = 1 + \bar{S} = 1.041$, then average price falls by about 3 per cent. The new variance will be

$$\tfrac{1}{2} \frac{\bar{p}^2 \sigma^2}{\epsilon^2}\left\{1 + \left(\frac{\beta}{1 + \beta}\right)^2\right\}$$

or, for $\beta = 0.95$, just 62 per cent of its original value. (In fact, this underestimates the reduction in variance as the supply-price schedule of Fig. 30.3 becomes progressively more elastic more effectively eliminating extreme low prices. If we take the average slope of $f(x)$ as 0.6 instead of 0.51 then the reduction in variance is 42 per cent.)

30.2.3 *The cost of increased price stability*

One of the key policy questions raised by those mainly interested in *price* instability is the minimum cost of reducing its instability by a given amount. As formulated, our storage rule is optimal for evening out *consumption* instability, but it is interesting to ask what is the cost of a further reduction in price variance. The logical way to achieve this is to subsidize storage (*not* the discount rate, since we wish the optimal intertemporal pattern of stabilization to be retained). If storage costs are reduced to $(1-\tau)\gamma/\bar{p}$, where τ is the proportional subsidy, the effect will be to lower x_0, raise $\bar{S}$, and lower the variance of prices. The new price distribution is as shown in Fig. 30.4.

The left hand (lower) part has been compressed by a factor $\alpha(=\beta/(1+\beta)$, or $1-f'$ for some average slope of the stocking function, $f' = df/dx$). Calculating the variance is slightly more complicated now that $\bar{S}$ and x_0 no longer coincide, but is not difficult. The cost of this extra price stabilization is just the cost of the increase in average stock:

$$\left(r + \frac{\gamma}{\bar{p}}\right)(\bar{S} - S_0).$$

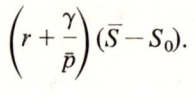

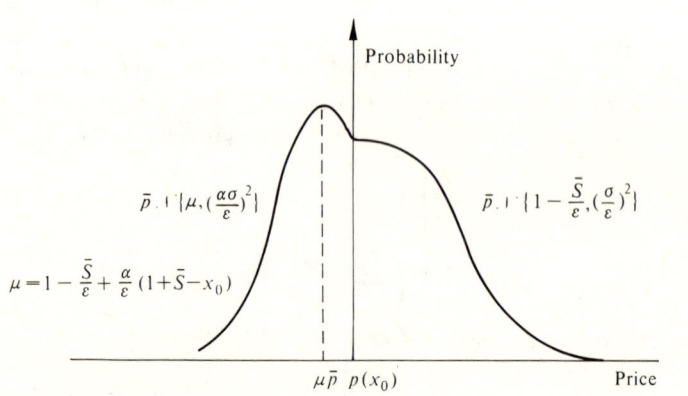

Fig. 30.4 New price distribution

30.3 The benefits of price stabilization

In order to calculate the benefits of price stabilization we need to use dynamic programming arguments, which are set out more fully and justified in Gustafson (1958), Samuelson (1971) or Newbery and Stiglitz (1977, Appendix F). Nevertheless, we can summarize the argument as follows.

The expected present value of stabilization can be written as a function of initial supply, x:

$$J(x) = U\{x - f(x)\} - \gamma f(x) + \beta E J\{\tilde{h} + f(x)\} \qquad (30.15)$$

where $U(C)$ is the total value of consuming C in money units. (This equation defines $J(x)$ recursively, and is the first step in the dynamic programming approach.)

The function $f(x)$ is chosen to maximize $J(x)$, from which it follows by the envelope theorem that at the optimum the value of extra supply is equal to its value in consumption, i.e.

$$\frac{dJ}{dx} = p\{x - f(x)\}, \quad \text{where } p(C) \equiv \frac{dU}{dC}. \tag{30.16}$$

Thus, integrating equation (30.16) gives

$$J(x) = \int_0^x p\{z - f(z)\}dz + K \tag{30.17}$$

for some constant K to be determined. Define

$$W(x) \equiv J(x) - K$$

and observe that for $x < x_0$, so $f(x) = 0$:

$$W(x) = \int_0^x \frac{dU}{dC} \cdot dC = U(x)$$

Substitute the expression for $J(x)$ into equation (30.15) for $x < x_0$:

$$U(x) + K = U(x) + \beta(EW(h) + K)$$

or

$$K = \frac{\beta}{1-\beta} \int_0^\infty \int_0^h p\{z - f(z)\}dz dF(h). \tag{30.18}$$

The present discounted benefit of stabilizing versus not stabilizing is then

$$B = J(x) - U(x) - \frac{\beta}{1-\beta} EU(h). \tag{30.19}$$

Equation (30.19) can be solved once f has been found or approximated. Notice that for $x \leq x_0$ the benefit is independent of x:

$$B = K - \left(\frac{\beta}{1-\beta}\right) EU(h) = B_0 \tag{30.20}$$

and that B increases with initial supply, x. It is thus much more attractive to start a buffer scheme in a year of massive surplus. Gustafson (1958, App. 2) calculates the expected returns for different initial supplies. With the data given above ($\epsilon = 0.5275$, $\sigma = 0.103$, $\gamma/\bar{p} = 6.4$ per cent, $\beta = 0.95$), $B_0/\bar{p} = 20.6$ per cent, or equivalent to a steady annual benefit of 1 per cent. At an initial supply of 120 per cent average harvest this rises to 60 per cent whilst at 142 per cent it reaches 267 per cent, or 13.4 per cent p.a. With $\epsilon = 0.3$, $\gamma/\bar{p} = 2.7$ per cent, $\bar{S} = 9$ per cent, $\sigma = 0.1$, $\beta = 0.98$, $B_0/\bar{p} = 7.6$, or an annual equivalent of 19.3 per cent at initial supply of 120 per cent average harvest. Lowering the costs of storage thus has a dramatic effect on the amount of and benefits from storage. The minimum benefits of the optimal policy, B_0 (starting with zero carry-over from last year) can easily be calculated for the case of linear demand. From equations (30.18) and (30.20)

$$B_0 = \frac{\beta}{1-\beta} \int_0^\infty \int_0^h [p\{z - f(z)\} - p(z)] \, dz \, dF(h)$$

$$= \frac{\beta}{1-\beta} \frac{\bar{p}}{\epsilon} \int_{x_0}^\infty \int_{x_0}^h f(z) \, dz \, dF(h)$$

since the two terms cancel when $f(z) = 0$, i.e. for $z \leq x_0$. In particular, if $f(z)$ is approximated by the piecewise linear function

$$f(z) = \alpha(z - x_0), \quad z \geq x_0$$

then

$$\frac{B_0}{\bar{p}} = \frac{\beta}{1-\beta} \frac{\alpha}{2\epsilon} \int_{x_0}^\infty (h - x_0)^2 \, dF(h). \quad (30.21)$$

This is readily evaluated once the probability density function is specified. Then if h is normal, this can be evaluated with equations similar to (30.A14). Thus for $\sigma = 0.2$, $\epsilon = 0.6$, $\gamma/\bar{p} = 1.7$ per cent, $\beta = 0.95$, $x_0 = 1.01$ (our representative primary commodity) the minimum present discounted benefits are 21 per cent of mean expenditure, equivalent to an annual benefit of 1 per cent.

30.4 The bias in the competitive stock rule

The competitive stock rule is optimal if we ignore risk benefits and the distribution of income. Now it could be argued that the distribution of income should be ignored, since price stabilization is likely to be an inefficient method of influencing it, but in international negotiations alternative more efficient methods may not be available. We therefore ask, under the competitive stock rule, would producers benefit from an increase in price stabilization (achieved, for example, by a subsidy on storage costs). The methods of Chapter 18 can be employed, once the form of the optimal rule has been found; except that we now have to take account of dynamic considerations, in particular, discounting future benefits. For example, consider the effect of storing an extra δQ units at date 0 when price is low and the harvest high to the following year, date 1, where the harvest is lower and price higher. The effect on expected present discounted profits is, from equation (18.1)

$$\delta Y = \Delta = \left\{ \frac{p_0 Q_0^s}{\epsilon_0 Q_0^c} - \beta E\left(\frac{p_1 Q_1^s}{\epsilon_1 Q_1^c}\right) \right\} \delta Q \quad (30.22)$$

Optimal Commodity Stockpiling Rules   431

(To preserve a logical time sequence, the low price state 2 of Chapter 17 has been replaced by date 0, since the transfer is from the present to the future.) If the amount of storage in the competitive equilibrium was small, and if the elasticity of the consumer demand schedule is constant, and if the optimum stock rule can be approximated as

$$f(x) = \alpha(x - x_0), \quad x \geqslant x_0,$$

then

$$Q_1^s \sim Q_1^c; \quad Q_0^c \sim (1-\alpha)Q_0^s + \alpha x_0,$$

$$p_0 + \gamma = \beta E p_1$$

and

$$\beta E \left(\frac{p_1 Q_1^s}{\epsilon Q_1^c} \right) \simeq \frac{\beta E p_1}{\epsilon}$$

so, substituting these in equation (30.22) gives

$$\delta Y \simeq \frac{p_0}{\epsilon} \left\{ \frac{2\alpha(Q_0^s - x_0)}{Q_0^c} - \frac{\gamma}{p_0} \right\} \delta Q.$$

The first term is twice the ratio of the amount stored to current consumption, and if this is small relative to storage costs then producers would lose from further stabilization, just as the effect of introducing a small amount of stabilization into an unstabilized market is to lower undiscounted producer's profits, as shown in Chapter 18.

A similar argument shows that producers benefit from increased storage if the demand schedule is linear; in this case the transfer benefits are

$$\delta Y = \frac{\bar{p}}{\epsilon \bar{Q}} \left\{ Q_0^s - \beta E Q_1^s \right\} \delta Q$$

where ϵ is the elasticity at the (unstabilized) mean price, $\bar{p}$. Since Q_0^s must be greater than x_0 for current storage to take place, and since $x_0 = a$ is greater than $\beta \bar{Q}$ (from equations (30.A3) and (30.A4)) this expression is unambiguously positive. If, therefore, producers are thought to be more deserving than consumers, then (ignoring risk aversion for the moment) there is a case for increasing storage beyond the competitive level, perhaps by subsidizing storage costs.

The risk benefits are easier to handle, since income risk is reduced if $\epsilon < 1$ and risk is on the supply side. Consumer risks can usually be ignored, since the marginal utility of consumers' income is typically insensitive to price fluctuations, except for major foodstuffs near subsistence levels. For such commodities there is an additional argument for providing a 'famine reserve', or food stocks over and above the competitive level.

We can thus summarize these findings as follows, assuming that the social weight on producers' income exceeds that on consumers.

(i) With constant linear demand, inelastic over the relevant range, competitive price stabilization should be subsidized or supplemented.

(ii) With constant elastic consumer demand of elasticity $\epsilon \geq 1$, it may be desirable to reduce competitive price stabilization if storage costs are high.

The determination of the optimal degree of intervention can be found by calculating the increased cost of further subsidization and the increased benefit in reduced producer income risk and increased transfers (weighted by the difference in producer and consumer weights).

30.4.1 Extensions

It is feasible, though computationally more demanding, to allow for supply responses, serial correlation in output, demand variabilities, and more complex storage costs and constraints (e.g. in maximum storage capacity). Gustafson discusses these and other extensions, including the practically important one of the optimum location of storage with costly transport.

30.4.2 Comparisons with alternative stocking rules

Once the alternative stocking rule has been specified its stochastic consequences can be evaluated and compared with the present value of the optimum rule. It is important in this comparison to compare like with like by starting each at the same initial stock. As an example, consider the four point probability distribution for which the band width rule is readily calculated. If the harvest can take values $1 \pm u$, $1 \pm 2u$ with equal probability, and if the social welfare function is

$$U(C) = \left(1 + \frac{1}{\epsilon}\right)C - \frac{1}{2\epsilon}C^2, \quad EC = 1,$$

the demand schedule will be linear, with $\bar{p} = 1$. If the parameters take values $\epsilon = 0.5$, $u = 0.15$ (so that the CV output is 23.7 per cent, and of price is 47.43 per cent), β (the discount factor) $= 0.95$, $c = 1 - \beta + \gamma/\bar{p} = 0.1$ (the annual storage cost) then $x_0 \simeq 0.98$ and the linear approximation to the optimum stocking rule derived in the Appendix is

$$f(x) = 0.6(x - 0.98) \quad x \geq 0.98.$$

(Unfortunately the parameters do not satisfy the restrictions for this to be the exact solution, but it is a close approximation). The average optimum stock $\bar{S}$, is about 11 per cent of the average harvest, and the present value of the optimum stock starting in a year of below average harvest (and zero stock) is from equation (30.21)

$$\frac{B_0}{\bar{p}} = 0.3742$$

equivalent to 1.9 per cent p.a. If the price were to be costlessly and perfectly stabilized from next year the annual equivalent benefit would be 5.34 per cent, so that the optimum role achieves 36 per cent of such costless gains. (The average annual storage cost under the optimum rule is itself about 1.1 per cent so that the gross benefits ignoring storage costs are 56 per cent of the gross benefits of perfect stabilization. Clearly it is very misleading to ignore storage costs.)

Now compare this with the bandwidth rule in which the stock is increased by u units of output in bumper years ($h = 1 + 2u$) and drawn down by u units in famine years ($h = 1 - 2u$). If we calculate the optimum maximal size of the stockpile using the methods of Chapter 29, restricting attention to integral numbers of the u units, we find that the optimal maximal size is $K = 1$ unit of storage, i.e. u units of output, so the average stock is

$$\bar{S}_b = \tfrac{1}{2}u = 7\tfrac{1}{2} \text{ per cent of annual supply.}$$

The net gains in steady state are readily calculated as

$$G = \frac{1}{2\epsilon}(\tfrac{3}{4}u^2) - \tfrac{1}{2}cu = 0.94 \text{ per cent p.a.}$$

There is a 50 per cent chance of reaching steady state in each successive year, starting from zero stock, and the effect of this is to lower the present equivalent annual gain to 0.87 of 1 per cent or 46 per cent of those achievable by the optimum rule. Gustafson has also compared his optimum rule with various alternatives, and finds even more dramatic examples of the inefficiencies of typical popular rules. (Note that we compared our rule with the *best* bandwidth rule — if the bandwidth rule were chosen with other criteria in mind it could typically be considerably more costly to operate.)

30.5 Conclusions

This chapter had two objectives. The first was to outline some simple procedures by which (approximations) to the optimal buffer stock rule could be derived. The second was to use these techniques to say something about the nature of the optimal buffer stock, both its form and consequences.

For reasonable values of the parameters, it appears that the optimal buffer stock can be characterized by an (approximately) piecewise linear function: no storage when the stock carried over plus the harvest is below a critical number, with a constant fraction of the excess over this critical amount being placed into storage. Very roughly the optimal storage rule is to carry forward slightly more than one-half of the excess of initial supply (including stocks on band) over some critical level, itself slightly greater than the average harvest. The exact form can be found by a sequence of successively more accurate iterations starting from such an approximation. It also appears that the critical value is sufficiently high that the average amount to be placed into storage is relatively small. The net gains from the optimal storage scheme, though small, are significantly greater than those obtained from the alternative storage policies (e.g. maintaining prices within a band width) often proposed. It should be observed, however, that the optimal buffer stock scheme leaves considerable remaining price variability.

One of the important results of this chapter was to show that the results of our earlier non-dynamic analysis can be extended to an explicitly dynamic context. We show, in particular, that with risk-neutral speculators, the amount of storage will not be socially optimal, in the absence of perfect risk markets. The exact nature of the bias, as in our earlier discussions, depends critically on properties of consumers' demand functions.

This chapter thus lays the foundation of the general dynamic-stochastic theory of optimal governmental intervention in agricultural markets.

Appendix. Derivation of approximate stock rule

Gustafson (1958) found that the optimal stock rule, $f(x)$, had a form which was relatively insensitive to the various parameters and, in particular, to the degree of harvest variability. Different coefficients of variation of harvest essentially displaced the function horizontally. He therefore suggested a short cut for obtaining an approximate solution — first calculate an approximate function $\phi(x)$ assuming no variability in harvest, and then use this approximation to estimate an accurate value of x_0 using equation (30.5). If the demand schedule is linear, then the approximation can be shown to be piecewise linear. To see this, note that the approximate function must satisfy equation (30.8) with the size of the harvest replaced by its expected value, so $h = 1$:

$$\phi(x) = \frac{1}{1+\beta}[x - a + \beta\phi\{1 + \phi(x)\}], \quad x \geqslant x_0, \tag{30.A1}$$
$$= 0, \quad x \leqslant x_0.$$

Piecewise linearity follows by observing that a piecewise linear function of a piecewise linear function is also piecewise linear, hence both sides of equation (30.A1) are piecewise linear. The only remaining problem is to find the values of x, x_i, at which the kinks occur, as shown in Fig. 30.A1.

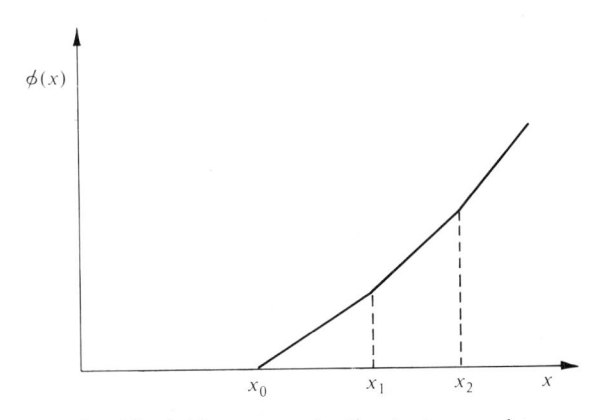

Fig. 30.A1 Linear approximation to storage rule

Let $\phi_i(x)$ be the linear segment between x_{i-1} and x_i, and let its slope be α_i, so that

$$\phi_i = \alpha_i(x - x_{i-1}) + \phi_{i-1}(x_{i-1}). \tag{30.A2}$$

The value of x_0 is by definition the value for which $\phi(x) = 0$:

$$0 = \frac{1}{1+\beta}\{x_0 - a + \beta\phi(1)\}$$

or
$$x_0 = a - \beta\phi(1), \quad a \equiv 1 + \epsilon(1 - \beta + \gamma/\bar{p}). \tag{30.A3}$$

The obvious solution is $x_0 = a > 1$, in which case $\phi(1) = 0$ as required. It is easy but tedious to show that there is no solution with $x_0 < 1$. The first segment can thus be written

$$\phi_1(x) = \alpha_1(x - x_0), \quad \alpha_1 = \frac{1}{1+\beta}, \quad x_0 = a. \tag{30.A4}$$

Define x_1 to be the point at which

$$x_0 = 1 + \phi_1(x_1) \tag{30.A5}$$

so that for x in the range $[x_0, x_1]$

$$\phi\{1 + \phi(x)\} = 0.$$

Substitute (30.A4) into (30.A5)

$$\alpha_1 x_1 = (1 + \alpha_1)x_0 - 1$$

so

$$x_1 = (2 + \beta)x_0 - (1 + \beta). \tag{30.A6}$$

The point x_2 is likewise defined to be the point at which

$$1 + \phi_2(x_2) = x_1 \tag{30.A7}$$

where, over the interval $[x_1, x_2]$ from (30.A2)

$$\phi(x) = \phi_2(x) = \alpha_2(x - x_1) + \alpha_1(x_1 - x_0).$$

But, from (30.A1), on this interval, since $1 + \phi_2(x) - x_0 < x_1$,

$$(1 + \beta)\phi_2(x - a + \beta\phi_1\{1 + \phi_2(x)\}$$

so, using (30.A4)

$$\{1 + \beta(1 - \alpha_1)\}\phi_2(x) = x - a + \alpha_1\beta(1 - x_0).$$

Hence

$$\alpha_2 = \{1 + \beta(1 - \alpha_1)\}^{-1} = \frac{1 - \beta^2}{1 - \beta^3}. \tag{30.A8}$$

Successive segments can be found from equation (30.A1)

$$(1 + \beta)\phi_i(x) = x - a + \beta\phi_{i-1}\{1 + \phi_i(x)\} \tag{30.A9}$$

which, together with (30.A2) gives

$$\{1 + \beta(1 - \alpha_{i-1})\}\phi_i(x) = x - a + \beta\alpha_{i-1}(1 - x_{i-2}) + \beta\phi_{i-2}(x_{i-2}) \tag{30.A10}$$

whence

$$\alpha_i = \{1 + \beta(1 - \alpha_{i-1})\}^{-1} = \frac{1 - \beta^i}{1 - \beta^{i+1}}. \tag{30.A11}$$

The values of x_i are found from the equation

$$1 + \phi_i(x_i) = x_{i-1} \tag{30.A12}$$

which, with (30.A2) gives

$$x_i - x_{i-1} = \frac{1}{\alpha_i}(x_{i-1} - x_{i-2}) = \frac{1-\beta^{i+1}}{1-\beta}(a-1). \tag{30.A13}$$

These equations define successive segments and hence build up the linear approximation $\phi(x)$. The second step is to calculate x_0 more accurately as the solution to

$$x_0 = a - \beta E \phi(h)$$

$$\cong a - \frac{\beta}{1+\beta} \int_a^{h_m} (h-a) dF(h) \tag{30.A14}$$

where $F(h)$ is the distribution function of h, and f has been approximated by the first line segment, ϕ_1. (If, as in Gustafson, dF is specified numerically, then f can be specified by the piecewise linear approximation.) Notice that the expectation is taken only over the non-negative values of $\phi(h)$. For example, if h is normally distributed as $N(1, \sigma^2)$ then the second term of equation (30.A13) is approximately

$$\psi(a) = \frac{\beta}{1+\beta}\left[\frac{\sigma}{\sqrt{(2\pi)}} \exp\left\{-\tfrac{1}{2}\left(\frac{a-1}{\sigma}\right)^2\right\} - (a-1)\left\{1 - \Phi\left(\frac{a-1}{\sigma}\right)\right\}\right] \tag{30.A14}$$

so

$$x_0 = a - \psi(a)$$

where ϕ is the normal distribution function for $N(0, 1)$.

Optimum Linear Rules

Under what conditions will the stock rule be linear over the interval $I = [x_0, x_m]$ where x_m is the maximum supply, given by equation (30.A6)?

Suppose that

$$f(x) = \alpha(x - x_0), \quad x_0 \leq x \leq x_m \equiv I.$$

In this case equation (30.A8) reduces to

$$(1+\beta)f(x) = x - a + \beta E f\{\bar{h} + \alpha(x-x_0)\} \quad \text{on } I$$

Define

$$\text{Prob}\{\bar{h} \geq x_0 - \alpha(x-x_0)\} = \pi(x)$$

$$E\bar{h}|\bar{h} \geq x_0 - \alpha(x-x_0) = \hat{h}(x)$$

then

$$(1 + \beta)f(x) = x - a + \alpha\beta\pi(x)\{\hat{h}(x) + \alpha(x - x_0) - x_0\} \quad \text{on } I.$$

The stock rule can only be linear if $\pi(x)$ is independent of x on I, and $\hat{h}(x)$ is constant or linear in x. This is equivalent to requiring

$$\text{Prob}\{\tilde{h} \mid (1 + \alpha)x_0 - \alpha x_m \leq \tilde{h} \leq x_0\} = 0. \qquad (30.\text{A}15)$$

This will be satisfied for the uniform discrete four point distribution $1 \pm u$, $1 \pm 2u$, if

$$\pi(x) = \tfrac{1}{2}, \quad \hat{h} = 1 + \frac{3u}{2},$$

and, from equation (30.A6)

$$x_m = \frac{1 + 2u - \alpha x_0}{1 - \alpha}$$

Condition (30.A15) will be satisfied if

$$1 - u < (1 + \alpha)x_0 - \alpha x_m < x_0 < 1 + u.$$

If $a = 1.05$, $\beta = 0.95$, $u = 0.05$, then $\alpha = 0.6$, $x_0 = 1.04$, $x_m = 1.19$ and all the conditions are satisfied.

Chapter 31

Epilogue

The analysis of any important and interesting policy question in economics is complex. This is almost a matter of definition, for were it simple, the effects of the policy could easily be analysed, and the problem would (at least from the analytical economist's perspective) not be interesting. Implicitly or explicitly, in evaluating any important policy, such as a commodity stabilization scheme, policy-makers must use a model – the model is often not articulated, but it is there none the less. The role of the economic theorist is to help bring out into the open the hidden assumptions and to detect errors in logic which all too often creep into this kind of analysis. In doing this, theorists are all too often accused, on the one hand, of oversimplifying what is really a complex matter, and on the other, of introducing unnecessary and irrelevant complications. It is a fine line that we must tread. We suspect that both accusations may be made against our earlier analysis. We have greatly simplified; but any theory must simplify, must represent an abstraction from reality if it is to offer insight.

Of course, whether a commodity stabilization scheme be adopted or not depends not only on economic but on political considerations. Nevertheless, the economic consequences must form a central part of any discussion of such proposals, and we believe that the distinctions we have drawn are essential for any meaningful assessment of these economic consequences:

1. We have argued that one needs to distinguish between *pure* stabilization schemes, in which there are no output restrictions, and proposals which involve the producing nations acting collusively to raise the average price. We suspect that much of the popularity of stabilization schemes among producing nations arises not from the reduction in risk but from the cartel prices which they hope will thereby be generated. When the maintenance of this cartel requires the co-operation of the consuming nations, as it often does, the consuming nations need to ask themselves whether this is the appropriate form in which to make transfers to developing countries.

2. We have argued that one needs to be careful in distinguishing between transfer effects and efficiency gains from any pure price stabilization scheme. We have argued that, in the short run, there is a presumption that the transfer effects will be deleterious to the producing nations. Average expenditure by consuming nations, under reasonable hypotheses concerning the shape of demand curves and the nature of the supply disturbances, will be reduced by a pure stabilization scheme.

The principal efficiency gains, in turn, are divided into two kinds: the gains from risk reduction (variability in the marginal utility of consumption of the producers) and the gains from intertemporal arbitrage (variability in the marginal utility of the good to consumers).

Producers are not directly concerned with price variability but rather with consumption variability. This may actually be increased by a commodity price stabilization programme and, in any case, there are likely to be more effective methods of directly treating consumption variability. Moreover, consumption variability may be less of a problem than it seems at first sight, because of the variety of methods by which risk is reduced, transferred, and shared.

The gains from intertemporal arbitrage could be significant and it is important to note that while the other gains and losses depend sensitively on the detailed specification of the relevant functions, the arbitrage gains appear to be less sensitive, and hence can be estimated more reliably. On the other hand, the gains from arbitrage need to be offset against the costs of storage. When reasonable estimates of the latter are employed, the optimal amount of storage (stabilization) appears to be rather small. We shall return to this later.

3. We have distinguished between the effects of partial and total stabilization schemes. The distinction is important because the benefits and costs of a partial stabilization scheme are not just equal to a fraction of those of total stabilization. The relationships are not only non-linear, but the qualitative effects (e.g. whether producers are better off or worse off) may also differ. Since total stabilization is not feasible, it will only be possible to achieve partial stabilization, and it will be inappropriate to justify price stabilization by referring to the results of a model which only analyses complete stabilization.

4. We have distinguished between the short-run and the long-run impact of price stabilization schemes. In the long run, there are likely to be a variety of responses of producers to the change in the price distribution resulting from price stabilization. To predict these long-run effects requires more detailed information about the form of demand functions, utility functions, and production functions than the kind of information required to predict the short-run effects (just as the kind of information required to predict the transfer effects is more detailed than the kind required to predict the arbitrage effect).

5. We have distinguished between the partial equilibrium and general equilibrium impact. The effects of price variability (and therefore the effects of price stabilization) are felt not only by the producers of the commodities concerned, but, as we have repeatedly emphasized, the risks may be shared (e.g. by sharecropping, or with futures markets), and shifted forward (to consumers), and backwards (to producers of commodities purchased by the farmers). As a result, the beneficiaries of commodity price stabilization may not be restricted to those directly in the sector itself. Our calculations suggest that although the benefits may thus be more diffuse, the aggregate magnitude may be less than if the risk were borne within the sector alone, provided that wages and prices are reasonably flexible. If they are not, there may be important macroeconomic benefits from stabilization, and the partial equilibrium analysis may understate the total benefits.

6. We have distinguished between the microeconomic benefits and the macroeconomic benefits. Many programmes which would, for instance, reduce the balance-of-payments difficulties of producing countries may have little impact on the producers within those countries; some programmes which would reduce the risk faced by producers might exacerbate the macroeconomic problems by increasing the variability in government deficits.

Our judgement is that programmes (like extended IMF credits) aimed at reducing the problems of fluctuations in balance of payments arising from unstable commodity prices will have little effect on the producers, unless they are directly linked to domestic programmes, aimed at stabilizing incomes (prices) of the producers themselves. Moreover, for most (but not all) countries there is sufficient diversity in exports that the elimination of fluctuations in export earnings arising from one crop alone would have minimal effects. Thus, whether there should be an improved international credit market is essentially a question which we believe should be assessed on its own merits and not related directly to the fluctuations in prices of agricultural commodities.

At the same time, our analysis does suggest that there are some significant macroeconomic benefits that might be derived from price (or income) stabilization in the presence of wage and price rigidities in other parts of the economy.

7. Finally, we have emphasized the dynamic and stochastic nature of any buffer stock stabilization schemes, and argued that most simple rules for stabilizing prices are very inefficient methods of improving welfare and very costly methods of achieving price stability. We argue that a more constructive approach is to ask first what the competitive stocking policy would be, and then enquire whether this generates too much or too little stabilization, using the techniques developed earlier for the study of partial stabilization schemes. As a rough approximation, the optimum buffer stock rule places one-half of the excess of total supply (harvest plus stocks on hand) over some critical level into store. This rule is quite different from the normal rule of attempting to keep prices within a pre-set band width, and is quite effective at reducing fluctuations at very modest cost. Moreover, with constant storage costs, the competitive rule breaks even on average, though increased stabilization will require subsidy.

Of course, this is not an exhaustive summary of the issues discussed in the book, nor would there be much point in repeating the distinctions we drew in Chpater 2 or the summary of results set out in Chapter 3, both of which might repay re-reading at this point. While we believe that our models and analysis are well designed to bring out the importance of these distinctions we must plead guilty to oversimplifying in three important respects: almost all of our analysis has assumed that the information (beliefs) of the producers is given, or changes, in response to a commodity price stabilization programme, so that eventually expectations are rational, i.e. the beliefs about the price distribution and its correlation with output correspond to the empirical distribution. We have ignored, in other words, the dynamics of adjustment and the benefits that might accrue in improved resource allocation from the greater ease of forecasting correct prices if prices were less volatile. (Many of those benefits, we have argued, might be more easily obtained by other methods.) This is not to say that we have not discussed these issues in some detail (in Chapters 10, 11, and 16), merely that we are unable to quantify their importance except in very simple models.

Second, we have not discussed in sufficient detail the structure of the optimal buffer stock programme taking into account (a) the effects of price variability on the income variability and hence the costs of risk on producers; and (b) the interaction between speculative activity and the design of the buffer stock scheme, although we show qualitatively how these factors will influence the design of the scheme.

Third, we have not discussed in detail the difficulties likely to be associated with determining *empirically* the relevant parameters (production functions, stochastic disturbances, demand functions) required for the design of a commodity price stabilization programme and the rules by which the policy of the stabilization authority might be revised as additional information about the structure of the economy (or about changes in the structure of the economy) became available. These difficulties are real, for if not properly designed, a buffer stock scheme could well prove extremely costly, with the benefits accruing to speculators who can perceive the defects in its design and producers actually being made worse off. This problem is particularly acute for buffer stocks attempting to stabilize prices within a fixed band width.

Although we have greatly simplified, we are equally afraid that our analysis will be said to be overly complicated. There are two reasons for this.

First, there will be those who will look upon our study as a typical theorist's study, showing that 'anything can happen' — welfare of producers could increase or it could decrease, output could increase or it could decrease, consumers might be better off or they might be worse off, etc. How, out of the myriad of possibilities, is the policy economist to know what it is reasonable to expect? Is it reasonable to assume, since output could go up or down, that it remains unchanged? Do we know any more than we did before undertaking the study, when we didn't know what would happen, to be told that anything could happen? Surely, all of this is the result of the theorist's penchant for making basic economics unnecessarily complicated? What is wrong with the simple view that if risk reduction is good, it improves the welfare of producers and raises the certainty equivalent return to farming. They therefore produce a little more. Their increase in production lowers prices and reduces the gains from risk reduction but does not eliminate them.

As much as we would have liked to have been able to say that this simple story is valid with all reasonable assumptions concerning the behaviour of farmers, we cannot. If, for instance, farmers are very risk averse, they may work very hard to be sure that their income, in their worst possible situation (when prices are the lowest) is sufficient for subsistence; a reduction in the variability of prices will, therefore, lead to a reduction in work effort. Thus, under conditions which may be quite normal in LDCs, a reduction in risk may led to either an increase or a decrease in output. Similarly, the possibility that risk reduction in the long run leads to a reduction in welfare is not necessarily a perversity; it can happen with quite reasonable utility and production functions. Our analysis has attempted to provide conditions under which different patterns of effects may be expected to follow.

In some contexts, this analysis might enable one to predict the effects of a particular price stabilization programme. There may be other situations, however, where the effects may be ambiguous. It seems to us important that the policy-maker be aware of this ambiguity; that he should not rely on overly simple (and incorrect) models to predict the benefits and costs of such a programme; and that he should realize that, with the present state of knowledge, there is a range of responses that might result.

This also suggests that an experimental approach might prove useful. It is already recognized that where the success of a programme depends sensitively on the magnitude of some imprecisely known response, it may be desirable to monitor a pilot programme, as has been done for studying the supply response to a negative income tax. The costs of such an experiment are likely to be significantly lower than the costs of a full-scale programme, and the experiments might not only provide information about whether it was worth while to have a price stabilization programme, but also provide information about the relative merits of different programmes or alternative rules for operating a commodity price stabilization scheme. The government could, for example, guarantee the price to all the farmers in a randomly selected district and observe their supply reponse (at different levels of prices). It could offer to buy their crop at the beginning of the production period at whatever price was then prevailing on the futures market. Although such experiments would not enable us to know for sure the general equilibrium effects of these alternative programmes, by assessing the supply responses of the producers we would be able to obtain a far better prediction of these effects than is available at present. At a minimum, it seems to us before any large commitment of resources is made to a commodity price stabilization scheme there should be some experimentation of the kind described above.

Second, there will be those who will agree with our analysis concerning the complexity of the patterns of response, but say it is all irrelevant: it only shows the futility of attempts by the government to interfere with the market. The great advantage of the market mechanism is that no one needs to make the complicated calculations we have engaged in in this book. These economists argue that the basic economics of commodity price stabilization is simply this: if it were socially profitable to engage in commodity price stabilization, then it would be privately profitable to do so, and, to the extent that it is privately profitable, it is already done. We hope our analysis has cast some light on the validity of this widespread view: the assumptions required for establishing the optimality of the market equilibrium – the existence of perfect information and complete risk markets – simply are not satisfied. The market does not even attain a constrained optimum, constrained that is, by the absence of the appropriate insurance markets and the absence of perfect information. The directions of bias in the market allocation and the appropriate remedies for the inefficiencies can be calculated, but require the same, currently imprecisely known, empirical estimates needed for the design of stabilization schemes.

Although we find this argument for not intervening in the market allocation of resources far from persuasive, our analysis has suggested that the conclusion may not be far from correct: our back-of-the-envelope calculations suggest that the optimal buffer stock is very small; indeed sufficiently small that it is not obvious that the amount of stabilization presently being provided is significantly below the optimal level.

Moreover, the traditional competitive market argument against commodity price stabilization, though incorrect, does serve to remind us that any government stabilization scheme must take account of the fact that the private sector is already engaged in arbitrage and storage activities. Consequently, attempts at further stabilization may not significantly increase the total amount of storage, but may simply transfer the locus of the storage from private to public hands. Moreover, most of the proposed rules for running buffer stock schemes seem vulnerable to speculative attack.

Although the private market does not provide perfect insurance against the risks associated with price and output variability in agriculture, there are a number of ways in which the risks are reduced, shared, and transferred, so that the social cost of imperfect risk markets may not be as great as it might seem at first sight. This implies that the gains from risk reduction from a commodity price stabilization scheme are likely to be smaller than might at first seem to be the case. In this book, we have explored a number of these mechanisms; and although we have not been able to quantify the extent to which they serve as a substitute for price stabilization (except in one case, to be noted below), we are convinced that they reduce considerably the magnitude of social gains which might result from the reduction of risks provided by a commodity price stabilization scheme.

There are two markets which are *potentially* particularly effective in reducing the costs of risks – futures markets and credit markets. We are not convinced that, within most LDCs, the potential of these markets is as yet fully realized; even in the more developed countries, the minimal size of units in which trade occurs on the futures markets is so large that small farmers may not be able to avail themselves of it although, as we point out, merchants may intermediate by buying forward from farmers and hedging the risks on the futures markets. Our analysis suggests that futures markets are not only a good substitute for price stabilization; they in fact are likely to be superior to it, since they allow the individual to *choose* the amount of stabilization he wants. If quantities are variable, and there is no output insurance, then if price and quantities are negatively correlated, he will not choose to sell all of his expected output on the futures market; but he would be effectively forced to do this under a price stabilization scheme. To the extent that futures markets can be made more accessible to potential participants, this would therefore seem desirable. It may be desirable to establish futures markets for crops currently not covered in some countries, and it may also be desirable for governments to promote more distant futures markets.

Improvements in the futures markets would also have some of the other information benefits associated with price stabilization: by knowing at what price they could sell their output, producers will be able to make better resource-allocation decisions.

Credit markets allow the transfer of income from dates when it is less valuable (where the marginal utility of income is low) to dates when it is more valuable (the marginal utility of income is high). This means that the variability in consumption may be much less than the variability in income, and hence the social loss from variable prices will be much smaller.

Although the improvement of rural credit markets would, like the improvement of futures markets, have benefits in addition to those directly related to risk reduction, we are less sanguine about the possibility of improving these in a significant way. The problems of imperfect information, adverse selection, and moral hazard, which seem to account for the limitations on rural credit markets, are not easily overcome.

In short, although the market does not necessarily provide an efficient allocation of resources, we believe that the gains to be had from a commodity price stabilization programme are likely to be small, and that most of the benefits in risk reduction may be had by improving the workings of the market, for example, by making futures markets more readily accessible (directly or indirectly) to small producers. This is not to say that a commodity programme will have little extra effect compared with improving the working of the market, for it may have quite different distributional consequences, but it does say that commodity programmes are likely to be a relatively expensive way of improving efficiency.

References

We have not attempted to provide a comprehensive bibliography on commodity price stabilization, for which the interested reader is referred to Turnovsky (1978). Stein and Smith (1977) survey the analysis of buffer stocks, Wilson (1977) surveys the macroeconomic aspects, Peck (1977) and Goss and Yamey (1976) provide reprints of articles on futures markets, while Adams and Klein (1978) present the papers given at a recent conference on price stabilization.

Adams, F. G. and Klein, S. A. (1978) *Stabilising World Commodity Markets*, Lexington, Heath-Lexington.

Aitcheson, J. and Brown, J. A. C. (1957) *The Lognormal Distribution*, Cambridge, England, Cambridge University Press.

Anderson, J. R. (1979) 'Perspective on Models of Uncertain Decisions', Ch. 3 of Roumasset *et al.* (1979).

Arrow, K. J. (1951) 'An Extension of the Basic Theorems of Classical Welfare Economics', in J. Neyman (ed.), *Proceedings of the Second Berkeley Symposium on Mathematical Statistics and Probability*, Berkeley, University of California Press, 507–32.

Arrow, K. J. (1953) 'Le Role des Valeurs Boursières pour la Répartition la Meilleure des Risques', *Centre National de la Recherche Scientifique*, Paris, translated as 'The Role of Securities in the Optimal Allocation of Risk-Bearing', *Review of Economic Studies*, 31 (April 1964), 91–6.

Arrow, K. J. (1965) *Aspects of the Theory of Risk-Bearing*, Helsinki, Academic Bookstore, reprinted in Arrow (1970).

Arrow, K. J. (1970) *Essays in the Theory of Risk Bearing*, Amsterdam, North-Holland.

Atkinson, A. B. and Stiglitz, J. E. (1980) *Lectures on Public Economics*, New York, McGraw-Hill.

Behrman, J. R. (1977) *International Commodity Agreements*, Overseas Development Council, Washington D.C. See also Behrman (1978).

Behrman, J. R. (1978) 'International Commodity Agreements: An Evaluation of the UNCTAD Integrated Programme for Commodities', Ch. 16 in Adams and Klein (1978).

Binswanger, H. P. (1978a) 'Attitudes towards Risk: Experimental Measurement Evidence in Rural India', *American Journal of Agricultural Economics*, 62, No. 3, Aug. 1980, 395–407.

Binswanger, H. P. (1978b) 'Attitudes towards Risk: Implications and Psychological Theories of an Experiment in Rural India', New Haven, Yale Growth Center DP 286.

Boadway, R. W. (1974) 'The Welfare Foundations of Cost–Benefit Analysis', *Economic Journal*, 84 (Dec.), 926–39.

Borch, K. (1968) *The Economics of Uncertainty*, Princeton, Princeton University Press.

Bray, M. (1979) 'Futures Trading, Rational Expectations and the Efficient Markets Hypothesis', Research Paper 516, Stanford, Graduate School of Business.

Cass, D. and Stiglitz, J. E. (1970) 'The Structure of Investor Preferences and

Asset Returns and Separability in Portfolio Allocation: A Contribution to the Pure Theory of Mutual Funds', *Journal of Economic Theory*, 2, 122–60.

Coase, R. H. and Fowler, R. F. (1937) 'The Pig Cycle in Great Britain', *Economica*, 4 (NS), 55–82.

Cooper, R. N. and Lawrence, R. Z. (1975) 'The 1972–75 Commodity Boom', *Brookings Papers on Economic Activity*, 3, 671–715.

Danin, Y., Sumner, D., and Johnson, D. Gale (1975) 'Determination of Optimal Grain Carryovers', Paper 74.12, Chicago, University of Chicago Office of Agricultural Economics Research.

Dasgupta, P. and Stiglitz, J. E. (1977) 'Tariffs vs Quotas as Revenue Raising Devices under Uncertainty', *American Economic Review*, 67, 975–81.

Davidson, J. E., Hendry, D. F., Srba, F., and Yeo, S. (1978) 'Econometric Modelling of the Aggregate Time Series Relationship Between Consumers' Expenditure and Income in the United Kingdom', *Economic Journal* 88 (Dec.), 661–92.

Debreu, G. (1959) *Theory of Value*, New York, Wiley.

Diamond, P. (1967) 'The Role of a Stock Market in a General Equilibrium Model with Technological Uncertainty', *American Economic Review*, 57, 759–76.

Diamond, P. A. and Stiglitz, J. E. (1975) 'Increases in Risk and Risk Aversion', *Journal of Economic Theory*, 8 (July), 337–60.

Dillon, J. L. and Scandizzo, P. L. (1978) 'Risk Attitudes of Subsistence Farmers in NorthEast Brazil: A Sampling Approach', *American Journal of Agricultural Economics*, 60, 425–35.

Drèze, J. H. (1974) 'Investment Under Private Ownership: Optimality, Equilibrium and Stability', in *Allocation under Uncertainty: Equilibrium and Optimality*, J. Drèze, editor, Ch. 9, Macmillan, New York.

Ezekial, M. (1938) 'The Cobweb Theorem', *Quarterly Journal of Economics*, 52 (Feb.), 255–80.

FAO (1975) 'Food Reserve Policies for World Food Security: A Consultant Study of Alternative Approaches', ESC:CSP/75/2, Rome, Food and Agriculture Organisation.

FAO, *Trade Yearbook*, Rome, Food and Agriculture Organisation (published annually).

Gardner, B. L. (1979) *Optimal Stockpiling of Grain*, Lexington, D. C. Heath.

Gelb, A. H. (1979) 'On the Definition and Measurement of Instability and the Costs of Buffering Export Fluctuations', *Review of Economic Studies*, 46 (Jan.), 149–62.

Girao, J. A., Tomek, W. G., and Mount, T. D. (1974) 'The Effect of Income Instability on Farmer's Consumption and Investment', *Review of Economics and Statistics*, 56 (May), 141–9.

Goreux, L. M. (1978) 'Optimal Rule of Buffer Stock Intervention', Washington, D.C., International Monetary Fund Research Department, mimeo DM/78/7.

Gorman, W. M. (1976) 'Tricks with Utility Functions', Ch. 11 in M. Parkin and A. R. Nobay, *Current Economic Problems*, Cambridge, England, Cambridge University Press.

Goss, B. A. and Yamey, B. S. (1976) *The Economics of Futures Trading*, London, Macmillan.

Gray, R. W. (1960) 'The Characteristic Bias on some Thin Futures Markets', *Food Research Institute Studies* (Nov.), reprinted in Peck (1977).

Gray, R. W. (1972) 'The Futures Market for Maine Potatoes: An Appraisal', *Food Research Institute Studies*, 9, reprinted in Peck (1977).

Green, H. A. J. (1971) *Consumer Theory*, Harmondsworth, Penguin.

Green, J. R. (1978) 'Value of Information with Sequential Futures Markets', Discussion Paper 631, Cambridge, Mass., Harvard Institute of Economic Research.

Grossman, S. J. and Stiglitz, J. E. (1976) 'Information and Competitive Price Systems', *American Economic Review*, 66, 246-53.

Grossman, S. J. and Stiglitz, J. E. (1980) 'On the Impossibility of Informationally Efficient Markets', *American Economic Review*, 70, 393-409.

Gustafson, R. L. (1958) *Carryover Levels for Grains*, US Department of Agriculture, Technical Bulletin No. 1178.

Hall, R. E. (1978) 'Stochastic Implications of the Life Cycle-Permanent Income Hypothesis: Theory and Evidence', *Journal of Political Economy*, 86 (Dec.), 971-87.

Harberger, A. C. (1964) 'Taxation, Resource Allocation and Welfare', in NBER and Brookings Institution, *The Role of Direct and Indirect Taxes in the Federal Revenue System*, Princeton, Princeton University Press.

Harberger, A. C. (1971) 'Three Basic Postulates for Applied Welfare Economics: An Interpretative Essay', *Journal of Economic Literature*, 9 (Sept.), 785-97.

Hart, O. D. (1975) 'On the Optimality of Equilibrium when the Market Structure is Incomplete', *Journal of Economic Theory*, 11, 418-43.

Hart, O. D. (1977) 'On the Profitability of Speculation', *Quarterly Journal of Economics*, 91, 579-97.

Hazell, P. B. R. and Scandizzo, P. L. (1975) 'Market Intervention Policies when Production is Risky', *American Journal of Agricultural Economics*, 57, 641-49.

Heady, E. O. (1952) *Economics of Agricultural Production and Resource Use*, Englewood Cliffs, Prentice Hall.

Helleiner, G. K. (1966) *Peasant Agriculture, Government, and Economic Growth in Nigeria*, Homewood, Richard Irwin.

House of Lords (1977) *Report of the Select Committee on Commodity Prices*, HMSO (165-i), 18 May.

IMF (1977) *International Financial Statistics* (May issue), Washington, D.C., International Monetary Fund (published annually).

Johnson, A. C. (1973) 'Effects of Futures Trading on Price Performance in the Cash Onion Market, 1930-68', USDA ERS. Technical Bulletin 1470, partially reprinted in Peck (1977).

Johnson, D. Gale (1975) *World Food Problems and Prospects*, Washington, D.C., American Enterprise Institute for Public Policy Research.

Kaldor, N. (1976) 'Inflation and Recession in the World Economy', *Economic Journal*, 86 (Dec.), 703-14.

Keynes, J. M. (1927) 'Some Aspects of Commodity Markets', *Manchester Guardian Commercial*, European Reconstruction Series, 29 Mar.

Knudsen, O. and Parnes, A. (1975) *Trade Instability and Economic Development*, Lexington, Heath-Lexington.

Larson, A. B. (1967) 'Price Prediction on the Egg Futures Market', *Food Research Institute Studies*, 7 (Supp.), reprinted in Peck (1977).

Lawson, C. W. (1974) 'The Decline in World Export Instability: A Reappraisal', *Bulletin of the Oxford University Institute of Economics and Statistics*, 36 (Feb.), 53-65.

Lewis, Sir A. (1978) 'The Less Developed Countries and Stable Exchange Rates', *Third World Quarterly*, 1 (Jan.), 18-29.

Lin, W., Dean, G., and Moore, C. (1974) 'An Empirical Test of Utility vs Profit Maximization in Agricultural Production', *American Journal of Agricultural Economics*, 56, 497-508.

Little, I. M. D. and Mirrlees, J. A. (1974), *Project Appraisal and Planning for Developing Countries*, London, Heinemann.

Luce, D. R. and Suppes, P. (1965) 'Preference, Utility and Subjective Probability', in D. R. Luce, R. R. Bush, and E. Galanther, *Handbook of Mathematical Psychology*, New York, John Wiley.

MacBean, A. (1966) *Export Instability and Economic Development*, Cambridge, Mass., Harvard University Press.

McKinnon, R. I. (1967) 'Futures Markets, Buffer Stocks, and Income Stability for Primary Producers', *Journal of Political Economy*, 75 (Dec.), 844–61.

McNicol, D. L. (1978) 'Political Economy of an Integrated Commodity Program', Ch. 10 in Adams and Klein (1978).

Massell, B. F. (1969) 'Price Stabilization and Welfare', *Quarterly Journal of Economics*, 83, 284–98.

Massell, B. F. (1970) 'Some Welfare Implications of International Price Stabilization', *Journal of Political Economy*, 78, 404–17.

Menezes, C. F. and Hanson, D. L. (1970) 'On the Theory of Risk Aversion', *International Economic Review*, vol. 11 (Oct.), 481–7.

Moscardi, E. and de Janvry, A. (1977) 'Attitudes toward Risk Among Peasants: An Econometric Approach', *American Journal of Agricultural Economics*, 59, 710–16.

Muth, J. F. (1961) 'Rational Expectations and the Theory of Price Movements', *Econometrica*, 29 (July), 315–35.

Nerlove, M. (1958) 'Adaptive Expectations and the Cobweb Phenomenon', *Quarterly Journal of Economics*, 73 (May), 227–40.

Newbery, D. M. G. (1976) 'Price Stabilisation with Risky Production', Institute for Mathematical Studies in the Social Sciences, Economic Series No. 69, Stanford, Stanford University.

Newbery, D. M. G. (1978) 'Stochastic Limit Pricing', *Bell Journal of Economics*, 9, 260–9.

Newbery, D. M. G. and Stiglitz, J. E. (1977) *The Economic Impact of Price Stabilization*, A Report presented to the Agency for International Development, Washington, D.C.

Newbery, D. M. G. and Stiglitz, J. E. (1979a) 'Sharecropping, Risk Sharing and the Importance of Imperfect Information', Ch. 17 (311–40), of Roumasset et al. (1979).

Newbery, D. M. G. and Stiglitz, J. E. (1979b) 'The Theory of Commodity Price Stabilisation Rules: Welfare Impacts and Supply Responses', *Economic Journal*, 89 (Dec.), 799–817.

Newbery, D. M. G. and Stiglitz, J. E. (1981) 'Pareto Inferior Trade and Optimal Trade Policy' (mimeo), Princeton University.

Oi, W. Y. (1961) 'The Desirability of Price Instability under Perfect Competition', *Econometrica*, 29, 58–64.

Peck, A. E. (ed.) (1977) *Selected Writings on Futures Markets*, Vol. II, Chicago, Chicago Board of Trade.

Powers, M. J. (1970) 'Does Futures Trading Reduce Price Fluctuations in the Cash Market?', *American Economic Review*, 60, 460–4, reprinted in Goss and Yamey (1976).

Pratt, J. W. (1964) 'Risk Aversion in the Small and in the Large', *Econometrica*, 32 (Jan.), 122–36.

Reutlinger, S. (1976) 'A Simulation Model for Evaluating Worldwide Buffer Stocks of Wheat', *American Journal of Agricultural Economics*, 58 (Feb.), 1-12.

Rothschild, M. and Stiglitz, J. E. (1970) 'Increasing Risk I: A Definition', *Journal of Economic Theory*, 2, 225–43.

Rothschild, M. and Stiglitz, J. E. (1971) 'Increasing Risk II: Its Economic Consequences', *Journal of Economic Theory*, 3, 66-84.

Roumasset, J. (1976) *Rice and Risk: Decison Making among Low-Income Farmers*, Amsterdam, North-Holland.

Roumasset, J. A., Boussard, J.-M., and Singh, I. J. (1979) *Risk, Uncertainty and Agricultural Development*, New York, Agricultural Development Council.

Salant, S. W. (1979) 'The Vulnerability of Price Stabilization Programs to Speculative Attack', mimeo.

Samuelson, P. A. (1942) 'Constancy of the Marginal Utility of Income', in O. Lange et al. (eds.) *Studies in Mathematical Economics and Econometrics in Memory of Henry Schultz*. Chicago, University of Chicago Press, 75-91, reprinted in Samuelson (1966), vol. I.

Samuelson, P. A. (1947) *Foundations of Economic Analysis*, Cambridge, Mass., Harvard University Press.

Samuelson, P. A. (1966) *The Collected Scientific Papers of Paul A. Samuelson*, vol. I, ed. J. E. Stiglitz, Cambridge, Mass., MIT Press.

Samuelson, P. A. (1967) 'General Proof that Diversification Pays', *Journal of Financial and Quantitative Analysis* 2 (Mar.), 1-13, reprinted in Samuelson (1972b).

Samuelson, P. A. (1970) 'The Fundamental Approximation Theorem of Portfolio Analysis in Terms of Means, Variances, and Higher Moments', *Review of Economic Studies*, 37 (Oct.), 537-42, reprinted in Samuelson (1972b).

Samuelson, P. A. (1971) 'Stochastic Speculative Price', *Proc. Nat. Acad. Sci.*, 68 (Feb.), 335-7, reprinted in Samuelson (1972b).

Samuelson, P. A. (1972a) 'The Consumer Does Benefit from Feasible Price Stability', *Quarterly Journal of Economics*, 86, 476-93.

Samuelson, P. A. (1972b) *The Collected Scientific Papers of Paul A. Samuelson*, vol. III, ed. R. C. Merton, Cambridge, Mass., MIT Press.

Sarris, A. H. and Taylor, L. (1978) 'Buffer Stock Analysis for Agricultural Products: Theoretical Murk or Empirical Resolution', Ch. 7 (149-60), in Adams and Klein (1978).

Savage, L. J. (1954) *Foundations of Statistics*, New York, John Wiley & Son.

Schechtman, J. (1977) 'A Grain Storage Problem, with Random Production', Operations Research Centre (mimeo), Berkeley, University of California.

Schluter, M. G. G. and Mount, T. D. (1976) 'Some Management Objectives of Risk Aversion in the Choice of Cropping Patterns, Surat District, India', *Journal of Development Studies*, 12, 246-61.

Scitovsky, T. (1943) 'A Note on Profit Maximisation and its Implications', *Review of Economic Studies*, 9, 57-60.

Simon, H. A. (1959) 'Theories of Decision-Making in Economics', *American Economic Review*, 49 (June), 223-83.

Slutzky, E. (1937) 'The Summation of Random Causes as the Source of Cyclic Processes', *Econometrica*, 5 (April), 105-14.

Stein, J. P. and Smith, R. T. (1977) 'The Economics of United States Grain Stock Policy', Rand Corporation R-1861-CIEP, March.

Stiglitz, J. E. (1969) 'Behaviour Towards Risk with Many Commodities', *Econometrica*, 37, 660-7.

Stiglitz, J. E. (1970) 'A Consumption Oriented Theory of the Demand for Financial Assets and the Term Structure of Interest Rates', *Review of Economic Studies*, 37, 321-51.

Stiglitz, J. E. (1972a) 'Taxation, Risk taking and the Allocation of Investment in a Risky Economy', in M. C. Jensen (ed.), *Studies in the Theory of Capital Markets*, New York.

Stiglitz, J. E. (1972b) 'On the Optimality of the Stock Market Allocation of Investment', *Quarterly Journal of Economics*, 86 (Feb.), 25-60.

Stiglitz, J. E. (1972c) 'Portfolio Allocation with Many Risky Assets', in Szegö and Shell (eds.), *Mathematical Methods in Investment and Finance*, Amsterdam, North Holland.

Stiglitz, J. E. (1974) 'Incentives and Risk Sharing in Sharecropping', *Review of Economic Studies*, 41(2), 219-56.

Stiglitz, J. E. (1975) 'The Efficiency of Market Prices in Long Run Allocations in the Oil Industry', in G. Brannon (ed.), *Studies in Energy Tax Policy*, Cambridge, Mass., Ballinger Publishing Co., 55-99.

Stiglitz, J. E. (1978) 'The Inefficiency of the Competitive Stock Market and its Implications for the Depletion of Exhaustible Resources', in *The Effects of Risk on Prices and Quantities Energy Supplies*, vol. 4, Palo Alto, Ca., Electric Power Research Institute.

Theil, H. (1958) *Economic Forecasts and Policy*, Amsterdam, North Holland.

Tomek, W. G. and Gray, R. W. (1970) 'Temporal Relationships among Prices on Commodity Futures Markets: Their Allocative and Stabilizing Roles', *American Journal of Agricultural Economics*, 52(3) (Aug.), reprinted in Peck (1977).

Turnovsky, S. J. (1974) 'Price Expectations and the Welfare Gains from Price Stabilization', *American Journal of Agricultural Economics*, 56, 706-16.

Turnovsky, S. J. (1976). 'The Distribution of Welfare Gains from Price Stabilization: the Case of Multiplicative Disturbances', *International Economic Review*, 17, 133-48.

Turnovsky, S. J. (1978) 'The Distribution of Welfare Gains from Price Stabilization: A Survey of Some Theoretical Issues', in Adams and Klein (1978).

Tversky, A. (1969) 'Intransitivity of Preferences', *Psychological Review*, 76, 31-48.

UNCTAD (1974) 'An Integrated Programme for Commodities', TD/B/C.1/166, Trade and Development Board, Committee on Commodities, Geneva, United Nations Conference on Trade and Development.

UNCTAD (1975a) 'Compensatory Financing of Export Fluctuations', TD/B/C.1/195, Trade and Development Board, Committee on Commodities, Geneva, United Nations Conference on Trade and Development.

UNCTAD (1975b) 'Second Progress Report on Storage Costs and Warehouse Facilities', TD/B/C.1/198, Trade and Development Board, Committee on Commodities, Geneva, United Nations Conference on Trade and Development.

Von Neumann, J. and Morgenstern, O. (1947) *The Theory of Games and Economic Behavior*, Princeton, Princeton University Press.

Waugh, F. V. (1944) 'Does the Consumer Benefit from Price Instability?', *Quarterly Journal of Economics*, 58, 602-14.

Willig, R. D. (1976) 'Consumer's Surplus without Apology', *American Economic Review*, 66, 589-97.

Wilson, P. R. D. (1977) 'Export Instability and Economic Development: A Survey', Parts I and II, Warwick University Economic Discussion Paper.

World Bank (1977a) 'Commodity Price Stabilization and Developing Countries: The Problem of Choice', by E. M. Brook, E. R. Grilli, and J. Waelbroek, Staff Working Paper No. 262, Washington, D.C., World Bank.

World Bank (1977b) *Commodity Trade and Price Trends* (1977 edn.), Report EC-166/77, Washington, D.C., World Bank (published annually by the Commodities and Export Projection Division of the World Bank).

Yule, G. U. (1927) 'On a Method of Investigating Periodicity in Disturbed Series', *Trans. Royal Soc. London*, A.226: 267-98.

Zeckhauser, R. and Keeler, E. (1970) 'Another Type of Risk Aversion', *Econometrica*, 38 (Sept.), 661-5.

Author Index

Adams, F. G. 18
Aitcheson, J. 89
Anderson, J. R. 103
Arrow, K. J. 72, 97, 207, 210
Atkinson, A. B. 7

Behrman, J. R. 44, 293, 409
Binswanger, H. P. 100, 101, 103, 104, 105, 106
Boadway, R. W. 275
Borch, K. 210
Bray, M. 240
Brown, J. A. C. 89

Cass, D. 74
Coase, R. H. 152
Cooper, R. N. 401

Danin, Y. 409
Dasgupta, P. 336
Davidson, J. E. 400
Deane, G. 100
Debreu, G. 206, 210
Diamond, P. 72, 210, 225, 226, 250, 344
Dillon, J. L. 100, 105
Drèze, J. 210

Ezekial, M. 152

Food and Agriculture Organization 274, 275, 291
Fowler, R. F. 152

Gardner, B. L. 409, 423
Gelb, A. H. 285, 286
Girao, J. A. 109
Goreux, L. M. 409, 423
Gorman, W. M. 111
Goss, B. A. 178, 179
Gray, R. W. 179, 180, 187, 274
Green, H. A. J. 112
Green, J. R. 148
Grossman, S. J. 51, 52, 240
Gustafson, R. L. 18, 404, 409, 422-6, 428-9, 432, 435, 437

Hall, R. E. 155
Hanson, D. L. 102
Harberger, A. C. 7, 275
Hart, O. D. 150, 210, 211, 274
Hazell, P. B. R. 143, 145
Heady, E. O. 8, 109
Helleiner, G. K. 288
Hendry, D. F. 400
House of Lords 286

International Monetary Fund 291

de Janvry, A. 101, 106, 107
Johnson, A. C. 180
Johnson, D. Gale 274, 409

Kaldor, N. 36, 375-6, 399
Keeler, E. 102

Keynes, J. M. 185
Klein, S. A. 18
Knudsen, O. 377, 395

Larson, A. B. 152, 181
Lawrence, R. Z. 401
Lawson, C. W. 286
Lewis, Sir A. 402
Lin, W. 100
Little, I. M. D. 396
Luce, D. R. 97

MacBean, A. 395
McKinnon, R. I. 177, 183
McNicol, D. L. 2
Massell, B. F. 17, 59
Menezes, C. F. 102
Mirrlees, J. A. 396
Moore, C. 100
Morgenstern, O. 100
Moscardi, E. 101, 106, 107
Mount, T. D. 107, 108, 109
Muth, J. F. 132, 133, 135, 152, 155

Nerlove, M. 148
Newbery, D. M. G. vi, 24n., 150, 293, 319, 369, 424, 428

Oi, W. Y. 17, 59, 318

Parnes, A. 377, 395
Peck, A. E. 178, 180, 185
Powers, M. J. 180
Pratt, J. W. 72

Reutlinger, S. 409
Rothschild, M. 72, 79, 182, 250, 344
Roumasset, J. 109

Salant, S. W. 413
Samuelson, P. A. 83, 91, 306, 318, 326, 340, 422, 428
Sarris, A. H. 276
Savage, L. J. 48, 97
Scandizzo, P. L. 100, 105, 143, 145
Schechtman, J. 409, 422
Schluter, M. G. G. 107-8, 109
Scitovsky, T. 63
Simon, H. A. 135
Slutzky, E. 152
Smith, Adam 24
Smith, R. T. 409
Srba, F. 400
Stein, J. P. 409
Stiglitz, J. E. vi, 7, 51, 52, 72, 74, 76, 79, 111, 116, 182, 210, 211, 213, 240, 250, 293, 336, 340, 342, 344, 369, 424, 428
Sumner, D. 409
Suppes, P. 97

Taylor, L. 276
Theil, H. 152
Tomek, W. G. 109, 179, 180

Turnovsky, S. J. 120, 305
Tversky, A. 98

United Nations Conference on Trade and Development 13, 290, 295

von Neumann, J. 100

Waugh, F. V. 17, 59, 318

Willig, R. D. 122
Wilson, P. R. D. 285
World Bank 13, 17, 287, 289, 290-1

Yamey, B. S. 178, 179
Yeo, S. 400
Yule, G. U. 152

Zeckhauser, R. 102

Subject Index

A, coefficient of absolute risk aversion, *see* risk aversion
accounting prices 396
action certainty equivalent, *see* certainty equivalent
adaptive expectations, *see* expectations
additive risk, *see* risk
additive separability, *see* separability
adequacy of private price stabilization 24, 46, 158, 244, 322, 331-2, 356, 371
adjustment process 306: *see also* stability; to disturbances 142-52; *see also* lags, learning
adverse selection 40, 166-7, 176, 208, 338, 414, 445
agreements: commodity 2, 259, 282, 286-7; intergovernmental 402
agricultural commodity prices 13-14, 36, 290-9: *see also under individual commodities*
agricultural economics, contributions of 8-10
agricultural economists, guide for 8-10
aid, economic 356, 439
alternatives: to buffer stocks 3, 22, 39-43, 297-9, 444-5; to price stabilization 20, 24, 39-43, 46, 248, 273, 297-9, 440, 444; *see also* credit markets; futures markets; income stabilization
arbitrage 16, 35, 42, 51-2, 166, 179, 244, 254, 371: relationships 179, 198, 411, 421-2; benefits, *see* benefits
arbitrageurs, influence on price stabilization 51-2; errors by 51-2; stabilizing effect of 24, 34; *see also* speculators
asset demand functions (linearity of) 74-6, 88
asset integration hypothesis 100, 103-5, 204-6: and perceived cost of risk 204-6
autarky 6, 337-71 *passim*: v. free trade 338-50, 355; trade policy near 362

backwardation, in futures market 184-6: evidence for 185
balance of payments: deficits 373, 392, 400; equilibrium in 365, 378-9, 399; policy 392-4, 400, 441; problems 402, 441; variations in 392, 394
band width rules 21, 405, 408-9, 413, 432-3, 441-2
Bangladesh 290-1, 296
basis (in futures market) 179n
bauxite 2
beef 178, 180
benefit-cost analysis, *see* cost-benefit
benefits: of borrowing 206; of eliminating competitive inefficiency 231; of increasing investment 396; of increasing storage, *see* storage; of operating buffer stock, *see* buffer stock schemes; of trade liberalization 20, 272, 575, *see also* trade; of trading on futures market: formula 187
benefits of commodity price stabilization 5, 18, 25-35, 92-5, 122-9, 147-8, 253-5, 278-80, 313-16, 373, 390: additivity of 126-8; aggregate net 19, 23, 34, 94-5, 125, 255-8, 295, 297; alternative methods of achieving 440, 444; arbitrage 21, 188, 254-5, 258, 269-70, 299, 440; to buffer stock operators 252-3, 255, 266; to consumers 18, 23, 33, 49, 57, 111, 120, 122-30, 147-8, 252, 254, 258, 269-71, 295, 314; affected by distortions 20, 276-83; distributional, *see* transfer, *below*; effect of futures markets on 184, 191; effect of risk reducing options on 166, 168-9, 172; effect of supply response on 19, 255; efficiency 21, 25-6, 33, 39, 43, 93-5, 123-4, 138, 141, 148, 255-8, 275, 346, estimates of 284-98: efficiency v. distributional 21, 92, 247, 249, 254-5, 259, 299, 354, 439, sensitivity to specification 247, 249, 259, 354; formulae for 5, 29, 93-5, 124-9, 187, 253-8, 260-1, 266-71, 279-80, 293, 312-15; from improved resource allocation 231, 441-2, *see also* intervention, consequences of; long run 252, 310-17, 327-34; macroeconomic 16, 20, 35, 380, 383-7, 390, 393, 440; magnitude of 23, 27, 29, 33-4, 43-6, 169, 187, 247-8, 254, 256, 259, 279, 285, 293-8, 440, 444; measurement of 18, 23, 49, 92-5, 111, 122, 163, 169, 172, 247-9, 293-7; prejudging 20, 163, 191, 249, 259; to producers 19, 23, 92, 147, 252-5, 260-8, 295, 314; risk (of risk reduction) 18, 21, 29, 43-5, 94-5, 125, 187, 249, 256, 267-9, 283, 285, 293, 295, 298, 337-8, 345-6; short run 92-5, 270, 326-7, *see also* impact; in small country 27; transfer/distributional 21, 25, 33, 39-40, 44-5, 92-5, 123-4, 188, 247, 255, 258, 259, 269-71, 285, 295, 317; *see also* buffer stock
bias: of competitive markets 137, 211, 228-31, 235, 275, 373, 444; of competitive stock rule 430-4, 441; of conventional parameterizations 3, 20, 209, 215, *see also* specification; of futures markets 184-92 *passim*, 197; in collection of information 243-4
borrowing 43, 99, 175, 201; constraints on 7, 28, 205-6; international 375

Brazil 44, 68, 95, 100, 289, 290-1, 296, 299
buffer fund 286
buffer profits, allocation of 266, 332-5
buffer stock rules (*see also* competitive storage rules; optimum buffer stock rules): bandwith 21, 405, 408-9, 413, 432-3, 441, 442; benefits of 403-4, 417, 419-20, 428-33; characterization of 404-5, 410-11, 433; choice of 308-10, 404-5, 409-20; comparisons between 404-5, 416-20; competitive, *see* competitive storage rule; consequences of 53, 199, 403-34 *passim*; difficulties in design of 45, 48, 442; efficiency of 404, 441; examples of 405, 410-20; 'famine' rule 418-20; feasibility of 288, 404, 407; 'flood' rule 418-20; numerical solution of 406, 409, 421, 423-6; optimum, *see* optimum buffer stock rule; 'random walk' rule 416-18; simulations of 409
buffer stocks (*see also* stocks; storage; buffer stock rules; buffer stock schemes): as means of price stabilization 3, 12, 15, 250, 259, 275, 356; as solution to macro-shock 376, 402; behaviour of 34, 406-20; consequences of 275, 403-33 *passim*; effect on harvests 427; following stochastic process 294, 406-9, 416-20
buffer stock schemes (*see also* buffer stock rules): alternatives to 3, 22, 39-43, 297-9, 444-5; costs of 39, 294-5, 403, 417, 419, 427-30, 433; design of 48, 403-6; desirability of 46, 356-7, 404; dynamic analysis of 5, 7, 37, 39, 406-20, 441; effect of private storage on 199-201, 404; effect on private storage 35, 37-8, 195, 199-201, 238, 259, 404; importance of costs for 16, 37, 252, 254, 299, 321, 403, 414, 417, 420, 429-30, 432-3, 440; optimum, *see* optimum buffer stock rule; as source of revenue 16-17
buffer stock size: average 39, 46, 198-9, 294, 406, 416-18, 420, 426, 432-3, 444; critical size for speculative attack 413; distribution of 294, 403, 408, 416-19, 427; importance of initial size for benefits 429-30; to avoid shortfalls 286, 295
butter 181

capital asset pricing model 85-9, 183
carryover, carryforward 195, 198, 412, 421; *see also* stocks
cartel 12, 14, 54, 439
caveats 4, 5, 10-11, 46, 203, 304, 317, 353, 371; *see also* robustness; specification
certainty equivalent 57, 59, 64, 66-8, 71, 83, 132-5; action certainty equivalent 59, 64, 66-8, 83, 89, 138, 140-1, 145-7, 151, 156, 190-1; danger in use of 59, 83, 319, 442; price 59, 64-8, 132, 138-9, 156, 277; price, estimation of 156, 159; price, formulae for 66-7, 138-9, 156, 191; relation to rational expectations 132-3, 135-6, 139; return 71-2, 83, 89, 159, 319; return, formulae for 89; utility certainty equivalent 59, 64, 83, 140
choice of technique 170, 172-5, 209, 212 (*see also* supply, theory of); bias in 211, 228-31; costless 227-8; by government 209, 215, 223, 231, 236; by market 224; model of 212-14, 221-5; optimality of 209-35; parameterizing 229; to reduce risk, 170; *see also* supply, theory of
cobweb 10, 29, 50-1, 148-53, 180, 244
cobweb stability, *see* stability
cocoa 2, 13, 43-5, 95, 122, 285, 287-8, 290-9
coefficient of variation: reasons for use 106, 123, 285-92; relation to mean average deviation 107-8, 286
coffee 13, 43-5, 122, 192, 285-8, 290-9
Colombia 289, 290-1, 296
commodity price stabilization: adequacy of private supply of 24, 46, 158, 244, 322, 330-2, 356, 371; alternatives to 20, 24, 39-43, 46, 248, 273, 297-9; benefits of, *see* benefits; characterization of 308-12, 316; consequences of 14, 17, 26-33, 36, 49, 52-3, 69, 172, 176-7, 301-3, 373, *see also* commodity price stabilization, effects of; conventional analysis of 10, 12, 17-23, 46, 172, 249, 285; costs of 19, 23, 25, 29, 34, 36-9, 45, 172, 285, 293-5, 373, 403; definition of 249-52; degree of 94-5, 259, 293, 295, 308-10, 313-16; and free trade 336-61; objectives of 1, 12-17, 298, 316, 403, 439; optimal level of 34, *see also* optimum buffer stock rule; theory of 18, 57
commodity price stabilization, effects of on: average price 17-18, 20, 68, 122, 187; average producer income 30-3, 439; consumers 16, 33-4, 147, 255, 329; consumption variability 297, 440; demand 53-4; distribution of income 18, 21, 23, 25-6, 33, 43, 92, 153, 161, 247, 259-70, 294, 304, 315-6, 340, 354; expectations 132; futures markets 53, 177, 181; governments 54, 275; income variability 15, 18, 170, 284, 297, 319; information collection 52-3, 99, 162, 238, 244; macroeconomic aggregates 373; market efficiency 169, 176, 204, 282, 305; misperceptions 132; output variability 19, 29-30, 38, 172-5; price distribution 8, 68, 69, 301; private storage 35, 37-8, 53, 195, 199-201, 238, 259, 404; producers 68, 147, 204, 255, 326-9; risk bearing 10, 18, 26, 33, 38, 168; supply 19, 38, 68, 171, *see also* supply
commodity price stabilization schemes (*see also* buffer stock schemes): analysis of effects of 76, 92, 163, 168-9, 249-58; beneficiaries of 19; comparison with other instruments 22, 39-43, 161, 177, 181, 248, 297-9; choice of 313-16, 443; choice of numeraire for 28, 287-9; design of 5, 48, 249, 313-16; desirability of 3, 10-11, 23, 26, 29, 43, 46, 238, 244-5, 259, 273, 299, 318-19, 334-5, 356; difficulty in design of 45, 205; domestic 14, 16-17, 28, 167-8, 192, 273, 275, 276, 298, 336, 375, 392; effectiveness of 286-7; equilibrium 304, 309-13, 320, 325; experiments to help design of 443; feasible 34, 39, 247, 250, 321, 325-6, 328, 332; homothetic 304, 309-13; interest in 2, 12; international 168-9, 259, 298; justification for 10, 20, 24, 175; macro aspects of 373; official discussions of 12, 249, 298, 373; partial

Subject Index 455

247, 249-58; pure 12, 14, 17, 47, 249, 439; responses to 25, 35, 37, 52, 195, 238, 440, 444
commodity stabilization policies 320-1, 374
Common Agricultural Policy of EEC 336
compact probabilities 91
comparative advantage 342, 355-6, 371
comparative statics 57, **80-4**, 329
compensated demand schedule **114-16**, 122
Compensatory Financing Facility of IMF 16, 287, 394
compensatory foreign borrowing 375
compensatory scheme for domestic producers 14
competitive market efficiency, *see* efficiency
competitive markets, agricultural as 8, 23, 207
competitive paradigm 5, 6, 23
competitive storage rule (*see also* buffer stock rules): as bench mark 404, 412, 421, 440; bias in 430-3; characterization of 411-13; consequences of 405; definition of 404, 411; implications of 412-14; optimality of 404-5, 411, 421-2, 430; solution of 412, 421, 423-8
complementary inequalities, defined 196
completeness of markets 6, 25, 137, 177, 207-8, 210, 235-6, 338, 356, 370, 440, 444
complete stabilization 21, 262, 264, 266, 276, 314-15, 403; impossibility of 21, 34-5, 76, 247, 403-4, 440; *see also* partial price stabilization; feasibility of complete price stabilization
concave, concavity: defined 30, 60-1; properties of 79-81, 83, 85, 251-2, 262, *see also* mean preserving spreads; Jensen's inequality; of cost function 61; of demand schedule 264-5; of expenditure function 113, 334; of first order condition 344; of probability density 281-2; of production function 60, 319, 356; of revenue 30-1, 354; of social welfare 216-17, 235; of utility function 71, 83, 116-17, 212, 319, 368
conditional probabilities 193-4
constrained Pareto optimality/efficiency 162, 209-37, 301; characterized 215-17, 220, 227-8, 233; necessary conditions for 211, 218-25, 227-8, 232-4; relation to Pareto efficiency 218, 233; special cases of 209; sufficient conditions for 211, 215-20, 226-8, 232-4; *see also* efficiency; inefficiency of market equilibrium
constraints: facing buffer stock schemes 414; facing farmers 108; facing government 209, 392
consumer demand, theory of **111-21**
consumers, effect of price stabilization on 16, 33-4, 142, 255, 329
consumption, planning 201
consumption function 392-3, 397, 400-1
consumption variability 15, 26, 28, 41, 195, 201, 389, 395, 440, 445; methods of treating 201-6, 440
convenience yields of stocks 178, 195-7
conventional analysis, difference between our approach and 10, 12, 17-22, 285; limitations of 23, 46, 172, 249
convergence of probabilities 90-1
convex, convexity: defined 30, 61; of demand 32, 137, 264-5; of expenditure 334; of indirect utility 113-14, 116,
152, 319; of profit 319; of revenue 31, 354; properties of 61, 79-81, 85, 262, *see also* mean preserving spreads; Jensen's inequality; quasi-convex, defined 113, 117
copper 13, 285, 375
'core' commodities vii, 10, 12-13, 29, 108, 285-99
corn, *see* grain
correspondence principle 83-4
cost: of additional price stabilization 404, 427-8, 432; of buffer stocks, *see* buffer stocks; of price stabilization, *see* commodity price stabilization; of price variability, *see* price variability; of risk, *see* risk
cost-benefit analysis 3-4, 7, 18-19, 23-4, 45, 256, 275, 284, 294-5; *see also* benefit; cost; of intervention, 432; macro 373-4, 390, 395; of partial v. total stabilization 440
cost function 60-1, 112
cotton 2, 12-13, 43, 285, 287, 289-93, 295-9
covariance, importance of 27, 64, 88, 95, 164-5; magnitude of 291
credit 15, 54
credit markets 43, 55, 162, 201, 205-6, 209, 284, 444-5; importance of 162, 201, 205; international 394, 441

decisions of farmers: affecting risk 163, 169-76; borrowing 161, 175, 201-6; choice of crops 161, 163, 170, 172, 204, 336, 340; choice of techniques 163, 170-2, 212; collection of information 161, 175; scale of output 161, 304, 320; storage 161, 175, 195-6; trade on futures markets 161, 172, 181-2
demand, theory of **111-21**
demand risk, specification of 118-21, 262-7
demand variability: benefits from stabilizing 18, 33-4, 48, 122-30, 258, 262-6, 268, 270-1, *see also* benefits; causes of 49-50; consequences of 63, 316-17; difficulty in welfare analysis of 122
density function (probability) 134, 250-1, 257, 281; definition 77-9
Depression, Great 2, 399
destabilizing prices, desirability of 157-8, 319, 332, 335
destabilizing speculation 51, 150
development, relation to export instability 17, 377, 395
diffusion process 408
disequilibrium 20, 36, 47; in labour market 381; *see also* macroeconomics
distortions 247, **272-83**, 284-5; consequences of reducing 272; dismantling 273, 275; effect on level of trade 278; importance of for price stabilization 373-5; magnitude of 228-31; in markets 9, 15, 20, 47, 285; *see also* market failure; quotas; tariffs; taxes; trade
distribution (probability): changes in, *see* mean preserving spreads; effects of changes of 84, 88, 96, 306, 309; comparing 76-9, 90-1, 250-2, 364-5; functions, defined 77-9, 133-4, used 257-8, 281, 408, 413, 437; of buffer stocks 294, 403, 408, 416-19, 427; of prices 9, 29, 76, 96, 133-4, 161, 175, 210, 212, 236, 250, 260, 427; of prices, determination of 214, 236; of returns 85-9, 182-3, 365; of supply 134, 183,

456 Commodity Price Stabilization

distribution (probability) (*cont.*)
   251, 413, 427, 430; *see also* lognormal; normal
distributional consequences of improved forecasting 148, 152-3, 158; of choice of technique 211; of supply responses 33
distributional consequences of price stabilization, *see* benefits; commodity price stabilization
distributional considerations: with distorted markets 270, 280; importance of for the choice of buffer scheme 409, 411, 421, 430; prejudging 10, 20, 249, 259; sensitivity to specification 247, 249, 258, 294
diversification of crops 27, 29, 86-9, 170-1
diversity of exports 441
duality 57, **111-16**
dynamic adjustment 441: *see also* cobwebs; expectations; learning
dynamic analysis 5, 7, 11, 21, 37, 39, 135, 137, **142-59**, 195, 403-5: of buffer stocks 5, 7, 37, 39, 406-20 *passim*, 441; of increased price stabilization 430-2
dynamic models, sensitivity to specification 132, 135
dynamic programming 421, 428-9

econometric estimation 9, 65, 107, 118, 120, 132, 155-6, 247, 285-93: of parameters 44-5
econometric models: of agricultural market 132; bias in 20, 259; difficulty in estimation of 106; used for analysis of price stabilization 3; of supply response 9, 159, 175
econometric specification 65, 89, 120, 139, 247, 249, 259: importance of and sensitivity to 3-5, 65, 89, 120, 139, 249, 255-68 *passim*, 271
economy, effects of instability on 374: *see also* macroeconomics, instability
EEC, *see* Common Agricultural Policy of
efficiency (*see also* inefficiency of market equilibrium; constrained Pareto optimality/efficiency): in collection and use of information 21-2, 134-7, 143, 157-9, 180, 238, 240, 243; of competitive markets 6, 23-5, 42, 137, 143-4, 158-9, 177, 207-37, 238, 243, 318, 329-32, 338, 356, 370, 411, 443-4, assumptions required for 6, 25, 207-8, 338, 443-4, *see also* completeness of markets; co-incidence of private and social profitability 24, 38, 207, 436, 443, decentralization theorem 231, 404, intervention to improve 7, 25, 42, 162, 208-9, 231-2, 237, 244, 336, 373, 404, 432, 'invisible hand' conjecture 24, 207, necessary conditions for 210, 220, 338, perfect market hypothesis 6, 24, 243, sufficient conditions for 210, 215, 218, 236; of trade 20, **336-61**
efficiency benefits of price stabilization, *see* benefits of commodity price stabilization, efficiency
eggs 178, 181
Egypt 290-2, 296
empirical estimates of benefits of price stabilization 21, 43-6, **284-99**: evidence for rational expectations 142, 152-3
empirical measurement: of bias in futures market 185; of key parameters 10, 44-5, 442; of risk aversion 96-110

empirical research, directions for future 4, 284
empirical specification of utility function 100, 118-20
empirical studies: of instability 374; of supply 9, 159, 175
empirical tests: of consistency of choice 97, 119; of consequences of instability 374, 395
employment: determination of sectoral levels of 379-82, 385, 388; fluctuations in 36, 375, 399; *see also* labour markets; macroeconomics; unemployment
energy 8
envelope theorem 310, 321, 324, 366, 429
equilibrium: adjustments to 142-59; under autarky 342; boundary 350, 358-9; in capital market 379, 382, 385, 388; in commodity market 411; effect of information on 238-46; efficiency of, *see* efficiency; in futures markets **177-93**, 239-45, *see also* futures markets; in international trade 339, 341-3, 358; in international trade with distortions 301, 309; in labour market 379, 381-3, 385-6, 388; long run 7, 19, 32, 175, 301-17, 318-34, 440; in markets with incorrect expectations 146-7, with price stabilization 301, 309-13, with rational expectations 131-41, 207-35; multiple 348-53; effect of response to risk on 161-76; response to changes in degree of price stabilization 3, 176, 249-58, 259-71, 305-17; stability of, *see* stability; with storage 195-200
equilibrium stabilization scheme, *see* commodity price stabilization schemes
expectations 9, 21, 32, 50, 64, **131-59**, 239, 306; adaptive, 143, **148-52**, 155, 306, 308, *see also* cobweb; efficiency in use of information 134-7, 180; efficiency of 157-8; errors in 10, 148, 150, 180; formulation of 131-2, 305; of future prices 179, 241; rational, *see* rational expectations; reasonable 153-7; relevance of for production decisions 131; specification of 132, 136; stability in 118; *see also* forecasts; price expectations
expectations operator xvii
expected utility, axiom of 97: testing of 96-7
expected utility hypothesis 57, 70, 96-105
expenditure function **112-16**
experiments to determine attitudes to risk 97-8, 100-5; to improve price stabilization schemes 443
export of domestic instability 278, 402
export earnings, fluctuations in 16, 43, 285, 375, 392-3, 395, 400-2, 441; stabilization of 393, 441
export price, instability of 375, **377-91**, 392
export quotas 12, 14
export unit value 288
exports: agricultural 2, 14, 290; correlation between 291, 399; instability of 17, 285, 375, 395; role of in international instability 399-402
externalities 25, 207

famine reserve 431
'famine' stock rule, *see* buffer stock rules
feasibility of complete price stabilization 21, 34-5, 76, 247, 403-4, 440

Subject Index 457

feasibility of intervention to eliminate inefficiency 232-3
feasibility locus 321, 325-9
feasible stabilization schemes, see commodity price stabilization schemes
financial markets 370-1: see also stockmarket
fiscal policy, coordination of 400
flexibility of wages and prices: compared with rigidity 3, 375, see also rigidities; macro-model of 377-80; required for efficiency 25
fluctuations, see price instability; demand variability; export instability; national income; trade cycle
forecasts, forecasting 131-59: actions of government 274; of average returns 135; bias or error in 22-3, 29, 51, 136, 148, 158; effects of price stabilization on 22, 29, 441-2; equation 155; with futures markets 179, 241-2; improvements of 136, 404; magnitude of bias in 188, 198, 287-8, 299, 305; modification of 10, 51; price 132, 142, 146-51
foreign borrowing 375
foreign: capital 377: as absorber of risk 377, 384, 395; earnings, variations in 15-17, 43, 285, 375, 392-3, 395, 400-2, 441; exchange, stabilizing role of 36, 392
free trade 6, 336-62; barriers to 336; bias in 337; compared with autarky 339-50, 355; desirability of restrictions on 336, 362, 368-9; inefficiency of 336, 339, 345-50, 362; stabilizing effect of 336
futures markets 177-92, 239-43; absence of 10, 25, 42; benefit of 41, 168, 184, 187, 191; bias in 184-7, 192, 197; compared with price stabilization 22, 161, 177, 181, 187-8, 192, 444; contracts 192; coordination of storage 178, 180, 192; determination of price on 179, 239; effect: on cobwebs 180-1, on market equilibrium 162, 177, 187-8, of price stabilization on 181, on supply 187, 190-1, on producer's income risk 178-9, 181, 186-7, 189, 192; efficiency of 41, 177, 243-4; empirical evidence on effect of 180-1; equilibrium in 88, 92, 179, 184, 185-91, 239, 241-2; role of expectations in 179, 241; importance of 28, 177, 440, 444-5; improvement of 22, 41-2, 192, 244, 445; insurance role of 41, 165, 167, 177, 178-83, 191-2; role in disseminating information 10, 51, 180, 239, 242, 244, 356; role in aggregating information 239, 243; informational efficiency 240; magnitude of trade on 165, 168, 172,181, 184-6, 195, 241-2, 370; risk reducing role 181-3, 288; stabilizing role of 180-1; relevance of storability for 178-80, 188-9, 191-2; and storage 178, 188, 195, 197; unbiased 153, 158, 177, 181, 185-8, 196, 243; variability of futures price on 179, 198; see also arbitrage; backwardation; basis; forecasting; hedging; information; speculation

general equilibrium analysis v, 6, 7, 19, 96, 172, 336, 352-3, 440: of wage rigidities, 379-90 passim; v. partial equilibrium analysis 352-3; see also partial equilibrium analysis; impact
Ghana 44, 95, 290-1, 296
government: concern with price instability 2; creation of more distant future markets by 445; domestic demand management by 37, 402; expenditure, determination of 16, 17, 392-4, 400; justification for intervention by 25, 273, see also intervention; programmes 167; response to price stabilization 54; role in causing price instability 52, 274, 375; role in transmission mechanism 375, 392, 402
grain 15, 20, 50, 106, 109, 178-80, 188-9, 274, 409: optimal stock of 424-5; price rises of 274, 401
growth, effects of price instability on 27, 375, 377, 395-8

hedge, hedging 64, 74, 131, 172, 180-92 passim, 200, 242, 274, 284, 288, 444; optimal hedge 186-7, 189
homothetic price stabilization scheme, see commodity price stabilization schemes

IMF 43, 287, 297, 356, 394, 441
impact effect of price stabilization: as benchmark 93, 247, 284; long run 301, 304, 312, 327-9; short run 7, 19, 29, 32, 53, 92, 247-99, 240; short run v. long run 7, 10, 19, 29, 136, 172, 247, 301-3, 310-13, 319-34, 440
imperfect risk markets, see market incompleteness
imports: adjustments in 399; competition from 396-7;fluctuations in 393, 400-2
incidence analysis of price stabilization 7, 10, 19, 53, 317, 440
income instability, see income variability
income insurance 42, 177, 337-8, 388, 411
income risk 6, 15, 16, 108-10, 204, 344: concern for 96, 104, 206, 244; effects of collective choices on 236; effect of futures market on 178-9, 181, 186-7, 189; effect of savings on 201-6; effect of storage on 195
income stabilization 15, 29, 39, 40, 42-3, 166, 248, 297-9, 316, 414, 441: measuring benefits of 92, 169, 298-9; superiority of future markets in providing 187-8, 191; role of labour markets in 388
income stabilization scheme 40, 42-3, 46, 166, 244, 297-9, 316, 414: vulnerability to speculative attack 414
income variability 28, 42, 49, 99: effect of on benefits 124-5; effect of change of price distribution on 96, 354; effect of price stabilization on 15, 18, 170, 284, 297, 319; effect on savings 202, 397; effect on utility 99, 201: of exporters 19; of farmers 2, 15, 18, 26-7, 201-6, 288-9, 319; importance of borrowing for 99
incompleteness of markets, see market incompleteness
inconsistencies in behaviour 97-8
index of instability, see measurement of variability
India 100-1, 107-9
indirect utility function 112-16: attitudes to risk of 116-18, 213-14, 312; derivation of 112-13; functional forms 116, 118-19, 219, 226, 229, 339; properties of 113-15, quasi-convexity of 113-14;

458 *Commodity Price Stabilization*

indirect utility function (*cont.*)
  separability of 111, 219–20; treatment of wage income in 113, 378; usefulness of 111, 254, 329
industrial economies: assumption of price rigidity in 374; fluctuations in 400–2; interaction with primary producers 375, 399–402
inefficiency of market equilibrium 7, 25, 59, 214–17: arising from market incompleteness 137, 143–4, 177, 208–37, 338, 356; importance of 211; presumption of in competitive market 162, 208–10, 232, 235, 238, 336, 339, 345, 356–7; structural v. marginal 211
inflation 15, 289, 375, 381, 388–9: correcting for 287; and unemployment 388–9
information: absence of perfect 51, 243, 444; aggregating 143, 184, 239–43; assumed constancy of 51, 441; benefits of 51, 58, 136–7, 141–2, 147–8, 152, 158–9, 197, 441; changes in 132, 137, 154; collecting 21, 51–2, 154, 162, 238, 243; costly 42, 244; role in credit markets 445; disseminating 158, 162, 243; effect of price stabilization on 52–3, 99, 162, 238, 244; efficiency in collection of 143, 157–8, 243; efficiency in transmission of 143, 240, 243; efficiency in use of 21, 134–7, 157–9, 180, 238; use in forecasting 132, 158, 442; role of futures markets 239; role of government 192, 238; imperfection of 25; incompleteness of as source of macro response 373–4; in past prices 155, 239; processing, 153–4, 156–7, 243; relevance of for price stabilization 154, 238, 244; sources of 10, 156; summarizing in certainty equivalents 135–6, 138–41; value of, *see* benefits of, *above*
instability (*see also* consumption variability; demand variability; export instability; income variability; price instability; investment): international 375, 399–402; of national economies 399–402
insurance 161, 163, 165–7, 348
insurance: absence of 8, 10, 54, 207–9, 235, 298, 444; consequences of absence of 338–9; contracts 40, 48, 169, 298; crop 40, 131, 167, 208; role of futures market 41, 165, 167, 177–83, 191–2; income 42, 177, 337–8, 388, 411; markets 8, 38, 48, 54, 143, 166, 207–9, 235–6; output 338; price 183, 338, *see also* hedging; reasons for limited use 166–7; *see also* adverse selection; market failure; market incompleteness; risk; moral hazard
Integrated Programme for Commodities v, 12, 14, 285
International Bank for Reconstruction and Development, *see* World Bank
international commodity agreements 2, 259, 282, 286–7
international negotiations 430
intertemporal aspects 5, 9, 395, 428: *see also* dynamic analysis
intervention: consequences of 54; to correct inefficiency 7, 25, 42, 162, 208–9, 231–2, 237, 244, 336, 373, 404, 432, 434; to improve information 244; justification for 6, 10, 208–9, 245, 356–7; magnitude of gain from 141, 211, 231, 371, 373; optimal degree of 432, 434; to

increase storage 404–5, 412, 428, 430, 432
investment: determination of level of 392–4, 397; effect of export instability on 375, 377, 392; effect of price stabilization on 373, 396–8; effect of savings on 397; fluctuations in 395, 401–2; shadow price of 396; as source of instability 375, 401–2
invisible hand 24, 207
Ivory Coast 290–1, 296

Jensen's inequality 79, 113, 137, 262
joint normality, lognormality 94–5, 190, 193–4, 240–1
jute 2, 13, 43–5, 54, 285–99

Keynesian: multiplier 375, 393, 400–1; theory 402

labour: allocation of 379–82, 385, 388; markets 55, 377–91 *passim*, 396–8; supply of 378, 385
lags, 402: *see also* cobwebs
landlords 164, 166–7
learning 10, 35, 99, 134, 138, 153–7, 284, 306; relation to rational expectations 134; speed of 10, 39, 151, 284, 301; *see also* cobweb; expectations; information
lending 20: *see also* borrowing; credit
less developed countries (LDCs): access to credit by 16, *see also* IMF; Stabex; credit markets in 55, 444–5; effect of export instability on 15, 375–6, 392; effect of price stabilization on 23, 334; importance of agricultural exports for 2, 14, 377; importance of futures markets for 444–5; macroeconomic responses in 374, 399; problems facing 15; severity of instability in 374, 395, 402; welfare of 14, 20, 47
linear expenditure system 119
linearity: importance of assumption of 17–18, 20, 30, 122, 132, 156, 184, 190, 240–1, 276; of asset demands 74–6; of demand for futures 184–91, 240–1; of trade policy 276
linkages 374, 377–88 *passim*, 396
lognormal distribution 65, 88–95, 107, 139–41, 184, 194, 257: joint 94–5, 194; properties of 88–90, 194, 286
long run equilibrium 7, 19, 32, 175, 301–17, 318–34, 440

macroeconomics: analysis 5, 7, 10, 20, 25, 373–4, 381; benefits 16, 20, 35–6, 168, 373, 380, 383–7, 390, 393, 440–1; effects 7, 16–17, 19–20, 47, 333–6, 392–402; instability 15, 384–9, 392–402, 441; models 7, 168, 373–4, 377–90, 397–8, 399–402; policy 20, 36, 392, 400, 402; responses to price changes 374, 381, 399; stabilization 15, 392, 400; welfare analysis 374, 380
Malayasia 290–1, 296
market, changes in allocative efficiency of 177, 209–10
market equilibrium, *see* equilibrium
market failure 6, 10, 24, 41, 210, 244
market fragmentation 15, 50, 274, 291
market imperfections 24, 291, 319, 373
market incompleteness vii, 6, 8, 10, 25, 63, 137, 143–4, 177, 208, 338, 356, 373, 443–5: reasons for 207–8, 338, 370;

Subject Index 459

consequences of 208-32, 244, 334-5, 356; inefficiency arising from 137, 143, 177, **208-37**, 334-5, 338, 356, 443-5; multiple role of markets with 177, 209-10, 338
markets: actuals 183; futures, *see* futures markets; insurance, *see* insurance; right set of 208, 215
marketing boards 16, 192, 288, 298, 375, 392
Marshallian analysis 10, 17: *see also* surplus; unsatisfactory nature of 122, 143, 249, 272
maturity basis 179n
Mauritius 290-1, 296
mean absolute deviation 107-8, 286
mean preserving spreads 79-81, 83, 85, 90, 116, 250-2, 338, 340, 343, 366, 368-70, 396
mean quantity preserving changes in price risk 21, 32, 171, 247, 250-2, 254, 260, 312-15, 317, 368
mean value theorem 336: *see also* Taylor series expansions
mean-variance analysis 57, 69, 75-7, **85-91**, 170-1, 183
measurement of variability 76, 249, 285-92
methodology 3, 7, 119, 252-3, 285-9, 301-2
Mexico 44, 290-1, 296
middlemen (merchants) 54-5, 164, 192, 195-7, 444
models: of distorted trade 276-81; of futures markets 183-7; of incorrect expectations 143-51; of inflation and unemployment 388-9; of informational role of futures markets 240-2; of instability and growth 396-8; in international instability 399-402; of intersectoral linkages with flexible prices 377-80; of intersectoral linkages with rigidities 381-8; of investment instability 393-400; lessons from 384-90; mean-variance models 85-8; micro v. macro 373; of multiple equilibria 348-57; need for 439, 443; of optimal savings 201-4; of optimal storage 410-11, 422-5; philosophy of 302-3, 406; of portfolio choice 85-7, 171; random walk model 416-17; robustness of 406; of supply 59-67, 80-4, 304-6; of supply responses to stabilization 304-7, 320-5; of trade 339-47; usefulness of 301-2
moment generating function 75, 85, 89, **193-4**
monopoly 24, 54-5, 139
moral hazard 40, 42, 165-6, 176, 207, 338, 370, 414, 445
multiple equilibria 211, 339, 348-53
multiplicative risk, *see* risk
multiplier 375, 393, 400-1

national income: level of 2, 378; effect of price instability on 373; fluctuations in 35-6, 375, 400-2; identity 393, 399, 401-2; stabilization of 394, 400
Nigeria 288-91, 296
non-traded goods 375-91 *passim*
normal distribution 75, 85-90, 183, 190, 193-4, 197-200, 361, 427: conditional distribution 193-4, 240; formulae using 199, 240-1, 286, 294, 426, 437; joint normal 190, 193-4, 240-1
normality: of buffer stock 294, 408; of supply 413, 425, 427
numeraire, choice of 28, 287-9, 297

oil 12, 16, 400-1
onion market 180
OPEC vii, 12, 14
optimality of markets, *see* efficiency
optimum buffer stock 7, 321
optimum buffer stock rule 21, 199, 206, 252, 254, **421-38**: accuracy of 425; analytical solution 425, 430, 437-8; approximate solution 423-8, 431, 435-8, 441; benefits of 404, 428-33; comparison with other rules 404, 432-3, 441; relation to competitive rule 404, 411, 412, 430-1; degree of price stabilization achieved by 404, 426-7, 433; derivation of 21, 74, 405, 410-11, 413, 421-5; effects of 425-7, 431-2; implementation of 404, 412, 442; nature of 199, 404, 406, 411, 422-3, 430-4, 441
optimum savings 7, **201-6**
optimum storage 404
output, *see* supply

Pareto efficiency 6, 24, 137, 207-8, 318, 329, 338, 356: *see also* efficiency
Pareto improvement 7, 209-11, 223, 318, 336, 362
Pareto inferiority of free trade 6, **336-56**
partial equilibrium analysis of price stabilization 6-7, 51, 172, 339, 352-3
partial equilibrium effect 375, 440
partial price stabilization 21, 34, 39, 247, **249-58, 259-71**, 293, 313-15, 440-1
perfect market hypothesis 6, 24-5, 243
permanent income hypothesis 28, 395, 400
Philippines 109, 290-1, 296
Phillips curve 389-90
policy: analysis of small change in 366-9; choices 19, 96, 98-9, 231-2; guide for the policy economist 5; questions 3, 6, 8-11, 20, 231: *see also* intervention; government; taxes; trade policy
pork bellies 180
portfolio choice 74-6, 85-9, 161, 170
portfolio separation theorems 87, 167
potatoes 179-80, 189
price, cash 179, 181, 188
price, distribution of 9, 29, 76, 96, 133, 210-14, 236, 250, 260
price expectations: adjustment of 29; effect on demand 133; effect on supply 9, 19, 32, 50, 149-52, 213, 305; formation of 9, 64, 132, 155, 239, 241; variations in 50, *see also* cobwebs
price, futures, *see* futures markets
price index, choice of 28, 287-9, 297
price instability: causes of 1, 4, 15, 34, 47-52, 63, 89, 120, 122, 124, 149-51, 274, 336, 393, 399; consequences of 1, 4, 15, 17, 19, 36, 50-5, 289; costs of 19, 377, 380, 383-4, 386-7, 390, 392, 395; effect on consumers 16, 34, 116-8; effect on countries 289; effect on producers 16; effect on supply 59, *see also* supply; effect of trade on 336; export-led 377-91, 393; importance of identifying source of 47-8, 59, 93, 155, 188-9, 263-9, 271; impossibility of completely eliminating 21, 34-5, 76, 247, 403-4, 440; magnitude of 2, 12-13, 34, 44, 108-9, 180, 198, 274, 285-8, 291; measurement of 76, 249, 285-92; responses to changes in 92, *see* commodity price stabilization; systematic v. non-systematic 120

price of primary products 13, 14, 36, 289–99, 399–402
price risk 7, 116–19, 180, 342
price stabilization, *see* commodity price stabilization
primary commodity markets, role in transmission mechanism 374, 399–401
private sector responses: to credit 394; to price stabilization 25, 35, 37, 52, 195, 238, 444; of storage to price stabilization 35, 37–8, 53, 195, 199–201, 238, 259, 404
probability: compact 91; conditional 193–4; convergence of 90–1; density functions 77–9, 134, 250–1, 257, 281; distribution, *see* distribution; objective 98–9; subjective 48, 98–9; of buffer stock exhaustion 294, 403, 408
producer surplus, *see* surplus
production, *see* supply
production function, specification of 57, 60–1, 65, 107, 111, 218, 221, 225, 304
profit function 60, 111–12
protection 14, 275, 368
public expenditure (*see* government): destabilization of 375, 392–4
public good 210, 236, 244

quotas 14, 20, 247, 272, 275, 277, 279–83, 336–7, 362–71: v. tariffs 363–4, 369–70

R, coefficient of relative risk aversion, *see* risk aversion
random walk 34, 204, 294–5, 388–9, 407–8, 414, 416–18
rational expectations: as benchmark 10, 21–2, 58, 131, 136–7, 142, 207; benefits of moving to 143, 148; characterization 137–41; concept of 131, 133–5; efficiency of markets with 6, 136–7, 143–4, 158, 162, 207, **209–37**; equilibrium 29, 58, 131–5, 151, 158, 207, **209–37**, 305–6, 340; evidence for 132, 142, 152–3; formulation of 64, 138; realism of 135, 142; relation to information 134, 136, 142, 203, 236; with storage 195, 321, 411
rationality 204
rationing, in labour market 385
reaction functions 348–52, 360
real income, variability in 28–9, 33, 39, 388–9, 375, 377, 380, 389
recession, causes of 36, 376, 399, 401–2
redistributive policies 6
rent, *see* surplus
rental, land 55: *see also* landlords; share cropping; tenants
rice 109
rigidities (wage and price) 7, 25, 47, 374, **381–91**, 392, 397–8, 441; welfare effects of 374, 383–4, 386–7, 390
risk: allocation of 6, 210, 235–6, 337; analysis of 4, 7, 18, 48, 57, 76–85, 122, 340; attitudes to 64, 96–110, 111, 116–17, 164, 175, 305; aversion, *see* risk aversion; bearing 6, 161, 164–5, 168, 175; benefits, *see* benefits; choice of 107–8; concept of 8, 18, 26, 57, 344; cost of 18–19, 72, 110, 163–4, 168, 175–6, 203–6, 342, 380, 395, 404, 444, *see also* benefits; instability; diversifiability of 29; magnitude of 96, 108–110; markets 6, 216, 444, *see also* insurance; measures of 76–9; nature of 118; neutrality, *see* risk neutrality; pooling 55;

price risk 116–19, 180, 342; premium 8, 59, 72–4, 77, 109–10, 164–5, 185, 203–4; reducing 9, 15–16, 161, 163, 169–75, 177, 181–3, 238, 282–3, 439–40, 444; responses to 9, 63–8, 69–84, 161, 163; sharing 8–9, 28, 161, 163–9, 175–7, 180, 238, 248, 282–3, 389, 440, 444; shifting 9; specification *see* risk specification; systematic v. non-systematic 48–51, 120, 156; taking, in multi-period context 99; transferring 161, 163–9, 175, 342; types of 63; effect on welfare 83, *see also* benefits, risk
risk aversion: coefficient of absolute risk aversion, A: defined 72, 102, 341, in formulae 73, 81–2, 165, 169, 184–91, 200–1, 203, 295, 341, importance of assumption of constancy of 74–6, 82, 85–8, 183–9, 200, 241–3, 331; coefficient of partial risk aversion 102–5; coefficient of relative risk aversion, R: defined 72, 102, 117, 268, 344, effect on magnitude of benefits 44, 45–6, 296–8, in formulae 73, 93–6, 141, 156, 191, 206, 219, 268–9, 307, 310–15, 344–5, importance of constancy of 73–6, 84–5, 119, 141, 175, 303, 305, 311–12, 317, 331, relevance of for savings 396; consequences of extreme 33, 82; magnitude of 101, 105, 107–9; meaning of 8–9, 57, 69–71, 79, 116–18; measurement of 70, 72, 101–8; and supply responses **318–35**
risk neutrality: consequences of assumption for efficiency 218–20, 228, 232, 404, 411, 421, 434; income 64–7, 72, 166, 168, 186, 196, 218, 220, 228, 232, 236, 255, 259, 383, 350; price 118, 122, 143–5, 218–20, 228, 232, 236, 313, 331, 340, 370, 411
risk market redundancy 144, 215, 217–28, 232–3
risk specification: additive 20, 60, 65–6, 120–1, 132, 140, 150, 152, 263; multiplicative 20, 65–6, 80, 89, 94, 120–1, 124, 135, 138–40, 181, 200, 209–10, 225, 228, 263, 295, 305, 309; importance of for results 17–18, 65, 119–20, 140, 276, 355
robustness: of analysis 3, 247, 338–40, 353–56, 406; of inefficiency results 338–40; of measures of total benefit 258, 278, *see also* specification
Roy's identity, derived 115: used 116–17, 123, 129, 214, 216, 223, 254, 270, 312, 329, 367, 378
rubber 2, 13, 43, 45, 167, 192, 285, 287–8, 290–9

savings 28, 161, 175, 195, **201–6**, 395–8
second-best, theory of 6
securities market 370: *see also* portfolio choice; stock-market
security motive 103, 105, 106
sensitivity, *see* robustness; specification
separability 57, 81, **111–16**, 305, 307, 320
serial correlation 151, 155, 432
sharecropping 166–9, 440
shocks: effect on fixed price economy 7; effect of with distorted trade 274
simulations 3, 409
sisal 2, 13, 28, 192, 285
Slutsky's theorem 83, 115
soybeans 179–80, 189

Subject Index 461

specification, functional 20-1, 100, 118-21, 302-3, 338: implications for presumed efficiency 209, 215, 237; importance of for results 3, 9, 10, 57, 107, 133, 137, 209-10, 215, 237, 247, 255, 258-9, 264, 271, 284, 302-3, 371, 380, 434, 440; robustness to alternative 247, 338-40, 353-6, *see also* econometric specification; robustness
spectral analysis 152, 285-7
speculative attack 35, 404, 413-14, 444
speculators, speculation 51-3: adequacy of 274; amount of 186; attitudes to government intervention 192, 274; and buffer stock policy 35, 42, 52, 442; in cobweb model 180; in foreign exchange markets 392; in futures markets 28, 41, 88, 181, 242; compared with hedging 181, 183-9; role in providing information 239, 241-2, 244; restricting 7, 208, 244, 371; risk bearing 164, 167; risk premium for 185, 332; stabilizing role of 150, 274; with storage 27, 199, 274, 434
Sri Lanka 290-1, 296
Stabex 16, 394
stability: cobweb 83, 149, 151, 306-8; conditions 81, 83, 149, 306-8, 320, 326, 329-30, 333, 339, 343, 348-53, 360-1, 368-9; Marshallian 83, 306; Walrasian 83, 306, 326
stabilization of consumption 15, 409, 416-18, 428
stabilization schemes, general characterization 308-10, 320-1: *see also* buffer stocks; commodity price stabilization; income stabilization
stochastic: process 21, 34, 39, 403, 405-9, 416-20; programming 421, 428-9
stock-market 167, 210: *see also* securities market
stockpiling 196, 199, 274
stocks: average size of 39, 46, 198-9, 406, 416-18, 420, 426, 432-3, 444; continuously held 178-80, 188-9, 191-2; convenience yield 178, 195-7; critical size at which vulnerable 413; demand for 196; discontinuously held 178-80, 183-8, 192; distribution of size of 294, 403, 408, 416-19, 427; effect on harvests 427; effect on price variability 180, 195, 374; importance of size for benefit 429-30; price movements with 178-9, *see also* buffer stocks; storage
storage 161, 173-5, 178-80, 188-9, **191-200**, 250-2, 257, 259-60, 321, 334: adequacy of private 24, 46, 199, 441; arbitrage benefits from 188; dynamic study of 195, *see also* dynamic analysis; effects on price stability 197-9; effect of price instability on 92; relation to futures market 178-80, 188-9, 197-201; magnitude of 197-207; interaction with price stabilization 161-2, 199-201; private 46, 195, 199-201, 238, 274-5, 276, 356, 404, 412-14, 443-4; subsidization of 46
storage costs: assumptions about 321, 424, 426, 430; estimates of 295, 408; in formulae 195-7, 294-5, 410-11, 417, 419, 421-8, 431-3; importance of for stabilization 252, 254, 299, 321, 403, 414, 417, 420, 429-30, 432-3, 440; importance of for storage 197
structural changes 48: consequences of price stabilization for 47, 54-5, 157-9; difficulty of distinguishing from fluctuations 394, 442
subjective probability 48, 98-9
Sudan 290-2, 296
sufficient statistic 154-5: *see also* information, aggregating; certainty equivalent
sugar 2, 13, 20, 34, 43-5, 272, 285, 287, 289-99, 413
supply: dependence on source of risk 59, 66; effect of buffer stock on 425; effect of changes of risk on 81-2, 337-8, 354; effect of risk on 57, 59, **63-85**, 92, 96, 163, 168-9, 171, 304, **318-35**; elasticity 84, 306-7, 310-12, 325-6; *ex ante* v. *ex post* 19, 67-8, 305; functions, estimation of 9, 159, 175; long run v. short run 19, 172, 175, 301; management of 14; probability distribution of 134, 183, 251, 413, 427, 430; response to futures markets 161, 190-1; response to price stabilization 4-5, 15, 19, 32-3, 37-9, 59, 68, 161, 163, 168-175, 177, 188, 190-1, 255, 275, 284, **304-17**, 326-34; response to trade policy 272, 275, 282-3; schedule 62-3, 67; pseudo supply schedule 68, 139; on hand for storage 406, 421; theory of **57-95**
supply variability 137-41: benefits from stabilizing 125-8, 262-6, 269; effect of price stabilization on 19, 29-30, 38, 172-5; sources of 50-1, 63, 336
surplus: consumer 18, 26, 33, 49, 110-11, 114-15, 120, 122, 143, 272, 340; Marshallian analysis 10, 122, 143, 256-8, 293, 340, unsatisfactory nature of 122, 143, 249, 272; net social 143-4, 256; producer 18, 26, 62, 143

tariffs 54, 247, 272, 255, 277, 279-80, 336-7, **363-71**: *see also* trade policy; compared with quotas 275, 336-7, 362-5, 369-70; effect on price instability 15, 20, 50, 276-80; effect on profits, consumption 396-7; reform 14-15, 20
taxes 19, 20, 50, 54: to improve efficiency 209, **231-2**, 237, 432, *see also* intervention; lump sum 211, 215-17, 223-4, 230-1, 234, 332, 364, 369, 380
Taylor series expansions 37, 69, 85, 90-3, 123, 129, 140, 164, 184, 187, 203, 227, 230-1, 249, 268, 313-14, 345, 361, 366, 386, 424, 435-8: accuracy of 69, 90-4, 184, 227, 256-7, 285-6, 387
tea 2, 12-13, 122, 167, 192, 285
tenants 164, 169
Thailand 290-1, 296
tin 2, 13, 285
trade: barriers 15; distortions 14-15, 20, 44, **272-83**; effect of opening 345, 352-6, 366; inefficiency of free trade 6, 137, 303, **336-56**; international 9, 20, 272-3, 399-402; model of 272-8, 336-57; theory 355
trade cycle 49, 120, 124, 126, 155, 401-2
trade liberalization 272-3, 275, 336, 352, 356, 366: benefits of 272-3, 366-8
trade policy 275-6, 283, 303, 340, 357, 362-71: choice of 275, 362, 369; linear v. non-linear 275, 279-83
transmission mechanism 375: between economies 374-5, 399-401; importance of price rigidities in 374; role in propagating disturbances 373-4
transport costs 50, 288, 370-1, 432

UNCTAD vii, 12, 130, 290, 295
uncertainty v. risk 48: *see also* risk
unemployment, level of 15, 36, 375, 381, **384-91**: effect of wage rigidity on 377, 381-91, 392; trade-off with inflation 375, 381, 388-90; welfare analysis of 374, 380, 383-90 *passim*
utility function: argument of 99; choice of 100, 218, 225, 232, 339-40, 355; constant absolute risk aversion 74-5, 82, 85-8, 102; constant relative risk aversion 73-6, 84-5, 89, 102-3, 399, 415-20; constrained 385; deriving 69, 102-3; 'famine' 415-20; 'flood' 415-20; indirect, *see* indirect utility function; logarithmic 74, 122, 144-5, 215, 217, 324, 339, 355, 370, 378-90; ordinal v. cardinal 112, 116, 118-19; parameterizing 73-5, 100, 116-21, 209; prejudging efficiency by choice of 209, 215, 232; quadratic 74, 76-7, 88, 202, 432; reflecting attitude to risk 70-6, 96-9; restrictions on 77; separability 57, 81, **111-16**, 305, 307, 320; Stone–Geary 118-19

variability: difficulty in assessing changes in 92, 105, 286; measuring 96, 249, 285-9; sensitivity of results to measurement of 293; *see also* instability

wages: contracts for 379; determination of 379, 382, 385-6, 397-8; fluctuations in 382, 384; minimum 381-91; shadow 396
wealth, contrasted with income 99-101: *see also* asset integration hypothesis
welfare: analysis 5, 60, 83, 110, 161, 204, 338, 345, *see also* cost-benefit analysis; economics 70, 338; effects of price stabilization 33, 48, 252-5, 321-13, *see also* benefits; effects of wage rigidity 383-90
wheat, *see* grain
World Bank v, 13, 17, 287, 289, 290-1

Zambia 375